ROTHMANS RUGBY LEAGUE YEARBOOK 1990-91

**Raymond Fletcher
and David Howes**

ROTHMANS

Queen Anne Press

A *Queen Anne Press* **BOOK**

© **Rothmans Publications Ltd**

First published in Great Britain in 1990 by
Queen Anne Press, a division of
Macdonald & Co (Publishers) Ltd
1 New Fetter Lane
London EC4A 1AR

A member of Maxwell Macmillan Pergamon Publishing Corporation

COVER PHOTOGRAPHS
Front Cover: Great Britain and Wigan skipper Ellery Hanley.
Back Cover: Great Britain and Bradford Northern prop forward Kelvin Skerrett on international duty in Perpignan in January 1990.

ACKNOWLEDGEMENTS
The compilers would like to acknowledge the assistance of the Rugby League Record Keepers' Club, club secretaries and individuals in providing material as a further source of reference for accuracy.

PHOTOGRAPHS
Modern day domestic photographs in this *Rothmans Rugby League Yearbook* are from the files of the *Rugby Leaguer.* The compilers acknowledge the co-operation of Chief Photographer Gerald Webster and his staff.
The colour photographs on the front and back covers, plus a number of black-and-white contributions, are by freelance photographer Andrew Varley.

British Library Cataloguing in Publication Data
Rothmans Rugby League Yearbook — 1990-91
   1. Rugby football — Great Britain —
   Periodicals
   796.33.3.0941 GV945.9.G7

ISBN 0 356 17851 X

Photoset by New Rush Filmsetters, London

Reproduced, printed and bound in Great Britain by
BPCC Hazell Books
Aylesbury, Bucks, England
Member of BPCC Ltd.

Rothmans Rugby League Yearbook 1990-91

CONTENTS

EDITORIAL PREFACE

As regular compilers of the *Rothmans Rugby League Yearbook*, we have always taken pride in heralding the publication as the most accurate statistical review of the game. There is equal satisfaction that the Yearbook has become the best-selling and longest-running annual of its kind in the history of the 13-a-side code, this 1990-91 Yearbook reaching the notable landmark of being the 10th edition.

We take extra pride that the *Rothmans Rugby League Yearbook* has for more than a decade received the seal of approval from, not only the sponsor and the publisher, but the Rugby League public ... one of the most knowledgeable and discerning sectors of sports followers.

One of the major changes during the past ten years has been the introduction of the contract system. Regrettably, this has not yet had the desired effect of tightening up the administration of players, either their registration or playing records. In the constant bid for the highest degree of accuracy we again thank club officials, RLHQ staff, the RL Record Keepers Club and a few individuals for their assistance.

While the task of compiling the Yearbook has not become any less arduous, nor has the support of our wives waned, their constant understanding and encouragement being especially appreciated. House editor Celia Kent has yet again provided a buffer of personable professionalism to keep us on the rails.

● Facts and figures in this *Rothmans Rugby League Yearbook* as at 1 June 1990.

RAYMOND FLETCHER, of the *Yorkshire Post*

DAVID HOWES, Rugby League Public Affairs Executive

COACHES SELECT XIII

For the second time, the coaches of the 14 clubs in the Stones Bitter Championship were invited to select their form team of the season as an exclusive feature of the 1990-91 *Rothmans Rugby League Yearbook*.

The coaches were asked not to include members of their own club sides and to base their choice on opposition performances during the 1989-90 campaign, while taking general form into account. It is based on individual form and does not necessarily represent their best team.

A total of 69 players were nominated by the 13 coaches taking part, Peter Fox of Featherstone Rovers again declining the invitation. This compared with the 54 players put forward in the first-ever ballot at the end of the 1988-89 season.

Nine players were chosen in more than one position, while 16 nominees were from overseas — one more than the previous year. Wigan provided a total of 13 players in the selection process, Widnes having 11 players nominated, while single votes were registered for Second Division outfits Hull K.R. and Oldham.

No player received 100 per cent support, the top individual rating being gained by Widnes winger Martin Offiah with 10 nominations, followed by teammate Alan Tait and Wigan centre Kevin Iro, who polled eight votes apiece, the latter also getting one wing vote.

Compared with the previous season, there was a wider spread of voting in each position. A total of 13 names were put forward for the two second row berths, with 12 candidates for the wing spots and the prop forward roles, 11 for the centre positions. The least number of nominees was the five in contention for the full back jersey.

The 1989-90 Coaches Select XIII featured a three-man tie for the hooking role. There was also a three-man tie for one of the prop positions between Karl Harrison, Dean Sampson and George Mann but Mann was given the casting vote because he had also been awarded a further nomination, in the second row.

There were seven changes from the previous selection of 12 months earlier with Tait, Des Drummond, Offiah, Shaun Edwards, Andy Gregory and Ellery Hanley retaining favour, while Phil McKenzie, having been the top hooker in 1988-89, now ties for the honour with Paul Groves of St. Helens and Hull's Lee Jackson.

Of the 15 players in the Select line-up, including the tied position, three were from overseas — Kiwis Kevin Iro and George Mann plus Australian import McKenzie. There were also three overseas players last year.

Great Britain full back and 1990 tourist, Alan Tait.

COACHES SELECT XIII

1. **Alan Tait** (Widnes)
2. **Des Drummond** (Warrington)
3. **Kevin Iro** (Wigan)
4. **Paul Loughlin** (St. Helens)
5. **Martin Offiah** (Widnes)
6. **Shaun Edwards** (Wigan)
7. **Andy Gregory** (Wigan)

8. **Kelvin Skerrett** (Bradford N.)
9. { **Paul Groves** (St. Helens)
     Lee Jackson (Hull)
     Phil McKenzie (Widnes)
10. **George Mann** (St. Helens)
11. **Denis Betts** (Wigan)
12. **Karl Fairbank** (Bradford N.)
13. **Ellery Hanley** (Wigan)

Great Britain wingman Des Drummond.

New Zealand centre Kevin Iro, a 1989 Kiwi tourist.

Great Britain centre Paul Loughlin.

Great Britain winger Martin Offiah, a 1990 tourist in New Zealand.

Great Britain half back Shaun Edwards.

Great Britain scrum half Andy Gregory.

GARY HETHERINGTON, Sheffield E.

1. Bibb (Featherstone R.)
2. Drummond (Warrington)
3. Iro (Wigan)
4. Loughlin (St. Helens)
5. Offiah (Widnes)
6. Schofield (Leeds)
7. Gregory (Wigan)
8. Harrison (Hull)
9. Maskill (Leeds)
10. Sampson (Castleford)
11. Cleal (Hull)
12. Fairbank (Bradford N.)
13. Goodway (Wigan)

DAVID HOBBS, Bradford N.

1. Bibb (Featherstone R.)
2. Bentley (Leeds)
3. Gibson (Leeds)
4. Loughlin (St. Helens)
5. Quirk (St. Helens)
6. Turner (Warrington)
7. Fox (Featherstone R.)
8. Dannatt (Hull)
9. Jackson (Hull)
10. Mann (St. Helens)
11. Jackson (Warrington)
12. Platt (Wigan)
13. Goodway (Wigan)

DENNIS JACKSON, Barrow

1. Tait (Widnes)
2. Eastwood (Hull)
3. Iro (Wigan)
4. Loughlin (St. Helens)
5. Offiah (Widnes)
6. Edwards (Wigan)
7. D. Hulme (Widnes)
8. Skerrett (Bradford N.)
9. Groves (St. Helens)
10. Mann (St. Helens)
11. Eyres (Widnes)
12. Betts (Wigan)
13. Cooper (St. Helens)

BRIAN JOHNSON, Warrington

1. Tait (Widnes)
2. Devereux (Widnes)
3. Iro (Wigan)
4. Wright (Widnes)
5. Offiah (Widnes)
6. Schofield (Leeds)
7. Aston (Sheffield E.)
8. Skerrett (Bradford N.)
9. B. Conway (Wakefield T.)
10. Harrison (Hull)
11. Fairbank (Bradford N.)
12. Betts (Wigan)
13. Hanley (Wigan)

Great Britain prop Kelvin Skerrett, a 1990 tourist.

11

Great Britain hooker Paul Groves.

DOUG LAUGHTON, Widnes

1. Blake (Wigan)
2. Cordle (Bradford N.)
3. Iro (Wigan)
4. Schofield (Leeds)
5. Fawcett (Leeds)
6. Edwards (Wigan)
7. Gregory (Wigan)
8. Skerrett (Bradford N.)
9. Groves (St. Helens)
10. Davidson (Wigan)
11. Cleal (Hull)
12. Platt (Wigan)
13. Hanley (Wigan)

Great Britain hooker Lee Jackson, a 1990 tourist.

MIKE McCLENNAN, St. Helens

1. Tait (Widnes)
2. Drummond (Warrington)
3. Iro (Wigan)
4. Schofield (Leeds)
5. Forster (Warrington)
6. Steadman (Castleford)
7. Bishop (Hull K.R.)
8. Ward (Castleford)
9. Mann (Warrington)
10. Dannatt (Hull)
11. Kuiti (Leeds)
12. Goodway (Wigan)
13. Holliday (Widnes)

Australian import, hooker Phil McKenzie.

JOHN MONIE, Wigan

1. Tait (Widnes)
2. Drummond (Warrington)
3. Schofield (Leeds)
4. Mercer (Warrington)
5. Offiah (Widnes)
6. Steadman (Castleford)
7. Cooper (St. Helens)
8. Skerrett (Bradford N.)
9. Groves (St. Helens)
10. Sorensen (Widnes)
11. Mann (St. Helens)
12. G. Price (Wakefield T.)
13. Gregory (Warrington)

ALEX MURPHY, Leigh

1. Tait (Widnes)
2. Bell (Wigan)
3. Iro (Wigan)
4. Loughlin (St. Helens)
5. Offiah (Widnes)
6. Edwards (Wigan)
7. Gregory (Wigan)
8. Skerrett (Bradford N.)
9. McKenzie (Widnes)
10. Shelford (Wigan)
11. Kuiti (Leeds)
12. Fairbank (Bradford N.)
13. Hanley (Wigan)

BRIAN SMITH, Hull

1. Larder (Castleford)
2. Drummond (Warrington)
3. Iro (Wigan)
4. Irwin (Castleford)
5. Offiah (Widnes)
6. Powell (Sheffield E.)
7. Fox (Featherstone R.)
8. Sampson (Castleford)
9. Cook (Sheffield E.)
10. Mann (St. Helens)
11. Betts (Wigan)
12. Dixon (Leeds)
13. Hardy (Castleford)

KEVIN TAMATI, Salford

1. Tait (Widnes)
2. Drummond (Warrington)
3. Newlove (Featherstone R.)
4. Bell (Wigan)
5. Offiah (Widnes)
6. Myler (Widnes)
7. D. Hulme (Widnes)
8. Grima (Widnes)
9. McKenzie (Widnes)
10. Casey (Oldham)
11. Platt (Wigan)
12. Betts (Wigan)
13. Goodway (Wigan)

New Zealand prop George Mann, a 1989 Kiwi tourist.

Great Britain second row man Denis Betts, a 1990 tourist.

13

DAVID TOPLISS, Wakefield T.

1. Tait (Widnes)
2. Lydon (Wigan)
3. Iro (Wigan)
4. Loughlin (St. Helens)
5. Offiah (Widnes)
6. Edwards (Wigan)
7. Gregory (Wigan)
8. Harrison (Hull)
9. Jackson (Hull)
10. Sampson (Castleford)
11. Goodway (Wigan)
12. Fairbank (Bradford N.)
13. Hanley (Wigan)

DARRYL VAN DE VELDE, Castleford

1. Tait (Widnes)
2. Iro (Wigan)
3. Bell (Wigan)
4. Wright (Widnes)
5. Offiah (Widnes)
6. Edwards (Wigan)
7. Gregory (Wigan)
8. Skerrett (Bradford N.)
9. Jackson (Hull)
10. Platt (Wigan)
11. Nickle (Sheffield E.)
12. Fairbank (Bradford N.)
13. Hanley (Wigan)

DAVID WARD, Leeds

1. Hampson (Wigan)
2. Drummond (Warrington)
3. Tait (Widnes)
4. Loughlin (St. Helens)
5. Offiah (Widnes)
6. Edwards (Wigan)
7. Gregory (Wigan)
8. Skerrett (Bradford N.)
9. McKenzie (Widnes)
10. Platt (Wigan)
11. Gregory (Warrington)
12. Goodway (Wigan)
13. Hanley (Wigan)

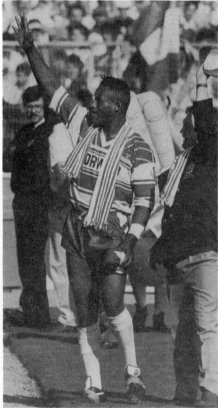

Great Britain loose forward Ellery Hanley.

Great Britain second row man Karl Fairbank, a 1990 tourist.

Man of the Decade . . . 80s superstar Ellery Hanley in 1989 vintage action for Great Britain in Avignon.

THE 1980s

THE 1980s

THE 1980s

This 10th edition of the *Rothmans Rugby League Yearbook* coincides with the end of the 1980s, the first annual covering the 1980-81 season. This special chapter celebrates the landmark with the Editors presenting a statistical and personal review of the 10 seasons covered.

SCORING ACHIEVEMENTS OF THE 1980s

Most tries in a match
6 by Vince Gribbin (Whitehaven) v. Doncaster (JP) ....18 Nov. 1984
6 by Shane Cooper (St. Helens) v. Hull (D1) ....17 Feb. 1988
6 by Chris Bibb (Featherstone R.) v. Keighley (YC) ....17 Sep. 1989

Most goals in a match
16 by Paul Loughlin (St. Helens) v. Carlisle (LC) ....14 Sep. 1986

Most points in a match
40 by Paul Loughlin (St. Helens) v. Carlisle (LC) ....14 Sep. 1986

Highest score
St. Helens 112 v. Carlisle 0 (LC)14 Sep. 1986

Highest away score
Runcorn H. 2 v. Leigh 88 (D2)15 Jan. 1989

Highest score by a losing team
Hunslet 40 v. Barrow 41 (D1) 9 Sep. 1984

Highest score draw
Hunslet 32 v. Swinton 32 (D1)20 Sep. 1988
Huddersfield B. 32 v. Keighley 32 (D2) ..
...................................17 Apr 1986

*Most tries in the decade
249 by Ellery Hanley (Bradford N., Wigan)

*Most goals in the decade
966 by John Woods (Leigh, Bradford N., Warrington, Rochdale H.)

*Most points in the decade
2,450 by John Woods (Leigh, Bradford N., Warrington, Rochdale H.)

*Most appearances in the decade
345 (+5 sub) by Tony Burke (Bramley, Leeds, St. Helens, Warrington)
*Club matches only

Featherstone Rovers full back Chris Bibb, joint top tryscorer in a 1980's match.

St. Helens skipper Shane Cooper, scorer of six tries against Hull in 1988.

Tony Burke, top club appearance tally in the 1980s.

TEST TEAM OF THE 1980s

Ellery Hanley made most appearances for Great Britain during the decade with 29, including one as substitute. He played in four different positions — centre, loose forward, wing and stand off.

Selecting Hanley at centre, this would be the Great Britain team of the decade based on most appearances in each positions.

1. Mick Burke
2. Des Drummond
3. Garry Schofield
4. Ellery Hanley
5. Henderson Gill
6. Tony Myler
7. Andy Gregory
8. Kevin Ward
9. David Watkinson
10. Lee Crooks
11. Andy Goodway
12. Mike Gregory
13. Harry Pinner

Great Britain full back Mick Burke in goalkicking action against New Zealand at Leeds in 1985.

Stand off Tony Myler tears through the New Zealand defence in the first 1985 Test at Leeds.

EDITORS' PERSONAL REVIEW OF THE 1980s

It has been a general editorial policy to allow the records to speak for themselves but to celebrate this 10th edition of *Rothmans Rugby League Yearbook* the editors have indulged in a little nostalgia and come up with what they consider the most memorable moments of a magnificent decade of Rugby League.

Most memorable match

Two games stand out for different reasons . . . the 1985 Wembley final between Wigan and Hull for the non-stop exhibition of modern Rugby League at its spectacular best; and the 1988 third Test when Great Britain ended a decade of defeats against Australia with a stunning 26-12 upset at Sydney.

Most memorable try

Even during a long run of Test defeats, Great Britain managed to score several magnificent tries and two stand out above them all.

The best team effort was the 80-yard move completed by Garry Schofield in the second Test at Brisbane in 1984. Schofield was involved three times as the attack swept from left to right and back left again in glorious style, Des Drummond and Andy Goodway also playing prominent parts.

Martin Offiah's extraordinary 80-yard try in the first British Coal Test against New Zealand rates as the most memorable solo touchdown of the 80s. The Widnes winger's try lit up a dismal British display as he shot through from acting half-back at a play-the-ball inside his own 25. A trail of defenders were left groping thin air on his winding run to the posts.

Des Drummond (left) congratulates 1984 tour colleague Garry Schofield after his second Test touchdown against Australia in Brisbane.

Most memorable goal

Joe Lydon's incredible drop goal for Wigan in the 1989 Silk Cut Challenge Cup semi-final at Maine Road, Manchester, was generally accepted as the greatest of all time. It was officially recorded at 61 yards and sunk Warrington's hopes of a shock victory as it edged Wigan 7-6 ahead in the 73rd minute and they never looked back.

The most memorable place-kicked goal was Lee Crooks' touchline penalty that snatched Great Britain a last minute 6-6 draw and levelled the series in the third Test against New Zealand at Elland Road, Leeds, in 1985.

Outstanding player

The outstanding player and personality of the decade has to be Ellery Hanley. After missing the first season recorded by the *Rothmans Rugby League Yearbook* he began to dominate the pages with a succession of records and awards, with Bradford Northern and then Wigan. The Great Britain captain's international status was confirmed in 1989 when he won the Adidas Golden Boot award as the world's outstanding player, only weeks after receiving the Man of Steel title as Britain's top personality for a record-extending third time.

Outstanding team

Facts support our choice of Widnes and Wigan as the outstanding teams in two categories.

Widnes were the most successful league side in Division One throughout the era, winning the Championship twice and totalling most points of 376 from 182 wins and 12 draws.

Wigan finished second in Division Two in 1980-81 and went on to become the Cup Kings of the decade with a total of 19 trophies as follows: Division One champions (2), RL Challenge Cup (4), Premiership (1), John Player/Regal Trophy (5), Lancashire Cup (4), Charity Shield (2) and World Club Challenge (1).

Great Britain substitute Lee Crooks kicks the memorable equalising goal in the third Test against New Zealand at Elland Road, Leeds, in 1985.

Widnes top of world

Crackdown on headhunters

Leeds swoop for All Black

OUT! Murphy goes in Saints shock

Soviets welcome the 13-man code

MEMORIES

1989-90 HEADLINES
Behind the scoring feats and records of the 1989-90 season were a number of stories which made the headlines:

ALL BLACK SENSATION
Leeds shook the Rugby Union world when they signed New Zealand All Black full back John Gallagher. The signing hit the headlines on 21 May 1990 when his world record deal was estimated to be £350,000 over five years.

London-born Gallagher had emigrated to New Zealand six years earlier and became one of their greatest ever number ones. Two weeks before his signing Gallagher had met Leeds officials when he came over to England to receive the RU International Player of the Year award.

TEAMS COOL OFF
Widnes referee Dave Carter caused heated controversy when he took off the Castleford and Hull teams for a five-minute cooling down period following a first half brawl in their Stones Bitter Championship match at Wheldon Road on 24 September. The League fined each club £3,000 for bringing the game into disrepute, suspending all but £500 for a year pending good behaviour.

ST. HELENS' RECORD FINE
St. Helens were fined a record £10,000 for postponing their Stones Bitter Championship home match against Bradford Northern that had been rescheduled for Friday 29 December. The club had claimed they could not field a team because of injuries and illness. The match had been switched from 17 December when St. Helens were involved in the Regal Trophy third round. The fine was reduced to £8,000 on appeal.

Bradford protested that the fine was comparatively low. Earlier in the season

Northern had fielded a near reserve side against New Zealand five days before they were due to meet Halifax in a Yorkshire Cup semi-final replay. Their punishment was to lose a game against the Australian tourists the following season which, they claimed, would cost them about £20,000 in lost revenue.

CLAMPDOWN ON HEAD HUNTERS
A campaign to clamp down on illegal head tackles resulted in total dismissals for all offences shooting up to 172 — almost double the previous season's total of 91 and the highest figure for many years.

The campaign began in November with Widnes forward Paul Moriarty of Widnes and Shane Cooper of St. Helens banned for eight matches. That became the customary sentence after Controller of Referees Fred Lindop called for all illegal head tacklers to be sent off.

Although there was general approval for the campaign it was not without controversy as many felt the ruling left referees with little chance to use discretion. There was certainly cause for great concern that 34 sent off players were later found not guilty.

USA EXHIBITION MATCH
Warrington and Wigan financed an American exhibition match in Milwaukee on 10 June. Warrington contributed £50,000 and Wigan £100,000, with the aid of sponsorship, Wigan winning the historic encounter 12-5. The official crowd return at the County Stadium was 7,773.

RUSSIAN INVASION
The most exciting international expansion plans for 50 years came with the sudden disclosure in January that Russia was preparing to take up Rugby League for the first time.

Remarkably, there was no great fanfare of announcements in this country but just a trickle of news items telling of Russian plans to encourage professional sport in the wake of historic political changes which brought wider freedom.

The first match was reported to be between Moscow and Leningrad in March and others took place before a squad of about 90 players and officials, including referees and coaches, arrived in Britain in May for a three-match trip and training course.

They were led by Edward Taturyan, the chief administrator, and based at Pontins holiday camp in Blackpool. The party included three teams who played three matches as follows:
Leningrad 43 v. Oulton amateurs 20 on 2 May; Moscow Magicians 16 v. Leeds reserves 34 on 4 May; and Tiraspol 24 v. Wigan reserves 24 on 5 May.

RECORD TRANSFER FEE

Graham Steadman was transferred from Featherstone Rovers to Castleford in a unique delayed record transfer deal of £170,000.

The stand off was originally listed at £185,000 on 7 May 1989 after he had agreed terms with Castleford, who offered Rovers about £100,000. It was then a case for the transfer tribunal and on 7 June 1989 they fixed a transfer fee of £145,000, plus £25,000 if and when he played in a Test for Great Britain.

The deal became a record £170,000 when Steadman made his Test debut against France at Leeds on 7 April 1990. It beat the previous record of £155,000 when Test centre Garry Schofield moved from Hull to Leeds in October 1987.

NEW CHORLEY CLUB

A new Chorley club had its first season and caused much confusion over its name. The Rugby League officially sanctioned a change of title and ground for the Chorley Borough club which changed its name to Trafford Borough and moved to Altrincham. Trafford Borough thus became a continuation of the Old Blackpool Borough club which became Springfield Borough and then Chorley Borough.

Although the new Chorley club adds Borough to its title on programmes, etc. and has the support of the old Blackpool/Springfield supporters' club this is unofficial recognition. Scoring records for Chorley begin from the start of 1989-90, while Trafford Borough's go back to Blackpool Borough days.

CHARLTON SUSPENDED *SINE DIE*

Gary Charlton of Whitehaven was suspended *sine die* after an off-the-ball high tackle which left Castleford stand-off Graham Steadman with a broken nose and cheekbone. The forward was not sent off but penalised by referee Paul Crashley of Wakefield after the foul had been reported by a touch judge early in the Regal Trophy first round match at Whitehaven on 10 December which Castleford won 62-2.

Castleford reported the incident to the League and Whitehaven instituted an indefinite club suspension. The League's *sine die* ban came on 5 January after they studied video evidence.

Charlton, the 22-year-old son of former Test full back Paul, appealed against the decision. Although the sentence was upheld, Charlton was told he could continue to appeal at regular intervals for the ban to be lifted. He had won an appeal against an eight-month ban imposed in Australia in 1989 after a player had received a broken jaw.

JUNE

Out-of-contract Kevin Iro chased by Warrington and Wigan, plus Australian clubs Canterbury-Bankstown, Penrith and Balmain .... David Ward resigns as Hunslet coach to be assistant to Malcolm Reilly at Leeds .... Castleford referee Ray Tennant appointed for the New Zealand Test series with Australia .... Leeds list scrum half Ray Ashton at £25,000 .... Hull K.R. grant hooker David Watkinson a free transfer .... The League decide to stage new style CIS Insurance Charity Shield at Liverpool FC's Anfield .... Keighley sign Army winger Owen Simpson .... Sheffield Eagles snap up teenager David Mycoe from Crigglestone All Blacks .... Bramley offer Peter Lister at £48,000 .... The Tribunal orders Castleford to pay £145,000 to Featherstone Rovers for stand off Graham Steadman, plus a further £25,000 if selected for Great Britain .... Runcorn Highfield appoint Dave Chisnall as coach .... Hull K.R. recruit Brisbane Broncos prop Bryan Niebling .... Wigan persuade Kevin Iro to sign a two-year contract .... Wigan beat Warrington 12-5 in American exhibition encounter in Milwaukee .... Rochdale Hornets sack coach Jim Crellin .... Parramatta back row forward Mark Laurie rejoins Leeds for a second spell .... Wigan appoint Australian John Monie as coach .... Keighley promote Colin Dixon to the board leaving Les Coulter in sole charge as coach .... Bramley winger Peter Lewis offered at £100,000 .... Hull land former Australian Test forward Noel Cleal from Manly .... Chorley appoint Stan Gittins as coach .... Australian packman Graeme Jennings named as coach of Hunslet .... League Chief Executive David Oxley awarded the OBE .... Leeds seal a 10-year £1.5m sponsorship and ground development deal with brewers Bass .... Frank Barrow resigns as coach of Swinton to become assistant to Alex Murphy at St. Helens .... Featherstone Rovers list

prop forward Karl Harrison at £95,000 .... Hull put price tag of £180,000 on loose forward Gary Divorty .... Great Britain skipper Ellery Hanley is awarded the Adidas Golden Boot as the best player in the world .... Castleford scrum half Bob Beardmore joins Leigh in £30,000-plus deal .... Halifax place hooker Seamus McCallion on the list at £100,000 .... Released to play Test trials in New Zealand, Joe Grima and Emosi Koloto anger Widnes by turning out in club games .... Barrow chase £65,000-rated St. Helens scrum half Neil Holding .... Bradford Northern sign Canberra half back Ivan Henjak .... League AGM decides that 50 per cent of transfer fees must be paid immediately, with the remainder settled inside a year .... Also postponed League fixtures must be played on or before the following Thursday.

JULY

Brisbane Broncos half back Gary French joins Castleford for the season .... Leeds ask £60,000 for forward Gary Price .... Former Wigan coach Graham Lowe appointed to the Manly role .... St. Helens rejected by Welsh RU star Mark Jones .... Widnes anger as Warrington announce the signing of Naughton Park utility back David Myers .... Swinton appoint Jim Crellin as coach for a second stint .... Chorley pay Trafford Borough £35,000 for Carl Briscoe, Mike Smith, Billy Price, David Bacon and Paul Broxton .... Carlisle pay Bradford Northern £20,000 for loose forward Harry Pinner .... Warrington reduce the asking price for winger Mark Forster from £85,000 to £40,000 .... Oldham and ex-Widnes full back Mick Burke announces his retirement at 30 years of age .... Mansfield Marksman change club title to Nottingham City and move to the Harvey Hadden Stadium in Nottingham .... St. Helens pursue star RU duo Jeremy Guscott, of Bath, and Australian international winger

David Campese .... Allan Agar takes over as coach of Rochdale Hornets .... Sheffield Eagles offered the hire of soccer stadiums by both Sheffield United and Wednesday .... Featherstone Rovers sign New Zealand centre Iva Ropati .... Swinton ask £60,000 for Steve Snape .... Bradford Northern recruit Welsh RU winger Gerald Cordle on a five-year £100,000 contract .... St Helens half back Neil Holding turns down a move to Barrow .... Illawara full back Steve Larder signs for Castleford .... Whitehaven shocked by prop Jeff Simpson's decision to retire .... Leigh sign New Zealand Test prop Peter Brown .... Australian RU star David Campese rejects a £250,000 contract from St. Helens .... Damaged ankle ligaments threaten Australian Test scrum half Peter Sterling's move to Leeds .... Barrow recruit Brisbane Broncos centre Chris Johns .... Leigh offer nine players for a total of £180,000, headed by John Westhead at £75,000 .... Oldham price prop Ian Sherratt at £75,000, winger Kevin Meadows at £30,000 and up Terry Flanagan's fee to £60,000 .... Oldham capture utility back Richard Russell from Wigan .... Hunslet sign Australians Brett Welch and John Adams .... Carlisle scrum half Dean Carroll joins Nottingham City .... Halifax turn down a £100,000 Bradford Northern bid for second row forward Paul Medley .... Carlisle's Steve Langton is offered at £42,000 .... Runcorn Highfield tempt Warrington half back Ken Kelly out of retirement .... Test centre David Stephenson priced at £75,000 by Leeds .... Hunslet utility back Warren Wilson moves to Leeds in a £30,000 deal .... Full back Paul Fletcher listed at £120,000 by Hull .... Hull K.R. raise asking price for prop forward Zook Ema by £60,000 to £140,000 .... Rochdale Hornets sign Warrington half back John Woods for £50,000.

AUGUST

Bath RU centre Jeremy Guscott rejects St.

Helens .... Leeds list centre Mark Lord at £15,000 .... New Zealand prop George Mann agrees to join St. Helens .... York offer Gary Atkins at £40,000 .... Oldham re-sign centre Des Foy seven months after his emigrating to Australia to play for Newcastle Knights .... New Zealander Tony Botica signs for Hull K.R. .... Featherstone Rovers hand over £50,000 for Leeds packman Gary Price .... Hull pay £57,500 for Featherstone Rovers prop Karl Harrison .... Castleford list prop Dean Sampson at £75,000, full back David Rockley at £40,000, prop Dean Mountain at £12,500, wingers Neil Greatbach at £5,000 and Tony Spears at £3,000 .... Wigan offer former Test packman Ian Potter at £45,000 .... Castleford reject a Hull proposal to part exchange Test winger David Plange for Gary Divorty .... St. Helens bid for Australian RU half back Michael Lynagh .... Bradford Northern hand over a club record £110,000 for Halifax's Paul Medley .... Hull K.R. complete their overseas quota by recruiting Australian centre Greg Austin .... Swinton list stand off Tommy Frodsham at £95,000 .... Rochdale Hornets sign Widnes scrum half Andy Sullivan for £20,000 .... Halifax sign South Sydney prop forward Lindsey Johnston .... Hull reject Castleford bid of £90,000 for Gary Divorty .... Barrow centre Tony Kay joins St. Helens on a three-month trial .... Australian Michael Lynagh turns down St. Helens .... Oldham's Tony Morrison joins Swinton for £8,000 .... Chorley sign Warrington's Mark Knight for £11,000 .... Warrington approach French Test full back David Fraisse after a starring role in the Student World Cup competition .... Salford recruit New Zealand back row forward Mark Brooke-Cowden from Leeds .... Salford veteran back Keiron O'Loughlin moves to Leigh .... New Zealander Dean Lonergan signs for Rochdale Hornets .... Wakefield Trinity secure Australian centre Brian Jackson .... Hull sign Australian utility back David Liddiard and Fulham winger Andrew Mighty .... Oldham sell Ian Sherratt to Salford and buy John Fieldhouse from St. Helens .... Rochdale Hornets hand over £30,000 for Warrington prop forward Tony Humphries .... Widnes physiotherapist Viv Gleave is Rugby League's first woman representative appointment with a call up to serve Lancashire in the Rodstock War of the Roses .... The League launch a new logo based on the number 13 .... Record £40,000 prize money put on offer for the 1989-90 Stones Bitter Champions .... Leigh pull off a double deal with Wigan for Ian Potter and Brian Case .... Wales and Bridgend RU centre John Devereux signs for Widnes .... Neil Fox MBE installed in the Whitbread Trophy Hall of Fame .... The League announce a new 12-match agreement with Granada Television for live coverage of a Stones Bitter Championship match to be played on Saturdays.

SEPTEMBER

Warrington sign Australian scrum half Greg Mackey .... Halifax hooker Seamus McCallion asks to come off the transfer list .... Wigan skipper Ellery Hanley is ruled out long term with a pelvic injury sustained on club duty in Sydney .... The Tribunal rules that David Myers is contracted with Warrington .... Bradford Northern coach Barry Seabourne resigns after a strike by A-team players .... Opening day attendances are the best since the re-introduction of two divisions in 1973 .... Tommy Smales and skipper David Hobbs appointed caretaker coaches at Bradford Northern .... Hull K.R. sign second row man Paul Vannett from Workington Town, winger Garry Clark and prop Zook Ema asking to come off the list .... Parramatta forward Craig Izzard joins Leeds .... Local authorities ban Sheffield Eagles from using Owlerton Stadium for safety reasons .... Bradford Northern centre Steve McGowan fined £200 by the League for signing contracts with both Northern and

Hull .... Oldham duo Neil Clawson and Kevin Meadows make their peace .... League Chief Executive David Oxley flies to France for a press conference denouncing French RU's signing of League players .... Whitehaven coach Barry Smith quits after just over a year in the post .... Dewsbury snap up former Hull K.R. hooker David Watkinson on a free transfer .... St. Helens recruit Swinton prop Ian Connor in a £27,000 deal .... Malcolm Reilly resigns as coach of Leeds after 14 months at the helm .... British Coal launch a four-year £750,000 sponsorship of Great Britain .... Leeds appoint David Ward as their new coach .... Leeds centre David Stephenson moves to Leigh .... Hull K.R. sign Whitehaven full back David Lightfoot, on offer at £48,000 .... The League prevent Lancashire coach Doug Laughton from playing Warrington's David Myers in the Rodstock War of the Roses while in dispute with his club .... Fulham hire Hendon FC ground for staging second round Lancashire Cup tie with Wigan .... Yorkshire hammer Lancashire 56-12 at Wigan .... Leeds join in the chase for Gary Divorty .... Whitehaven offer Oldham's Terry Flanagan the role of player-coach .... Hull K.R. celebrate the opening of their new ground with a 48-8 success over Trafford Borough .... Widnes referee Dave Carter orders off Castleford and Hull players for a five-minute cooling down period in the League fixture at Wheldon Road .... Wigan recruit Australians Phil Blake and Les Davidson as short-term replacements for Kiwi tourists Adrian Shelford and Kevin Iro .... Swinton list hooker Gary Ainsworth at £37,000 and prop Steve O'Neil at £30,000 .... Canberra Raiders insist on a neutral referee for the Foster's World Club Challenge encounter with Widnes, Frenchman Francis Desplas being appointed .... Former Australian Test forward Ray Price launches a comeback with Wakefield Trinity .... Leeds sign up South Sydney scrum half Craig Coleman.

OCTOBER

Makeshift St. Helens defeat New Zealand 27-26 in the opening tour fixture .... Foster's World Club Challenge contenders Canberra Raiders warn British clubs not to poach their players on short-term contracts .... Castleford and Hull each fined £3,000 — £2,500 suspended for a year — on a disrepute charge for brawling .... New Zealand beat Castleford 22-20 .... Widnes lift the Foster's World Club Challenge title with a thrilling 30-18 defeat of Canberra in front of 30,000-plus fans at Old Trafford .... Kevin Ashcroft resigns as coach of Salford, anchored at the bottom of the Stones Bitter Championship without a point .... Warrington reserve team coach Kevin Tamati appointed as new Salford coach .... Doncaster sign Wakefield Trinity forward Dick Jasiewicz .... Bradford Northern appoint ex-Penrith supremo Ron Willey as coach .... Wigan beat New Zealand 24-14 .... 18-year-old Paul Newlove called up in the Great Britain squad for the first British Coal Test .... Salford sign Lancashire and Orrell RU centre David Fell .... Keighley reject a £40,000 Bradford Northern bid for Terry Manning .... Weakened Bradford Northern defeated 26-8 by New Zealand .... Salford turn down two bids from Leeds for centre Ian Bragger .... Fitness checks rule out Joe Lydon and Tony Myler from Great Britain training squad, Sheffield Eagles captain Daryl Powell being called in .... Keighley centre Terry Manning joins Featherstone Rovers for £40,000 .... Warrington beat Oldham 24-16 in the Grunhalle Lager Lancashire Cup final .... New Zealand defeat Leeds 34-4 .... Warrington skipper Mike Gregory appointed captain of Great Britain .... New Zealand call Wigan's Dean Bell and Widnes skipper Kurt Sorensen into their Test Squad .... Widnes centre Andy Currier hands in a transfer request .... Cumbria lose 28-2 to New Zealand .... David Hulme preferred to Shaun Edwards at stand off in Great Britain first Test line-up, with debuts for Andy Currier and Kelvin Skerrett .... Injury rules out New Zealand Test men Adrian Shelford and Mark Elia .... Bradford Northern offer £150,000 contract to British Lions utility back Tony Clement .... New Zealand win the first British Coal Test 24-16 .... Fears that Great Britain and Wigan skipper Ellery Hanley may be ruled out for the season with a pelvic injury .... Bramley fail in cheeky bid to take unsettled Lee Crooks on loan from Leeds .... Wakefield Trinity sign up Queensland RU full back Chris Perry, having paid his own way from Australia .... Warrington anger as Hull swoop to sign Australian scrum half Greg Mackey, David Liddiard being released to make room on the Boulevard overseas quota .... Great Britain drop Andy Currier and Andy Gregory for the second British Coal Test .... Tribunal orders Leeds to pay £120,000 to Hull for Gary Divorty .... League bar Bradford Northern from staging a 1990 Australian tour fixture as punishment for fielding a weakened side against New Zealand .... Tribunal orders Warrington to pay up to £80,000 to Widnes for David Myers: £35,000 immediately, plus £20,000 after 25 games and £25,000 after a further 30 matches .... Injury rules Kevin Beardmore and Alan Tait out of second Test, being replaced by Paul Hulme and Steve Hampson .... Castleford list Kenny Hill at £100,000 .... Steve Hampson sent off after only two minutes in Great Britain's 26-6 victory over New Zealand at Elland Road .... The Wigan full back is dismissed for the second time in 24 hours in home league encounter with Castleford .... Leeds offer unhappy Lee Crooks at £250,000.

NOVEMBER

New Zealand take prop forward George Mann from St. Helens as replacement for James Goulding, returned home with a broken wrist .... Widnes list centre Andy Currier at £185,000 .... New Zealand defeat Hull 44-8 .... Hull K.R. offer scrum half Steve Robinson at £35,000 .... Andy Currier makes his peace at Widnes .... New Zealand fly in Wellington winger David Ewe to replace the injured Tea Ropati .... Alex Murphy found not guilty of verbally abusing Cumbrian referee Colin Steele .... Bradford Northern beat Featherstone Rovers 20-14 in the John Smiths Yorkshire Cup final .... New Zealand beat Widnes 26-18 .... Hull bid for former skipper Lee Crooks described as derisory by Leeds .... Workington Town players ask not to be paid after a humiliating 35-8 home defeat by Trafford Borough .... New Zealand defeat Featherstone Rovers 44-20 .... Great Britain recall Alan Tait and Joe Lydon for the third British Coal Test .... Salford chairman John Wilkinson calls for two referees to share match duties .... New Zealand make four changes for the deciding third Test, calling up Tony Kemp and Esene Faimalo .... British coach Malcolm Reilly puts a press gag on his players in build-up to the Wigan Test .... Salford centre Ian Bragger joins Castleford for £60,000 .... Second row man Mick Worrall listed at £65,000 by Salford .... Great Britain clinch their first home series win over New Zealand for 24 years with a 10-6 victory at Wigan .... League selects Doncaster as the venue for the Under-21 international .... Britain's Shaun Edwards and Kiwi Gary Mercer chosen as British Coal Men of the Series .... Four Kiwi tourists sign for British clubs: David Watson (York), Kelly Shelford (Whitehaven), Duane Mann and Gary Mercer (Warrington) .... Welsh RU star Mike Hall turns down a £150,000 contract with St. Helens .... Released by Warrington, New Zealander Joe Ropati joins Swinton .... Salford sign Swinton half back Frank Cassidy for £35,000 .... Bottom-of-the-table Barrow sack Australian coach Rod Reddy and appoint Dennis Jackson as caretaker .... Silk Cut Challenge

Great Britain skipper Mike Gregory holds aloft the British Coal Trophy after the third Kiwi Test at Wigan.

Cup prize money increased by 50 per cent with a record £30,000 for the Wembley winners .... Lee Crooks decides to stay at Leeds .... St. Helens recruit New Zealand tour centre Tea Ropati .... Widnes packman Paul Moriarty and St. Helens skipper Shane Cooper both suspended for eight matches as the League impose a clampdown on illegal high tackles .... Keighley price prop forward Gary Rose at £70,000 .... Widnes fail in double bid to reduce their overseas quota, the League rejecting their application to exempt Emosi Koloto, due to long-term injury, and Australian-born Phil McKenzie, he having obtained British citizenship .... Featherstone Rovers and Salford fail in bids to sign Halifax loose forward Les Holliday.

DECEMBER

The League rule that players turning down an invitation to tour Papua New Guinea and New Zealand the following summer will not be allowed to play club football in Australia .... Sheffield Eagles recruit New Zealand tour duo Francis Leota and Tawere Nikau .... Ruled by the Tribunal to be a free agent, Barrow centre Tony Kay joins St. Helens .... The Board of Directors reappoint Malcolm Reilly as Great Britain coach, but replace manager Les Bettinson with Wigan chairman Maurice Lindsay, carrying the new title of Tour Director .... Castleford offer winger Chris Chapman at £45,000 .... Hull list 1984 tourist Wayne Proctor at £15,000, plus fellow forwards Neil Puckering and Alan Tomlinson .... Halifax, Leeds and Wakefield Trinity chase Barrow's Australian forward Cavill Heugh .... Castleford renew interest in Leeds prop Lee Crooks with a cash-and-player offer .... Hull sign Doncaster winger Neil Turner in a £50,000-rated deal involving the part exchange of Wayne Proctor and Neil Puckering .... Swinton price Mark Viller at £20,000 .... Controversy as Silk Cut Challenge Cup preliminary round draw pairs Leeds and

Bradford Northern, plus St. Helens and Castleford .... Castleford's Great Britain threequarter Tony Marchant moves to Bradford Northern for £35,000 plus utility player Neil Roebuck .... Whitehaven indefinitely suspend back row forward Gary Charlton after a tackle which broke Graham Steadman's nose and cheekbone in the Regal Trophy tie with Castleford .... Widnes take eight-match ban Joe Grima off their register and give debut to Tongan Boblin Tuavao .... Wigan dramatically recall skipper Ellery Hanley after injury for the Regal Trophy replay with Leeds .... The League suspend a referee and two judges for poor performances as part of a new policy .... The League rule that Joe Grima cannot be deregistered by Widnes while serving a suspension and that Boblin Tuavao was played unregistered .... Widnes offer Joe Grima at £40,000, arousing interest from a host of clubs, including St. Helens, Oldham and Rochdale Hornets .... Hull trim £30,000 off Paul Fletcher's £120,000 asking price .... Bradford Northern sign Wigan winger Henderson Gill for £30,000 .... St. Helens call off their rearranged home fixture with Bradford Northern because of injury and illness .... Great Britain's 1990 British Coal Tests with Australia to be staged at Wembley, Old Trafford, Manchester and Elland Road, Leeds .... Great Britain and Wigan skipper Ellery Hanley awarded the MBE in the New Year's honours list .... Leeds sign Barrow packman Cavill Heugh, cross off Australian forward Craig Izzard and confirm recruitment of Kiwi tourist Mike Kuiti .... Oldham list Paul Round at a club record £95,000.

JANUARY

Ten-cap Welsh RU winger Glen Webbe turns down a £90,000 contract from Hull .... Joe Grima decides to stay at Widnes .... Wigan deny interest in Welsh RU full back Paul Thorburn .... St. Helens fined £10,000 for non-fulfilment of Championship fixture at home to Bradford Northern .... Alex Murphy parts company with St. Helens .... Whitehaven forward Gary Charlton banned *sine die* in trial by video for a high tackle on Castleford's Graham Steadman in a Regal Trophy first round tie .... Swinton sign Paris Chatillon scrum half Ronel Xenon .... Batley complete the signing of Halifax prop forward Andrew Parkinson .... Salford stand off David Needham joins Halifax .... Leeds recruit Whitehaven's Welsh centre Rob Ackerman .... Castleford fork out £150,000 for Leeds Test forward Lee Crooks in Challenge Cup deadline deal .... Salford swoop for Swinton scrum half Darren Bloor and St. Helens hooker Mark Lee .... Swinton pay £25,000 for Warrington scrum half Keith Holden .... Hull recruit Dewsbury centre Marquis Charles for £15,000 and Barrow skipper Russ Walker for £40,000 .... £90,000-rated Paul Round settles his differences at Oldham .... Batley fend off £50,000 bids for Paul Gearey from Salford, Leigh and Oldham .... Swinton full back Mark Viller joins Rochdale Hornets in exchange for Logan Edwards .... Leeds sign South Sydney scrum half David Cruickshank .... Wigan extend their Regal Trophy final record to five wins with a 24-12 success over Halifax .... Carlisle start legal proceedings against stay-away skipper Harry Pinner .... Tommy Dawes resigns as coach of Carlisle .... St. Helens appoint New Zealander Mike McClennan as coach .... Oldham offer prop forward Neil Clawson for £30,000 and scrum half Alan Bates at £10,000 .... The League agree a contract with satellite television company BSB with Sunday matches kicking off live at 6.30pm .... Salford sign Army under-21 captain Tony Howard .... St. Helens chase £95,000-tagged Widnes winger Brimah Kebbie .... Workington Town fail in bid for Swinton utility man John Myler .... Businessman Ken Balmforth, preparing to launch a bid for a club at Brighouse, approaches Alex Murphy to be manager .... Auckland coach Cameron Bell, in line for the New Zealand national post, opts to take charge at Carlisle .... Great Britain Under-21s record a 22-0 victory over their French counterparts in Villeneuve .... Rochdale Hornets reject a Swinton swap proposal of stand off Steve Snape for Spotland prop forward Neil Cowie .... Rochdale Hornets fail in a bid to recruit Widnes forward Boblin Tuavea .... St. Helens have £10,000 fixture fine reduced to £8,000 on appeal .... Leeds in bid for Welsh RU double, Swansea's Tony Clement and Cardiff's David Young .... England B and Headingley centre Simon Irving joins Leeds .... Great Britain wingman Phil Ford listed at £90,000 after losing his first team place at Leeds.

FEBRUARY

Warrington transfer list David Myers only three months after his capture from Widnes .... Castleford offer Great Britain Under-21 packman Kenny Hill at £45,000 .... Leeds fail in £145,000 bid for Swansea stand off Tony Clement .... Hull K.R. winger Anthony Sullivan follows in the footsteps of late father Clive with Great Britain selection for the Under-21s .... Leeds sign 14-cap Welsh RU forward David Young on five-year £165,000 contract .... Wigan announce a record £280,000 profit .... Leigh fail to sign Hull's £90,000-rated full back Paul Fletcher on loan .... Wakefield Trinity trim asking price on full back Kevin Harcombe from £90,000 to £50,000 .... Alex Murphy offered job as coach of Barrow .... Hull K.R. line up Parramatta prop forward Peter Martin as replacement for New Zealander Tony Botica .... Halifax list want-away prop Brendan Hill at £105,000 .... Hull K.R. sign Kiwi tourist Dave Watson, currently serving Ryedale-York, on a five-year contract .... Featherstone Rovers recruit New Zealander Aaron Palelei from Nottingham City .... Oldham clinch signing of schoolboy star Chris Eckersley .... Ryedale-York offer to extend the contract of coach Gary Stephens until the end of 1992 .... Following secret talks with Soviet officials in London, the League reveals that Rugby League was being played by 11 Russian clubs with International Board recognition being sought in July .... Great Britain Under-21s gain a 1990 double with a 20-6 victory over France at Doncaster, the international celebrating the opening of floodlights at Tattersfield .... Featherstone Rovers sign Doncaster hooker Mark Gibbons for £20,000 .... Doncaster take Castleford's Kenny Hill on loan .... St. Helens sign New Zealander winger Mark Bourneville, currently serving French club Villeneuve .... Halifax list second row man Peter Bell at £20,000 .... Widnes and Andy Currier fail in a High Court action to secure an injunction against the League's eight-match ban .... Gary Charlton is unsuccessful in appeal against *sine die* ban .... David Cairns listed at £25,000 by Salford .... Dewsbury hand over £10,000 for Bradford Northern's Dean Hall .... Kiwi stand off Kelly Shelford fails to return from a trip home for Whitehaven's third round Silk Cut Challenge Cup tie at St. Helens .... Oldham agree terms with Widnes for winger Brimah Kebbie .... Leigh stand off David Ruane ruled out for the rest of the season with a punctured lung .... Oldham sign £100,000-rated Bramley winger Peter Lewis on loan until the end of the season with Neil Clawson going to McLaren Field .... Oldham coach Tony Barrow blasts the League for agreeing with BBC Television to a three-week gap between the Silk Cut Challenge Cup semi-finals.

MARCH

St. Helens' home fixture with Warrington abandoned after only four minutes when part

of the stand roof fell onto the pitch during a gale .... Oldham pull out of the race to sign Widnes winger Brimah Kebbie .... Nottingham City offer Chris Willis at £10,000 .... Bradford Northern part company with Australian coach Ron Willey and reappoint Tommy Smales and David Hobbs as caretaker coaches .... Halifax offer Australian centre Tony Anderson to Featherstone Rovers for £90,000, while placing price tags of £40,000 on John Lyons and £30,000 on Wilf George .... Alex Murphy rejoins Leigh as coach for the fourth time .... Oldham coach Tony Barrow fined £250, suspended for a year, for bringing the game into disrepute for comments regarding the staging of the Silk Cut Challenge Cup semi-finals .... Barrow appoint Steve Norton as coach .... Ryedale-York take Hull duo Paul Doherty and Paul Fletcher on loan .... Halifax reduce the asking price on prop forward Brendan Hill to £80,000 .... Oldham sign Halifax centre Tony Anderson for £70,000, a target for neighbours Rochdale .... Sheffield Eagles swoop to capture Leeds Test prop forward Hugh Waddell .... Leigh show an interest in French Test centre David Fraisse .... Nigel Stephenson resigns at Huddersfield after 18 months as coach .... Sacked Leigh coach Billy Benyon decides to take legal action .... Great Britain made to work hard for a record eighth successive win over France, by 8-4 .... Three Soviet teams to visit Britain in April, with two British club sides to play in Russia in the autumn .... Brimah Kebbie joins St. Helens .... Batley sign scrum half Paul Kay from Nottingham City for £10,000 .... Wakefield Trinity snap up Parramatta utility man Paul Taylor, surplus to the Australian salary cap system .... Australian coach Darryl Van de Velde signs a new two-year contract at Castleford .... Whitehaven agree to transfer requests from seven players after a 92-10 defeat at Hull K.R., captain Steve Howse topping the total of £280,000 fees at £90,000 .... Widnes discuss a deal with Australian Test skipper Wally Lewis .... Barry Seabourne appointed coach of Huddersfield .... Paul Daley decides to leave Batley at the end of the season .... Whitehaven sack coach Eric Fitzsimons .... Leeds cut the fee on Ray Ashton from £20,000 to £15,000 .... Rochdale Hornets hand over £20,000 for Castleford forward John Blackburn .... Halifax receive £100,000 from Widnes for loose forward Les Holliday .... Huddersfield offer England RU centre Jeremy Guscott a £300,000 package .... Warrington sign Kiwi hooker Duane Mann on a new two-year contract.

APRIL

BSB announce first-ever live television coverage of the summer tour of New Zealand .... Oldham skipper John Cogger returns to Australia because of his father's illness .... Under a Tribunal ruling, selection for his Great Britain debut raises Graham Steadman's transfer fee from Featherstone Rovers to Castleford to a record £170,000 .... Castleford's Australian trio Gary French, Jeff Hardy and Steve Larder re-sign for another season .... France pull off a shock 25-18 victory over Great Britain at Leeds .... Surprise Great Britain tour squad features nine uncapped players including Rugby Union converts Jonathan Davies and David Bishop, plus a record 10 Wigan players .... Featherstone Rovers veteran prop forward Jeff Grayshon plays against his 22-year old son Paul, propping for Bradford Northern .... Wigan lift the Stones Bitter Championship Trophy and £40,000 prize money, Hull K.R. taking the Second Division Bowl and £18,000 .... Injured Ellery Hanley, plus Steve Hampson and Les Holliday for personal reasons, withdraw from the British tour squad .... Malcolm Reilly calls in Chris Bibb, Karl Fairbank and Gary Price .... Widnes transfer list Mike O'Neill for £90,000 as a disciplinary

French captain Hugues Ratier shows off the British Coal Trophy after their shock victory over Great Britain at Leeds

measure .... Halifax players threaten to strike because of unpaid wages .... Leeds sign Halifax forward Neil James for £20,000 .... Halifax use the cash to pay outstanding players' payments .... Barrow list 10 players for a total of £330,000, loose forward Steve Maguire being top-priced at £90,000 .... Castleford put a £120,000 asking price on Test prop forward Kevin Ward .... Huddersfield loose forward Peter Subritzky joins Swinton for £10,000 .... The League provide their Australian counterparts with a list of players rejecting an invitation to tour Down Under, blocking any moves to play club football in Australia .... Wigan clinch a record club sponsorship worth up to £750,000 with bonuses over three years from current backer Norweb .... Rochdale Hornets agree a club record £75,000 for Widnes forward Mike O'Neill .... Debt-ridden Halifax face a £70,000 tax demand from the Inland Revenue .... Second Division champions Hull K.R. sign French Test second row man Daniel Divet .... Oldham offer £20,000 for St. Helens prop forward Austin Donegan .... Police drop assault charges against Hull K.R.'s David Bishop, clearing him for the British tour .... Wigan lift the Silk Cut Challenge Cup for a record third successive year, scrum half Andy Gregory earning the Lance Todd Trophy for a record-equalling second time .... Wigan stand off Shaun Edwards ruled out of the summer tour with a double fracture of the eye socket, having played in the Wembley final with a broken hand .... Warrington captain Mike Gregory declares himself doubtful for the tour with persistent ankle trouble .... Nearly 90 Russians arrive in Britain for a week-long education programme, including first-ever games against Leeds and Wigan reserves, plus Oulton amateurs.

MAY

Warrington prop forward Steve Molloy asks for a transfer after being dropped for the Silk Cut Challenge Cup final .... Troubled by a toe injury, Widnes winger Martin Offiah pledges to join the Great Britain tour party for the three British Coal Tests in New Zealand .... Nearly 90 Russians spend a week in Britain learning the basics of Rugby League .... In the first-ever Soviet game on British soil, Leningrad gain a 40-23 victory over Oulton amateurs in Leeds .... Wigan having won both the League and the Challenge Cup, the League decide that the Stones Bitter Premiership winners will meet them in the 1990 CIS Insurance Charity Shield .... Leigh recruit £120,000-rated Swinton full back Paul Topping, in exchange for £100,000-tagged prop Tim Street, ex-Great Britain full back Chris Johnson and stand off John Kerr .... Oldham beat neighbours Rochdale Hornets for St. Helens prop forward Austin Donegan, paying the full fee of £20,000 .... Having left Batley, Paul Daley returns to Hunslet for a third spell as coach, having previously served a total of eight years .... The Australian League pull out of the 1990 Foster's World Club Challenge against newly-crowned British Champions Wigan because of Kangaroo tour commitments .... Injured British Lion tourists Shaun Edwards and Andy Platt replaced by Daryl Powell and Paul Dixon .... Russians' first experience of professional Rugby League is gained at Headingley where Moscow Magicians are defeated 34-16 by a Leeds reserve team .... In the last of three matches, Russian side Tiraspol register a 24-24 draw at Central Park against a Wigan reserve side .... Australian Premiership outfit Gold Coast sign Leeds loose forward Gary Divorty and Castleford prop forward Dean Sampson on summer contracts .... Wakefield Trinity skipper Keith Rayne appointed player-coach of Batley .... Warrington cite Wigan's Joe Lydon for an illegal tackle on scrum half Paul Bishop in the Silk Cut Challenge Cup final .... Leeds, Widnes and Sydney club Manly show interest in out-of-contract Wigan stand off Shaun Edwards ....

Warrington captain Mike Gregory named as skipper of the Great Britain touring party with Garry Schofield as vice-captain .... Wakefield Trinity ask £60,000 for centre Phil Eden and put Kiwi James Leuluai on offer .... Huddersfield hand over £8,000 for Ryedale-York prop forward Dean Mountain .... Prop Ian Fletcher priced at £15,000 by Doncaster .... Great Britain call up Hull K.R. winger Anthony Sullivan and Bradford Northern utility back Roger Simpson for tour duty .... Bradford Northern officially confirm the coaching appointment of David Hobbs .... An ankle operation rules Joe Lydon out of the Papua New Guinea leg of the tour Down Under .... Great Britain and Wigan stand off Shaun Edwards named as 1990 Stones Bitter Man of Steel .... Hull K.R. plans to sign Carcassonne second row man Daniel Divet hit by Rugby League Council's decision not to exempt EEC players from the quota system .... Widnes full back Alan Tait becomes the first player to be awarded the Harry Sunderland Trophy twice as Widnes record a first-ever hat-trick of Stones Bitter Premiership titles, beating Bradford Northern 28-6 at Manchester United's Old Trafford .... In the Second Division Premiership final, Oldham come back from trailing 29-8 to register a 30-29 victory .... Wigan decide not to re-engage out-of-contract New Zealand Test prop Adrian Shelford .... Wigan selected as Stones Bitter Team of the Year, receiving a prize cheque for £1,500 .... Utility back David Myers, subject of a tug-of-war between Widnes and Warrington, joins Wigan .... Carlisle put eight players on offer, headed by top-priced Dave Kendall and Gary Murdock at £60,000 each .... Rugby League Board of Directors decide that Warrington's citation of Joe Lydon should not proceed further .... Huddersfield pay a club record £12,500 for Castleford winger Chris Chapman .... Great Britain open their five-match tour of Papua New Guinea with a 40-18 success over Southern Zone at Port Moresby .... Hull K.R.'s Anthony Sullivan sent home from the tour Down Under with a torn hamstring .... All Black full back John Gallagher, newly-crowned International RU Player of the Year, signs for Leeds in a five-year £350,000 deal .... Great Britain call up Widnes threequarter John Devereux for tour duty .... Great Britain tourist Kelvin Skerrett sent to Sydney for an exploratory operation on an injured knee .... Locked out crowds riot as Britain beat Northern Zones 24-10 at Lae .... Jonathan Davies selected for his Test debut against Papua New Guinea along with Paul Eastwood, Bobby Goulding and Lee Jackson .... Leeds target Balmain half back Gary Freeman .... Financial crisis club Halifax face winding-up action .... Great Britain suffer shock 20-18 defeat by Papua New Guinea in the first British Coal Test at Goroka amid scenes of tear gas and crowd riots .... The Rugby League World Cup, stolen in 1970, is found in a ditch near Bingley by Stephen Uttley of Bradford .... Great Britain beat Island Zones 50-4 at Raboul .... Wigan sign All Black RU utility player Frano Botica .... Warrington recruit Wales B and Bridgend scrum half Kevin Ellis .... Headingley RU scrum half Neil Summers turns professional with Bradford Northern .... Ryedale-York sign Kiwi pair James Leuluai, from Wakefield Trinity, and Tawera Nikau, who had played for Sheffield Eagles in the latter part of the 1989-90 season.

Centre Steve McGowan, scorer of 14 tries in 36 games for Bradford Northern, finalists in the Stones Bitter Premiership and the John Smiths Yorkshire Cup.

Prop forward Jeff Grayshon, who made 36 appearances for Featherstone Rovers in 1989-90 despite celebrating his 41st birthday in March.

Evergreen half back Neil Holding, four tries in 19 appearances for St. Helens.

CLUBS

The following is a focus on the 35 professional Rugby League clubs, the section providing each club with a profile and an analysis of their 1989-90 campaign on a match by match basis with a summary for each first team player.

KEY

In the individual club profiles the following headings are featured:

First season refers to when the club gained senior league status. In some instances clubs have disbanded and re-formed, sometimes under different titles. For record purposes these changes are ignored except where there has been a break of more than one full season.

Honours. Until they were scrapped in 1970, the Yorkshire and Lancashire Leagues were among the honours in the professional game. Before 1903 they operated under the title of the Yorkshire and Lancashire Senior Competitions. Winners of these senior competitions are listed under Yorkshire and Lancashire League Champions. The pre-1903 Yorkshire Senior Competition should not be confused with the league operating for A-teams in Yorkshire which had the same title.

Regal Trophy is the new title for the John Player/Player's No. 6 Trophy competition.

Coaches. Changes in the appointment of a club's coach since 1 June 1989 are shown in brackets.

Attendances. Crowds in brackets are at neutral venue.

Appearances. Players' totals are based on official teamsheets submitted to the League after each first team match. + indicates playing substitute appearance.

In the match by match review for each club the following abbreviations are used:

YC	—	Yorkshire Cup	A	—	Away
LC	—	Lancashire Cup	W	—	Won
SBC	—	Stones Bitter Championship	L	—	Lost
SD	—	Second Division	D	—	Drawn
RT	—	Regal Trophy	dg	—	Drop goal
CC	—	Challenge Cup	Fr	—	France
PT	—	Premiership Trophy	Aus	—	Australia
SDP	—	Second Division Premiership	NZ	—	New Zealand
P	—	Preliminary Round	PNG	—	Papua New Guinea
H	—	Home	Pr	—	Probationer

CLUBS

BARROW

Ground: Craven Park
Colours: Royal blue
First Season: 1900-01
Nickname: Shipbuilders
Chairman: John Gilbert
Coach: Rod Reddy (Nov 1987-Nov 1989)
Dennis Jackson (Nov 1989-Apr 1990)
Steve Norton (May 1990-)
Honours: **Challenge Cup** Winners, 1954-55
Beaten finalists, 1937-38, 1950-51, 1956-57, 1966-67
Regal Trophy Beaten finalists 1980-81
Lancashire Cup Winners, 1954-55, 1983-84
Beaten finalists, 1937-38
Division Two Champions, 1975-76, 1983-84
Records: Attendance: 21,651 v. Salford (League) 15 Apr, 1938
Season
Goals: 135 by J. Ball, 1956-57
Tries: 50 by J. Lewthwaite, 1956-57
Points: 305 by I. Ball, 1979-80
Match
Goals: 12 by F. French v. Maryport, 19 Feb, 1938; W. Horne v. Cardiff, 8 Sep, 1951; S. Tickle v. Kent Invicta, 8 Apr, 1984
Tries: 6 by V. Cumberbatch v. Batley, 21 Nov, 1936; J. Thornburrow v. Maryport, 19 Feb, 1938; F. Castle v. York, 29 Sep, 1951
Points: 28 by K. Jarrett v. Doncaster, 25 Aug, 1970; S. Tickle v. Kent Invicta, 8 Apr, 1984; D. Marwood at Runcorn H., 16 Apr, 1989
Highest score: 83-3 v. Maryport, 1937-38
Highest against: 90-0 v. Leeds, 1989-90

1989-90 PLAYERS' SUMMARY

	App	Tries	Goals	Dr	Pts
Beckwith, Mark	21	2	—	—	8
Blackwood, Mark	1	—	—	—	—
Burney, Steve	1 + 1	—	—	—	—
Burns, Paul	12 + 2	2	—	—	8
Clayton, Steve	22 +1	—	—	—	—
Crarey, Paul	29	1	—	—	4
Creary, Richard	1	—	—	—	—
Cummings, Robert	0 + 2	1	—	—	4
Cussack, Jeremy	8	1	—	—	4
Freeman, Ian	1	—	—	—	—
Godfrey, Heath	1	—	—	—	—
Hadley, Derek	5 + 1	—	—	—	—
Heugh, Cavill	14	8	—	—	32
Irving, Paul	3	—	—	—	—
James, Mick	5 + 1	—	—	—	—
Johns, Chris	12	3	—	—	12
Kendall, Gary	19 + 3	3	—	—	12
Livesey, Dave	5 + 1	—	—	—	—
Maguire, Steve	19 + 3	1	9	—	22
Marshall, Ken	5	—	4	—	8
Marwood, Dean	20 + 3	1	23	1	51
Morrison, Steve	8 + 1	1	—	—	4
Moses, Alan	0 + 1	—	—	—	—
Mossop, Steve	9 + 1	—	—	—	—
O'Neill, Ian	16	2	—	—	8
O'Neill, Kevin	4 + 1	—	—	—	—
Pemberton, Keith	9 + 8	1	—	—	4
Phillips, Joe	3	1	—	—	4
Potts, Martin	1	—	—	—	—
Richardson, Dave	1 + 3	—	—	—	—
Roper, Kevin	1	—	—	—	—
Ross, Lachlan	2 + 2	1	—	—	4
Rowan, Steve	7 + 7	—	—	—	—
Shaw, Neil	21 + 3	1	—	—	4
Stott, Phil	16 + 1	—	—	—	—
Tees, Gary	6 + 2	3	—	—	12
Thompson, Phil	5	—	—	—	—
Thurlow, Jason	3 + 2	—	—	—	—
Tickle, Steve	2 + 1	—	—	—	—
Trainor, Patrick	27	2	—	—	8
Tuavao, Boblin	9	2	—	—	8
Tuavao, Hami	4	—	—	—	—
Walker, Russ	16	—	—	—	—
Williams, Stewart	3	—	—	—	—

TOTALS:
44 players...................... | | 37 | 36 | 1 | 221 |

Former Test loose forward Steve Norton, who took over as coach of Barrow in May 1990.

1989-90 MATCH ANALYSIS

Date	Com-petition	H/A	Opponent	Rlt	Score	Tries	Goals	Atten-dance	Referee
3.9.89	SBC	A	Leigh	L	16-42	Heugh, Tees, Kendall	Marwood (2)	—	—
10.9.89	SBC	H	Leeds	L	10-32	Tees, Kendall	Marwood	3143	Tennant
17.9.89	LC(1)	H	Oldham	L	2-46	—	Maguire	2253	Carter
24.9.89	SBC	H	Sheffield E.	L	10-22	Shaw, Morrison	Maguire	1417	Cross
1.10.89	SBC	H	Wigan	L	0-66	—	—	4972	Galtress
8.10.89	SBC	A	Bradford N.	L	24-36	Phillips, Heugh, Pemberton, Kendall	Marshall (4)	—	—
15.10.89	SBC	A	Wigan	L	6-62	Trainor	Maguire	—	—
24.10.89	SBC	H	Warrington	L	0-9	—	—	1909	Crashley
29.10.89	SBC	A	Featherstone R.	W	29-22	Johns (2), Maguire, Beckwith, Heugh	Marwood (4, 1dg)	—	—
5.11.89	SBC	H	Wakefield T.	L	10-26	Beckwith, Tees	Marwood	2107	McCallum (Aus)
12.11.89	SBC	A	St. Helens	L	18-62	Heugh (3)	Maguire (3)	—	—
19.11.89	SBC	H	Salford	L	2-36	—	Maguire	1801	Crashley
26.11.89	SBC	A	Wakefield T.	L	16-30	Heugh (2), Johns	Maguire (2)	—	—
3.12.89	RT(1)	A	Hunslet	L	6-10	Cussack	Marwood	—	—
17.12.89	SBC	H	Widnes	L	4-34	—	Marwood (2)	2124	Kendrew
21.12.89	SBC	A	Widnes	L	0-48	—	—	—	—
7.1.90	SBC	A	Hull	L	0-48	—	—	—	—
14.1.90	SBC	A	Warrington	L	6-58	I. O'Neill	Marwood	—	—
21.1.90	SBC	H	Featherstone R.	L	0-46	—	—	1289	Crashley
28.1.90	CC(1)	H	Sheffield E.	L	12-22	Trainor, I. O'Neill	Marwood (2)	—	Whitfield
2.2.90	SBC	A	Salford	L	4-36	Burns	—	—	—
11.2.90	SBC	A	Leeds	L	0-90	—	—	—	—
18.2.90	SBC	H	St. Helens	L	6-46	B. Tuavao	Marwood	2168	Crashley
25.2.90	SBC	A[1]	Sheffield E.	L	2-40	—	Marwood	—	—
4.3.90	SBC	H	Hull	L	6-38	B. Tuavao	Marwood	1080	Holdsworth
11.3.90	SBC	H	Leigh	L	6-44	Crarey	Marwood	1293	Campbell
18.3.90	SBC	H	Castleford	L	14-42	Marwood, Burns	Marwood (3)	1170	Cross
25.3.90	SBC	A	Castleford	L	6-58	Cummings	Marwood	—	—
1.4.90	SBC	H	Bradford N.	L	6-60	Ross	Marwood	1483	Tennant

[1] at Doncaster

BATLEY

Ground: Mount Pleasant
Colours: Cerise and fawn
First Season: 1895-96
Nickname: Gallant Youths
Chairman: Stephen Ball
Coach: Paul Daley (July 1987-Apr 1990)
Keith Rayne (May 1990-)
Honours: **Championship** Winners, 1923-24
Challenge Cup Winners, 1896-97,
1897-98, 1900-01
Yorkshire League Winners,
1898-99, 1923-24
Yorkshire Cup Winners, 1912-13
Beaten finalists, 1909-10, 1922-23,
1924-25, 1952-53
Records: Attendance: 23,989 v. Leeds
(RL Cup) 14 Mar, 1925
Season
Goals: 120 by S. Thompson,
1958-59
Tries: 29 by J. Tindall, 1912-13
Points: 281 by J. Perry, 1950-51
Match
Goals: 9 by W. Davies v. Widnes,
27 Mar, 1909; S. Thompson v.
Keighley, 20 Sep, 1958
Tries: 5 by J. Oakland v. Bramley,
19 Dec, 1908; T. Brannan v.
Swinton, 17 Jan, 1920; J. Wale v.
Bramley, 4 Dec, 1926 and v.
Cottingham, 12 Feb, 1927
Points: 26 by J. Perry v. Liverpool
C., 16 Sep, 1951
Highest score: 52-8 v. Widnes,
1908-09
Highest against: 78-9 v. Wakefield
T., 1967-68

1989-90 PLAYERS' SUMMARY

	App	Tries	Goals	Dr	Pts
Arnold, Derek	1	—	—	—	—
Bowness, Mark	5	1	—	—	4
Cook, Mark	16 + 8	4	—	—	16
Fortis, Mark	10 + 6	2	—	—	8
Gearey, Paul	29	22	—	—	88
Halloran, Paul	1 + 4	—	—	1	1
Hartley, Neil	5 + 9	1	—	—	4
Heron, Wayne	4	1	—	—	4
Hinchliffe, Mark	26 + 1	1	—	—	4
Kay, Paul	2 + 2	3	—	—	12
Langton, Steve	1	—	—	—	—
Mackay, Gary	0 + 4	—	—	—	—
Marshall, Paul	17	2	—	—	8
McGowan, John	13	5	—	—	20
McGrath, Damien	8	2	15	—	38
Parkinson, Andy	6 + 5	1	—	—	4
Perry, David	4	1	—	—	4
Sanderson, Mark	0 + 1	—	—	—	—
Scott, Mark	28	8	—	—	32
Smith, Gary	10 + 10	3	—	—	12
Speight, Mark	30 + 2	—	—	—	—
Spendler, Mark	33	2	—	—	8
Stainburn, John	33	1	42	6	94
Storey, Paul	33	—	—	—	—
Subritzky, Dean	2 + 1	1	—	—	4
Waites, Brian	31	10	—	—	40
Wilkinson, Mark	2	—	—	—	—
Williams, Andrew	33	16	—	—	64
Wilson, Simon	30	11	20	1	85
Wood, Mark	0 + 4	—	—	—	—
Wragg, Nicky	16 + 5	4	—	—	16

TOTALS:
31 players		102	77	8	570

Former Test forward Keith Rayne, appointed Batley coach in May 1990.

1989-90 MATCH ANALYSIS

Date	Competition	H/A	Opponent	Rlt	Score	Tries	Goals	Attendance	Referee
3.9.89	SD	H	Nottingham C.	W	20-11	Wilson (2), Scott	Stainburn (4)	1022	Bowman
6.9.89	SD	A	Runcorn H.	W	9-0	McGowan, Waites	Stainburn (dg)	—	—
10.9.89	SD	H	Ryedale-York	L	8-18	Waites	McGrath (2)	1417	Smith
17.9.89	YC(1)	H	Sheffield E.	L	5-36	Smith	Halloren (dg)	1299	Smith
24.9.89	SD	H	Bramley	W	30-12	Waites (2), Wragg, Williams, Scott	Stainburn (5)	1046	Whitelam
1.10.89	SD	A	Hunslet	W	23-12	Smith (2), Williams, McGowan	Stainburn (3, 1dg)	—	—
8.10.89	SD	H	Swinton	L	0-18	—	—	1396	Crashley
15.10.89	SD	A	Nottingham C.	W	29-10	Williams (3), Wilson, McGrath	Stainburn (4, 1dg)	—	—
22.10.89	SD	H	Whitehaven	W	21-6	Waites, Gearey, Williams	Stainburn (4, 1dg)	987	Burke
29.10.89	SD	A	Oldham	L	4-22	McGowan		—	—
5.11.89	SD	A	Keighley	W	22-8	Wilson, Gearey, Spendler	Stainburn (3), Wilson (2)	—	—
12.11.89	SD	H	Runcorn H.	W	46-14	Williams (4), Wilson (2), Hartley, McGowan, Scott	Stainburn (5)	1090	Galtress
19.11.89	RT(P)	H	West Hull	W	28-14	Gearey (2), McGowan, Williams, Scott, Perry	Stainburn, Wilson	844	Steele
26.11.89	SD	H	Fulham	L	10-12	Williams	Stainburn (3)	997	K. Morris
3.12.89	RT(1)	A	Swinton	L	16-18	Wilson, Bownass, Williams	Stainburn, McGrath	—	—
10.12.89	SD	A	Workington T.	W	28-17	Scott (2), Fortis, Williams, Wilson	McGrath (4)	—	—
17.12.89	SD	H	Trafford B.	W	12-11	Fortis, Cook	McGrath (2)	876	Burke
26.12.89	SD	H	Dewsbury	W	18-6	Williams, Marshall, Gearey, Waites	McGrath	3248	Allatt
31.12.89	SD	A	Dewsbury	L	8-22	Gearey (2)	—	—	—
7.1.90	SD	A	Bramley	L	10-18	Gearey (2)	Stainburn	—	—
12.1.90	CC(P)	A[1]	Thatto Heath	W	45-2	Gearey (3), Cook, Wilson, Waites, Spendler, Scott, Wragg	Stainburn (4, 1dg)	—	—
21.1.90	SD	A	Fulham	L	14-17	Gearey, Wilson	Stainburn (3)	—	—
28.1.90	CC(1)	A	Widnes	L	10-26	Gearey (2)	Wilson	—	—
4.2.90	SD	A	Trafford B.	L	12-18	Gearey, Scott	Wilson (2)	—	—
11.2.90	SD	H	Hunslet	L	16-22	Gearey (2), Stainburn	Wilson (2)	1207	Tidball
25.2.90	SD	H	Workington T.	W	46-6	Gearey (4), Williams, Waites, Cook, Subritzky	Wilson (7)	859	Carter
4.3.90	SD	A	Swinton	L	3-20	—	Wilson (1, 1dg)	—	—
11.3.90	SD	H	Oldham	L	14-30	Wilson, Marshall, Waites	Wilson	2800	Kershaw
18.3.90	SD	A	Halifax	L	12-42	Waites, Heron	Wilson (2)	—	—
25.3.90	SD	H	Halifax	L	2-16	—	Wilson	3200	Holdsworth
1.4.90	SD	A	Whitehaven	L	6-30	Kay	Stainburn	—	—
4.4.90	SD	H	Keighley	W	37-16	Kay (2), Wragg (2), McGrath, Cook, Parkinson	McGrath (4, 1dg)	944	Simpson
16.4.90	SD	A	Ryedale-York	L	6-44	Hinchcliffe	McGrath	—	—

[1] at St. Helens

BRADFORD NORTHERN

Ground: Odsal Stadium
Colours: White, red, amber and black
First Season: 1895-96 as "Bradford". Disbanded
             and became Bradford Northern in
             1907-08. Disbanded during 1963-64
             and re-formed for start of 1964-65
Nickname: Northern
Chairman: Chris Caisley
Secretary: Gary Tasker
Coach: Barry Seabourne (May 1985-Sep
             1989)
             Ron Willey (Oct 1989-Mar 1990)
             David Hobbs (Mar 1990-)
Honours: **Challenge Cup** Winners, 1905-06,
             1943-44, 1946-47, 1948-49
             Beaten finalists, 1897-98, 1944-45,
             1947-48, 1972-73
             Championship Beaten finalists,
             1947-48, 1951-52
             Division One Champions, 1903-04,
             1979-80, 1980-81
             Division Two Champions, 1973-74
             War-time Emergency League
             Championship winners, 1939-40,
             1940-41, 1944-45
             Beaten finalists, 1941-42
             Yorkshire League Winners,
             1899-1900, 1900-01, 1939-40,
             1940-41, 1947-48
             Yorkshire Cup Winners, 1906-07,
             1940-41, 1941-42, 1943-44,
             1945-46, 1948-49, 1949-50,
             1953-54, 1965-66, 1978-79,
             1987-88, 1989-90
             Beaten finalists, 1913-14, 1981-82,
             1982-83
             Premiership Winners, 1977-78
             Beaten finalists, 1978-79, 1979-80,
             1989-90
             Regal Trophy Winners, 1974-75,
             1979-80
Records: Attendance: 102,569 Warrington v.
             Halifax (RL Cup Final replay)
             5 May, 1954
             Home: 69,429 v. Huddersfield
             (RL Cup) 14 March, 1953

Season
Goals: 173 by E. Tees, 1971-72
Tries: 63 by J. McLean, 1951-52
Points: 364 by E. Tees, 1971-72
Match
Goals: 14 by J. Phillips v. Batley,
6 Sep, 1952
Tries: 7 by J. Dechan v. Bramley,
13 Oct, 1906
Points: 36 by J. Woods v. Swinton,
13 Oct, 1985
Highest score: 72-9 v. Doncaster,
1973-74; 72-12 v. Hunslet, 1984-85
Highest against: 75-18 v. Leeds,
1931-32

1989-90 PLAYERS' SUMMARY

	App	Tries	Goals	Dr	Pts
Barnett, Steve	0 + 2	—	—	—	—
Barraclough, Glenn	23 + 1	1	—	—	4
Cooper, David	2 + 5	—	3	1	7
Cordle, Gerald	36	31	—	—	124
Croft, David	4 + 1	—	—	—	—
Fairbank, Karl	29 + 2	11	—	—	44
Francis, Richard	23 + 5	9	—	—	36
Gill, Henderson	8 + 2	6	—	—	24
Grayshon, Paul	4	—	—	—	—
Green, Alex	0 + 1	—	—	—	—
Hall, Darren	0 + 1	—	—	—	—
Hall, Steve	1 + 1	1	—	—	4
Hamer, Jon	11	1	—	—	4
Harkin, Paul	37	7	1	12	42
Hellewell, Phil	1 + 2	1	—	—	4
Henjak, Ivan	15	1	—	—	4
Hobbs, David	35 + 1	5	95	5	215
Johnson, Errol	4 + 2	—	—	—	—
Mackay, Graham	17 + 1	—	—	—	—
Marchant, Tony	22	12	—	—	48
McGowan, Steve	36	14	—	—	56
Medley, Paul	21 + 6	13	—	—	52
Moxon, Darren	1 + 1	1	—	—	4
Mumby, Keith	24 + 3	1	26	—	56
Noble, Brian	23	—	—	—	—
Pendlebury, John	16 + 1	3	1	—	14
Rhodes, Paul	1	—	—	—	—
Richards, Craig	7 + 6	—	—	—	—
Roebuck, Neil	5	2	—	—	8
Simpson, Roger	32 + 1	8	—	—	32
Skerrett, Kelvin	27 + 2	6	—	—	24
Snee, Gavin	5 + 1	—	—	—	—
Stewart, Russell	24 + 4	—	—	—	—
Tuffs, Neil	6 + 4	1	—	—	4
Wilkinson, Ian	28	4	—	—	16
Wilson, Mark	3 + 9	2	—	—	8
TOTALS:					
36 players		150	131	18	880

1989-90 MATCH ANALYSIS

Date	Competition	H/A	Opponent	Rlt	Score	Tries	Goals	Attendance	Referee
3.9.89	SBC	H	Hull	W	30-12	Medley (2), Cordle, Mackay, Harkin	Hobbs (5)	6458	Tennant
10.9.89	SBC	A	Warrington	L	17-18	Medley, Fairbank	Hobbs (3, 1dg), Harkin (2dg)	—	—
17.9.89	YC(1)	A	Leeds	W	15-8	Wilkinson, Cordle	Hobbs (3), Harkin (dg)	—	—
24.9.89	SBC	H	St. Helens	W	28-18	McGowan, Mackay, Hamer, Fairbank, Pendlebury	Hobbs (4)	6552	Whitfield
27.9.89	YC(2)	H	Sheffield E.	W	19-6	Francis, Harkin, McGowan	Hobbs (3), Harkin (dg)	4210	Tennant
1.10.89	SBC	A	Salford	W	36-12	Cordle, Medley, Fairbank, Francis, Hobbs, Wilson	Hobbs (6)	—	—
5.10.89	YC(SF)	A	Halifax	D	16-16	McGowan, Medley, Wilkinson	Hobbs, Mackay	—	—
8.10.89	SBC	H	Barrow	W	36-24	Cordle (2), McGowan (2), Simpson, Francis, Henjak	Mumby (2), Harkin, Pendlebury	3747	Kershaw
11.10.89	Tour	H	New Zealand	L	8-26	Mackay (2)	—	3498	Kendrew
15.10.89	YC(SF) Replay	H	Halifax	W	26-4	Cordle, Fairbank, Pendlebury, Medley	Hobbs (5)	12,748	Kershaw
29.10.89	SBC	H	Leigh	W	30-10	Hobbs, Medley, Fairbank, Pendlebury, Cordle, Francis	Hobbs (3)	3990	Crashley
5.11.89	YC(F)	Leeds	Featherstone R.	W	20-14	Harkin (2), Cordle (2)	Hobbs (2)	(12,607)	Whitfield
8.11.89	SBC	A	Castleford	L	13-32	Mackay, Simpson	Mackay (2), Harkin (dg)	—	—
15.11.89	SBC	H	Wigan	L	15-16	Roebuck, Fairbank	Hobbs (3, 1dg)	6930	Tennant
19.11.89	SBC	A¹	Sheffield E.	W	34-14	Simpson (2), Cordle (2), McGowan (2)	Hobbs (5)	—	—
26.11.89	SBC	H	Leeds	W	14-13	Roebuck, Cordle	Hobbs (2, 1dg), Harkin (dg)	11,441	Whitfield
3.12.89	RT(1)	H	Keighley	W	38-10	Cordle (4), Wilkinson, McGowan, Francis, Mackay	Hobbs (3)	3260	Burke
10.12.89	RT(2)	A	Leeds	L	8-27	—	Hobbs (4)	—	—
3.1.90	SBC	H	Castleford	W	24-16	Mackay (3), Marchant	Hobbs (4)	5065	C. Morris
7.1.90	SBC	A	Wigan	L	0-12	—	—	—	—
14.1.90	CC(P)	A	Leeds	W	24-8	McGowan (2), Harkin, Skerrett	Hobbs (3, 1dg), Harkin (dg)	—	—
17.1.90	SBC	H	Widnes	W	16-6	McGowan, Marchant, Skerrett	Mackay (2)	5279	Crashley
21.1.90	SBC	A	Leeds	L	8-13	Cordle, Simpson	—	—	—
28.1.90	CC(1)	A	Runcorn H.	W	22-12	Marchant, McGowan, Tuffs	Hobbs (5)	—	—
31.1.90	SBC	A	St. Helens	L	10-32	Wilson, Moxon	Hobbs	—	—
4.2.90	SBC	A	Leigh	L	16-22	Marchant, Hall, Hobbs	Hobbs (2)	—	—
11.2.90	CC(2)	A	Fulham	W	20-2	Cordle (3), Gill	Hobbs (2)	—	—
18.2.90	SBC	H	Featherstone R.	W	32-10	Cordle (2), Marchant, Gill, Hobbs, Medley	Hobbs (4)	5745	Holdsworth
25.2.90	CC(3)	H	Warrington	L	10-12	Cordle, Gill	Hobbs	9114	Whitfield
28.2.90	SBC	A	Hull	L	0-24	—	—	—	—
4.3.90	SBC	H	Salford	W	18-12	Cordle, Gill	Hobbs (5)	3459	C. Morris
11.3.90	SBC	A	Widnes	W	40-14	Fairbank (2), Marchant, Cordle, Simpson, Wilkinson	Hobbs (7), Harkin (2dg)	—	—
18.3.90	SBC	H	Sheffield E.	W	28-16	Marchant (2), Simpson (2), Hellewell	Hobbs (4)	4354	Holdsworth
25.3.90	SBC	H	Warrington	W	38-10	Skerrett (2), Gill, Marchant, Fairbank, Medley	Hobbs (5), Mumby (2)	4293	Whitfield
1.4.90	SBC	A	Barrow	W	60-6	McGowan (2), Marchant, Fairbank, Medley, Hobbs, Harkin, Gill, Mumby, Cordle, Francis	Mumby (8)	—	—

(continued on page 108)

BRAMLEY

Ground:	McLaren Field
Colours:	Amber and black
First Season:	1896-97
Nickname:	Villagers
Chairman:	Jeff Wine
Secretary:	Barry Rennison
Coach:	Barry Johnson (Mar 1989-)
Honours:	**BBC2 Floodlit Trophy** Winners, 1973-74
Records:	Attendance: 12,600 v. Leeds (League) 7 May, 1947

Season
Goals: 130 by J. Wilson, 1961-62
Tries: 34 by P. Lister, 1985-86
Points: 276 by G. Langfield, 1956-57

Match
Goals: 11 by B. Ward v. Doncaster, 1 Sep, 1974
Tries: 7 by J. Sedgewick v. Normanton, 16 Apr, 1906
Points: 28 by B. Ward v. Doncaster, 1 Sep, 1974
Highest score: 62-14 v. Dewsbury, 1988-89
Highest against: 92-7 v. Australia, 1921-22

1989-90 PLAYERS' SUMMARY

	App	Tries	Goals	Dr	Pts
Atkins, Ken	0 + 2	—	—	—	—
Barnett, Gary	16 + 6	2	—	—	8
Bibb, Trevor	4 + 1	—	—	—	—
Bowie, Iain	1	—	—	—	—
Brentley, Gary	28 + 1	3	—	—	12
Carroll, Steve	29	7	68	11	175
Clawson, Neil	7	2	—	—	8
Cook, Terry	10 + 1	4	—	—	16
Crawford, Adrian	2 + 1	—	—	—	—
Durham, Steve	18 + 2	5	—	—	20
Edmondson, Steve	8 + 6	—	—	—	—
Ellis, Andy	5 + 1	—	—	—	—
Fletcher, Paul	1 + 5	1	—	—	4
Fraser, Paul	26 + 2	1	—	—	4
Gascoigne, Andy	6 + 2	1	—	—	4
Gibson, Andy	0 + 1	—	—	—	—
Greentree, William	1	—	—	—	—
Gutherson, John	0 + 1	—	—	—	—
Hart, Alan	2 + 1	—	—	—	—
Harwood, Dean	2 + 1	—	—	—	—
Hemingway, Neil	9 + 1	—	—	—	—
Hobbs, Gary	3	—	—	—	—
Holden, Barry	2 + 1	—	—	—	—
Hopkins, Calvin	21	4	—	—	16
Hunter, Damian	8 + 1	4	—	—	16
Illingworth, Neil	11	1	—	—	4
Johnson, Barry	8	—	—	—	—
Kain, John	15 + 1	4	—	—	16
Kilner, Shaun	4 + 5	—	—	—	—
Korn, Steve	7	2	—	—	8
Langley, Paul	2	—	—	—	—
Lewis, Peter	4 + 1	—	—	—	—
Lidbury, Steve	7	2	—	—	8
Lister, Peter	22	8	—	1	33
Neal, Lex	29	6	—	1	25
Olpherts, Eric	0 + 1	—	—	—	—
Owen, Phil	3 + 2	—	—	—	—
Pitts, David	5 + 2	2	5	—	18
Race, Wayne	23 + 1	2	—	—	8
Robinson, Steve	2 + 6	—	—	—	—
Rodgers, Jeremy	7	2	10	—	28
Sharp, Ronnie	14	5	—	—	20
Spedding, Paul	27	1	—	—	4
Thornton, Wayne	4 + 2	—	—	—	—

TOTALS:
44 players		69	83	13	455

Winger Steve Lidbury, two tries in seven appearances.

1989-90 MATCH ANALYSIS

Date	Com-petition	H/A	Opponent	Rlt	Score	Tries	Goals	Atten-dance	Referee
3.9.89	SD	A	Hunslet	L	14-22	Rogers, Hunter	Rogers (3)	–	–
10.9.89	SD	H	Doncaster	L	2-12	–	Rogers	1433	Kendrew
17.9.89	YC(1)	H	Hull K.R.	L	12-54	Hunter, Carroll	Rogers (2)	1545	Tennant
24.9.89	SD	A	Batley	L	12-30	Lister, Durham	Rogers (2)	–	–
1.10.89	SD	H	Rochdale H.	L	17-46	Durham (2), Carroll	Rogers (2), Carroll (dg)	1084	Campbell
8.10.89	SD	H	Chorley	W	46-10	Neal (2), Hunter, Illingworth, Durham, Race, Gascoigne, Carroll	Carroll (7)	569	Smith
15.10.89	SD	A	Workington T.	W	20-12	Carroll, Hunter, Frazer	Carroll (4)	–	–
22.10.89	SD	A	Fulham	L	6-16	Brentley	Carroll	–	–
29.10.89	SD	H	Halifax	L	10-46	Neal	Carroll (3)	2872	K. Morris
5.11.89	SD	A	Swinton	L	11-30	Carroll, Kain	Carroll, Neal (dg)	–	–
12.11.89	SD	H	Fulham	L	0-17	–	–	574	Cross
19.11.89	SD	A	Runcorn H.	W	12-11	Kain, Hopkins	Carroll (2)	–	–
26.11.89	SD	H	Huddersfield	L	2-14	–	Carroll	910	Holgate
3.12.89	RT(1)	H	Oldham	L	16-48	Cook, Sharp	Carroll (4)	1632	Asquith
17.12.89	SD	A	Rochdale H.	W	25-18	Neal (2), Lister, Cook	Carroll (4, 1dg)	–	–
26.12.89	SD	H	Keighley	W	15-8	Cook	Carroll (5, 1dg)	832	Whitelam
31.12.89	SD	A	Halifax	L	10-30	Carroll	Carroll (3)	–	–
7.1.90	SD	H	Batley	W	18-10	Kain, Barnett, Lister	Carroll (3)	1046	Carter
14.1.90	SD	H	Workington T.	W	27-18	Durham, Kain, Race, Spedding	Carroll (5, 1dg)	450	Tickle
21.1.90	SD	A	Carlisle	W	21-18	Sharp (2), Cook, Hopkins	Carroll (2, 1dg)	–	–
28.1.90	CC(1)	H	St. Helens	L	14-22	Hopkins, Neal	Carroll (3)	2710	Tidball
4.2.90	SD	H	Hull K.R.	L	2-60	–	Carroll	1392	Holgate
18.2.90	SD	A	Doncaster	L	14-27	Fletcher, Lister	Carroll (2, 2dg)	–	–
25.2.90	SD	H	Hunslet	L	10-23	Carroll, Rodgers	Carroll	917	Steele
11.3.90	SD	H	Runcorn H.	W	29-6	Lister, Lidbury, Brentley, Barnett	Carroll (6), Lister (dg)	534	Burke
18.3.90	SD	A	Huddersfield	W	16-12	Hopkins, Sharp, Barnett	Carroll (2)	–	–
21.3.90	SD	A	Chorley	L	18-26	Korn, Lister, Lidbury, Pitts	Pitts	–	–
25.3.90	SD	H	Carlisle	L	18-24	Lister, Pitts, Clawson	Pitts (3)	469	C. Morris
1.4.90	SD	A	Hull K.R.	L	10-42	Lister, Clawson	Pitts	–	–
13.4.90	SD	A	Keighley	W	17-13	Korn	Carroll (5, 3dg)	–	–
16.4.90	SD	H	Swinton	L	11-22	Brentley	Carroll (3, 1dg)	666	Ollerton (Pr)

CARLISLE

Ground: Gillford Park
Colours: Blue, red and white
First Season: 1981-82. A Carlisle City team entered the League in 1928-29 but withdrew after 10 matches, winning one
Chairman: Alan Tucker
Secretary: Robert Taylor
Coach: Tommy Dawes (Dec 1988-Jan 1990) Cameron Bell (Feb 1990-)
Records: Attendance: 5,903 v. Workington T. (Div. 2) 6 Sep, 1981

Season
Goals: 113 by S. Ferres, 1981-82
Tries: 25 by M. Morgan, 1981-82; G. Peacham, 1984-85
Points: 242 by S. Ferres, 1981-82

Match
Goals: 10 by B. Vickers at Nottingham C., 11 Mar, 1990
Tries: 4 by G. Peacham v. Workington T., 25 Jan, 1987 and K. Pape v. Rochdale H., 11 Feb, 1987
Points: 24 by B. Vickers at Nottingham C., 11 Mar, 1990
Highest score: 60-0 v. Nottingham C., 1989-90
Highest against: 112-0 v. St. Helens, 1986-87

1989-90 PLAYERS' SUMMARY

	App	Tries	Goals	Dr	Pts
Armstrong, Ian	0 + 1	—	—	—	—
Bowness, Chris	3 + 2	—	—	—	—
Brierley, Steve	30	2	—	—	8
Coles, Colin	22	7	1	—	30
Cubiss, George	1	—	1	—	2
Doyle, Mark	16	3	7	—	26
Graham, John	2 + 2	—	—	—	—
Hepi, Brad	25	3	—	—	12
Kavanagh, Michael	7 + 4	3	1	—	14
Kendall, Dave	15 + 2	2	—	—	8
Kohlass, Darren	2	—	—	—	—
Lithgow, Paul	9 + 2	3	—	—	12
Little, Alan	9 + 2	4	—	—	16
MacLagan, Alan	0 + 1	—	—	—	—
McNichol, Tony	19 + 2	9	—	—	36
Murdock, Gary	24 + 1	2	—	—	8
Murdock, Paul	1 + 2	—	—	—	—
Nicholson, Gerry	12 + 3	3	—	—	12
Okesene, Hitro	16 + 2	3	—	—	12
Pape, Kevin	27	16	—	—	64
Pinner, Harry	10	1	—	—	4
Pollard, Damien	5 + 5	1	—	—	4
Rea, Steve	20 + 1	8	—	—	32
Robinson, Paul	5 + 7	—	—	—	—
Schubert, Gary	26	2	—	—	8
Scott, Ian	0 + 4	—	—	—	—
Scott, Tony	20 + 4	2	—	—	8
Southwell, Eddie	12 + 4	5	—	—	20
Thomason, Malcolm	31	7	—	—	28
Tunstall, Brian	0 + 1	—	1	—	2
Vickers, Barry	25	4	72	1	161
Whitchurch, Duncan	2	—	—	—	—
Williams, Barry	6	—	—	—	—

TOTALS:
33 players		90	83	1	527

Malcolm Thomason, seven tries in 31 appearances for Carlisle.

Former Great Britain skipper Harry Pinner, scorer of one try in 10 games for Carlisle after moving from Bradford Northern.

1989-90 MATCH ANALYSIS

Date	Competition	H/A	Opponent	Rlt	Score	Tries	Goals	Attendance	Referee
3.9.89	SD	H	Runcorn H.	W	54-14	Rae (2), Pape (2), Southwell (2), Thomason, Doyle, Kendall, Brierley	Vickers (7)	707	Tidball
10.9.89	SD	A	Workington T.	L	22-30	Lithgow (2), Pape, Southwell	Vickers (3)	—	—
17.9.89	LC(1)	H[1]	Widnes	L	6-46	Pinner	Vickers	4329	Simpson
1.10.89	SD	A	Fulham	L	6-50	—	Vickers (3)	—	—
8.10.89	SD	H	Workington T.	L	12-14	Doyle, Hepi	Vickers (2)	768	Kendrew
15.10.89	SD	A	Swinton	L	14-26	Rea, Kendall, Thomason	Doyle	—	—
22.10.89	SD	H	Oldham	L	10-32	Southwell	Vickers (3)	1059	Kendrew
29.10.89	SD	A	Hunslet	L	12-26	Pollard, McNichol	Doyle (2)	—	—
5.11.89	SD	A	Dewsbury	L	12-20	Nicholson, Thomason	Doyle (2)	—	—
12.11.89	SD	H	Ryedale-York	L	12-22	McNichol, Pape	Doyle (2)	446	Whitelam
19.11.89	SD	A	Keighley	L	22-30	McNichol (2), Coles, Pape	Vickers (3)	—	—
26.11.89	SD	H	Halifax	W	30-20	Rea (3), Pape, Coles	Vickers (5)	1102	Campbell
3.12.89	RT(1)	A	Dewsbury	L	4-14	Vickers	—	—	—
17.12.89	SD	H	Nottingham C.	W	15-14	Pape, McNichol	Vickers (3, 1dg)	360	Tickle
26.12.89	SD	A	Runcorn H.	W	18-9	Okesene, Kavanagh, Brierley	Vickers (3)	—	—
29.12.89	SD	A	Trafford B.	L	12-36	Thomason, Vickers	Vickers (2)	—	—
1.1.90	SD	A	Whitehaven	L	12-24	Pape, Coles	Vickers, Kavanagh	—	—
7.1.90	SD	H	Swinton	L	10-28	Doyle, Rea	Cubiss	425	Simpson
14.1.90	SD	A	Ryedale-York	L	14-52	Thomason (2), McNichol	Turnstall	—	—
21.1.90	SD	H	Bramley	L	18-21	Okesene, Nicholson, Rea, Little	Vickers	419	Smith
30.1.90	CC(1)	A	Rochdale H.	L	6-38	Thomason	Coles	—	—
18.2.90	SD	H	Keighley	W	38-9	Pape (3), Coles, McNichol, Scott, Murdock	Vickers (5)	354	Carter
25.2.90	SD	A	Halifax	L	4-32	Pape	—	—	—
4.3.90	SD	H	Dewsbury	L	12-22	Vickers, Schubert	Vickers (2)	520	Kendrew
11.3.90	SD	A	Nottingham C.	W	60-0	Pape (2), Hepi (2), Schubert, Lithgow, Murdock, Okesene, Vickers, Nicholson	Vickers (10)	—	—
18.3.90	SD	H	Hunslet	L	2-4	—	Vickers	495	Burke
25.3.90	SD	A	Bramley	W	24-18	Pape (2), Coles, Scott	Vickers (4)	—	—
1.4.90	SD	H	Fulham	L	2-14	—	Vickers	492	Whitelam
4.4.90	SD	H	Trafford B.	W	24-6	Little, Southwell, Kavanagh	Vickers (6)	355	Burke
8.4.90	SD	A	Oldham	L	16-48	Coles, Kavanagh, McNichol	Vickers (2)	—	—
16.4.90	SD	H	Whitehaven	W	24-4	Little (2), McNichol, Coles	Vickers (4)	530	Tidball

[1] at Carlisle FC

CASTLEFORD

Ground:	Wheldon Road
Colours:	Yellow and black
First Season:	1926-27. There was also a Castleford team from 1896-97 to 1905-06, inclusive
Nickname:	Glassblowers
Chairman:	David Poulter
Secretary:	Denise Cackett
Coach:	Darryl Van de Velde (July 1988-)
Honours:	**Championship** Beaten finalists, 1938-39, 1968-69
	Challenge Cup Winners, 1934-35, 1968-69, 1969-70, 1985-86
	Yorkshire League Winners, 1932-33, 1938-39, 1964-65
	Yorkshire Cup Winners, 1977-78, 1981-82, 1986-87
	Beaten finalists, 1948-49, 1950-51, 1968-69, 1971-72, 1983-84, 1985-86, 1987-88, 1988-89
	Eastern Division Championship Beaten finalists, 1963-64
	BBC2 Floodlit Trophy Winners, 1965-66, 1966-67, 1967-68, 1976-77
	Regal Trophy Winners, 1976-77
	Premiership Beaten finalists, 1983-84
	Charity Shield Beaten finalists 1986-87
Records:	Attendance: 25,449 v. Hunslet (RL Cup) 3 Mar, 1935
	Season
	Goals: 158 by S. Lloyd, 1976-77
	Tries: 36 by K. Howe, 1963-64
	Points: 334 by R. Beardmore, 1983-84
	Match
	Goals: 17 by S. Lloyd v. Millom, 16 Sep, 1973

Tries: 5 by D. Foster v. Hunslet, 10 Nov, 1972; J. Joyner v. Millom, 16 Sep, 1973; S. Fenton v. Dewsbury, 27 Jan, 1978; I. French v. Hunslet, 9 Feb, 1986; S. Ellis at Whitehaven, 10 Dec, 1989
Points: 43 by S. Lloyd v. Millom, 16 Sep, 1973
Highest score: 94-12 v. Huddersfield, 1988-89
Highest against: 62-12 v. St. Helens, 1985-86

1989-90 PLAYERS' SUMMARY

	App	Tries	Goals	Dr	Pts
Anderson, Grant	23	8	—	—	32
Battye, Neil	12 + 3	3	—	—	12
Beardmore, Kevin	28 + 1	3	—	—	12
Blackburn, John	1	—	—	—	—
Blankley, Dean	1	—	—	—	—
Boothroyd, Giles	1 + 2	—	—	—	—
Bragger, Ian	12	3	—	—	12
Chapman, Chris	2 + 1	1	—	—	4
Clarke, Andy	4 + 4	1	—	—	4
Crabtree, Paul	4 + 5	1	—	—	4
Crooks, Lee	6 + 1	1	14	—	32
Ellis, St. John	26	23	9	—	110
England, Keith	32 + 1	2	—	—	8
French, Gary	29	9	1	1	39
Gibbs, Ronnie	18	8	—	—	32
Gibson, Mark	3 + 2	1	—	—	4
Hardy, Jeff	15	9	—	—	36
Hill, Kenny	0 + 2	—	—	—	—
Irwin, Shaun	34 + 1	16	—	—	64
Joyner, John	32 + 2	3	—	—	12
Ketteridge, Martin	22	—	42	—	84
Larder, Steve	35	29	10	—	136
Marchant, Tony	9 + 3	—	—	—	—
McAllister, Terry	1 + 3	—	—	—	—
Mirfin, Phil	1	—	—	—	—
Plange, David	27	17	—	—	68
Price, Darren	4 + 3	1	—	—	4
Roebuck, Neil	5 + 10	2	—	—	8
Sampson, Dean	29 + 5	8	—	—	32
Smith, Tony	4 + 2	2	—	—	8
Southernwood, Graham	13 + 3	4	—	—	16
Southernwood, Roy	2	—	—	—	—
Steadman, Graham	26	17	75	2	220
Thornton, Wayne	0 + 1	—	—	—	—
Ward, Kevin	20 + 3	2	—	—	8
Whitehead, Paul	0 + 1	—	—	—	—
TOTALS:					
36 players		174	151	3	1,001

1989-90 MATCH ANALYSIS

Date	Competition	H/A	Opponent	Rlt	Score	Tries	Goals	Attendance	Referee
3.9.89	SBC	H	Featherstone R.	L	20-22	Gibbs, Plange, Irwin	Ketteridge (2), Steadman (2)	8487	Whitfield
10.9.89	SBC	A	St. Helens	W	26-24	Irwin, Gibbs, Larder, Plange	Ketteridge (5)	—	—

(continued)

MATCH ANALYSIS (continued)

Date	Com-petition	H/A	Opponent	Rlt	Score	Tries	Goals	Atten-dance	Referee
17.9.89	YC(1)	A	Hunslet	W	44-0	Plange (4), Steadman (2), French, Irwin, Gibson	Ketteridge (2), Steadman (2)	—	—
24.9.89	SBC	H	Hull	W	18-10	Larder (3)	Steadman (3)	7297	Carter
27.9.89	YC(2)	H	Hull K.R.	W	28-12	Steadman (3), Plange, French	Steadman (4)	6250	Tidball
30.9.89	SBC	A	Warrington	L	10-32	Irwin	Steadman (2), Larder	—	—
3.10.89	Tour	H	New Zealand	L	20-22	French, Clarke, Crabtree	Ellis (4)	5993	Whitfield
12.10.89	YC(SF)	A	Featherstone R.	D	18-18	Larder (2), Plange	Steadman (3)	—	—
15.10.89	SBC	H	Sheffield E.	W	24-22	Larder, Joyner, Smith, Irwin	Steadman (4)	6582	Bowman
22.10.89	YC(SF) Replay	H	Featherstone R.	L	26-28	Irwin (2), Steadman, Plange, Smith	Ellis (2), Steadman	9065	C. Morris
29.10.89	SBC	A	Wigan	W	22-20	French (2), Plange, Irwin	Steadman (3)	—	—
8.11.89	SBC	H	Bradford N.	W	32-13	Gibbs, Ellis, Sampson, G. Southernwood, Larder	Steadman (4), Ketteridge (2)	5171	Whitfield
12.11.89	SBC	A	Wakefield T.	L	14-22	Gibbs, Plange	Ketteridge (2), Steadman	—	—
19.11.89	SBC	H	Warrington	W	40-6	Larder (3), Irwin (2), French, Steadman, Plange	Ketteridge (4)	5274	C. Morris
25.11.89	SBC	A	Widnes	L	16-24	Sampson, Ellis. G. Southernwood	Ketteridge (2)	—	—
3.12.89	RT(1)	A	Chorley	W	42-18	Gibbs (2), Beardmore (2), Larder (2), Ellis, Irwin	Ketteridge (5)	—	—
10.12.89	RT(2)	A	Whitehaven	W	62-2	Ellis (5), Larder (3), Bragger, G. Southernwood, Beardmore	Ketteridge (9)	—	—
17.12.89	RT(3)	A[1]	Sheffield E.	W	18-2	Ellis (3), Larder	Ketteridge	—	—
26.12.89	SBC	A	Leeds	L	18-25	Gibbs, Ward, Ellis	Larder (2), Ketteridge	—	—
30.12.89	RT(SF)	Leeds	Wigan	L	10-24	Larder, Ellis	Larder	(10,193)	Whitfield
3.1.90	SBC	A	Bradford N.	L	16-24	Roebuck, Gibbs	Ketteridge (4)	—	—
7.1.90	SBC	H	Wakefield T.	W	16-18	Bragger (2), Price	Ketteridge (2)	7017	Whitelam
14.1.90	CC(P)	A	St. Helens	L	12-39	Anderson, Irwin	Ketteridge, Larder	—	—
20.1.90	SBC	H	Widnes	L	22-30	Chapman, Hardy, Larder, Crooks	Crooks (3)	5203	Kershaw
4.2.90	SBC	A	Hull	L	6-16.	Steadman	Larder	—	—
11.2.90	SBC	A	Featherstone R.	L	6-12	Larder	Steadman	—	—
18.2.90	SBC	H	Leigh	W	44-18	Hardy (2), Ellis, Joyner, Steadman, French, Ward	Steadman (8)	5053	Asquith
25.2.90	SBC	A	Salford	W	24-18	Plange, Hardy, Ellis, Larder	Steadman (4)	—	—
4.3.90	SBC	H	St. Helens	W	34-24	Sampson (3), Battye, Larder	Steadman (7)	6739	Whitfield
9.3.90	SBC	A[2]	Sheffield E.	W	18-14	Ellis, Larder, Sampson	Steadman (3)	—	—
18.3.90	SBC	A	Barrow	W	42-14	Anderson, Hardy, Irwin, Plange, G. Southernwood, Battye, Ellis	Larder (4), Ellis (3)	—	—
25.3.90	SBC	H	Barrow	W	58-6	Steadman (3), Irwin (3), Hardy (2), Anderson (2), Ellis, French, Larder	Steadman (2), French	4028	Kershaw
28.3.90	SBC	H	Wigan	W	34-10	Ellis, Steadman, Hardy, French, Anderson	Steadman (6, 2dg)	8895	Cross
1.4.90	SBC	H	Salford	W	65-0	Larder (4), Steadman (3), Ellis (2), Plange	Steadman (12), French (dg)	4756	Campbell
12.4.90	SBC	A	Leigh	W	40-6	Plange (2), Anderson (2), Joyner, Ellis, Steadman, Battye	Steadman (3), Crooks	—	—
16.4.90	SBC	H	Leeds	W	38-18	Sampson, Larder, Anderson, Hardy, England, Roebuck	Crooks (7)	9060	C. Morris
22.4.90	PT(1)	A	Leeds	L	18-24	England, Sampson, Ellis	Crooks (3)	—	—

[1] at Chesterfield FC   [2] at Doncaster

CHORLEY

Ground: Victory Park
Colours: Black and white
First Season: 1989-90
Chairman: Syd Secker
Secretary: George Lunn
Coach: Stan Gittins (Jun 1989-Apr 1990)
Bob Eccles (May 1990-)
Records: Attendance: 2,851 v. Oldham (League) 21 Jan, 1990. There was a crowd of 5,026 for a 'home' Lancashire Cup-tie against Wigan played at Wigan on 15 Sep, 1989
Season
Goals: 73 by M. Smith, 1989-90
Tries: 10 by D. Bacon, 1989-90
Points: 142 by M. Smith, 1989-90
Match
Goals: 6 by M. Smith v. Runcorn H., 1 Jan, 1990 and v. Nottingham C., 8 Apr, 1990
Tries: No player has scored more than 3
Points: No player has scored more than 12
Highest score: 46-12 v. Runcorn H., 1989-90
Highest against: 66-16 v. Oldham, 1989-90

1989-90 PLAYERS' SUMMARY

	App	Tries	Goals	Dr	Pts
Aylward, John	1	—	—	—	—
Bacon, David	31	10	—	—	40
Bimson, Jeff	25	8	—	—	32
Briscoe, Carl	30	4	—	—	16
Broxton, Paul	1	—	—	—	—
Burnette, Kurt	17	4	—	—	16
Cheetham, Mike	7 + 2	—	—	—	—
Chisnall, Chris	1	—	—	—	—
Cinnanon, Stan	0 + 1	—	—	—	—
Copeland, Terry	0 + 1	—	—	—	—
Duffy, John	27	8	—	—	32
Edwards, Mark	13 + 9	2	—	—	8
Ellis, Jeff	2 + 11	—	—	—	—
Evans, Alan	8	1	—	—	4
Galbraith, Stuart	1	—	—	—	—
Gittins, Stan	0 + 1	—	—	—	—
Gittins, Tom	21 + 3	3	—	—	12
Grundy, Tracy	3 + 4	—	—	—	—
Hodson, Tony	29	1	—	—	4
Jones, David	6	1	—	—	4
Knight, Mark	28 + 3	7	—	—	28
Lee, Martin	4	1	—	—	4
Marshall, Ken	15 + 1	1	—	—	4
Massey, Peter	1 + 1	—	—	—	—
Mayo, John	9	—	—	—	—
Meyrick, Martin	7 + 7	4	—	—	16
Nanyn, Mick	1 + 7	—	—	—	—
O'Hara, Mike	1	1	—	—	4
Price, Billy	24 + 7	1	4	7	19
Roberts, Paul	0 + 2	—	—	—	—
Robinson, Darren	2 + 1	—	—	—	—
Schofield, Colin	2	—	—	—	—
Smith, Mike	30	—	69	4	142
Torpy, Brian	22 + 1	2	—	—	8
Whittaker, Aaron	16	7	—	—	28
Williams, Stuart	16	4	—	—	16
Wood, David	15	—	1	—	2
TOTALS:					
37 players		70	74	11	439

New Zealander Aaron Whittaker, scorer of seven tries for Chorley.

Half back Jeff Bimson, eight tries in 25 appearances for Chorley.

1989-90 MATCH ANALYSIS

Date	Competition	H/A	Opponent	Rlt	Score	Tries	Goals	Attendance	Referee
30.8.89	LC(P)	H	Trafford B.	W	12-6	Duffy	Price (3, 2dg)	628	Holgate
3.9.89	SD	A	Swinton	L	4-48	—	Smith (1, 2dg)	—	—
10.9.89	SD	H	Whitehaven	W	13-9	Meyrick, Jones	Smith (2, 1dg)	520	K. Morris
15.9.89	LC(1)	H[1]	Wigan	L	4-50	Lee	—	5026	Burke
24.9.89	SD	H	Fulham	L	8-20	Bacon	Smith (2)	442	Holgate
1.10.89	SD	H	Keighley	L	12-25	Gittins, Knight, Meyrick	—	585	Simpson
3.10.89	SD	A	Bramley	L	10-46	Burnett, Bacon	Smith	—	—
15.10.89	SD	H	Hunslet	W	16-8	Bacon, Duffy, Edwards	Smith (2)	663	Cross
29.10.89	SD	A	Dewsbury	L	16-32	Bimson, Bacon	Smith (4)	—	—
5.11.89	SD	H	Nottingham C.	W	22-8	Whittaker (2), Hodson, Bacon	Smith (3)	626	Galtress
12.11.89	SD	H	Dewsbury	L	6-22	Burnette	Smith	655	Holdsworth
19.11.89	SD	A	Halifax	L	16-26	Gittins, Bacon	Smith (4)	—	—
24.11.89	SD	A	Ryedale-York	L	10-28	Whittaker, Knight	Smith	—	—
3.12.89	RT(1)	H	Castleford	L	18-42	Duffy, O'Hara, Price	Smith (3)	1256	Galtress
17.11.89	SD	H	Swinton	L	10-22	Williams, Whittaker	Smith	722	Carter
26.12.89	SD	A	Hunslet	W	14-2	Williams, Burnette	Smith (3),	—	—
1.1.90	SD	H	Runcorn H.	W	46-12	Bimson (3), Bacon (2), Torpy, Briscoe, Duffy	Smith (6), Price	548	Smith
7.1.90	SD	A	Workington T.	W	12-6	Bacon, Knight	Smith (2)	—	—
14.1.90	SD	A	Trafford B.	L	6-14	Duffy	Smith	—	—
21.1.90	SD	H	Oldham	L	6-44	Torpy	Wood	2851	Steele
30.1.90	CC(1)	H	Keighley	L	6-12	Whittaker	Smith	552	Smith
4.2.90	SD	H	Workington T.	L	14-17	Whittaker (2)	Smith (3)	380	Cross
18.2.90	SD	A	Oldham	L	16-66	Williams (2), Burnette	Smith (2)	—	—
25.2.90	SD	H	Ryedale-York	W	10-6	Bimson	Smith (3)	491	Galtress
4.3.90	SD	H	Halifax	L	2-34	—	Smith	1885	Burke
11.3.90	SD	A	Whitehaven	L	4-16	—	Smith (2)	—	—
21.3.90	SD	H	Bramley	W	26-18	Duffy (2), Evans, Briscoe	Smith (4), Price (2dg)	420	Steele
25.3.90	SD	A	Keighley	L	9-11	Gittins	Smith (2), Price (dg)	—	—
1.4.90	SD	H	Trafford B.	L	28-30	Knight, Duffy, Edwards, Marshall, Bimson	Smith (4)	496	Tidball
8.4.90	SD	A	Nottingham C.	W	42-8	Knight (3), Briscoe, Bimson, Bacon, Meyrick	Smith (6), Price (2dg)	—	—
13.4.90	SD	A	Fulham	L	10-38	Bimson, Meyrick	Smith	—	—
16.4.90	SD	A	Runcorn	W	11-2	Briscoe	Smith (3, 1dg)	—	—

[1] at Leigh

DEWSBURY

Ground: Crown Flatt
Colours: Red, amber and black
First Season: 1901-02
Chairman: Rodney Hardcastle
Secretary: Ken Croft
Coach: Maurice Bamford (Dec 1988-)
Honours: **Championship** Winners, 1972-73
Beaten finalists, 1946-47
Division Two Champions, 1904-05
Challenge Cup Winners, 1911-12, 1942-43
Beaten finalists, 1928-29
Yorkshire League Winners, 1946-47
Yorkshire Cup Winners, 1925-26, 1927-28, 1942-43
Beaten finalists, 1918-19, 1921-22, 1940-41, 1972-73
BBC2 Floodlit Trophy Beaten finalists, 1975-76
War League Championship Winners, 1941-42. (1942-43 won final but championship declared null and void because Dewsbury played an ineligible player.)
Beaten finalists, 1943-44
Records: Attendance: 26,584 v. Halifax (Yorkshire Cup) 30 Oct, 1920
Season
Goals: 145 by N. Stephenson, 1972-73
Tries: 40 by D. Thomas, 1906-07
Points: 368 by N. Stephenson, 1972-73
Match
Goals: 10 by J. Ledgard v. Yorkshire Amateurs, 13 Sep, 1947; N. Stephenson v. Blackpool B, 28 Aug, 1972; C. Wilkinson v. Huddersfield, 27 Mar, 1989
Tries: 8 by D. Thomas v. Liverpool C, 13 Apr, 1907
Points: 29 by J. Lyman v. Hull, 22 Apr, 1919
Highest score: 72-0 v. Doncaster, 1984-85
Highest against: 82-0 v. Widnes, 1986-87

1989-90 PLAYERS' SUMMARY

	App	Tries	Goals	Dr	Pts
Bailey, Dennis	33	19	—	—	76
Bailey, Howard	15 + 8	2	1	—	10
Bloor, Andrew	18 + 2	3	—	—	12
Burgess, Mark	17 + 4	—	—	—	—
Butler, Tim	20 + 2	4	—	—	16
Carroll, John	11 + 5	—	—	—	—
Charles, Marquis	11	4	10	—	36
Cocks, Gary	35	1	—	—	4
Coen, Darren	25	2	—	—	8
Cooper, Andy	1 + 1	—	—	—	—
Coughlan, Glen	33	10	—	—	40
Deakin, Keiron	0 + 3	—	—	—	—
Durnin, Paul	11	4	—	—	16
Elsey, Richard	6	2	—	—	8
Graham, Nathan	27	7	16	—	60
Gregoire, Don	3	1	—	—	4
Haigh, Chris	3 + 3	—	—	—	—
Hall, Dean	8 + 3	5	—	—	20
Howley, Pat	16 + 5	2	—	—	8
Hughes, Lee	2	—	—	—	—
Jennings, Paul	5	—	—	—	—
Johnson, Willie	31 + 2	8	—	3	35
Jones, Kevin	2 + 1	—	—	—	—
Kelly, Neil	23	3	—	3	15
Kelly, Richard	1	—	—	—	—
Manners, Simon	1 + 1	—	—	—	—
Moore, Gary	9 + 3	2	—	—	8
Moore, John	3	—	—	—	—
O'Hara, Jock	2	—	—	—	—
Parkinson, Andy	2	—	—	—	—
Parrish, Steve	1 + 1	—	—	—	—
Shuttleworth, Paul	32	4	—	10	26
Squires, Chris	19 + 1	6	—	—	24
Trembath, Dennis	13 + 11	4	—	—	16
Watkinson, David	5 + 1	1	—	—	4
Whitehead, Craig	10	—	—	—	—
Wilkinson, Chris	27 + 3	8	70	2	174
TOTALS: 37 players		102	97	18	620

Former Great Britain skipper David Watkinson, one try in six appearances for Dewsbury.

1989-90 MATCH ANALYSIS

Date	Competition	H/A	Opponent	Rlt	Score	Tries	Goals	Attendance	Referee
27.8.89	YC (P)	H	Wakefield T.	W	18-17	Squires, Bloor, Charles	Charles (2), N. Kelly (dg), Johnson (dg)	2246	Asquith
3.9.89	SD	A	Doncaster	W	21-10	Charles, D. Bailey, Squires	Charles (4), Kelly (dg)	—	—
10.9.89	SD	H	Keighley	W	29-6	Coughlan, Gregoire, D. Bailey, Trembath, Charles	Charles (3), H. Bailey, Shuttleworth (dg)	915	Bowman
17.9.89	YC(1)	H	Halifax	L	7-22	Watkinson	Charles, Johnson (dg)	3604	C. Morris
24.9.89	SD	A	Rochdale H.	L	20-46	Johnson, Shuttleworth, D. Bailey	Wilkinson (4)	—	—
1.10.89	SD	H	Swinton	L	12-17	Wilkinson, Trembath	Wilkinson (2)	905	Holgate
8.10.89	SD	A	Hunslet	W	24-19	D. Bailey (2), Charles, Bloor	Wilkinson (4)	—	—
15.10.89	SD	H	Runcorn H.	W	34-10	Trembath (2), Shuttleworth, Cocks, Coughlan	Wilkinson (7)	615	Holgate
22.10.89	SD	A	Halifax	L	9-25	D. Bailey	Wilkinson (2), Shuttleworth (dg)	—	—
29.10.89	SD	H	Chorley	W	32-16	Johnson (2), Bloor, Howley, Squires, D. Bailey	Wilkinson (4)	533	Steele
5.11.89	SD	H	Carlisle	W	20-12	D. Bailey, Squires, Graham, H. Bailey	Wilkinson (2)	542	Simpson
12.11.89	SD	A	Chorley	W	22-6	Coughlan, Johnson, D. Bailey	Wilkinson (5)	—	—
19.11.89	SD	H	Hunslet	W	13-10	Graham (2)	Wilkinson (2), Johnson (dg)	792	K. Morris
26.11.89	SD	A	Hull K.R.	L	6-54	D. Bailey	Wilkinson	—	—
3.12.89	RT(1)	H	Carlisle	W	14-4	D. Bailey, Wilkinson	Wilkinson (3)	631	Whitelam
10.12.89	RT (2)	A	St. Helens	D	12-12	D. Bailey, Graham	Wilkinson (2)	—	—
13.12.89	RT(2) Replay	H[1]	St. Helens	L	0-14	—	—	1981	Kershaw
26.12.89	SD	A	Batley	L	6-18	Moore	Wilkinson	—	—
31.12.89	SD	H	Batley	W	22-8	D. Bailey (2), G. Moore	Graham (5)	2469	Campbell
7.1.90	SD	H	Doncaster	L	0-16	—	—	1322	Steele
14.1.90	SD	A	Runcorn H.	W	28-6	Wilkinson (2), Kelly, Coen, Coughlan	Wilkinson (4)	—	—
21.1.90	SD	H	Halifax	W	24-16	Wilkinson (2), Graham, D. Bailey	Wilkinson (4)	3576	Carter
28.1.90	CC(1)	A	Nottingham C.	W	32-2	D. Bailey (2), Elsey (2), Butler	Wilkinson (5), Shuttleworth (2)	—	—
4.2.90	SD	A	Keighley	W	20-6	Coen, Graham, Wilkinson	Wilkinson (4)	—	—
11.2.90	CC(2)	A	Wigan	L	6-30	Coughlan	Graham	—	—
18.2.90	SD	H	Rochdale H.	L	8-10	Coughlan	Wilkinson (2)	1508	Tickle
25.2.90	SD	A	Huddersfield	W	13-0	N. Kelly, Johnson	Wilkinson (2), Shuttleworth	—	—
4.3.90	SD	A	Carlisle	W	22-12	Howley, Durnin, Butler, H. Bailey, Squires	Wilkinson	—	—
11.3.90	SD	H	Workington T.	W	32-4	Squires, Coughlan, Durnin, D. Bailey, Butler, Hall	Graham (2), Wilkinson (1, 1dg), N. Kelly (dg)	722	Simpson
18.3.90	SD	A	Swinton	L	12-36	Durnin, Graham	Wilkinson (2)	—	—
25.3.90	SD	A	Workington T.	W	9-8	Wilkinson	Wilkinson, Shuttleworth (3dg)	—	—
1.4.90	SD	H	Huddersfield	W	26-8	Shuttleworth (2), Johnson (2)	Graham (4), Shuttleworth (2dg)	1186	Cross
8.4.90	SD	A	Fulham	D	14-14	N. Kelly, Wilkinson	Wilkinson (3)	—	—
11.4.90	SD	H	Hull K.R.	W	3-2		Wilkinson (1, 1dg)	1346	Tidball
16.4.90	SD	H	Fulham	W	22-16	Hall (2), D. Bailey, Johnson	Graham (3)	742	Holgate
22.4.90	SDP(1)	A	Rochdale H.	W	20-18	D. Hall, Butler, Durnin Coughlan,	Graham, Wilkinson	—	—
6.5.90	SDP(SF)	A	Hull K.R.	L	8-36	Hall, Coughlan	—	—	—

[1] at Wakefield T.

DONCASTER

Ground: Tattersfield
Colours: Blue and yellow
First Season: 1951-52
Nickname: Dons
Chairman: John Desmond
Secretary: Granville Bowen
Coach: Dave Sampson (May 1989-)
Records: Attendance: 5,274 v. Wigan (RL Cup) 29 Jan, 1989. There was an attendance of 10,000 for a Challenge Cup tie against Bradford N. at York Road Stadium on 16 Feb, 1952

Season
Goals: 118 by D. Noble, 1985-86
Tries: 21 by M. Roache, 1989-90
Points: 250 by D. Noble, 1986-87

Match
Goals: 9 by D. Towle v. York, 9 Sep, 1967
Tries: 4 by V. Grace v. Rochdale H, 4 Oct, 1952; B. Tasker v. Leeds, 26 Oct, 1963; J. Buckton v. Rochdale H., 30 Aug, 1981; T. Kemp v. Carlisle, 23 Nov, 1986; N. Turner v. Keighley, 22 Oct, 1989
Points: 20 by K. Jones v. Whitehaven, 13 Mar, 1988; D. Noble v. Dewsbury, 2 Oct, 1988
Highest score: 50-6 v. Keighley, 1986-87; 50-6 v. Nottingham C., 1989-90
Highest against: 75-3 v. Leigh, 1975-76

1989-90 PLAYERS' SUMMARY

	App	Tries	Goals	Dr	Pts
Abraham, Steve	5	—	—	—	—
Beardsmore, Paul	0 + 1	—	—	—	—
Carroll, Dean	14	3	—	7	19
Chappell, Tony	5 + 1	1	—	—	4
Ellis, Mark	0 + 1	—	—	—	—
Evans, John	6 + 9	1	—	—	4
Fletcher, Ian	13 + 7	2	—	—	8
Gibbon, Mark	23	2	—	—	8
Green, John	3 + 4	1	—	—	4
Hall, Carl	30	16	—	—	64
Hermannson, Terry	18 + 1	2	—	—	8
Hill, Kenny	4	—	—	—	—
Hutchinson, Lee	0 + 1	—	—	—	—
Idle, Graham	21 + 2	—	—	—	—
Jasiewicz, Dick	26 + 2	5	—	—	20
Jones, Keith	22 + 10	7	50	—	128
Jones, Kevin	6 + 10	6	1	—	26
Kemp, Tony	10	11	—	1	45
Livingstone, Mark	1 + 3	1	—	—	4
Parkhouse, Kevin	0 + 1	—	—	—	—
Pennant, Audley	31	3	—	—	12
Pickerill, Neil	15	—	—	—	—
Proctor, Wayne	16	3	—	—	12
Puckering, Neil	14 + 2	2	—	—	8
Rayne, Kevin	24 + 2	7	—	—	28
Roache, Mark	32 + 1	21	—	—	84
Sampson, Lee	8 + 4	1	—	—	4
Sheldon, Ian	4	—	—	—	—
Shillito, Alan	12 + 1	1	—	—	4
Sygrove, Andy	26	6	22	—	68
Timpson, Andy	0 + 1	—	—	—	—
Turner, Neil	16	9	—	—	36
Vincent, Andy	20	2	—	—	8
Zelei, Tony	3	1	8	—	20

TOTALS:
34 players		114	81	8	626

New Zealand Test back Tony Kemp, scorer of 45 points in 10 games for Doncaster.

1989-90 MATCH ANALYSIS

Date	Competition	H/A	Opponent	Rlt	Score	Tries	Goals	Attendance	Referee
3.9.89	SD	H	Dewsbury	L	10-21	Pennant, Rayne	Kevin Jones	2335	Campbell
10.9.89	SD	A	Bramley	W	12-2	Turner, Jasiewicz, Roache	—	—	—
17.9.89	YC(1)	H	Huddersfield	W	23-4	Roache (2), Kemp	Keith Jones (5), Kemp (dg)	2341	Whitelam
24.9.89	SD	H	Runcorn H.	W	46-6	Kevin Jones (2), Roache, Turner, Gibbon, Hall, Kemp, Jasiewicz	Keith Jones (7)	1949	Smith
27.9.89	YC(2)	A	Featherstone R.	L	22-37	Hall, Roache, Keith Jones, Kevin Jones	Keith Jones (3)	—	—
1.10.89	SD	H	Whitehaven	W	30-9	Turner, Fletcher, Hall, Gibbon, Kevin Jones	Keith Jones (5)	2136	Tidball
8.10.89	SD	A	Halifax	L	12-20	Roache, Hermansson	Keith Jones (2)	—	—
15.10.89	SD	H	Ryedale-York	D	12-12	Jasiewicz	Keith Jones (2), Sygrove (2)	2610	Campbell
22.10.89	SD	A	Keighley	W	34-6	Turner (4), Hall, Jasiewicz, Shillito	Keith Jones (3)	—	—
29.10.89	SD	H	Workington T.	W	26-4	Hall (2), Roache, Kevin Jones	Keith Jones (5)	2092	Burke
5.11.89	SD	H	Oldham	L	20-22	Vincent, Rayne, Turner, Hall	Keith Jones (2)	3460	Smith
12.11.89	SD	A	Whitehaven	W	28-12	Hall (2), Roache, Turner, Green	Keith Jones (2), Sygrove (2)	—	—
19.11.89	RT(P)	A[1]	Kells	W	28-2	Rayne (2), Roache, Hall, Sygrove	Keith Jones (4)	—	—
26.11.89	SD	A	Oldham	L	8-30	Keith Jones	Keith Jones (2)	—	—
3.12.89	RT(1)	A	Wigan	L	4-62	Fletcher	—	—	—
10.12.89	SD	H	Trafford B.	L	2-27	—	Keith Jones	1554	Whitelam
17.12.89	SD	H	Hunslet	W	12-2	Proctor, Roache, Kemp	—	1388	Sampson
26.12.89	SD	A	Nottingham C.	W	50-6	Hall (3), Kemp (2), Roache (2), Sygrove, Kevin Jones	Keith Jones (7)	—	—
31.12.89	SD	H	Fulham	D	8-8	Hermansson, Hall	—	1911	Whitelam
7.1.90	SD	A	Dewsbury	W	16-0	Kemp (2), Pennant	Sygrove, Carroll (2dg)	—	—
14.1.90	CC(P)	A	Fulham	L	16-23	Kemp (2), Carroll	Sygrove (2)	—	—
21.1.90	SD	H	Keighley	W	28-14	Rayne (2), Kemp (2), Chappell, Hall	Sygrove (2)	1756	Simpson
4.2.90	SD	A	Hunslet	L	12-27	Roache, Keith Jones	Sygrove (2)	—	—
11.2.90	SD	A	Swinton	L	22-34	Roache, Puckering, Carroll, Keith Jones	Sygrove (3)	—	—
18.2.90	SD	H	Bramley	W	27-14	Roache (2), Sampson, Sygrove, Proctor	Sygrove (3), Carroll (dg)	1632	K. Morris
25.2.90	SD	A	Fulham	L	12-28	Roache, Sygrove	Sygrove (2)	—	—
4.3.90	SD	A	Trafford B.	L	14-29	Roache, Livingstone, Hall	Sygrove	—	—
11.3.90	SD	H	Swinton	L	5-38	Vincent	Carroll (dg)	1687	Carter
16.3.90	SD	A	Ryedale-York	L	5-12	Jasiewicz	Carroll (dg)	—	—
25.3.90	SD	A	Runcorn H.	W	29-2	Sygrove (2), Keith Jones (2), Roache	Zelei (4), Carroll (dg)	—	—
28.3.90	SD	H	Halifax	W	8-6	Carroll	Sygrove (2)	1999	Kershaw
8.4.90	SD	A	Workington T.	W	11-0	Puckering, Zelei	Zelei, Carroll (dg)	—	—
16.4.90	SD	H	Nottingham C.	W	34-8	Roache (2), Proctor, Evans, Keith Jones, Rayne, Pennant	Zelei (3)	1005	K. Morris

[1] at Whitehaven

FEATHERSTONE ROVERS

Ground:	Post Office Road
Colours:	Blue and white
First Season:	1921-22
Nickname:	Colliers
Chairman:	Eric Gardner
Secretary:	Terry Jones
Coach:	Peter Fox (May 1987-)

Honours: **Challenge Cup** Winners, 1966-67, 1972-73, 1982-83
Beaten finalists, 1951-52, 1973-74
Championship Beaten finalists, 1927-28
Division One Champions, 1976-77
Division Two Champions, 1979-80
Second Division Premiership Beaten finalists, 1987-88
Yorkshire Cup Winners, 1939-40, 1959-60
Beaten finalists, 1928-29, 1963-64, 1966-67, 1969-70, 1970-71, 1976-77, 1977-78, 1989-90
Captain Morgan Trophy Beaten finalists, 1973-74

Records: Attendance: 17,531 v. St. Helens (RL Cup) 21 Mar, 1959
Season
Goals: 163 by S. Quinn, 1979-80
Tries: 31 by C. Woolford, 1958-59
Points: 375 by S. Quinn, 1979-80
Match
Goals: 13 by M. Knapper v. Keighley, 17 Sep, 1989
Tries: 6 by M. Smith v. Doncaster, 13 Apr, 1968; C. Bibb v. Keighley, 17 Sep, 1989
Points: 30 by M. Knapper v. Keighley, 17 Sep, 1989
Highest score: 86-18 v. Keighley, 1989-90
Highest against: 70-2 v. Halifax, 1940-41

1989-90 PLAYERS' SUMMARY

	App	Tries	Goals	Dr	Pts
Banks, Alan	28 + 6	5	—	—	20
Bell, Glenn	18 + 2	1	—	—	4
Bell, Keith	1	—	—	—	—
Bibb, Chris	31	16	—	—	64
Booth, Glen	10 + 2	1	—	—	4
Bugg, David	0 + 1	—	—	—	—
Burton, Chris	28 + 2	—	—	—	—
Clark, Trevor	36	11	—	—	44
Dakin, Alan	11 + 6	—	—	—	—
Davies, Richard	2 + 2	—	—	—	—
Drummond, Barry	14	2	—	—	8
Fisher, Andy	15 + 16	12	—	—	48
Fox, Deryck	34	3	70	8	160
Gibbon, Mark	0 + 3	—	—	—	—
Grayshon, Jeff	35 + 1	1	—	—	4
Hall, Gary	2 + 3	1	—	—	4
Hughes, Paul	12 + 4	5	—	—	20
Knapper, Mark	16	6	43	—	110
Love, Brett	1	—	—	—	—
Manning, Terry	25	11	—	—	44
Newlove, Paul	30	18	—	—	72
Newlove, Shaun	2 + 2	—	—	—	—
Palelei, Aaron	4 + 1	1	—	—	4
Pearson, Martin	0 + 2	—	—	—	—
Powell, Paul	2	1	—	—	4
Price, Gary	18 + 1	2	—	—	8
Ropati, Iva	26	15	—	—	60
Rose, Gary	14 + 1	4	—	—	16
Sharp, Tim	20 + 2	4	—	—	16
Smales, Ian	23 + 2	11	4	—	52
Smith, Peter	9 + 1	2	—	—	8
Staniforth, Tony	1 + 1	—	—	—	—
Whiteley, Les	0 + 2	—	—	—	—
TOTALS:					
33 players		133	117	8	774

Featherstone Rovers utility man Ian Smales, a 1990 Great Britain tourist.

1989-90 MATCH ANALYSIS

Date	Competition	H/A	Opponent	Rlt	Score	Tries	Goals	Attendance	Referee
3.9.89	SBC	A	Castleford	W	22-20	P. Newlove, Bibb, Clark, Hughes	Fox (3)	—	—
10.9.89	SBC	H	Sheffield E.	L	12-37	Knapper, Hughes	Fox (2)	3573	Tickle
17.9.89	YC(1)	H	Keighley	W	86-18	Bibb (6), P. Newlove (2), Banks (2), Knapper, Hughes, Fox, Clark, Fisher	Knapper (13)	2209	Cross
24.9.89	SBC	A	Widnes	L	8-59	Booth	Knapper (2)	—	—
27.9.89	YC(2)	H	Doncaster	W	37-22	Ropati (2), Bibb, Clark, Hughes, Fisher	Knapper (6), Fox (dg)	3526	Galtress
1.10.89	SBC	H	Leigh	L	16-30	P. Newlove (3)	Knapper (2)	3206	Cross
8.10.89	SBC	H	Leeds	L	20-22	Smales (2), Smith	Knapper (4)	6287	Steele
12.10.89	YC(SF)	H	Castleford	D	18-18	P. Newlove, Knapper, Bibb	Knapper (3)	6227	C. Morris
15.10.89	SBC	A	St. Helens	L	11-50	Bibb, Knapper	Knapper, Fox (dg)	—	—
22.10.89	YC(SF) Replay	A	Castleford	W	28-26	P. Newlove (2), Bell, Price, Knapper	Knapper (4)	—	—
29.10.89	SBC	H	Barrow	L	22-29	Knapper, Drummond, Bibb, Smales	Knapper (2), Fox	2530	Asquith
5.11.89	YC(F)	Leeds	Bradford N.	L	14-20	Smith, Ropati	Fox (3)	(12,607)	Whitfield
7.11.89	Tour	H	New Zealand	L	20-44	Clark, Manning, Fisher	Smales (4)	2773	Bowman
12.11.89	SBC	H	Hull	L	10-24	Smales	Fox (3)	3509	Burke
15.11.89	SBC	A	Leigh	L	26-35	P. Newlove (2), Sharp, Smales, Ropati	Fox (3)	—	—
18.11.89	SBC	A	Wigan	L	14-40	Ropati, Fisher	Fox (3)	—	—
26.11.89	SBC	H	St. Helens	L	23-24	Fisher (2), Bibb, P. Newlove	Fox (3, 1dg)	3849	Cross
3.12.89	RT(1)	A	Trafford B.	W	36-18	Fisher, Ropati, Clark, Price, Fox, Hall	Fox (6)	—	—
10.12.89	RT (2)	A	Hunslet	W	34-4	Manning (2), P. Newlove (2), Ropati (2), Fisher, Drummond	Fox	—	—
17.12.89	RT(3)	A	Halifax	L	10-23	Clark, Fisher	Fox	—	—
26.12.89	SBC	H	Wakefield T.	W	15-8	Ropati (2), Fox	Fox (1, 1dg)	5898	Kershaw
31.12.89	SBC	A	Wakefield T.	L	14-22	Ropati (2), Clark	Fox	—	—
3.1.90	SBC	A[1]	Sheffield G.	W	30-20	Manning (2), Smales (2), Sharp	Fox (5)	—	—
7.1.90	SBC	A	Salford	W	15-14	Sharp, Manning	Fox (3, 1dg)	—	—
21.1.90	SBC	A	Barrow	W	46-0	Manning (2), Rose (2), Smales, Clark, Sharp, Banks, Bibb	Fox (5)	—	—
27.1.90	CC(1)	A	Warrrington	L	12-20	Smales, Bibb	Fox (2)	—	—
4.2.90	SBC	H	Warrington	W	20-13	Ropati (2), Clark	Fox (4)	3183	Whitelam
11.2.90	SBC	H	Castleford	W	12-6	Ropati, Palelei	Fox (2)	6166	Whitfield
18.2.90	SBC	A	Bradford N	L	10-32	Rose, Fisher	Fox	—	—
4.3.90	SBC	A	Warrington	W	15-9	Manning, P. Newlove	Fox (3, 1dg)	—	—
7.3.90	SBC	H	Widnes	W	30-22	Rose, Powell, Clark, P. Newlove, Manning	Fox (4), Knapper	3525	C. Morris
11.3.90	SBC	H	Salford	L	20-33	Grayshon, Manning, Fisher	Fox (4)	3318	Allatt
20.3.90	SBC	H	Wigan	L	20-26	P. Newlove, Hughes, Bibb	Knapper (4)	5507	Bowman
25.3.90	SBC	A	Hull	L	10-36	Banks, Fisher	Knapper	—	—
8.4.90	SBC	H	Bradford N.	W	24-16	Smales (2), Bibb, P. Newlove	Fox (3, 2dg)	4879	Kershaw
13.4.90	SBC	A	Leeds	L	14-25	Clark, Banks	Fox (3)	—	—

[1] at Wakefield T.

FULHAM

Ground: Moved to Crystal Palace National Sports Centre for 1990-91 season
Colours: Black, red and white
First Season: 1980-81
Chairman: David Price
Secretary: David Oakes
Coach: Ross Strudwick (June 1989-)
Honours: **Division Two** Champions, 1982-83
Records: Attendance: 15,013 v. Wakefield T. (RL Cup) 15 Feb, 1981 at Fulham FC
Season
Goals: 136 by S. Diamond, 1982-83
Tries: 27 by J. Crossley, 1982-83
Points: 308 by S. Diamond, 1982-83
Match
Goals: 11 by S. Guyett v. Huddersfield, 23 Oct, 1988
Tries: No player has scored more than 3
Points: 22 by A. Platt, v. Mansfield M., 10 May, 1986
Highest score: 61-22 v. Huddersfield, 1988-89
Highest against: 72-6 v. Whitehaven, 1986-87

1989-90 PLAYERS' SUMMARY

	App	Tries	Goals	Dr	Pts
Best, Tony	1	—	—	—	—
Bridge, Russ	29	1	—	—	4
Browning, Russell	22 + 2	4	—	—	16
Bush, Peter	3 + 1	1	—	—	4
Callow, Steve	1 + 1	—	—	—	—
Coutts, Jeff	15	8	10	—	52
Daunt, Brett	26	12	—	3	51
Gillan, Dave	21 + 2	8	—	—	32
Guyett, Steve	22 + 2	5	33	—	86
Johannson, Lawrence	6 + 2	1	—	—	4
Keating, Noel	16 + 7	2	—	—	8
Kennedy, Eric	21	6	—	—	24
Leslie, Roy	16 + 2	4	—	—	16
Look, Tim	23 + 2	3	—	—	12
M'Barki, Hussein	11 + 11	11	—	—	44
McCabe, Redvers	18	8	—	—	32
Mellors, Ian	21 + 7	1	—	—	4
Murphy, Keiron	26 + 4	4	—	—	16
Noble, Mick	8 + 1	1	—	—	4
Pearce, Greg	22	2	47	—	102
Pitt, Darryl	5	1	—	—	4
Rees, Huw	3 + 6	1	—	—	4
Roberts, Steve	6 + 2	1	—	—	4
Robertson, Karl	4 + 2	1	—	—	4
Rotherham, David	1	—	—	—	—
Sanchez, Wayne	21	3	9	—	30
Scott, Conrad	7 + 6	—	—	—	—
Taylor, Mick	31	12	—	—	48
Wightman, Ian	2	—	—	—	—
Williams, Brett	26 + 1	1	—	—	4
Wright, Rob	4 + 2	—	—	—	—
Zillman, Andrew	30	—	—	—	—
TOTALS:					
32 players		102	99	3	609

Fulham threequarter Mick Taylor, an August 1989 recruit from Halifax.

1989-90 MATCH ANALYSIS

Date	Competition	H/A	Opponent	Rlt	Score	Tries	Goals	Attendance	Referee
3.9.89	SD	H	Ryedale-York	W	10-9	Taylor, Robertson	Guyett	794	K. Morris
10.9.89	SD	A	Huddersfield	W	8-6	Noble	Guyett (2)	—	—
17.9.89	LC(1)	A	Workington T.	W	30-24	Gillan (2), Bridge, Sanchez, Guyett	Guyett (5)	—	—
24.9.89	SD	A	Chorley	W	20-8	Murphy (2), Guyett, Coutts	Guyett (2)	—	—
27.9.89	LC(2)	H[1]	Wigan	L	4-34	—	Guyett (2)	3204	Whitfield
1.10.89	SD	H	Carlisle	W	50-6	Gillan (3), M'Barki (2), Taylor, Williams, Murphy, Browning	Guyett (7)	1014	C. Morris
8.10.89	SD	A	Whitehaven	L	14-15	Gillan, Daunt	Guyett (3)	—	—
15.10.89	SD	H	Rochdale H.	L	4-18	Johannson	—	1184	Simpson
22.10.89	SD	H	Bramley	W	16-6	Murphy, Sanchez, Kennedy	Guyett (2)	758	Tickle
29.10.89	SD	A	Hull K.R.	L	0-44	—	—	—	—
5.11.89	SD	H	Whitehaven	W	24-0	Guyett, Gillan, M'Barki, Daunt	Guyett (4)	706	Stokes (NZ)
12.11.89	SD	A	Bramley	W	17-0	M'Barki, Kennedy	Guyett (4), Daunt (dg)	—	—
19.11.89	SD	H	Oldham	L	10-40	Taylor, McCabe	Guyett	1440	Carter
26.11.89	SD	A	Batley	W	12-10	Daunt (2)	Sanchez (2)	—	—
3.12.89	RT(1)	H	Halifax	L	18-32	McCabe (2), Rees	Sanchez (3)	1549	Cross
17.12.89	SD	H	Hull K.R.	L	6-60	Gillan	Sanchez	1009	Smith
31.12.89	SD	A	Doncaster	D	8-8	Daunt	Sanchez (2)	—	—
7.1.90	SD	H	Trafford B.	L	10-20	Keating, Taylor	Sanchez	—	Tidball
14.1.90	CC(P)	H	Doncaster	W	23-16	Daunt, Leslie, McCabe	Pearce (5), Daunt (dg)	898	Burke
17.1.90	SD	A	Rochdale H.	L	8-42	Pitt	Pearce (2)	—	—
21.1.90	SD	H	Batley	W	17-14	Browning (2), Taylor	Pearce (2), Daunt (dg)	692	Galtress
28.1.90	CC(1)	H	Ryedale-York	D	14-14	Taylor (2)	Pearce (3)	856	Allatt
31.1.90	CC(1) Replay	A	Ryedale-York	W	16-12	Pearce, Taylor	Pearce (4)	—	—
4.2.90	SD	A	Oldham	L	4-52	Daunt	—	—	—
11.2.90	CC(2)	H	Bradford N.	L	2-20	—	Pearce	1685	Whitelam
18.2.90	SD	A	Nottingham C.	W	34-14	Coutts (2), Daunt (2), Guyett, Kennedy	Pearce (5)	—	—
25.2.90	SD	H	Doncaster	W	28-12	Coutts, Kennedy, Roberts, Guyett, Daunt	Pearce (4)	652	Tickle
4.3.90	SD	A	Ryedale-York	L	14-18	M'Barki, Kennedy	Pearce (3)	—	—
11.3.90	SD	H	Huddersfield	W	34-10	Leslie (2), Coutts, Daunt, Kennedy	Pearce (7)	804	Asquith
18.3.90	SD	A	Trafford B.	W	22-18	Coutts (2), Daunt, McCabe	Coutts (3)	—	—
25.3.90	SD	H	Nottingham C.	W	44-10	Taylor (2), M'Barki (2), Coutts, Look, Keating, Browning	Coutts (6)	617	Burke
1.4.90	SD	A	Carlisle	W	14-2	Pearce, Taylor	Pearce (2), Coutts	—	—
8.4.90	SD	H	Dewsbury	D	14-14	McCabe (2), Mellors	Pearce	732	K. Morris
13.4.90	SD	H	Chorley	W	38-10	M'Barki (3), Look, Bush, Sanchez, Leslie	Pearce (5)	717	Tidball
16.4.90	SD	A	Dewsbury	L	16-22	M'Barki, Look, Taylor	Pearce (2)	—	—
22.4.90	SDP(1)	A	Hull K.R.	L	6-40	McCabe	Pearce	—	—

[1] at Hendon FC

59

HALIFAX

Ground: Thrum Hall
Colours: Blue and white
First Season: 1895-96
Nickname: Thrum Hallers
Secretary: David Tomlinson
Coach: John Dorahy (June 1989-)
Honours: **Championship** Winners, 1906-07, 1964-65
Beaten finalists, 1952-53, 1953-54, 1955-56, 1965-66
Division One Champions, 1902-03, 1985-86
War League Beaten finalists, 1942-43, 1944-45
Challenge Cup Winners, 1902-03, 1903-04, 1930-31, 1938-39, 1986-87
Beaten finalists, 1920-21, 1940-41, 1941-42, 1948-49, 1953-54, 1955-56, 1987-88
Yorkshire League Winners, 1908-09, 1920-21, 1952-53, 1953-54, 1955-56, 1957-58
Eastern Division Championship Winners, 1963-64
Yorkshire Cup Winners, 1908-09, 1944-45, 1954-55, 1955-56, 1963-64
Beaten finalists, 1905-06, 1907-08, 1941-42, 1979-80
Regal Trophy Winners, 1971-72
Beaten finalists, 1989-90
Premiership Trophy Beaten finalists, 1985-86
Charity Shield Winners, 1986-87
Beaten finalists, 1987-88
Records: Attendance: 29,153 v. Wigan (RL Cup) 21 Mar, 1959
Season
Goals: 147 by T. Griffiths, 1955-56
Tries: 48 by J. Freeman, 1956-57
Points: 298 by C. Whitfield, 1986-87

Match
Goals: 14 by B. Burton v. Hunslet, 27 Aug, 1972
Tries: 8 by K. Williams v. Dewsbury, 9 Nov, 1957
Points: 31 by B. Burton v. Hunslet, 27 Aug, 1972
Highest score: 76-8 v. Hunslet, 1972-73
Highest against: 64-0 v. Wigan, 1922-23

1989-90 PLAYERS' SUMMARY

	App	Tries	Goals	Dr	Pts
Anderson, Tony	24	13	—	—	52
Atkins, Gary	2	1	—	—	4
Atkinson, Colin	26	6	—	—	24
Beevers, Graham	9 + 1	—	—	—	—
Bell, Peter	9 + 3	1	—	—	4
Carroll, Jason	7 + 3	1	—	—	4
Dick, Kevin	3 + 2	—	—	—	—
Dickinson, Roy	12 + 5	2	—	—	8
Dorahy, John	22 + 1	5	10	—	40
Fairbank, Dick	18 + 1	2	—	—	8
George, Wilf	30	24	—	—	96
Heatherington, Brian	33	14	—	—	56
Hill, Brendan	24 + 6	9	—	—	36
Holliday, Les	29	3	53	1	119
Holmes, David	9 + 1	2	—	—	8
Hutchinson, Rob	11 + 3	2	—	—	8
James, Neil	13 + 3	5	—	—	20
Johnston, Lindsey	20 + 4	1	—	—	4
Longstaff, Simon	1	—	—	—	—
Lyons, John	28 + 4	3	—	2	14
McCallion, Seamus	23 + 4	2	—	2	10
Milner, Richard	37	10	—	—	40
Moore, Darren	3	1	—	—	4
Needham, David	11 + 1	3	—	—	12
Parkinson, George	0 + 1	—	—	—	—
Ramshaw, Jason	19 + 2	12	—	3	51
Rawlinson, Scott	5 + 1	1	—	—	4
Riddlesden, Eddie	23	10	—	—	40
Roberts, Lee	5 + 2	2	6	—	20
Scott, Mick	7 + 8	2	—	—	8
Smith, Steve	15 + 8	6	6	—	36
Whitfield, Colin	24 + 2	11	55	—	154
Wood, Martin	5 + 12	4	—	—	16

TOTALS:
33 players		158	130	8	900

1989-90 MATCH ANALYSIS

Date	Com-petition	H/A	Opponent	Rlt	Score	Tries	Goals	Atten-dance	Referee
3.9.89	SD	H	Rochdale H.	W	36-12	Milner (2), Holmes (2), Holliday, Riddlesden	Whitfield (6)	6761	Burke
10.9.89	SD	H	Oldham	W	22-12	Whitfield, Atkinson, Milner	Whitfield (5)	8612	Campbell
17.9.89	YC(1)	A	Dewsbury	W	22-7	Dorahy, Whitfield, Milner, Wood	Whitfield (3)	—	—
27.9.89	YC(2)	H	Hull	W	13-2	George, Riddlesden	Whitfield (2), Holliday (dg)	8087	Kendrew
1.10.89	SD	A	Nottingham C.	W	72-20	Anderson (4), Wood (2), Hill, Riddlesden, Whitfield, Ramshaw, Milner, Hetherington, George	Whitfield (10)	—	—
5.10.89	YC(SF)	H	Bradford N.	D	16-16	George, Anderson, Smith	Dorahy (2)	9454	Kershaw
8.10.89	SD	H	Doncaster	W	20-12	McCallion, George, Hetherington, Holliday	Dorahy, Holliday	7400	Holgate
15.10.89	YC(SF) Replay	A	Bradford N.	L	4-26	Dickinson	—	—	—
18.10.89	SD	A	Oldham	L	3-14	—	Dorahy, McCallion (dg)	—	—
22.10.89	SD	H	Dewsbury	W	25-9	George (2), Atkins, Carroll	Holliday (4), Lyons (dg)	5610	Tidball
29.10.89	SD	A	Bramley	W	46-10	James (2), George (2), Hutchinson (2), Lyons, Whitfield, Dickinson	Whitfield (5)	—	—
5.11.89	SD	H	Hull K.R.	L	6-20	Johnston	Whitfield	9050	Holdsworth
12.11.89	SD	A	Trafford B.	W	9-6	Wood	Holliday (2), Ramshaw (dg)	—	—
19.11.89	SD	H	Chorley	W	26-16	George, Whitfield, Anderson, Ramshaw	Whitfield (5)	4733	Holgate
26.11.89	SD	A	Carlisle	L	20-30	Hetherington, George, Anderson, Lyons	Whitfield, Holliday	—	—
3.12.89	RT(1)	A	Fulham	W	32-18	George (3), Whitfield (2), Hetherington	Dorahy (4)	—	—
10.12.89	RT(2)	H	Salford	W	20-6	Hetherington (2), George (2)	Whitfield, Dorahy	6005	C. Morris
17.12.89	RT(3)	H	Featherstone R.	W	23-10	Dorahy, George, Smith	Whitfield (4), Dorahy, Lyons (dg)	6075	Bowman
23.12.89	RT(SF)	Wigan	St. Helens	W	10-9	Riddlesden, Scott	Whitfield	(6085)	Kershaw
26.12.89	SD	H	Huddersfield	W	28-4	Anderson (2), Smith, Dorahy, Milner	Holliday (4)	9103	Tidball
31.12.89	SD	H	Bramley	W	30-10	George (2), Scott, Anderson, Riddlesden, Atkinson	Holliday (3)	6155	Asquith
5.1.90	SD	A	Ryedale-York	L	14-18	Anderson, Milner	Holliday (3)	—	—
13.1.90	RT(F)	Leeds	Wigan	L	12-24	Hill	Holliday (4)	(17,810)	Kershaw
17.1.90	SD	A	Whitehaven	W	17-12	Riddlesden, Milner, Atkinson	Holliday (2), Ramshaw (dg)	—	—
21.1.90	SD	A	Dewsbury	L	16-24	Hetherington, Anderson, Hill	Holliday (2)	—	—
28.1.90	CC(1)	A	Hull	L	0-46	—	—	—	—
11.2.90	SD	H	Nottingham C.	W	60-4	Fairbank (2), Ramshaw (2), James (2), Riddlesden, Holliday, Hetherington, Moore, Needham	Holliday (8)	4157	Galtress
18.2.90	SD	H	Ryedale-York	W	22-14	Ramshaw, Atkinson, Riddlesden	Holliday (5)	6065	Bowman
25.2.90	SD	H	Carlisle	W	32-4	Ramshaw (2), Needham, Milner, Hetherington, Dorahy	Holliday (4)	4273	Whitelam

(continued on page 108)

61

HUDDERSFIELD

Ground:	Fartown
Colours:	Claret and gold
First Season:	1895-96; added Barracudas to title from 1984-85 to 1987-88 inclusive
Nickname:	Fartowners
Chairman:	Jim Collins
Secretary:	David Parker
Coaches:	Nigel Stephenson (Nov 1988-Mar 1990) Barry Seabourne (Mar 1990-)
Honours:	**Championship** Winners, 1911-12, 1912-13, 1914-15, 1928-29, 1929-30, 1948-49, 1961-62 Beaten finalists, 1913-14, 1919-20, 1922-23, 1931-32, 1945-46, 1949-50 **Division Two** Champions, 1974-75 **Challenge Cup** Winners, 1912-13, 1914-15, 1919-20, 1932-33, 1944-45, 1952-53 Beaten finalists, 1934-35, 1961-62 **Yorkshire League** Winners, 1911-12, 1912-13, 1913-14, 1914-15, 1919-20, 1921-22, 1928-29, 1929-30, 1948-49, 1949-50, 1951-52 **Eastern Division** Beaten finalists, 1962-63 **Yorkshire Cup** Winners, 1909-10, 1911-12, 1913-14, 1914-15, 1918-19, 1919-20, 1926-27, 1931-32, 1938-39, 1950-51, 1952-53, 1957-58 Beaten finalists, 1910-11, 1923-24, 1925-26, 1930-31, 1937-38, 1942-43, 1949-50, 1960-61
Records:	Attendance: 35,136 Leeds v. Wakefield T. (RL Cup SF) 19 April 1947. Home: 32,912 v. Wigan (League) 4 Mar, 1950 **Season** Goals: 147 by B. Gronow, 1919-20 Tries: 80 by A. Rosenfeld, 1913-14 Points: 330 by B. Gronow, 1919-20

Match
Goals: 18 by M. Holland v. Swinton Park, 28 Feb, 1914
Tries: 10 by L. Cooper v. Keighley, 17 Nov, 1951
Points: 39 by M. Holland v. Swinton Park, 28 Feb, 1914
Highest score: 119-2 v. Swinton Park, 1913-14
Highest against: 94-12 v. Castleford, 1988-89

1989-90 PLAYERS' SUMMARY

	App	Tries	Goals	Dr	Pts
Bannister, Andy	6	1	—	—	4
Boothroyd, Alan	17 + 4	2	—	—	8
Brooks, Kevin	0 + 1	—	—	—	—
Chatterton, Ian	0 + 1	—	—	—	—
Cocker, Stuart	22 + 4	13	6	1	65
Cook, Billy	3	—	—	—	—
Coulter, Stuart	1	—	—	—	—
Dick, Kevin	2 + 1	1	7	3	21
Dickinson, Andy	28 + 2	4	—	—	16
Diskin, Tony	7	—	—	—	—
Edwards, Anthony	27 + 1	8	—	—	32
Farrell, Anthony	6	1	—	—	4
Fitzpatrick, Dennis	0 + 2	—	—	—	—
Gibson, Wally	31	19	12	—	100
Grayshon, Paul	1 + 2	—	—	—	—
Huck, Phil	28 + 1	4	—	—	16
Jowett, Bob	20 + 5	1	—	—	4
Kenworthy, Simon	20 + 2	—	61	—	122
Lee, Bryan	1	—	—	—	—
Mackintosh, Andy	19 + 1	1	—	—	4
Mountain, Dean	3 + 1	—	—	—	—
Nadiole, Joe	4 + 1	1	—	—	4
Nelson, Dave	6 + 6	—	—	—	—
O'Donnell, Damien	2	—	—	—	—
Power, Anthony	1 + 7	—	—	—	—
Royston, Paul	1 + 2	—	—	—	—
St. Hilaire, Lee	29 + 1	4	—	—	16
Senior, Gary	10 + 1	—	—	—	—
Shuttleworth, Greg	28	1	1	1	7
Siddall, Gary	22 + 3	4	—	—	16
Simpson, Andy	6 + 1	3	—	—	12
Simpson, Frank	15 + 1	—	—	—	—
Staniforth, Tony	4 + 1	—	—	—	—
Stephenson, Nigel	0 + 1	—	—	—	—
Subritzky, Peter	24 + 1	7	3	—	34
Thomas, Ian	17 + 1	7	—	—	28
Wardle, Chris	0 + 1	—	—	—	—
Whitehead, Craig	3 + 1	—	—	—	—
Wilson, Mick	2 + 1	1	—	—	4

TOTALS:
39 players		83	90	5	517

1989-90 MATCH ANALYSIS

Date	Com-petition	H/A	Opponent	Rlt	Score	Tries	Goals	Atten-dance	Referee
3.9.89	SD	A	Whitehaven	W	34-22	Gibson (3), Thomas, Cocker	Kenworthy (7)	—	—
10.9.89	SD	H	Fulham	L	6-8	Farrell	Kenworthy	1852	Allatt
13.9.89	SD	H	Hunslet	W	14-10	Edwards, Thomas	Subritzky (2), Shuttleworth	1311	Holgate
17.9.89	YC(1)	A	Doncaster	L	4-23	—	Kenworthy (2)	—	—
24.9.89	SD	H	Workington T.	L	16-21	Cocker (2), Gibson	Gibson, Subritzky	1049	K. Morris
1.10.89	SD	A	Runcorn H.	W	42-0	Subritzky (3), Cocker (2), St. Hilaire, Dickinson	Kenworthy (7)	—	—
8.10.89	SD	H	Trafford B.	W	22-18	Subritzky (2), Gibson	Kenworthy (5)	1085	Asquith
15.10.89	SD	H	Whitehaven	W	31-12	Boothroyd (2), Huck, Jowett, Edwards	Kenworthy (5), Shuttleworth (dg)	1202	Holdsworth
27.10.89	SD	A	Ryedale-York	W	10-6	Thomas	Kenworthy (3)	—	—
12.11.89	SD	A	Hunslet	W	14-10	Cocker (2), Siddall	Kenworthy	—	—
19.11.89	SD	H	Nottingham C.	W	16-10	Edwards, Mackintosh, Thomas	Kenworthy (2)	1348	Allatt
26.11.89	SD	A	Bramley	W	14-2	Dickinson, Siddall	Gibson (2), Kenworthy	—	—
3.12.89	RT(1)	A	Workingon T.	W	28-4	Gibson (3), Huck, Dickinson	Kenworthy (4)	—	—
10.12.89	RT(2)	A	Oldham	L	8-22	Gibson	Kenworthy (2)	—	—
17.12.89	SD	H	Ryedale-York	L	8-16	—	Kenworthy (4)	1174	Steele
26.12.89	SD	A	Halifax	L	4-28	St. Hilaire	—	—	—
31.12.89	SD	H	Keighley	L	10-11	Thomas, Edwards	Gibson	1685	K. Morris
7.1.90	SD	H	Runcorn H.	W	22-10	Simpson (2), Subritzky, Edwards	Kenworthy (3)	922	Tickle
14.1.90	CC(P)	A	Oldham	L	8-30	—	Kenworthy (4)	—	—
17.1.90	SD	A	Swinton	L	10-26	Subritzky, Simpson	Kenworthy	—	—
21.1.90	SD	A	Trafford B.	L	18-28	St. Hilaire, Gibson, Edwards	Kenworthy (3)	—	—
4.2.90	SD	A	Nottingham C.	W	42-4	Gibson (2), Huck (2), Cocker (2), Edwards, St. Hilaire	Gibson (5)	—	—
18.2.90	SD	A	Workington T.	W	24-8	Gibson (3), Dickinson, Cocker	Gibson (2)	—	—
25.2.90	SD	H	Dewsbury	L	0-13	—	—	1630	Burke
4.3.90	SD	A	Oldham	L	8-23	Thomas	Gibson, Kenworthy	—	—
11.3.90	SD	A	Fulham	L	10-34	Thomas	Kenworthy (3)	—	—
18.3.90	SD	H	Bramley	L	12-16	Gibson, Shuttleworth	Kenworthy (2)	898	Whitelam
24.3.90	SD	H	Oldham	L	14-22	Bannister, Gibson, Nadiole	Cocker	4943	Simpson
1.4.90	SD	A	Dewsbury	L	8-26	Gibson	Dick (1, 2dg)	—	—
8.4.90	SD	H	Swinton	W	14-9	Cocker, Gibson	Dick (2, 2dg)	743	Bowman
13.4.90	SD	H	Halifax	L	15-28	Siddall, Dick	Dick (3, 1dg)	3174	Burke
16.4.90	SD	A	Keighley	W	31-20	Cocker (2), Edwards, Wilson, Siddall	Cocker (5, 1dg)	—	—

HULL

Ground:	The Boulevard
Colours:	Black and white
First Season:	1895-96
Nickname:	Airlie Birds
Chairman:	Roy Waudby
Secretary:	Ian Pickering
Coach:	Brian Smith (July 1988-)
Honours:	**Championship** Winners, 1919-20, 1920-21, 1935-36, 1955-56, 1957-58
	Beaten finalists, 1956-57
	Division One Champions, 1982-83
	Division Two Champions, 1976-77, 1978-79
	Challenge Cup Winners, 1913-14, 1981-82
	Beaten finalists, 1907-08, 1908-09, 1909-10, 1921-22, 1922-23, 1958-59, 1959-60, 1979-80, 1982-83, 1984-85
	Yorkshire League Winners, 1918-19, 1922-23, 1926-27, 1935-36
	Yorkshire Cup Winners, 1923-24, 1969-70, 1982-83, 1983-84, 1984-85
	Beaten finalists, 1912-13, 1914-15, 1920-21, 1927-28, 1938-39, 1946-47, 1953-54, 1954-55, 1955-56, 1959-60, 1967-68, 1986-87
	Regal Trophy Winners, 1981-82
	Beaten finalists, 1975-76, 1984-85
	BBC2 Floodlit Trophy Winners, 1979-80
	Premiership Beaten finalists, 1980-81, 1981-82, 1982-83, 1988-89
Records:	Attendance: 28,798 v. Leeds (RL Cup) 7 Mar, 1936
	Season
	Goals: 170 by S. Lloyd, 1978-79
	Tries: 52 by J. Harrison, 1914-15
	Points: 369 by S. Lloyd, 1978-79
	Match
	Goals: 14 by J. Kennedy v. Rochdale H., 7 Apr, 1921; S. Lloyd v. Oldham, 10 Sep, 1978
	Tries: 7 by C. Sullivan v. Doncaster, 15 Apr, 1968
	Points: 36 by J. Kennedy v. Keighley, 29 Jan, 1921

Highest score: 86-0 v. Elland, 1898-99
Highest against: 64-2 v. St. Helens, 1987-88

1989-90 PLAYERS' SUMMARY

	App	Tries	Goals	Dr	Pts
Blacker, Brian	24	3	—	—	12
Charles, Marquis	13 + 1	4	—	—	16
Cleal, Noel	24 + 1	9	—	—	36
Crooks, Steve	10 + 1	—	—	—	—
Dannatt, Andy	31	4	—	—	16
Dixon, Michael	1 + 4	2	—	—	8
Doherty, Paul	6 + 1	1	1	—	6
Eastwood, Paul	31 + 1	22	101	—	290
Fletcher, Paul	6	1	—	—	4
Folkes, Steve	24	2	—	—	8
Gay, Richard	25 + 1	6	—	—	24
Harrison, Karl	28 + 3	2	—	—	8
Harrison, Paul	0 + 2	—	—	—	—
Hick, Steve	6 + 1	1	—	—	4
Jackson, Lee	31 + 1	6	—	—	24
Jackson, Tony	6 + 4	6	—	—	24
Khan, Patrick	1	—	—	—	—
Liddiard, David	7	4	—	—	16
Mackey, Greg	25	6	—	3	27
McNamara, Steve	6 + 1	2	—	—	8
Mighty, Andrew	3 + 2	1	—	—	4
Nolan, Robert	11 + 12	3	5	—	22
O'Hara, Dane	10	1	—	—	4
Patrick, Shaun	2	—	—	—	—
Pearce, Gary	12 + 1	5	17	3	57
Price, Richard	16 + 1	3	—	—	12
Puckering, Neil	0 + 1	—	—	—	—
Sharp, Jon	28 + 2	6	—	—	24
Turner, Neil	17	12	—	—	48
Walker, Russ	6 + 7	4	—	—	16
Welham, Paul	13 + 12	4	—	—	16
Wilby, Tim	13 + 2	1	—	—	4
Windley, Phil	19 + 4	7	—	—	28

TOTALS:
33 players		128	124	6	766

Australian Test packman Noel Cleal, scorer of nine tries in 25 appearances for Hull.

1989-90 MATCH ANALYSIS

Date	Competition	H/A	Opponent	Rlt	Score	Tries	Goals	Attendance	Referee
27.8.89	YC(P)	A	Nottingham C.	W	56-6	Nolan (2), Pearce (2), Welham, Fletcher, Dannatt, O'Hara, Windley, Price	Pearce (5), Eastwood (2), Nolan	—	—
3.9.89	SBC	A	Bradford N.	L	12-30	McNamara	Eastwood (4)	—	—
10.9.89	SBC	H	Widnes	L	11-26	Welham	Pearce (3, 1dg)	8298	Steele
17.9.89	YC(1)	H	Ryedale-York	W	20-10	Liddiard (2), L. Jackson (2),	Nolan (2)	4317	Galtress
24.9.89	SBC	A	Castleford	L	10-18	Cleal	Pearce, Doherty, Nolan	—	—
27.9.89	YC(2)	A	Halifax	L	2-13	—	Nolan	—	—
1.10.89	SBC	H	Leeds	W	8-7	Sharp, Liddiard	—	7741	Tickle
8.10.89	SBC	A	Warrington	D	12-12	Gay, Liddiard	Eastwood (2)	—	—
15.10.89	SBC	H	Salford	W	44-8	Eastwood (2), A. Jackson (2), Cleal, Doherty, Welham	Eastwood (8)	5858	Asquith
29.10.89	SBC	A	Wakefield T.	L	14-30	A. Jackson (2), L. Jackson	Eastwood	—	—
1.11.89	Tour	H	New Zealand	L	8-44	Eastwood	Eastwood (2)	5894	C. Morris
12.11.89	SBC	A	Featherstone R.	W	24-10	Pearce, Folkes, Welham, Nolan	Pearce (3), Eastwood	—	—
19.11.89	RT(P)	A	Wakefield T.	W	19-12	A. Jackson (2), Mackey	Pearce (3, 1dg)	—	—
21.11.89	SBC	H	St. Helens	L	24-34	Eastwood (2), Price, Sharp	Pearce (2), Eastwood (2)	6124	Whitfield
26.11.89	SBC	A	Wigan	L	2-30	—	Eastwood	—	—
3.12.89	RT(1)	H	Salford	L	18-21	Eastwood (2)	Eastwood (5)	4587	Bowman
17.12.89	SBC	H	Leigh	W	28-24	Turner (2), Eastwood, Mighty, Harrison	Eastwood (4)	4287	Holdsworth
26.12.89	SBC	H	Sheffield E.	W	15-6	Eastwood, Pearce	Eastwood (3), Pearce (dg)	5752	Kendrew
1.1.90	SBC	A	Leeds	L	2-18	—	Eastwood	—	—
7.1.90	SBC	H	Barrow	W	48-0	Eastwood (3), Mackey, Dixon, Blacker, Pearce, Turner	Eastwood (8)	4355	Kershaw
17.1.90	SBC	A	St. Helens	L	12-19	Cleal	Eastwood (4)	—	—
21.1.90	SBC	H	Wigan	W	30-20	Dannatt, Eastwood, Charles, Gay, Windley	Eastwood (5)	8065	Bowman
28.1.90	CC(1)	H	Halifax	W	46-0	L. Jackson (2), Mackey, Windley, Blacker, Charles	Eastwood (7)	7574	Kendrew
4.2.90	SBC	H	Castleford	W	16-6	Mackey, Windley, Dixon	Eastwood (2)	7497	Campbell
10.2.90	CC(2)	H	St. Helens	L	12-24	Dannatt, McNamara	Eastwood (2)	8066	Kershaw
18.2.90	SBC	A	Widnes	L	12-30	Turner, Cleal	Eastwood (2)	—	—
28.2.90	SBC	H	Bradford N.	W	24-0	Turner, Walker, Charles, Gay	Eastwood (4)	3976	Campbell
4.3.90	SBC	A	Barrow	W	38-6	Turner (3), Eastwood (2), Walker, Wilby	Eastwood (5)	—	—
11.3.90	SBC	H	Wakefield T.	W	34-17	Eastwood (2), Sharp (2), Turner (2), Gay	Eastwood (3)	6749	Whitfield
18.3.90	SBC	A	Salford	W	21-5	Turner, Walker, Dannatt, Charles	Eastwood (2), Mackey (dg)	—	—
25.3.90	SBC	H	Featherstone R.	W	36-10	Cleal (2), Eastwood (2), Windley, Folkes	Eastwood (6)	6242	Crashley
1.4.90	SBC	A	Leigh	W	24-14	Eastwood (2), Cleal, Hick, Turner	Eastwood (2)	—	—
8.4.90	SBC	H	Warrington	W	44-16	Windley (2), L. Jackson, Blacker, Eastwood, Sharp, Walker, Price	Eastwood (6)	5890	Mairs (Pr)
15.4.90	SBC	A[1]	Sheffield E.	W	32-4	Mackey (2), Harrison, Cleal, Sharp	Eastwood (5), Mackey (2dg)	—	—
22.4.90	PT(1)	A	Widnes	L	8-18	Cleal	Eastwood (2)	—	—

[1] at Sheffield U. FC

CLUBS

HULL KINGSTON ROVERS

Ground:	Craven Park
Colours:	Red, blue and white
First Season:	1899-1900
Nickname:	Robins
Chairman:	Malcolm West
Secretary:	Ron Turner
Coach:	Roger Millward (Mar 1977-)
Honours:	**Championship** Winners, 1922-23, 1924-25 Beaten finalists, 1920-21, 1967-68 **First Division** Champions, 1978-79, 1983-84, 1984-85 **Second Division** Champions, 1989-90 **Challenge Cup** Winners, 1979-80 Beaten finalists, 1904-05, 1924-25, 1963-64, 1980-81, 1985-86 **Regal Trophy** Winners, 1984-85, Beaten finalists, 1981-82, 1985-86 **Premiership** Winners, 1980-81, 1983-84, Beaten finalists, 1984-85 **Second Division Premiership** Beaten finalists, 1989-90 **Yorkshire League** Winners, 1924-25, 1925-26 **Yorkshire Cup** Winners, 1920-21, 1929-30, 1966-67, 1967-68, 1971-72, 1974-75, 1985-86 Beaten finalists, 1906-07, 1911-12, 1933-34, 1962-63, 1975-76, 1980-81, 1984-85 **BBC2 Floodlit Trophy** Winners, 1977-78 Beaten finalists, 1979-80 **Eastern Division** Championship Winners, 1962-63 **Charity Shield** Beaten finalists, 1985-86
Records:	Attendance: 22,282 v. Hull, 7 October, 1922. There was a crowd of 27,670 for a League match v. Hull at Hull City FC's Boothferry Park on 3 April, 1953

Season
Goals: 199 by M. Fletcher, 1989-90
Tries: 45 by G. Prohm, 1984-85
Points: 450 by M. Fletcher, 1989-90
Match
Goals: 14 by A. Carmichael v. Merthyr Tydfil, 8 Oct, 1910; M. Fletcher v. Whitehaven, 18 Mar, 1990
Tries: 11 by G. West v. Brookland R., 4 Mar, 1905
Points: 53 by G. West v. Brookland R., 4 Mar, 1905
Highest score: 92-10 v. Whitehaven, 1989-90
Highest against: 68-0 v. Halifax, 1955-56

1989-90 PLAYERS' SUMMARY

	App	Tries	Goals	Dr	Pts
Armstrong, Colin	25 + 7	6	5	—	34
Austin, Greg	34	38	—	—	152
Beall, Malcolm	0 + 1	—	—	—	—
Bishop, David	26 + 2	19	—	—	76
Botica, Tony	26	17	—	—	68
Clark, Garry	35	22	—	—	88
Ema, Asuquo	24 + 2	4	—	—	16
Fairbairn, George	12	2	—	—	8
Fletcher, Mike	35	13	199	—	450
Fletcher, Paul	0 + 6	1	—	—	4
Hallas, Graeme	3	—	—	—	—
Harrison, Des	10 + 1	5	—	—	20
Irvine, Jimmy	10 + 18	9	—	—	36
Lightfoot, David	23	6	—	—	24
Lydiat, John	0 + 1	—	—	—	—
Lyman, Paul	21 + 8	14	—	—	56
Niebling, Bryan	30 + 1	1	—	—	4
O'Brien, Craig	0 + 1	—	—	—	—
Parker, Wayne	14 + 11	8	—	3	35
Pratt, Richard	4	—	—	—	—
Robinson, Steve	2 + 1	—	—	—	—
Rudd, Chris	35	9	—	—	36
Smith, Mike	32	9	—	—	36
Speckman, Paul	0 + 1	—	—	—	—
Sullivan, Anthony	28	34	—	—	136
Thompson, Andy	28 + 4	4	—	—	16
Vannet, Paul	2 + 5	2	—	—	8
TOTALS: 27 players		223	204	3	1,303

1989-90 MATCH ANALYSIS

Date	Competition	H/A	Opponent	Rlt	Score	Tries	Goals	Attendance	Referee
3.9.89	SD	A	Keighley	W	50-16	Lyman (2), Harrison (2), Botica, M. Fletcher, Bishop, Clark	M. Fletcher (8), Armstrong	—	—
17.9.89	YC(1)	A	Bramley	W	54-12	Austin (2), Bishop, Lyman, Botica, Smith, Sullivan, Clark, M. Fletcher	M. Fletcher (9)	—	—
24.9.89	SD	H	Trafford B.	W	48-8	Clark (2), Austin (2), M. Fletcher, Botica, Rudd, Bishop	M. Fletcher (8)	8095	C. Morris
27.9.89	YC(2)	A	Castleford	L	12-28	Bishop, W. Parker	M. Fletcher (2)	—	—
1.10.89	SD	A	Oldham	L	4-12	—	M. Fletcher (2)	—	—
8.10.89	SD	H	Nottingham C.	W	54-4	Clark (3), Austin (2), Bishop, Rudd, M. Fletcher, Vannet	M. Fletcher (9)	4886	Campbell
22.10.89	SD	H	Swinton	W	38-16	Clark (2), Botica, Austin, Bishop, W. Parker	M. Fletcher (7)	4688	Whitfield
29.10.89	SD	H	Fulham	W	44-0	Botica (2), M. Fletcher (2), Clark, Ema, Irvine	M. Fletcher (8)	4272	Tidball
5.11.89	SD	A	Halifax	W	20-6	Botica (2), Sullivan, Bishop	M. Fletcher (2)	—	—
12.11.89	SD	H	Workington T.	W	34-0	Irvine (2), Clark, Botica, Rudd, W. Parker	M. Fletcher (5)	4558	Simpson
19.11.89	SD	A	Swinton	W	30-10	Clark (2), Lightfoot, Sullivan, Lyman	M. Fletcher (5)	—	—
26.11.89	SD	H	Dewsbury	W	54-6	Armstrong (2), Bishop (2), Botica, Lightfoot, Sullivan, Niebling, Lyman, Smith	M. Fletcher (7)	4318	Steele
2.12.89	RT(1)	A	St. Helens	L	26-40	Armstrong, Irvine, Bishop	Armstrong (4), M. Fletcher (3)	—	—
17.12.89	SD	A	Fulham	W	60-6	Austin (2), Sullivan (2), M. Fletcher (2), Lightfoot (2), Clark, Bishop	M. Fletcher (10)	—	—
26.12.89	SD	H	Ryedale-York	W	12-0	Austin, Sullivan	M. Fletcher (2)	4994	Bowman
31.12.89	SD	A	Hunslet	W	36-10	Austin (4), Irvine, Smith, Clark	M. Fletcher (4)	—	—
7.1.90	SD	A	Nottingham C.	W	58-0	Sullivan (3), Austin (2), Smith (2), Irvine, Lyman, Botica, M. Fletcher	M. Fletcher (7)	—	—
17.1.90	SD	H	Oldham	L	6-9	Sullivan	M. Fletcher	6425	Tidball
21.1.90	SD	A	Workington T.	W	40-6	Austin (3), Bishop, Smith, Sullivan, M. Fletcher	M. Fletcher (6)	—	—
28.1.90	CC(1)	H	Wigan	L	4-6	—	M. Fletcher (2)	8473	Tennant
4.2.90	SD	A	Bramley	W	60-2	Bishop (3), Austin (2), Sullivan (2), Lightfoot, Botica, Lyman	M. Fletcher (10)	—	—
18.2.90	SD	H	Runcorn H.	W	36-6	Austin (2), Sullivan (2), Botica, Ema, Armstrong	M. Fletcher (4)	3712	Simpson
4.3.90	SD	H	Keighley	W	66-10	Sullivan (5), Austin (2), Fairbairn, M. Fletcher, Botica, Thompson, P. Fletcher	M. Fletcher (9)	3643	K. Morris
7.3.90	SD	A	Whitehaven	W	46-2	Rudd (2), Clark (2), Sullivan (2), Austin, Bishop, Irvine	M. Fletcher (5)	—	—
18.3.90	SD	H	Whitehaven	W	92-10	Austin (3), Sullivan (3), Bishop (3), Botica (3), Armstrong (2), Smith, Thompson	M. Fletcher (14)	3691	Galtress

(continued on page 108)

HUNSLET

Ground:	Elland Road
Colours:	Myrtle, flame and white
First Season:	1895-96. Disbanded at end of 1972-73. Re-formed as New Hunslet in 1973-74. Retitled Hunslet from start of 1979-80
Chairman:	Graham Lisle
Secretary:	Mabel Grainger
Coaches:	Graeme Jennings (Sep 1989-Apr 1990) Paul Daley (May 1990-)
Honours:	**Challenge Cup** Winners, 1907-08, 1933-34 Beaten finalists, 1898-99, 1964-65 **Championship** Winners, 1907-08, 1937-38 Beaten finalists, 1958-59 **Division Two** Champions, 1962-63, 1986-87 **Second Division Premiership** Beaten finalists, 1986-87 **Yorkshire Cup** Winners, 1905-06, 1907-08, 1962-63 Beaten finalists, 1908-09, 1929-30, 1931-32, 1944-45, 1956-57, 1965-66 **Yorkshire League** Winners, 1897-98, 1907-08, 1931-32
Records:	Attendance: 54,112 v. Leeds (Championship final) 30 Apr, 1938 **Season** Goals: 181 by W. Langton, 1958-59 Tries: 34 by A. Snowden, 1956-57 Points: 380 by W. Langton, 1958-59 **Match** Goals: 12 by W. Langton v. Keighley, 18 Aug, 1959 Tries: 7 by G. Dennis v. Bradford N., 20 Jan, 1934 Points: 27 by W. Langton v. Keighley, 18 Aug, 1959 Highest score: 75-5 v. Broughton Rec., 1896-97 Highest against: 76-8 v. Halifax, 1972-73

1989-90 PLAYERS' SUMMARY

	App	Tries	Goals	Dr	Pts
Adams, John	17	1	1	—	6
Bateman, Andy	5	1	—	—	4
Bowden, Chris	21 + 7	3	—	—	12
Brook, Richard	4 + 1	1	—	—	4
Burrow, Paul	7 + 1	1	—	—	4
Carter, Paul	0 + 2	—	—	—	—
Coates, Jed	16 + 4	4	—	—	16
Evans, Gary	2	—	—	—	—
Jackson, Michael	20	6	—	1	25
Jennings, Graeme	12	1	—	—	4
Kay, Andy	9	2	8	—	24
King, Graham	6 + 4	3	—	—	12
Langton, Steve	24 + 1	5	—	1	21
Lay, Steve	10	1	25	—	54
Lowes, James	24 + 1	6	1	—	26
Lumb, Tim	10 + 8	3	28	4	72
Lyons, Paddy	21 + 6	5	—	2	22
Marson, Andrew	8	—	—	—	—
Mason, Andrew	23 + 1	—	—	—	—
Mitchell, Keith	11 + 5	3	—	—	12
Morgan, Paul	6 + 1	—	—	—	—
Oldroyd, Tom	8 + 3	1	—	—	4
Penola, Colin	20 + 1	3	—	—	12
Petch, Andrew	18 + 5	4	—	—	16
Raw, Andy	23	6	—	—	24
Sampson, Roy	19 + 2	3	—	—	12
Tate, Phil	4	—	—	—	—
Warrener, Stan	14 + 1	3	5	—	22
Welsh, Brett	17 + 3	—	—	—	—
Whittington, Mark	18	3	—	—	12
Wilby, Simon	0 + 4	—	—	—	—
Wilkinson, Shaun	19	7	2	—	32
TOTALS:					
32 players		76	70	8	452

Roy Sampson, three tries in 21 games for Hunslet.

1989-90 MATCH ANALYSIS

Date	Competition	H/A	Opponent	Rlt	Score	Tries	Goals	Attendance	Referee
3.9.89	SD	H	Bramley	W	22-14	Wilkinson, Jackson, Mitchell	Lumb (5)	1048	Allatt
6.9.89	SD	H	Ryedale-York	L	16-36	Lowes, Bowden	Lumb (4)	1059	Crashley
10.9.89	SD	A	Nottingham C.	W	23-12	Wilkinson, Coates, Mitchell, Bateman	Lumb (3, 1dg)	—	—
13.9.89	SD	A	Huddersfield	L	10-14	Adams	Lumb (2, 2dg)	—	—
17.9.89	YC(1)	H	Castleford	L	0-44	—	—	3180	Kershaw
24.9.89	SD	A	Whitehaven	L	11-22	Jennings	Lumb (3), Jackson (dg)	—	—
1.10.89	SD	H	Batley	L	12-23	Wilkinson, Kay	Lumb (2)	1128	Bowman
8.10.89	SD	H	Dewsbury	L	19-24	Jackson, Lumb, Raw	Lumb (3, 1dg)	1046	K. Morris
15.10.89	SD	A	Chorley	L	8-16	Kay	Lumb (2)	—	—
22.10.89	SD	A	Trafford B.	W	32-0	Jackson (2), Raw (2), Bowden, Lumb	Kay (4)	—	—
29.10.89	SD	H	Carlisle	W	26-12	Lowes (2), Wilkinson, Lyons, Oldroyd	Kay (3)	597	Allatt
5.11.89	SD	A	Ryedale-York	L	0-20	—	—	—	—
12.11.89	SD	H	Huddersfield	L	10-14	Jackson	Lumb (2), Kay	1241	Smith
19.11.89	SD	A	Dewsbury	L	10-13	Lowes, Jackson	Lowes	—	—
26.11.89	SD	H	Rochdale H.	L	20-26	Penola (3), Burrows	Wilkinson (2)	1320	Tickle
3.12.89	RT(1)	A	Barrow	W	10-6	Lowes, Brook	Adams	537	Holdsworth
10.12.89	RT(2)	H	Featherstone R.	L	4-34	Langton	—	2031	Tidball
17.12.89	SD	A	Doncaster	L	2-12	—	Lumb	—	—
26.12.89	SD	H	Chorley	L	2-14	—	Warrener	606	Campbell
31.12.89	SD	H	Hull K.R.	L	10-36	Wilkinson, Sampson	Lumb	1718	Burke
7.1.90	SD	A	Oldham	L	10-48	Bowden, Whittington	Warrener	—	—
14.1.90	SD	H	Nottingham C.	W	32-8	Wilkinson (2), Coates, King, Raw, Lyons	Lay (4)	478	Galtress
28.1.90	CC(1)	A	Trafford B.	L	7-14	Whittington	Lay, Lyons (dg)	—	—
4.2.90	SD	H	Doncaster	W	27-12	Sampson, Raw, Lyons, Langton, Coates	Warrener (3), Lyons (dg)	1260	Carter
11.2.90	SD	A	Batley	W	22-16	Warrener, Whittington, Sampson, Coates	Lay (3)	—	—
25.2.90	SD	A	Bramley	W	23-10	Langton, Petch, King, Lyons	Lay (3), Langton (dg)	—	—
4.3.90	SD	H	Whitehaven	W	32-16	Langton (2), Lay, Lowes, Warrener, Petch	Lay (4)	609	Whitelam
11.3.90	SD	H	Trafford B.	L	14-25	Lyons, Mitchell	Lay (3)	767	K. Morris
18.3.90	SD	A	Carlisle	W	4-2	Petch	—	—	—
21.3.90	SD	H	Oldham	L	14-42	Warrener, King	Lay (3)	1772	Allatt
25.3.90	SD	A	Rochdale H.	L	14-40	Raw, Lumb	Lay (3)	—	—
16.4.90	SD	A	Hull K.R.	L	6-58	Petch	Lay	—	—

KEIGHLEY

Ground:	Lawkholme Lane
Colours:	Green, scarlet and white
First Season:	1901-02
Nickname:	Lawkholmers
Chairman:	Colin Farrar
Secretary:	Betty Spencer
Coaches:	Colin Dixon (July 1986-June 1989)
	Les Coulter (July 1986-Apr 1990)
	Tony Fisher (June 1990-)
Honours:	**Division Two** Champions, 1902-03
	Challenge Cup Beaten finalists, 1936-37
	Yorkshire Cup Beaten finalists, 1943-44, 1951-52
Records:	Attendance: 14,500 v. Halifax (RL Cup) 3 Mar, 1951

Season
Goals: 155 by B. Jefferson, 1973-74
Tries: 30 by J. Sherburn, 1934-35
Points: 331 by B. Jefferson, 1973-74

Match
Goals: 11 by R. Walker v. Castleford, 13 Jan, 1906; H. Cook v. Hull K.R., 31 Oct, 1953
Tries: 5 by I. Jagger v. Castleford, 13 Jan, 1906; S. Stacey v. Liverpool C., 9 Mar, 1907
Points: 24 by J. Phillips v. Halifax, 5 Oct, 1957
Highest score: 67-0 v. Castleford, 1905-06
Highest against: 92-2 v. Leigh, 1985-86

1989-90 PLAYERS' SUMMARY

	App	Tries	Goals	Dr	Pts
Ambler, Andy	0 + 2	—	—	—	—
Badger, Warwick	10 + 4	—	—	—	—
Bardgett, Joe	15 + 3	2	—	—	8
Bardgett, Paul	9	—	—	—	—
Butterfield, Jeff	21 + 1	5	—	—	20
Collis, John	19	4	1	—	18
Coop, Chris	0 + 4	—	—	—	—
Coulter, Gary	23 + 1	4	—	—	16
Cox, Dave	4 + 2	—	—	—	—
Cudmore, Mark	2	—	—	—	—
Delman, Robert	1	—	—	—	—
Dixon, Keith	27	11	62	6	174
Dixon, Paul	7	1	1	—	6
Fairbank, Andy	10 + 1	1	—	—	4
Fairbank, Mark	14 + 3	4	—	—	16
Fallon, Tony	0 + 1	—	—	—	—
Goodier, Frank	4 + 1	—	—	—	—
Hirst, Carl	9	1	1	—	6
Johnson, Dave	7 + 7	1	—	—	4
Kemp, Martin	5 + 3	—	—	—	—
Manning, Terry	6	2	—	—	8
Mason, Max	0 + 1	—	—	—	—
Moorby, Gary	14 + 3	1	—	—	4
Moses, Paul	27 + 2	5	8	2	38
Okesene, Paul	20 + 1	5	—	—	20
Porter, Dave	1	—	—	—	—
Proctor, Rob	23	—	—	—	—
Ragan, Mark	6	1	—	—	4
Richardson, Peter	10 + 1	4	—	—	16
Rose, Gary	9	—	—	—	—
Rose, Kevin	2	—	—	—	—
St. Hilaire, Darren	22 + 1	3	—	—	12
Simpson, Owen	30 + 1	24	—	—	96
Smith, Phil	1 + 3	—	—	—	—
Thompson, Julian	11	1	—	—	4
Tyers, Andy	2 + 2	1	—	—	4
Waller, Vince	4	—	—	—	—
Wardle, Chris	4 + 3	1	—	—	4
White, Brendan	12 + 1	—	—	—	—
Widdop, Garry	6 + 1	1	—	—	4
Wilson, Shaun	10 + 2	—	—	—	—
Winterbottom, Ricky	7 + 5	—	—	—	—
Trialists (2)	2	—	—	—	—
TOTALS:					
44 players		83	73	8	486

Keith Dixon, scorer of 174 points for Keighley.

1989-90 MATCH ANALYSIS

Date	Com-petition	H/A	Opponent	Rlt	Score	Tries	Goals	Atten-dance	Referee
3.9.89	SD	H	Hull K.R.	L	16-50	Ragan, Coulter, K. Dixon	K. Dixon (2)	1981	Asquith
10.9.89	SD	A	Dewsbury	L	6-29	Moses	K. Dixon	—	—
13.9.89	SD	H	Whitehaven	W	31-24	St. Hilaire (2), K. Dixon, Moses, Simpson	K. Dixon (5, 1dg)	581	Asquith
17.9.89	YC(1)	A	Featherstone R.	L	18-86	Simpson (2), Thompson	Moses (2), K. Dixon	—	—
24.9.89	SD	H	Nottingham C.	W	51-16	Simpson (3), Manning, Bardgett, K. Dixon, Butterfield, Collis	K. Dixon (9, 1dg)	681	Allatt
1.10.89	SD	A	Chorley	W	25-12	Bardgett, Manning, Widdot, Simpson	K. Dixon (4, 1dg)	—	—
8.10.89	SD	A	Ryedale-York	L	6-16	K. Dixon	K. Dixon	—	—
15.10.89	SD	A	Trafford B.	L	19-25	Moses, K. Dixon, Collis	K. Dixon (3, 1dg)	—	—
22.10.89	SD	H	Doncaster	L	6-34	—	K. Dixon (3)	1427	Campbell
29.10.89	SD	H	Trafford B.	L	16-25	Simpson, Okesene, K. Dixon	K. Dixon (2)	577	Holdsworth
5.11.89	SD	H	Batley	L	8-22	Simpson	K. Dixon (2)	997	Tickle
12.11.89	SD	A	Oldham	L	34-50	Simpson (2) Okesene, K. Dixon, Butterfield, Collis	K. Dixon (3), Moses (2)	—	—
19.11.89	SD	H	Carlisle	W	30-22	K. Dixon (2), Simpson, Okesene, Butterfield	K. Dixon (4), Collis	621	Cross
26.11.89	SD	A	Whitehaven	L	18-22	Moses, Okesene, M. Fairbank	K. Dixon (3)	—	—
3.12.89	RT(1)	A	Bradford N.	L	10-38	Richardson, Simpson	K. Dixon	—	—
26.12.89	SD	A	Bramley	L	8-15	Okesene, Simpson	—	—	—
31.12.89	SD	A	Huddersfield	W	11-10	Wardle, Moorby	K. Dixon (1, 1dg)	—	—
7.1.90	SD	H	Rochdale H.	L	12-38	Butterfield, Simpson	K. Dixon (2)	1377	Burke
21.1.90	SD	A	Doncaster	L	14-28	Simpson, Butterfield, Collis	K. Dixon	—	—
30.1.90	CC(1)	A	Chorley	W	12-6	K. Dixon, Coulter	K. Dixon (2)	—	—
4.2.90	SD	H	Dewsbury	L	6-20	St. Hilaire	K. Dixon	998	Galtress
11.2.90	CC(2)	A	Whitehaven	L	10-46	M. Fairbank, Simpson	K. Dixon	—	—
18.2.90	SD	A	Carlisle	L	9-38	Simpson, Hirst	Moses (dg)	—	—
4.3.90	SD	A	Hull K.R.	L	10-66	Richardson (2)	Hirst	—	—
7.3.90	SD	H	Oldham	L	10-30	Richardson, Simpson	P. Dixon	1366	Holgate
11.3.90	SD	H	Ryedale-York	L	8-70	Simpson, Coulter	—	797	Steele
18.3.90	SD	A	Nottingham C.	L	22-29	Simpson (3)	K. Dixon (5)	—	—
25.3.90	SD	H	Chorley	W	11-9	Moses, M. Fairbank	K. Dixon, Moses (dg)	447	Kendrew
4.4.90	SD	A	Batley	L	16-37	M. Fairbank, Tyas	Moses (4)	—	—
8.4.90	SD	A	Rochdale H.	L	0-52	—	—	—	—
13.4.90	SD	H	Bramley	L	13-17	P. Dixon, A. Fairbank, Simpson	K. Dixon (dg)	513	Asquith
16.4.90	SD	H	Huddersfield	L	20-31	K. Dixon, Coulter, Johnson	K. Dixon (4)	744	Carter

LEEDS

Ground: Headingley
Colours: Blue and amber
First Season: 1895-96
Nickname: Loiners
Chief Exec: Alf Davies
Coach: Malcolm Reilly
(Aug 1988-Sep 1990)
David Ward (Sep 1990-)
Honours: **Championship** Winners, 1960-61,
1968-69, 1971-72
Beaten finalists, 1914-15, 1928-29,
1929-30, 1930-31, 1937-38, 1969-70,
1972-73
League Leaders Trophy Winners,
1966-67, 1967-68, 1968-69, 1969-70,
1971-72
Challenge Cup Winners, 1909-10,
1922-23, 1931-32, 1935-36, 1940-41,
1941-42, 1956-57, 1967-68, 1976-77,
1977-78
Beaten finalists, 1942-43, 1946-47,
1970-71, 1971-72
Yorkshire League Winners,
1901-02, 1927-28, 1930-31, 1933-34,
1934-35, 1936-37, 1937-38, 1950-51,
1954-55, 1956-57, 1960-61, 1966-67,
1967-68, 1968-69, 1969-70
Yorkshire Cup Winners, 1921-22,
1928-29, 1930-31, 1932-33, 1934-35,
1935-36, 1937-38, 1958-59, 1968-69,
1970-71, 1972-73, 1973-74, 1975-76,
1976-77, 1979-80, 1980-81, 1988-89
Beaten finalists, 1919-20, 1947-48,
1961-62, 1964-65
BBC2 Floodlit Trophy Winners,
1970-71
Regal Trophy Winners, 1972-73,
1983-84
Beaten finalists, 1982-83, 1987-88
Premiership Winners, 1974-75,
1978-79
Records: Attendance: 40,175 v. Bradford N.
(League) 21 May, 1947

Season
Goals: 166 by B.L. Jones, 1956-57
Tries: 63 by E. Harris, 1935-36
Points: 431 by B.L. Jones, 1956-57
Match
Goals: 13 by B.L. Jones v.
Blackpool B., 19 Aug, 1957
Tries: 8 by F. Webster v. Coventry,
12 Apr, 1913; E. Harris v. Bradford
N., 14 Sep, 1931
Points: 31 by B.L. Jones v.
Bradford N., 22 Aug, 1956
Highest score: 102-0 v. Coventry,
1912-13
Highest against: 71-0 v. Wakefield
T., 1945-46

1989-90 PLAYERS' SUMMARY

	App	Tries	Goals	Dr	Pts
Ackerman, Rob	11 + 1	4	—	—	16
Bentley, John	20 + 3	10	15	—	70
Butt, Ikram	0 + 1	—	—	—	—
Coleman, Craig	17	3	—	2	14
Creasser, David	12 + 1	5	1	—	22
Crooks, Lee	9	—	—	—	—
Cruickshank, David	8	3	—	—	12
Delaney, Paul	13 + 7	6	—	—	24
Divorty, Gary	27 + 1	6	1	5	31
Dixon, Paul	34	6	—	—	24
Fawcett, Vince	26 + 1	8	—	—	32
Ford, Phil	23	11	1	1	47
Francis, Norman	9 + 3	3	—	—	12
Gibson, Carl	36	12	—	—	48
Gunn, Richard	4 + 17	3	—	—	12
Heron, David	23 + 1	5	—	—	20
Heugh, Cavill	18	6	—	—	24
Holmes, John	0 + 1	—	—	—	—
Izzard, Craig	12 + 1	3	—	—	12
James, Neil	0 + 1	—	—	—	—
Kuiti, Mike	12	5	—	—	20
Laurie, Mark	11	1	—	—	4
Lord, Gary	20 + 11	4	—	—	16
Maskill, Colin	35	7	114	—	256
Powell, Roy	17 + 7	1	—	—	4
Schofield, Garry	29	20	2	5	89
Spencer, Gary	9	3	—	—	12
Terp, Rex	1	—	—	—	—
Vasey, Chris	5 + 2	2	—	1	9
Waddell, Hugh	17 + 5	2	—	—	8
Wilson, Mark	7 + 4	3	—	—	12
Worthy, Paul	1	—	—	—	—
Young, David	2 + 1	—	—	—	—
TOTALS:					
33 players		142	134	14	850

1989-90 MATCH ANALYSIS

Date	Competition	H/A	Opponent	Rlt	Score	Tries	Goals	Attendance	Referee
3.9.89	SBC	H	Wakefield T.	L	14-22	Ford, Schofield	Bentley (3)	11,658	Carter
10.9.89	SBC	A	Barrow	W	32-10	Vasey (2), Wilson (2), Fawcett, Delaney	Bentley (4)	—	—

(continued)

MATCH ANALYSIS (continued)

Date	Competition	H/A	Opponent	Rlt	Score	Tries	Goals	Attendance	Referee
17.9.89	YC(1)	H	Bradford N.	L	8-15	Francis, Bentley	—	13,214	Holdsworth
24.9.89	SBC	H	Salford	W	34-28	Maskill (2), Dixon, Powell, Gunn, Fawcett	Bentley (5)	8575	Kershaw
1.10.89	SBC	A	Hull	L	7-8	Izzard	Bentley, Vasey (dg)	—	—
8.10.89	SBC	A	Featherstone R.	W	22-20	Spencer (2), Francis	Maskill (3), Divorty (1, 1dg), Coleman (dg)	—	—
15.10.89	Tour	H	New Zealand	L	4-34	—	Maskill (2)	9632	Burke
29.10.89	SBC	A[1]	Sheffield E.	W	27-16	Spencer, Heron, Dixon, Gibson	Maskill (5), Coleman (dg)	—	—
2.11.89	SBC	H	Warrington	W	30-6	Ford, Heron, Gunn, Gibson, Fawcett	Maskill (3), Bentley (2)	8673	Asquith
8.11.89	RT(P)	H	Ryedale-York	W	32-2	Schofield (4), Dixon	Maskill (6)	4979	Crashley
12.11.89	SBC	A	Salford	W	38-18	Divorty (2), Schofield, Dixon, Fawcett, Lord	Maskill (7)	—	—
19.11.89	SBC	H	Widnes	W	26-12	Heron (2), Lord, Izzard, Schofield	Maskill (3)	14,111	Tennant
26.11.89	SBC	A	Bradford N.	L	13-14	Ford (2)	Maskill (2), Schofield (dg)	—	—
3.12.89	RT(1)	H	Leigh	W	26-12	Coleman, Maskill, Izzard, Fawcett	Maskill (5)	7712	Tidball
10.12.89	RT(2)	H	Bradford N.	W	27-8	Coleman, Maskill, Divorty, Wilson	Maskill (5), Schofield (dg)	14,459	Whitfield
16.12.89	RT(3)	H	Wigan	D	10-10	Gibson	Maskill (3)	9310	Kershaw
21.12.89	RT(3) Replay	A	Wigan	L	0-8	—	—	—	—
26.12.89	SBC	H	Castleford	W	25-18	Heron, Delaney, Gibson, Creasser	Maskill (4), Divorty (dg)	18,350	Cross
1.1.90	SBC	H	Hull	W	18-2	Coleman, Heugh	Maskill (4), Divorty (2dg)	11,298	Crashley
7.1.90	SBC	A	Widnes	W	20-8	Lord, Schofield, Laurie	Maskill (4)	—	—
14.1.90	CC(P)	H	Bradford N.	L	8-24	Gibson, Divorty	—	14,152	C. Morris
17.1.90	SBC	H	Leigh	W	38-16	Maskill (2), Bentley, Ford, Creasser	Maskill (9)	6529	Campbell
21.1.90	SBC	H	Bradford N.	W	13-8	Kuiti (2), Francis	Schofield (dg)	12,403	Holdsworth
4.2.90	SBC	A	St. Helens	L	26-32	Gibson (2), Creasser, Dixon, Schofield	Maskill (3)	—	—
11.2.90	SBC	H	Barrow	W	90-0	Heugh (2), Gibson (2), Ackerman (2), Kuiti (2), Schofield (2), Bentley (2), Delaney (2), Cruickshank, Divorty, Maskill	Maskill (11)	8502	Asquith
18.2.90	SBC	H	Sheffield E.	W	44-2	Schofield (2), Waddell, Gibson, Cruickshank, Kuiti, Lord, Creasser	Maskill (6)	10,023	Cross
25.2.90	SBC	A	Leigh	W	26-14	Schofield (2), Cruickshank, Waddell, Fawcett	Maskill (3)	—	—
4.3.90	SBC	H	Wigan	L	14-21	Creasser, Fawcett	Maskill (2), Creasser	23,570	Bowman
11.3.90	SBC	A	Warrington	L	6-9	Gibson	Schofield (dg), Divorty (dg)	—	—
25.3.90	SBC	A	Wakefield T.	W	36-17	Bentley (3), Delaney, Heugh, Dixon, Schofield	Maskill (4)	—	—
1.4.90	SBC	H	St. Helens	W	50-14	Ford (3), Bentley (2), Schofield, Heugh, Divorty, Ackerman	Maskill (5), Schofield (2)	14,020	Bowman
10.4.90	SBC	A	Wigan	L	12-16	Heugh	Maskill (4)	—	—
13.4.90	SBC	H	Featherstone R.	W	25-14	Bentley, Gunn, Gibson, Schofield	Maskill (3), Ford (1,1dg)	11,320	Campbell
16.4.90	SBC	A	Castleford	L	18-38	Ford (2), Delaney	Maskill (3)	—	—
22.4.90	PT(1)	H	Castleford	W	24-18	Schofield (2), Ford, Fawcett	Maskill (4)	14,700	Whitfield
6.5.90	PT(SF)	H	Widnes	L	7-27	Ackerman	Maskill, Schofield (dg)	17,082	Allatt

[1] at Chesterfield FC

LEIGH

Ground: Hilton Park
Colours: Red and white
First Season: 1895-96
Chairman: Keith Bell
Secretary: John Clark
Coach: Billy Benyon (Dec 1986-Mar 1990)
Alex Murphy (Mar 1990-)
Honours: **Championship** Winners, 1905-06
Division One Champions, 1981-82
Division Two Champions, 1977-78, 1985-86, 1988-89
Challenge Cup Winners, 1920-21, 1970-71
Lancashire Cup Winners, 1952-53, 1955-56, 1970-71, 1981-82
Beaten finalists, 1905-06, 1909-10, 1920-21, 1922-23, 1949-50, 1951-52, 1963-64, 1969-70
BBC2 Floodlit Trophy Winners, 1969-70, 1972-73
Beaten finalists, 1967-68, 1976-77
Records: Attendance: 31,324 v. St. Helens (RL Cup) 14 Mar, 1953
Season
Goals: 173 by C. Johnson, 1985-86
Tries: 49 by S. Halliwell, 1985-86
Points: 400 by C. Johnson, 1985-86
Match
Goals: 15 by M. Stacey v. Doncaster, 28 Mar, 1976
Tries: 6 by J. Wood v. York, 4 Oct, 1947
Points: 38 by J. Woods v. Blackpool B., 11 Sep, 1977
Highest score: 92-2 v. Keighley, 1985-86
Highest against: 60-8 v. Salford, 1940

1989-90 PLAYERS' SUMMARY

	App	Tries	Goals	Dr	Pts
Beardmore, Bob	25	12	—	—	48
Brown, Peter	19 + 3	3	3	—	18
Burrill, Craig	3	2	—	—	8
Case, Brian	13 + 1	1	—	—	4
Collier, Andy	15 + 4	3	—	—	12
Cooper, Mark	2	—	—	—	—
Cottrell, Tony	8 + 10	1	—	—	4
Dean, Mick	18 + 6	5	—	—	20
Doherty, Paul	1	—	—	—	—
Donohue, Jason	2 + 3	—	—	—	—
Dunn, Brian	2 + 6	—	—	—	—
Evans, David	0 + 1	—	—	—	—
Gore, Mike	1	—	—	—	—
Herbert, Graham	2 + 1	1	—	—	4
Hill, David	10 + 1	1	—	—	4
Jeffrey, Ian	30	12	—	—	48
Johnson, Chris	17	—	50	—	100
Johnson, Phil	6 + 1	—	7	—	14
Kerr, John	2	—	—	—	—
Ledger, Barry	22 + 1	11	—	—	44
McCulloch, Neil	1 + 1	—	—	—	—
McGrory, Paul	1	—	—	—	—
Moimoi, Robert	19	3	—	—	12
Ogden, Mike	1 + 1	1	—	—	4
O'Loughlin, Keiron	3	—	—	—	—
Platt, Alan	25 + 3	4	20	1	57
Potter, Ian	25	1	—	—	4
Ropati, Peter	26	6	—	—	24
Round, Mike	7	—	—	—	—
Ruane, David	21 + 3	13	—	1	53
Standish, Wayne	21	4	—	—	16
Stephenson, David	19	3	2	—	16
Street, Tim	16 + 2	—	—	—	—
Westhead, John	7 + 7	—	—	—	—

TOTALS:
34 players		87	82	2	514

Re-signed from Wigan in August 1989, 25 Leigh appearances for back row forward Ian Potter.

1989-90 MATCH ANALYSIS

Date	Competition	H/A	Opponent	Rlt	Score	Tries	Goals	Attendance	Referee
3.9.89	SBC	H	Barrow	W	42-16	Beardmore (4), Platt, Dean, Hill, Ledger	P. Johnson (5)	2497	Tickle
6.9.89	SBC	H	Wigan	L	7-44	Beardmore	P. Johnson, Platt (dg)	10,136	Burke
10.9.89	SBC	A	Wakefield T.	L	0-32	—	—	—	—
17.9.89	LC(1)	H	Whitehaven	W	26-8	Jeffrey, Ruane, Herbert, Ogden, Ledger	C. Johnson (3)	2039	Campbell
24.9.89	SBC	H	Warrington	L	10-25	Ruane	C. Johnson (3)	5170	Holdsworth
27.9.89	LC(2)	H	Widnes	L	12-34	Platt, Ruane	C. Johnson (2)	6748	Tickle
1.10.89	SBC	A	Featherstone R.	W	30-16	Brown (2), Beardmore (2), Collier	C. Johnson (4), Brown	—	—
7.10.89	SBC	A	Salford	L	6-19	Ruane	Stephenson	—	—
29.10.89	SBC	A	Bradford N.	L	10-30	Ledger, Jeffrey	Platt	—	—
12.11.89	SBC	A	Widnes	W	18-16	Standish, Jeffrey, Beardmore	C. Johnson (3)	—	—
15.11.89	SBC	H	Featherstone R.	W	35-26	Stephenson (2), Moimoi, Potter, Dean, Jeffrey	C. Johnson (5), Ruane (dg)	2681	Kershaw
22.11.89	SBC	H	Wakefield T.	L	6-24	Ledger	C. Johnson	3479	Holdsworth
26.11.89	SBC	A	Warrington	L	8-16	Ledger, Ruane	—	—	—
3.12.89	RT(1)	A	Leeds	L	12-26	Standish, Ledger	Platt (2)	—	—
17.12.89	SBC	A	Hull	L	24-28	Dean, Brown, Beardmore, Jeffrey	C. Johnson (4)	—	—
26.12.89	SBC	H	Salford	W	18-10	Ropati, Case, Ruane	C. Johnson (3)	4123	C. Morris
7.1.90	SBC	H	St. Helens	W	30-18	Platt, Collier, Ropati, Standish, Beardmore	C. Johnson (5)	5829	Whitfield
17.1.90	SBC	A	Leeds	L	16-38	Ruane, Stephenson, Moimoi	C. Johnson (2)	—	—
21.1.90	SBC	H	Sheffield E.	W	28-16	Jeffrey, Ledger, Collier, Ruane, Ropati	C. Johnson (4)	3207	Whitelam
28.1.90	CC(1)	A	Whitehaven	L	22-23	Ruane (2), Jeffrey, Dean	C. Johnson (3)	—	—
4.2.90	SBC	H	Bradford N.	W	22-16	Ruane (2), Moimoi	C. Johnson (5)	3759	Bowman
18.2.90	SBC	A	Castleford	L	18-44	Beardmore, Jeffrey, Ruane	C. Johnson (3)	—	—
25.2.90	SBC	H	Leeds	L	14-26	Beardmore, Ropati	Platt (3)	5211	Holdsworth
4.3.90	SBC	A[1]	Sheffield E.	L	4-46	Standish	—	—	—
11.3.90	SBC	A	Barrow	W	44-6	Jeffrey (3), Ledger (3), Dean, Cottrell	Platt (5), Stephenson	—	—
18.3.90	SBC	H	Widnes	D	20-20	Ropati, Ledger, Jeffrey	Platt (4)	4848	Crashley
25.3.90	SBC	A	St. Helens	L	6-12	—	Brown (2), Platt	—	—
1.4.90	SBC	H	Hull	L	14-24	Burrill (2)	Platt (2), P. Johnson	5211	Whitfield
12.4.90	SBC	H	Castleford	L	6-40	Ropati	Platt	4097	Smith
16.4.90	SBC	A	Wigan	L	6-34	Platt	Platt	—	—

[1] at Doncaster

NOTTINGHAM CITY

Ground:	Harvey Hadden Stadium
Colours:	Green and yellow
First Season:	1984-85 as Mansfield Marksman. Moved and became Nottingham City at start of 1989-90.
Chairman:	Paul Tomlinson
Secretary:	David Fleming
Coach:	Lee Greenwood (Feb 1989-Mar 1990)
	Mel Wibberley (Mar 1990-)
Records:	Attendance: 2,291 v. Wakefield T. (Div. 2) 9 Sep, 1984

Season
Goals: 63 by C. Sanderson, 1984-85
Tries: 13 by S. Nicholson,
K. Whiteman, 1984-85
Points: 136 by C. Sanderson,
1984-85

Match
Goals: 7 by B. Holden v. Keighley,
10 Mar, 1985; W. Sanchez v.
Hunslet, 2 Oct, 1988
Tries: 4 by K. Whiteman v.
Doncaster, 4 Nov, 1984
Points: 18 by B. Holden v.
Keighley, 10 Mar, 1985;
M. Howarth v. Dewsbury, 17 Jan,
1988
Highest score: 54-10 v. Doncaster,
1984-85
Highest against: 76-6 v. Leigh,
1985-86

1989-90 PLAYERS' SUMMARY

	App	Tries	Goals	Dr	Pts
Andrews, Brent	25 + 1	4	—	—	16
Bowie, Iain	8	1	—	—	4
Carroll, Dean	12	—	24	3	51
Cockayne, Phil	4	—	—	—	—
Crellin, Martin	3 + 5	—	—	—	—
Cummins, Shane	27	1	—	—	4
Dalton, Alan	3	—	—	—	—
Davis, Maurice	1 + 1	—	—	—	—
Faumuina, Mark	14	—	—	—	—
Foley, Tommy	1 + 2	—	—	—	—
Frankland, Nick	1 + 9	—	—	—	—
Garforth, Dave	4 + 2	—	—	—	—
Greenwood, Brandon	0 + 4	—	—	—	—
Grimes, David	1 + 1	—	—	—	—
Hale, Chris	3 + 1	—	—	—	—
Hema, Arnold	29	3	—	—	12
Hough, Mick	22 + 2	—	—	—	—
Hoyle, Bob	6 + 1	—	—	—	—
Jackson, Dean	1 + 1	—	—	—	—
James, Tony	1	—	—	—	—
Johnson, Jimmy	1 + 1	—	—	—	—
Kay, Paul	25	1	—	—	4
Kellett, Brian	3 + 1	1	—	—	4
Kemp, Martin	9	1	—	—	4
King, David	1	—	—	—	—
Lidbury, Steve	4	—	—	—	—
Longville, Dean	5	1	—	—	4
Mitchell, Pat	3	2	—	—	8
Moulden, Darren	17 + 2	4	—	—	16
Nickle, Vince	1	—	—	—	—
Oates, David	24 + 2	4	5	—	26
Palelei, Aaron	6 + 4	1	—	—	4
Peacham, Gary	0 + 1	—	—	—	—
Perry, Mark	0 + 1	—	—	—	—
Powell, Paul	10	2	—	—	8
Pritchard, Neil	0 + 1	—	—	—	—
Robson, Duncan	4	2	1	—	10
Rogers, Darren	1	1	—	—	4
Rudd, Neil	22 + 1	4	—	—	16
Shrewsbury, Ian	4	1	—	—	4
Sidebottom, Gary	16	3	—	—	12
Simpson, Andy	8 + 1	3	—	—	12
Stones, Chris	27 + 2	5	—	—	20
Subritzky, Dean	2 + 1	1	—	—	4
Toder, Jai	1 + 1	—	—	—	—
Whitehead, Craig	4 + 1	—	—	—	—
Williams, Tony	0 + 1	—	—	—	—
Willis, Chris	27 + 4	10	30	2	102
Wrigley, Jamie	12 + 1	—	—	—	—

TOTALS:
49 players		56	60	5	349

Brent Andrews, four tries in 26 appearances for Nottingham City.

1989-90 MATCH ANALYSIS

Date	Competition	H/A	Opponent	Rlt	Score	Tries	Goals	Attendance	Referee
27.8.89	YC(P)	H	Hull	L	6-56	Kellett	Oates	902	Crashley
3.9.89	SD	A	Batley	L	11-20	Andrews, Mitchell	Oates, Willis (dg)	—	—
10.9.89	SD	H	Hunslet	L	12-23	Willis, Hema	Oates (2)	617	Asquith
24.9.89	SD	A	Keighley	L	16-51	Hema, Kay, Mitchell	Carroll (2)	—	—
1.10.89	SD	H	Halifax	L	20-72	Palelei, Oates, Willis	Carroll (4)	2545	Crashley
8.10.89	SD	A	Hull K.R.	L	4-54	Oates	—	—	—
15.10.89	SD	H	Batley	L	10-29	Sidebottom, Willis	Carroll	437	Allatt
22.10.89	SD	A	Runcorn H.	W	17-14	Andrews, Willis	Carroll (4, 1dg)	—	—
29.10.89	SD	H	Rochdale H.	L	24-50	Andrews, Stone, Willis	Carroll (6)	536	Whitelam
5.11.89	SD	A	Chorley	L	8-22	Andrews, Rudd	—	—	—
12.11.89	SD	H	Swinton	L	11-27	Stones	Carroll (3, 1dg)	446	K. Morris
19.11.89	SD	A	Huddersfield	L	10-16	Willis, Kemp	Carroll	—	—
26.11.89	SD	H	Runcorn H.	W	13-6	Sidebottom, Cummins	Carroll (2, 1dg)	389	Asquith
3.12.89	RT(1)	H	Widnes	L	18-48	Willis, Powell, Oates, Moulden	Willis	2246	Kendrew
17.12.89	SD	A	Carlisle	L	14-15	Powell, Moulden	Willis (3)	—	—
26.12.89	SD	H	Doncaster	L	6-50	Stones	Carroll	567	Steele
7.1.90	SD	H	Hull K.R.	L	0-58	—	—	873	Allatt
14.1.90	SD	A	Hunslet	L	8-32	Willis	Willis (2)	—	—
21.1.90	SD	A	Swinton	L	10-46	Willis, Rudd	Willis	—	—
28.1.90	CC(1)	H	Dewsbury	L	2-32	—	Willis	529	Cross
4.2.90	SD	H	Huddersfield	L	4-42	—	Willis (2)	440	K. Morris
11.2.90	SD	A	Halifax	L	4-60	Rudd	—	—	—
18.2.90	SD	H	Fulham	L	14-34	Bowie, Hema, Simpson	Willis	285	Steele
25.2.90	SD	A	Rochdale H.	L	20-70	Oates, Rudd, Simpson	Willis (3), Oates	—	—
4.3.90	SD	A	Workington T.	L	14-27	Shrewsbury, Simpson	Willis (3)	—	—
11.3.90	SD	H	Carlisle	L	0-60	—	—	200	Galtress
18.3.90	SD	H	Keighley	W	29-22	Sidebottom, Willis, Stones, Moulden	Willis (6, 1dg)	250	Tidball
25.3.90	SD	A	Fulham	L	10-44	Robson, Subritzky	Willis	—	—
1.4.90	SD	H	Workington T.	W	18-12	Longville, Moulden, Robson	Willis (2), Robson	220	Kendrew
8.4.90	SD	H	Chorley	L	8-42	Stones	Willis (2)	266	Campbell
16.4.90	SD	A	Doncaster	L	8-34	Rogers	Willis (2)	—	—

OLDHAM

Ground:	Watersheddings
Colours:	Red and white
First Season:	1895-96
Nickname:	Roughyeds
Chairman:	John Chadwick
Secretary:	Fred Howarth
Coach:	Tony Barrow (Nov 1988-)

Honours: **Championship** Winners, 1909-10, 1910-11,1956-57

Beaten finalists, 1906-07, 1907-08, 1908-09, 1921-22, 1954-55

Division One Champions, 1904-05

Division Two Champions, 1963-64, 1981-82, 1987-88

Second Division Premiership Winners, 1987-88, 1989-90

Challenge Cup Winners, 1898-99, 1924-25, 1926-27

Beaten finalists, 1906-07, 1911-12, 1923-24, 1925-26

Lancashire League Winners, 1897-98, 1900-01, 1907-08, 1909-10, 1921-22, 1956-57, 1957-58

Lancashire Cup Winners, 1907-08, 1910-11, 1913-14, 1919-20, 1924-25, 1933-34, 1956-57, 1957-58, 1958-59

Beaten finalists, 1908-09, 1911-12, 1918-19, 1921-22, 1954-55, 1966-67, 1968-69, 1986-87, 1989-90

Records: Attendance: 28,000 v. Huddersfield (League) 24 Feb, 1912

Season
Goals: 200 by B. Ganley, 1957-58
Tries: 49 by R. Farrar, 1921-22
Points: 412 by B. Ganley, 1957-58

Match
Goals: 14 by B. Ganley v. Liverpool C., 4 Apr, 1959
Tries: 7 by Miller v. Barry, 31 Oct, 1908
Points: 30 by A. Johnson v. Widnes, 9 Apr, 1928
Highest score: 67-6 v. Liverpool C., 1958-59
Highest against: 67-11 v. Hull K.R., 1978-79

1989-90 PLAYERS' SUMMARY

	App	Tries	Goals	Dr	Pts
Allen, Shaun	32 + 3	6	—	—	24
Anderson, Tony	3	1	—	—	4
Atkinson, Keith	10 + 15	2	16	—	40
Bardsley, Mick	2	—	—	—	—
Bates, Ian	1	—	—	—	—
Casey, Leo	30 + 1	8	—	—	32
Clark, Brett	36 + 2	17	—	—	68
Clawson, Neil	4 + 1	2	—	—	8
Cogger, John	34	24	—	—	96
Croston, Trevor	5 + 3	2	—	—	8
Fairbank, John	16 + 12	8	—	—	32
Fieldhouse, John	37 + 1	5	—	—	20
Flanagan, Neil	1 + 1	1	—	—	4
Ford, Mike	37	8	—	2	34
Foy, Des	18	10	—	—	40
Henderson, John	23 + 2	17	—	—	68
Hyde, Gary	21 + 3	5	30	—	80
Irving, Richard	33 + 2	17	—	—	68
Joynt, Chris	0 + 1	—	—	—	—
Lewis, Peter	2	1	—	—	4
Lord, Paul	40	29	—	—	116
Martyn, Tommy	5 + 5	6	3	1	31
Maxwell, John	0 + 1	—	—	—	—
McAlister, Charlie	20 + 7	8	16	—	64
Meadows, Kevin	5 + 5	6	—	—	24
Newton, Keith	30 + 2	7	—	—	28
Platt, Duncan	30	8	125	1	283
Robinson, Steve	13 + 4	5	—	—	20
Round, Paul	9 + 2	3	—	—	12
Ruane, Andy	25 + 2	9	1	—	38
Russell, Richard	37 + 4	8	—	—	32
Sanderson, Ian	1	—	—	—	—
TOTALS:					
32 players		223	191	4	1,278

New Zealander Charlie McAlister, 64 points in 27 appearances for Oldham.

1989-90 MATCH ANALYSIS

Date	Competition	H/A	Opponent	Rlt	Score	Tries	Goals	Attendance	Referee
3.9.89	SD	H	Workington T.	W	40-8	Henderson (2), Cogger (2), Lord, McAlister, Ruane, Russell	Platt (4)	3743	C. Morris
10.9.89	SD	A	Halifax	L	12-22	Platt, Cogger	Platt (2)	—	—
17.9.89	LC(1)	A	Barrow	W	46-2	Platt (2), Lord (2), Ford, Casey, Allen, Hyde, Cogger	Platt (5)	—	—
27.9.89	LC(2)	A	St. Helens	W	36-6	Robinson, Ford, Platt, Cogger, Allen, Newton	Platt (6)	—	—
1.10.89	SD	H	Hull K.R.	W	12-4	Lord	Platt (4)	5797	Crashley
5.10.89	LC(SF)	H	Wigan	W	19-18	Fieldhouse, Newton, Ford	Hyde (2), Platt, Ford (dg)	8603	Whitfield
8.10.89	SD	A	Runcorn H.	W	34-6	Meadows (2), Clarke (2), Russell, Clawson, Irving	Hyde (3)	—	—
14.10.89	LC(F)	St. Helens	Warrington	L	16-24	Irving, Robinson, Lord	Platt, Hyde	(9990)	Tennant
18.10.89	SD	H	Halifax	W	14-3	Lord, Fairbank	Hyde (3)	6953	McCallum (Aus)
22.10.89	SD	A	Carlisle	W	32-10	Fieldhouse (2), Cogger, Hyde, Meadows, Fairbank	Hyde (2), McAlister (2)	—	—
29.10.89	SD	H	Batley	W	22-4	Ruane, Martyn, Meadows, Irving	Martyn (3)	4120	Holgate
5.11.89	SD	A	Doncaster	W	22-20	Casey, Lord, Hyde, Fairbank	Hyde (3)	—	—
12.11.89	SD	H	Keighley	W	50-34	Clark, Hyde, Irving, Ford, McAlister, Meadows, Ruane, Lord, Russell	Hyde (7)	4113	Campbell
19.11.89	SD	A	Fulham	W	40-10	Ruane (2), Cogger, Allen, Ford, Clark, McAlister	McAlister (6)	—	—
26.11.89	SD	H	Doncaster	W	30-8	Lord, Meadows, Ruane, Robinson, Clark	McAlister (5)	4914	Asquith
3.12.89	RT(1)	A	Bramley	W	48-16	Cogger (2), Robinson, Lord, McAlister, Clawson, Clark, Croston	Platt (8)	—	—
10.12.89	RT(2)	H	Huddersfield	W	22-8	Cogger (2), Croston	Platt (5)	5292	Tickle
17.12.89	RT(3)	A	St. Helens	L	18-32	Cogger (2), Lord, Fairbank	McAlister	—	—
26.12.89	SD	A	Rochdale H.	L	12-24	McAlister, Lord	McAlister (2)	—	—
1.1.90	SD	H	Swinton	W	29-14	Lord (2), Ford, Russell, Cogger	Platt (4), Ford (dg)	4934	Kendrew
7.1.90	SD	H	Hunslet	W	48-10	Foy (5), Cogger (3), Fairbank	Platt (6)	3672	Cross
14.1.90	CC(P)	H	Huddersfield	W	30-8	Clark, Allen, Newton, Cogger, Fairbank	Platt (5)	4593	Allatt
17.1.90	SD	A	Hull K.R.	W	9-6	Irving	Platt (2, 1dg)	—	—
21.1.90	SD	A	Chorley	W	44-6	Irving (3), Foy (2), Cogger (2), Newton	Platt (6)	—	—
28.1.90	CC(1)	H	Workington T.	W	30-8	Henderson (3), Platt, Clark	Atkinson (4), Platt	3710	Simpson
4.2.90	SD	H	Fulham	W	52-4	Henderson (4), Newton (2), Foy, Casey, Lord, Platt	Platt (6)	3549	Smith
11.2.90	CC(2)	A	Salford	W	18-7	Russell, Clark	Platt (5)	—	—
18.2.90	SD	H	Chorley	W	66-16	Clark (3), Russell (2), Martyn, McAlister, Casey, Cogger, Irving, Round, Foy	Platt (9)	3576	Whitelam
25.2.90	CC(3)	A	Widnes	W	16-4	Henderson, Newton	Platt (4)	—	—
4.3.90	SD	H	Huddersfield	W	23-8	Cogger, Lewis, Lord, Martyn	Platt (2), Atkinson, Martyn (dg)	5615	Steele

(continued on page 109)

ROCHDALE HORNETS

Ground: Spotland
Colours: White, blue and red
First Season: 1895-96
Nickname: Hornets
Chairman: Len Stansfield
Secretary: Paul Reynolds
Coach: Jim Crellin (June 1988-June 1989)
Allan Agar (July 1989-)
Honours: **Challenge Cup** Winners, 1921-22
Lancashire League Winners, 1918-19
Lancashire Cup Winners, 1911-12, 1914-15, 1918-19
Beaten finalists, 1912-13, 1919-20, 1965-66
Regal Trophy Beaten finalists 1973-74
BBC2 Floodlit Trophy Beaten finalists 1971-72
Records: Attendance: 41,831 Wigan v. Oldham (RL Cup Final) 12 Apr 1924
Home: 26,664 v. Oldham (RL Cup) 25 Mar, 1922
Season
Goals: 115 by K. Harcombe, 1985-86
Tries: 30 by J. Williams, 1934-35
Points: 243 by S. Turner, 1988-89
Match
Goals: 14 by S. Turner v. Runcorn H., 5 Nov, 1989
Tries: 5 by J. Corsi v. Barrow, 31 Dec, 1921 and v. Broughton Moor, 25 Feb, 1922; J. Williams v. St. Helens, 4 Apr, 1933; N. Brelsford v. Whitehaven, 3 Sep, 1972

Points: 32 by S. Turner v. Runcorn H., 5 Nov, 1989
Highest score: 92-0 v. Runcorn H., 1989-90
Highest against: 79-2 v. Hull, 1920-21

1989-90 PLAYERS' SUMMARY

	App	Tries	Goals	Dr	Pts
Bamber, Simon	7 + 7	2	—	—	8
Barratt, Dave	4 + 1	—	—	—	—
Blackburn, John	2 + 4	—	—	—	—
Clucas, Geoff	0 + 1	—	—	—	—
Cowie, Neil	29 + 2	6	—	—	24
Edwards, Logan	7 + 3	7	—	—	28
Fox, Phil	8	7	—	—	28
Gamble, Paul	6	2	—	—	8
Garritty, Brian	18 + 1	10	—	—	40
Hall, Martin	33	10	—	—	40
Higgins, John	26	13	—	—	52
Humphries, Tony	26 + 4	6	—	—	24
Lonergan, Dean	24	12	—	—	48
Lord, Mark	31	24	—	—	96
Lowe, Kevin	0 + 2	—	—	—	—
Malloy, Dale	0 + 1	—	—	—	—
Marriott, Karl	11 + 2	7	—	—	28
Marsden, Bob	7 + 8	1	—	—	4
McCormack, Kevin	3	6	—	—	24
McDermott, Paul	29 + 1	15	—	—	60
Myler, Chris	21 + 2	5	—	—	20
Myler, John	12 + 1	4	6	2	30
Nixon, Mark	27 + 1	19	—	—	76
Sanderson, Mark	0 + 1	—	—	—	—
Sullivan, Andy	31 + 1	1	—	—	4
Turner, Steve	16 + 10	4	97	1	211
Viller, Mark	12 + 2	5	—	—	20
Webb, Vince	0 + 1	—	—	—	—
Wood, David	11 + 1	4	—	—	16
Woods, John	28	16	65	—	194
TOTALS:					
30 players		186	168	3	1,083

1989-90 MATCH ANALYSIS

Date	Competition	H/A	Opponent	Rlt	Score	Tries	Goals	Attendance	Referee
3.9.89	SD	A	Halifax	L	12-36	Lord, McDermott	Woods, Turner	—	—
6.9.89	SD	A	Whitehaven	W	36-16	Nixon (2), C. Myler, Higgins, Lord, Humphries, McDermott	Turner (4)	—	—
10.9.89	SD	H	Swinton	W	26-22	Cowie, Higgins, Lord, Turner	Turner (5)	2025	Tidball

(continued)

MATCH ANALYSIS (continued)

Date	Com-petition	H/A	Opponent	Rlt	Score	Tries	Goals	Atten-dance	Referee
17.9.89	LC(1)	A	Salford	L	12-52	McDermott	Turner (4)	—	—
24.9.89	SD	H	Dewsbury	W	46-20	McCormack (3), Lonergan (2), Lord, Hall, McDermott, Higgins	Turner (5)	1576	Galtress
1.10.89	SD	A	Bramley	W	46-17	McCormack (3), Humphries, Lonergan, Wood, Nixon, Cowie	Turner (6), Woods	—	—
15.10.89	SD	A	Fulham	W	18-4	Edwards (2), Woods	Turner (3)	—	—
22.10.89	SD	H	Workington T.	W	52-14	Woods (2), Edwards, Nixon, Lord, Marriott, Woods, Cowie, Lonergan	Turner (8)	1237	Stokes (NZ)
29.10.89	SD	A	Nottingham C.	W	50-24	Woods (2), Lord, Lonergan, Turner, Higgins, Marriott, Marsden	Turner (9)	—	—
5.11.89	SD	H	Runcorn H.	W	92-0	Hall (3), Edwards (3), Lord (3), Marriott (2), Higgins (2), Nixon, Turner, Woods	Turner (14)	1663	Campbell
19.11.89	SD	H	Ryedale-York	W	47-8	Wood, Lord, Cowie, Edwards, Higgins, Nixon, Woods	Turner (9, 1dg)	2370	Bowman
26.11.89	SD	A	Hunslet	W	26-20	Lord (2), Woods, Higgins, Humphries	Turner (3)	—	—
1.12.89	RT(1)	A¹	Sheffield E.	L	22-36	Nixon, McDermott, Lord, Humphries	Turner (3)	—	—
17.12.89	SD	H	Bramley	L	18-25	Higgins (2), Woods	Turner (3)	1277	Galtress
26.12.89	SD	H	Oldham	W	24-12	Lonergan, Woods, Gamble, McDermott	Turner (3), Woods	8061	Holdsworth
1.1.90	SD	A	Trafford B.	W	18-4	Nixon, Woods	Woods (5)	—	—
7.1.90	SD	A	Keighley	W	38-12	Nixon (3), Lord (2), Lonergan, Woods	Woods (3), Turner (2)	—	—
17.1.90	SD	H	Fulham	W	42-8	Nixon (2), McDermott, Lonergan, Woods, Viller	Woods (9)	1589	Holgate
21.1.90	SD	H	Whitehaven	W	28-18	McDermott (2), Lord (2), Woods, Garritty	Woods (2)	2054	Asquith
30.1.90	CC(1)	H	Carlisle	(W)	38-6	Nixon (2), Gamble, Garritty, Cowie, Lord	Turner (7)	1609	K. Morris
4.2.90	SD	A	Ryedale-York	L	10-20	Garritty, J. Myler	Woods	—	—
11.2.90	CC(2)	A	Widnes	L	16-22	Nixon, Hall	Turner (4)	—	—
18.2.90	SD	A	Dewsbury	W	10-8	Lonergan, Higgins	Woods	—	—
25.2.90	SD	H	Nottingham C.	W	70-20	Lonergan (3), Marriott (3), McDermott (3), Nixon, Lord, J. Myler, Hall	Woods (9)	1707	Simpson
4.3.90	SD	A	Runcorn H.	W	28-0	Garritty (2), Hall, Woods, Viller	Woods (4)	—	—
11.3.90	SD	H	Halifax	W	23-12	Higgins, Fox, Nixon	Woods (5), J. Myler (dg)	5923	Kendrew
18.3.90	SD	A	Workington T.	W	16-14	Garritty, Viller, Woods	Woods (2)	—	—
25.3.90	SD	H	Hunslet	W	40-14	Nixon, Hall, C. Myler, Cowie, Humphries, Higgins, Fox	J. Myler (6)	1987	Tickle
1.4.90	SD	A	Swinton	W	37-16	Lord (2), C. Myler, Fox, Sullivan, J. Myler	Woods (6), J. Myler (dg)	—	—
8.4.90	SD	H	Keighley	W	52-0	Lord (2), Fox (2), Bamber (2), C. Myler, Viller, Hall, Garritty	Woods (6)	1737	J.Connolly (Pr)
13.4.90	SD	H	Trafford B.	W	70-28	McDermott (3), Garritty (3), Hall, Woods, Lord, Fox, J. Myler, Humphries, Viller	Woods (5), Turner (4)	1936	Whitelam
16.4.90	SD	A	Oldham	L	2-30	—	Woods	—	—
22.4.90	SDP(1)	H	Dewsbury	L	18-20	C. Myler, Fox, Turner	Woods (3)	2096	Kershaw

¹ at Halifax

RUNCORN HIGHFIELD

Ground: Canal Street
Colours: Black
First Season: 1922-23 as Wigan Highfield.
Became London Highfield in
1933-34. Became Liverpool Stanley
in 1934-35 and changed to
Liverpool City in 1951-52. Became
Huyton in 1968-69 and changed to
Runcorn Highfield in 1984-85.
Chairman: Terry Hughes
Secretary: Ian Swann
Coach: Dave Chisnall (June 1989-)
Honours: **Lancashire League** Winners,
1935-36
Records: Attendance: 14,000 v. Widnes
(Championship semi-final) 2 May,
1936 at Prescott Road
Season
Goals: 126 by P. Wood, 1984-85
Tries: 28 by J. Maloney, 1930-31
Points: 240 by P. Wood, 1984-85
Match
Goals: 11 by P. Wood v. Batley,
21 Oct, 1984
Tries: 5 by J. Maloney v. Bramley,
25 Apr, 1931
Points: 24 by T. Rose v.
Workington T., 4 Oct, 1987
Highest score: 59-11 v. Bramley,
1933-34
Highest against: 92-2 v. Wigan,
1988-89; 92-0 v. Rochdale H.,
1989-90

1989-90 PLAYERS' SUMMARY

	App	Tries	Goals	Dr	Pts
Adams, Dave	3	—	—	—	—
Ashcroft, Keith	13 + 5	—	—	—	—
Ashcroft, Simon	31	3	1	—	14
Ball, Jimmy	12 + 2	—	—	—	—
Barrow, Shaun	29	4	—	—	16
Basnett, Keith	0 + 1	—	—	—	—
Beckett, Peter	8 + 11	—	—	—	—
Campbell, Danny	3 + 2	—	—	—	—
Dean, Geoff	16	1	—	—	4
Deeks, Shane	3	1	—	—	4
Dolan, Shaun	22 + 3	5	—	—	20
Dooley, Jimmy	4 + 5	1	—	—	4
Fenney, Paul	25 + 4	—	—	—	—
Fyles, Anthony	2	—	—	—	—
Fraser, Paul	20 + 4	3	4	—	20
Goodier, Frank	16 + 2	1	—	—	4
Grady, Mike	11	1	—	—	4
Hine, David	23 + 3	3	—	—	12
Hoey, Robert	18 + 2	1	—	—	4
Hunt, Dave	1 + 1	—	—	—	—
Jones, Charlie	29	5	—	—	20
Kelly, Ken	5	1	—	—	4
Marsden, Peter	5	—	—	—	—
Milner, John	4	—	—	—	—
Natoli, Joe	2	—	—	—	—
O'Garra, Kevin	6 + 6	—	6	—	12
Platt, Billy	22	5	19	4	62
Platt, Brian	16	1	13	—	30
Rawlinson, Tommy	25 + 2	1	—	—	4
Rose, Terry	6 + 3	2	—	—	8
Simms, Stephen	1 + 1	—	—	—	—
Southward, Phil	21 + 1	1	—	—	4
Walls, David	1 + 2	—	—	—	—
TOTALS:					
33 players		40	43	4	250

*Former Great Britain forward Dave Chisnall, who joined
Runcorn Highfield as coach in June 1989.*

1989-90 MATCH ANALYSIS

Date	Com-petition	H/A	Opponent	Rlt	Score	Tries	Goals	Atten-dance	Referee
3.9.89	SD	A	Carlisle	L	14-54	Dooley, S. Ashcroft, Barrow	O'Garra	—	—
6.9.89	SD	H	Batley	L	0-9	—	—	423	Holgate
10.9.89	SD	A	Trafford B.	L	10-46	Jones, Dean	O'Garra	—	—
17.9.89	LC(1)	A	St. Helens	L	10-78	S. Ashcroft	O'Garra (3)	—	—
24.9.89	SD	A	Doncaster	L	6-46	Southwood	S. Ashcroft	—	—
1.10.89	SD	H	Huddersfield	L	0-42	—	—	500	Whitelam
8.10.89	SD	H	Oldham	L	6-34	Kellett	Fraser	1621	Simpson
15.10.89	SD	A	Dewsbury	L	10-34	Dolan, Hine	Fraser	—	—
22.10.89	SD	H	Nottingham C.	L	14-17	Brady, Deeks, Jones	Fraser	250	Cross
5.11.89	SD	A	Rochdale H.	L	0-92	—	—	—	—
12.11.89	SD	A	Batley	L	14-46	Goodier, Dolan	W. Platt (2), O'Garra	—	—
19.11.89	SD	H	Bramley	L	11-12	Barrow, Fraser	W. Platt (1, 1dg)	200	Simpson
26.11.89	SD	A	Nottingham C.	L	6-13	Jones	W. Platt	—	—
3.12.89	RT(1)	A	Whitehaven	L	10-20	Fraser	B. Platt (3)	—	—
17.12.89	SD	H	Whitehaven	L	10-28	Dolan, W. Platt	Fraser	140	Whitelam
26.12.89	SD	H	Carlisle	L	9-18	W. Platt	B. Platt (2), W. Platt (dg)	230	Simpson
1.1.90	SD	A	Chorley	L	12-46	Barrow, Rawlinson	B. Platt (2)	—	—
7.1.90	SD	A	Huddersfield	L	10-22	W. Platt	W. Platt (2), B. Platt	—	—
14.1.90	SD	H	Dewsbury	L	6-28	Jones	B. Platt	425	Holgate
21.1.90	SD	H	Ryedale-York	L	24-27	W. Platt, Hoey, Dolan, Hine	B. Platt (4)	516	Crashley
28.1.90	CC(1)	H	Bradford N.	L	12-22	B. Platt, Rose	W. Platt (2)	—	—
4.2.90	SD	A	Whitehaven	L	8-20	Hine	W. Platt (2)	—	—
18.2.90	SD	A	Hull K.R.	L	6-36	S. Ashcroft	W. Platt	—	—
25.2.90	SD	H	Trafford B.	L	7-18	W. Platt	W. Platt (1, 1dg)	220	Smith
4.3.90	SD	H	Rochdale H.	L	0-28	—	—	816	Holgate
11.3.90	SD	A	Bramley	L	6-29	Rose	W. Platt	—	—
18.3.90	SD	A	Oldham	L	2-60	—	W. Platt	—	—
25.3.90	SD	H	Doncaster	L	2-29	—	W. Platt	300	Smith
1.4.90	SD	A	Ryedale-York	L	11-52	Barrow, Jones	W. Platt (1, 1dg)	—	—
8.4.90	SD	H	Hull K.R.	L	12-38	Fraser, Dolan	W. Platt (2)	500	Asquith
16.4.90	SD	H	Chorley	L	2-11	—	W. Platt	206	Hunter (Pr)

RYEDALE-YORK

Ground:	Monks Cross Stadium
Colours:	Amber and black
First Season:	1901-02 as York. Moved and became Ryedale-York at start of 1989-90
Nickname:	Wasps
Chairman:	John Stabler
Secretary:	Ian Clough
Coach:	Gary Stephens (Apr 1988-)
Honours:	**Division Two** Champions, 1980-81
	Challenge Cup Beaten finalists, 1930-31
	Yorkshire Cup Winners, 1922-23, 1933-34, 1936-37
	Beaten finalists, 1935-36, 1957-58, 1978-79
Records:	Attendance: 14,689 v. Swinton (RL Cup) 10 Feb, 1934
	Season
	Goals: 146 by V. Yorke, 1957-58
	Tries: 35 by J. Crossley, 1980-81
	Points: 318 by G. Steadman, 1984-85
	Match
	Goals: 11 by V. Yorke v. Whitehaven, 6 Sep, 1958; C. Gibson v. Dewsbury, 28 Sep, 1980
	Tries: 6 by R. Hardgrave v. Bramley, 5 Jan, 1935; D. Kettlestring at Keighley, 11 Mar, 1990
	Points: 26 by G. Steadman v. Batley, 25 Nov, 1984; G. Sullivan at Keighley, 11 Mar, 1990
	Highest score: 70-8 v. Keighley, 1989-90
	Highest against: 75-3 v. Warrington 1950-51

1989-90 PLAYERS' SUMMARY

	App	Tries	Goals	Dr	Pts
Ake, Basil	34	18	—	—	72
Arrundale, Stuart	1 + 1	1	—	—	4
Atkins, Gary	20	6	—	—	24
Bleakley, Steve	13	1	—	—	4
Carlyle, Brendan	31	8	12	—	56
Crossley, John	17 + 3	4	2	—	20
Dickenson, Robert	0 + 1	—	—	—	—
Dobson, Steve	4	2	—	1	9
Doherty, Paul	3	1	—	—	4
Dyson, Jeremy	1	—	—	—	—
Ellis, St. John	3	1	9	—	22
Fagan, Gary	1	—	—	—	—
Faumuina, Mark	6	—	—	—	—
Fletcher, Paul	3	—	—	—	—
Hammerton, Chris	17 + 2	5	—	1	21
Hayes, Richard	33 + 1	—	—	—	—
Horton, Stuart	33	5	—	1	21
Hughes, Ian	3 + 5	1	—	—	4
Hutchinson, Paul	9 + 4	—	—	—	—
Kettlestring, David	18	14	—	—	56
Laws, David	0 + 2	1	—	—	4
Maxwell, Paul	17 + 8	—	—	—	—
Miles, Paul	1 + 5	—	—	—	—
Morris, Stuart	22 + 2	15	—	—	60
Mountain, Dean	5	—	—	—	—
Mulherin, Paul	9	3	—	—	12
Olsen, Steve	15 + 1	1	—	—	4
Pavor, Ian	13 + 8	1	—	—	4
Payne, Phil	8	1	—	—	4
Pinkney, Nick	7	2	—	—	8
Poole, Phil	1	—	—	—	—
Pryce, Geoff	24 + 4	8	—	—	32
Render, Steven	0 + 3	—	—	—	—
Smith, Adrian	6 + 6	1	—	—	4
Sullivan, Graham	29	13	83	—	218
Warters, Nick	0 + 2	—	—	—	—
Watson, David	12	8	—	—	32
White, Brendan	1	—	—	—	—
White, Paul	10	3	—	—	12
Willey, Sean	5	1	—	—	4
Williams, Dean	7	2	—	—	8

TOTALS:					
41 players		127	106	3	723

Forward Dean Mountain, a September 1989 Ryedale-York signing from Castleford who made five appearances.

1989-90 MATCH ANALYSIS

Date	Competition	H/A	Opponent	Rlt	Score	Tries	Goals	Attendance	Referee
3.9.89	SD	A	Fulham	L	9-10	Ake	Ellis (2), Dobson (dg)	—	—
6.9.89	SD	A	Hunslet	W	36-16	Ake (2), Ellis, Williams, Atkins, Dobson	Ellis (6)	—	—
10.9.89	SD	A	Batley	W	18-8	Morris, Ake, Mulherin, Dobson	Ellis	—	—
17.9.89	YC(1)	A	Hull	L	10-20	White, Horton	Sullivan	—	—
24.9.89	SD	A	Swinton	W	17-8	Williams, Morris	Sullivan (4), Horton (dg)	—	—
1.10.89	SD	A	Workington T.	W	42-2	Morris (2), Carlyle (2), Crossley, Payne, Hughes	Sullivan (7)	—	—
8.10.89	SD	H	Keighley	W	16-6	Mulherin, Sullivan, Carlyle	Sullivan (2)	4803	Tidball
15.10.89	SD	A	Doncaster	D	12-12	Mulherin	Sullivan (4)	—	—
27.10.89	SD	H	Huddersfield	L	6-10	—	Sullivan (3)	1909	Cross
5.11.89	SD	H	Hunslet	W	20-0	Sullivan, Ake, Crossley, Bleakley	Sullivan (2)	1939	Holgate
8.11.89	RT(P)	A	Leeds	L	2-32	—	Sullivan	—	—
12.11.89	SD	A	Carlisle	W	22-12	Sullivan, Pryce, Hammerton, Willey	Sullivan (3)	—	—
19.11.89	SD	A	Rochdale H.	L	8-47	Hammerton	Sullivan (2)	—	—
24.11.89	SD	H	Chorley	W	28-10	Ake, Crossley, Hammerton, Morris, Pinkney	Sullivan (4)	1115	Carter
17.12.89	SD	A	Huddersfield	W	16-8	Carlyle, Crossley, Pryce	Sullivan (2)	—	—
26.12.89	SD	A	Hull K.R.	L	0-12	—	—	—	—
31.12.89	SD	H	Workington T.	W	44-12	Watson (2), Morris (2), Carlyle, Ake, Sullivan, Hammerton, Horton	Sullivan (4)	1686	Allatt
5.1.90	SD	H	Halifax	W	18-14	Atkins, Hammerton, Sullivan	Sullivan (3)	4977	Crashley
14.1.90	SD	H	Carlisle	W	52-14	Watson (4), Kettlestring (2), Pryce (2), Sullivan	Sullivan (8)	2128	Cross
21.1.90	SD	A	Runcorn H.	W	27-24	Ake (2), Atkins, Kettlestring, Arrondel	Carlyle (3), Hammerton (dg)	—	—
28.1.90	CC(1)	A	Fulham	D	14-14	Watson, Ake, Morris	Carlyle	—	—
31.1.90	CC(1) Replay	H	Fulham	L	12-16	Ake, Carlyle, Pryce	—	2059	Allatt
4.2.90	SD	H	Rochdale H.	W	20-10	Morris (3), Carlyle	Carlyle (2)	2868	Tidball
18.2.90	SD	A	Halifax	L	14-22	White, Morris	Sullivan (3)	—	—
25.2.90	SD	A	Chorley	L	6-10	Sullivan	Sullivan	—	—
4.3.90	SD	H	Fulham	W	18-14	Sullivan, White, Horton	Carlyle (2) Sullivan	1515	Crashley
11.3.90	SD	A	Keighley	W	70-8	Kettlestring (6), Sullivan (2), Doherty, Atkins, Ake, Watson	Sullivan (9), Crossley (2)	—	—
16.3.90	SD	H	Doncaster	W	12-5	Kettlestring, Sullivan	Sullivan (2)	1792	Whitfield
25.3.90	SD	H	Swinton	W	18-10	Kettlestring, Ake, Pinkney, Sullivan	Sullivan	1934	Tidball
1.4.90	SD	H	Runcorn H.	W	52-11	Ake (2), Morris (2), Kettlestring, Atkins, Paver, Laws, Sullivan	Sullivan (8)	1508	Steele
13.4.90	SD	H	Hull K.R.	L	8-17	Horton	Sullivan (2)	4186	Tickle
16.4.90	SD	H	Batley	W	44-6	Pryce (2), Horton, Kettlestring (2), Morris, Atkins, Carlyle, Olsen	Carlyle (4)	1702	Galtress
21.4.90	SDP(1)	H	Halifax	W	24-7	Ake (3), A. Smith	Sullivan (4)	2340	Tennant
6.5.90	SDP(SF)	A	Oldham	L	8-32	Pryce	Sullivan (2)	—	—

ST. HELENS

Ground:	Knowsley Road
Colours:	Red and white
First Season:	1895-96
Nickname:	Saints
Chairman:	Eric Latham
Secretary:	Geoff Sutcliffe
Coach:	Alex Murphy (Nov 1985-Jan 1990)
	Mike McClennan (Feb 1990-)

Honours: **Championship** Winners, 1931-32, 1952-53, 1958-59, 1965-66, 1969-70, 1970-71

Beaten finalists, 1964-65, 1966-67, 1971-72

Division One Champions, 1974-75

League Leaders Trophy Winners, 1964-65, 1965-66

Club Championship (Merit Table) Beaten finalists, 1973-74

Challenge Cup Winners, 1955-56, 1960-61, 1965-66, 1971-72, 1975-76

Beaten finalists, 1896-97, 1914-15, 1929-30, 1952-53, 1977-78, 1986-87, 1988-89

Lancashire Cup Winners, 1926-27, 1953-54, 1960-61, 1961-62, 1962-63, 1963-64, 1964-65, 1967-68, 1968-69, 1984-85

Beaten finalists, 1932-33, 1952-53, 1956-57, 1958-59, 1959-60, 1970-71, 1982-83

Lancashire League Winners, 1929-30, 1931-32, 1952-53, 1959-60, 1964-65, 1965-66, 1966-67, 1968-69

Regal Trophy Winners, 1987-88

Premiership Winners, 1975-76, 1976-77, 1984-85

Beaten finalists, 1974-75, 1987-88

Western Division Championship Winners, 1963-64

BBC2 Floodlit Trophy Winners, 1971-72, 1975-76

Beaten finalists, 1965-66, 1968-69, 1970-71, 1977-78, 1978-79

Records: Attendance: 35,695 v. Wigan (League) 26 Dec, 1949

Season

Goals: 214 by K. Coslett, 1971-72

Tries: 62 by T. Van Vollenhoven, 1958-59

Points: 452 by K. Coslett, 1971-72

Match

Goals: 16 by P. Loughlin v. Carlisle, 14 Sep, 1986

Tries: 6 by A. Ellaby v. Barrow, 5 Mar, 1932; S. Llewellyn v. Castleford, 3 Mar, 1956 and v. Liverpool C., 20 Aug, 1956; T. Vollenhoven v. Wakefield T., 21 Dec, 1957 and v. Blackpool B., 23 Apr, 1962; F. Myler v. Maryport, 1 Sep, 1969; S. Cooper v. Hull, 17 Feb, 1988

Points: 40 by P. Loughlin v. Carlisle, 14 Sep, 1986

Highest score: 112-0 v. Carlisle, 1986-87

Highest against: 78-3 v. Warrington, 1908-09

1989-90 PLAYERS' SUMMARY

	App	Tries	Goals	Dr	Pts
Arkwright, Chris	7	1	—	—	4
Atherton, Peter	0 + 1	—	—	—	—
Bailey, Mark	24 + 13	13	—	—	52
Bateman, Andy	20 + 2	4	—	—	16
Bourneville, Mark	2 + 3	—	—	—	—
Carrington, Mike	0 + 1	1	—	—	4
Connolly, Gary	24 + 1	3	—	—	12
Connor, Ian	2 + 2	—	—	—	—
Cooper, Shane	33	11	—	3	47
Cosgrove, David	14 + 4	2	—	—	8
Devine, Sean	17 + 2	4	26	—	68
Donegan, Austin	1 + 3	—	—	—	—
Dwyer, Bernard	9 + 1	3	—	—	12
Evans, Stuart	11	2	—	—	8
Forber, Paul	34 + 1	11	2	—	48
Frodsham, Tommy	21	8	—	—	32
Griffiths, Jonathan	11 + 3	7	—	—	28
Groves, Paul	37	9	—	—	36
Haggerty, Roy	32 + 3	7	—	2	30
Harrison, John	5 + 4	2	—	—	8
Holding, Neil	18 + 1	4	—	2	18
Hunte, Allan	35	21	—	—	84
Jones, Paul	11 + 12	2	—	—	8
Kay, Tony	14 + 2	—	—	—	—
Kebbie, Brimah	5	—	—	—	—
Large, David	10	4	—	—	16
Lee, Mark	0 + 2	—	—	—	—
Lever, David	1 + 1	—	—	—	—
Loughlin, Paul	32	17	135	—	338
Mann, George	22 + 1	3	—	—	12
McCormack, Kevin	1	1	—	—	4
Quirk, Les	17 + 4	15	—	—	60
Roach, Jason	2	—	—	—	—
Ropati, Tea	1	—	—	—	—
Tanner, David	21	4	15	—	46
Veivers, Phil	39	21	—	—	84

TOTALS:

36 players		180	178	7	1,083

1989-90 MATCH ANALYSIS

Date	Com-petition	H/A	Opponent	Rlt	Score	Tries	Goals	Atten-dance	Referee
3.9.89	SBC	A[1]	Sheffield E.	W	36-20	Griffiths (2), Forber, Loughlin, Veivers	Loughlin (8)	—	—
10.9.89	SBC	H	Castleford	L	24-26	Groves, Griffiths, Veivers, Harrison	Loughlin (4)	8859	Galtress
17.9.89	LC(1)	H	Runcorn H.	W	78-10	Veivers (3), Hunter (3), Loughlin (2), Forber, Bailey, Cooper, Frodsham, Griffiths, Cosgrove	Loughlin (11)	5498	Bowman
24.9.89	SBC	A	Bradford N.	L	18-28	Bailey, Cooper	Loughlin (5)	—	—
27.9.89	LC(2)	H	Oldham	L	6-36	Carrington	Tanner	7834	Steele
1.10.89	Tour	H	New Zealand	W	27-26	Hunte, Evans, Forber, Tanner	Tanner (5), Holding (dg)	7040	Tennant
8.10.89	SBC	A	Wakefield T.	W	24-21	Loughlin (2), Bailey, Large, Hunte	Loughlin (2)	—	—
15.10.89	SBC	H	Featherstone R.	W	50-11	Frodsham (2), Loughlin, Mann, Forber, Veivers, Hunte, Groves	Loughlin (9)	7267	Tidball
29.10.89	SBC	A	Warrington	W	15-3	Forber, Holding	Loughlin (3), Holding (dg)	—	—
4.11.89	SBC	H	Salford	W	40-16	Cooper, Cosgrove, Veivers, Bailey, Groves, Forber, Dwyer	Loughlin (6)	4437	Tidball
12.11.89	SBC	H	Barrow	W	62-18	Veivers (3), Holding (3), Hunte (2), Loughlin, Frodsham	Loughlin (10), Tanner	6130	C. Morris
21.11.89	SBC	A	Hull	W	34-24	Groves (3), Tanner, Loughlin, Frodsham	Loughlin (5)	—	—
26.11.89	SBC	A	Featherstone R.	W	24-23	Hunte, Harrison, Bailey, Connolly	Loughlin (4)	—	—
2.12.89	RT(1)	H	Hull K.R.	W	40-26	Hunte (3), Loughlin (2), Tanner, Veivers	Loughlin (6)	4888	C. Morris
10.12.89	RT(2)	H	Dewsbury	D	12-12	Hunte, Tanner	Loughlin (2)	5847	Kershaw
13.12.89	RT(2) Replay	A[2]	Dewsbury	W	14-0	Griffiths, Quirk, Connolly	Tanner	—	—
17.12.89	RT(3)	H	Oldham	W	32-18	Hunte (2), Loughlin, Frodsham, Bailey, Groves	Loughlin (4)	7742	Whitfield
23.12.89	RT(SF)	Wigan	Halifax	L	9-10	Bateman	Loughlin (2), Haggerty (dg)	(6085)	Kershaw
26.12.89	SBC	A	Wigan	L	6-38	Quirk	Tanner	—	—
1.1.90	SBC	H	Widnes	L	8-18	Veivers	Loughlin (2)	12,375	Cross
7.1.90	SBC	A	Leigh	L	18-30	Loughlin (2), Veivers	Loughlin (3)	—	—
14.1.90	CC(P)	H	Castleford	W	39-12	Bateman (2), Haggerty, Devine, Evans	Devine (9), Cooper (dg)	8662	Bowman
17.1.90	SBC	H	Hull	W	19-12	McCormack, Arkwright, Jones	Devine (3), Cooper (dg)	6304	Holdsworth
21.1.90	SBC	A	Salford	W	25-10	Cooper (2), Quirk, Large	Devine (4), Cooper (dg)	—	—
28.1.90	CC(1)	A	Bramley	W	22-14	Quirk (2), Cooper, Loughlin	Loughlin (3)	—	—
31.1.90	SBC	H	Bradford N.	W	32-10	Devine, Forber, Hunte, Jones, Bailey	Loughlin (6)	6981	Crashley
4.2.90	SBC	H	Leeds	W	32-26	Veivers (2), Bailey, Quirk, Dwyer	Loughlin (6)	11,235	Holdsworth
10.2.90	CC(2)	A	Hull	W	24-12	Dwyer, Connolly, Veivers, Haggerty, Quirk	Loughlin (2)	—	—
18.2.90	SBC	A	Barrow	W	46-6	Haggerty (2), Veivers (2), Forber, Hunte, Cooper, Devine	Loughlin (7)	—	—
25.2.90	CC(3)	H	Whitehaven	W	44-10	Hunte (2), Loughlin (2), Quirk, Cooper, Groves, Forber	Loughlin (6)	9253	Bowman

(continued on page 109)

SALFORD

Ground:	The Willows
Colours:	Red and white
First Season:	1896-97
Nickname:	Red Devils
Chairman:	John Wilkinson
Secretary:	Graham McCarty
Coach:	Kevin Ashcroft (May 1984-Oct 1989)
	Kevin Tamati (Oct 1989-)
Honours:	**Championship** Winners, 1913-14, 1932-33, 1936-37, 1938-39
	Beaten finalists, 1933-34
	Division One Champions, 1973-74, 1975-76
	Challenge Cup Winners, 1937-38
	Beaten finalists, 1899-1900, 1901-02, 1902-03, 1905-06, 1938-39, 1968-69
	Lancashire League Winners, 1932-33, 1933-34, 1934-35, 1936-37, 1938-39
	Lancashire Cup Winners, 1931-32, 1934-35, 1935-36, 1936-37, 1972-73
	Beaten finalists, 1929-30, 1938-39, 1973-74, 1974-75, 1975-76, 1988-89
	Premiership Beaten finalists, 1975-76
	Regal Trophy Beaten finalists 1972-73
	BBC2 Floodlit Trophy Winners, 1974-75
Records:	Attendance: 26,470 v. Warrington (RL Cup) 13 Feb, 1937
	Season
	Goals: 221 by D. Watkins, 1972-73
	Tries: 46 by K. Fielding, 1973-74
	Points: 493 by D. Watkins, 1972-73
	Match
	Goals: 13 by A. Risman v. Bramley, 5 Apr, 1933 and v. Broughton R., 18 May, 1940; D. Watkins v. Keighley, 7 Jan, 1972; S. Rule v. Doncaster, 4 Sep, 1981

Tries: 6 by F. Miles v. Lees, 5 Mar, 1898; E. Bone v. Goole, 29 Mar, 1902; J. Hilton v. Leigh, 7 Oct, 1939

Points: 39 by J. Lomas v. Liverpool C., 2 Feb, 1907

Highest score: 78-0 v. Liverpool C., 1906-07

Highest against: 65-0 v. Castleford, 1989-90

1989-90 PLAYERS' SUMMARY

	App	Tries	Goals	Dr	Pts
Barrett, Mark	3	—	—	—	—
Bentley, Keith	7 + 1	1	—	—	4
Birkett, Martin	11 + 1	—	5	—	10
Blease, Ian	24 + 5	1	—	—	4
Bloor, Darren	0 + 1	—	—	—	—
Bradshaw, Arthur	2 + 1	—	—	—	—
Bragger, Ian	9	6	—	—	24
Brooke-Cowden, Mark	18 + 2	2	—	—	8
Brown, Shaun	11 + 2	4	3	1	23
Burgess, Andrew	8 + 10	4	5	—	26
Cairns, David	23	1	—	1	5
Cassidy, Frank	19	4	—	—	16
Chick, Stuart	2	—	—	—	—
Clare, Jeff	1 + 2	1	—	—	4
Conroy, Tony	1 + 1	—	—	—	—
Disley, Gary	0 + 1	—	—	—	—
Evans, Tex	21 + 2	10	—	—	40
Fell, David	16	3	—	—	12
Gibson, Steve	26 + 3	13	—	—	52
Gill, Mick	1 + 1	—	—	—	—
Gormley, Ian	28 + 2	4	—	—	16
Hadley, Adrian	20	7	1	—	30
Havard, Keiron	2	—	—	—	—
Herbert, Steve	2 + 1	—	—	—	—
Howard, Tony	3	1	—	—	4
Jones, Ken	2 + 5	—	1	—	2
Kerry, Steve	27 + 4	16	70	5	209
Lee, Mark	13 + 1	1	—	1	5
McTigue, Mick	1	—	—	—	—
Mercer, Andy	6 + 6	2	—	—	8
Moran, Mark	17 + 1	—	—	—	—
Needham, David	0 + 1	—	—	—	—
O'Neill, Steve	13	1	—	1	5
Rampling, Tony	11	2	—	—	8
Regan, Peter	0 + 1	—	—	—	—
Sherratt, Ian	14	1	—	—	4
Walsh, Joe	1 + 2	—	—	—	—
Whiteley, Chris	12	—	—	—	—
Williams, Peter	20	4	—	—	16
Worrall, Mick	20 + 1	8	—	—	32
Trialist	1	—	—	—	—
TOTALS:					
41 players		97	85	9	567

1989-90 MATCH ANALYSIS

Date	Competition	H/A	Opponent	Rlt	Score	Tries	Goals	Attendance	Referee
3.9.89	SBC	A	Widnes	L	18-46	Sherratt, Williams, Evans, Hadley	Kerry	—	—
10.9.89	SBC	H	Wigan	L	12-56	Burgess, Bragger	Kerry (2)	7318	Whitfield
17.9.89	LC(1)	H	Rochdale H.	W	52-12	Bragger (4), Kerry (2), Gibson (2), Gormley	Kerry (8)	3094	Tickle
24.9.89	SBC	A	Leeds	L	28-34	Evans, Kerry, Blease, Hadley	Kerry (6)	—	—
27.9.89	LC(2)	H	Warrington	L	4-27	—	Kerry (2)	4994	Allatt
1.10.89	SBC	H	Bradford N.	L	12-36	Worrall, Gibson	Kerry, Jones	4059	Carter
7.10.89	SBC	H	Leigh	W	19-6	Kerry, Evans	Kerry (5, 1dg)	2241	Galtress
15.10.89	SBC	A	Hull	L	8-44	Hadley, Evans	—	—	—
31.10.89	SBC	H	Widnes	L	16-28	Gibson, Worrall	Kerry (4)	5453	Asquith
4.11.89	SBC	A	St. Helens	L	16-40	Bragger, Cairns, Bentley	Hadley, Kerry	—	—
12.11.89	SBC	H	Leeds	L	18-38	Williams, Hadley, Brown	Brown (3)	4624	Kershaw
19.11.89	SBC	A	Barrow	W	36-2	Kerry (2), Rampling, Burgess, Hadley, Gibson	Kerry (6)	—	—
26.11.89	SBC	H	Sheffield E.	D	20-20	Hadley, Gormley, Fell, Kerry	Kerry (2)	3020	Tennant
3.12.89	RT(1)	A	Hull	W	21-18	Kerry (2), Brooke-Cowden	Kerry (4, 1dg)	—	—
10.12.89	RT(2)	A	Halifax	L	6-20	Evans	Kerry	—	—
17.12.89	SBC	A	Warrington	L	15-18	Rampling, Williams	Kerry (3, 1dg)	—	—
26.12.89	SBC	A	Leigh	L	10-18	Gibson	Kerry (2, 2dg)	—	—
7.1.90	SBC	H	Featherstone R.	L	14-15	Cassidy, Williams, Evans	Kerry	3104	Campbell
14.1.90	SBC	A	Wakefield T.	L	4-28	Hadley	—	—	—
21.1.90	SBC	H	St. Helens	L	10-25	Gormley	Gormley (3)	5187	Whitfield
28.1.90	CC(1)	H	Bisons	W	56-6	Worrall (3), Cassidy (2), Gormley, Evans, Burgess, O'Neill, Mercer, Lee	Birkett (4), Burgess (2)	1935	Asquith
2.2.90	SBC	H	Barrow	W	36-4	Evans (2), Burgess, Kerry, Cassidy, Gibson, Worrall	Kerry (4)	2167	Tennent
11.2.90	CC(2)	H	Oldham	L	7-18	Brown	Birkett, Lee (dg)	6472	Holdsworth
18.2.90	SBC	A	Wigan	L	26-32	Gibson (2), Kerry (2), Evans	Kerry (3)	—	—
25.2.90	SBC	H	Castleford	L	18-24	Howard, Brown, Kerry	Kerry (3)	3178	Allatt
4.3.90	SBC	A	Bradford N.	L	12-18	Gibson (2)	Kerry (2)	—	—
11.3.90	SBC	A	Featherstone R.	W	33-20	Gibson (2), Kerry (2), Brooke-Cowden, Worrall	Kerry (4), O'Neill (dg)	—	—
18.3.90	SBC	H	Hull	L	5-21	Mercer	Cairns (dg)	2829	Kershaw
25.3.90	SBC	A[1]	Sheffield E.	L	12-17	Worrall, Kerry	Kerry (2)	—	—
1.4.90	SBC	A	Castleford	L	0-65	—	—	—	—
8.4.90	SBC	H	Wakefield T.	L	18-28	Fell (2), Brown	Kerry (3)	2217	Smith
16.4.90	SBC	H	Warrington	L	5-16	Clare	Brown (dg)	2960	Crashley

[1] at Doncaster

SHEFFIELD EAGLES

Ground:	No home ground in 1989-90 after Owlerton Stadium was declared unsafe. Moved to Don Valley Stadium for 1990-91
Colours:	Red and black
First Season:	1984-85
Nickname:	Eagles
Managing Director:	Gary Hetherington
Secretary:	Julie Bush
Coach:	Gary Hetherington (July 1986-)
Honours:	**Second Division Premiership** Winners, 1988-89
Records:	Attendance: 8,636 v. Widnes (League) at Sheffield U. FC, 8 Oct, 1989

Season

Goals: 148 by M. Aston, 1988-89
Tries: 28 by D. Powell, 1988-89
Points: 307 by M. Aston, 1988-89

Match

Goals: 12 by R. Rafferty at Fulham, 21 Sep, 1986
Tries: 5 by D. Powell at Mansfield M., 2 Jan, 1989
Points: 32 by R. Rafferty at Fulham, 21 Sep, 1986
Highest score: 80-8 v. Wigan St. Patricks, 1988-89
Highest against: 62-11 v. Warrington, 1985-86

1989-90 PLAYERS' SUMMARY

	App	Tries	Goals	Dr	Pts
Aston, Mark	29	1	94	5	197
Branton, Richard	0 + 1	—	—	—	—
Broadbent, Paul	23	2	—	—	8
Cartwright, Phil	2 + 2	—	—	—	—
Cator, Lance	1	—	—	—	—
Close, David	11 + 1	—	2	2	6
Cook, Mick	30	—	—	—	—
Dickinson, Andy	29 + 1	14	—	—	56
Dobson, Steve	2	—	—	—	—
Farrell, Anthony	8 + 4	—	—	—	—
Fleming, Mark	0 + 1	1	—	—	4
Gamson, Mark	33 + 1	8	—	—	32
Grimoldby, Nick	18 + 7	4	—	—	16
Halafihi, Nick	0 + 6	1	—	—	4
Hardy, Jeff	20	13	—	—	52
Kellett, Neil	9 + 18	7	—	—	28
Ketteridge, Martin	3	—	9	—	18
Leota, Francis	11	1	—	—	4
Lidbury, Steve	0 + 3	—	—	—	—
McGuire, Bruce	15 + 1	2	—	—	8
Mycoe, David	23 + 6	8	—	—	32
Nelson, Dave	32 + 1	8	—	—	32
Nickle, Sonny	28 + 2	11	—	—	44
Nikau, Tawera	10	5	—	—	20
Picksley, Richard	7	3	—	—	12
Powell, Darryl	33	16	—	2	66
Smiles, Warren	17 + 1	1	—	—	4
Van Bellen, Gary	22 + 4	—	—	—	—
Waddell, Hugh	5	—	—	—	—
Willey, Sean	8 + 1	2	—	—	8
Young, Andy	13 + 5	5	—	—	20
TOTALS:					
31 players		113	105	9	671

David Mycoe, a July 1989 Sheffield Eagles signing from amateur football, graduating to Great Britain Under-21 honours.

1989-90 MATCH ANALYSIS

Date	Com-petition	H/A	Opponent	Rlt	Score	Tries	Goals	Atten-dance	Referee
3.9.89	SBC	H[1]	St. Helens	L	20-36	Broadbent, Nickle, Hardy	Aston (3, 1dg), Powell (dg)	6200	Holdsworth
10.9.89	SBC	A	Featherstone R.	W	37-12	Dickinson (2), Powell, Young, Hardy, Nickle, Grimoldby	Aston (4, 1dg)	—	—
17.9.89	YC(1)	A	Batley	W	36-5	Hardy (3), Young (2), Nickle, Fleming	Aston (4)	—	—
24.9.89	SBC	A	Barrow	W	22-10	Dickinson (2), Hardy, Nickle	Aston (3)	—	—
27.9.89	YC(2)	A	Bradford N.	L	6-19	Powell	Aston	—	—
1.10.89	SBC	A	Wakefield T.	W	28-16	Powell, McGuire, Young, Nelson	Aston (6)	—	—
8.10.89	SBC	H[2]	Widnes	W	31-6	Hardy (2), McGuire, Grimoldby, Nickle	Aston (5, 1dg)	8636	Tennant
15.10.89	SBC	A	Castleford	L	22-24	Mycoe (2), Dickinson	Aston (5)	—	—
29.10.89	SBC	H[3]	Leeds	L	16-27	Dickinson, Nelson, Gamson	Aston (2)	4622	Whitfield
5.11.89	SBC	H[1]	Wigan	L	10-22	Nelson, Nickle	Aston	7642	C. Morris
8.11.89	RT(P)	A	Warrington	W	12-4	Powell, Gamson	Aston (2)	—	—
12.11.89	SBC	A	Warrington	W	36-22	Gamson, Nelson, Aston, Kellett, Nickle, Mycoe	Aston (6)	—	—
19.11.89	SBC	H[3]	Bradford N.	L	14-34	Kellett, Powell	Aston (3)	2986	Kershaw
26.11.89	SBC	A	Salford	D	20-20	Kellett, Smiles, Powell	Aston (4)	—	—
1.12.89	RT(1)	H[4]	Rochdale H.	W	36-22	Hardy (2), Kellett, Nelson, Dickinson, Nickle, Gamson	Aston (4)	2307	Kershaw
10.12.89	RT(2)	A	Swinton	W	28-6	Dickinson, Nelson, Powell, Grimoldby, Hardy	Aston (4)	—	—
17.12.89	RT(3)	H[3]	Castleford	L	2-18	—	Aston	3014	C. Morris
26.12.89	SBC	A	Hull	L	6-15	Nelson	Aston	—	—
3.1.90	SBC	H[5]	Featherstone R.	L	20-30	Hardy (2), Mycoe	Aston (4)	2756	Crashley
7.1.90	SBC	H[6]	Warrington	L	8-12	Powell	Aston (2)	1298	Bowman
16.1.90	SBC	A	Wigan	L	2-30	—	Aston	—	—
21.1.90	SBC	A	Leigh	L	16-28	Powell (2), Dickinson	Aston (2)	—	—
28.1.90	CC(1)	A	Barrow	W	22-12	Mycoe, Powell, Willey	Aston (5)	—	—
4.2.90	SBC	H[7]	Wakefield T.	W	24-10	Powell (2), Nikau	Aston (5, 1 dg), Powell (dg)	5104	Kendrew
11.2.90	CC(2)	A	Wakefield T.	L	12-27	Powell, Nikau	Aston (2)	—	—
18.2.90	SBC	A	Leeds	L	2-44	—	Aston	—	—
25.2.90	SBC	H[6]	Barrow	W	40-2	Grimoldby, Broadbent, Gamson, Nikau, Powell, Dickinson, Young	Aston (6)	1002	Asquith
4.3.90	SBC	H[6]	Leigh	W	46-4	Dickinson (3), Mycoe, Nikau, Kellett, Powell, Halafihi, Gamson	Aston (5)	1106	Allatt
9.3.90	SBC	H[6]	Castleford	L	14-18	Leota, Mycoe	Aston (2, 1 dg), Close (dg)	4169	Crashley
18.3.90	SBC	A	Bradford N.	L	16-28	Picksley (2), Gamson, Nickle	—	—	—
25.3.90	SBC	H[6]	Salford	W	17-12	Picksley, Nikau, Kellett	Close (2, 1dg)	1121	Asquith
1.4.90	SBC	A	Widnes	L	20-52	Willey, Gamson, Nickle, Mycoe	Ketteridge (2)	—	—
8.4.90	SBC	A	St. Helens	L	26-42	Nickle, Nelson, Dickinson, Kellett	Ketteridge (5)	—	—
15.4.90	SBC	H[2]	Hull	L	4-32	—	Ketteridge (2)	5856	Crashley

[1] at Sheffield W. FC   [4] at Halifax   [6] at Doncaster
[2] at Sheffield U. FC   [5] at Wakefield T.   [7] at Barnsley FC
[3] at Chesterfield FC

SWINTON

Ground:	Station Road
Colours:	Blue and white
First Season:	1896-97
Nickname:	Lions
Chairman:	John Way
Secretary:	Wayne Dore
Coach:	Frank Barrow (Oct 1987-June 1989)
	Jim Crellin (July 1989-)

Honours: **Championship** Winners, 1926-27, 1927-28, 1930-31, 1934-35
Beaten finalists, 1924-25, 1932-33
War League Beaten finalists, 1939-40
Division One Champions, 1962-63, 1963-64
Division Two Champions, 1984-85
Second Division Premiership Winners, 1986-87
Beaten finalists, 1988-89
Challenge Cup Winners, 1899-1900, 1925-26, 1927-28
Beaten finalists, 1926-27, 1931-32
Lancashire League Winners, 1924-25, 1927-28, 1928-29, 1930-31, 1960-61
Lancashire War League Winners, 1939-40
Lancashire Cup Winners, 1925-26, 1927-28, 1939-40, 1969-70
Beaten finalists, 1910-11, 1923-24, 1931-32, 1960-61, 1961-62, 1962-63, 1964-65, 1972-73
BBC2 Floodlit Trophy Beaten finalists, 1966-67
Western Division Championship Beaten finalists, 1963-64

Records: Attendance: 44,621 Wigan v. Warrington (RL Cup SF) 7 Apr, 1951
Season
Goals: 128 by A. Blan, 1960-61
Tries: 42 by J. Stopford, 1963-64
Points: 283 by A. Blan, 1960-61
Match
Goals: 12 by K. Gowers v. Liverpool C., 3 Oct, 1959
Tries: 5 by T. Bevan v. Morecambe, 10 Sep, 1898; W. Wallwork v. Widnes, 15 Dec, 1900; J. Evans v. Bradford N., 30 Sep, 1922; H. Halsall v. St. Helens, 24 Jan, 1925; R. Cracknell v. Whitehaven Rec., 11 Feb, 1928; R. Lewis v. Keighley, 12 Jan, 1946; J. Stopford v. Bramley, 22 Dec, 1962; A. Buckley v. Salford, 8 Apr, 1964; J. Ropati v. Nottingham C., 21 Jan, 1990
Points: 29 by B. McMahon v. Dewsbury, 15 Aug, 1959
Highest score: 76-4 v. Pontefract, 1906-07
Highest against: 76-3 v. Huddersfield, 1945-46; 76-16 v. Castleford, 1987-88

1989-90 PLAYERS' SUMMARY

	App	Tries	Goals	Dr	Pts
Ainsworth, Gary	5 + 4	3	—	—	12
Allen, John	3 + 1	1	—	—	4
Ashall, Barry	6	2	2	—	12
Bate, Derek	10	6	—	—	24
Berry, John	2	—	—	—	—
Bloor, Darren	7	—	—	—	—
Capewell, Philip	19 + 1	2	—	—	8
Cassidy, Frank	10 + 1	2	—	1	9
Chadwick, Les	6 + 2	2	—	—	8
Edwards, Logan	0 + 3	2	—	—	8
Flanagan, Terry	11 + 1	3	—	—	12
Graziano, Joe	0 + 1	—	—	—	—
Hancock, Mike	4	—	—	—	—
Hewitt, Tony	4 + 3	—	—	—	—
Holden, Keith	7	1	—	—	4
Hudson, Julian	2 + 1	—	—	—	—
Hudson, Mark	2	—	—	—	—
Jackson, Steve	3	1	—	—	4
Linton, Ralph	9 + 1	3	—	—	12
Maloney, David	1	—	—	—	—
McCue, Vince	3	1	—	—	4
Melling, Alex	32	8	—	—	32
Mellor, Paul	4 + 4	—	—	—	—
Mooney, Frank	2 + 1	—	—	—	—
Morrison, Tony	22 + 1	4	—	—	16
Myler, John	13	2	43	2	96
O'Neill, Steve	4	1	—	—	4
Partington, Carl	0 + 1	—	—	—	—
Peacham, Gary	7	4	—	—	16
Peters, Barry	13	4	—	—	16
Pickavance, Ian	17 + 4	6	—	—	24
Pucill, Andy	30 + 3	2	—	1	9
Rabbitt, Jacent	0 + 1	—	—	—	—
Ranson, Scott	34	22	—	—	88
Ropati, Joe	22	14	5	—	66
Scott, Terry	6	3	—	—	12
Sheals, Mark	23 + 5	8	—	—	32
Skeech, Ian	5 + 1	—	—	—	—
Snape, Steve	17	2	—	—	8
Sutton, Gary	3 + 2	—	—	—	—
Topping, Paul	31	7	48	2	126
Tupaea, Shane	29 + 1	13	—	—	52
Viller, Mark	12 + 2	2	—	—	8
Waterworth, Keith	1	—	—	1	1
Zenon, Ronel	0 + 1	—	—	—	—
Trialist	1	—	—	—	—

TOTALS:
	App	Tries	Goals	Dr	Pts
46 players		131	98	7	727

1989-90 MATCH ANALYSIS

Date	Competition	H/A	Opponent	Rlt	Score	Tries	Goals	Attendance	Referee
3.9.89	SD	H	Chorley	W	48-4	Ranson (4), Melling (2), Snape, Scott, Ainsworth	Myler (6)	1320	Whitelam
6.9.89	SD	A	Trafford B.	W	33-18	Melling, Cassidy, Viller, Scott, Allen	Myler (6, 1dg)	—	—
10.9.89	SD	A	Rochdale H.	L	22-26	O'Neill, Topping, Ranson	Myler (5)	—	—
17.9.89	LC(1)	A	Warrington	L	6-16	Myler	Myler	—	—
24.9.89	SD	H	Ryedale-York	L	8-17	Ranson	Myler (2)	1518	Kendrew
1.10.89	SD	A	Dewsbury	W	17-12	Chadwick, Tupaea	Myler (4, 1dg)	—	—
8.10.89	SD	A	Batley	W	18-0	Snape, Chadwick, Ranson	Topping (2, 2dg)	—	—
15.10.89	SD	H	Carlisle	W	26-14	Ranson, Tupaea, Morrison, Topping, Pucill	Topping (3)	1369	Whitelam
22.10.89	SD	A	Hull K.R.	L	16-38	Bate, Topping, Tupaea	Topping (2)	—	—
29.10.89	SD	A	Whitehaven	W	14-7	McCue, Tupaea, Jackson	Topping	—	—
5.11.89	SD	H	Bramley	W	30-11	Bate (3), Cassidy, Ainsworth	Topping (5)	1334	Steele
12.11.89	SD	A	Nottingham C.	W	27-11	Bate (2), Topping, Ranson, Ainsworth	Topping (3), Cassidy (dg)	—	—
19.11.89	SD	H	Hull K.R.	L	10-30	Tupaea, Linton	Topping	2362	Smith
3.12.89	RT(1)	H	Batley	W	18-16	Sheals, Ranson, Tupaea	Myler (3)	1359	Tickle
10.12.89	RT(2)	H	Sheffield E.	L	6-28	Tupaea	Myler	1925	Tennant
17.12.89	SD	A	Chorley	W	22-10	Ropati (2), Linton, Sheals	Myler (3)	—	—
26.12.89	SD	H	Trafford B.	W	28-10	Topping, Scott, Myler, Ranson, Ropati, Melling	Myler (2)	1302	Carter
1.1.90	SD	A	Oldham	L	14-29	Tupaea, Linton	Myler (3)	—	—
7.1.90	SD	A	Carlisle	W	28-10	Ranson (2), Topping, Viller, Ropati	Myler (4)	—	—
17.1.90	SD	H	Huddersfield	W	26-10	Sheals (3), Tupaea, Ranson	Myler (3)	1287	Smith
21.1.90	SD	H	Nottingham C.	W	46-10	Ropati (5), Capewell, Ranson, Holden, Flanagan	Topping (5)	1102	Burke
28.1.90	CC(1)	H	Wakefield T.	D	10-10	Tupaea	Topping (3)	3330	Whitelam
31.1.90	CC(1) Replay	A	Wakefield T.	L	4-32	Pickavance	—	—	—
11.2.90	SD	H	Doncaster	W	34-22	Ropati (2), Tupaea, Peters, Flanagan, Morrison	Topping (5)	1266	Holgate
18.2.90	SD	H	Whitehaven	W	40-4	Melling (2), Ropati (2), Sheals, Flanagan, Pickavance, Ranson	Topping (2), Ropati (2)	1254	Smith
4.3.90	SD	H	Batley	W	20-3	Ranson (2), Morrison, Pucill	Topping (2)	1412	Tickle
11.3.90	SD	A	Doncaster	W	38-5	Edwards (2), Ashall, Morrison, Tupaea, Capewell, Pickavance	Topping (5)	—	—
18.3.90	SD	H	Dewsbury	W	36-12	Peters (2), Ranson, Peacham, Melling, Topping	Topping (6)	1361	Steele
25.3.90	SD	A	Ryedale-York	L	10-18	Sheals, Tupaea	Topping	—	—
1.4.90	SD	H	Rochdale H.	L	16-37	Ranson, Ropati, Peacham	Topping (2)	3189	Stokes (NZ)
8.4.90	SD	A	Huddersfield	L	9-14	Pickavance, Peacham	Waterworth (dg)	—	—
13.4.90	SD	H	Oldham	W	15-12	Peters, Ranson, Ashall	Ropati, Pucill (dg)	3417	Tennent
16.4.90	SD	A	Bramley	W	22-11	Pickavance (2), Ranson, Sheals	Ropati (2), Ashall	—	—
22.4.90	SDP (1)	A	Oldham	L	10-32	Peacham, Melling	Ashall	—	—

TRAFFORD BOROUGH

Ground:	Moss Lane, Altrincham
Colours:	Blue and crimson
First Season:	1954-55 as Blackpool Borough; changing to Springfield Borough in 1987-88; Chorley Borough in 1988-89; and Trafford Borough from 1989-90
Chairman:	Mike Marsland
Secretary:	Alan Sherratt
Coach:	Mike Peers (Aug 1987-)
Honours:	**Regal Trophy** Beaten finalists, 1976-77
Records:	Attendance: 7,614 v. Castleford (RL Cup) 14 Mar, 1964. There was an attendance of 21,000 in an RL Cup-tie against Leigh on Blackpool FC ground on 9 Mar, 1957

Season
Goals: 98 by M. Smith, 1987-88
Tries: 30 by T. Frodsham, 1985-86
Points: 201 by P. Fearis, 1957-58
Match
Goals: 11 by N. Turley v. Carlisle, 26 Apr, 1984;
Tries: 4 by T. Wilkshire v. Bradford N, 14 Jan, 1961;
J. Stockley v. Doncaster, 1 Apr, 1984
T. Frodsham v. Bridgend, 14 Apr, 1985 and v. Mansfield M., 30 Nov, 1986
Points: 27 by N. Turley v. Carlisle, 26 Apr, 1984
Highest score: 56-2 v. Runcorn H., 1988-89
Highest against: 77-8 v. Wigan, 1963-64

1989-90 PLAYERS' SUMMARY

	App	Tries	Goals	Dr	Pts
Abram, Dane	30	18	—	—	72
Brown, David	7 + 1	3	—	—	12
Cole, Keith	5	1	—	—	4
Connor, Steve	23	9	—	—	36
Eccles, Bob	12 + 8	1	—	—	4
Eccles, Cliff	32	4	—	—	16
Feasey, Tony	2 + 1	—	—	—	—
Galbraith, Stuart	18	12	—	—	48
Garner, Steve	21	5	—	—	20
Glynn, Peter	2 + 1	—	—	—	—
Green, Andy	4 + 6	—	—	—	—
Griffiths, Steve	1 + 3	1	—	—	4
Herbert, Steve	20 + 1	2	—	—	8
Hewitt, David	18 + 1	6	—	—	24
Higgins, Brian	2	—	—	—	—
Horrocks, John	17 + 1	1	—	—	4
Iddon, Jimmy	3 + 2	3	—	—	12
Jones, Ken	20	5	2	1	25
Litz, Terry	3 + 8	—	—	—	—
Meadows, Kevin	6 + 2	—	—	—	—
Meadows, Mark	27 + 4	8	—	—	32
Mellor, Terry	3	—	—	—	—
Morris, Darren	2	1	—	—	4
O'Rourke, Mike	8 + 2	1	—	—	4
Perenara, Tom	4	—	2	—	4
Pugsley, Stuart	1	—	—	—	—
Reynolds, Paul	15	6	—	—	24
Rippon, Andrew	15 + 4	1	17	—	38
Robwell, Paul	0 + 2	—	—	—	—
Smith, Graham	10 + 1	3	—	—	12
Spicer, Adam	4 + 2	—	—	—	—
Stewart, Mike	24 + 2	10	—	—	40
Thompson, Courtney	3	1	—	—	4
Tickle, Steve	24	1	65	2	136
Turley, Norman	30	—	2	9	13

TOTALS:
35 players		103	88	12	600

1989-90 MATCH ANALYSIS

Date	Com-petition	H/A	Opponent	Rlt	Score	Tries	Goals	Atten-dance	Referee
30.8.89	LC(P)	A	Chorley	L	6-12	M. Meadows	Rippon	—	—
6.9.89	SD	H	Swinton	L	18-33	M. Meadows (2), Morris	Rippon (3)	1089	Asquith
10.9.89	SD	H	Runcorn H.	W	46-10	Abrams (3), Stewart, Brown, Cole, O'Rourke, M. Meadows, Rippon	Rippon (5)	537	Crashley
24.9.89	SD	A	Hull K.R.	L	8-48	Smith	Rippon (2)	—	—
8.10.89	SD	A	Huddersfield	L	18-22	Thompson, M. Meadows, Connor	Rippon (2), Turley (2dg)	—	—
15.10.89	SD	H	Keighley	W	25-19	Connor (3), Reynolds (2)	Rippon (2), Turley (dg)	814	Smith
22.10.89	SD	H	Hunslet	L	0-32	—	—	600	Crashley
29.10.89	SD	A	Keighley	W	25-16	Brown, Stewart, Abrams, Galbraith	Rippon (2), Perenara (2), Turley (dg)	—	—
5.11.89	SD	A	Workington T.	W	35-8	Galbraith (2), Reynolds (2), Connor, Brown	Tickle (5), Turley (dg)	—	—
12.11.89	SD	H	Halifax	L	6-9	Stewart	Tickle	2000	Allatt
26.11.89	SD	H	Workington T.	W	24-10	Jones, Connor, Reynolds, Galbraith	Tickle (4)	474	Smith
3.12.89	RT(1)	H	Featherstone R.	L	18-36	Garner, Galbraith, Jones	Tickle (3)	934	Crashley
10.12.89	SD	A	Doncaster	W	27-2	Galbraith (2), Abrams, Garner	Tickle (4, 1dg), Turley	—	—
17.12.89	SD	A	Batley	L	11-12	Connor, Galbraith	Tickle, Jones (dg)	—	—
26.12.89	SD	A	Swinton	L	10-28	Smith	Tickle (3)	—	—
29.12.89	SD	H	Carlisle	W	36-12	Horrocks, Reynolds, Hewitt, Garner, C. Eccles, Herbert, M. Meadows	Tickle (4)	620	Asquith
1.1.90	SD	H	Rochdale H.	L	4-18	—	Jones (2)	1088	Holgate
7.1.90	SD	A	Fulham	W	20-10	Abrams (2), Jones, C. Eccles	Tickle (2)	—	—
14.1.90	SD	H	Chorley	W	14-6	Garner, Hewitt	Tickle (3)	587	K. Morris
21.1.90	SD	H	Huddersfield	W	28-18	Abrams (2), Stewarts (2), Hewitt	Tickle (4)	635	Allatt
28.1.90	CC(1)	H	Hunslet	W	14-7	Connor, Abrams	Tickle (3)	379	Tickle
4.2.90	SD	H	Batley	W	18-12	Stewart, Garner, Jones, Hewitt	Tickle	675	Steele
11.2.90	CC(2)	A	Warrington	L	11-20	Hewitt, M. Meadows	Tickle, Turley (dg)	—	—
25.2.90	SD	A	Runcorn H.	W	18-7	Jones, Hewitt, Abram	Tickle (3)	—	—
4.3.90	SD	H	Doncaster	W	29-14	Galbraith (2), Eccles, Stewart, Abram	Tickle (4, 1 dg)	465	Asquith
11.3.90	SD	A	Hunslet	W	25-14	Stewart (2), Herbert, Galbraith	Tickle (3), Turley (1 dg)	—	—
18.3.90	SD	H	Fulham	L	18-22	Abram (2), Tickle, Galbraith	Tickle	400	Kendrew
25.3.90	SD	H	Hull K.R.	L	6-28	Griffiths	Tickle	1030	Carter
1.4.90	SD	A	Chorley	W	30-28	Conner, Eccles, Iddon, Stewart	Tickle (6), Turley (2 dg)	—	—
13.4.90	SD	A	Rochdale H.	L	28-70	Iddon (2), Abram (2), Eccles, Meadows	Tickle (2)	—	—
16.4.90	SD	A	Halifax	L	18-19	Abram (2), Smith	Tickle (3)	—	—

WAKEFIELD TRINITY

Ground: Belle Vue
Colours: Red, white and blue
First Season: 1895-96
Nickname: Dreadnoughts
Chairman: Rodney Walker
General
Manager: Neil Cadigan
Coach: David Topliss (May 1987-)
Honours: **Championship** Winners, 1966-67, 1967-68
Beaten finalists, 1959-60, 1961-62
Division Two Champions, 1903-04
Challenge Cup Winners, 1908-09, 1945-46, 1959-60, 1961-62, 1962-63
Beaten finalists, 1913-14, 1967-68, 1978-79
Yorkshire League Winners, 1909-10, 1910-11, 1945-46, 1958-59, 1959-60, 1961-62, 1965-66
Yorkshire Cup Winners, 1910-11, 1924-25, 1946-47, 1947-48, 1951-52, 1956-57, 1960-61, 1961-62, 1964-65
Beaten finalists, 1926-27, 1932-33, 1934-35, 1936-37, 1939-40, 1945-46, 1958-59, 1973-74, 1974-75
Regal Trophy Beaten finalists, 1971-72
Records: Attendance: 37,906 Leeds v. Huddersfield (RL Cup SF) 21 March, 1936
Home: 28,254 v. Wigan (RL Cup) 24 Mar, 1962
Season
Goals: 163 by N. Fox, 1961-62
Tries: 38 by F. Smith, 1959-60, D. Smith, 1973-74
Points: 407 by N. Fox, 1961-62
Match
Goals: 12 by N. Fox v. Workington T., 19 Sep, 1970 and v. Batley, 26 Aug, 1967; B. Ward v. Hunslet, 6 Feb, 1971
Tries: 7 by F. Smith v. Keighley, 25 Apr, 1959; K. Slater v. Hunslet, 6 Feb, 1971
Points: 33 by N. Fox v. Batley, 26 Aug, 1967
Highest score: 78-9 v. Batley, 1967-68

Highest against: 72-6 v. Wigan, 1986-87

1989-90 PLAYERS' SUMMARY

	App	Tries	Goals	Dr	Pts
Bell, Nigel	13 + 8	1	—	—	4
Conway, Billy	16 + 7	4	—	—	16
Conway, Mark	31 + 1	6	104	3	235
Douglas, Ian	0 + 2	—	—	—	—
Eden, Phil	28 + 3	12	—	—	48
Fletcher, Andrew	0 + 1	—	—	—	—
Fox, Phil	14 + 1	5	—	—	20
Glancy, John	21 + 1	—	—	—	—
Haggerty, Gary	1 + 1	—	—	—	—
Hirst, John	1 + 5	—	—	—	—
Jackson, Brian	17	3	—	—	12
Jowitt, Ian	0 + 1	—	—	—	—
Kelly, Andy	32	6	—	—	24
Lazenby, Tracy	26	5	—	3	23
Leuluai, James	23 + 4	6	—	—	24
Mallinder, Paul	1	—	—	—	—
Mason, Andy	31	17	—	—	68
Perry, Chris	14 + 2	3	—	—	12
Potts, Steven	0 + 1	—	—	—	—
Price, Gary	30	8	—	—	32
Price, Ray	25	6	—	—	24
Rayne, Keith	12 + 3	—	—	—	—
Reeves, Mark	0 + 1	—	—	—	—
Sheldon, Ian	1 + 2	—	—	—	—
Slater, Richard	5 + 3	2	—	—	8
Sygrove, Andy	5 + 1	1	—	—	4
Taylor, Paul	1	—	—	—	—
Thompson, John	28	4	—	—	16
Thompson, Mike	1 + 2	—	—	—	—
Timmins, Jason	3 + 1	—	—	—	—
Walker, Andrew	1	—	—	—	—
Wilson, Andy	30	9	—	—	36
Zelei, Tony	5 + 5	2	—	—	8
TOTALS:					
33 players		100	104	6	614

Coaxed out of retirement by Wakefield Trinity, Australian Test forward Ray Price, scorer of six tries in 25 appearances.

1989-90 MATCH ANALYSIS

Date	Competition	H/A	Opponent	Rlt	Score	Tries	Goals	Attendance	Referee
27.8.89	YC(P)	A	Dewsbury	L	17-18	Fox, Leuluai	M. Conway (4, 1dg)	—	—
3.9.89	SBC	A	Leeds	W	22-14	Eden, Fox, Sygrove, Zelei	M. Conway (3)	—	—
10.9.89	SBC	H	Leigh	W	32-0	B. Conway (2), M. Conway, G. Price, Lazenby	M. Conway (6)	4115	Cross
24.9.89	SBC	A	Wigan	L	10-38	Zelei, Fox	M. Conway	—	—
1.10.89	SBC	H	Sheffield E.	L	16-28	Mason, Kelly	M. Conway (4)	4882	Burke
8.10.89	SBC	H	St. Helens	L	21-24	G. Price (2), Lazenby	M. Conway (4), Lazenby (dg)	5053	Holdsworth
15.10.89	SBC	A	Widnes	L	12-30	Slater, Wilson	M. Conway (2)	—	—
29.10.89	SBC	H	Hull	W	30-14	Mason, G. Price, Jackson, Wilson, M Conway	M. Conway (5)	4839	Bowman
5.11.89	SBC	A	Barrow	W	26-10	Leuluai (2), G. Price, R. Price, Mason	M. Conway (3)	—	—
12.11.89	SBC	H	Castleford	W	22-14	Mason, Leuluai, Jackson	M. Conway (5)	7159	Asquith
19.11.89	RT(P)	H	Hull	L	12-19	G. Price	M. Conway (4)	4731	Burke
22.11.89	SBC	A	Leigh	W	24-6	Fox, Mason, Perry, Wilson	M. Conway (4)	—	—
26.11.89	SBC	H	Barrow	W	30-16	Mason (2), Lazenby, Perry, Eden	M. Conway (5)	5271	Holdsworth
26.12.89	SBC	A	Featherstone R.	L	8-15	R. Price	M. Conway (2)	—	—
31.12.89	SBC	H	Featherstone R.	W	22-14	Eden (2), Perry, Mason	M. Conway (3)	6794	Bowman
7.1.90	SBC	A	Castleford	W	18-16	Eden (2), G. Price	M. Conway (3)	—	—
14.1.90	SBC	H	Salford	W	28-4	Wilson (2), Mason (2), Kelly	M. Conway (4)	4119	Kendrew
21.1.90	SBC	H	Warrington	W	32-8	M. Conway, Eden, Leuluai, Kelly, B. Conway	M. Conway (6)	5120	Campbell
28.1.90	CC(1)	A	Swinton	D	10-10	Mason, Jackson	M. Conway	—	—
31.1.90	CC(1) Replay	H	Swinton	W	32-4	B. Conway, M. Conway, Mason, Thompson, Kelly	M. Conway (6)	4741	Whitelam
4.2.90	SBC	A¹	Sheffield E.	L	10-24	M. Conway, Wilson	M. Conway	—	—
11.2.90	CC(2)	H	Sheffield E.	W	27-12	Lazenby, Wilson, Eden, Thompson, Mason	M. Conway (3, 1dg)	5359	C. Morris
17.2.90	SBC	A	Warrington	L	2-33	—	M. Conway	—	—
24.2.90	CC(3)	H	Wigan	L	14-26	Kelly, G. Price	M. Conway (3)	8033	Campbell
4.3.90	SBC	H	Widnes	D	10-10	Fox, Wilson	M. Conway	5293	Kershaw
11.3.90	SBC	A	Hull	L	17-34	Mason (3)	M. Conway (2, 1dg)	—	—
17.3.90	SBC	A	St. Helens	L	21-44	R. Price, Thompson, M. Conway	M. Conway (4), Lazenby (dg)	—	—
25.3.90	SBC	H	Leeds	L	17-36	Thompson, Kelly, Lazenby	M. Conway (2), Lazenby (dg)	6837	Campbell
1.4.90	SBC	H	Wigan	L	14-23	Bell, R. Price	M. Conway (3)	6075	C. Morris
8.4.90	SBC	A	Salford	W	28-18	Eden (3), Leuluai, Mason	M. Conway (4)	—	—
13.4.90	SBC	A	Bradford N.	L	18-19	R. Price, Slater	M. Conway (5)	—	—
16.4.90	SBC	H	Bradford N.	L	12-36	Wilson, R. Price, Eden	—	5006	Holdsworth

¹at Barnsley FC

WARRINGTON

Ground:	Wilderspool
Colours:	Primrose and blue
First Season:	1895-96
Nickname:	Wire
Chairman:	Peter Higham
General Manager:	Ron Close
Coach:	Brian Johnson (Nov 1988-)

Honours: **Championship** Winners, 1947-48, 1953-54, 1954-55
Beaten finalists, 1925-26, 1934-35, 1936-37, 1948-49, 1950-51, 1960-61
League Leaders Trophy Winners, 1972-73
Club Championship (Merit Table) Winners, 1973-74
Challenge Cup Winners, 1904-05, 1906-07, 1949-50, 1953-54, 1973-74
Beaten finalists, 1900-01, 1903-04, 1912-13, 1927-28, 1932-33, 1935-36, 1974-75, 1989-90
Lancashire League Winners, 1937-38, 1947-48, 1948-49, 1950-51, 1953-54, 1954-55, 1955-56, 1967-68
Lancashire Cup Winners, 1921-22, 1929-30, 1932-33, 1937-38, 1959-60, 1965-66, 1980-81, 1982-83, 1989-90
Beaten finalists, 1906-07, 1948-49, 1950-51, 1967-68, 1985-86, 1987-88
Regal Trophy Winners, 1973-74, 1977-78, 1980-81
Beaten finalists, 1978-79, 1986-87
Premiership Trophy Winners, 1985-86
Beaten finalists 1976-77, 1986-87
Captain Morgan Trophy Winners, 1973-74
BBC2 Floodlit Trophy Beaten finalists, 1974-75

Records: Attendance: 35,000 Wigan v. Leigh (Lancs. Cup Final) 29 Oct, 1949
Home: 34,304 v. Wigan (League) 22 Jan, 1949

Season
Goals: 170 by S. Hesford, 1978-79
Tries: 66 by B. Bevan, 1952-53
Points: 363 by H. Bath, 1952-53
Match
Goals: 14 by H. Palin v. Liverpool C., 13 Sep, 1950
Tries: 7 by B. Bevan v. Leigh, 29 Mar, 1948 and v. Bramley, 22 Apr, 1953
Points: 33 by G. Thomas v. St. Helens, 12 Apr, 1909
Highest score: 78-3 v. St. Helens, 1908-09
Highest against: 68-14 v. Hunslet, 1927-28

1989-90 PLAYERS' SUMMARY

	App	Tries	Goals	Dr	Pts
Bacon, Mike	0 + 1	—	—	—	—
Bishop, Paul	16 + 2	2	6	10	30
Burke, Tony	31	1	—	—	4
Chambers, Gary	0 + 3	—	—	—	—
Crompton, Martin	15	5	—	—	20
Cullen, Paul	8 + 3	3	—	—	12
Darbyshire, Paul	14 + 7	2	12	—	32
Drummond, Des	37	14	—	—	56
Duane, Ronnie	2 + 4	1	—	—	4
Forster, Mark	35 + 1	15	—	—	60
Gregory, Mike	27	2	—	—	8
Harmon, Neil	21 + 7	—	—	—	—
Jackson, Bob	22 + 2	6	—	—	24
Kenyon, Neil	4 + 2	5	—	—	20
Lyon, David	32	6	2	—	29
Mackey, Greg	9	2	—	4	12
Mann, Duane	19 + 2	1	—	—	4
McGinty, Billy	8 + 3	2	—	—	8
Mercer, Gary	17	5	—	—	20
Molloy, Steve	24 + 6	—	—	—	—
Muller, Roby	2 + 1	—	—	—	—
Myers, David	4 + 2	—	—	—	—
Myler, Robert	2 + 1	1	—	—	4
Peters, Barry	1 + 2	—	—	—	—
Richards, Basil	0 + 1	—	—	—	—
Roberts, Mark	3	—	—	—	—
Ropati, Joe	10 + 1	5	—	—	20
Roskell, Mark	20	—	—	—	—
Rudd, Chris	5 + 1	1	9	—	22
Sanderson, Gary	32	—	—	—	—
Sumner, Phil	8 + 3	—	—	—	—
Thomas, Mark	12 + 8	1	—	—	4
Thorniley, Tony	25 + 2	12	—	—	48
Turner, Robert	27	3	85	—	182
Wernham, Mike	1	—	1	—	2
Williamson, Paul	1 + 1	—	—	—	—
TOTALS:					
36 players		95	115	15	625

1989-90 MATCH ANALYSIS

Date	Com-petition	H/A	Opponent	Rlt	Score	Tries	Goals	Atten-dance	Referee
3.9.89	SBC	A	Wigan	W	18-6	Thorniley, Lyon, Mackey	Turner (3)	—	—
10.9.89	SBC	H	Bradford N	W	18-17	Drummond, Jackson, Forster	Turner (3)	5529	Kershaw
17.9.89	LC(1)	H	Swinton	W	16-6	Lyon, Drummond	Turner (4)	4055	Whitfield
24.9.89	SBC	A	Leigh	W	25-10	Thorniley, Mackey, Turner	Turner (5), Mackey (3dg)	—	—
27.9.89	LC(2)	A	Salford	W	27-4	Drummond (2), Ropati, Duane	Turner (5), Mackey (dg)	—	—
30.9.89	SBC	H	Castleford	W	32-10	Lyon (2), Thorniley (2), Jackson	Turner (6)	4076	Steele
8.10.89	SBC	H	Hull	D	12-12	Thorniley, Ropati	Turner (2)	5084	Kershaw
10.10.89	LC(SF)	H	Widnes	W	28-6	Thorniley (2), Forster, Ropati	Turner (6)	10,240	Bowman
14.10.89	LC(F)	St. Helens	Oldham	W	24-16	Jackson (2), Ropati, Forster	Turner (4)	(9990)	Tennant
24.10.89	SBC	A	Barrow	W	9-0	Drummond	Turner (2), Lyon (dg)	—	—
29.10.89	SBC	H	St. Helens	L	3-15		Lyon, Bishop (dg)	8420	Tennant
2.11.89	SBC	A	Leeds	L	6-30	Thorniley	Turner	—	—
8.11.89	RT(P)	H	Sheffield E.	L	4-12	—	Turner, Darbyshire	2507	C. Morris
12.11.89	SBC	H	Sheffield E.	L	22-36	Drummond, Ropati, Thomas	Darbyshire (5)	3710	Whitfield
19.11.89	SBC	A	Castleford	L	6-40	Crompton	Darbyshire	—	—
26.11.89	SBC	H	Leigh	W	16-8	Drummond, Forster	Darbyshire (3), Lyon	3941	Crashley
17.12.89	SBC	H	Salford	W	18-15	Drummond (2), Darbyshire	Turner (3)	3910	Cross
26.12.89	SBC	A	Widnes	L	20-32	Mercer (2), Forster	Turner (4)	—	—
1.1.90	SBC	H	Wigan	L	2-8	—	Turner	9629	Holdsworth
7.1.90	SBC	A[1]	Sheffield E.	W	12-8	Turner, Thorniley	Turner (2)	—	—
14.1.90	SBC	H	Barrow	W	58-6	Kenyon (3), Cullen (2), Drummond, Mercer, Thorniley, Crompton, Mann, Forster	Turner (7)	3504	Whitelam
21.1.90	SBC	A	Wakefield T.	L	8-32	Lyon	Turner (2)	—	—
27.1.90	CC(1)	A	Featherstone R.	W	20-12	Gregory, McGinty	Turner (5), Bishop (2dg)	3435	Bowman
4.2.90	SBC	A	Featherstone R.	L	13-20	Burke, McGinty	Turner (2), Bishop (dg)	—	—
11.2.90	CC(2)	H	Trafford B.	W	20-11	Thorniley (2), Forster, Bishop	Turner (2)	3448	Crashley
17.2.90	SBC	H	Wakefield T.	W	33-2	Forster, Drummond, Turner, Bishop, Mercer	Turner (5), Darbyshire, Bishop (dg)	3305	Campbell
25.2.90	CC(3)	A	Bradford N.	W	12-10	Jackson	Turner (4)	—	—
1.3.90	SBC	A	St. Helens	*Aban	—			—	—
4.3.90	SBC	H	Featherstone R.	L	9-15	Forster	Turner (2), Bishop (dg)	6711	Cross
11.3.90	SBC	H	Leeds	W	9-6	Drummond	Bishop (2, 1dg)	4802	Holdsworth
14.3.90	SBC	A	St. Helens	W	23-14	Drummond (2), Cullen, Forster	Bishop (2, 3dg)	—	—
25.3.90	SBC	A	Bradford N.	L	10-38	Forster	Turner (3)	—	—
31.3.90	CC(SF)	Wigan	Oldham	W	10-6	Crompton, Forster	Turner	(15,631)	Holdsworth
8.4.90	SBC	A	Hull	L	16-44	Rudd, Forster, Darbyshire	Rudd, Wernham	—	—
13.4.90	SBC	H	Widnes	L	10-22	Mercer	Rudd (3)	7740	Kershaw
16.4.90	SBC	A	Salford	W	16-5	Jackson, Kenyon, Crompton, Myler	—	—	—
22.4.90	PT(1)	A	Wigan	L	26-28	Forster (2), Kenyon, Crompton	Rudd (5)	—	—

[1] at Doncaster
*Abandoned after three minutes due to gale damage.

WHITEHAVEN

Ground:	Recreation Ground
Colours:	Chocolate, blue and gold
First Season:	1948-49
Nickname:	Haven
Chairman:	Keith Irving
Secretary:	Keith Nelson
Coach:	Barry Smith (July 1988-Sep 1989)
	Eric Fitzsimons (Oct 1989-Mar 1990)
	Norman Turley (June 1990-)
Records:	Attendance: 18,500 v. Wakefield T. (RL Cup) 19 Mar, 1960

Season
Goals: 141 by J. McKeown, 1956-57
Tries: 29 by W. Smith, 1956-57
Points: 291 by J. McKeown, 1956-57

Match
Goals: 11 by W. Holliday v. Hunslet, 31 Mar, 1962
Tries: 6 by V. Gribbin v. Doncaster, 18 Nov, 1984
Points: 25 by W. Holliday v. Hunslet, 31 Mar, 1962
Highest score: 72-6 v. Fulham, 1986-87
Highest against: 92-10 v. Hull K.R., 1989-90

1989-90 PLAYERS' SUMMARY

	App	Tries	Goals	Dr	Pts
Ackerman, Rob	18	5	—	—	20
Blaney, Ged	13 + 4	5	—	—	20
Branthwaite, Steve	16 + 4	2	—	—	8
Burney, Phil	11	—	—	—	—
Burns, Bill	6 + 6	1	—	—	4
Butler, Tim	1	—	—	—	—
Cameron, Graham	26	3	26	2	66
Charlton, Gary	7	—	—	—	—
Clucas, Geoff	1 + 1	—	—	—	—
Davidson, Alan	2 + 2	—	—	—	—
D'leny, Tony	14 + 2	—	—	—	—
Dover, Peter	11 + 3	1	—	—	4
Fisher, Billy	29	7	—	—	28
Fryer, Mark	7 + 4	—	—	—	—
Fryer, Steve	13 + 6	2	—	—	8
Gribbin, Vince	6 + 4	2	1	—	10
Hetherington, Gary	14 + 3	2	—	—	8
Hewer, Gary	7	—	—	—	—
Howland, Kevin	13	2	—	—	8
Howse, Steve	32	4	—	—	16
Johnston, Frank	7	1	—	—	4
King, Dave	3 + 1	1	—	—	4
Lofthouse, Norman	22 + 4	6	4	—	32
McCartney, Duncan	21	1	—	—	4
Milburn, Ray	0 + 1	—	—	—	—
Mounsey, Gary	25	3	—	—	12
Petrie, Steve	12	2	—	—	8
Phillips, Joe	1	—	—	—	—
Rawling, Shane	1	—	—	—	—
Richardson, Willie	25 + 4	7	46	—	120
Rushton, Brad	9	2	—	—	8
Ryan, Mark	13 + 8	2	6	2	22
Sanderson, Kevin	2	—	—	—	—
Shelford, Kelly	9	4	—	—	16
Solarie, Tony	22	11	—	—	44
Sparks, Brian	2 + 1	—	—	—	—
Symes, Jeff	1 + 1	—	—	—	—
Telford, Robert	0 + 3	1	—	—	4
Tunstall, Brian	3 + 1	—	—	—	—
Ward, James	17	6	—	3	27

TOTALS:
40 players		83	83	7	505

New Zealand Test stand off Kelly Shelford, who joined Whitehaven for a second spell of duty, scoring four tries in nine games.

1989-90 MATCH ANALYSIS

Date	Com-petition	H/A	Opponent	Rlt	Score	Tries	Goals	Atten-dance	Referee
3.9.89	SD	H	Huddersfield	L	22-34	Richardson (2), Telford, Solarie, McCarthy	Richardson	1167	Smith
6.9.89	SD	H	Rochdale H.	L	16-36	Johnstone, Richardson	Richardson (4)	821	C. Morris
10.9.89	SD	A	Chorley	L	9-13	Rushton	Richardson (2), Ryan (dg)	—	—
13.9.89	SD	A	Keighley	L	24-31	Fisher, Gribbin, Rushton, Cameron	Richardson (4)	—	—
17.9.89	LC(1)	A	Leigh	L	8-26	Howland	Richardson (2)	—	—
24.9.89	SD	H	Hunslet	W	22-11	Ackerman, Fisher, Branthwaite, Richardson	Richardson (3)	986	Simpson
1.10.89	SD	A	Doncaster	L	9-30	Cameron	Richardson (2), Cameron (dg)	—	—
8.10.89	SD	H	Fulham	W	15-14	Ackerman, Ryan	Richardson (3), Ryan (dg)	940	Whitelam
15.10.89	SD	A	Huddersfield	L	12-31	Fisher	Richardson (3), Ryan	—	—
22.10.89	SD	A	Batley	L	6-21	King	Lofthouse	—	—
29.10.89	SD	H	Swinton	L	7-14	Howland	Lofthouse, Ward (dg)	1016	Carter
5.11.89	SD	A	Fulham	L	0-24	—	—	—	—
12.11.89	SD	H	Doncaster	L	12-28	Lofthouse, Ward	Lofthouse (2)	781	Tickle
26.11.89	SD	H	Keighley	W	22-18	Howse, Blaney, Fisher, Gribbin	Ryan (3)	602	Simpson
3.12.89	RT(1)	H	Runcorn H.	W	20-10	Dover, Ryan, Ward	Ryan (2), Gribbin, Richardson	603	Allatt
10.12.89	RT(2)	H	Castleford	L	6-62	—	Richardson	1838	Crashley
17.12.89	SD	A	Runcorn H.	W	28-10	Shelford, Ward, Richardson, Lofthouse, Ackerman	Richardson (4)	—	—
26.12.89	SD	A	Workington T.	W	19-8	Ackerman, Shelford	Richardson (5), Ward (dg)	—	—
1.1.90	SD	H	Carlisle	W	24-12	Mounsey (2), Richardson, Ackerman, Howse	Richardson (2)	1258	Galtress
17.1.90	SD	H	Halifax	L	12-17	Lofthouse, Cameron	Richardson (2)	1477	Steele
21.1.90	SD	A	Rochdale H.	L	18-28	Ward, Richardson, Petrie, Hetherington	Richardson	—	—
28.1.90	CC(1)	H	Leigh	W	23-22	Fisher, Ward, Fryer, Shelford	Cameron (3), Ward (dg)	1528	Kershaw
4.2.90	SD	H	Runcorn H.	W	20-8	Solarie (2), Petrie, Fisher	Cameron (2)	818	Burke
11.2.90	CC(2)	H	Keighley	W	46-10	Howse (2), Blaney (2), Fisher, Shelford, Fryer, Ward	Cameron (5), Richardson (2)	1653	Kendrew
18.2.90	SD	A	Swinton	L	4-40	Solarie	—	—	—
25.2.90	CC(3)	A	St. Helens	L	10-44	Lofthouse	Cameron (3)	—	—
4.3.90	SD	A	Hunslet	L	16-32	Solarie (2), Branthwaite	Richardson (2)	—	—
7.3.90	SD	H	Hull K.R.	L	2-46	—	Cameron	986	Holdsworth
11.3.90	SD	H	Chorley	W	16-4	Burns, Lofthouse	Cameron (3), Richardson	648	Tidball
18.3.90	SD	A	Hull K.R.	L	10-92	Solarie, Mounsey	Cameron	—	—
1.4.90	SD	H	Batley	W	30-6	Solarie (3), Blaney, Lofthouse	Cameron (4), Richardson	587	Carter
8.4.90	SD	A	Halifax	L	0-74	—	—	—	—
13.4.90	SD	H	Workington T.	W	17-4	Hetherington, Blaney, Solarie	Cameron (2, 1 dg)	1498	Steele
16.4.90	SD	A	Carlisle	L	4-24	—	Cameron (2)	—	—

WIDNES

Ground: Naughton Park
Colours: Black and white
First Season: 1895-96
Nickname: Chemics
Chairman: Ray Owen
General
  Manager: John Stringer
Coach: Doug Laughton (Jan 1986-)
Honours: **Division One** Champions, 1977-78, 1987-88, 1988-89
Championship Beaten finalists, 1935-36
Challenge Cup Winners, 1929-30, 1936-37, 1963-64, 1974-75, 1978-79, 1980-81, 1983-84
Beaten finalists, 1933-34, 1949-50, 1975-76, 1976-77, 1981-82
Lancashire League Winners, 1919-20
Lancashire Cup Winners, 1945-46, 1974-75, 1975-76, 1976-77, 1978-79, 1979-80
Beaten finalists, 1928-29, 1939-40, 1955-56, 1971-72, 1981-82, 1983-84
Regal Trophy Winners, 1975-76, 1978-79
Beaten finalists, 1974-75, 1977-78, 1979-80, 1983-84, 1988-89
Premiership Winners, 1979-80, 1981-82, 1982-83, 1987-88, 1988-89, 1989-90
Beaten finalists, 1977-78
BBC2 Floodlit Trophy Winners, 1978-79
Beaten finalists, 1972-73, 1973-74
Western Division Championship Beaten finalists, 1962-63
Charity Shield Winners, 1988-89, 1989-90
World Cup Challenge Winners, 1989-90

Records: Attendance: 24,205 v. St. Helens (RL Cup) 16 Feb, 1961
Season
Goals: 140 by M. Burke, 1978-79
Tries: 58 by M. Offiah, 1988-89
Points: 316 by M. Burke, 1978-79
Match
Goals: 11 by R. Whitfield v. Oldham, 28 Oct, 1965
Tries: 5 by E. Cunningham v. Doncaster, 15 Feb, 1981; J. Basnett v. Hunslet, 17 Oct, 1981 and v. Hull K.R., 2 Nov, 1986; D. Hulme v. Dewsbury, 30 Nov, 1986; A. Currier v. Featherstone R., 25 Sept, 1988; M. Offiah v. Warrington, 15 Mar, 1989
Points: 34 by A. Currie v. Featherstone R., 25 Sept, 1988
Highest score: 82-0 v. Dewsbury, 1986-87
Highest against: 60-5 v. Oldham, 1927-28

1989-90 PLAYERS' SUMMARY

	App	Tries	Goals	Dr	Pts
Ashurst, Chris	3 + 1	—	—	—	—
Critchley, Jason	5 + 5	1	—	—	4
Currier, Andy	27	13	37	—	126
Davies, Jonathan	29 + 1	16	98	—	260
Devereux, John	23 + 2	12	—	—	48
Dowd, Barry	2 + 3	—	—	—	—
Eyres, Andy	0 + 2	—	—	—	—
Eyres, Richard	32	4	—	—	16
Grima, Joe	21 + 11	2	—	—	8
Holliday, Les	6 + 1	1	—	1	5
Hulme, David	38	10	—	—	40
Hulme, Paul	27	7	—	—	28
Kebbie, Brimah	14 + 1	16	—	—	64
Koloto, Emosi	16 + 3	3	—	—	12
Marsh, David	8 + 8	2	—	—	8
McCurrie, Steve	2 + 2	—	—	—	—
McKenzie, Phil	37	11	—	—	44
Moriarty, Paul	13 + 11	3	5	—	22
Myler, Tony	25 + 5	1	—	—	4
Offiah, Martin	32	40	—	—	160
O'Neill, Mike	28	5	—	—	20
Pyke, Derek	21 + 3	—	—	—	—
Sarsfield, Mark	1	—	—	—	—
Smith, David	12 + 9	1	—	—	4
Sorensen, Kurt	29 + 2	4	—	—	16
Spruce, Stuart	1	—	—	—	—
Tait, Alan	36	17	1	2	72
Tuavao, Boblin	1	—	—	—	—
Wright, Darren	31 + 1	8	—	—	32

TOTALS:
| 29 players | | 177 | 141 | 3 | 993 |

1989-90 MATCH ANALYSIS

Date	Competition	H/A	Opponent	Rlt	Score	Tries	Goals	Attendance	Referee
27.8.89	CS	Liverpool FC	Wigan	W	27-22	Kebbie, Davies, Offiah, D. Hulme	Davies (5), Tait (dg)	(17,263)	Holdsworth
3.9.89	SBC	H	Salford	W	46-18	Offiah (2), P. Hulme, Kebbie, Davies, Sorensen, Grima, Koloto	Davies (7)	8591	Kershaw
10.9.89	SBC	A	Hull	W	26-11	Offiah (2), Kebbie, Myler, O'Neill,	Davies (3)	—	—
17.9.89	LC(1)	A[1]	Carlisle	W	46-6	Kebbie (4), Davies (2), Offiah, McKenzie, Koloto	Davies (5)	—	—
24.9.89	SBC	H	Featherstone R.	W	59-8	Kebbie (4), Offiah (4), McKenzie, Davies	Davies (9), Tait (dg)	8008	Tickle
27.9.89	LC(2)	A	Leigh	W	34-12	Offiah (2), Tait (2), D. Hulme, Davies	Davies (5)	—	—
4.10.89	WCC	Man U. FC	Canberra	W	30-18	Offiah (2), P. Hulme, Davies, Eyres, Wright	Davies (3)	(30,786)	Desplas (Fr)
8.10.89	SBC	A[2]	Sheffield E.	L	6-31	McKenzie	Davies	—	—
10.10.89	LC(SF)	A	Warrington	L	6-28	Currier	Davies	—	—
15.10.89	SBC	H	Wakefield T.	W	30-12	Offiah (3), P. Hulme, Currier	Davies (5)	7488	C. Morris
31.10.89	SBC	A	Salford	W	28-16	Currier (2), Offiah, Kebbie, Smith	Davies (4)	—	—
5.11.89	Tour	H	New Zealand	L	18-26	Tait, D. Hulme, O'Neill, Kebbie	Davies	9905	Crashley
12.11.89	SBC	H	Leigh	L	16-18	Tait, O'Neill	Davies (4)	7104	Tidball
19.11.89	SBC	A	Leeds	L	12-26	Offiah (2)	Davies (2)	—	—
25.11.89	SBC	H	Castleford	W	24-16	Currier, Sorensen, Devereux, Davies	Davies (4)	5122	Kershaw
3.12.89	RT(1)	A	Nottingham C.	W	48-18	Kebbie (3), Offiah (2), Currier, Davies, McKenzie, P. Hulme	Davies (3), Currier (3)	—	—
9.12.89	RT(2)	A	Wigan	L	0-18	—	—	—	—
17.12.89	SBC	A	Barrow	W	34-4	Sorensen (2), Tait, Devereux, D. Hulme	Currier (7)	—	—
21.12.89	SBC	H	Barrow	W	48-0	Devereux (2), McKenzie (2), Critchley, Tait, D. Hulme, Currier, Offiah	Currier (6)	3782	Holdsworth
26.12.89	SBC	H	Warrington	W	32-20	Offiah (3), Devereux (2), R. Eyres	Currier (4)	10,179	Crashley
1.1.90	SBC	A	St. Helens	W	18-8	Davies (2), Tait	Davies (3)	—	—
7.1.90	SBC	H	Leeds	L	8-20	P. Hulme	Currier (2)	10,232	Holdsworth
17.1.90	SBC	A	Bradford N.	L	6-16	Moriarty	Davies	—	—
20.1.90	SBC	A	Castleford	W	30-22	Offiah (4), Currier, P. Hulme	Currier (3)	—	—
28.1.90	CC(1)	H	Batley	W	26-10	Tait, Devereux, Offiah, D. Hulme, O'Neill	Currier (2), Tait	5801	Holdsworth
3.2.90	SBC	H	Wigan	L	10-11	Marsh, Offiah	Davies	9542	Morris
11.2.90	CC(2)	H	Rochdale	W	22-16	Davies, Devereux, O'Neill, Offiah	Davies (3)	6956	Bowman
18.2.90	SBC	H	Hull	W	30-12	Offiah (3), Tait, Wright, McKenzie	Davies (3)	7356	Allatt
25.2.90	CC(3)	H	Oldham	L	4-16	—	Davies (2)	11,802	Bowman
4.3.90	SBC	A	Wakefield T.	D	10-10	Davies, Wright	Davies	—	—
7.3.90	SBC	A	Featherstone R.	L	22-30	Moriarty, Davies, Devereux, Tait	Davies (3)	—	—
11.3.90	SBC	H	Bradford N.	L	14-40	Offiah (2), Wright	Moriarty	6605	Cross
18.3.90	SBC	A	Leigh	D	20-20	P. Hulme, D. Hulme, Moriarty	Moriarty (4)	—	—

(continued on page 110)

WIGAN

Ground:	Central Park
Colours:	Cherry and white
First Season:	1895-96
Nickname:	Riversiders
Chairman:	Maurice Lindsay
Secretary:	Mary Charnock
Coach:	John Monie (Sep 1989-)

Honours: **Championship** Winners, 1908-09, 1921-22, 1925-26, 1933-34, 1945-46, 1946-47, 1949-50, 1951-52, 1959-60 Beaten finalists, 1909-10, 1910-11, 1911-12, 1912-13, 1923-24, 1970-71 **League Leaders Trophy** Winners, 1970-71 **Division One** Champions 1986-87, 1989-90 **Challenge Cup** Winners, 1923-24, 1928-29, 1947-48, 1950-51, 1957-58, 1958-59, 1964-65, 1984-85, 1987-88, 1988-89, 1989-90 Beaten finalists, 1910-11, 1919-20, 1943-44, 1945-46, 1960-61, 1962-63, 1965-66, 1969-70, 1983-84 **Lancashire League** Winners, 1901-02, 1908-09, 1910-11, 1911-12, 1912-13, 1913-14, 1914-15, 1920-21, 1922-23, 1923-24, 1925-26, 1945-46, 1946-47, 1949-50, 1951-52, 1958-59, 1961-62, 1969-70 **Lancashire War League** Winners, 1940-41 **Lancashire Cup** Winners, 1905-06, 1908-09, 1909-10, 1912-13, 1922-23, 1928-29, 1938-39, 1946-47, 1947-48, 1948-49, 1949-50, 1950-51, 1951-52, 1966-67, 1971-72, 1973-74, 1985-86, 1986-87, 1987-88, 1988-89 Beaten finalists, 1913-14, 1914-15, 1925-26, 1927-28, 1930-31, 1934-35, 1935-36, 1936-37, 1945-46, 1953-54, 1957-58, 1977-78, 1980-81, 1984-85 **Regal Trophy** Winners, 1982-83, 1985-86, 1986-87, 1988-89, 1989-90 **Premiership Winners** 1986-87 **BBC2 Floodlit Trophy** Winners, 1968-69 Beaten finalists, 1969-70 **Charity Shield** Winners, 1985-86, 1987-88

Beaten finalists, 1988-89, 1989-90 **War League Championship** Winners, 1943-44 Beaten finalists, 1940-41

Records: Attendance: 47,747 v. St. Helens (League) 27 Mar, 1959 **Season** Goals: 176 by F. Griffiths, 1958-59 Tries: 62 by J. Ring, 1925-26 Points: 394 by F. Griffiths, 1958-59 **Match** Goals: 22 by J. Sullivan v. Flimby & Fothergill, 14 Feb, 1925 Tries: 7 by J. Ring v. Flimby & Fothergill, 14 Feb, 1925; v. Salford, 13 Apr, 1925 and v. Pemberton R., 12 Feb, 1927; G. Ratcliffe v. Liverpool S., 23 Aug, 1947; W. Boston v. Dewsbury, 20 Aug, 1955 and v. Salford, 30 Apr, 1962; G. Vigo v. St. Helens, 21 Aug, 1976 Points: 44 by J. Sullivan v. Flimby & Fothergill, 14 Feb, 1925 Highest score: 116-0 v. Flimby & Fothergill, 1924-25 Highest against: 58-3 v. Leeds, 1972-73

1989-90 PLAYERS' SUMMARY

	App	Tries	Goals	Dr	Pts
Bell, Dean	33	10	—		40
Betts, Denis	32 + 1	11	—		44
Blake, Phil	10 + 1	7	17	—	62
Byrne, Ged	28 + 9	10	—		40
Clarke, Phil	8 + 10	2	—	—	8
Davidson, Les	10 + 1	2	—	—	8
Dermott, Martin	30 + 1	3	—	1	13
Edwards, Shaun	32 + 1	25	10	—	120
Forshaw, Mike	0 + 3	—	—	—	—
Gildart, Ian	30 + 6	1	—	—	4
Gilfillan, John	6 + 6	2	—	—	8
Gill, Henderson	5 + 1	2	—	—	8
Goodway, Andy	38 + 1	22	—	—	88
Goulding, Bobby	14 + 11	7	28	1	85
Gregory, Andy	31 + 2	3	4	—	20
Hampson, Steve	27 + 2	5	3	1	27
Hanley, Ellery	19 + 1	10	—	—	40
Iro, Kevin	26	16	—	—	64
Kiss, Nicky	6	—	—	—	—
Lucas, Ian	25 + 4	4	—	—	16
Lydon, Joe	30 + 1	10	83	—	206
Marshall, David	13 + 4	7	—	—	28
O'Donnell, Augustine	0 + 3	—	1	—	2
Platt, Andy	35 + 1	8	—	—	32
Preston, Mark	41	32	—	—	128
Shelford, Adrian	22	1	—	—	4
Stazicker, Ged	10 + 14	3	—	—	12
Tyrer, Sean	3	1	12	—	28
Wane, Shaun	7 + 1	1	—	—	4
West, Graeme	1	—	—	—	—
TOTALS:					
30 players		205	158	3	1,139

1989-90 MATCH ANALYSIS

Date	Competition	H/A	Opponent	Rlt	Score	Tries	Goals	Attendance	Referee
27.8.89	CS	Liverpool FC	Widnes	L	22-27	Platt, Lydon, Iro	Lydon (5)	(17,263)	Holdsworth
3.9.89	SBC	H	Warrington	L	6-18	Preston	Lydon	14,741	Cross
6.9.89	SBC	A	Leigh	W	44-7	Preston (3), Gregory, Iro, Lydon, Platt, Goodway	Lydon (6)	—	—
10.9.89	SBC	A	Salford	W	56-12	Betts (2), Bell (2), Staziger, Iro, Goodway, Preston, Platt, Hampson	Lydon (6), Gregory (2)	—	—
15.9.89	LC(1)	A[1]	Chorley	W	50-4	Iro (4), Betts (2), Bell (2), Byrne, Goodway, Preston	Lydon (3)	—	—
24.9.89	SBC	H	Wakefield T.	W	38-10	Preston (2), Iro (2), Tyrer, Shelford	Tyrer (7)	11,739	Steele
27.9.89	LC(2)	A[2]	Fulham	W	34-4	Goodway (2), Bell, Platt, Blake, Gill	Tyrer (5)	—	—
1.10.89	SBC	A	Barrow	W	66-0	Gilfillan (2), Edwards (2), Staziker (2), Byrne (2), Blake, Preston, Marshall, Bell	Edwards (7), Blake (2)	—	—
5.10.89	LC(SF)	A	Oldham	L	18-19	Blake, Edwards, Platt	Edwards (3)	—	—
8.10.89	Tour	H	New Zealand	W	24-14	Lydon, Platt, Byrne, Davidson	Blake (4)	15,013	Carter
15.10.89	SBC	H	Barrow	W	62-6	Preston (5), Edwards (4), Goodway, Davidson	Blake (9)	9051	McCallum (Aus)
29.10.89	SBC	H	Castleford	L	20-22	Preston, Lydon, Goodway, Edwards	Blake, Lydon	11,073	Kershaw
5.11.89	SBC	A[3]	Sheffield E.	W	22-10	Bell, Blake, Edwards, Platt	Lydon (3)	—	—
15.11.89	SBC	A	Bradford N.	W	16-15	Lucas, Goodway, Edwards	Lydon, Blake	—	—
18.11.89	SBC	H	Featherstone R.	W	40-14	Preston (2), Betts, Blake, Byrne, Goodway, Gildart, Lydon	Lydon (4)	6742	Asquith
26.11.89	SBC	H	Hull	W	30-2	Blake, Dermott, Gregory, Preston, Goodway	Lydon (5)	10,728	C. Morris
3.12.89	RT(1)	H	Doncaster	W	62-4	Goodway (3), Preston (2), Lydon (2), Edwards (2), Lucas, Blake, Marshall	Lydon (7)	7854	Tennant
9.12.89	RT(2)	H	Widnes	W	18-0	Goodway, Lydon, Wane, Preston	Lydon	12,398	Bowman
16.12.89	RT(3)	A	Leeds	D	10-10	Gill, Preston	Lydon	—	—
21.12.89	RT(3) Replay	H	Leeds	W	8-0	Edwards	Goulding (2)	20,111	Kershaw
26.12.89	SBC	H	St. Helens	W	38-6	Preston (2), Bell, Marshall, Lydon, Edwards, Lucas, Betts	Goulding (2), Lydon	27,075	Whitfield
30.12.89	RT(SF)	Leeds	Castleford	W	24-10	Lydon, Betts, Edwards, Marshall	Lydon (4)	(10,193)	Whitfield
1.1.90	SBC	A	Warrington	W	8-2	Edwards	Gregory, Lydon	—	—
7.1.90	SBC	H	Bradford N.	W	12-0	Hanley, Marshall Dermott	—	13,443	Kendrew
13.1.90	RT(F)	Leeds	Halifax	W	24-12	Hanley (3), Edwards, Goodway	Lydon (2)	(17,810)	Kershaw
16.1.90	SBC	H	Sheffield E.	W	30-2	Bell, Edwards, Goodway, Hanley, Byrne	Lydon (5)	10,668	Kershaw
21.1.90	SBC	A	Hull	L	20-30	Gregory, Preston, Iro, Marshall	Lydon (2)	—	—
28.1.90	CC(1)	A	Hull K.R.	W	6-4	Marshall	Lydon	—	—
3.2.90	SBC	A	Widnes	W	11-10	Hanley	Goulding (3, 1dg)	—	—
11.2.90	CC(2)	H	Dewsbury	W	30-6	Edwards (2), Bell, Iro, Lucas, Betts	Goulding (2), Lydon	11,113	Campbell
18.2.90	SBC	H	Salford	W	32-26	Edwards (2), Iro (2), Preston, Goodway	Lydon (4)	11,368	C. Morris

(continued on page 110)

WORKINGTON TOWN

Ground: Derwent Park
Colours: Blue and white
First Season: 1945-46
Nickname: Town
Chairman: Kevin Gorge
Secretary: John Bell
Coach: Phil Kitchin (Dec 1988-May 1990)
Ray Ashton (June 1990-)
Honours: **Championship** Winners, 1950-51
Beaten finalists, 1957-58
Challenge Cup Winners, 1951-52
Beaten finalists, 1954-55, 1957-58
Lancashire Cup Winners, 1977-78
Beaten finalists, 1976-77, 1978-79,
1979-80
Western Division Championship
Winners, 1962-63
Records: Attendance: 17,741 v. Wigan
(RL Cup) 3 Mar, 1965. There was a
crowd of 20,403 at Borough Park
for a RL Cup-tie v. St. Helens on 8
Mar, 1952
Season
Goals: 186 by L. Hopkins, 1981-82
Tries: 49 by J. Lawrenson, 1951-52
Points: 438 by L. Hopkins, 1981-82
Match
Goals: 11 by I. MacCorquodale v.
Blackpool B., 6 Jan, 1973
Tries: 7 by I. Southward v.
Blackpool B., 17 Sep, 1955
Points: 33 by I. Southward v.
Blackpool B., 17 Sep, 1955
Highest score: 62-15 v. Hunslet,
1963-64
Highest against: 68-0 at Wigan,
1986-87

1989-90 PLAYERS' SUMMARY

	App	Tries	Goals	Dr	Pts
Ainsworth, Gary	10 + 1	1	—	—	4
Armstrong, Malcolm	8	4	—	—	16
Barker, Brian	2 + 2	—	—	—	—
Beattie, John	12 + 2	—	1	—	2
Beck, David	2	—	—	—	—
Bower, Ian	7 + 1	—	—	—	—
Brake, Greg	23 + 4	7	—	—	28
Burgess, Glen	12 + 6	—	—	1	1
Dockery, Darryl	1 + 2	—	—	—	—
Falcon, Colin	17	2	—	—	8
Gorge, Paul	12	2	—	—	8
Henney, Russell	2 + 4	—	—	—	—
Higgins, Michael	0 + 1	—	—	—	—
Kitchen, Wayne	15 + 2	2	22	—	52
Lamb, Keith	1 + 1	—	—	—	—
Law, Andrew	21 + 1	1	—	—	4
Little, Andrew	7 + 1	1	—	—	4
Lowden, David	27 + 2	3	24	4	64
Lynch, Keith	2 + 5	—	—	—	—
Matache, Michael	14	2	—	—	8
Mawson, Mark	19 + 1	3	—	—	12
McGuirk, Gary	2 + 4	—	—	—	—
McMullen, Alan	19 + 1	1	—	—	4
Newall, John	17 + 2	4	—	1	17
Nixon, Gary	24	3	—	—	12
O'Loughlin, Keiron	6	—	—	—	—
Penman, Daniel	4	—	—	—	—
Penrice, Paul	29	12	—	—	48
Phillips, Graeme	12 + 1	—	—	—	—
Pickering, Brendan	1	—	—	—	—
Riley, Peter	31	3	—	—	12
Rooney, Neil	19 + 1	4	—	—	16
Smith, Gary	11	1	10	3	27
Sullivan, Joe	6 + 3	—	—	—	—
Torley, Ian	1	—	—	—	—
Tubman, Keith	18 + 8	2	1	—	10
Walker, William	0 + 1	—	—	—	—
Wear, Steve	2 + 4	2	—	1	9

TOTALS:
| 38 players | | 60 | 58 | 10 | 366 |

1989-90 MATCH ANALYSIS

Date	Competition	H/A	Opponent	Rlt	Score	Tries	Goals	Attendance	Referee
3.9.89	SD	A	Oldham	L	8-40	Lowden	Lowden (2)	—	—
10.9.89	SD	H	Carlisle	W	30-22	Penrice, Falcon, Nixon, Smith, Newall	Lowden (4, 1dg), Newall (dg)	1005	Simpson
17.9.89	LC(1)	H	Fulham	L	24-30	Penrice (2), Rooney (2), Law	Lowden (2)	702	K. Morris
24.9.89	SD	A	Huddersfield	W	21-16	Penrice (2), Nixon	Lowden (3), Smith (1, 1dg)	—	—
1.10.89	SD	H	Ryedale-York	L	2-42	—	Lowden	784	Allatt
8.10.89	SD	A	Carlisle	W	14-12	Little, Brake	Smith (2, 2dg)	—	—
15.10.89	SD	H	Bramley	L	12-20	Brake	Smith (4)	683	Galtress
22.10.89	SD	A	Rochdale H.	L	14-52	Brake, Tubman	Smith (3)	—	—
29.10.89	SD	A	Doncaster	L	4-26	Penrice	—	—	—
5.11.89	SD	H	Trafford B.	L	8-35	Penrice	Lowden (2)	509	Carter
12.11.89	SD	A	Hull K.R.	L	0-34	—	—	—	—
19.11.89	RT(P)	A[1]	Crosfields	W	19-14	Nixon, Penrice, Brake, Wear	Lowden (1, 1dg)	—	—
26.11.89	SD	A	Trafford B.	L	10-24	Rooney	Lowden (2), Beatty	—	—
3.12.89	RT(1)	H	Huddersfield	L	4-28	Lowden	—	571	Smith
10.12.89	SD	H	Batley	L	17-28	Riley, Penrice, Rooney	Lowden (2), Burgess (dg)	413	Steele
26.12.89	SD	H	Whitehaven	L	8-19	Tubman	Kitchin (2)	1604	Burke
31.12.89	SD	A	Ryedale-York	L	12-44	George, Brake	Lowden (2)	—	—
7.1.90	SD	H	Chorley	L	6-12	Matache	Kitchin	378	Asquith
14.1.90	SD	A	Bramley	L	18-27	Kitchin, George, Riley	Kitchin (3)	—	—
21.1.90	SD	H	Hull K.R.	L	6-40	Matache	Kitchin	888	K. Morris
28.1.90	CC(1)	A	Oldham	L	8-30	Riley	Kitchin (2)	—	—
4.2.90	SD	A	Chorley	W	17-14	McMullen, Penrice	Kitchin (4), Wear (dg)	—	—
18.2.90	SD	H	Huddersfield	L	8-24	Ainsworth	Kitchin (2)	517	Tidball
25.2.90	SD	A	Batley	L	6-46	Kitchin	Kitchin	—	—
4.3.90	SD	H	Nottingham C.	W	27-14	Newell (2), Armstrong (2), Penrice	Kitchin (3), Lowden (dg)	448	Smith
11.3.90	SD	A	Dewsbury	L	4-32	Mawson	—	—	—
18.3.90	SD	H	Rochdale H.	L	14-16	Falcon, Armstrong	Kitchin (3)	661	Campbell
25.3.90	SD	H	Dewsbury	L	8-9	Penrice, Mawson	—	469	Galtress
1.4.90	SD	A	Nottingham C.	L	12-18	Lowden, Brake	Lowden, Tubman	—	—
4.4.90	SD	H	Oldham	W	21-14	Brake, Mawson, Newell, Armstrong	Lowden (2, 1dg)	780	Carter
8.4.90	SD	H	Doncaster	L	0-11	—	—	535	Burke
13.4.90	SD	A	Whitehaven	L	4-17	Wear	—	—	—

[1] at Warrington

BRADFORD NORTHERN MATCH ANALYSIS (continued)

Date	Com-petition	H/A	Opponent	Rlt	Score	Tries	Goals	Atten-dance	Referee
8.4.90	SBC	A	Featherstone R	L	16-24	Cordle, Medley, Francis	Mumby (2)	—	—
13.4.90	SBC	H	Wakefield T.	W	19-18	Cordle, Skerrett, Barraclough	Cooper (3, 1dg)	5274	Smith
16.4.90	SBC	A	Wakefield T.	W	36-12	Cordle (2), Medley (2), Francis, Marchant	Mumby (6)	—	—
22.4.90	PT(1)	H	St. Helens	W	25-8	Cordle, Francis, Skerrett, Fairbank	Mumby (4), Harkin (dg)	6725	Crashley
6.5.90	PT(SF)	A	Wigan	W	9-0	Harkin	Mumby, Harkin (2dg), Hobbs (dg)	—	—
13.5.90	PT(F)	Man U FC	Widnes	L	6-28	Marchant	Mumby	(40,796)	C. Morris

[1] at Chesterfield FC

HALIFAX MATCH ANALYSIS (continued)

Date	Com-petition	H/A	Opponent	Rlt	Score	Tries	Goals	Atten-dance	Referee
4.3.90	SD	A	Chorley	W	34-2	Riddlesden (2), Anderson, Whitfield, Needham, Hetherington, Ramshaw	Holliday (3)	—	—
11.3.90	SD	A	Rochdale H.	L	12-23	Whitfield, Dorahy	Holliday (2)	—	—
18.3.90	SD	H	Batley	W	42-12	Ramshaw (2), Hetherington (2), James, Whitfield, Smith, George	Holliday (5)	4257	Holgate
25.3.90	SD	A	Batley	W	16-2	Atkinson, George, Rawlinson	Whitfield (2)	—	—
28.3.90	SD	A	Doncaster	L	6-8	Ramshaw	Whitfield	—	—
4.4.90	SD	A	Hull K.R.	L	6-29	Hill	Whitfield	—	—
8.4.90	SD	H	Whitehaven	W	74-0	George (4), Hill (2), Smith (2), Whitfield, Roberts, Atkinson, McCallion, Lyons, Bell	Whitfield (7), Roberts (2)	3236	Royales (Pr)
13.4.90	SD	A	Huddersfield	W	28-15	Roberts, Hill, Hetherington	Smith (5), Roberts (3)	—	—
16.4.90	SD	H	Trafford B.	W	19-18	Hill (2), Milner, Hetherington	Roberts, Ramshaw (dg)	3488	Whitelam
21.4.90	SDP(1)	A	Ryedale-York	L	7-24	Ramshaw	Smith, McCallion (dg)	—	—

HULL K.R. MATCH ANALYSIS (continued)

Date	Com-petition	H/A	Opponent	Rlt	Score	Tries	Goals	Atten-dance	Referee
25.3.90	SD	A	Trafford B.	W	28-6	Sullivan (2), Thompson, Smith, Clark	M. Fletcher (4)	—	—
1.4.90	SD	H	Bramley	W	42-10	Austin (2), Lyman (2), Sullivan, W. Parker, Smith	M. Fletcher (7)	3751	Simpson
4.4.90	SD	H	Halifax	W	29-6	Ema, Rudd, Lyman, Austin, M. Fletcher	M. Fletcher (4), W. Parker (dg)	5291	Crashley
8.4.90	SD	A	Runcorn H.	W	38-12	Harrison, Austin, Lyman, Rudd, Fairbairn, Thompson, Vannet	M. Fletcher (5)	—	—
11.4.90	SD	A	Dewsbury	L	2-3	—	M. Fletcher	—	—
13.4.90	SD	A	Ryedale-York	W	17-8	Austin (2)	M. Fletcher (4), W. Parker (dg)	—	—
16.4.90	SD	H	Hunslet	W	58-6	Lyman (2), Sullivan (2), Austin (2), Rudd (2), Irvine, M. Fletcher	M. Fletcher (9)	5591	Simpson

(continued)

HULL K.R. MATCH ANALYSIS (continued)

22.4.90	SDP(1)	H	Fulham	W	40-6	Clark (2), Sullivan (2), Ema, Harrison, Austin	M. Fletcher (6)	4308	Allatt
6.5.90	SDP(SF)	H	Dewsbury	W	36-8	W. Parker (2), Lightfoot, Clark, Sullivan, Irvine	M. Fletcher (6)	5189	C. Morris
13.5.90	SDP(F)	Man U. FC	Oldham	L	29-30	W. Parker (2), Clark, Lyman, Austin	M. Fletcher (4), W. Parker (dg)	—	Whitfield

OLDHAM MATCH ANALYSIS (continued)

Date	Competition	H/A	Opponent	Rlt	Score	Tries	Goals	Attendance	Referee
7.3.90	SD	A	Keighley	W	30-10	Lord (3), Ruane, Martyn, Irving	Platt (3)	—	—
11.3.90	SD	A	Batley	W	30-14	Lord (2), Casey, Clark	Hyde (7)	—	—
18.3.90	SD	H	Runcorn H.	W	60-2	Allen (2), Casey (2), Cogger (2), Lord, Irving, Anderson, Clark, Hyde	Platt (8)	4406	K. Morris
21.3.90	SD	A	Hunslet	W	42-14	Lord (2), Platt, Fieldhouse, Russell, Henderson, McAlister	Platt (7)	—	—
24.3.90	SD	A	Huddersfield	W	22-14	Ruane, Robinson, Fairbank, Irving	Atkinson (3)	—	—
31.3.90	CC(SF)	at Wigan	Warrington	L	6-10	Irving	Platt	(15,631)	Holdsworth
4.4.90	SD	A	Workington T.	L	14-21	Atkinson, Fairbank	Atkinson (2), Ruane	—	—
8.4.90	SD	H	Carlisle	W	48-16	Henderson (2), Clark (2), McAlister, Atkinson, Lord, Irving, Flanagan	Atkinson (6)	2885	Galtress
13.4.90	SD	A	Swinton	L	12-15	Foy, Casey	Platt (2)	—	—
16.4.90	SD	H	Rochdale H.	W	30-2	Round (2), Platt, Henderson	Platt (7)	6332	Whitfield
22.4.90	SDP(1)	H	Swinton	W	32-10	Henderson (2), Fieldhouse, Ford, Martyn	Platt (6)	4540	Bowman
6.5.90	SDP(SF)	H	Ryedale-York	W	32-8	Lord (3), Irving (2), Clark	Platt (4)	5159	Crashley
13.5.90	SDP(F)	Man U. FC	Hull K.R.	W	30-29	Lord, Ford, Henderson, Irving, Ruane, Martyn	Hyde (2), Platt	—	Whitfield

ST. HELENS MATCH ANALYSIS (continued)

Date	Competition	H/A	Opponent	Rlt	Score	Tries	Goals	Attendance	Referee
1.3.90	SBC	H	Warrington	*Aban	—	—	—	—	Bowman
4.3.90	SBC	A	Castleford	L	24-34	Frodsham, Bailey, Quirk, Bateman	Loughlin (4)	—	—
10.3.90	CC(SF)	Man U FC	Wigan	L	14-20	Devine, Quirk	Loughlin (3)	(26,489)	Whitfield
14.3.90	SBC	H	Warrington	L	14-23	Cooper, Haggerty	Devine (3)	10,270	Bowman
17.3.90	SBC	H	Wakefield T.	W	44-21	Quirk, Griffiths, Groves, Cooper, Frodsham, Bailey, Large, Veivers	Devine (6)	4742	Morris
25.3.90	SBC	H	Leigh	W	12-6	Large, Haggerty	Loughlin (2)	9189	Cross
1.4.90	SBC	A	Leeds	L	14-50	Haggerty, Loughlin	Loughlin (3)	—	—
8.4.90	SBC	H	Sheffield E.	W	42-26	Forber (2), Veivers, Griffiths, Bailey, Hunte, Mann	Tanner (6), Devine	6256	Tennant
13.4.90	SBC	H	Wigan	W	35-10	Quirk (3), Mann, Hunte, Bailey	Loughlin (5), Haggerty (dg)	17,176	Holdsworth
16.4.90	SBC	A	Widnes	L	16-34	Quirk, Veivers, Cooper	Loughlin (2)	—	—
22.4.90	PT(1)	A	Bradford N.	L	8-25	Bailey	Forber (2)	—	—

[1] at Sheffield W. FC   [2] at Wakefield T.   *Abandoned after three minutes because of gale damage

WIDNES MATCH ANALYSIS (continued)

Date	Competition	H/A	Opponent	Rlt	Score	Tries	Goals	Attendance	Referee
24.3.90	SBC	A	Wigan	W	22-8	Tait (3), D. Hulme	Currier (3)	—	—
1.4.90	SBC	H	Sheffield E.	W	52-20	Wright (3), Currier (2), McKenzie (2), Tait, Marsh, Devereux, D. Hulme	Currier (4)	6212	Smith
13.4.90	SBC	A	Warrington	W	22-10	McKenzie, Wright, R. Eyres, Devereux	Davies (3)	—	—
16.4.90	SBC	H	St. Helens	W	34-16	Devereux, Currier, D. Hulme, Grima, Davies	Davies (7)	11,931	Bowman
22.4.90	PT(1)	H	Hull	W	18-8	Tait, Koloto, Offiah	Currier (3)	8672	Holdsworth
6.5.90	PT(SF)	A	Leeds	W	27-7	Davies, McKenzie, R. Eyres, Offiah	Davies (5), Holliday (dg)	—	—
13.5.90	PT(F)	Man U. FC	Bradford N.	W	28-6	Tait (2), Currier (2), Holliday	Davies (4)	(40,796)	C. Morris

[1] at Carlisle FC
[2] at Sheffield U. FC

WIGAN MATCH ANALYSIS (continued)

Date	Competition	H/A	Opponent	Rlt	Score	Tries	Goals	Attendance	Referee
24.2.90	CC(3)	A	Wakefield T.	W	26-14	Edwards (2), Iro, Hanley	Lydon (5)	—	—
4.3.90	SBC	A	Leeds	W	21-14	Goulding, Platt, Preston	Lydon (3), Goulding, Hampson (dg)	—	—
10.3.90	CC(SF)	Man U FC	St. Helens	W	20-14	Hampson, Byrne, Goodway	Lydon (4)	26,489	Whitfield
20.3.90	SBC	A	Featherstone R.	W	26-20	Goulding (2), Betts, Hampson, Clarke	Goulding (2), Gregory	—	—
24.3.90	SBC	H	Widnes	L	8-22	Byrne	Goulding, Hampson	10,916	Stokes (NZ)
28.3.90	SBC	A	Castleford	L	10-34	Clarke, Goulding	Goulding	—	—
1.4.90	SBC	A	Wakefield T.	W	23-14	Dermott, Hanley, Edwards, Preston	Hampson (2), Goulding, Dermott (dg)	—	—
10.4.90	SBC	H	Leeds	W	16-12	Preston (2)	Goulding (4)	24,462	Whitfield
13.4.90	SBC	A	St. Helens	L	10-35	Betts, Goodway	O'Donnell	—	—
16.4.90	SBC	H	Leigh	W	34-6	Goodway (2), Hampson, Byrne, Goulding, Hanley	Goulding (5)	19,641	Allatt
22.4.90	PT(1)	H	Warrington	W	28-26	Goulding (2), Hampson, Bell, Goodway	Goulding (4)	10,768	C. Morris
6.5.90	PT(SF)	H	Bradford N.	L	0-9	—	—	18,835	Whitfield

[1] at Leigh
[2] at Hendon FC
[3] at Sheffield W. FC

Martin Offiah, top try scorer for the third successive season.

RECORDS

LEADING SCORERS FOR 1989-90

TOP TEN TRIES

1. Martin Offiah (Widnes) 45
2. Greg Austin (Hull K.R.) 38
3. Anthony Sullivan (Hull K.R.)..................... 35
4. Mark Preston (Wigan)............................... 33
5. Gerald Cordle (Bradford N.)........................ 32
6. Steve Larder (Castleford) 29
   Paul Lord (Oldham) 29
8. Shaun Edwards (Wigan)............................. 26
   Andy Goodway (Wigan)............................. 26
10. John Cogger (Oldham) 24
    St. John Ellis (Castleford) 24
    Wilf George (Halifax)................................ 24
    Mark Lord (Rochdale H.).......................... 24
    Owen Simpson (Keighley).......................... 24
● Others with 20 or more: Garry Clark (Hull K.R.), Paul Eastwood (Hull), Paul Gearey (Batley), Jeff Hardy (Castleford), Alan Hunte (St. Helens), Scott Ranson (Swinton) 22; Paul Newlove (Featherstone R.), Mark Roache (Doncaster), Garry Schofield (Leeds), Neil Turner (Hull), Phil Veivers (St. Helens) 21; Kevin Iro (Wigan) 20.

TOP TEN GOALS
(Including drop goals)

1. Mike Fletcher (Hull K.R.) 199
2. Paul Loughlin (St. Helens) 145
3. Duncan Platt (Oldham)............................. 126
4. Colin Maskill (Leeds) 114
5. Mark Conway (Wakefield T.)...................... 107
6. David Hobbs (Bradford N.)........................ 104
7. Paul Eastwood (Hull) 101
8. Mark Aston (Sheffield E.) 99
9. Jonathan Davies (Widnes) 98
   Steve Turner (Rochdale H.)........................ 98

TOP FIVE DROP GOALS

1. Paul Harkin (Bradford N.)'............................ 12
2. Steve Carroll (Bramley) 11
3. Paul Bishop (Warrington)........................... 10
   Dean Carroll (Doncaster)............................ 10
   Paul Shuttleworth (Dewsbury)..................... 10

TOP FIVE POINTS

	T	G	DG	Pts
1. Mike Fletcher (Hull K.R.).	13	199	0	450
2. Paul Loughlin (St. Helens).	17	145	0	358
3. Paul Eastwood (Hull)........	22	101	0	290
4. Duncan Platt (Oldham)	8	125	1	283
5. Jonathan Davies (Widnes)..	16	98	0	260

Key:
SBC .... Stones Bitter Championship
SD.............. Second Division
PT.............. Premiership Trophy
SDP............ Second Division Premiership
LC.............. Lancashire Cup
YC.............. Yorkshire Cup
RT .... Regal Trophy
CC.............. Challenge Cup
NA .... Non-appearance

OUTSTANDING SCORING FEATS IN 1989-90

INDIVIDUAL

Most tries in a match:
6 by Chris Bibb (Featherstone R.) v. Keighley ... YC
   David Kettlestring (Ryedale-York) at
   Keighley .... SD
5 by Mark Preston (Wigan) v. Barrow .... SBC
   St. John Ellis (Castleford) at Whitehaven.... RT
   Des Foy (Oldham) v. Hunslet .... SD
   Joe Ropati (Swinton) v. Nottingham C. .... SD
   Anthony Sullivan (Hull K.R.) v. Keighley .. SD

Most goals in a match:
14 by Mike Fletcher (Hull K.R.) v. Whitehaven. SD
   Steve Turner (Rochdale H.) v.
   Runcorn H. .... SD
13 by Mark Knapper (Featherstone R.) v.
   Keighley .... YC
12 by Graham Steadman (Castleford) v. Salford .. SBC
11 by Paul Loughlin (St. Helens) v. Runcorn H . LC
   Colin Maskill (Leeds) v. Barrow.............. SBC
10 by Keith Dixon (Keighley) v. Nottingham C.. SD
   Colin Whitfield (Halifax) v. Nottingham C SD
   Paul Loughlin (St. Helens) v. Barrow....... SBC
   Steve Turner (Rochdale H.) v. Ryedale-
   York .... SD
   Mike Fletcher (Hull K.R.) at Fulham ...... SD
   Mike Fletcher (Hull K.R.) at Bramley...... SD
   Barry Vickers (Carlisle) at Nottingham C .. SD

Most points in a match:
36 by Graham Steadman (Castleford) v. Salford .. SBC
32 by Steve Turner (Rochdale H.) v. Runcorn H. SD
30 by Mark Knapper (Featherstone R.) v.
   Keighley .... YC
   Paul Loughlin (St. Helens) v. Runcorn H . LC

TEAM

Highest score:
Rochdale H. 92 v. Runcorn H. 0..................... SD
Hull K.R. 92 v. Whitehaven 10 .... SD
● There was a total of 52 matches in which a team scored 50 points or more, compared with 29 in the previous season. The other 60-plus scores were:

Home:

Leeds 90 v. Barrow 0	SBC
Featherstone R. 86 v. Keighley 18	YC
St. Helens 78 v. Runcorn H. 10	LC
Halifax 74 v. Whitehaven 0	SD
Rochdale H. 70 v. Nottingham C. 20	SD
Rochdale H. 70 v. Trafford B. 28	SD
Oldham 66 v. Chorley 16	SD
Hull K.R. 66 v. Keighley 10	SD
Castleford 65 v. Salford 0	SBC
Wigan 62 v. Barrow 6	SBC
St. Helens 62 v. Barrow 18	SBC
Wigan 62 v. Doncaster 6	RT
Halifax 60 v. Nottingham C. 4	SD
Oldham 60 v. Runcorn H. 2	SD

Away:

Nottingham C. 20 v. Halifax 72	SD
Keighley 8 v. Rydedale-York 70	SD
Barrow 0 v. Wigan 66	SBC
Whitehaven 2 v. Castleford 62	RT
Fulham 6 v. Hull K.R. 60	SD
Bramley 2 v. Hull K.R. 60	SD
Nottingham C. 0 v. Carlisle 60	SD
Barrow 6 v. Bradford N. 60	SBC

Highest score by losing team:

Oldham 50 v. Keighley 34	SD

● There was a total of 61 matches in which a team scored 20 points or more and lost, compared with 64 the previous season.

High-scoring draws:

Salford 20 v. Sheffield E. 20	SBC
Leigh 20 v. Widnes 20	SBC

● There were only two matches in which both teams scored 20 points or more, compared with none the previous season.

● From the start of the 1983-84 season, the value of a try was raised from three points to four points. It was decided officially that records for most points in a match, season or career would subsequently include the four-point try and that no attempt would be made to adjust existing records featuring the three-point try. This rule applies to all other changes in scoring values.
● Substitute appearances do not count towards players' full appearance records.

RECORD-BREAKING FEATS 1989-90

MARK ROACHE scored a Doncaster record of 21 tries in a season.

NEIL TURNER reached a Doncaster career record of 72 tries including a record equalling four in a match.

CHRIS BIBB equalled the Featherstone Rovers record of six tries in a match.

DAVID KETTLESTRING equalled the Ryedale-York record of six tries in a match.

JOE ROPATI equalled the Swinton record of five tries in a match.

ST. JOHN ELLIS equalled the Castleford record of five tries in a match.

DAVID GILLAN AND HUSSEIN M'BARKI equalled the Fulham record of three tries in match.

ELLERY HANLEY of Wigan scored a Regal Trophy final record three tries.

JOHN WOODS of Rochdale Hornets set a Division Two record of scoring a try in 12 successive league matches.

MIKE FLETCHER of Hull K.R. scored a club record 199 goals and 450 points in a season, including a record equalling 14 goals in a match and a Division Two record total of 167 in a season. He also joined the few who have scored in every match throughout a season.

MARK KNAPPER scored a Featherstone Rovers record 13 goals and 30 points in a match.

STEVE TURNER scored a Rochdale Hornets record 14 goals and 32 points in a match.

BARRY VICKERS scored a Carlisle record 10 goals and 24 points in a match.

GRAHAM SULLIVAN scored a Ryedale-York record equalling 26 points in a match.

LEEDS ran up a Division One record score of 90-0 which was Barrow's biggest defeat.

ROCHDALE HORNETS achieved a club record score of 92-0 which equalled the most points conceded by Runcorn Highfield. It also set a Division Two record margin and equalled the division's highest score which was matched by HULL K.R.'s 92-10 defeat of Whitehaven — a record win and defeat for the two clubs.

WIGAN equalled the Divison One record away winning margin with a 66-0 win at Barrow.

FEATHERSTONE ROVERS had a club record 86-18 win over Keighley.

RYEDALE-YORK ran up a club record 70-8 victory against Keighley.

DONCASTER equalled their record score with a 50-6 victory at Nottingham City which was their highest away score.

CARLISLE scored a club record 60-0 win over Nottingham City.

KEIGHLEY equalled Division Two record score by a beaten team when they lost 50-34 at Oldham.

NEW RECORDS IN DETAIL . . .

MARK ROACHE broke the Doncaster try record for a season with two tries in their final match giving the winger a total of 21 tries. His tries in the 34-8 home defeat of Nottingham City took him past the previous record of 20 by winger Neil Turner in 1985-86 and 1988-89. Roache played in all 33 of Doncaster's matches, including one as substitute, compared with Turner's 35 and 30 matches. Roache's match-by-match figures were:

Doncaster		Tries
Dewsbury	(H)	0
Bramley	(A)	1
Huddersfield (YC)	(H)	2
Runcorn H.	(H)	1
Featherstone R. (YC)	(A)	1
Whitehaven	(H)	0
Halifax	(A)	1
Ryedale-York	(H)	0
Keighley	(A)	0
Workington T.	(H)	1
Oldham	(H)	0
Whitehaven	(A)	1
Kells (RT)	(A)	1
Oldham	(A)	0
Wigan (RT)	(A)	0
Trafford B.	(H)	0
Hunslet	(H)	1
Nottingham C.	(A)	2
Fulham	(H)	0
Dewsbury	(A)	0
Fulham (CC)	(A)	0
Keighley	(H)	0
Hunslet	(A)	1
Swinton	(A)	1
Bramley	(H)	2
Fulham	(A)	1
Trafford B.	(A)	1
Swinton	(H)	0
Ryedale-York	(A)	0
Runcorn H.	(A)	1
Halifax	(H)	0
Workington T.	(A)	0
Nottingham C.	(H)	2
Total		**21**

NEIL TURNER finished with a Doncaster career record of 72 tries, including a record-equalling four in one match, before being transferred to Hull. He broke the Doncaster try career record of 66 tries with a club record equalling four in a match in a 34-6 Division Two win at Keighley on 22 October. The winger had begun the match level with the 66 scored by stand off John Buckton between 1980 and 1984.

His four tries equalled the record by Vernon Grace v. Rochdale Hornets, 4 October 1952; Brian Tasker v. Leeds, 26 October 1963; John Buckton v. Rochdale Hornets, 30 August 1981; Tony Kemp v. Carlisle, 23 November 1986.

Turner made his debut for Doncaster as an unnamed trialist from Wheatley Hills Rugby Union club in an 11-14 Division Two home defeat against Fulham on 8 September 1985. He finished that season with the old club record 20 tries which he equalled in 1988-89. Turner's career record total had reached 72 tries when he was transferred to Hull in December 1989.

His total included three hat-tricks plus one four-try feat and was made up as follows:

1985-86	20
1986-87	12
1987-88	11
1988-89	20
1989-90	9
Total	**72**

CHRIS BIBB equalled the Featherstone Rovers record of six tries in a match in an 86-18 Yorkshire Cup first round home win over Keighley on 17 September. It is also believed to be the best match feat by any full back. The club record was set by stand off Mick Smith in a 44-2 home league defeat of Doncaster on 13 April 1968.

DAVID KETTLESTRING equalled the Ryedale-York record of six tries in a match in a 70-8 Division Two win at Keighley on 11 March. The former amateur winger achieved the feat in only his 11th senior match after the record had stood since winger R. Hardgrave scored six in a 40-11 home league defeat of Bramley on 5 January 1935.

JOE ROPATI equalled the Swinton record of five tries in a match in a 46-10 Divison Two home win over Nottingham City on 21 January. The New Zealand centre achieved the feat in only his ninth match after being transferred from Warrington. Eight other players had scored five tries in a match for Swinton, the previous one being centre Alan Buckley against Salford on 8 April 1964.

ST. JOHN ELLIS equalled the Castleford record of five tries in a match in a 62-2 Regal Trophy second round win at Whitehaven on 10 December. The winger achieved the feat in only his 10th match after being transferred from Ryedale-York. Others who have scored five in a match for Castleford are: Derek Foster v. Hunslet, 10 November 1972; John Joyner v. Millom Amateurs, 16 September 1973; Steve Fenton v. Dewsbury, 27 January 1978; Ian French v. Hunslet, 9 February 1986.

DAVID GILLAN AND HUSSEIN M'BARKI took the number of times the Fulham record of three tries has been scored in a match to 12. Loose forward Gillan did it in the 50-6 Division Two home win over Carlisle on 1 October and M'Barki went on as substitute to score three in a 38-10 Division Two home win over Chorley on 13 April. Gillan and M'Barki join David Allen as the only players to score two hat-tricks for Fulham.

ELLERY HANLEY of Wigan became the first player to score three tries in a Regal Trophy, previously John Player, final as Halifax were beaten 24-12 at Headingley, Leeds on 13 January. The hat-trick helped the loose forward to win the Man of the Match award.

JOHN WOODS of Rochdale Hornets set a Divison Two record of scoring at least one try in 12 successive league matches. The stand off's sequence was made up of singles except for two in a match and brought him a total of 13 tries. Woods began the tryscoring run on 15 October and scored a 12th successive time on 21 January.

The previous record of 10 successive tryscoring Division Two matches was set by stand off Roger Millward who touched down in the last 10 matches of 1974-75 for Hull K.R. before they were promoted.

Hull K.R. centre Mike Fletcher.

MIKE FLETCHER of Hull K.R. scored a club record of 199 goals and 450 points in a season, including a record-equalling 14 goals in a match and a Division Two record total of 167 goals in a season. He also joined the few who have scored in every match throughout a season.

The centre equalled the match record with 14 goals in the 92-10 Divison Two home defeat of Whitehaven on 18 March. It had stood since 8 October 1910, when Alf Carmichael included four drops in the 70-13 home league defeat of Merthyr Tydfil on 8 October 1910.

Fletcher broke the points record of 366 by winger Steve Hubbard in 1979-80 with an early try followed by four goals in a 29-6 Division Two home defeat of Halifax on 4 April. Hubbard's total was made up of 30 tries and 138 goals.

Fletcher broke the club goals record in his next match with five in the 38-12 Division Two win at Runcorn Highfield on 8 April taking him past George Fairbairn's 166 in 1981-82.

The Division Two goals record went with Fletcher's last league goal of the season on 16 April when he landed nine in a 58-6 home defeat of Hunslet to edge him past the 166 by Workington Town's Lynn Hopkins in 1981-82, which included three drop goals.

Fletcher scored in all 35 of Rovers' matches — the 14th feat of scoring in every match throughout a season.

His match-by-match record was as follows:

		T	G	Pts
Keighley	(A)	1	8	20
Bramley (YC)	(A)	1	9	22
Trafford B	(H)	1	8	20
Castleford (YC)	(A)	0	2	4
Oldham	(A)	0	2	4
Nottingham C	(H)	1	9	22
Swinton	(H)	0	7	14
Fulham	(H)	2	8	24
Halifax	(A)	0	2	4
Workington T	(H)	0	5	10
Swinton	(A)	0	5	10
Dewsbury	(H)	0	7	14
St. Helens (RT)	(A)	0	3	6
Fulham	(A)	2	10	28
Ryedale-York	(H)	0	2	4
Hunslet	(A)	0	4	8
Nottingham C	(A)	1	7	18
Oldham	(H)	0	1	2
Workington T	(A)	1	6	16
Wigan (CC)	(H)	0	2	4
Bramley	(A)	0	10	20
Runcorn H	(H)	0	4	8
Keighley	(H)	1	9	22
Whitehaven	(A)	0	5	10
Whitehaven	(H)	0	14	28
Trafford B	(A)	0	4	8
Bramley	(H)	0	7	14
Halifax	(H)	1	4	12
Runcorn H	(A)	0	5	10
Dewsbury	(A)	0	1	2
Ryedale-York	(A)	0	4	8
Hunslet	(H)	1	9	22
Fulham (SDP)	(H)	0	6	12
Dewsbury (SDP)	(H)	0	6	12
Oldham (SDP)	*	0	4	8

Totals
	T	G	Pts
35 appearances	13	199	450

* At Manchester U. FC

MARK KNAPPER scored a Featherstone Rovers record 13 goals and 30 points in the 86-18 Yorkshire Cup first round home win over Keighley on 17 September. The centre also scored a try in only his third senior match since leaving the amateur ranks and his first as goalkicker.

Loose forward Don Fox had set the old goals record with 12 in a 60-4 home defeat of Stanningley Amateurs in the first round of the Challenge Cup on 8 February 1964. Steve Quinn held the previous points record with 20 from 10 goals and a hat-trick of three-point tries in a 47-7 Division Two home defeat of Doncaster on 4 November 1979.

STEVE TURNER scored a Rochdale Hornets record 14 goals and 32 points in a match when they beat Runcorn Highfield in a Division Two home match on 5 November. The loose forward included one try in beating the 27 points, from nine goals and three tries, by centre F. Blincow in a 51-0 home league defeat of Normanton on 17 October 1903. Full back Herbert Lees held the previous goals record with 10 in a 50-2 home defeat of Glasshoughton Amateurs in the first round of the Challenge Cup on 19 February 1938.

BARRY VICKERS scored a Carlisle record 10 goals and 24 points in a match when they won 60-0 at Nottingham City on 11 March. The previous records were also set by Vickers against Nottingham in their Mansfield Marksman days.

Vickers' total included a try and beat the club points record of 22 he set himself with nine goals and a try in the 58-1 Silk Cut Challenge Cup first round home defeat of Mansfield on 29 January 1989.

The goals tally then was also the previous record he shared with Dean Carroll, who kicked nine including a drop in a 45-13 Division Two home defeat of Mansfield on 16 March 1986.

GRAHAM SULLIVAN scored a Ryedale-York record-equalling 26 points in a match with nine goals and two tries in a 70-8 Division Two win at Keighley on 11 March. The second row forward's total equalled stand off Graham Steadman's nine goals and two tries in a 54-4 Division Two home defeat of Batley on 25 November 1984.

LEEDS ran up a Division One record score and inflicted Barrow's biggest-ever defeat with a 90-0 home win on 11 February.

The previous Division One record was Castleford's 76-16 home defeat of Swinton on 6 March 1988, when they scored 14 tries compared with 17 by Leeds.

Leeds also hold the record for the biggest score in any league match with their 102-0 defeat of Coventry under the old one division system on 12 April 1913, when they scored 24 tries.

Barrow's previous biggest defeat was 71-15 at St. Helens in a league match on 14 February 1959, when they conceded 15 tries.

ROCHDALE HORNETS achieved a club record score of 92-0 which equalled the most points conceded by Runcorn Highfield. It also set a Division Two record margin and equalled the division's highest score which was matched by Hull K.R.'s 92-10 defeat of Whitehaven — a record win and defeat for the two clubs.

Rochdale's home victory on 5 November beat the club record 75-13 home Challenge Cup-tie defeat of Broughton Moor amateurs on 13 March 1915, when they scored 17 tries, compared with 16 against Runcorn.

It was the widest margin defeat for Runcorn and equalled the most points conceded. Previously, they lost 92-2 at Wigan in a first round John Player Special Trophy

tie on 13 November 1988. Wigan scored 18 tries.

The previous widest margin in a Division Two match was Leigh's 92-2 home defeat of Keighley on 30 April 1986, when they scored 16 tries.

Hull K.R.'s 16-try, 92-10 defeat of Whitehaven on 18 March, beat the club record highest score and winning margin of 73-5 in a Challenge Cup first round home defeat of Brookland Rovers amateurs on 4 March 1905, when they scored 17 tries.

Whitehaven's prevous biggest defeat was 74-6 at home to Wigan in the second round of the Lancashire Cup when they conceded 14 tries.

WIGAN equalled the Division One record away winning margin with a 66-0 win at Barrow on 1 October when they scored 12 tries. They had set the record with a 72-6 win at Wakefield Trinity on 29 March 1987. The 72 points remains the highest Division One away score and included 14 tries. The defeat was Barrow's biggest ever at home.

FEATHERSTONE ROVERS had a club record 86-18 win over Keighley in the second round of the Yorkshire Cup on 17 September. The 15-try home win beat the 66-14 Division One home defeat of Barrow on 12 April 1987, when they scored 12 tries.

RYEDALE-YORK ran up a club record score of 70-8 at Keighley in a Division Two match on 11 March when they scored 12 tries.

York's previous highest score was 60 points twice. They beat Barrow 60-0 in a home league match on 3 April 1972, when they scored 14 tries and then beat Workington Town 60-10, with 11 tries, in a Division Two home game on 2 November 1986.

DONCASTER equalled their record score with a 50-6 Division Two win at Nottingham City on 26 December, their best away win. They also won 50-6 at home to Keighley in a Division Two home match on 22 March 1987. Doncaster scored nine tries in each match.

CARLISLE had a club record 60-0 win at Nottingham City on 11 March in a Division Two match which produced 10 tries. The previous highest win of 58-1 was against Nottingham in their Mansfield Marksman days on 29 January 1989, in a Silk Cut Challenge Cup first round home tie, when Carlisle also scored 10 tries.

KEIGHLEY equalled the Division Two record score for a beaten team when they lost 50-34 at Oldham on 12 November. The record was set when Rochdale Hornets lost 36-34 at Dewsbury in a Division Two match on 9 October 1988.

WIGAN's home game against St. Helens attracted a Division One record crowd of 27,075 on 26 December when the Saints were beaten 38-6. The previous record was 23,809 for the corresponding fixture on 27 December 1988. Under the old one-league system the record league crowd was 47,747 for Wigan v. St. Helens on 27 March 1959.

MILESTONES . . .

BOB BEARDMORE scored the 100th try of his career with the first of four on his debut for Leigh in a 42-16 Stones Bitter Championship home defeat of Barrow on 3 September. The scrum half's 99 previous tries had all been scored for Castleford, who had transferred him during the close season for £35,000.

Beardmore began his professional career with Castleford, making his debut in a 10-8 Division One defeat at Workington Town on 18 November 1979. After failing to score a try in his first season, in which he played only four matches, Beardmore followed up with 17 in his first full campaign and that remains his best total. Apart from his four-try debut for Leigh, Beardmore also scored four in a match and one other hat-trick.

His grand total of 111 career tries is made up as follows:

Castleford

1979-80	0
1980-81	17
1981-82	13
1982-83	14
1983-84	13
1984-85	6
1985-86	13
1986-87	14
1987-88	6
1988-89	3

Leigh

1989-90	12

Totals

Castleford	99
Leigh	12

GRAND TOTAL **111**

Scrum half Bob Beardmore, 100th career try on his debut for Leigh.

KEVIN PAPE scored the 100th try of his career with the second of two for Carlisle in a 54-14 Division Two home defeat of Runcorn Highfield on 3 September.

The centre's total of 114 is made up of 113 for Carlisle and one for Cumbria. Pape is the only Carlisle player to total a century of tries since the club was formed in 1981 and also shares the club record for most in one match. He scored four tries in a 30-22 Challenge Cup first round home victory over Rochdale Hornets on 11 February 1987 and has also notched three other hat-tricks.

A former player with Cumbrian amateurs Glasson Rangers, Pape made his senior debut on 2 September 1984 when he scored a try in a 31-15 Division Two home defeat of Doncaster. His most prolific campaign was 1987-88 when he scored 23, including one for Cumbria, to be fifth in the try chart, the only time he has finished in the top ten.

Pape's season-by-season totals are as follows:

Carlisle

1984-85	19	
1985-86	20	
1986-87	22	
1987-88	22	+1 Cumbria
1988-89	14	
1989-90	16	

Totals

Carlisle	113
Cumbria	1

GRAND TOTAL **114**

SHAUN EDWARDS of Wigan scored the 100th try of his career with one in the 19-18 Lancashire Cup semi-final defeat at Oldham on 5 October. The Test stand off's total of 123 is made up of 112 for Wigan and 11 in representative matches.

Edwards signed for Wigan on his 17th birthday before the TV cameras on 17 October 1983 after captaining England schoolboys at both Rugby Union and League. He made his debut at stand off in a 30-13 John Player Special Trophy first round home win over York on 6 November 1983.

His best season's totals were 26 in 1986-87, when he finished seventh in the try chart, and last season when he was eighth. His other top 10 placing was seventh with 21 in 1987-88. Edwards has scored four hat-tricks for Wigan including one four-try feat.

Although Edwards went on the Great Britain 1988 tour of Papua New Guinea and Australasia he was injured in the first game and returned home without playing again.

His season-by-season try figures are as follows:

Wigan

1983-84	6	
1984-85	11	
1985-86	14	+1 GB Under-21s
1986-87	24	+2 Gt Britain

1987-88	17	+2 Gt Britain, 2 Lancs
1988-89	15	+3 Gt Britain
1989-90	25	+1 Gt Britain

Totals

Wigan	112
Great Britain	8
GB Under-21	1
Lancashire	2

GRAND TOTAL...... 123

DAVID HOBBS of Bradford Northern scored the 100th try of his career with one in the 22-16 Stones Bitter Championship defeat at Leigh on 3 February. The Test forward's total of 102 at the end of the season was made up of Featherstone Rovers 66, Oldham 11, Bradford Northern 21 and four in representative matches.

A former Featherstone junior, Hobbs made his senior debut in the centre with a try and three goals in a 32-15 Division One home defeat against Castleford on 27 March 1978. He was transferred to Oldham for £40,000 and made his debut for them at prop in a 44-6 Division One home victory over Workington Town on 31 March 1985. Hobbs then moved to Bradford in a cash-plus-Ian Sherratt deal, making his debut in the second row at home to Warrington in an 11-10 Division One home win.

Hobbs' 21 tries for Featherstone in 1981-82 is a club record for a forward, since equalled by Peter Smith. He is also the only forward to score more than one try in a Challenge Cup final this century, his two against Hull in 1983 helping him to the Lance Todd Trophy as Man of the Match. Hobbs' total of 102 tries includes only two hat-tricks, both for Featherstone.

His season-by-season totals are as follows:

Featherstone R.

1977-78	1
1978-79	2
1979-80	4
1980-81	4
1981-82	21
1982-83	18
1983-84	9
1984-85	7

Oldham

1984-85	0	
1985-86	4	+1 Yorks
1986-87	7	

Bradford N.

1986-87	0	
1987-88	6	
1988-89	10	
1989-90	5	+1 Yorks

Totals

Featherstone R.	66
Oldham	11
Bradford N.	21
Yorkshire	2
1984 GB Tour	2

GRAND TOTAL...... 102

COLIN WHITFIELD took his career try total past the century mark with two in Halifax's 32-18 Regal Trophy first round home win at Fulham on 3 December. Whitfield's total at the end of the season of 105 is made up of Halifax 48, Salford 11 and Wigan 46.

He made his senior professional debut in the centre for Salford when they lost 13-14 at home to Rochdale Hornets in Division One on 23 January 1979. Wigan signed him in a £65,000 deal with Roy Heaney and Trevor Stockley joining Salford. He made his debut for Wigan at full back when they lost 24-20 in a Division One match at York on 8 November 1981, kicking four goals. Halifax paid a then club record £25,000 to sign Whitfield and he made his debut in the centre when they lost 15-8 in a Division One match against Widnes at the Halifax Town soccer ground on 22 January 1986. He kicked one goal.

Whitfield's most prolific tryscoring season was 1986-87 when he touched down 21 times for Halifax, helping him to a club record 298 points in a season.

His total of 105 tries includes only one hat-trick, for Wigan, and is made up as follows:

Salford

1978-79	0
1979-80	8
1980-81	2
1981-82	1

Wigan

1981-82	6
1982-83	12
1983-84	13
1984-85	4
1985-86	11

Halifax

1985-86	3
1986-87	21
1987-88	7
1988-89	6
1989-90	11

Totals

Salford	11
Wigan	46
Halifax	48

GRAND TOTAL 105

JOHN HENDERSON of Oldham took his career tries total past the century mark with four in the 52-4 Division Two home win over Fulham on 3 February. His total of 110 at the end of the season was made up of 84 Leigh, 25 Oldham and one for Lancashire.

The former Saddleworth Rangers amateur made his senior debut for Leigh in the centre at home to St. Helens on 22 August 1982 when they drew 19-19 in a Division One match. His most prolific season was 1985-86 as he scored 31 tries and finished fourth in the try chart. He was sixth the following season with 27 but has not finished in the top 10 since.

Henderson moved to Oldham for £50,000 and made his debut at Castleford on 25 September 1988. Playing in the centre, he scored a try in a 22-19 Division One victory. He has scored eight hat-tricks, two for Oldham including a four-try feat. Henderson's total of 110 tries is made up as follows:

Leigh

1982-83	5	
1983-84	7	
1984-85	8	
1985-86	31	
1986-87	27	
1987-88	5	+ 1 Lancs
1988-89	1	

Oldham

1988-89	8
1989-90	17

Totals

Leigh	84
Oldham	25
Lancashire	1

GRAND TOTAL...... 110

ANDY GOODWAY of Wigan scored the 100th try of his career with one in the 30-2 Division One home defeat of Hull on 26 November. The Test forward's total of 112 at the end of season was made up of 30 for Oldham, 68 for Wigan and 14 in representative matches.

Castleford-born Goodway played for local junior side Redhill before signing for Oldham and making his senior debut as a substitute at home to Dewsbury in a 19-5 Division Two win on 13 September 1981. His full debut followed on 4 October 1981 when he played second row in a 15-9 league defeat at Halifax.

He moved to Wigan in July 1985 for a then record £65,000 for a forward and made his debut on 15 September 1985 in the second row in a 24-13 Lancashire Cup first round home win over Fulham. Goodway's best match feat is four tries and he has scored one other hat-trick. His season-by-season totals are as follows:

Oldham

1981-82	3	
1982-83	8	+ 1 Great Britain
1983-84	10	+ 1 Great Britain
1984-85	9	

Wigan

1985-86	8	+ 1 Great Britain, 1 Yorks
1986-87	11	+ 1 Great Britain
1987-88	23	
1988-89	4	
1989-90	22	+ 2 Great Britain, 2 Yorks

Totals

Oldham	30
Wigan	68
Great Britain	6
1984 Tour	5
Yorkshire	3

GRAND TOTAL...... 112

Kiwi utility back James Leuluai, scorer of 100 tries in British club football.

JAMES LEULUAI scored the 100th try of his British-based career with the first of two tries in Wakefield Trinity's 26-10 Division One win at Barrow on 5 November. His total of 104 at the end of the season was made up of 85 for Hull, 6 Leigh, 12 Wakefield Trinity and one in a Test match for New Zealand.

Leuluai was one of three Kiwis signed by Hull after the 1980 tour of Britain. The others in one of the biggest signing coups of all time were Gary Kemble and O'Hara. O'Hara and Leuluai, at centre, made their debuts for Hull on 27 September 1981 in a 42-24 Division One home defeat of Castleford.

The centre had one season with Leigh in 1986-87, making his debut at stand off in a 35-20 Division One defeat at Hull K.R. on 26 October 1986. Leuluai returned to Hull for the 1987-88 season and then joined Wakefield Trinity. He made a one-try debut for Trinity at full back in a 34-12 Division One away defeat against Wigan on 16 October 1988. His total of 104 tries includes two hat-tricks and a four-try feat, all for Hull. At the end of last season he signed for Ryedale-York.

Leuluai's season-by-season totals are as follows:

Hull

1981-82	10	
1982-83	21	
1983-84	23	
1984-85	15	
1985-86	13	+1 New Zealand

Leigh

1986-87	6

Hull

1987-88	3

Wakefield T.

1988-89	6
1989-90	6

Totals

Hull	85
Leigh	6
Wakefield T.	12
New Zealand	1

GRAND TOTAL...... 104

DES FOY scored the 100th try of his career with the first of two for Oldham in a 44-6 Division Two win at Chorley on 21 January. The centre or stand off's total of 104 tries at the end of the season was made up of 89 for Oldham, seven for Widnes and eight in representative matches.

A former England schoolboy international, Foy was only 16 when he signed for Widnes in July 1980, for a reported then record amateur contract of £17,000. He made his senior debut as a substitute in a 14-9 Division One home defeat of Featherstone Rovers on 7 September 1980. His full debut came on the wing in Widnes' next match, a 14-10 Lancashire Cup semi-final home defeat against Wigan on 10 September 1980.

Foy moved to Oldham and was signed after an earlier loan spell when he made his debut on the wing in a 23-10 Division One home win at Bradford Northern on 29 August 1982. His most prolific season was 1987-88 when he scored 21 tries to finish seventh, his only top 10 placing. Foy missed the whole of the following season when he emigrated to Australia, but returned to Oldham in 1989 and scored five tries in one match. He has scored three other hat-tricks.

Foy's total of 104 tries is made up as follows:

Widnes

1980-81	0	
1981-82	7	

Oldham

1982-83	4	
1983-84	13	+1 Great. Britain, 1 Gt Britain U-24
1984-85	15	+1 Great. Britain
1985-86	10	
1986-87	16	
1987-88	21	
1989-90	10	

Totals

Widnes	7
Oldham	89
1984 Tour	5
Great Britain	2
Under-24s	1

GRAND TOTAL...... 104

Wingman Garry Clark, a ton-up try merchant for Hull K.R.

GARRY CLARK scored his 100th try for Hull K.R. with the second of two in the 48-8 Division Two defeat of Trafford Borough in the inaugural match at Rovers' new Craven Park Stadium on 24 September.

A former Hull K.R. Colt, Clark signed for Rovers after touring Australia and Papua New Guinea with the 1982 Great Britain Colts squad. Clark was still only 17 when he made his senior debut with a try in the 33-10 Division One home defeat of Workington Town on 22 August 1982. In the next match the winger scored the first of three hat-tricks for Rovers.

In addition to his 118 tries for Rovers, the Test winger has also scored 14 in representative matches, including seven on Britain's 1984 tour of Australasia.

Clark's season-by-season total for Rovers are as follows:

1982-83	17
1983-84	24
1984-85	16
1985-86	11
1986-87	10
1987-88	12
1988-89	6
1989-90	22
Total	**118**

GED BYRNE scored the 100th try of his career with one in Wigan's 50-4 Lancashire Cup first round defeat of Chorley at Leigh on 15 September. The utility back's end of season total of 109 was made up of 84 for Salford and 25 for Wigan.

Byrne made his senior debut for Salford as a substitute in a 19-3 Lancashire Cup second round home win over Fulham on 23 August 1981. He made his full debut centre on 4 September 1981, in a 59-13 Division Two home win against Doncaster.

Byrne's move to Wigan in August 1987 was the first involving the new independent transfer tribunal, who fixed his fee at £40,000 after Salford had sought £75,000 and Wigan offered £20,000. Byrne had already made his debut for Wigan in the Charity Shield match at Douglas, Isle of Man, on 23 August 1987, when Halifax were beaten 44-12. Byrne's most prolific season was 1984-85 when he scored 25 tries and was eighth in the try chart, the only time he has finished in the top 10. He has scored four hat-tricks, including one four-try feat, all for Salford.

His season-by-season totals are as follows:

Salford

1981-82	7
1982-83	18
1983-84	18
1984-85	25
1985-86	6
1986-87	10

Wigan

1987-88	7
1988-89	8
1989-90	10

Totals

Salford	84
Wigan	25
GRAND TOTAL	**109**

Wigan utility player Ged Byrne, scorer of 100 career tries, getting to grips with Widnes full back Alan Tait.

DAVID CREASSER of Leeds took his club points career total past the 1,000 mark with a try in the 38-16 Division One home win over Leigh on 17 January. The centre or stand off's total of 1,017 at the end of the season was made up of 76 tries and 357 goals, including one drop goal.

A former Hunslet Parkside junior, Creasser signed for his hometown club after touring with the Great Britain Youth squad to New Zealand in 1983. He made his debut for Leeds as a substitute in a 30-14 Yorkshire Cup first round win at Batley on 4 September 1983. His first full senior game was in the second round 24-16 win at York when he played centre on 14 September 1983.

Creasser's most prolific season was 1984-85 when he totalled 218 points. His best match tally is 28 points from 10 goals and two tries in a 60-6 Division One home defeat of Salford on 27 September 1987. He has also scored 22 and 24 points in a match. In addition to his 1,017 points for Leeds, Creasser has also totalled 40 in representative matches.

His season-by-season totals for Leeds are as follows:

	T	G	Pts
1983-84	16	76	216
1984-85	12	85	218
1985-86	12	84	216
1986-87	13	48	148
1987-88	14	43	142
1988-89	4	19(1)	55
1989-90	5	1	22
Totals	**76**	**356(1)**	**1,017**

David Creasser, scorer of more than 1,000 points for Leeds.

CHRIS JOHNSON scored the 1,000th point of his career for Leigh in an 18-16 Division One win at Widnes on 12 November. At the end of the season the full back's total of 1,073 was made up of 38 tries and 467 goals, including 13 drop goals.

Johnson holds two club records for a season with 173 goals and 400 points in 1985-86 when he finished at the top of the two charts. His top match tally is 32 points twice. He made his senior debut for Leigh in the centre on 12 February 1984 when they lost 16-10 at St. Helens in a Challenge Cup first round tie.

Johnson's season-by-season totals are as follows:

	T	G	DG	Pts
1983-84	3	0	0	12
1984-85	5	0	0	20
1985-86	14	171	2	400
1986-87	1	84	2	174
1987-88	3	35	6	88
1988-89	12	114	3	279
1989-90	0	50	0	100
Totals	**38**	**454**	**13**	**1,072**

Full back Chris Johnson, who passed the 1,000-point mark at Leigh before moving to Swinton.

LEADING SCORERS 1895-1971

	TRIES	GOALS	POINTS
1895-96	Hurst (Oldham) 28	Lorimer (Manningham) 35	Cooper (Bradford)..........106
			Lorimer (Manningham)...106
1896-97	Hannah (Hunslet)............19	Goldthorpe (Hunslet) 26	Rigg (Halifax) 112
		Sharpe (Liversedge) 26	
1897-98	Hoskins (Salford) 30	Goldthorpe (Hunslet) 66	Goldthorpe (Hunslet)......135
1898-99	Williams (Oldham) 39	Goldthorpe (Hunslet) 67	Jaques (Hull) 169
1899-00	Williams (Oldham) 36	Cooper (Bradford) 39	Williams (Oldham).........108
1900-01	Williams (Oldham) 47	Goldthorpe (Hunslet) 44	Williams (Oldham).........141
1901-02	Wilson (Broughton R.).....38	James (Broughton R.) 75	Lomas (Salford).............172
1902-03	Evans (Leeds).................27	Goldthorpe (Hunslet) 48	Davies (Batley)..............136
1903-04	Hogg (Broughton R.).......34	Lomas (Salford) 66	Lomas (Salford).............222
1904-05	Dechan (Bradford)...........31	Ferguson (Oldham)..........50	Lomas (Salford).............146
1905-06	Leytham (Wigan) 40	Ferguson (Oldham)..........49	Leytham (Wigan)...........160
1906-07	Eccles (Halifax)...............41	Lomas (Salford) 86	Lomas (Salford).............280
1907-08	Leytham (Wigan) 44	Goldthorpe (Hunslet)......101	Goldthorpe (Hunslet)......217
1908-09	Miller (Wigan)................49	Lomas (Salford) 88	Lomas (Salford).............272
	Williams (Halifax) 49		
1909-10	Leytham (Wigan) 48	Carmichael (Hull K.R.)....78	Leytham (Wigan)...........232
1910-11	Kitchen (Huddersfield).....40	Carmichael (Hull K.R.)...129	Carmichael (Hull K.R.)...261
	Rosenfeld (Huddersfield) ..40		
	Miller (Wigan)................40		
1911-12	Rosenfeld (Huddersfield) ..78	Carmichael (Hull K.R.)...127	Carmichael (Hull K.R.)...254
1912-13	Rosenfeld (Huddersfield) ..56	Carmichael (Hull K.R.)....93	Thomas (Wigan)............198
1913-14	Rosenfeld (Huddersfield) ..80	Holland (Huddersfield) ...131	Holland (Huddersfield) ...268
1914-15	Rosenfeld (Huddersfield) ..56	Gronow (Huddersfield) ...136	Gronow (Huddersfield) ...284
● Competitive matches suspended during war years			
1918-19	Francis (Hull).................25	Kennedy (Hull) 54	Kennedy (Hull) 135
1919-20	Moorhouse (Huddersfield).39	Gronow (Huddersfield) ...148	Gronow (Huddersfield) ...332
1920-21	Stone (Hull)...................41	Kennedy (Hull) 108	Kennedy (Hull) 264
1921-22	Farrar (Oldham) 49	Sullivan (Wigan)............100	Farrar (Oldham) 213
1922-23	Ring (Wigan) 41	Sullivan (Wigan)............161	Sullivan (Wigan)............349
1923-24	Ring (Wigan) 49	Sullivan (Wigan)............158	Sullivan (Wigan)............319
1924-25	Ring (Wigan) 54	Sullivan (Wigan)............138	Sullivan (Wigan)............282
1925-26	Ring (Wigan) 63	Sullivan (Wigan)............131	Sullivan (Wigan)............274
1926-27	Ellaby (St. Helens) 55	Sullivan (Wigan)............149	Sullivan (Wigan)............322
1927-28	Ellaby (St. Helens) 37	Thompson (Leeds) 106	Thompson (Leeds) 233
1928-29	Brown (Wigan)...............44	Sullivan (Wigan)............107	Sullivan (Wigan)............226
	Mills (Huddersfield)........44		
1929-30	Ellaby (St. Helens) 39	Thompson (Leeds) 111	Thompson (Leeds) 243
1930-31	Harris, E. (Leeds)...........58	Sullivan (Wigan)............133	Sullivan (Wigan)............278
1931-32	Mills (Huddersfield)........50	Sullivan (Wigan)............117	Sullivan (Wigan)............249
1932-33	Harris, E. (Leeds)...........57	Sullivan (Wigan)............146	Sullivan (Wigan)............307
1933-34	Brown (Salford) 45	Sullivan (Wigan)............193	Sullivan (Wigan)............404

	TRIES	GOALS	POINTS
1934-35	Morley (Wigan) 49	Sullivan (Wigan)............165	Sullivan (Wigan)............348.
1935-36	Harris, E. (Leeds)...........63	Sullivan (Wigan)............117	Sullivan (Wigan)............246
1936-37	Harris, E. (Leeds)...........40	Sullivan (Wigan)............120	Sullivan (Wigan)............258
1937-38	Harris, E. (Leeds)...........45	Sullivan (Wigan)............135	Sullivan (Wigan)............285
1938-39	Markham (Huddersfield)...39	Sullivan (Wigan)............124	Risman (Salford)............267

● For the next six seasons emergency war-time competitions resulted in a reduction of matches and players were allowed to 'guest' for other clubs

	TRIES	GOALS	POINTS
1939-40	Batten (Hunslet) 38	Hodgson (Swinton)..........98	Hodgson (Swinton) 208
1940-41	Walters (Bradford N.)......32	Lockwood (Halifax) 70	Belshaw (Warrington) 174
1941-42	Francis (Barrow) 30	Lockwood (Halifax) 91	Lockwood (Halifax)........185
1942-43	Batten (Hunslet) 24	Lockwood (Halifax) 65	Lockwood (Halifax)........136
1943-44	Lawrenson (Wigan) 21	Horne (Barrow) 57	Horne (Barrow)..............144
1944-45	Batten (Bradford N.)........41	Stott (Wakefield T.).........51	Stott (Wakefield T.) 129

● Normal peace-time rugby resumed

	TRIES	GOALS	POINTS
1945-46	Batten (Bradford N.)........35	Ledgard (Dewsbury)........89	Bawden (Huddersfield) ...239
1946-47	Bevan (Warrington) 48	Miller (Hull).................103	Bawden (Huddersfield) ...243
1947-48	Bevan (Warrington) 57	Ward (Wigan) 141	Ward (Wigan) 312
1948-49	Cooper (Huddersfield)......60	Ward (Wigan) 155	Ward (Wigan) 361
1949-50	Nordgren (Wigan) 57	Gee (Wigan) 133	Palin (Warrington) 290
		Palin (Warrington) 133	
1950-51	Bevan (Warrington) 68	Cook (Leeds) 155	Cook (Leeds) 332
1951-52	Cooper (Huddersfield)......71	Ledgard (Leigh) 142	Horne (Barrow).............313
1952-53	Bevan (Warrington) 72	Bath (Warrington)..........170	Bath (Warrington)..........379
1953-54	Bevan (Warrington) 67	Metcalfe (St. Helens)......153	Metcalfe (St. Helens)......369
		Bath (Warrington)..........153	
1954-55	Cooper (Huddersfield)......66	Ledgard (Leigh) 178	Ledgard (Leigh) 374
1955-56	McLean (Bradford N.) 61	Ledgard (Leigh) 155	Bath (Warrington)..........344
1956-57	Boston (Wigan)...............60	Jones (Leeds)................194	Jones (Leeds)................496
1957-58	Sullivan (Wigan) 50	Ganley (Oldham) 219	Ganley (Oldham) 453
1958-59	Vollenhoven (St. Helens) ..62	Ganley (Oldham) 190	Griffiths (Wigan) 394
1959-60	Vollenhoven (St. Helens) ..54	Rhodes (St. Helens) 171	Fox (Wakefield T.) 453
		Fox (Wakefield T.) 171	
1960-61	Vollenhoven (St. Helens) ..59	Rhodes (St. Helens) 145	Rhodes (St. Helens) 338
1961-62	Boston (Wigan)...............51	Fox (Wakefield T.) 183	Fox (Wakefield T.) 456
1962-63	Glastonbury (Work'ton T.)41	Coslett (St. Helens)........156	Coslett (St. Helens)........321
1963-64	Stopford (Swinton) 45	Coslett (St. Helens)........138	Fox (Wakefield T.) 313
1964-65	Lake (Wigan) 40	Kellett (Hull K.R.) 150	Killeen (St. Helens)........360
1965-66	Killeen (St. Helens) 32	Killeen (St. Helens)........120	Killeen (St. Helens)........336
	Lake (Wigan) 32		
1966-67	Young (Hull K.R.)...........34	Risman (Leeds) 163	Killeen (St. Helens)........353
	Howe (Castleford) 34		
1967-68	Millward (Hull K.R.).......38	Risman (Leeds) 154	Risman (Leeds) 332
1968-69	Francis (Wigan) 40	Risman (Leeds) 165	Risman (Leeds) 345
1969-70	Atkinson (Leeds).............38	Tyrer (Wigan)...............167	Tyrer (Wigan)...............385
1970-71	Haigh (Leeds) 40	Coslett (St. Helens)........183	Coslett (St. Helens)........375
1971-72	Atkinson (Leeds).............36	Costlett (St. Helens).......214	Watkins (Salford)..........473
	Lamb (Bradford N.) 36		
1972-73	Atkinson (Leeds).............39	Watkins (Salford)...........221	Watkins (Salford)..........493

LEADING SCORERS 1973-89

TRIES

1973-74

Fielding (Salford)..49
Mathias (St. Helens)..40
D. Smith (Wakefield T.)....................................38
Eckersley (St. Helens)......................................26
Fleay (Swinton)...26
Jones (St. Helens)..25
Wilson (St. Helens)..25
Watkins (Salford)..24
Atkinson (Leeds)...23
Lamb (Bradford N.)...22
A. Smith (Leeds)...22
Bevan (Warrington)...22
Ayres (Wigan)...22

1974-75

Dunn (Hull K.R.)..42
Fielding (Salford)..35
Bevan (Warrington)...31
A. Smith (Leeds)...30
Millward (Hull K.R.).......................................30
Atkinson (Leeds)...29
Richards (Salford)..28
Sullivan (Hull K.R.)..28
Mathias (St. Helens)..27
Dyl (Leeds)..26

1975-76

Richards (Salford)..37
Fielding (Salford)..33
Jones (St. Helens)..31
Briggs (Leigh)...27
D. Smith (Wakefield T.)....................................26
Burton (Castleford)..25
Clark (Hull)..23
Wright (Workington T.).....................................22
Barends (York)..21
Boxall (Hull)..21
Holmes (Leeds)...21
Mathias (St. Helens)..21
Butler (Salford)...21

1976-77

Wright (Widnes)..31
Burton (Castleford)..29
D. Smith (Leeds)...28
Fielding (Salford)..27
Dunn (Hull K.R.)..26
Cunningham (St. Helens)...................................26

Topliss (Wakefield T.).......................................24
Richards (Salford)..23
Mathias (St. Helens)..23
Barends (York)..22

1977-78

Wright (Widnes)..33
Fielding (Salford)..31
Cunningham (St. Helens)...................................30
Bevan (Warrington)...30
Fenton (Castleford)..30
Vigo (Wigan)..29
Glynn (St. Helens)...28
D. Smith (Leeds)...28
T. Morgan (York)..27
Burton (Castleford)..27

1978-79

Hartley (Hull K.R.)...35
Wright (Widnes)..28
Barends (Bradford N.)......................................25
Lowe (Hull K.R.)..25
Prendiville (Hull)..25
Fielding (Salford)..24
D. Redfearn (Bradford N.)................................23
Mathias (St. Helens)..22
Bray (Hull)..21
O'Loughlin (Wigan)...21
Sullivan (Hull K.R.)..21

1979-80

Fielding (Salford)..30
Hubbard (Hull K.R.)..30
Munro (Oldham)..29
Ball (Barrow)...27
Bentley (Widnes)...27
Glynn (St. Helens)...27
Mathias (St. Helens)..27
Bevan (Warrington)...26
D. Redfearn (Bradford N.)................................26
D. Smith (Leeds)...24

1980-81

Crossley (York)...35
Richardson (Castleford).....................................28
Hubbard (Hull K.R.)..25
Hartley (Hull K.R.)...23
McDermott (York)...23
Slater (Huddersfield)..23
Drummond (Leigh)...20
Ball (Barrow)...19
Bevan (Warrington)...19
Cramp (Huddersfield).......................................19
Hyde (Castleford)..19
Ramsdale (Wigan)..19

1981-82

Jones (Workington T.)	31
Drummond (Leigh)	26
Basnett (Widnes)	26
Ashton (Oldham)	26
Morgan (Carlisle)	25
Hartley (Hull K.R.)	23
Hopkins (Workington T.)	23
Day (Hull)	23
Evans (Hull)	22
D. Hobbs (Featherstone R.)	21
Moll (Keighley)	21

1982-83

Eccles (Warrington)	37
Evans (Hull)	28
Crossley (Fulham)	27
David (Cardiff C.)	26
Topliss (Hull)	24
M'Barki (Fulham)	23
Hyde (Castleford)	22
McDermott (York)	22
Leuluai (Hull)	21
Phil Ford (Warrington)	20
Clark (Hull K.R.)	20

1983-84

Schofield (Hull)	38
Lydon (Widnes)	28
King (Hunslet)	28
Woods (Leigh)	27
Basnett (Widnes)	26
Gibson (Batley)	26
Herbert (Barrow)	25
Steadman (York)	25
Prohm (Hull K.R.)	25
Clark (Hull K.R.)	24

1984-85

Hanley (Bradford N.)	55
Prohm (Hull K.R.)	45
Gill (Wigan)	34
Ledger (St. Helens)	30
Meninga (St. Helens)	28
Gibbin (Whitehaven)	27
Gibson (Batley)	26
G. Peacham (Carlisle)	25
Byrne (Salford)	25
Evans (Hull)	24
Ferguson (Wigan)	24

1985-86

Halliwell (Leigh)	49
Hanley (Wigan)	38
Lister (Bramley)	34
Henderson (Leigh)	31
Frodsham (Blackpool B.)	30
Fox (Leigh)	29
Williams (Barrow)	27
Garrity (Runcorn H.)	24
Gibson (Leeds)	23
Beck (Workington T.)	23

1986-87

Hanley (Wigan)	63
Schofield (Hull)	37
Gill (Wigan)	32
Bate (Swinton)	31
Ford (Bradford N.)	30
Henderson (Leigh)	27
Edwards (Wigan)	26
Johnson (Warrington)	25
Lydon (Wigan)	24
Dunn (Rochdale H.)	23
Ledger (St. Helens)	23
McCormack (St. Helens)	23

1987-88

Offiah (Widnes)	44
Hanley (Wigan)	36
Schofield (Leeds)	25
Gibson (Leeds)	24
Goodway (Wigan)	23
Pape (Carlisle)	23
Edwards (Wigan)	21
Foy (Oldham)	21
Smith (Featherstone R.)	21
Bibb (Featherstone R.)	20
M. Conway (Wakefield T.)	20
Elia (St. Helens)	20
Quirk (St. Helens)	20

1988-89

Offiah (Widnes)	60
Ledger (Leigh)	34
Bate (Swinton)	32
Hanley (Wigan)	29
Lister (Bramley)	28
Powell (Sheffield E.)	28
Lewis (Bramley)	26
Quirk (St. Helens)	24
Anderson (Castleford)	24
Burns (Barrow)	24

GOALS
(including drop goals)

1973-74
Watkins (Salford) 183
Whitehead (Warrington) 168
Jefferson (Keighley)......................................165
Coslett (St. Helens) 134
Mumby (Bradford N.).................................131
Dutton (Widnes)...129
Lloyd (Castleford) 121
Quinn (York) 112
Fiddler (Leigh)...111
Holliday (Rochdale H.) 107

1974-75
Fox (Hull K.R.) 146
Coslett (St. Helens) 129
Dutton (Widnes)...122
Lloyd (Castleford) 112
Quinn (York) 112
Hartley (Huddersfield) 110
MacCorquodale (Workington T.) 107
Marshall (Leeds)...107
Mumby (Bradford N.)................................. 96
Fiddler (Salford, Leigh)............................... 85

1975-76
Watkins (Salford) 175
Pimblett (St. Helens) 149
Lloyd (Castleford) 149
Dutton (Widnes)...148
Fairbairn (Wigan)..146
Stacey (Leigh) 137
MacCorquodale (Workington T.) 130
Fox (Hull K.R., York)..................................102
Marshall (Leeds)...101
Gaitley (New Hunslet)..................................100

1976-77
Lloyd (Castleford) 163
Quinn (Featherstone R.)...............................152
Pimblett (St. Helens) 152
Hesford (Warrington)....................................132
MacCorquodale (Workington T.) 128
Watkins (Salford) 125
Stephenson (Dewsbury) 106
Fairbairn (Wigan)..105
Dutton (Widnes)... 97
Woods (Leigh)... 90

1977-78
Pimblett (St. Helens) 178
Hesford (Warrington)....................................158
Woods (Leigh)...149
MacCorquodale (Workington T.) 138
Woods (Widnes) 122
Watkins (Salford) 110
Mumby (Bradford N.).................................107
Lloyd (Castleford) 104
Fox (Bradford N.).. 95
Oulton (Leeds) 80

1978-79
Lloyd (Hull) 172
Hesford (Warrington)....................................170
Burke (Widnes) 140
MacCorquodale (Workington T.) 114
Pimblett (St. Helens) 105
Beale (Keighley)... 96
Woods (Leigh)... 96
Birts (Halifax) 86
Fairbairn (Wigan)... 86
Norton (Castleford)...................................... 82

1979-80
Quinn (Featherstone R.)...............................163
Hubbard (Hull K.R.)....................................138
Rule (Salford)...134
Hesford (Warrington)....................................128
Burke (Widnes) 127
Ball (Barrow)..119
Diamond (Wakefield T.)...............................116
Fitzsimons (Oldham).....................................108
Parrish (Hunslet)... 98
Birts (Halifax) 97

1980-81
Hesford (Warrington)....................................147
Quinn (Featherstone R.)...............................123
Diamond (Wakefield T.)...............................112
Burke (Widnes) 110
Hubbard (Hull K.R.)....................................109
Ball (Barrow)..104
Birts (Halifax) 100
Beale (Keighley)... 97
Parrish (Oldham) 95
Fairbairn (Wigan)... 94

1981-82
Hopkins (Workington T.) 190
Fairbairn (Hull K.R.) 168
Parrish (Oldham) 164
Woods (Leigh)...158
Rule (Salford)...130
Dick (Leeds) 125
Quinn (Featherstone R.)...............................120
Agar (Halifax) 119
Crooks (Hull) 118
Hesford (Warrington)....................................116

1982-83

Diamond (Fulham)..136
Fitzsimons (Hunslet)..121
Crooks (Hull)..120
R. Beardmore (Castleford)................................117
Hesford (Warrington)......................................113
Fenwick (Cardiff C.).......................................111
Jones (Swinton)..110
Whitfield (Wigan)...104
Kilner (Bramley)...104
Quinn (Featherstone R.)................................... 98

1983-84

Hesford (Warrington)......................................142
R. Beardmore (Castleford)................................142
Hallett (Cardiff C.)..140
Fitzsimons (Hunslet)..131
Woods (Leigh)...124
Whitfield (Wigan) 122
Ball (Barrow)..104
Parrish (Oldham) 101
Agar (Halifax) 94
Tickle (Barrow) 91

1984-85

Day (St. Helens)..157
Fairbairn (Hull K.R.) 141
Wood (Runcorn H.) 126
Steadman (York)...122
Griffiths (Salford)..118
Parrish (Oldham) 117
Schofield (Hull)...105
Creasser (Leeds)..102
Agar (Halifax) 87
Jones (Swinton) 87

1985-86

C. Johnson (Leigh)...173
Stephenson (Wigan)...128
Noble (Doncaster) 118
Harcombe (Rochdale H.) 115
Kilner (Bramley)..110
Dorahy (Hull K.R.)...101
Woods (Bradford N.) 98
Creasser (Leeds).. 84
Carroll (Carlisle).. 83
Smith (Workington T.) 83

1986-87

Loughlin (St. Helens) 190
Bishop (Warrington) 117
Noble (Doncaster) 114
Whitfield (Halifax) 109
Platt (Hunslet) 102
Topping (Swinton) 100
C. Johnson (Leigh)... 86
Ketteridge (Castleford) 80
Wood (Rochdale H.).. 80
Quinn (Featherstone R.) 77

1987-88

Woods (Warrington) 152
Quinn (Featherstone R.)....................................128
Harcombe (Wakefield T.) 116
Loughlin (St. Helens) 114
Pearce (Hull)..111
Smith (Springfield B.)....................................... 98
Stephenson (Leeds).. 95
M. Fletcher (Hull K.R.)...................................... 94
Hobbs (Bradford N.) 83
Jones (Salford).. 79

1988-89

Aston (Sheffield E.)..148
Ketteridge (Castleford) 129
Hobbs (Bradford N.) 118
C. Johnson (Leigh)...117
Marwood (Barrow)...115
Loughlin (St. Helens) 113
Noble (Doncaster) 110
Woods (Warrington) 107
Currier (Widnes)..107
Turner (Rochdale H.) 104

DROP GOALS

1974-75 Seabourne (Bradford N.) 10
1975-76 Hancock (Hull)....................................10
1976-77 N. Stephenson (Dewsbury) 16
1977-78 Fiddler (Bramley, Leigh) 10
1978-79 Turley (Blackpool B.) 18
1979-80 Dean (Hunslet) 18
1980-81 Walker (Whitehaven) 22
1981-82 Agar (Halifax) 17
           Donlan (Leigh) 17
1982-83 Pinner (St. Helens)................................13
1983-84 Hallett (Cardiff C.) 29
1984-85 Wood (Runcorn H.) 28
1985-86 Bishop (Warrington) 13
1986-87 Platt (Mansfield M.) 18
1987-88 W. Parker (Hull K.R.)............................15
1988-89 Pearce (Hull).....................................16

POINTS

1973-74 Watkins (Salford)................................438
1974-75 Fox (Hull K.R.)...................................333
1975-76 Watkins (Salford)................................385
1976-77 Lloyd (Castleford)................................341
1977-78 Pimblett (St. Helens)............................381
1978-79 Lloyd (Hull).......................................373
1979-80 Quinn (Featherstone R.)........................375
1980-81 Hesford (Warrington)............................310
1981-82 Hopkins (Workington T.).......................446
1982-83 Diamond (Fulham)...............................308
1983-84 Woods (Leigh)....................................355
1984-85 Day (St. Helens) 362
1985-86 C. Johnson (Leigh) 400
1986-87 Loughlin (St. Helens)............................424
1987-88 Woods (Warrington).............................351
1988-89 Aston (Sheffield E.) 307

ALL TIME RECORDS

Most goals in a match:
22 by Jim Sullivan (Wigan) v. Flimby & Fothergill (Challenge Cup), 14th February 1925

Most goals in a season:
DAVID WATKINS holds the record for most goals in a season with 221 — all for Salford — in 1972-73. Watkins played and scored a goal in every match that season as follows:

1972

Aug.	19	Leeds ....(H)	5
	23	Featherstone R. ....(A)	3
	26	Whitehaven.............................(A)	4
	28	Swinton ....(H)	1
Sept.	1	Oldham ....(LC) (H)	10
	9	Leeds.....................................(A)	2
	15	Rochdale H. ....(LC) (H)	11
	17	Leigh.....................................(A)	6
	24	Barrow...........................(JP) (A)	4
	29	Huyton ....(H)	10
Oct.	3	Oldham...........................(FT) (A)	4
	6	Wigan............................(LC) (A)	4
	8	Blackpool B. ....(A)	5
	13	Blackpool B. ....(H)	8
	21	Swinton ....(LCF)	5
Nov.	5	Huyton ....(A)	8
	10	Rochdale H. ....(H)	6
	17	Warrington ....(A)	4
	19	New Zealand..........................(H)	10
	24	Dewsbury ....(JP) (H)	4
	26	Workington T. ....(H)	6
Dec.	1	Barrow..................................(H)	9
	10	Bradford N. ....(JP) (H)	9
	13	Oldham..................................(A)	4
	15	Leigh ....(H)	3
	24	Bradford N. ....(A)	5
	26	Workington T. ....(A)	3
	30	Hull K.R. ....(JP) (A)	5

1973

Jan.	3	Bradford N............................(H)	6
	7	Rochdale H. ....(A)	2
	12	Featherstone R. ....(H)	4
	28	Featherstone R...........(RL Cup) (A)	4
Feb.	2	Whitehaven............................(H)	4
	11	Barrow..................................(A)	5
	23	St. Helens ....(H)	3
Mar.	7	Widnes..................................(A)	3
	9	Dewsbury..............................(H)	3
	16	St. Helens..............................(A)	2
	24	Leeds........................(JP Final)	2
	30	Warrington ....(H)	1
Apr.	6	Widnes ....(H)	4
	13	Oldham..................................(H)	3
	15	Dewsbury ....(A)	2

17	Wigan....................................(A)	3
20	Swinton..................................(A)	7
23	Wigan....................................(H)	3
29	Rochdale H. ....(top 16) (H)	2

	App	Gls
League	34	147
Lancs Cup..............................	4	30
John Player.............................	5	24
Tour match	1	10
RL Cup.................................	1	4
Floodlit Cup	1	4
Top 16	1	2
Totals	**47**	**221**

Fastest goals century:
Three players share the record of scoring the fastest 100 goals from the start of a season in terms of number of matches played. They are Bernard Ganley, David Watkins and Steve Quinn, who achieved the century in 18 matches.

Ganley reached 100 goals on 16 November 1957, after playing 17 matches for Oldham and one for Great Britain.

Watkins scored his 100th goal on 17 November 1972, all for Salford.

Quinn scored his 100th goal on 16 December 1979, all for Featherstone Rovers.

Most goals in a career:
JIM SULLIVAN holds the record for most goals in a career with 2,867 between 1921-22 and 1945-46. He scored a century of goals in every season after leaving Welsh Rugby Union for Wigan until the War interrupted the 1939-40 campaign.

The Test full back played all of his club rugby for Wigan apart from War-time appearances with Bradford Northern, Dewsbury and Keighley.

Sullivan's total includes 441 in representative matches, including three tours of Australasia. These figures are accepted by the Record Keepers' Club following research by James Carter and Malcolm Bentley.

Most one-point drop goals in a match:
5 by Danny Wilson (Swinton) v. Hunslet (John Player Special), 6 November 1983.
Peter Wood (Runcorn H.) v. Batley, 21 October 1984.
Paul Bishop (Warrington) at Wigan (Premiership semi-final), 11 May 1986.

Most one-point drop goals in a season:
29 by Lyn Hallett (Cardiff C.).....................1983-84

Most one-point drop goals in a career:
94 by Norman Turley (Warrington, Runcorn H., Swinton, Blackpool B., Rochdale H., Barrow, Workington T., Trafford B.) 1974-90

Most tries in a match:
11 by George West (Hull K.R.) v Brookland Rovers
Challenge Cup ....4 March 1905

Most tries in a career:
BRIAN BEVAN holds the record for most tries in a career
with 796 between 1946 and 1964. His season-by-season
record is:

1946-47	48
1947-48	57
1948-49	56
1949-50	33
1950-51	68
1951-52	51
1952-53	72
1953-54	67
1954-55	63
1955-56	57
1956-57	17
1957-58	46
1958-59	54
1959-60	40
1960-61	35
1961-62	15
1962-63	10
1963-64	7

Totals

Warrington	740
Blackpool Borough	17
Other Nationalities	26
Other representative matches	13
Grand Total	**796**

The Australian winger played his first game for
Warrington on 17 November 1945 and his last on 23 April
1962 before having two seasons at Blackpool Borough.
His last match for Borough was on 22 February, 1964.

Most tries in a season:
ALBERT ROSENFELD holds the record for most tries
in a season with 80 — all for Huddersfield — in 1913-14.

Rosenfeld's match-by-match record:
1913

Sept. 6	York	(A)	4
8	Warrington	(H)	2
13	Leeds	(H)	5
20	Halifax	(A)	1
27	Batley	(A)	0
Oct. 4	Oldham	(H)	2
11	Rochdale H.	(A)	0
18	Bramley	(YC) (H)	2
25	Dewsbury	(A)	4
Nov. 1	Halifax	(YC) (A)	2
8	Wigan	(A)	1
15	Dewsbury	(YC) (H)	3

19	Bradford N.	(H)	3
22	Leeds	(A)	3
29	Bradford N.	(Halifax, YCF)	1
Dec. 3	Halifax	(H)	3
6	Hunslet	(A)	2
13	Rochdale H.	(H)	3
20	Hull K.R.	(A)	2
25	Hull	(A)	1
26	Wakefield T.	(H)	3
27	Hunslet	(H)	0
1914			
Jan. 1	St. Helens	(A)	0
3	Warrington	(A)	0
10	York	(H)	3
17	Keighley	(A)	2
24	Dewsbury	(H)	1
31	Batley	(H)	0
Feb. 7	Oldham	(A)	0
14	Bramley	(H)	5
21	Wigan	(H)	3
28	Swinton Park R.	(RL Cup) (H)	7
Mar. 7	Wakefield T.	(A)	2
14	Hull K.R.	(RL Cup) (A)	2
18	Bramley	(A)	3
21	Widnes	(RL Cup) (H)	0
25	Keighley	(H)	3
28	Hull K.R.	(H)	1
30	Bradford N.	(A)	1
Apr. 4	Hull	(Leeds, RL Cup SF)	0
11	Hull	(H) did not play	
13	St. Helens	(H)	0
20	Hull	(Play-off) (H) did not play	
25	Salford	(Leeds, Championship final)	0

	App	Tries
League	33	63
Yorks Cup	4	8
RL Cup	4	9
Play Off	1	0
Totals	**42**	**80**

Most points in a season:
LEWIS JONES holds the record for most points in a
season with 496 from 194 goals and 36 tries for Leeds and
representative teams in 1956-57.

Jones' match-by-match record:

For Leeds
1956

			Gls	Tries	Pts
Aug. 17	Halifax	(H)	3	0	6
22	Bradford N.	(A)	11	3	31
25	Wigan	(A)	4	0	8
27	Featherstone R.	(H)	4	1	11
Sept. 1	Wakefield	(YC) (A)	3	1	9
8	Dewsbury	(A)	6	0	12
15	Warrington	(H)	7	0	14
22	Huddersfield	(A)	3	0	6
29	York	(H)	6	0	12

Oct.	6	Batley.........................(A)	4	2	14
	13	Australia.....................(H)	Did not play		
	20	Hull K.R. ....(A)	Did not play		
	27	Wigan ....(H)	2	0	4
Nov.	3	Hunslet ....(A)	1	0	2
	10	Barrow ....(H)	3	2	12
	17	Halifax ....(A)	4	0	8
	24	Keighley.....................(H)	3	3	15
Dec.	1	Barrow ....(A)	4	0	8
	8	Bramley......................(A)	5	0	10
	15	Doncaster ....(H)	1	2	8
	22	Bradford N (abandoned) (H)	1	1	5
	25	Batley ....(H)	8	1	19
	29	Keighley ....(A)	3	0	6
1957					
Jan.	5	Hull ....(H)	5	2	16
	12	Warrington...................(A)	0	3	9
	19	St. Helens...................(H)	5	1	13
	26	Doncaster....................(A)	Did not play		
Feb.	2	Huddersfield ....(H)	6	0	12
	9	Wigan ....(RL Cup) (H)	2	1	7
	16	York ....(A)	7	1	17
	23	Warrington....(RL Cup) (H)	5	1	13
	27	Castleford ....(H)	4	1	11
Mar.	9	Halifax ....(RL Cup) (A)	5	0	10
	16	Wakefield T. ....(H)	5	1	13
	20	Bradford N ....(H)	5	1	13
	23	Hull ....(A)	2	0	4
	30	Whitehaven			
		.........(Odsal, RL Cup SF)	1	0	2
Apr.	3	Wakefield T. ....(A)	3	0	6
	6	St. Helens...................(A)	0	0	0
	12	Hull K.R.....................(H)	Did not play		
	13	Dewsbury ....(H)	6	2	18
	19	Hunslet ....(H)	5	2	16
	20	Featherstone R.............(A)	2	0	4
	22	Castleford...................(A)	2	0	4
	23	Bramley......................(H)	7	1	17
May	4	Oldham ....(Play-off) (A)	3	0	6
	11	Barrow			
		...(Wembley, RL Cup final)	0	0	0

Representative matches
For Great Britain:

Jan.	26	France..............(at Leeds)	9	1	21
Mar.	3	France..........(at Toulouse)	5	1	13
Apr.	10	France.........(at St. Helens)	7	1	17

For The Rest:

Oct.	3	Britain XIII .....(at Bradford)	4	0	8

For RL XIII:

Oct.	29	Australia................(Leigh)	3	0	6

	App	Gls	Tries	Pts
League	36	147	30	384
RL Cup.............................	5	13	2	32
Yorks Cup............................	1	3	1	9
Play-off..............................	1	3	0	6
Representative......................	5	28	3	65
Totals	**48**	**194**	**36**	**496**

Most points in a match:
53 (11t, 10g) by George West (Hull K.R.) v. Brookland Rovers (RL Cup)..............................4 March, 1905

Most points in a career:
NEIL FOX holds the record for most points in a career with 6,220 between 1956 and 1979. This total does not include points scored during a spell of club rugby in New Zealand.

Fox was a month short of his 17th birthday when he made his debut for Wakefield Trinity on 10 April, 1956. Apart from a brief time at Bradford Northern Fox had 19 seasons at Wakefield before moving to a succession of clubs in later years.

After a long career as an international centre Fox moved into the forwards and played his last professional match for Bradford in their opening fixture of the 1979-80 season, on 19 August. That match enabled him to join the elite few who have played first team rugby at 40 years of age.

Fox's season-by-season tally is as follows:

	Gls	Tries	Pts
1955-56..............................	6	0	12
1956-57..............................	54	10	138
1957-58..............................	124	32	344
1958-59..............................	148	28	380
1959-60....:........................	171	37	453
1960-61..............................	94	20	248
1961-62..............................	183	30	456
1962 Tour			
Australasia...........................	85	19	227
South Africa	19	4	50
1962-63..............................	125	14	292
1963-64..............................	125	21	313
1964-65..............................	121	13	281
1965-66..............................	98	11	229
1966-67..............................	144	16	336
1967-68..............................	98	18	250
1968-69..............................	95	9	217
1969-70..............................	17	5	49
1970-71..............................	110	12	256
1971-72..............................	84	6	186
1972-73..............................	138	8	300
1973-74..............................	62	8	148
1974-75..............................	146(1)	14	333
1975-76..............................	102(1)	4	215
1976-77..............................	79(1)	6	175
1977-78..............................	95(1)	9	216
1978-79..............................	50	4	112
1979-80..............................	2	0	4

A breakdown of Fox's club and representative totals is as follows:

	App	Gls	Tries	Pts
Wakefield T.	574	1,836	272	4,488
Bradford N.	70	85(1)	12	205
Hull K.R.	59	212(2)	16	470
York.......................	13	42	2	90
Bramley...................	23	73	6	164
Huddersfield..............	21	73(1)	5	160
Club Totals	**760**	**2,321(4)**	**313**	**5,577**
				(cont)

131

Yorkshire..................	17	60	9	147
Britain v. Australia	8	26	3	61
New Zealand.	4	11	1	25
France.........	17	56	10	142
Other representative games including tour	22	101	22	268
Representative Totals.	**68**	**254**	**45**	**643**
Grand Totals	**828**	**2,575(4)**	**358**	**6,220**

( ) Figures in brackets are one point drop goals included in total.

Score-a-match:
The following players have appeared and scored in all of their club's matches in one season:

Jim Hoey (Widnes) 1932-33
Billy Langton (Hunslet) 1958-59
Stuart Ferguson (Leigh) 1970-71
David Watkins (Salford)..............................1972-73
David Watkins (Salford)..............................1973-74
John Woods (Leigh)....................................1977-78
Steve Quinn (Featherstone R.) 1979-80
Mick Parrish (Hunslet) 1979-80
John Gorton (Swinton)................................1980-81
Mick Parrish (Oldham) 1981-82
Peter Wood (Runcorn H.) 1984-85
David Noble (Doncaster)............................1986-87
Mark Aston (Sheffield E.) 1988-89
Mike Fletcher (Hull K.R.) 1989-90

Longest scoring run:
DAVID WATKINS holds the record for the longest scoring run, playing and scoring in 92 consecutive matches for Salford from 19 August 1972 to 25 April 1974. He totalled 403 goals, 41 tries and 929 points.

Longest run of appearances:
KEITH ELWELL holds the record for the longest run of appearances with one club with a total of 239 for Widnes. The consecutive run started at Wembley in the 1977 Challenge Cup final against Leeds on 7 May, and ended after he played in a Lancashire Cup-tie at home to St. Helens on 5 September 1982. He was dropped for the match at Featherstone Rovers a week later. Although he went on as a substitute the record refers to full appearances only.

Elwell played as a substitute in the next match and then made a full appearance before his run of all appearances ended at 242.

Highest score:
Huddersfield 119 v. Swinton Park 2 (RL Cup)
.......28 February 1914

Most points in all matches in a season:
1,436 by Leigh from 43 matches in 1985-86 as follows:
34 Division Two matches 1,156
2 Lancashire Cup 54
4 John Player Special Trophy 161
3 RL Challenge Cup 65

Most League points in a season:
1,156 by Leigh from 34 Division Two matches in 1985-86.

Longest winning run:
29 by Wigan from February to October 1987, as follows:
20 Division One, 3 Premiership, 4 Lancashire Cup, 1 Charity Shield and 1 World Club Challenge.

Longest unbeaten run:
38 Cup and League matches by Huddersfield in 1914-15, including three draws. After the interruption by the First World War Huddersfield won their next five competitive matches — 4 Yorkshire Cup ties in 1918-19 and the opening league match of 1919-20.

Longest winning run in the League:
31 matches by Wigan. Last 8 matches of 1969-70 and first 23 of 1970-71.
● In 1978-79 Hull won all of their 26 Division Two matches, the only time a club has won all its league matches in one season.

Longest losing run:
41 Cup and League matches by Runcorn Highfield since an 8-8 Division Two home draw against Workington Town on 22 January 1989. Made up of 37 Division Two, 2 Challenge Cup, 1 Regal Trophy, 1 Lancashire Cup.

Longest run without a win:
52 Cup and League matches by Runcorn Highfield since a 20-12 Division Two home win over Fulham on 30 October 1988. Including one draw and made up as follows: 47 Division Two, 2 Challenge Cup, 2 Regal Trophy, 1 Lancashire Cup.

Longest League losing run:
40 Division Two matches by Doncaster between November 1975 and April 1977.

Longest League run without a win:
47 by Runcorn Highfield since a 20-12 Division Two home win over Fulham on 30 October 1988.

● Only two teams have lost all their matches in a season: Liverpool City and Runcorn Highfield.
In 1906-07 Liverpool City lost all 30 of their league matches. Liverpool also lost their two cup ties and dropped out after only one season. They did manage a home league draw against Bramley, but when they were unable to fulfil a return fixture the match was expunged from league records.
In 1989-90 Runcorn Highfield lost all 28 of their league matches, plus three cup ties.

Cup of joy . . . for 1990 Lance Todd Trophy winner Andy Gregory, also celebrating a record fifth victory at Wembley.

RUGBY LEAGUE CHALLENGE CUP

1990 Final

Cup Kings Wigan returned to their second home, Wembley, to launch an assault on both opponents Warrington and the record books.

The relentless Riversiders became the first side to lift the coveted Silk Cut Challenge Cup for a third successive time, a triple trophy success in the season adding to the Stones Bitter Championship and the Regal Trophy.

The 36-14 demolition of Warrington, struck by nerves after a 15-year absence from the twin towers, fell only two points short of the Wembley record score by Wakefield Trinity in 1960.

Having battled all week to overcome serious injury threats to Test men Ellery Hanley, Joe Lydon, Kevin Iro, Andy Platt and others, Wigan took full advantage of Warrington's nervousness in a disastrous opening 35 minutes before turning on full throttle to take their tally of scoring in the Wembley treble to a remarkable 95 points, conceding only 26.

Wembley records were breached as often as the Wire's defence as Rugby League's first all-seater crowd were regularly brought to their feet with a powerful, professional display on both attack and defence.

The Riversiders became the most successful side in Challenge Cup history with their 11th victory, extending the records for most finals to 20 and most at Wembley to 16, including a record 10 wins.

Andy Gregory cast aside the prospects of a summer operation on a groin injury which had cost him a tour Down Under by becoming the first player to win the Lance Todd Trophy twice at Wembley, giving him a special place ahead of Gerry Helme as the second of the former Warrington scrum half's Man of the Match awards was for the 1954 replay at Odsal Stadium, Bradford.

Gregory gathered further Wembley fame by collecting a record fifth winner's medal, including two with Widnes with whom he also played in a drawn 1982 final. Six appearances at Wembley without tasting defeat is a just testimony to his big match temperament.

New Zealand centre Kevin Iro scored two tries for the third successive year, his record tally of six Wembley touchdowns being twice as many as any other player in the stadium's Challenge Cup final history. Runner-up for the Lance Todd Trophy, Iro had another try disallowed, robbing him of the distinction of being the first player to score a hat-trick at Wembley.

If the record books reflected deeds of bravery, Wigan's Shaun Edwards would have earned immediate entry. After pre-match injections for a broken hand, the stand-off received a facial injury in the 10th minute. Edwards refused to come off until a few minutes from the end to learn that he had suffered a double fracture of the eye socket and a depressed cheekbone, ruling him out of the British Coal tour to Papua New Guinea and New Zealand.

Central Park skipper Ellery Hanley also passed through the pain barrier to lift the Cup for the second time after a week-long stay in a London clinic for treatment on a pelvic injury which had stopped him training and forced him to relinquish the tour captaincy.

Warrington also provided central characters in the Wembley drama. Robbed of a semi-final appearance by a domestic accident on the morning of the match, scrum half Paul Bishop overcame a nightmare start to his Wembley debut, missing two comfortable penalty goal attempts before hitting the target twice, the second after creating the space for skipper Mike Gregory to power his way over for a 39th minute try to cut the interval scoreline to 16-8.

On the hour, Bishop's growing influence was halted by a bone-jarring tackle from Joe Lydon which flattened the half back, who was helped off with concussion.

Mike Gregory played a captain's role in his best performance of the season, scoring Warrington's first touchdown and creating the 70th minute consolation try for full back David Lyon, breaking from the base of the scrum to send him on a 40-yard run to the line. Aggravation of a season-long Achilles' heel injury left him facing both Wembley disappointment and the prospect of crying off the tour.

Both of Wigan's first half tries, from Denis Betts and Mark Preston, came from kicking mistakes by Warrington, whose fierce opening onslaught of tackles fully tested the Cup-holders' injury risk policy.

Lydon's fourth goal in the 37th minute put Wigan ahead 16-2 with a now traditional air of inevitability and, although Mike Gregory's try on the stroke of half-time added interest, a 15-minute spell brought three tries from Preston, Iro and Hanley to take Wigan clear at 32-8 with a quarter of an hour remaining.

It was during the uncertain opening period that scrum half Andy Gregory laid the foundations for his Man of the Match rating. His prompting and probing helped Wigan gain total control, while keeping things ticking over smoothly as they moved into top gear after the break. Then Hanley and Iro unleashed powerful, damaging runs on a tiring Wire defence.

Other Wigan star performers were full back Steve Hampson, forceful Kiwi centre Dean Bell and prop forward Andy Platt, playing his first full game for six weeks after a knee injury. Lydon was on target with six goals.

A crowd of nearly 78,000 paid a world record £1,360,000 to witness Wigan's record-breaking success. With a scoring average of 32 points a match during the three-year span, the punters were left pining for only one element. . . a competitive challenge to Rugby League's version of the Liverpool soccer machine.

Warrington scrum half Paul Bishop before suffering concussion after a 60th minute Joe Lydon tackle.

SILK CUT CHALLENGE CUP FINAL
28 April   **Wembley**
WIGAN 36   **WARRINGTON 14**

Steve Hampson	1.	David Lyon
Joe Lydon	2.	Des Drummond
Kevin Iro	3.	Gary Mercer
Dean Bell	4.	Paul Darbyshire
Mark Preston	5.	Mark Forster
Shaun Edwards	6.	Martin Crompton
Andy Gregory	7.	Paul Bishop
Adrian Shelford	8.	Tony Burke
Martin Dermott	9.	Duane Mann
Andy Platt	10.	Neil Harmon
Denis Betts	11.	Bob Jackson
Andy Goodway	12.	Gary Sanderson
Ellery Hanley, Capt	13.	Mike Gregory, Capt
Bobby Goulding	14.	Billy McGinty
Ian Gildart	15.	Mark Thomas

T: Iro (2), Preston (2), Betts,
    Hanley
G: Lydon (6)
Substitutions:
Goulding for Dermott (31 min.)
Gildart for Preston (70 min.)
Half-time: 16-8
Referee: John Holdsworth (Kippax)

T: M. Gregory, Lyon
G: Bishop (2), Darbyshire
Substitutions:
Thomas for Jackson (35 min.)
McGinty for Bishop (61 min.)
Attendance: 77,729
Receipts: £1,360,000

Scorechart

Minute	Score		Wigan	Warrington
11:	Lydon (P)		2	0
22:	Betts (T)			
	Lydon (G)		8	0
25:	Bishop (P)		8	2
34:	Preston (T)			
	Lydon (G)		14	2
37:	Lydon (P)		16	2
39:	M. Gregory (T)			
	Bishop (G)		16	8
49:	Iro (T)			
	Lydon (G)		22	8
53:	Preston (T)		26	8
64:	Hanley (T)			
	Lydon (G)		32	8
70:	Lyon (T)			
	Darbyshire (G)		32	14
77:	Iro (T)		36	14
	Scrums		8	8
	Penalties		5	10

Wigan tryscorer Ellery Hanley.

1990 Round by Round

The six-tie preliminary round draw brought calls for seeding as it meant two top sides must drop out before the first round. Scrum half Paul Harkin was the architect of Bradford Northern's 24-8 success at Leeds as he scored one of Northern's four tries after a month's absence through illness. In the other all-First Division encounter, St. Helens, under caretaker-coach Shane Cooper, hammered Castleford 39-12. Fielding Cup deadline £150,000 signing Lee Crooks, Castleford were taken apart by teenage scrum half Sean Devine, who amassed 22 points to take the Silk Cut Award. Led by former Great Britain forward Trevor Skerrett, Leeds amateur side Bison disposed of Cumbrian Cup winners Millom 4-0, while Lancashire amateurs Thatto Heath fell to Batley 45-2 at St. Helens, the Second Division side running in nine tries with forward Paul Gearey claiming a hat-trick. Fulham recovered from a 16-11 deficit with 10 minutes left of their home tie with Doncaster to record a 23-16 success. Oldham, reduced to 12 men after the sending off of Keith Atkinson 17 minutes from the end, scored three tries in the final minutes to register a flattering 30-8 triumph over visiting Huddersfield.

In the first round, holders Wigan survived a scare at Second Division leaders Hull K.R., the only try of the match, from winger David Marshall, helping secure a 6-4 victory. In the televised tie at Wilderspool, Warrington held off a brave comeback by Featherstone Rovers to win 20-12. An inept first half performance saw the Colliers trailing 17-0 at the break before pulling back to 17-12. Second Division Whitehaven pulled off the shock of the round with a 23-22 home success over First Division Leigh. The Cumbrians led 18-4 before a pair of David Ruane tries eased Leigh to within two points, the scoreline moving to 22-all

before Australian James Ward hit the winning drop goal in the dying minutes. Regal Trophy finalists Halifax, without six regulars through injury, conceded eight tries at Hull in a 46-0 defeat.

Bottom of the table Runcorn Highfield, without a win for over a year, made Yorkshire Cup winners Bradford Northern work hard for a 22-12 away victory. Sheffield Eagles recorded their fourth success at Craven Park in 10 months with a 22-12 defeat of Barrow. Struggling Nottingham City were beaten 32-2 by visitors Dewsbury, Dennis Bailey grabbing two tries. Second Division Batley were not outclassed on their visit to World Club Champions Widnes, going down 26-10 with second row man Gearey continuing his consecutive scoring run with two tries.

St. Helens had to work hard for a 22-14 win at Bramley after pulling away 16-0 early in the second half. Bramley rallied to 16-14 with tries from Calvin Hopkins and Lex Neal, plus three Steve Carroll goals. Amateurs Bison did not concede a penalty for foul play in a 56-6 trouncing at First Division Salford, who led 28-0 at the break. A quagmire at Moss Lane turned the Trafford Borough and Hunslet tie into a lottery, Borough's Darren Abrams being the match winner in a 14-7 success. Centre John Henderson contributed a hat-trick of tries in Oldham's 30-8 victory over visitors Workington Town.

Keighley gained a hard-fought 12-6 success at Chorley, their tries coming from Keith Dixon and Gary Coulter, while at Rochdale the Hornets ran in five tries in the last 20 minutes to secure a 38-6 victory over Carlisle.

Fulham centre Mike Taylor scored his second try to draw level with visitors Ryedale-York in the Chiswick encounter, the score finishing 14-all. Wakefield Trinity squandered an early 10-0 lead at Second Division Swinton, who earned a replay with a last minute try from Shane Tupaea, goalled by full back Paul Topping to level at 10-10.

In the replays, Fulham sprang the shock of the round by winning at Ryedale-York 16-12 with a display of basic rugby against the off-form Yorkshiremen. At Belle Vue, visitors Swinton were the better side in the opening quarter before Wakefield Trinity pulled clear for a 32-4 success, highlighted by a Silk Cut Award performance from scrum half Mark Conway, scorer of a try and six goals.

In the second round, Second Division pacemakers Oldham travelled to First Division strugglers Salford to pull off an 18-7 success, their first Challenge Cup victory over the Red Devils for 63 years. Warrington prevented a similar shock by staging a second half rally in the home tie with Trafford Borough who led 7-6 at the break before going down 20-11. Wigan also entertained Second Division opponents, Maurice Bamford's Dewsbury holding the title favourites 2-0 into the second half. The Riversiders brought on Test stars Joe Lydon and Andy Gregory, to inspire a spell of three tries in 14 minutes towards a 30-6 win. Second Division tabletoppers Rochdale Hornets visited Division One title holders Widnes to pull back from 16-6 down and level the scores at 16-16 at the interval with tries from Martin Hall and Mark Wilson. Winger Martin Offiah ended their giant-killing hopes with a decisive 53rd minute touchdown in a 22-16 win.

Bradford Northern's Welsh winger Gerald Cordle finished Fulham's Cup hopes with a hat-trick of tries in a 20-2 away win. In the televised tie, Hull went down 24-12 at home to St. Helens, New Zealand coach Mike McClennan taking charge of his first British cup tie. Rival skippers Noel Cleal and Shane Cooper both played after being declared unfit, the New Zealander earned the Silk Cut Award with a masterful performance.

Wakefield Trinity gained revenge for a league double defeat from Sheffield Eagles with a 27-12 home victory. The Eagles led 6-0 after six minutes before Trinity ran in five tries. Keighley never looked like mastering the monsoon-like conditions at Whitehaven, especially after losing injured pack duo Gary Coulter and Warwick Badger, the Cumbrians' 46-10 win including eight tries.

Oldham sprung the shock of the third round with a 16-4 success at Widnes, who led 4-0 from two Jonathan Davies penalty goals before Keith Newton replied with a try against his old club. Fellow Widnes old boy Duncan Platt added four goals, centre John Henderson's second half touchdown sealing an Oldham victory. In the televised tie, Wigan equalled the Challenge Cup record of 13 consecutive wins by winning 26-14 at Wakefield Trinity. Trinity were badly hit when Ray Price was stretchered off with a back injury in the 37th minute as Wigan led only 12-10. Bradford Northern scored two tries to one at home to Warrington but went down 12-10. St. Helens ran in eight tries in a 44-10 home rout of Second Division Whitehaven, Alan Hunte and Paul Loughlin each collecting two tries, the latter adding six goals for a 20-point tally.

In the semi-finals, St. Helens were denied a replay with only 75 seconds left by the brilliance of Wigan skipper Ellery Hanley. At 14-14 Hanley beat four men before sending Andy Goodway between the posts. Lydon added a goal for a dramatic 20-14 success. Three weeks later Second Division Oldham were denied a similar finish as Warrington held on for a 10-6 win. Warrington's second half display was inspired by substitute Mark Thomas, who created tries for Martin Crompton and Mark Forster. Oldham had a last minute touchdown turned down by referee John Holdsworth who ruled winger Paul Lord to have been offside from a kick through by scrum half Mike Ford, winner of the Silk Cut Award.

1990 PRIZES

Round	Per Team			Total
Preliminary	12	×	£2,000	£24,000
First	16	×	£2,000	£32,000
Second	8	×	£3,250	£26,000
Third	4	×	£5,000	£20,000
Semi-Finals	2	×	£8,500	£17,000
Runners-up	1	×	£16,000	£16,000
Winners	1	×	£30,000	£30,000

Total Prize Money	£165,000
Capital Development Fund	£110,000
Grand Total	£275,000

1990 RESULTS

Preliminary Round

Fulham	23	Doncaster	16
Leeds	8	Bradford N.	24
Millom	0	Bison	4
Oldham	30	Huddersfield	8
St. Helens	39	Castleford	12
Thatto Heath	2	Batley	45

First Round

Barrow	12	Sheffield E.	22
Bramley	14	St. Helens	22
Chorley	6	Keighley	12
Fulham	14	Ryedale-York	14
Hull	46	Halifax	0
Hull K. R.	4	Wigan	6
Nottingham C.	2	Dewsbury	32
Oldham	30	Workington T.	8
Rochdale H.	38	Carlisle	6
Runcorn H.	12	Bradford N.	22
Salford	56	Bison	6
Swinton	10	Wakefield T.	10
Trafford B.	14	Hunslet	7
Warrington	20	Featherstone R.	12
Whitehaven	23	Leigh	22
Widnes	26	Batley	10

Replays

Ryedale-York	12	Fulham	16
Wakefield T.	32	Swinton	4

Second Round

Fulham	2	Bradford N.	20
Hull	12	St. Helens	24
Salford	7	Oldham	18
Wakefield T.	27	Sheffield E.	12
Warrington	20	Trafford B.	11
Whitehaven	46	Keighley	10
Widnes	22	Rochdale H.	16
Wigan	30	Dewsbury	6

Third Round

Bradford N.	10	Warrington	12
St. Helens	44	Whitehaven	10
Wakefield T.	14	Wigan	26
Widnes	4	Oldham	16

Semi-Finals

Wigan (at Man. Utd. FC)	20	St. Helens	14
Warrington (at Wigan)	10	Oldham	6

Final

Wigan (at Wembley)	36	Warrington	14

Wigan prop forward Adrian Shelford in 1990 Wembley action.

CHALLENGE CUP ROLL OF HONOUR

Year	Winners		Runners-up		Venue	Attendance	Receipts
1897	Batley	10	St Helens	3	Leeds	13,492	£624.17.7
1898	Batley	7	Bradford	0	Leeds	27,941	£1,586.3.0
1899	Oldham	19	Hunslet	9	Manchester	15,763	£946.16.0
1900	Swinton	16	Salford	8	Manchester	17,864	£1,100.0.0
1901	Batley	6	Warrington	0	Leeds	29,563	£1,644.16.0
1902	Broughton R.	25	Salford	0	Rochdale	15,006	£846.11.0
1903	Halifax	7	Salford	0	Leeds	32,507	£1,834.8.6
1904	Halifax	8	Warrington	3	Salford	17,041	£936.5.6
1905	Warrington	6	Hull K.R.	0	Leeds	19,638	£1,271.18.0
1906	Bradford	5	Salford	0	Leeds	15,834	£920.0.0
1907	Warrington	17	Oldham	3	Broughton	18,500	£1,010.0.0
1908	Hunslet	14	Hull	0	Huddersfield	18,000	£903.0.0
1909	Wakefield T.	17	Hull	0	Leeds	23,587	£1,490.0.0
1910	Leeds	7	Hull	7	Huddersfield	19,413	£1,102.0.0
Replay	Leeds	26	Hull	12	Huddersfield	11,608	£657.0.0
1911	Broughton R.	4	Wigan	0	Salford	8,000	£376.0.0
1912	Dewsbury	8	Oldham	5	Leeds	15,271	£853.0.0
1913	Huddersfield	9	Warrington	5	Leeds	22,754	£1,446.9.6
1914	Hull	6	Wakefield T.	0	Halifax	19,000	£1,035.5.0
1915	Huddersfield	37	St. Helens	3	Oldham	8,000	£472.0.0
1920	Huddersfield	21	Wigan	10	Leeds	14,000	£1,936.0.0
1921	Leigh	13	Halifax	0	Broughton	25,000	£2,700.0.0
1922	Rochdale H.	10	Hull	9	Leeds	32,596	£2,964.0.0
1923	Leeds	28	Hull	3	Wakefield	29,335	£2,390.0.0
1924	Wigan	21	Oldham	4	Rochdale	41,831	£3,712.0.0
1925	Oldham	16	Hull K.R.	3	Leeds	28,335	£2,879.0.0
1926	Swinton	9	Oldham	3	Rochdale	27,000	£2,551.0.0
1927	Oldham	26	Swinton	7	Wigan	33,448	£3,170.0.0
1928	Swinton	5	Warrington	3	Wigan	33,909	£3,158.1.11
1929	Wigan	13	Dewsbury	2	Wembley	41,500	£5,614.0.0
1930	Widnes	10	St. Helens	3	Wembley	36,544	£3,102.0.0
1931	Halifax	22	York	8	Wembley	40,368	£3,908.0.0
1932	Leeds	11	Swinton	8	Wigan	29,000	£2,479.0.0
1933	Huddersfield	21	Warrington	17	Wembley	41,874	£6,465.0.0
1934	Hunslet	11	Widnes	5	Wembley	41,280	£6,686.0.0
1935	Castleford	11	Huddersfield	8	Wembley	39,000	£5,533.0.0
1936	Leeds	18	Warrington	2	Wembley	51,250	£7,070.0.0
1937	Widnes	18	Keighley	5	Wembley	47,699	£6,704.0.0
1938	Salford	7	Barrow	4	Wembley	51,243	£7,174.0.0
1939	Halifax	20	Salford	3	Wembley	55,453	£7,681.0.0
1940	*No competition*						
1941	Leeds	19	Halifax	2	Bradford	28,500	£1,703.0.0
1942	Leeds	15	Halifax	10	Bradford	15,250	£1,276.0.0
1943	Dewsbury	16	Leeds	9	Dewsbury	10,470	£823.0.0
	Dewsbury		Leeds	6	Leeds	16,000	£1,521.0.0
	Dewsbury won on aggregate 16-15						
1944	Bradford	0	Wigan	3	Wigan	22,000	£1,640.0.0
	Bradford	8	Wigan	0	Bradford	30,000	£2,200.0.0
	Bradford won on aggregate 8-3						
1945	Huddersfield	7	Bradford N.	4	Huddersfield	9,041	£1,184.3.7
	Huddersfield	6	Bradford N.	5	Bradford	17,500	£2,050.0.0
	Huddersfield won on aggregate 13-9						

Year	Winners		Runners-up		Venue	Attendance	Receipts
1946	Wakefield T.	13	Wigan	12	Wembley	54,730	£12,013.13.6
1947	Bradford N.	8	Leeds	4	Wembley	77,605	£17,434.5.0
1948	Wigan	8	Bradford N.	3	Wembley	91,465	£21,121.9.9
1949	Bradford N.	12	Halifax	0	Wembley	*95,050	£21,930.5.0
1950	Warrington	19	Widnes	0	Wembley	94,249	£24,782.13.0
1951	Wigan	10	Barrow	0	Wembley	94,262	£24,797.19.0
1952	Workington T.	18	Featherstone R.	10	Wembley	72,093	£22,374.2.0
1953	Huddersfield	15	St. Helens	10	Wembley	89,588	£30,865.12.3
1954	Warrington	4	Halifax	4	Wembley	81,841	£29,706.7.3
Replay	Warrington	8	Halifax	4	Bradford	102,569	£18,623.7.0
1955	Barrow	21	Workington T.	12	Wembley	66,513	£27,453.16.0
1956	St. Helens	13	Halifax	2	Wembley	79,341	£29,424.7.6
1957	Leeds	9	Barrow	7	Wembley	76,318	£32,671.14.3
1958	Wigan	13	Workington T.	9	Wembley	66,109	£33,175.17.6
1959	Wigan	30	Hull	13	Wembley	79,811	£35,718.19.9
1960	Wakefield T.	38	Hull	5	Wembley	79,773	£35,754.16.0
1961	St. Helens	12	Wigan	6	Wembley	94,672	£38,479.11.9
1962	Wakefield T.	12	Huddersfield	6	Wembley	81,263	£33,390.18.4
1963	Wakefield T.	25	Wigan	10	Wembley	84,492	£44,521.17.0
1964	Widnes	13	Hull K.R.	5	Wembley	84,488	£44,840.19.0
1965	Wigan	20	Hunslet	16	Wembley	89,016	£48,080.4.0
1966	St. Helens	21	Wigan	2	Wembley	*98,536	£50,409.0.0
1967	Featherstone R.	17	Barrow	12	Wembley	76,290	£53,465.14.0
1968	Leeds	11	Wakefield T.	10	Wembley	87,100	£56,171.16.6
1969	Castleford	11	Salford	6	Wembley	*97,939	£58,848.1.0
1970	Castleford	7	Wigan	2	Wembley	95,255	£89,262.2.0
1971	Leigh	24	Leeds	7	Wembley	85,514	£84,452.15
1972	St. Helens	16	Leeds	13	Wembley	89,495	£86,414.30
1973	Featherstone R.	33	Bradford N.	14	Wembley	72,395	£125,826.40
1974	Warrington	24	Featherstone R.	9	Wembley	77,400	£132,021.05
1975	Widnes	14	Warrington	7	Wembley	85,098	£140,684.45
1976	St. Helens	20	Widnes	5	Wembley	89,982	£190,129.40
1977	Leeds	16	Widnes	7	Wembley	80,871	£241,488.00
1978	Leeds	14	St. Helens	12	Wembley	*96,000	£330,575.00
1979	Widnes	12	Wakefield T.	3	Wembley	94,218	£383,157.00
1980	Hull K.R.	10	Hull	5	Wembley	*95,000	£448,202.90
1981	Widnes	18	Hull K.R.	9	Wembley	92,496	£591,117.00
1982	Hull	14	Widnes	14	Wembley	92,147	£684,500.00
Replay	Hull	18	Widnes	9	Elland Rd., L'ds	41,171	£180,525.00
1983	Featherstone R.	14	Hull	12	Wembley	84,969	£655,510.00
1984	Widnes	19	Wigan	6	Wembley	80,116	£686,171.00
1985	Wigan	28	Hull	24	Wembley	*97,801	£760,322.00
1986	Castleford	15	Hull K.R.	14	Wembley	82,134	£806,676.00
1987	Halifax	19	St. Helens	18	Wembley	91,267	£1,009,206.00
1988	Wigan	32	Halifax	12	Wembley	*94,273	£1,102,247.00
1989	Wigan	27	St. Helens	0	Wembley	*78,000	£1,121,293.00
1990	Wigan	36	Warrington	14	Wembley	*77,729	£1,360,000.00

*Indicates a capacity attendance, the limit being fixed annually taking into account variable factors.

RUGBY LEAGUE CHALLENGE CUP .... A REVIEW

1967-68
Leeds 11 Risman (4g); Alan Smith, Hynes, Watson, Atkinson (1t); Shoebottom, Seabourne; Clark, Crosby, K. Eyre, Ramsey, A. Eyre, Batten
Wakefield T. 10 Cooper, Hirst (2t), Brooke, Coetzer, Batty; Poynton, Owen; Jeanes, Shepherd, D. Fox (2g), Haigh, McLeod, Hawley
Referee: J.P. Hebblethwaite (York)

1968-69
Castleford 11 Edwards; Briggs, Howe (1t), Thomas, Lowndes; Hardisty (1t), Hepworth (1t); Hartley, C. Dickinson, J. Ward, Redfearn (1g), Lockwood, Reilly
Salford 6 K. Gwilliam; Burgess, Whitehead, Hesketh, Jackson; Watkins, Brennan; Ogden, Dickens, Bott, Coulman, Dixon, Hill (3g)
Referee: D.S. Brown (Preston)

1969-70
Castleford 7 Edwards; Briggs, Thomas, Stenton, Lowndes (1t); Hardisty (Hargrave), Hepworth; Hartley, C. Dickinson, Redfearn (2g), Kirkbride, Lockwood, Reilly
Wigan 2 Tyrer (1g) (C. Hill); Jones, Francis, Rowe, Kevin O'Loughlin; D. Hill, Parr; Ashcroft, Burdell, Hogan, Ashurst, D. Robinson, Laughton
Referee: G.F. Lindop (Wakefield)

1970-71
Leigh 24 Eckersley (1t, 1g); Ferguson (5g), Dorrington (1t), Collins, Walsh; A. Barrow, Murphy (2g) (L. Chisnall); Watts, Ashcroft, Fiddler (1g), Grimes, Clarkson, Smethurst
Leeds 7 Holmes (2g); Langley, Hynes, Cowan (Dyl), Atkinson; Wainwright (1t), Seabourne; J. Burke, Fisher, Barnard, Hick, Haigh, Ramsey
Referee: W.H. Thompson (Huddersfield)

1971-72
St. Helens 16 G. Pimblett; L. Jones (1t), Benyon, Walsh, Wilson; K. Kelly, Heaton; Rees (1t), Greenall, J. Stephens, Mantle, E. Chisnall, Coslett (5g)
Leeds 13 Holmes; Alan Smith, Hynes (Langley), Dyl, Atkinson; Hardisty, Hepworth; Clawson (5g), Fisher, Ramsey, Cookson (1t), Haigh, Batten
Referee: E. Lawrinson (Warrington)

1972-73
Featherstone R. 33 C. Kellett (8g); Coventry, M. Smith (1t) (Hartley) (1t), Newlove (2t), K. Kellett; Mason, Nash (1g); Tonks, Bridges, Farrar (1t), Rhodes (Hollis), Thompson, Stone
Bradford N. 14 Tees (4g); Lamb, Stockwell, Watson, D. Redfearn (1t); Blacker (Treasure), Seabourne; Hogan, Dunn, Earl (Long), Joyce, W. Pattinson, Fearnley (1t)
Referee: M.J. Naughton (Widnes)

1973-74
Warrington 24 Whitehead (7g); M. Philbin, Noonan, Whittle, Bevan; Murphy (2g) (Pickup), Gordon; D. Chisnall, Ashcroft (1t), Brady (Wanbon), Wright, Nicholas (1t), B. Philbin
Featherstone R. 9 Box (3g); Dyas, M. Smith, Hartley, Bray; Newlove (1t), Nash; Tonks, Bridges, Harris, Rhodes (Busfield), Thompson (Stone), Bell
Referee: S. Shepherd (Oldham)

1974-75
Widnes 14 Dutton (5g, 1dg); A. Prescott, George, Aspey, Anderson; Hughes, Bowden; Mills (1t), Elwell, Sheridan, Foran, Adams, Laughton
Warrington 7 Whitehead (2g); M. Philbin, Noonan, Reynolds (W. Briggs), Bevan (1t); Whittle, Gordon; D. Chisnall, Ashcroft, Wanbon, Conroy, Martyn (Nicholas), B. Philbin
Referee: P. Geraghty (York)

1975-76
St. Helens 20 G. Pimblett (3g, 2dg); L. Jones, Cunningham (1t), Noonan, Mathias; Benyon (Glynn 2t), Heaton (1t); Mantle (James), A. Karalius, Coslett, Nicholls, E. Chisnall, Hull
Widnes 5 Dutton (2g); A. Prescott (D. O'Neill) Hughes, George, Jenkins; Eckersley, Bowden; Nelson, Elwell (1dg), Wood, Foran (Sheridan), Adams, Laughton
Referee: R. Moore (Wakefield)

1976-77
Leeds 16 Murrell; Alan Smith (D. Smith), Hague, Dyl (1t), Atkinson (1t); Holmes, Dick (1t, 3g, 1dg); Harrison, Ward, Pitchford, Eccles, Cookson, Fearnley (Dickinson)
Widnes 7 Dutton (2g); S. Wright (George), Aspey (1t), Eckersley, D. O'Neill; Hughes, Bowden; Ramsey, Elwell, Mills, Dearden (Foran), Adams, Laughton
Referee: V. Moss (Manchester)

1977-78
Leeds 14 Oulton (1g); D. Smith (1t), Hague, Dyl, Atkinson (1t); Holmes (1dg), J. Sanderson (Dick); Harrison (Dickinson), Ward (2dg), Pitchford, Cookson (1t), Eccles, Crane
St. Helens 12 G. Pimblett (3g), L. Jones, Noonan, Glynn, Mathias; Francis (1t), K. Gwilliam; D. Chisnall, Liptrot (1t), James, Nicholls, Cunningham, Pinner
Referee: W.H. Thompson (Huddersfield)

1978-79
Widnes 12 Eckersley (1dg); S. Wright (1t), Aspey, George (Hull), Burke (2g); Hughes (1t), Bowden; Mills, Elwell (1dg), Shaw, Adams, Dearden (M. O'Neill), Laughton
Wakefield T. 3 Sheard; Fletcher (1t), K. Smith, Diamond, Juliff; Topliss, Lampkowski; Burke, McCurrie, Skerrett, Ashurst, Keith Rayne, Idle
Referee: J.E. Jackson (Pudsey)

1979-80
Hull K.R. 10 Hall; Hubbard (3g, 1t) (Hogan),
M. Smith, Hartley, Sullivan; Millward (1dg),
Agar; Holdstock, Watkinson, Lockwood, Lowe,
Rose (Millington), Casey
Hull 5 Woods; Bray, Walters, Wilby (1t),
Prendiville; Newlove (Hancock), Pickerill;
Tindall, Wileman, Stone (Farrar), Birdsall,
Lloyd (1g), Norton
Referee: G.F. Lindop (Wakefield)
1980-81
Widnes 18 Burke (4g, 1t); S. Wright, George (1t),
Cunningham (J. Myler), Bentley; Hughes,
Gregory (1t); M. O'Neill (Shaw), Elwell,
Lockwood, L. Gorley, E. Prescott, Adams (1dg)
Hull K.R. 9 Hall; Hubbard (3g), M. Smith,
Hogan, Muscroft; Hartley, Harkin; Holdstock
(Millington), Watkinson, Crooks (Proctor), Lowe,
Burton (1t), Casey
Referee: D.G. Kershaw (Easingwold)
1981-82
Hull 14 Kemble; O'Hara (1t), Day, S. Evans,
Prendiville; Topliss, Harkin; Skerrett, Wileman,
Stone, Crane (Crooks), Lloyd (4g), Norton (1t)
Widnes 14 Burke (1g), (A. Myler); S. Wright (1t),
Keiron O'Loughlin, Cunningham (2t), Basnett;
Hughes, Gregory (1g); M. O'Neill, Elwell (1dg),
Lockwood (S. O'Neill), L. Gorley, E. Prescott,
Adams
Referee: G.F. Lindop (Wakefield)
Replay
Hull 18 Kemble (1t); Sullivan, Leuluai, S. Evans,
Prendiville; Topliss (2t), Dean; Tindall, Duke,
Stone, Skerrett, Crooks (1t, 3g), Norton (Crane)
Widnes 9 Burke (3g); S. Wright (1t), Keiron
O'Loughlin, Cunningham, Basnett; Hughes,
Gregory; M. O'Neill, Elwell, Lockwood,
L. Gorley, E. Prescott, Adams
Referee: G.F. Lindop (Wakefield)
1982-83
Featherstone R. 14 N. Barker; Marsden,
Quinn (4g), Gilbert (Lyman), K. Kellett;
A. Banks, Hudson; Gibbins, Handscombe,
Hankins, D. Hobbs (2t), Slatter (Siddall), Smith
Hull 12 Kemble; O'Hara, S. Evans, Leuluai (1t),
Prendiville; Topliss, Harkin (Day), (Crane);
Skerrett, Bridges, Stone, Rose, Crooks (1t, 3g),
Norton
Referee: M.R. Whitfield (Widnes)
1983-84
Widnes 19 Burke (3g); D. Wright, Hughes
(D. Hulme), Lydon (2t), Basnett;
Keiron O'Loughlin (1t), Gregory; S. O'Neill
(1dg), Elwell, K. Tamati, L. Gorley, M. O'Neill
(Whitfield), Adams

Wigan 6 Edwards; Ramsdale, Stephenson,
Whitfield (1g), (Elvin), Gill; Cannon, Stephens;
Hemsley (1t), H. Tamati, Case (Juliff), West,
Scott, Pendlebury
Referee: W.H. Thompson (Huddersfield)
1984-85
Wigan 28 Edwards (1t); Ferguson (2t),
Stephenson (1g), Donlan, Gill (1t, 3g);
Kenny (1t), M. Ford; Courtney, Kiss, Case
(Campbell), West, Dunn, Potter
Hull 24 Kemble; James (1t), S. Evans (1t),
Leuluai (2t), O'Hara (Schofield); Ah Kuoi,
Sterling; Crooks (2g), Patrick, Puckering
(Divorty 1t), Muggleton, Rose, Norton
Referee: R. Campbell (Widnes)
1985-86
Castleford 15 Lord (Roockley); Plange,
Marchant (1t), Hyde, Sandy (1t); Joyner,
R. Beardmore (1t, 1dg); Ward, K. Beardmore
(Horton), Johnson, England, Ketteridge (1g),
French
Hull K.R. 14 Fairbairn; Clark, M. Smith,
Prohm (2t), Laws; Dorahy (1g), Harkin; P.
Johnston, Watkinson, Ema, Kelly (G. Smith),
Des Harrison (Lydiat 1t), Miller
Referee: R. Whitfield (Widnes)
1986-87
Halifax 19 Eadie (1t); Wilson, Whitfield (3g),
Rix, George (1t); C. Anderson (Juliff), Stephens;
Beevers (James), McCallion (1t), Neller, Dixon,
Scott, Pendlebury (1dg)
St. Helens 18 Veivers; Ledger, Loughlin (1t, 3g),
Elia (1t), McCormack; Clark, Holding; Burke,
Liptrot, Fieldhouse, Platt, Haggerty (Round 1t),
Arkwright
Referee: J. Holdsworth (Kippax)
1987-88
Wigan 32 Lydon (1t, 1g); T. Iro (1t), K. Iro (2t),
Bell (1t), Gill (1t); Edwards (Byrne), Gregory
(1g); Case, Kiss, Shelford, Goodway, Potter
(Wane), Hanley (1t)
Halifax 12 Eadie; Meredith, T. Anderson (1t),
Wilkinson, Whitfield (2g); Grogan, Robinson
(Fairbank); James (1t), McCallion, Neller,
Holliday (Scott), Dixon, Pendlebury.
Referee: G. F. Lindop (Wakefield)
1988-89
Wigan 27 Hampson (1t); T. Iro, K. Iro (2t),
Bell, Lydon (3g); Edwards, Gregory (1t, 1dg);
Lucas, Kiss (Betts), Shelford, Platt, Potter
(Goodway), Hanley (1t)
St. Helens 0 Connolly; O'Connor, Veivers,
Loughlin (Bloor), Quirk; Cooper, Holding;
Burke, Groves, Forber, Dwyer (Evans),
Haggerty, Vautin
Referee: R. Tennant (Castleford)

143

THE LANCE TODD TROPHY

The Lance Todd Trophy is presented to the Man of the Match in the Rugby League Challenge Cup Final, the decision being reached by a ballot of members of the Rugby League Writers' Association present at the game.

Lance Todd made his name in Britain as a player with Wigan and as manager of Salford. His untimely death in a road accident on the return journey from a game at Oldham was commemorated by the introduction of the Lance Todd Trophy.

The award was instituted by Australian-born Harry Sunderland, Warrington director Bob Anderton and Yorkshire journalist John Bapty.

Around 1950, the Red Devils' Association at Salford, comprising players and officials who had worked with Todd, raised sufficient funds to provide a trophy and replica for each winner.

Len Killeen, of St. Helens, is the only winger to earn the title; Hull's Tommy Harris the only hooker; and Ray Ashby and Brian Gabbitas the only players to share the honour.

Following the 1954 replay, it was decided by the Red Devils that in future the trophy would be awarded for the Wembley game. In 1954, Gerry Helme had received the trophy for his performance in the Odsal replay. In the 1982 replay at Elland Road, Leeds, the Man of the Match award went to Hull skipper David Topliss, the Lance Todd Trophy having been awarded to Eddie Cunningham, of Widnes, in the drawn Wembley tie.

In 1990 Andy Gregory, of Wigan, became the first player to win the trophy twice at Wembley, having also won it two years earlier.

The Lance Todd Trophy Roll of Honour

Year	Winner	Team	Position
1946	Billy Stott	Wakefield Trinity (v Wigan)	Centre
1947	Willie Davies	Bradford Northern (v Leeds)	Stand off
1948	Frank Whitcombe	Bradford Northern (v Wigan)	Prop
1949	Ernest Ward	Bradford Northern (v Halifax)	Centre
1950	Gerry Helme	Warrington (v Widnes)	Scrum half
1951	Cec Mountford	Wigan (v Barrow)	Stand off
1952	Billy Ivison	Workington T. (v Featherstone R.)	Loose forward
1953	Peter Ramsden	Huddersfield (v St. Helens)	Stand off
1954	Gerry Helme	Warrington (v Halifax)	Scrum half
1955	Jack Grundy	Barrow (v Workington Town)	Second row
1956	Alan Prescott	St. Helens (v Halifax)	Prop
1957	Jeff Stevenson	Leeds (v Barrow)	Scrum half
1958	Rees Thomas	Wigan (v Workington Town)	Scrum half
1959	Brian McTigue	Wigan (v Hull)	Second row
1960	Tommy Harris	Hull (v Wakefield Trinity)	Hooker
1961	Dick Huddart	St. Helens (v Wigan)	Second row
1962	Neil Fox	Wakefield Trinity (v Huddersfield)	Centre
1963	Harold Poynton	Wakefield Trinity (v Wigan)	Stand off
1964	Frank Collier	Widnes (v Hull K.R.)	Prop

1965	Ray Ashby	Wigan	Full back
	Brian Gabbitas	Hunslet	Stand off
1966	Len Killeen	St. Helens (v Wigan)	Winger
1967	Carl Dooler	Featherstone Rovers (v Barrow)	Scrum half
1968	Don Fox	Wakefield Trinity (v Leeds)	Prop
1969	Malcolm Reilly	Castleford (v Salford)	Loose forward
1970	Bill Kirkbride	Castleford (v Wigan)	Second row
1971	Alex Murphy	Leigh (v Leeds)	Scrum half
1972´	Kel Coslett	St. Helens (v Leeds)	Loose forward
1973	Steve Nash	Featherstone R. (v Bradford N.)	Scrum half
1974	Derek Whitehead	Warrington (v Featherstone Rovers)	Full back
1975	Ray Dutton	Widnes (v Warrington)	Full back
1976	Geoff Pimblett	St. Helens (v Widnes)	Full back
1977	Steve Pitchford	Leeds (v Widnes)	Prop
1978	George Nicholls	St. Helens (v Leeds)	Second row
1979	David Topliss	Wakefield Trinity (v Widnes)	Stand off
1980	Brian Lockwood	Hull K.R. (v Hull)	Prop
1981	Mick Burke	Widnes (v Hull K.R.)	Full back
1982	Eddie Cunningham	Widnes (v Hull)	Centre
1983	David Hobbs	Featherstone Rovers (v Hull)	Second row
1984	Joe Lydon	Widnes (v Wigan)	Centre
1985	Brett Kenny	Wigan (v Hull)	Stand off
1986	Bob Beardmore	Castleford (v Hull K.R.)	Scrum half
1987	Graham Eadie	Halifax (v St. Helens)	Full back
1988	Andy Gregory	Wigan (v Halifax)	Scrum half
1989	Ellery Hanley	Wigan (v St. Helens)	Loose forward
1990	Andy Gregory	Wigan (v Warrington)	Scrum half

1990 Lance Todd Trophy winner, Andy Gregory.

145

CHALLENGE CUP RECORDS

ALL ROUNDS

TEAM
Highest score:
Huddersfield 119 v. *Swinton Park 2. 1914

INDIVIDUAL

Most goals in a match:
22 by Jim Sullivan (Wigan) v. *Flimby and Fothergill
. . . . 1925

Most tries in a match:
11 by George West (Hull K.R.) v. *Brookland Rovers
. . . . 1905

Most points in a match:
53 (11t,10g) by George West (Hull K.R.) as above.

*Amateur teams

FINAL RECORDS

TEAM

Most wins: 11 by Wigan

Most finals: 20 by Wigan

Highest score:
Wakefield T. 38 v. Hull 5. 1960

Widest margin:
Huddersfield 37 v. St. Helens 3. 1915

Biggest attendance:
102,569 Warrington v. Halifax (Replay) at Bradford
. . . . 1954

INDIVIDUAL

Most goals:
8 by Cyril Kellett (Featherstone R.) v. Bradford N.
. . . . 1973

Most tries:
3 by Bob Wilson (Broughton R.) v. Salford. 1902
    Stan Moorhouse (Huddersfield) v. Warrington. 1913
    Tom Holliday (Oldham) v. Swinton. 1927

Most points:
20 (7g,2t) by Neil Fox (Wakefield T.) v. Hull. . . 1960

WEMBLEY FACTS

WIGAN have made a record 16 appearances at Wembley and won there a record 10 times, including the only hat-trick in 1988, 1989 and 1990.

A RECORD 10 overseas players trod the Wembley turf in 1985. Hull fielded six — a record for one club. The Airlie Birds sextet were Australians Peter Sterling and John Muggleton, plus New Zealanders Gary Kemble, James Leuluai, Dane O'Hara and Fred Ah Kuoi. Wigan added Australians John Ferguson and Brett Kenny together with New Zealanders Graeme West and Danny Campbell, who went on as substitute. South African Nick Du Toit was substitute back but did not play.

THE 1985 aggregates of 10 tries and 52 points were both record totals for a Challenge Cup final with Hull's 24 points the most by a losing side. There were also 10 tries in the 1915 final when Huddersfield beat St. Helens 37-3, which is the widest margin. Wakefield Trinity ran up the highest Cup final score when they beat Hull 38-5 in 1960.

WORLD RECORD receipts of £1,360,000 were taken at the 1990 Final between Wigan and Warrington from a crowd of 77,729.

ANDY GREGORY holds the record for most Cup-winning appearances at Wembley with five. The scrum half has never been on a losing side at the stadium, having also been in the Widnes side that drew with Hull in 1982 before losing the replay at Elland Road, Leeds.
    Gregory's winning appearances were with Widnes (1981, 1984) and Wigan (1988, 1989, 1990).

THE Widnes trio of Eric Hughes, Keith Elwell and Mick Adams hold the record for most appearances at Wembley…seven. They earned winner's medals in 1975, 1979, 1981 and 1984, plus the drawn final of 1982. They were on the losing side in 1976 and 1977.

ERIC ASHTON captained a record six teams at Wembley — Wigan in 1958, 1959, 1961, 1963, 1965 and 1966. His record of three wins (in 1958, 1959, 1965) is shared with Derek Turner (Wakefield Trinity 1960, 1962, 1963) and Alex Murphy (St. Helens 1966, Leigh 1971 and Warrington 1974).

THE YOUNGEST player to appear in a Wembley Cup final was Shaun Edwards who was 17 years, 6 months and 19 days when he played full back for Wigan against Widnes in 1984. He was also the youngest captain at Wembley, leading Wigan to success in the 1988 final against Halifax at the age of 21 years, 6 months and 14 days.

ALEX MURPHY has been a record six times to Wembley as a coach. He was a winner as player-coach with Leigh (1971) and Warrington (1974), but losing each time when confined to the bench with Warrington (1975), Wigan (1984) and St. Helens (1987 and 1989). Murphy also went twice solely as a player, with St. Helens in 1961 and 1966.

MOST WINS as a coach at Wembley is three, by Jim Sullivan (Wigan 1948, 1951 and St. Helens 1956), Joe Egan (Wigan 1958, 1959 and Widnes 1964) and Ken Traill (Wakefield T. 1960, 1962 and 1963).

THE OLDEST player at Wembley was Gus Risman, who at 41 years 29 days led Workington Town to victory over Featherstone Rovers in 1952. He played full back.

THE TALLEST player at Wembley was New Zealand Test star Graeme West who captained Wigan in the 1984 and 1985 finals. He measured 6ft. 5in.

SCHOOLBOYS who have appeared in an Under-11 curtain-raiser at Wembley and gone on to play in the major final at the stadium are Joe Lydon, David Hulme, Mike Ford, Neil Puckering, David Plange, Denis Betts and Bobby Goulding. Lydon became the first to achieve the feat with Widnes in the 1984 final against Wigan, followed by teammate Hulme who went on as a 72nd minute substitute. Both had played in the first schoolboys' curtain-raiser in 1975 — Lydon for Wigan, and Hulme for Widnes.

CYRIL KELLETT holds the record for most goals in a Challenge Cup final with his eight for Featherstone Rovers in 1973.

In the most remarkable exhibition of kicking seen at Wembley, the veteran full back was successful with every one of his attempts as Bradford Northern crashed 33-14.

Nine years earlier he scored only one for Hull Kingston Rovers in the 13-5 defeat by Widnes.

NEIL FOX — the record aggregate points scorer of all time — piled up the most points in a Challenge Cup final in 1960. His 20 points helped Wakefield Trinity to a 38-5 defeat of Hull. Fox's points came from two tries and seven goals.

His three drop goals for Trinity in the 12-6 victory over Huddersfield two years later was another extraordinary feat in the days when the drop goal was a rarity.

NO player has scored a hat-trick of tries at Wembley, the feat being achieved only three times in the preceding era.

The last to do it was Oldham winger Tom Holliday in the 26-7 defeat of Swinton in 1927.

Bob Wilson, the Broughton Rangers centre and captain, was the first to score three tries, in the 25-0 victory over Salford in 1902.

In between, Stan Moorhouse's three-try feat accounted for all of Huddersfield's points when they beat Warrington 9-5 in 1913. Moorhouse was winger to Harold Wagstaff, recognised as the greatest centre of all time.

MANY great players have gone through an entire career without achieving their ambition of playing at Wembley. Hull's Mike Smith achieved it in his first senior game.

Smith made one of the most remarkable debuts in sporting history when he played in the second row of an injury-hit Boulevard side against Wakefield Trinity in 1960.

In contrast, Freddie Miller signed for Hull in 1932 and did not play at Wembley until 1952...two years after joining Featherstone Rovers.

A NOTABLE Wembley captain was Gus Risman who led two clubs to victory...14 years apart.

He was captain of Salford when they beat Barrow in 1938. At 41, he led Workington Town to their triumph over Featherstone Rovers in 1952.

PROBABLY the unluckiest Challenge Cup finalist was Dai Davies who appeared in four finals and was on the losing side each time. Three of those occasions were at Wembley with different clubs. He was a loser with Warrington (1933), Huddersfield (1935) and Keighley (1937). Before the Wembley era he was also in Warrington's beaten team of 1928.

Steve Norton has played at Wembley four times and has yet to be on the winning side. He was in the beaten Hull teams of 1980, 1983 and 1985 in addition to playing in the 1982 drawn final. In 1970 he was a non-playing substitute for Castleford who won the Cup.

Bill Ramsey was on the losing side in four Wembley finals but gained a winner's medal with Leeds in 1968. He picked up losers' medals with Hunslet (1965), Leeds (1971 and 1972) and Widnes (1977).

A TOTAL of 14 current clubs have yet to play at Wembley ...Batley, Bramley, Carlisle, Chorley, Doncaster, Fulham, Nottingham City, Oldham, Rochdale Hornets, Runcorn Highfield, Sheffield Eagles, Swinton, Trafford Borough and Whitehaven.

Fate seems to be against Swinton and Oldham. In the five years preceding the move to Wembley, one or the other appeared in the final, twice meeting each other. Oldham played in a record four successive finals in that period. Swinton's run of three finals ended when the first Wembley took place in 1929. They got through to the final three years later ...only for it to be played at Wigan!

CHALLENGE CUP

Wembley Era Semi-Finals

It is generally felt that it is better to have played at Wembley and lost than never to have played there at all. This makes the semi-final stage of the RL Challenge Cup almost as important as the final with no consolation for the losers.

Of the 14 current clubs who have never appeared at Wembley four have been beaten semi-finalists. They are Oldham (five times), Swinton, Rochdale Hornets (twice) and Whitehaven.

Probably the unluckiest are Oldham. They have reached the penultimate stage five times without being able to realise their ambition. Oldham almost made it in 1964. After drawing 5-5 with Hull K.R. they were winning 17-14 in extra time of the replay when bad light stopped play and they were beaten in the third game.

Swinton did win a semi-final in 1932 but the final that year was switched from Wembley to Wigan!

There have been three occasions when Yorkshire has provided all four semi-finalists in one year — in 1962, 1973 and 1983. Three times have all four semi-finalists come from west of the Pennines — in 1930, 1989 and 1990.

Until 1962 the two semi-finals were always played on the same Saturday, but with four Yorkshire clubs competing for the first time it was decided to play one mid-week. Both matches were played at Odsal Stadium, Bradford. The first was on a Wednesday evening — without floodlights — when 43,625 saw Wakefield Trinity beat Featherstone Rovers and on the following Saturday there were 31,423 to see Huddersfield beat Hull K.R.

The following year both semi-finals were again played on the same Saturday, but since then they have been staged on different Saturdays.

Some semi-final facts during the Wembley era are:

Biggest attendance: 69,898 Warrington v. Leeds at Bradford in 1950

Biggest aggregate: 104,453 in 1939 (Only other six-figure aggregate was 102,080 in 1951)

Record receipts: £177,161 St. Helens v. Wigan at Old Trafford, Manchester in 1990

Lowest attendance: 7,971 Featherstone R. v. Leigh at Leeds in 1974

Highest score and widest margin: Wigan 34 v. Salford 4 in 1988

CHALLENGE CUP SEMI-FINALS

Year	Winners		Runners-up		Venue	Attendance	Receipts
1929	Dewsbury	9	Castleford	3	Huddersfield	25,000	£1,562
	Wigan	7	St. Helens Recs.	7	Swinton	31,000	£2,209
Replay	Wigan	13	St. Helens Recs.	12	Leigh	21,940	£1,437
1930	Widnes	10	Barrow	3	Warrington	25,500	£1,630
	St. Helens	5	Wigan	5	Swinton	37,169	£2,666
Replay	St. Helens	22	Wigan	10	Leigh	24,000	£1,657
1931	Halifax	11	St. Helens	2	Rochdale	21,674	£1,498
	York	15	Warrington	5	Leeds	32,419	£2,329
1932	Leeds	2	Halifax	2	Huddersfield	31,818	£2,456
Replay	Leeds	9	Halifax	2	Wakefield	21,000	£1,417
	Swinton	7	Wakefield T.	4	Rochdale	21,273	£1,369
●	*Final was played at Wigan, not Wembley*						
1933	Huddersfield	30	Leeds	8	Wakefield	36,359	£2,299
	Warrington	11	St. Helens	5	Swinton	30,373	£2,055

Year	Winners		Runners-up		Venue	Attendance	Receipts
1934	Hunslet	12	Huddersfield	7	Wakefield	27,450	£1,797
	Widnes	7	Oldham	4	Swinton	17,577	£1,050
1935	Castleford	11	Barrow	5	Swinton	24,469	£1,534
	Huddersfield	21	Hull	5	Leeds	37,111	£2,753
1936	Leeds	10	Huddersfield	5	Wakefield	37,906	£2,456
	Warrington	7	Salford	2	Wigan	41,538	£2,796
1937	Keighley	0	Wakefield T.	0	Leeds	39,998	£2,793
Replay	Keighley	5	Wakefield T.	3	Huddersfield	14,400	£1,052
	Widnes	13	Wigan	9	Warrington	29,260	£1,972
1938	Barrow	4	Halifax	2	Huddersfield	31,384	£2,431
	Salford	6	Swinton	0	Belle Vue, Manchester	31,664	£2,396
1939	Halifax	10	Leeds	4	Bradford	64,453	£3,645
	Salford	11	Wigan	2	Rochdale	40,000	£2,154
●	*During the war the semi-finals were two-legged and the finals were not played at Wembley*						
1946	Wakefield T.	7	Hunslet	3	Leeds	33,000	£4,991
	Wigan	12	Widnes	5	Swinton	36,976	£4,746
1947	Bradford N.	11	Warrington	7	Swinton	33,474	£4,946
	Leeds	21	Wakefield T.	0	Huddersfield	35,136	£6,339
1948	Bradford N.	14	Hunslet	7	Leeds	38,125	£7,437
	Wigan	11	Rochdale H.	0	Swinton	26,004	£4,206
1949	Bradford N.	10	Barrow	0	Swinton	26,572	£4,646
	Halifax	11	Huddersfield	10	Bradford	61,875	£8,638
1950	Warrington	16	Leeds	4	Bradford	69,898	£9,861
	Widnes	8	Bradford N.	0	Wigan	25,390	£3,936
1951	Barrow	14	Leeds	14	Bradford	57,459	£8,248
Replay	Barrow	28	Leeds	13	Huddersfield	31,078	£5,098
	Wigan	3	Warrington	2	Swinton	44,621	£7,358
1952	Featherstone R.	6	Leigh	2	Leeds	35,621	£6,494
	Workington T.	5	Barrow	2	Wigan	31,206	£4,782
1953	Huddersfield	7	Wigan	0	Bradford	58,722	£10,519
	St. Helens	9	Warrington	3	Swinton	38,059	£7,768
1954	Halifax	18	Hunslet	3	Bradford	46,961	£8,243
	Warrington	8	Leeds	4	Swinton	36,993	£7,596
1955	Barrow	9	Hunslet	6	Wigan	25,493	£4,671
	Workington T.	13	Featherstone R.	2	Leeds	33,499	£7,305
1956	Halifax	11	Wigan	10	Bradford	51,889	£9,054
	St. Helens	5	Barrow	5	Swinton	38,897	£7,793
Replay	St. Helens	10	Barrow	5	Wigan	44,731	£7,750
1957	Barrow	2	Leigh	2	Wigan	34,628	£6,340
Replay	Barrow	15	Leigh	10	Swinton	28,081	£5,695
	Leeds	10	Whitehaven	9	Bradford	49,094	£8,987
1958	Wigan	5	Rochdale H.	3	Swinton	28,597	£6,354
	Workington T.	8	Featherstone R.	2	Bradford	31,517	£6,325
1959	Wigan	5	Leigh	0	Swinton	27,906	£6,068
	Hull	15	Featherstone R.	5	Bradford	52,131	£9,776
1960	Wakefield T.	11	Featherstone R.	2	Bradford	55,935	£10,390
	Hull	12	Oldham	9	Swinton	27,545	£6,093
1961	St. Helens	26	Hull	9	Bradford	42,935	£9,231
	Wigan	19	Halifax	10	Swinton	35,118	£7,557

Year	Winners		Runners-up		Venue	Attendance	Receipts
1962	Wakefield T.	9	Featherstone R.	0	Bradford	43,625	£8,496
	Huddersfield	6	Hull K.R.	0	Bradford	31,423	£6,685
1963	Wakefield T.	5	Warrington	2	Swinton	15,565	£3,530
	Wigan	18	Hull K.R.	4	Leeds	21,420	£6,029
1964	Widnes	7	Castleford	7	Swinton	25,603	£5,541
Replay	Widnes	7	Castleford	5	Wakefield	28,739	£5,313
	Hull K.R.	5	Oldham	5	Leeds	28,823	£7,411
Replay	Hull K.R.	14	Oldham	17	Swinton	27,209	£5,929

● *Score after 80 minutes was 14-14, then bad light caused match to be abandoned after 12 minutes of extra time with Oldham winning 17-14*

Second Replay	Hull K.R.	12	Oldham	2	Huddersfield	28,732	£6,183
1965	Wigan	25	Swinton	10	St. Helens	26,658	£6,384
	Hunslet	8	Wakefield T.	0	Leeds	21,262	£6,090
1966	St. Helens	12	Dewsbury	5	Swinton	13,046	£3,102
	Wigan	7	Leeds	2	Huddersfield	22,758	£5,971
1967	Featherstone R.	16	Leeds	8	Huddersfield	20,052	£6,276
	Barrow	14	Dewsbury	9	Swinton	13,744	£4,560
1968	Leeds	25	Wigan	4	Swinton	30,058	£9,845
	Wakefield T.	0	Huddersfield	0	Bradford	21,569	£6,196
Replay	Wakefield T.	15	Huddersfield	10	Leeds	20,983	£6,425
1969	Castleford	16	Wakefield T.	10	Leeds	21,497	£8,477
	Salford	15	Warrington	8	Wigan	20,600	£7,738
1970	Castleford	6	St. Helens	3	Swinton	18,913	£7,171
	Wigan	19	Hull K.R.	8	Leeds	18,495	£7,862
1971	Leeds	19	Castleford	8	Bradford	24,464	£9,120
	Leigh	10	Huddersfield	4	Wigan	14,875	£5,670
1972	St. Helens	10	Warrington	10	Wigan	19,300	£8,250
Replay	St. Helens	10	Warrington	6	Wigan	32,380	£12,604
	Leeds	16	Halifax	3	Bradford	16,680	£6,851
1973	Featherstone R.	17	Castleford	3	Leeds	15,369	£9,454
	Bradford N.	23	Dewsbury	7	Leeds	14,028	£9,221
1974	Warrington	17	Dewsbury	7	Wigan	11,789	£6,821
	Featherstone R.	21	Leigh	14	Leeds	7,971	£4,461
1975	Widnes	13	Wakefield T.	7	Bradford	9,155	£5,856
	Warrington	11	Leeds	4	Wigan	13,168	£9,581
1976	Widnes	15	Featherstone R.	9	Swinton	13,019	£9,078
	St. Helens	5	Keighley	4	Huddersfield	9,829	£6,113
1977	Leeds	7	St. Helens	2	Wigan	12,974	£11,379
	Widnes	14	Hull K.R.	5	Leeds	17,053	£16,068
1978	Leeds	14	Featherstone R.	9	Bradford	12,824	£11,322
	St. Helens	12	Warrington	8	Wigan	16,167	£13,960
1979	Widnes	14	Bradford N.	11	Swinton	14,324	£16,363
	Wakefield T.	9	St. Helens	7	Leeds	12,393	£14,195
1980	Hull K.R.	20	Halifax	7	Leeds	17,910	£31,650
	Hull	10	Widnes	5	Swinton	18,347	£29,415
1981	Widnes	17	Warrington	9	Wigan	12,624	£20,673
	Hull K.R.	22	St. Helens	5	Leeds	17,073	£30,616
1982	Hull	15	Castleford	11	Leeds	21,207	£41,867
	Widnes	11	Leeds	8	Swinton	13,075	£25,796

Year	Winners		Runners-up		Venue	Attendance	Receipts
1983	Featherstone R.	11	Bradford N.	6	Leeds	10,784	£22,579
	Hull	14	Castleford	7	Elland Rd., L'ds	26,031	£65,498
1984	Wigan	14	York	8	Elland Rd., L'ds	17,156	£52,888
	Widnes	15	Leeds	4	Swinton	14,046	£37,183
1985	Wigan	18	Hull K.R.	11	Elland Rd., L'ds	19,275	£70,192
	Hull	10	Castleford	10	Leeds	20,982	£64,163
Replay	Hull	22	Castleford	16	Leeds	20,968	£65,005
1986	Castleford	18	Oldham	7	Wigan	12,430	£38,296
	Hull K.R.	24	Leeds	24	Elland Rd., L'ds	23,866	£83,757
Replay	Hull K.R.	17	Leeds	0	Elland Rd., L'ds	32,485	£113,345
1987	St. Helens	14	Leigh	8	Wigan	13,105	£48,627
	Halifax	12	Widnes	8	Leeds	16,064	£61,260
1988	Wigan	34	Salford	4	Bolton W. FC	20,783	£95,876
	Halifax	0	Hull	0	Leeds	20,534	£82,026
Replay	Halifax	4	Hull	3	Elland Rd., L'ds	25,117	£113,679
1989	St. Helens	16	Widnes	14	Wigan	17,119	£70,411
	Wigan	13	Warrington	6	Man. C. FC	26,529	£144,056
1990	Wigan	20	St. Helens	14	Man. U. FC	26,489	£177,161
	Warrington	10	Oldham	6	Wigan	15,631	£80,500

NON-LEAGUE CLUBS IN THE CHALLENGE CUP

AMATEUR clubs were invited to compete in the 1986 Rugby League Challenge Cup after a five-year break. The League asked for two of the three county cup competition winners to enter the preliminary round.

The League later decided that from 1987 the Silk Cut Challenge Cup campaign would feature 38 teams, amateur clubs joining the professionals for a preliminary round of six ties.

In the early years of the Northern Union Challenge Cup — as it was then called — the line between professional and amateur was less clearly defined.

A variety of Leagues also make it difficult to set non-League clubs apart. Fifty-six clubs appeared in the inaugurating first round of 1897 and four others received byes. The complications continued until 1904 when the League format settled down and non-League clubs had to qualify for the first round.

Between 1904 and 1907 there was a preliminary round of up to 14 ties involving mostly non-league clubs. In 1906-07 SAVILLE GREEN beat Bramley 10-0, and NEWINGTON ROVERS drew 3-3 and 13-13 with York before losing 14-5.

Not since 1909 when BEVERLEY beat Ebbw Vale 7-2 has a senior team been knocked out by a non-League club although amateur teams twice had victories in the two-leg era of 1946-54.

NON-LEAGUE CLUB VICTORIES OVER SENIOR CLUBS SINCE 1904

(Excluding preliminary rounds before 1908)
Non-League Clubs in Capitals

1905-06
*FEATHERSTONE ROVERS 23 v. Widnes 2
(second round)

1907-08
WHITEHAVEN RECREATION 13 v. St. Helens 8
(Lost 33-5 at Merthyr Tydfil in second round)

1908-09
BEVERLEY 7 v. Ebbw Vale 2
(Lost 53-2 at Halifax in second round)

1945-46
SHARLSTON 12 v. Workington Town 7
(1st leg) (Workington Town won 2nd leg 16-2)

1947-48
RISEHOW and GILLHEAD 10 v. Keighley 2 (2nd leg)
(Keighley won 1st leg 11-0)

*FEATHERSTONE ROVERS are the only non-League club to appear in the third round when they lost 3-0 at Keighley. In the first round they beat BROOKLAND ROVERS 16-5.

There have been several other instances of non-League clubs meeting in the first round. The last occasion was in 1960 when WALNEY CENTRAL beat LOCK LANE 10-5 before losing at Oldham 55-4 in the second round.

In 1964 THAMES BOARD MILLS received a bye when Bradford Northern disbanded, but lost 48-8 at Blackpool Borough in the second round.

CHALLENGE CUP PROGRESS CHART

A 20-year review ....

Key: W — Winners. F — Beaten finalists. SF — Semi-final. P — Preliminary round.

	1989-90	1988-89	1987-88	1986-87	1985-86	1984-85	1983-84	1982-83	1981-82	1980-81	1979-80	1978-79	1977-78	1976-77	1975-76	1974-75	1973-74	1972-73	1971-72	1970-71
BARROW	1	2	1	2	2	P	1	2	2	1	2	3	1	2	1	1	1	1	2	1
BATLEY	1	1	1	1	1	1	1	1	2	1	1	1	1	1	1	1	1	1	1	1
BRADFORD N.	3	2	1	2	3	3	3	SF	3	1	3	SF	3	3	2	3	3	F	2	1
BRAMLEY	1	P	P	1	2	3	1	1	1	1	1	2	1	1	1	1	2	1	3	3
CARLISLE	1	2	1	2	1	1	P	1	1											
CASTLEFORD	P	2	1	1	W	SF	3	SF	SF	2	2	3	3	3	1	1	1	SF	2	SF
CHORLEY	1																			
DEWSBURY	2	1	1	1	1	1	1	1	1	2	1	2	1	3	1	1	SF	SF	1	2
DONCASTER	P	1	3	1	2	P	2	1	1	1	1	1	1	1	2	1	1	1	1	1
FEATHERSTONE R.	1	3	2	1	1	P	1	W	P	3	1	1	SF	2	SF	1	F	W	2	2
FULHAM	2	1	1	1	1	1	2	2	2	1										
HALIFAX	1	1	F	W	1	2	1	2	3	2	SF	1	1	1	1	1	1	1	SF	1
HUDDERSFIELD	P	1	P	1	1	1	1	1	1	2	3	3	1	1	1	1	1	2		SF
HULL	2	1	SF	3	1	F	2	F	W	2	F	3	2	2	1	2	1	2	2	3
HULL K.R.	1	3	3	3	F	SF	3	1	2	F	W	2	1	SF	2	3	2	2	1	1
HUNSLET	1	P	1	2	1	3	2	3	1	1	1	1	2	1	2	3	1	2	1	2
KEIGHLEY	2	2	2	2	1	1	1	1	1	2	1	2	1	1	SF	1	1	1	1	2
LEEDS	P	3	2	3	SF	1	SF	2	SF	1	2	1	W	W	3	SF	3	1	F	F
LEIGH	1	1	1	SF	3	2	1	1	3	2	1	2	1	1	3	2	SF	2	2	W
NOTTINGHAM C.	1	1	2	2	P	1														
OLDHAM	SF	3	1	2	SF	1	2	1	2	3	2	2	2	1	3	3	1	3	1	1
ROCHDALE H.	2	1	2	1	2	2	1	1	2	1	2	2	1	2	1	2	2	2	1	1
RUNCORN H.	1	1	1	1	1	2	1	2	1	1	1	1	1	1	1	1	2	1	1	1
RYEDALE-YORK	1	1	1	P	2	1	SF	1	1	2	2	1	1	1	2	2	1	1	3	1
ST. HELENS	SF	F	3	F	2	1	3	3	1	SF	2	SF	F	SF	W	2	3	2	W	2
SALFORD	2	1	SF	1	1	2	1	2	1	3	3	1	2	2	2	2	2	1	1	3
SHEFFIELD E.	2	2	2	1	1	1														
SWINTON	1	1	1	P	P	1	P	2	1	1	1	1	2	2	1	1	2	1	3	3
TRAFFORD B.	2	2	2	1	2	1	1	1	1	1	1	1	1	1	1	1	1	1	1	1
WAKEFIELD T.	3	2	1	2	1	2	2	2	3	3	3	F	2	2	1	SF	1	3	3	1
WARRINGTON	F	SF	2	1	2	2	2	3	1	SF	3	1	SF	1	3	F	W	3	SF	2
WHITEHAVEN	3	1	P	3	1	1	1	1	1	1	1	1	1	1	1	1	1	1	1	1
WIDNES	3	SF	3	SF	3	3	W	1	F	W	SF	W	3	F	F	W	2	2	1	2
WIGAN	W	W	W	1	3	W	F	1	2	1	1	2	2	2	2	3	3	2	2	
WORKINGTON T.	1	P	1	P	1	2	2	3	2	2	1	1	2	3	2	2	2	2	1	1

REGAL TROPHY

1989-90 Final

The first-ever Regal Trophy final was a triumph for the King of Rugby League — newly-crowned MBE Ellery Hanley — scorer of a hat-trick of tries in only his fifth comeback game after a five-month injury lay off.

With a change of title after 18 years under the John Player banner, the new trophy found a home on the Wigan sideboard after their fourth final success in five years, extending their record haul in the tournament to five victories.

Hanley became the first player to score three tries in the final of the competition as Halifax battled in their brave bid to become the first Second Division side to win the tournament. Instead the Thrum Hallers went down five tries to one to join Hull (1976) and Blackpool Borough (1977) as runner-up on the roll of honour.

Hat-trick hero Hanley also collected the £250 Man of the Match award for the second year in succession, emulating Hull K.R. scrum half Paul Harkin who performed the feat in 1985 and 1986.

Mingled with the top class football, the near-18,000 crowd also witnessed bouts of ill-temper, referee Gerry Kershaw despatching three players to the sin bin. Australian prop forward Lindsey Johnston was the first to go in the 38th minute for punching Martin Dermott, the former Under-21 hooker having to leave the field with a badly cut nose. After a 53rd minute dust-up, two more props — Halifax's Brendan Hill and Wigan Test man Andy Platt — spent 10 minutes in the dug out as the tense tie always threatened to bubble over.

Wigan's bonus yardage was evident as early as the fifth minute when Great Britain stand off Shaun Edwards sent centre Kevin Iro clear, the Kiwi bumping off Halifax full back Colin Whitfield before giving the ball back to Edwards to open the scoring.

As the Yorkshiremen sought their fourth First Division scalp in the competition, a kick ahead by skipper-coach John Dorahy, outstanding in the first half, led to Halifax's first score in the 15th minute, Dean Bell's high tackle on the Australian stand off resulting in a successful Holliday penalty goal. The Cumbrian levelled the scores 16 minutes later when Wigan full back Joe Lydon was penalised for treading on Dorahy after fielding his kick through.

Hanley broke the deadlock a minute from the break, Johnston just having taken his place in the sin bin. The Great Britain skipper followed up a glorious break by substitute Andy Goodway, returning after a compound dislocation of the finger in the third round, to touch down and give the Riversiders an 8-4 half-time lead.

The difference in pace was shown in direct contrast five minutes after the restart. Les Holliday and John Lyons kicked on from near their own line only for Wigan winger Mark Preston to win the race for possession. From the play-the-ball, wingman David Marshall sped clear on the counter attack to send Hanley on a 55-yard gallop to the line leaving centre Tony Anderson in his wake. Lydon added the goal to open up a 14-4 lead.

Holliday struck his third penalty goal before Hanley completed his hat-trick with a 59th minute touchdown. Lydon adding the goal before Goodway scored a 71st minute try created by Gregory.

Though unable to repeat their success in the inaugural Player's No.6 Trophy final of 1971-72, Halifax gained respectability with Hill's barging try four minutes from the end, Holliday tacking on his fourth goal for a final scoreline of 24-12.

REGAL TROPHY FINAL

13 January **Leeds**

WIGAN 24   **HALIFAX 12**

Joe Lydon	1.	Colin Whitfield
David Marshall	2.	Eddie Riddlesden
Kevin Iro	3.	Tony Anderson
Dean Bell	4.	Brian Hetherington
Mark Preston	5.	Wilf George
Shaun Edwards	6.	John Dorahy, Capt.
Andy Gregory	7.	John Lyons
Ian Lucas	8.	Brendan Hill
Martin Dermott	9.	Seamus McCallion
Andy Platt	10.	Lindsey Johnston
Denis Betts	11.	Peter Bell
Ian Gildart	12.	Richard Milner
Ellery Hanley, Capt.	13.	Les Holliday
Andy Goodway	14.	Steve Smith
Shaun Wane	15.	Mick Scott

T: Hanley (3), Edwards, Goodway

G: Lydon (2)

Substitutions:

Goodway for Gildart (21min.)

Wane for Lucas (21 min.)

Half-time: 8-4

Attendance: 17,810

T: Hill

G: Holliday (4)

Substitutions:

Smith for Whitfield (17 min.)

Scott for Smith (66 min.)

Referee: Gerry Kershaw (Easingwold)

Halifax hooker Seamus McCallion eludes Wigan second row man Denis Betts in the Headingley final.

1989-90 Round by Round

In the six-tie preliminary round, the three amateur representatives were all beaten. Warrington club Crosfields came closest to an upset, going down only 19-14 to Second Division Workington Town at Wilderspool, the scores being level 8-8 at half-time. National League champions West Hull were disposed of 28-14 at Batley, two tries from stand off Stuart Wainman keeping the Humbersiders in contention at 12-12. Doncaster trailed 2-0 to Cumbrians Kells at the interval at Whitehaven before cutting loose to win 28-2 with five tries, two from former Test forward Kevin Rayne. Great Britain centre Garry Schofield marked his comeback after a two-month injury lay off by scoring four tries in Leeds' 32-2 defeat of Ryedale-York at Headingley. Warrington's hangover from their Lancashire Cup success continued with visitors Sheffield Eagles gaining a 12-4 away victory. Scrum half Mark Aston was outstanding as the creator of tries for Daryl Powell and Mark Gamson. Only three weeks after beating Hull 30-14 in the league, Wakefield Trinity were beaten 19-12 by the Airlie Birds at Belle Vue.

In the first round, Second Division Hull K.R. were thwarted at St. Helens when centre Mike Fletcher was sent off for an alleged trip just before half-time with the Robins leading 16-12. Saints opened up in the second half to win 40-26, Alan Hunte completing a hat-trick of tries and centre Paul Loughlin amassing 20 points from two tries and six goals. Sheffield Eagles blitzed Rochdale Hornets with four tries to one in the first half of their tie staged at Halifax, the Eagles adding another three touchdowns before Hornets rallied with three tries in the last half hour for a final scoreline of 36-22. Lowly Nottingham City entertained the mighty Widnes, for whom Man of the Match Jonathan Davies scored a spectacular 100-yard try before retiring in the 55th minute with a hamstring injury, the Chemics claiming a 48-18 victory. Australian import Phil Blake maintained his record of scoring in his 11 appearances as Wigan disposed of Second Division Doncaster 62-4 at Central Park, Blake being overshadowed by Andy Goodway, with a hat-trick of tries, and 22-point Joe Lydon.

Great Britain scrum half Deryck Fox inspired six-try Featherstone Rovers to a 36-18 success at Trafford Borough. Bradford Northern's Welsh winger Gerald Cordle took the spotlight with a four-try haul in a 38-10 win against 12-man Keighley who had Mark Fairbank sent off after only four minutes for an off-the-ball incident. Bramley were tormented by New Zealand centre Charlie McAlister who set up Oldham's first three tries before scorching through for one himself, skipper John Cogger adding two touchdowns as the visitors went through 48-16. Salford's £35,000 signing Frank Cassidy paid back part of the fee by creating the match-winning try for Mark Brooke-Cowden seven minutes from time in the tie at Hull, Man of the Match Steve Kerry tallying 17 points in the 21-18 win.

Hooker Colin Maskill was the mainstay of Leeds' 26-12 success over visitors Leigh, setting up a try for Craig Coleman, scoring himself and kicking five goals. Coached by former Halifax supremo Ross Strudwick, Fulham were level with their Thrum Hall visitors until Hussein M'Barki was sent off for a high tackle in the 56th minute, Halifax making the tie safe with winger Wilf George completing a hat-trick of tries in the 32-18 success. Teenage prop Richard Brook helped Hunslet knock out Barrow with a second half try in only his second first-team appearance, in a 10-6 victory. Second Division hosts Chorley were swamped by Castleford 42-18, their eight-try haul featuring two each from Steve Larder, Ron Gibbs and Kevin Beardmore.

Huddersfield extended their winning run to eight with a 28-4 triumph at Workington, Australian full back Wally Gibson claiming a hat-trick of tries. Stand off Chris Wilkinson was the hero of Dewsbury's 14-4 home defeat of Carlisle, contributing a tally of 10 points and continually pushing the Cumbrians back with his kicking. Batley pulled back from a 10-0 deficit at Swinton to set up a grandstand finish, Damian McGrath's attempted goal kick to level the scores with only nine minutes left hitting the post. Swinton held on to win 18-16. Runcorn Highfield's losing sequence continued at Whitehaven where the Cumbrians scored three tries to one in a 20-10 success.

In the second round, Second Division Dewsbury shocked high-flying St. Helens by snatching a 12-12 draw at Knowsley Road. Inspired by Man of the Match Willie Johnson, the Yorkshiremen led 12-6 until the last 10 minutes when David Tanner scored a try for goalkicker Loughlin to equal the scores. The replay, staged in rain and sleet at Wakefield Trinity's Belle Vue, saw the Saints secure a 14-0 success. Sheffield Eagles reached the quarter-finals for the first time by defeating Swinton 28-6 at Station Road, Aston providing a five-star show including four goals as the Eagles ran in five tries. Salford were the livelier team in the first half at Halifax before player-coach John Dorahy masterminded the Thrum Haller's second half domination, scoring three tries without reply to clinch a 20-6 victory. In the televised tie, Wigan beat Widnes in a four-try 18-0 victory, the visitors losing prop Joe Grima for a high tackle when trailing 4-0 in the first half.

Hunslet conceded three tries in the first nine minutes as visitors Featherstone Rovers romped home 34-4, led by the inspirational Fox. Castleford's 11-try 62-2 victory at Whitehaven featured a club record-equalling five tries by winger St. John Ellis

and a hat-trick for Australian full back Larder. The success was marred by a fourth minute tackle by Gary Charlton breaking record signing Graham Steadman's nose and cheekbone. Charlton was later suspended *sine die*. Leeds rattled up 18 points in the last 15 minutes to dispose of Bradford Northern 27-8 in front of a 14,459 Headingley crowd, the scores having been level until Schofield's 55th minute drop goal broke the deadlock at 9-8. Oldham could not relax until the last 10 minutes in a 22-8 Watersheddings success over neighbours Huddersfield, well served by full back Gibson, scorer of their only try.

In the third round, holders Wigan put on a brave show at Leeds to earn a well deserved 10-10 draw. Without flu victim Gregory, the Riversiders had Steve Hampson sent off after only five minutes for an illegal high tackle on hooker Colin Maskill, then lost packman Goodway with a compound dislocation of a finger. In the Central Park replay, Wigan recorded an 8-0 victory, their hero being 17-year-old substitute Bobby Goulding, the scrum half coming on at hooker for the last 23 minutes to set up the only try and kick two goals. Castleford's Ellis and Larder maintained their try-a-match record in the competition in the 18-2 win against Sheffield Eagles at Chesterfield. Australian centre Brian Hetherington was the hero of Halifax's 23-10 home defeat of Featherstone Rovers, backed up by Dorahy and Les Holliday. Oldham were devastated at St. Helens by the sending off of goalkicker Duncan Platt in the first minute for a trip on Saints' hooker Paul Groves. St. Helens built up an 18-4 half-time lead before skipper Cogger grabbed two tries in a minute to raise hopes which were dashed when Hunte notched his second try in the 32-18 win.

In the semi-finals, Halifax became only the third Second Division side to reach the final of the competition with a 10-9 success over Alex Murphy's St. Helens. The Thrum

Hallers overcame a series of disallowed tries to capitalise on the efforts of bulldozing front row Brendan Hill, Seamus McCallion and Lindsey Johnston plus the silky skills of loose forward Holliday, winner of the Regal Man of the Match award. At Leeds, Wigan produced one of the most professional performances of the season to beat a disappointing Castleford, 24-10. Inspired by Man of the Match Gregory, Wigan ran in four tries, one by Lydon who added four goals despite a trip to the sin bin. The Glassblowers tries came from Ellis and Larder, maintaining their Regal Trophy tryscoring sequences.

1989-90 RESULTS

Preliminary Round

Batley	28	West Hull	14	
Crosfields	14	Workington T.	19	
(at Warrington)				
Kells	2	Doncaster	28	
(at Whitehaven)				
Leeds	32	Ryedale-York	2	
Wakefield T.	12	Hull	19	
Warrington	4	Sheffield E.	12	

First Round

Bradford N.	38	Keighley	10
Bramley	16	Oldham	48
Chorley	18	Castleford	42
Dewsbury	14	Carlisle	4
Fulham	18	Halifax	32
Hull	18	Salford	21
Hunslet	10	Barrow	6
Leeds	26	Leigh	12
Nottingham C.	18	Widnes	48
St. Helens	40	Hull K.R.	26
Sheffield E.	36	Rochdale H.	22
(at Halifax)			
Swinton	18	Batley	16
Trafford B.	18	Featherstone R.	36
Whitehaven	20	Runcorn H.	10
Wigan	62	Doncaster	4
Workington T.	4	Huddersfield	28

Second Round

Halifax	20	Salford	6
Hunslet	4	Featherstone R.	34
Leeds	27	Bradford N.	8
Oldham	22	Huddersfield	8
St. Helens	12	Dewsbury	12
Swinton	6	Sheffield E.	28
Whitehaven	2	Castleford	62
Wigan	18	Widnes	0

Replay

Dewsbury	0	St. Helens	14
(at Wakefield)			

Third Round

Halifax	23	Featherstone R.	10
Leeds	10	Wigan	10
St. Helens	32	Oldham	18
Sheffield E.	2	Castleford	18
(at Chesterfield)			

Replay

Wigan	8	Leeds	0

Semi-Finals

Halifax	10	St. Helens	9
(at Wigan)			
Castleford	10	Wigan	24
(at Leeds)			

Final

Wigan	24	Halifax	12
(at Leeds)			

1989-90 PRIZES

Round	Per Team		Total
Preliminary	12 ×	£1,740	£20,880
First	16 ×	£1,745	£27,920
Second	8 ×	£2,750	£22,000
Third	4 ×	£4,800	£19,200
Semi-Finals	2 ×	£8,250	£16,500
Runners-up	1 ×	£15,500	£15,500
Winners	1 ×	£28,000	£28,000

Total Prize Money	£150,000
Capital Development Fund	£100,000
Grand Total	£250,000

REGAL TROPHY ROLL OF HONOUR

Season	Winners		Runners-up		Venue	Attendance	Receipts
1971-72	Halifax	22	Wakefield T.	11	Bradford	7,975	£2,545
1972-73	Leeds	12	Salford	7	Huddersfield	10,102	£4,563
1973-74	Warrington	27	Rochdale H.	16	Wigan	9,347	£4,380
1974-75	Bradford N.	3	Widnes	2	Warrington	5,935	£3,305
1975-76	Widnes	19	Hull	13	Leeds	9,035	£6,275
1976-77	Castleford	25	Blackpool B.	15	Salford	4,512	£2,919
1977-78	Warrington	9	Widnes	4	St. Helens	10,258	£8,429
1978-79	Widnes	16	Warrington	4	St. Helens	10,743	£11,709
1979-80	Bradford N.	6	Widnes	0	Leeds	9,909	£11,560
1980-81	Warrington	12	Barrow	5	Wigan	12,820	£21,020
1981-82	Hull	12	Hull K.R.	4	Leeds	25,245	£42,987
1982-83	Wigan	15	Leeds	4	Elland Rd, Leeds	19,553	£49,027
1983-84	Leeds	18	Widnes	10	Wigan	9,510	£19,824
1984-85	Hull K.R.	12	Hull	0	Hull City FC	25,326	£69,555
1985-86	Wigan	11	Hull K.R.	8	Elland Rd, Leeds	17,573	£66,714
1986-87	Wigan	18	Warrington	4	Bolton W. FC	21,144	£86,041
1987-88	St. Helens	15	Leeds	14	Wigan	16,669	£62,232
1988-89	Wigan	12	Widnes	6	Bolton W.FC	20,709	£94,874
1989-90	Wigan	24	Halifax	12	Leeds	17,810	£73,688

REGAL TROPHY FINAL ....
A REVIEW

1971-72
Halifax 22 Hepworth; Rayner, Davies (1t), Willicombe (1t), Kelly (1t); Burton (5g), Baker (Sanderson); Dewhirst, Hawksley, Callon (1t), (Reeves), Fogerty, J. Martin, Halmshaw
Wakefield T. 11 Wraith (Ward); Slater (1t), Marston, Hegarty, Major; Topliss (1t), Harkin; Jeanes, Morgan, Lyons, Harrison (Spencer), Valentine (1t), N. Fox (1g)
Referee: S. Shepherd (Oldham)
1972-73
Leeds 12 Holmes (1g); Alan Smith, Hynes, Dyl, Atkinson (2t); Hardisty, Hepworth; Clawson (2g) (Ward), Fisher (Pickup), Jeanes, Haigh, Cookson, Eccles
Salford 7 Charlton; Colloby, Watkins (2g), Hesketh, Richards; Gill (P. Ward), Banner; Ramshaw, J. Ward, Mackay, Grice (Davies), Kirkbride, Dixon (1t)
Referee: W.H. Thompson (Huddersfield)
1973-74
Warrington 27 Whitehead (6g, 1t); M. Philbin, Noonan (2t), Reynolds (Pickup), Bevan (1t); Whittle, Gordon; D. Chisnall, (Nicholas 1t), Ashcroft, Brady, Wright, Wanbon, B. Philbin

Rochdale H. 16 Crellin; Brelsford (2t), Brophy (1t), Taylor (1t), Aspinall; Butler (Wood), Gartland; Holliday (2g), Harris, Whitehead, Fogerty, Sheffield, Halmshaw
Referee: D.G. Kershaw (York)
1974-75
Bradford N. 3 Carlton (1t); Francis, Ward, Gant, D. Redfearn; Blacker, Seabourne; Earl, Jarvis, Jackson, Joyce, Trotter, Fearnley
Widnes 2 Dutton (1g); A. Prescott, D.O'Neill, Aspey, Anderson; Hughes, Bowden; Mills, Elwell, Sheridan, Adams, Blackwood, Laughton
Referee: G.F. Lindop (Wakefield)
1975-76
Widnes 19 Dutton (3g); A. Prescott, George, Aspey, Jenkins (2t); Hughes, Bowden (1t, 1dg); Mills, Elwell, Wood, Foran, Sheridan, Adams (1t)
Hull 13 Stephenson; A. Macklin, Clark, Portz, Hunter (1t); Hancock, Foulkes (Davidson); Ramsey, Flanagan, Wardell, Boxall (2g), Walker, Crane (2t)
Referee: J.V. Moss (Manchester)
1976-77
Castleford 25 Wraith (1t); Fenton, Joyner (1t), P. Johnson (1t), Briggs; Burton (1t), Stephens (1t), Khan, Spurr, A. Dickinson, Reilly, Lloyd (5g), S. Norton

Blackpool B 15 Reynolds; Robinson, Heritage, Machen (1t), Pitman (Lamb); Marsh, Newall; Hamilton, Allen (1t), Egan (3g, 1t), Gamble, Groves (Hurst), M. Pattinson
Referee: M. J. Naughton (Widnes)
1977-78
Warrington 9 Finnegan; Hesford (3g), Benyon, Wilson, Bevan (1t); K. Kelly, Gordon; Lester, Dalgreen, Nicholas, Martyn, B. Philbin, Potter
Widnes 4 Eckersley; Wright, Aspey, George, Woods (2g); Hughes, Bowden; Ramsey, Elwell, Shaw (Dearden), Adams, Hull, Laughton
Referee: W.H. Thompson (Huddersfield)
1978-79
Widnes 16 Eckersley; Wright (1t), Aspey, Hughes, Burke (3g); Moran, Bowden; Mills, Elwell (2dg), Shaw, Dearden, Hull (1t), Adams (2dg)
Warrington 4 Finnegan; M. Kelly, Hesford (2g), Benyon, Sutton; K. Kelly, (Hunter), Gordon; Lester, Waller, Nicholas, Case, Martyn, A. Gwilliam
Referee: G.F. Lindop (Wakefield)
1979-80
Bradford N. 6 Mumby (1g); Barends, D. Redfearn, D. Parker (1t), Gant; Stephenson (1dg), A. Redfearn; Thompson, Bridges, Forsyth (I. Van Bellen), Grayshon, G. Van Bellen (Ferres), Casey
Widnes 0 Eckersley; Wright, Aspey, George, Burke; Hughes, Bowden; Hogan (Mills), Elwell, Shaw, L. Gorley, Hull, Adams
Referee: W.H. Thompson (Huddersfield)
1980-81
Warrington 12 Hesford (2g, 2dg); Thackray, I. Duane, Bevan (2t), M. Kelly; K. Kelly, A. Gwilliam; Courtney, Waller, Case, Martyn, Potter, Hunter (Eccles)
Barrow 5 Elliott; McConnell, French, Ball (1g), Wainwright; Mason (1t), Cairns; D. Chisnall, Allen (Szymala), Flynn, K. James, Kirkby, Hadley
Referee: W.H. Thompson (Huddersfield)
1981-82
Hull 12 Banks; O'Hara, Harrison, Leuluai, Prendiville; Day, Dean (1dg) (K. Harkin); Skerrett, Wileman (1t), Stone, Crane, L. Crooks (4g), Norton
Hull K.R. 4 Fairbairn (2g); Hubbard, M. Smith, Hogan, Muscroft; Hartley, P. Harkin (Burton); Holdstock (Millington), Watkinson, S. Crooks, Lowe, Casey, Hall
Referee: G.F. Lindop (Wakefield)

1982-83
Wigan 15 Williams; Ramsdale, Stephenson, Whitfield (4g, 1dg), Gill (1t) (Juliff 1t); M. Foy, Fairhurst; Shaw, Kiss, Campbell, West (Case), Scott, Pendlebury
Leeds 4 Hague; Campbell, Wilkinson, Dyl, Andy Smith; Holmes, Dick (2g); Dickinson, Ward, Burke, Sykes, W. Heron, D. Heron
Referee: R. Campbell (Widnes)
1983-84
Leeds 18 Wilkinson; Prendiville, Creasser (5g), D. Bell, Andy Smith; Holmes (1t), Dick (1t); Keith Rayne, Ward (Squire), Kevin Rayne, Moorby, Laurie, Webb
Widnes 10 Burke (1g); Wright, Keiron O'Loughlin, Lydon (1t), Linton (1t); Hughes, Gregory; S. O'Neill, Elwell, K. Tamati, L. Gorley, Whitfield, Adams
Referee: W.H. Thompson (Huddersfield)
1984-85
Hull K.R. 12 Fairbairn; Clark (1t), Robinson, Prohm (1t), Laws; M. Smith, Harkin; Broadhurst, Watkinson, Ema, Burton, Hogan (1t), Miller
Hull 0 Kemble (Schofield); S. Evans, Ah Kuoi, Leuluai, O'Hara; Topliss, Sterling; Edmonds (Dannatt), Patrick, Rose, L. Crooks, Proctor, Divorty
Referee: S. Wall (Leigh)
1985-86
Wigan 11 Hampson; Mordt, Stephenson (1g), Hanley, Gill (Edwards); Ella, M. Ford (1t); Dowling (1dg), Kiss, Wane (1t), West, Goodway, Potter (Du Toit)
Hull K.R. 8 Lydiat (1t); Clark, M. Smith, Dorahy, Laws (1t); G. Smith, Harkin; P. Johnston (Robinson), Watkinson, Ema, Burton, Kelly, Miller
Referee: J. Holdsworth (Kippax)
1986-87
Wigan 18 Hampson; Stephenson, Lydon, Bell (1t), Gill (2t, 1g); Hanley, Edwards; West, Dermott, Case, Roberts, Potter, Goodway (1t)
Warrington 4 Johnson; Meadows, Cullen, Ropati, Forster (1t); K. Kelly, Peters (Duane); Boyd, K. Tamati (Rathbone), Jackson, Sanderson, Roberts, M. Gregory
Referee: J. Holdsworth (Kippax)
1987-88
St. Helens 15 Veivers; Tanner, Loughlin (2t, 3g), Elia, Quirk; Cooper, Holding (1dg); Burke, Groves, Souto (Evans), Forber, Haggerty, Platt

Leeds 14 Gurr; Morris, Schofield, Jackson (1t), Basnett (Gibson); Creasser (1t, 3g), Ashton; Tunks, Maskill, Kevin Rayne (Fairbank), Powell, Medley, D. Heron
Referee: G.F. Lindop (Wakefield)
1988-89
Wigan 12 Hampson; Bell, K. Iro (1t), Lydon (2g) (Gregory), T. Iro; Byrne, Edwards; Shel-
ford (Goodway), Dermott, Wane, Betts, Potter, Hanley (1t)
Widnes 6 Tait; Thackray, Currier (1g), Wright (1t), Offiah; Myler, D. Hulme; Sorensen, McKenzie, Grima, O'Neill, Koloto (P. Hulme), Eyres
Referee: J. Holdsworth (Kippax)

REGAL TROPHY MAN OF THE MATCH

Season	Winner	Team	Position
1971-72	Bruce Burton	Halifax (v. Wakefield T.)	Stand off
1972-73	Keith Hepworth	Leeds (v. Salford)	Scrum half
1973-74	Kevin Ashcroft	Warrington (v. Rochdale H.)	Hooker
1974-75	Barry Seabourne	Bradford N. (v. Widnes)	Scrum half
1975-76	Reg Bowden	Widnes (v. Hull)	Scrum half
1976-77	Gary Stephens	Castleford	Scrum half
	Howard Allen	Blackpool B.	Hooker
1977-78	Steve Hesford	Warrington (v. Widnes)	Winger
1978-79	David Eckersley	Widnes (v. Warrington)	Full back
1979-80	Len Casey	Bradford N. (v. Widnes)	Loose forward
1980-81	Tommy Martyn	Warrington (v. Barrow)	Second row
1981-82	Trevor Skerrett	Hull (v. Hull K.R.)	Prop
1982-83	Martin Foy	Wigan (v. Leeds)	Stand off
1983-84	Mark Laurie	Leeds (v. Widnes)	Second row
1984-85	Paul Harkin	Hull K.R. (v. Hull)	Scrum half
1985-86	Paul Harkin	Hull K.R. (v. Wigan)	Scrum half
1986-87	Andy Goodway	Wigan (v. Warrington)	Loose forward
1987-88	Paul Loughlin	St. Helens (v. Leeds)	Centre
1988-89	Ellery Hanley	Wigan (v. Widnes)	Loose forward
1989-90	Ellery Hanley	Wigan (v. Halifax)	Loose forward

REGAL TROPHY RECORDS

ALL ROUNDS

TEAM
Highest score: Wigan 92 v. Runcorn H. 2 (1988-89)
Biggest attendance: 25,326 Hull v. Hull K.R.
(at Hull C. FC)....... Final 1984-85

INDIVIDUAL
Most tries: 6 by Vince Gribbin (Whitehaven) v. Doncaster 1984-85
*Most goals: 17 by Sammy Lloyd (Castleford)
*Most points: 43 (17g,3t) by Sammy Lloyd (Castleford)
*The above records were achieved in the Castleford v. Millom first round tie in 1973-74.

REGAL TROPHY FINAL RECORDS

Most final appearances: 7 by Widnes
Most wins: 5 by Wigan
Most tries: 3 by Ellery Hanley (Wigan) v. Halifax
.... 1989-90
Most goals: 6 by Derek Whitehead (Warrington) v. Rochdale H.............................. 1973-74
Most points: 15 (6g,1t) by Derek Whitehead (Warrington) v. Rochdale H......................... 1973-74
Highest score: Warrington 27 v. Rochdale H. 16 1973-74
Widest margin win: Wigan 18 v. Warrington 4 1986-87
Biggest attendance: 25,326 Hull v. Hull K.R.
(at Hull C. FC)...............1984-85
Biggest receipts: £94,874 Widnes v. Wigan
(at Bolton W. FC)............... 1988-89

NON-LEAGUE CLUBS IN THE REGAL TROPHY

Amateur clubs have entered the Regal tournament in every season apart from a period between 1981 and 1984. Two figured in the first round up to 1979-80 and one the following season. They were then left out from 1981-82 because the number of professional clubs had grown beyond the mathematically suitable 32.

But the amateurs returned in 1984-85 with two clubs joining the professionals in a small preliminary round, the number being increased to three in 1989-90.

The fate of the amateurs has varied from the record 88-5 hammering Millom received at Castleford to victories by Cawoods and Myson over Halifax and Batley respectively.

The full list of amateur clubs' results — all first round matches except where stated (P) Preliminary (2) Second Round — is:

●*BEFORE 1977-78 the competition was known as the Player's No. 6 Trophy, then the John Player Trophy. In 1983-84 it became the John Player Special Trophy, renamed the Regal Trophy in 1989-90. It was not until 1979-80 that semi-finals were played at neutral venues.*

Season							Attendance
1971-72		Wigan	33	v	Ace Amateurs (Hull)	9	2,678
		Thames Board Mill (Warr.)	7	v	Huddersfield	27	1,175
1972-73		Bramley	26	v	Pilkington Recs. (St. Helens)	5	616
		Dewsbury	22	v	Dewsbury Celtic	4	1,897
1973-74		Whitehaven	26	v	Dewsbury Celtic	3	1,276
		Castleford	88	v	Millom (Cumbria)	5	1,031
1974-75		Whitehaven	32	v	Lock Lane (Castleford)	6	537
		Doncaster	15	v	Kippax White Swan	6	453
1975-76		Salford	57	v	Mayfield (Rochdale)	3	3,449
		Barrow	16	v	Pilkington Recs. (St. Helens)	9	612
1976-77		Halifax	24	v	Ovenden (Halifax)	4	3,680
		Salford	39	v	Ace Amateurs (Hull)	15	3,037
1977-78		N.D.L.B. (Hull)	4	v	New Hunslet	18	3,845
		Halifax	8	v	Cawoods (Hull)	9	1,168
	(2)	Wakefield T.	31	v	Cawoods (Hull)	7	3,380
1978-79		Leigh Miners Welfare	9	v	Halifax	21	1,621
		Milford (Leeds)	5	v	Dewsbury	38	3,129
1979-80		Pilkington Recs. (St. Helens)	9	v	Wigan	18	6,707
		Blackpool B.	6	v	West Hull	3	555
1980-81		Castleford	30	v	Pilkington Recs. (St. Helens)	17	2,823
1984-85	(P)	Myson (Hull)	2	v	Dewsbury	8	1,572
	(P)	Keighley	24	v	Dudley Hill (Bradford)	10	1,570
1985-86	(P)	Keighley	24	v	Jubilee (Featherstone)	6	1,007
	(P)	West Hull	10	v	Castleford	24	2,500
1986-87	(P)	Batley	2	v	Myson (Hull)	8	687
	(P)	Millom (Cumbria)	4	v	Wakefield T.	18	2,000
		Myson (Hull)	11	v	Swinton	18	1,648
1987-88	(P)	Featherstone R.	34	v	Thatto Heath (St. Helens)	16	1,045
	(P)	Heworth (York)	5	v	Swinton	32	1,063
1988-89	(P)	Wigan St. Patricks	36	v	Elland (Halifax)	2	2,510
		Sheffield E.	80	v	Wigan St. Patricks	8	621
1989-90	(P)	Batley	28	v	West Hull	14	844
	(P)	Crosfields (Warrington)	14	v	Workington T.	19	942
	(P)	Kells (Whitehaven)	2	v	Doncaster	28	2,127

REGAL TROPHY PROGRESS CHART

Key: W — Winners. F — Beaten finalists. SF — Semi-final. P — Preliminary round.

	1989-90	1988-89	1987-88	1986-87	1985-86	1984-85	1983-84	1982-83	1981-82	1980-81	1979-80	1978-79	1977-78	1976-77	1975-76	1974-75	1973-74	1972-73	1971-72
BARROW	1	1	1	3	2	1	2	3	3	F	1	1	1	1	2	1	1	1	3
BATLEY	1	1	2	P	1	1	P	1	1	1	1	1	1	1	2	1	1	2	1
BRADFORD N.	2	SF	1	3	2	2	1	3	2	1	W	SF	SF	2	1	W	1	3	1
BRAMLEY	1	2	P	1	1	3	*	1	1	1	2	1	1	2	1	2	SF	2	2
CARLISLE	1	1	1	2	P	P	2	2	2										
CASTLEFORD	SF	2	2	2	1	2	1	1	2	SF	3	3	2	W	SF	1	2	1	2
CHORLEY	1																		
DEWSBURY	2	1	2	1	1	3	1	1	1	1	1	2	1	1	1	1	3	2	1
DONCASTER	1	2	1	2	2	1	1	1	1	1	1	1	1	1	1	2	1	1	1
FEATHERSTONE R.	3	1	1	2	P	2	3	1	2	2	2	2	3	2	1	1	1	2	1
FULHAM	1	P	P	1	1	1	1	1	1	2									
HALIFAX	F	2	2	2	1	SF	1	1	1	3	1	2	1	2	1	1	2	1	W
HUDDERSFIELD	2	1	1	P	1	1	1	2	2	2	1	1	3	1	3	1	1	2	2
HULL	1	2	3	SF	3	F	2	2	W	SF	1	2	1	3	F	1	1	3	3
HULL K.R.	1	3	2	1	F	W	2	3	F	2	1	SF	1	1	3	SF	1	SF	2
HUNSLET	2	P	1	1	2	P	1	1	1	2	1	1	2	1	2	1	1	1	1
KEIGHLEY	1	1	1	1	2	1	2	1	2	1	2	3	2	1	1	2	3	1	2
LEEDS	3	1	F	1	1	SF	W	F	3	1	2	1	1	3	2	3	3	W	SF
LEIGH	1	3	2	3	SF	1	SF	2	1	3	3	3	3	SF	2	1	2	2	1
NOTTINGHAM C.	1	1	2	1	1	1													
OLDHAM	3	1	SF	1	2	2	1	1	SF	1	1	1	2	2	2	2	1	1	1
ROCHDALE H.	1	2	1	1	1	2	1	2	1	1	1	1	1	1	1	1	F	1	2
RUNCORN H.	1	1	1	1	1	2	2	P	1	1	1	1	1	1	2	1	1	1	1
RYEDALE-YORK	P	1	1	P	3	1	1	2	1	2	2	1	3	1	2	2	2	2	2
ST. HELENS	SF	SF	W	3	SF	3	SF	2	1	1	2	2	2	2	3	1	SF	SF	SF
SALFORD	2	1	3	1	2	1	2	3	3	2	SF	2	2	2	SF	3	2	F	1
SHEFFIELD E.	3	2	1	2	1	1													
SWINTON	2	1	1	2	1	1	3	1	SF	1	1	1	1	1	1	3	1	3	1
TRAFFORD B.	1	2	3	2	1	1	1	2	P	2	2	1	1	F	1	1	1	1	3
WAKEFIELD T.	P	3	2	2	2	P	1	1	1	1	SF	3	SF	1	2	2	3	2	F
WARRINGTON	P	3	3	F	3	1	2	SF	2	W	3	F	W	1	1	3	W	1	1
WHITEHAVEN	2	1	1	1	1	2	P	1	1	3	1	1	1	1	1	SF	2	1	2
WIDNES	2	F	1	SF	3	3	F	SF	3	3	F	W	F	SF	W	F	1	3	1
WIGAN	W	W	SF	W	W	2	3	W	1	1	2	2	3	2	2	2	2	1	3
WORKINGTON T.	1	P	1	1	1	1	1	1	2	1	3	2	2	3	3	1	2	1	1

*Bramley withdrew from the Trophy while in liquidation, opponents Hull K.R. receiving a bye.

PREMIERSHIP TROPHY

1990 Final

Reduced to 12 men for the whole of the second half, Widnes outclassed Bradford Northern to race to a record third successive Stones Bitter Premiership Trophy triumph.

The Chemics were already 10-0 in front when scrum half Paul Hulme was sent off in the 39th minute for alleged gouging of Northern second row man Paul Medley. Three more second half touchdowns sealed a commanding victory, Bradford's sole response being a slick Tony Marchant try in the 63rd minute.

Widnes extended their Premiership record to six victories in seven appearances in the final.

The dismissal of Hulme on the stroke of half-time cast a cloud over a Widnes performance that so completely overwhelmed Bradford, impressive conquerors of newly-crowned Champions Wigan in the semi-finals a week earlier. Northern were a huge disappointment, never showing the pace or variety in attack to seriously trouble a Widnes defence whose tackling and covering was back to its best, earning a Stones Bitter prize cheque for £15,000 in front of a record Premiership crowd of 40,796, paying a record £273,877.

Widnes full back Alan Tait was the best of several outstanding individuals and became the first player twice to win the Harry Sunderland Trophy as Man of the Match after taking the award 12 months earlier. On the eve of departure of the 15-match tour of Papua New Guinea and New Zealand, the Great Britain number one had a big hand in the opening try by loose forward Les Holliday, scoring the next two himself to put Widnes well on the way to victory before Andy Currier finished with two more touchdowns.

That Holliday try came after only three minutes, Tait and the ex-Halifax and Swinton forward splitting Northern down the middle with Holliday handling twice before going between the posts for Jonathan Davies to add the goal.

With the Chemics over-elaborating and two or three players hesitating to add the vital finishing touch, Tait stepped up to take a more positive approach for his first try in the 27th minute. The Scot again timed his support to perfection to complete another bout of passing and go in for Widnes's opening touchdown of the second half.

With so many of the Widnes players capable of striking back from any distance, Northern's plan to pin them down with deep kicks never looked like being effective. Widnes also kept a close watch on Paul Harkin, the mainspring of Bradford's attacking machine rarely being given a chance to produce his usual big match performance. He still managed to provide one of Northern's few highlights when breaking brilliantly from a scrum, teasing and dummying on a 40-yard run before being smothered by the cover.

Ian Wilkinson was also prominent at full back with a series of thundering runs from his own line, while 1990 tourist Karl Fairbank justified his selection with a succession of punishing charges to be the best of the Bradford pack.

Only once did Northern combine effectively, Marchant racing round Tait in spectacular fashion for a 63rd minute touchdown after Harkin and Fairbank had made the initial impact 40 yards out.

Slack tackling that allowed Balmain-bound Currier to pick his way through for their last two tries, Davies adding both goals before completing the scoring with a 70th minute penalty goal.

With Bradford Northern hooker Brian Noble taken off at half-time with knee ligament trouble, Widnes went on to win the scrums 15-6, Northern having a 12-6 penalty count advantage.

STONES BITTER PREMIERSHIP FINAL

13 May   **Old Trafford, Manchester**

WIDNES 28		BRADFORD NORTHERN 6
Alan Tait	1.	Ian Wilkinson
Jonathan Davies	2.	Gerald Cordle
Andy Currier	3.	Steve McGowan
Darren Wright	4.	Tony Marchant
Martin Offiah	5.	Richard Francis
David Hulme	6.	Roger Simpson
Paul Hulme	7.	Paul Harkin
Kurt Sorensen, Capt.	8.	Kelvin Skerrett
Phil McKenzie	9.	Brian Noble
Mike O'Neill	10.	David Hobbs, Capt
Emosi Koloto	11.	Paul Medley
Richard Eyres	12.	Karl Fairbank
Les Holliday	13.	Keith Mumby
Tony Myler	14.	David Cooper
Joe Grima	15.	Craig Richards

T: Tait (2), Currier (2), Holliday   T: Marchant
G: Davies (4)   G: Mumby
Substitutions: Substitutions:
Myler for Sorensen (Half-time)   Richards for Noble (Half-time)
Grima for Koloto (64 min.)   Cooper for McGowan (69 min.)
Half-time: 10-0   Attendance: 40,796
Referee: Colin Morris (Huddersfield)   Receipts: £273,877

1990 Round by Round

A week before their Wembley meeting, Wigan and Warrington clashed in a Stones Bitter Premiership first round tie at Central Park. Short of six injured Test men, Wigan trailed 20-4 at the break, storming back with three tries in four minutes to leave the Wire leading 26-22. Substitute Bobby Goulding scored a 70th minute penalty goal before touching down three seconds from the end to clinch a 28-26 success for Wigan. Visitors St. Helens pulled back to 13-8 with only minutes left at Bradford Northern, the Yorkshiremen pulling clear with last ditch tries from Gerald Cordle and Karl Fairbank to seal a 25-8 victory. Leeds hooker Colin Maskill pulled off a sensational interception to set up a last minute 85-yard try for Vince Fawcett and clinch a 24-18 home win against a 12-man Castleford side who lost skipper John Joyner, sent off after 43 minutes. In a powerful second half display, Widnes scored tries through Emosi Koloto and Martin Offiah to add to an Alan Tait first half effort in an 18-8 success over visitors Hull, for whom Noel Cleal scored a consolation try.

Widnes clinched a record third successive Premiership final appearance with a convincing 27-7 semi-final triumph at Leeds, Welshman Jonathan Davies scoring all 10 first half points with a penalty try and three goals before setting up the Phil McKenzie try which killed off the Loiners. Scrum half Paul Harkin was the key figure in Bradford Northern's 9-0 success at champions Wigan, their first scoreless performance of the season. Harkin contributed a try and two drop goals, Keith Mumby adding a goal and David Hobbs a drop goal.

1990 Results

First Round

Bradford N.	25	St. Helens	8
Leeds	24	Castleford	18
Widnes	18	Hull	8
Wigan	28	Warrington	26

Semi-Finals

Leeds	7	Widnes	27
Wigan	0	Bradford N.	9

Final

Widnes	28	Bradford N.	6

(at Old Trafford, Manchester)

1990 Prizes

Winners: £15,000
Runners-up: £6,000

History

With the reintroduction of two divisions in 1973-74 there was no longer a need for a play-off to decide the championship.

However, it was decided to continue the tradition of an end-of-season play-off, the winners to receive the newly instituted Premiership Trophy.

In the first season of the Premiership, 1974-75, the top 12 Division One clubs and the top four from Division Two went into a first round draw, the luck of the draw operating through to the final, played on a neutral venue.

The following season the play-off was reduced to the top eight clubs in the First Division, the ties being decided on a merit basis i.e. 1st v. 8th, 2nd v. 7th etc. At the semi-final stage the highest placed clubs had the option of when to play at home in the two-legged tie.

In 1978-79 the two-leg system was suspended because of fixture congestion and the higher placed clubs had home advantage right through to the neutrally staged final.

Two legs returned the following season, but were finally abolished from 1980-81.

A Second Division Premiership tournament was introduced for the first time in 1986-87, Manchester United's Old Trafford being selected as a new fixed venue for a doubleheader final.

PREMIERSHIP ROLL OF HONOUR

Year	Winners		Runners-up		Venue	Attendance	Receipts
1975	Leeds	26	St. Helens	11	Wigan	14,531	£7,795
1976	St. Helens	15	Salford	2	Swinton	18,082	£13,138
1977	St. Helens	32	Warrington	20	Swinton	11,178	£11,626
1978	Bradford N.	17	Widnes	8	Swinton	16,813	£18,677
1979	Leeds	24	Bradford N.	2	Huddersfield	19,486	£21,291
1980	Widnes	19	Bradford N.	5	Swinton	10,215	£13,665
1981	Hull K.R.	11	Hull	7	Leeds	29,448	£47,529
1982	Widnes	23	Hull	8	Leeds	12,100	£23,749
1983	Widnes	22	Hull	10	Leeds	17,813	£34,145
1984	Hull K.R.	18	Castleford	10	Leeds	12,515	£31,769
1985	St. Helens	36	Hull K.R.	16	Elland Rd, Leeds	15,518	£46,950
1986	Warrington	38	Halifax	10	Elland Rd, Leeds	13,683	£50,879
1987	Wigan	8	Warrington	0	Old Trafford, Man'r	38,756	£165,166
1988	Widnes	38	St. Helens	14	Old Trafford, Man'r	35,252	£202,616
1989	Widnes	18	Hull	10	Old Trafford, Man'r	40,194	£264,242
1990	Widnes	28	Bradford N.	6	Old Trafford, Man'r	40,796	£273,877

PREMIERSHIP FINAL . . . . A REVIEW

1974-75

Leeds 26 Holmes (2g) (Marshall 3g); Alan Smith (1t), Hynes (1t, 1dg) (Eccles), Dyl, Atkinson (2t), Mason (1t), Hepworth; Dickinson, Ward, Pitchford, Cookson, Batten, Haigh
St. Helens 11 G. Pimblett; L. Jones (1t), Wilson, Hull, Mathias (1t); Walsh, Heaton (1t); Warlow (Cunningham), A. Karalius, Mantle (K. Gwilliam), E. Chisnall, Nicholls, Coslett (1g)
Referee: W.H. Thompson (Huddersfield)

1975-76

St. Helens 15 G. Pimblett (3g); L. Jones, Glynn (1t), Noonan, Mathias; Benyon, Heaton (K. Gwilliam); Mantle, A. Karalius (1t), James, Nicholls, E. Chisnall (1t), Coslett
Salford 2 Watkins (2dg); Fielding, Richards, Hesketh, Graham; Butler, Nash; Coulman, Raistrick, Sheffield, Knighton (Turnbull), Dixon, E. Prescott
Referee: M. J. Naughton (Widnes)

1976-77
St. Helens 32 G. Pimblett (7g, 1t); L. Jones, Benyon (1t), Cunningham (1t), Mathias (1t), Glynn (Ashton); K. Gwilliam (1t); D. Chisnall, Liptrot, James (1t), Nicholls (A. Karalius), E. Chisnall, Pinner
Warrington 20 Finnegan; Curling, Bevan (Cunliffe), Hesford (4g), M. Kelly; A. Gwilliam (1t), Gordon (1t); Weavill (1t), Price, Case, Martyn (Peers), Lester, B. Philbin (1t)
Referee: G.F. Lindop (Wakefield)
1977-78
Bradford N. 17 Mumby (2g); Barends (1t), Roe (1t), Austin, D. Redfearn (1t); Wolford (1dg), A. Redfearn; I. Van Bellen (Fox), Raistrick, Thompson, Joyce (Forsyth), Trotter, Haigh (1t)
Widnes 8 Eckersley; Wright, Hughes, Aspey (2t), Woods (1g); Gill, Bowden; Mills, Elwell, Shaw (Ramsey) (George), Adams, Hull, Laughton
Referee: J.E. Jackson (Pudsey)

1978-79
Leeds 24 Hague; Alan Smith (1t), D. Smith (1t), Dyl (Fletcher), Atkinson; Dick (7g, 1dg); J. Sanderson, Harrison, Ward (1t), Pitchford, Joyce, Eccles (Adams), Cookson
Bradford N. 2 Mumby; D. Parker, Okulicz, Gant, Spencer; Ferres (1g), A. Redfearn; Thompson, Bridges, Forsyth (I. Van Bellen), Trotter (Mordue), Grayshon, Casey
Referee: W.H. Thompson (Huddersfield)
1979-80
Widnes 19 Burke (1g); Wright (1t), George, Aspey (1t), Bentley (1t); Eckersley (1dg), Bowden; Shaw, Elwell (1t, 1dg), M. O'Neill, L. Gorley (1t), Hull (Hogan), Adams
Bradford N. 5 Mumby (1g); MacLean (Ferres), D. Redfearn (1t), D. Parker, Gant; Stephenson, A. Redfearn; Thompson, Bridges, Forsyth, Clarkson (G. Van Bellen), Grayshon, Hale
Referee: W.H. Thompson (Huddersfield)

Widnes skipper Kurt Sorensen lifts the Stones Bitter Premiership Trophy for a record third successive year.

1980-81
Hull K.R. 11 Proctor; Hubbard (1g), M. Smith
(1t), Hogan (1t), Muscroft; Hartley (1t), Harkin;
Holdstock, Watkinson, Millington, Lowe, Casey,
Hall (Burton)
Hull 7 Woods (2g); Peacham, Elliott, Wilby,
Prendiville; Banks, Dean; Tindall, Wileman,
Stone, Skerrett (Madley), Crane (1t), Norton
Referee: J. Holdsworth (Leeds)
1981-82
Widnes 23 Burke (4g, 1t); Wright (1t), Kieron
O'Loughlin, Cunningham (A. Myler), Basnett
(1t); Hughes (1t), Gregory; M. O'Neill, Elwell,
Lockwood (Whitfield), L. Gorley, E. Prescott,
Adams (1t)
Hull 8 Kemble; O'Hara (Day), Leuluai,
S. Evans, Prendiville; Topliss, Harkin; Tindall,
Wileman (Lloyd), Stone, Skerrett, Crooks
(1t, 2g, 1dg), Norton
Referee: S. Wall (Leigh)
1982-83
Widnes 22 Burke; Linton, Hughes, Lydon (5g),
Basnett (2t); A. Myler (1t), Gregory (1t) (Hulme);
M. O'Neill, Elwell, L. Gorley, Whitfield
(S. O'Neill), Prescott, Adams
Hull 10 Kemble; O'Hara (1t), Day (Solal),
Leuluai, S. Evans; Topliss (1t), Dean; Skerrett,
Bridges, Stone, Rose, Crooks (2g), Norton
(Crane)
Referee: F. Lindop (Wakefield)
1983-84
Hull K.R. 18 Fairbairn; Clark, M. Smith (1t),
Prohm (1t), Laws (1t); Dorahy (1t, 1g), Harkin;
Holdstock, Rudd, Millington (Robinson),
Burton (Lydiat), Broadhurst, Hall
Castleford 10 Roockley; Coen, Marchant, Hyde,
Kear (1t); Robinson, R. Beardmore (3g); Ward,
Horton, Connell, Crampton, Atkins, Joyner
Referee: R. Campbell (Widnes)
1984-85
St. Helens 36 Veivers (1t); Ledger (2t), Peters,
Meninga (2t) (Allen), Day (4g); Arkwright,
Holding; Burke (Forber), Ainsworth (1t),
P. Gorley, Platt, Haggerty, Pinner (1t)

Hull K.R. 16 Fairbairn (1t, 2g); Clark,
Robinson (1t), Prohm, Laws (1t); M. Smith,
G. Smith (Harkin); Broadhurst, Watkinson,
Ema (Lydiat), Kelly, Hogan, Hall
Referee: S. Wall (Leigh)
1985-86
Warrington 38 Paul Ford (Johnson 1t);
Forster (1t), Cullen, R. Duane, Carbert;
Bishop (1t, 5g), A. Gregory; Boyd (2t),
Tamati (1t), Jackson (1t), Sanderson (McGinty),
Roberts, M. Gregory
Halifax 10 Whitfield (3g) (Smith); Riddlesden,
T. Anderson, C. Anderson (1t), Wilson;
Crossley, Stephens; Scott, McCallion, Robinson,
Juliff, James (Bond), Dixon
Referee: F. Lindop (Wakefield)
1986-87
Wigan 8 Hampson; Gill (1g), Stephenson (1g),
Bell, Lydon (1t) (Russell); Edwards, Gregory;
Case, Kiss, Wane (West), Goodway, Potter,
Hanley
Warrington 0 Johnson; Drummond, Ropati, B.
Peters, Forster; Cullen, Bishop; Tamati, Roberts
(Eccles), Jackson, Humphries (M. Gregory),
Sanderson, Duane
Referee: K. Allatt (Southport)
1987-88
Widnes 38 Platt (1g); Thackray (Tait, 1t),
Currier (4g), Wright (2t), Offiah; Dowd,
D. Hulme (2t); Sorensen (1t), McKenzie (1t),
Grima (S. O'Neill),M. O'Neill, P. Hulme,
R. Eyres
St. Helens 14 Loughlin (3g); Ledger (1t),
Tanner, Elia, Quirk; Bailey, Holding; Burke,
Groves, Evans (Dwyer), Forber, Fieldhouse
(Allen), Haggerty (1t)
Referee: J. Holdsworth (Kippax)
1988-89
Widnes 18 Tait; Davies (3g), Currier (1t) (Pyke),
Wright (1t), Offiah (1t); D. Hulme (A. Myler),
P. Hulme; Sorensen, McKenzie, Grima, M.
O'Neill, Koloto, R. Eyres.
Hull 10 Fletcher; Eastwood, Blacker, Price
(Wilby), O'Hara; Pearce (3g), Windley (Nolan);
Dannatt, Jackson, S. Crooks, Welham (1t),
Sharp, Divorty.
Referee: J. Holdsworth (Kippax)

THE HARRY SUNDERLAND TROPHY

The trophy, in memory of the famous
Queenslander, a former Australian Tour
Manager, broadcaster and journalist, is
presented to the Man of the Match in the end
of season Championship or Premiership final.

The award is donated and judged by the
Rugby League Writers' Association and is
sponsored by Stones Bitter.

The Harry Sunderland Trophy Roll of Honour

Year	Winner	Team	Position
1965	Terry Fogerty	Halifax (v. St. Helens)	Second row
1966	Albert Halsall	St. Helens (v. Halifax)	Prop
1967	Ray Owen	Wakefield T. (v. St. Helens)	Scrum half
1968	Gary Cooper	Wakefield T. (v. Hull K.R.)	Full back
1969	Bev Risman	Leeds (v. Castleford)	Full back
1970	Frank Myler	St. Helens (v. Leeds)	Stand off
1971	Bill Ashurst	Wigan (v. St. Helens)	Second row
1972	Terry Clawson	Leeds (v. St. Helens)	Prop
1973	Mick Stephenson	Dewsbury (v. Leeds)	Hooker
1974	Barry Philbin	Warrington (v. St. Helens)	Loose forward
1975	Mel Mason	Leeds (v. St. Helens)	Stand off
1976	George Nicholls	St. Helens (v. Salford)	Second row
1977	Geoff Pimblett	St. Helens (v. Warrington)	Full back
1978	Bob Haigh	Bradford N. (v. Widnes)	Loose forward
1979	Kevin Dick	Leeds (v. Bradford N.)	Stand off
1980	Mal Aspey	Widnes (v. Bradford N.)	Centre
1981	Len Casey	Hull K.R. (v. Hull)	Second row
1982	Mick Burke	Widnes (v. Hull)	Full back
1983	Tony Myler	Widnes (v. Hull)	Stand off
1984	John Dorahy	Hull K.R. (v. Castleford)	Stand off
1985	Harry Pinner	St. Helens (v. Hull K.R.)	Loose forward
1986	Les Boyd	Warrington (v. Halifax)	Prop
1987	Joe Lydon	Wigan (v. Warrington)	Winger
1988	David Hulme	Widnes (v. St. Helens)	Scrum half
1989	Alan Tait	Widnes (v. Hull)	Full back
1990	Alan Tait	Widnes (v. Bradford N.)	Full back

PREMIERSHIP RECORDS First staged 1975

ALL ROUNDS

TEAM

Highest score: Hull K.R. 54 v. Leeds 0 1984
(Also widest margin)
Biggest attendance: 40,796 Bradford N. v. Widnes
..........Final at Old Trafford 1990

INDIVIDUAL

Most goals:
9 by Andy Gregory (Widnes) v. Leeds...Round 1 1982
Most points:
22 (7g, 2t) by John Dorahy (Hull K.R.) v. Leeds
.............Round 1 1984

Most tries:
4 by David Hall (Hull K.R.) v. Castleford
.............Round 1 1983
4 by Phil Ford (Wigan) v. Hull...........Round 1 1985
4 by Ellery Hanley (Wigan) v. Hull K.R.
.............Round 1 1986

PREMIERSHIP FINAL

TEAM

Most appearances: 7 by Widnes
Most wins: 6 by Widnes
Highest score:
Warrington 38 v. Halifax 10 (widest margin).......1986
Widnes 38 v. St. Helens 14 1988
Biggest attendance:
40,796 Bradford N. v. Widnes
(at Old Trafford, Man'r) 1990

INDIVIDUAL

Most tries:
No player has scored 3 or more
Most goals:
8 by Kevin Dick (Leeds) v. Bradford N.............1979
Most points: 17 (7g, 1t) by Geoff Pimblett (St. Helens)
v. Warrington..........1977

SECOND DIVISION PREMIERSHIP TROPHY

1990 Final

Oldham staged the most remarkable comeback in any cup final to snatch the Stones Bitter Second Division Premiership Trophy after trailing 29-8 early in the second half.

Teenage substitute Tommy Martyn — son of the former England forward, Tommy — was the match winner seven minutes from the end of a see-saw contest, selling a dummy to the weary Hull K.R. defence to complete Oldham's blistering scoring burst of five tries in 27 minutes.

The comeback rally was led by scrum half Mike Ford, who took the Tom Bergin Trophy as Man of the Match for scheming Rovers' amazing downfall in great style. The Roughyeds' skipper produced an inspired display, all the more satisfying for being opposite Great Britain tourist David Bishop.

Until Ford took control of the pulsating match, the reins had been in the hand of Robins' stand off Wayne Parker who had dominated the midfield in brilliant style. Parker overcame a foot injury, which needed a pre-match painkilling injection, and a late switch from scrum half to the number six jersey to set a marvellous example from the start.

He was the mainspring on attack as Rovers opened in the free-flowing style which had brought them the Second Division title. He led the Yorkshiremen into a 13-2 lead inside 15 minutes with two tries and a drop goal, centre Mike Fletcher adding two goals to join the elite band to have played and scored in every match in a season.

Parker was still bossing the show a minute after the break when he combined with skipper Bryan Niebling to send in second row man Des Harrison for Hull K.R.'s fifth try.

With the floodgates expected to open, Oldham suddenly came roaring back.

There seemed no cause for alarm when Ford sneaked in for his 46th minute try and Gary Hyde added the goal, nor when centre John Henderson scrambled over after a superb 50-yard move to make it 29-18 in the 56th minute. But when a glorious sweeping attack from a scrum sent Richard Irving winging in on the hour the Oldham players and fans sensed the near impossible.

Six minutes later hooker Andy Ruane squeezed in from a play-the-ball for a third consecutive unconverted touchdown, taking the scoreline to 29-24 and setting up the distinct possibility of the biggest turn around in cup history.

Oldham's sensational victory came with Rovers' defence in tatters, 18-year-old substitute Martyn taking full advantage, having come on for the concussed Duncan Platt after 19 minutes. Hyde's successful goal kick gave Oldham their second Division Two premiership title in three years, the only side to lift the trophy twice.

A total of 11 tries was amassed in yet another highly entertaining Second Division Premiership showpiece, taking the tally of points scored in the four-year history of the tournament to a massive 211, an average of 53 points per match.

The magnificent Oldham comeback was never on the cards as Hull K.R. swept ahead, seeking revenge for the home-and-away league defeats by the Roughyeds. With further tries from winger Garry Clark, created by Australian Greg Austin and an individual effort from Paul Lyman, the Robins held a half-time lead of 23-8.

Their bid to land a first-ever double haul of the First and Second Division Premiership titles, having taken the premier trophy in 1981 and 1985, floundered in tired fashion as Oldham added a major chapter in the history of cup final comebacks.

SECOND DIVISION PREMIERSHIP FINAL

13 May   **Old Trafford, Manchester**

OLDHAM 30   **HULL K.R. 29**

Duncan Platt	1.	David Lightfoot
Richard Irving	2.	Garry Clark
Gary Hyde	3.	Mike Fletcher
John Henderson	4.	Greg Austin
Paul Lord	5.	Anthony Sullivan
Brett Clark	6.	Wayne Parker
Mike Ford, Capt	7.	David Bishop
Leo Casey	8.	Bryan Niebling, Capt
Andy Ruane	9.	Chris Rudd
John Fieldhouse	10.	Asuquo Ema
Paul Round	11.	Des Harrison
Charlie McAlister	12.	Andy Thompson
Richard Russell	13.	Paul Lyman
Tommy Martyn	14.	Jimmy Irvine
Keith Newton	15.	Colin Armstrong

T: Lord, Ford, Henderson, Irving, Ruane, Martyn
G: Hyde (2), Platt
Substitutions:
Martyn for Platt (19 min)
Newton for Casey (31 min)
Half-time: 8-23

T: Parker (2), Clark, Lyman, Harrison
G: Fletcher (4), Parker (dg)
Substitutions:
Irvine for Bishop (60 min)
Armstrong for Harrison (74 min)
Referee: Robin Whitfield (Widnes)

1990 Round by Round

Seventh-placed Dewsbury pulled off the shock first round result with a 20-18 success at title runners-up Rochdale Hornets. Although the better side throughout, Dewsbury only took the lead for the first time with five minutes left, Paul Durnin finishing off a neat move. Hornets' marksman Steve Turner missed a last second goal kick attempt to level the scores. Table-toppers Hull K.R. scored seven tries — two apiece to wingmen Garry Clark and Anthony Sullivan — to dispose of Fulham 40-6 before receiving the Second Division Championship bowl in a post-match ceremony. Beaten 15-12 at Swinton to spoil their title bid, Oldham gained revenge with a five-try 32-10 victory at Watersheddings. After a week of strike threats, Halifax travelled to Ryedale-York to go down 24-7, New Zealand centre Basil Ake grabbing a hat-trick of tries for the home side.

In the semi-finals, Hull K.R. were inspired by two-try Man of the Match Wayne Parker in a 36-8 trouncing of Dewsbury at Craven Park. Rovers scored a total of six tries, three in each half. Visitors Ryedale-York trailed only 10-8 after an hour, Oldham running in four of their six tries in the last quarter to clinch a 32-8 passage to their second Old Trafford final in three years.

Hull K.R. two-try hero, stand off Wayne Parker.

Man of the Match, Oldham skipper Mike Ford.

1990 Results

First Round

Hull K.R.	40	Fulham	6
Oldham	32	Swinton	10
Rochdale H.	18	Dewsbury	20
Ryedale-York	24	Halifax	7

Semi-Finals

Hull K.R.	36	Dewsbury	8
Oldham	32	Ryedale-York	8

Final

Oldham	30	Hull K.R.	29

(at Old Trafford, Manchester)

1990 Prizes

Winners:	£8,000
Runners-up:	£3,000

SECOND DIVISION PREMIERSHIP.... A REVIEW

1986-87

Swinton 27 Viller; Bate (1t), Topping (Ratcliffe), Brown, Rippon (3g); Snape, Lee (1t); Grima (1t), Ainsworth (1t), Muller, Derbyshire (1t), M. Holliday (Allen), L. Holliday (1dg)
Hunslet 10 Kay; Tate, Penola, Irvine, Wilson; Coates, King; Sykes, Gibson (Senior), Bateman (2t), Platt (1g) (Mason), Bowden, Jennings
Referee: J. McDonald (Wigan)

1987-88

Oldham 28 Burke (Irving); Round, D. Foy (2t), McAlister (4g), Meadows (1t); Walsh (1t), Ford; Sherratt (Warnecke), Sanderson, Waddell, Hawkyard, Graham, Flanagan (1t)
Featherstone R. 26 Quinn (5g); Bannister (1t), Sykes (1t), Banks, Marsh (Crossley); Steadman (2t), Fox; Siddall (Bastian), K. Bell, Harrison, Hughes, Smith, Lyman
Referee: R. Whitfield (Widnes)

1988-89

Sheffield E. 43 Gamson; Cartwright, Dickinson, Powell (3t), Young; Aston (1t, 7g, 1dg), Close (Evans); Broadbent (1t), Cook (1t), Van Bellen, Nickle, Fleming (McDermott, 1t), Smiles
Swinton 18 Topping; Ranson (1t), Viller (Maloney), Snape, Bate; Frodsham (1t), Hewitt; Mooney, Melling (1t), S. O'Neill, Ainsworth, Allen (1t) (Horrocks), J. Myler (3g).
Referee: R. Whitfield (Widnes)

SECOND DIVISION PREMIERSHIP ROLL OF HONOUR

Year	Winners	Runners-up	Venue
1987	Swinton 27	Hunslet 10	Old Trafford, Manchester
1988	Oldham 28	Featherstone R. 26	Old Trafford, Manchester
1989	Sheffield E 43	Swinton 18	Old Trafford, Manchester
1990	Oldham 30	Hull K.R. 29	Old Trafford, Manchester

THE TOM BERGIN TROPHY

The trophy, in honour of the President of the Rugby League Writers' Association and former Editor of the *Salford City Reporter,* is presented to the Man of the Match in the end of season Second Division Premiership final. The award is donated and judged by the Association and sponsored by Stones Bitter.

The Tom Bergin Trophy Roll of Honour

Year	Winner	Team	Position
1987	Gary Ainsworth	Swinton (v. Hunslet)	Hooker
1988	Des Foy	Oldham (v. Featherstone R.)	Centre
1989	Mark Aston	Sheffield E. (v. Swinton)	Stand off
1990	Mike Ford	Oldham (v. Hull K.R.)	Scrum half

LANCASHIRE CUP

1989 Final

Riding high at the head of the Stones Bitter Championship, revitalised Warrington collected their first piece of silverware for more than three years by lifting the Grunhalle Lager Lancashire Cup.

The Wire overcame a spirited Second Division Oldham 24-16 at St. Helens, denying the Roughyeds their first county cup success for 31 years.

But it took Australian second row man Bob Jackson, coaxed out of premature retirement, to settle the issue after Oldham had battled their way back to 14-12 after an hour.

Warrington opened with all their new-found confidence and stormed into a 12-0 lead in the first 10 minutes. Inspired by the powerful running of skipper Mike Gregory, bidding for the role at national level with the first British Coal Test looming and Ellery Hanley out injured, Warrington scored two tries through the opportunism of New Zealander Joe Ropati and winger Mark Forster. Stand off Robert Turner added the first of his four goals.

The Second Division outfit refused to lie down and Tony Barrow's charges came back with tries by centre Richard Irving and winger Steve Robinson, while left winger Paul Lord was unfortunate to have a third disallowed by referee Ray Tennant.

Warrington's 14-12 lead was looking anything but secure until Jackson, in his second spell at the club, took over. In the 57th minute, the former Fulham packman caught the Oldham defence off guard with a 30-yard burst to the line.

A touchdown from Lord kept Oldham in the hunt but Jackson popped up again eight minutes from time to take a Des Drummond pass to crash over and earn the Man of the Match award, while praising the contribution of loose forward Gregory.

Warrington lifted the Lancashire Cup for the first time since 1982, but Oldham, having conquered St. Helens and Wigan en route to the final, were left to rue the disallowing of Lord's claim for a touchdown which would have given them a half-time lead.

Oldham were also disrupted by the loss through injury of goalkicking full back Duncan Platt, who had already hit the target once, centre Gary Hyde taking over to add a second.

The Knowsley Road success crowned Warrington's transformation of image under Australian coach Brian Johnson, the trophy being collected a month before his first anniversary at the helm. Jackson's individual match honour was a reward for alertness, pace and stamina, attributes characterising Warrington's new outlook.

Triumphant Warrington skipper Mike Gregory.

GRUNHALLE LAGER LANCASHIRE CUP FINAL

14 October   St. Helens

WARRINGTON 24   **OLDHAM 16**

David Lyon	1.	Duncan Platt
Des Drummond	2.	Steve Robinson
Joe Ropati	3.	Gary Hyde
Tony Thorniley	4.	Richard Irving
Mark Forster	5.	Paul Lord
Robert Turner	6.	Brett Clark
Greg Mackey	7.	Mike Ford
Tony Burke	8.	Leo Casey
Mark Roskell	9.	Andy Ruane
Steve Molloy	10.	John Fieldhouse
Bob Jackson	11.	Shaun Allen
Gary Sanderson	12.	Keith Newton
Mike Gregory, Capt.	13.	John Cogger, Capt.
Paul Darbyshire	14.	Richard Russell
Ronnie Duane	15.	John Fairbank

T: Jackson (2), Ropati, Forster
G: Turner (4)
Substitutions:
Darbyshire for Lyon (34 min.)
Duane for Sanderson (65 min.)
Half-time: 14-12
Attendance: 9,990

T: Irving, Robinson, Lord
G: Platt, Hyde
Substitutions:
Russell for Platt (34 min.)
Fairbank for Casey (58 min.)
Referee: Ray Tennant (Castleford)

1989 Round by Round

In the preliminary round Trafford Borough, ex-Chorley Borough, were drawn at Victory Park, their former home now occupied by newly-formed Chorley. Rugby League's latest club secured a 12-6 debut victory after the visitors had led 6-2 at the interval.

Chorley's cup success was shortlived for big spenders Wigan handed out a 50-4 drubbing in the first round tie staged at Leigh, Kevin Iro leading an 11-try rout with four touchdowns. Revitalised Rochdale Hornets also came down to earth with a 52-12 defeat at First Division Salford, Steve Kerry amassing 24 points and centre Ian Bragger running in four tries in the last 11 minutes. Hornets, despite missing new recruit John Woods, trailed only 12-10 five minutes after half-time. Troubled Barrow crashed 46-2 to

Second Division Oldham at Craven Park, the Shipbuilders opening the scoring with a Steve Maguire penalty goal, having conceded 74 points in their previous two league encounters. Leigh's 26-8 home success over Whitehaven was marred by the sending off of scrum half Phil Johnson for a high tackle plus hooker Mick Dean and Whitehaven's Frank Johnston for fighting after the final whistle. Bottom of the Second Division the previous season, Runcorn Highfield visited St. Helens to suffer their 25th successive defeat, the rampant Saints running in 14 tries in a 78-10 victory. Centre Paul Loughlin piled up 30 points, while Phil Veivers and Alan Hunte notched hat-tricks of tries.

A crowd of over 4,000 at Carlisle FC's Brunton Park watched Second Division Carlisle crash 46-6 to Championship-

Premiership double winners Widnes. Winger Brimah Kebbie bagged four tries and Jonathan Davies scored twice in a nine-try display, the Cumbrians' consolation try coming from skipper Harry Pinner. Warrington opened with a try from full back David Lyon and two Robert Turner goals before Second Division visitors Swinton consolidated to hold the Wire to a 10-0 interval lead, the home side running out 16-6 victors with a further try from Des Drummond and two more Turner goals. Fulham pulled off a shock 30-24 success at Workington, each side scoring five tries with the Londoners' Steve Guyett kicking five goals, while Town's David Lowden only hit the target twice.

In the second round, Second Division Oldham upset the form book by registering a 36-6 victory at St. Helens, who lost forward Roy Haggerty after only 10 minutes for punching ex-Saint colleague John Fieldhouse. Oldham ran in six tries including one from full back Duncan Platt who also added six goals, while St. Helens prop Stuart Evans was dismissed with a minute left for a late tackle on hooker Andy Ruane. Fulham attracted a crowd of 3,204 to Hendon FC for the visit of Wigan, who scored six tries in a comfortable 34-4 success which generated much needed publicity in the capital city. Fulham trailed to two touchdowns in the first nine minutes, their contribution to the scoreline being two Guyett goals. Widnes flier Martin Offiah scored twice in a 34-12 success at Leigh, his first coming after only 10 minutes, skipper Kurt Sorensen setting up the second midway through the second half. Warrington avenged the previous season's Lancashire Cup semi-final defeat by Salford by inflicting a 27-4 away success. Winger Drummond took the spotlight with two tries, the second a 70-yard sprint after intercepting Keith Bentley's pass.

In the semi-finals, Second Division Old-ham pulled off the shock of the tournament by defeating top-of-the-table Wigan 19-18 at Watersheddings. Deputy kicker Gary Hyde hit the winning goal five minutes from time. Moments later visiting stand off Shaun Edwards was sent off for tripping as Wigan went out after winning the Lancashire Cup in the past four seasons. World Club Champions Widnes continued their hangover to the Old Trafford celebrations, having lost in the league at Sheffield Eagles, by crashing 28-6 at Warrington, the Wire being lifted by Australian scrum half Greg Mackey, creator of their first two tries, plus the accurate boot of half back partner Turner, who kicked six goals.

Oldham hooker Andy Ruane.

1989 RESULTS

Preliminary Round

Chorley	12	Trafford B.	6

First Round

Barrow	2	Oldham	46
Carlisle	6	Widnes	46
(at Carlisle FC)			
Chorley	4	Wigan	50
(at Leigh)			
Leigh	26	Whitehaven	8
St Helens	78	Runcorn H.	10
Salford	52	Rochdale H.	12
Warrington	16	Swinton	6
Workington T.	24	Fulham	30

Second Round

Fulham	4	Wigan	34
(at Hendon FC)			
Leigh	12	Widnes	34
St. Helens	6	Oldham	36
Salford	4	Warrington	27

Semi-Finals

Oldham	19	Wigan	18
Warrington	28	Widnes	6

Final

Warrington	24	Oldham	16
(at St. Helens)			

LANCASHIRE CUP ROLL OF HONOUR

Season	Winners		Runners-up		Venue	Attendance	Receipts
1905-06	Wigan	0	Leigh	0	Broughton	16,000	£400
(replay)	Wigan	8	Leigh	0	Broughton	10,000	£200
1906-07	Broughton R.	15	Warrington	6	Wigan	14,048	£392
1907-08	Oldham	16	Broughton R.	9	Rochdale	14,000	£340
1908-09	Wigan	10	Oldham	9	Broughton	20,000	£600
1909-10	Wigan	22	Leigh	5	Broughton	14,000	£296
1910-11	Oldham	4	Swinton	3	Broughton	14,000	£418
1911-12	Rochdale H.	12	Oldham	5	Broughton	20,000	£630
1912-13	Wigan	21	Rochdale H.	5	Salford	6,000	£200
1913-14	Oldham	5	Wigan	0	Broughton	18,000	£610
1914-15	Rochdale H.	3	Wigan	2	Salford	4,000	£475
1915-16 to 1917-18 *Competition suspended*							
1918-19	Rochdale H.	22	Oldham	0	Salford	18,617	£1,365
1919-20	Oldham	7	Rochdale H.	0	Salford	19,000	£1,615
1920-21	Broughton R.	6	Leigh	3	Salford	25,000	£1,800
1921-22	Warrington	7	Oldham	5	Broughton	18,000	£1,200
1922-23	Wigan	20	Leigh	2	Salford	15,000	£1,200
1923-24	St. Helens Recs.	17	Swinton	0	Wigan	25,656	£1,450
1924-25	Oldham	10	St. Helens Recs.	0	Salford	15,000	£1,116
1925-26	Swinton	15	Wigan	11	Broughton	17,000	£1,115
1926-27	St. Helens	10	St. Helens Recs.	2	Warrington	19,439	£1,192
1927-28	Swinton	5	Wigan	2	Oldham	22,000	£1,275
1928-29	Wigan	5	Widnes	4	Warrington	19,000	£1,150
1929-30	Warrington	15	Salford	2	Wigan	21,012	£1,250
1930-31	St. Helens Recs.	18	Wigan	3	Swinton	16,710	£1,030
1931-32	Salford	10	Swinton	8	Broughton	26,471	£1,654
1932-33	Warrington	10	St. Helens	9	Wigan	28,500	£1,675
1933-34	Oldham	12	St. Helens Recs.	0	Swinton	9,085	£516
1934-35	Salford	21	Wigan	12	Swinton	33,544	£2,191
1935-36	Salford	15	Wigan	7	Warrington	16,500	£950
1936-37	Salford	5	Wigan	2	Warrington	17,500	£1,160
1937-38	Warrington	8	Barrow	4	Wigan	14,000	£800

Season	Winners		Runners-up		Venue	Attendance	Receipts
1938-39	Wigan	10	Salford	7	Swinton	27,940	£1,708
1939-40*	Swinton	5	Widnes	4	Widnes	5,500	£269
	Swinton	16	Widnes	11	Swinton	9,000	£446
	Swinton won on aggregate 21-15						
1940-41 to 1944-45 *Competition suspended during war-time*							
1945-46	Widnes	7	Wigan	3	Warrington	28,184	£2,600
1946-47	Wigan	9	Belle Vue R.	3	Swinton	21,618	£2,658
1947-48	Wigan	10	Belle Vue R.	7	Warrington	23,110	£3,043
1948-49	Wigan	14	Warrington	8	Swinton	39,015	£5,518
1949-50	Wigan	20	Leigh	7	Warrington	35,000	£4,751
1950-51	Wigan	28	Warrington	5	Swinton	42,541	£6,222
1951-52	Wigan	14	Leigh	6	Swinton	33,230	£5,432
1952-53	Leigh	22	St. Helens	5	Swinton	34,785	£5,793
1953-54	St. Helens	16	Wigan	8	Swinton	42,793	£6,918
1954-55	Barrow	12	Oldham	2	Swinton	25,204	£4,603
1955-56	Leigh	26	Widnes	9	Wigan	26,507	£4,090
1956-57	Oldham	10	St. Helens	3	Wigan	39,544	£6,274
1957-58	Oldham	13	Wigan	8	Swinton	42,497	£6,918
1958-59	Oldham	12	St. Helens	2	Swinton	38,780	£6,933
1959-60	Warrington	5	St. Helens	4	Wigan	39,237	£6,424
1960-61	St. Helens	15	Swinton	9	Wigan	31,755	£5,337
1961-62	St. Helens	25	Swinton	9	Wigan	30,000	£4,850
1962-63	St. Helens	7	Swinton	4	Wigan	23,523	£4,122
1963-64	St. Helens	15	Leigh	4	Swinton	21,231	£3,857
1964-65	St. Helens	12	Swinton	4	Wigan	17,383	£3,393
1965-66	Warrington	16	Rochdale H.	5	St. Helens	21,360	£3,800
1966-67	Wigan	16	Oldham	13	Swinton	14,193	£3,558
1967-68	St. Helens	2	Warrington	2	Wigan	16,897	£3,886
(replay)	St. Helens	13	Warrington	10	Swinton	7,577	£2,485
1968-69	St. Helens	30	Oldham	2	Wigan	17,008	£4,644
1969-70	Swinton	11	Leigh	2	Wigan	13,532	£3,651
1970-71	Leigh	7	St. Helens	4	Swinton	10,776	£3,136
1971-72	Wigan	15	Widnes	8	St. Helens	6,970	£2,204
1972-73	Salford	25	Swinton	11	Warrington	6,865	£3,321
1973-74	Wigan	19	Salford	9	Warrington	8,012	£2,750
1974-75	Widnes	6	Salford	2	Wigan	7,403	£2,833
1975-76	Widnes	16	Salford	7	Wigan	7,566	£3,880
1976-77	Widnes	16	Workington T.	11	Wigan	8,498	£6,414
1977-78	Workington T.	16	Wigan	13	Warrington	9,548	£5,038
1978-79	Widnes	15	Workington T.	13	Wigan	10,020	£6,261
1979-80	Widnes	11	Workington T.	0	Salford	6,887	£7,100
1980-81	Warrington	26	Wigan	10	St. Helens	6,442	£8,629
1981-82	Leigh	8	Widnes	3	Wigan	9,011	£14,029
1982-83	Warrington	16	St. Helens	0	Wigan	6,462	£11,732
1983-84	Barrow	12	Widnes	8	Wigan	7,007	£13,160
1984-85	St. Helens	26	Wigan	18	Wigan	26,074	£62,139
1985-86	Wigan	34	Warrington	8	St. Helens	19,202	£56,030
1986-87	Wigan	27	Oldham	6	St. Helens	20,180	£60,329
1987-88	Wigan	28	Warrington	16	St. Helens	20,237	£67,339
1988-89	Wigan	22	Salford	17	St. Helens	19,154	£71,879
1989-90	Warrington	24	Oldham	16	St. Helens	9,990	£41,804

*Emergency War-time competition

177

LANCASHIRE CUP FINAL .... A REVIEW

1967-68
St. Helens 2 F. Barrow; Vollenhoven, Whittle, Benyon, A. Barrow; Douglas, Bishop; Warlow, Sayer, Watson, Hogan, Mantle, Coslett (1g)
Warrington 2 Affleck; Coupe, Melling, Harvey (Pickavance), Glover; Aspinall (1g), Gordon; Ashcroft, Harrison, Brady, Parr, Briggs, Clarke
Referee: G.F. Lindop (Wakefield)
Replay
St. Helens 13 F. Barrow; Vollenhoven, Smith, Benyon, Jones (1t); Douglas (Houghton 2g), Bishop; Warlow (1t), Sayer, Watson, E. Chisnall (1t), Mantle, Coslett
Warrington 10 Conroy; Coupe, Melling (1t), Allen (2g), Glover; Scahill, Gordon (1t); Ashcroft, Harrison, Price, Parr, Briggs, Clarke
Referee: G.F. Lindop (Wakefield)
1968-69
St. Helens 30 Rhodes; F. Wilson (2t), Benyon, Myler, Williams (1t); Whittle, Bishop (1t); Warlow, Sayer, Watson, Rees (1t), E. Chisnall (1t) Coslett (6g)
Oldham 2 Murphy; Elliott, Larder, McCormack, Whitehead; Briggs (1g), Canning; K. Wilson, Taylor, Fletcher (Maders), Irving, McCourt, Hughes
Referee: W.H. Thompson (Huddersfield)

1969-70
Swinton 11 Gowers; Gomersall, Fleet, Buckley, M. Philbin (1t); Davies, Kenny (4g); Bate, D. Clarke, Mackay, Holliday, Smith, Robinson
Leigh 2 Grainey; Tickle, Warburton, Collins, Stringer (Brown); Eckersley, Murphy (1g); D. Chisnall, Ashcroft, Watts, Welding, Lyon, Fiddler
Referee: E. Clay (Leeds)
1970-71
Leigh 7 Ferguson (2g); Tickle (Canning), L. Chisnall, Collins, Walsh; Eckersley (1t), Murphy; D. Chisnall, Ashcroft, Watts, Grimes, Clarkson, Mooney
St. Helens 4 F. Barrow; L. Jones, Benyon, Walsh, Wilson; Myler, Whittle; Halsall, A. Karalius, Rees (Prescott), Mantle, E. Chisnall, Coslett (2g)
Referee: W.H. Thompson (Huddersfield)
1971-72
Wigan 15 Tyrer (3g); Eastham (1t), Francis (1t), Fuller, Wright (Gandy); D. Hill, Ayres (1t); Ashcroft, Clarke, Fletcher, Ashurst, Kevin O'Loughlin, Laughton
Widnes 8 Dutton; Brown, McLoughlin, Aspey (1g), Gaydon (1t); D. O'Neill (1t), Bowden; Warlow, Foran, Doughty, Kirwan, Walsh (Lowe), Nicholls
Referee: W.H. Thompson (Huddersfield)

1972-73
Salford 25 Charlton (1t); Eastham (1t), Watkins (1t, 5g), Hesketh, Richards (1t); Gill, Banner (1t); Mackay, Walker, Ward, Whitehead, Dixon, Prescott
Swinton 11 Jackson; Fleay (1t), Cooke, Buckley, Gomersall; Kenny (1g) (M. Philbin), Gowers (3g); Halsall, Evans, Bate, R. Smith (Holliday), Hoyle, W. Pattinson
Referee: W.H. Thompson (Huddersfield)
1973-74
Wigan 19 Francis; Vigo, D. Hill, Keiron O'Loughlin (2t), Wright (1t); Cassidy, Ayres (1g); Smethurst, Clarke, Gray (4g), Irving, D. Robinson, Cunningham
Salford 9 Charlton; Fielding, Watkins (1t, 3g), Hesketh, Holland; Gill, Banner; Mackay, Walker, Davies (Grice), Dixon, Kear (Knighton), E. Prescott
Referee: W.H. Thompson (Huddersfield)

1974-75
Widnes 6 Dutton (1g); George (1t), D. O'Neill, Aspey, A. Prescott; Hughes (1dg), Bowden, Mills, Elwell, J. Stephens, Adams, Blackwood, Laughton
Salford 2 Charlton; Fielding (1g), Dixon, Graham, Richards; Taylor, Banner; Mackay, Devlin, Grice, Knighton, Coulman, E. Prescott
Referee: G.F. Lindop (Wakefield)
1975-76
Widnes 16 Dutton (3g, 1dg); A. Prescott (1t), George (1t), Aspey (1t), Jenkins; Hughes, Bowden; Mills, Elwell, Nelson, Foran, Fitzpatrick (Sheridan), Adams
Salford 7 Watkins (2g); Fielding, Butler, Hesketh, Richards (1t); Gill, Nash; Fiddler, Hawksley, Dixon (Mackay), Turnbull, Knighton, E. Prescott
Referee: W.H. Thompson (Huddersfield)
1976-77
Widnes 16 Dutton (4g, 1dg); Wright (1t), Aspey, George (1t), A. Prescott; Eckersley, Bowden (1dg); Ramsey, Elwell, Nelson, Dearden, Adams, Laughton
Workington T. 11 Charlton; Collister, Wilkins (1t), Wright, MacCorquodale (4g); Lauder, Walker; Mills, Banks, Calvin, Bowman, L. Gorley, W. Pattinson (P. Gorley)
Referee: W.H. Thompson (Huddersfield)
1977-78
Workington T. 16 Charlton (Atkinson); Collister, Risman, Wright (1t), MacCorquodale (4g); Wilkins (1t), Walker (2dg); Watts, Banks, Bowman, L. Gorley, W. Pattinson, P. Gorley
Wigan 13 Swann; Vigo, Davies (Burke 1g), Willicombe (1t), Hornby; Taylor, Nulty (1t, 1g); Hogan, Aspinall, Irving, Ashurst (1t),

Blackwood, Melling (Regan)
Referee: W.H. Thompson (Huddersfield)
1978-79
Widnes 15 Eckersley; Wright (1t), Aspey,
George, Burke (3g); Hughes, Bowden; Mills,
Elwell, Shaw, Adams, Dearden (Hull),
Laughton (2t)
Workington T. 13 Charlton; Collister, Risman,
Wilkins (1t), MacCorquodale (1t, 2g), McMillan,
Walker; Beverley, Banks, Bowman, Blackwood,
P. Gorley, W. Pattinson (L. Gorley 1t)
Referee: W.H. Thompson (Huddersfield)
1979-80
Widnes 11 Eckersley; Wright, Aspey, Hughes
(George), Burke (2g), Moran (1t), Bowden;
Hogan, Elwell (1dg), Shaw, L. Gorley, Dearden,
Adams (1t)
Workington T. 0 Charlton; MacCorquodale,
Maughan, Thompson, Beck; Rudd, Walker
(Roper); Beverley, Banks, Wallbanks (Varty),
W. Pattinson, Lewis, Dobie
Referee: W.H. Thompson (Huddersfield)

1980-81
Warrington 26 Finnegan; Thackray (1t),
I. Duane, Bevan (1t), Hesford (7g, 1t);
K. Kelly, A. Gwilliam; Courtney, Waller, Case,
Martyn (1t), Eccles (Potter), Hunter
Wigan 10 Fairbairn (1t, 2g); Ramsdale (1t),
Willicombe, Davies, Hornby; M. Foy, Bolton
(Coyle); Breheny, Pendlebury (M. Smith),
S. O'Neill, Melling, Clough, Hollingsworth
Referee: D. G. Kershaw (York)
1981-82
Leigh 8 Hogan; Drummond, Bilsbury (1t),
Donlan (1dg), Worgan; Woods (2g), Green;
Wilkinson, Tabern, Cooke, Martyn (Platt),
Clarkson, McTigue
Widnes 3 Burke; George, Hughes,
Cunningham, Bentley (1t); Moran, Gregory;
M. O'Neill, Elwell, Lockwood, L. Gorley,
E. Prescott, Adams
Referee: W.H. Thompson (Huddersfield)
1982-83
Warrington 16 Hesford (2g); Fellows (1t),
R. Duane, Bevan, M. Kelly (1t); Cullen,
K. Kelly (1t); Courtney, Webb, Cooke
(D. Chisnall), Eccles (1t), Fieldhouse, Gregory
St. Helens 0 Parkes (Smith); Ledger,
Arkwright, Haggerty, Litherland; Peters,
Holding; James, Liptrot, Bottell (Mathias),
Moorby, P. Gorley, Pinner
Referee: J. Holdsworth (Leeds)
1983-84
Barrow 12 Tickle (1dg); Moore, Whittle,
Ball (3g, 1dg), Milby; McConnell (1t), Cairns;
Hodkinson, Wall, McJennett, Herbert, Szymala,
Mossop

Widnes 8 Burke; Lydon (1t, 2g), Hughes,
Keiron O'Loughlin, Basnett; A. Myler,
Gregory; S. O'Neill, Elwell, K. Tamati,
Whitfield, E. Prescott, Adams
Referee: K. Allatt (Southport)
1984-85
St. Helens 26 Veivers (Haggerty 1t); Ledger,
Allen, Meninga (2t), Day (1t, 5g); Arkwright,
Holding; Burke, Liptrot, P. Gorley, Platt,
Round, Pinner
Wigan 18 Edwards; Ferguson, Stephenson,
Whitfield (3g), Gill (1t) (Pendlebury); Cannon,
Fairhurst; Courtney, Kiss (1t), Case, West (1t),
Wane, Potter
Referee: R. Campbell (Widnes)
1985-86
Wigan 34 Edwards (1t); Henley-Smith
(Hampson), Stephenson (7g), Hanley (1t),
Whitfield; Ella (2t), M. Ford; Dowling, Kiss
(1t), Wane (Case), Du Toit, Goodway, Potter
Warrington 8 Johnson (1t); Carbert (2g), Cullen,
Blake (Forster), Thackray; Kelly, A. Gregory;
Eccles, Webb, Jackson, Boyd (Tamati),
M. Gregory, Rathbone
Referee: J. Holdsworth (Kippax)
1986-87
Wigan 27 Edwards (2t); Lydon (1t, 1dg),
Stephenson, Bell, Gill (5g); Hanley, M. Ford
(1t); West, Dermott, Case, Roberts (Louw),
Potter, Goodway
Oldham 6 M'Barki; Sherman, Bridge (1t),
Warnecke, Taylor; Topliss, Kirwan; Clark,
Flanagan, Hobbs (1g), Nadiole, Worrall, Raper
(Hawkyard)
Referee: J.E. Smith (Halifax)
1987-88
Wigan 28 Hampson; Russell, Stephenson (1g)
(Bell), Lydon (5g), Gill (1t); Edwards, A.
Gregory; Case, Kiss, Wane (West, 1t),
Goodway, Potter, Hanley (2t)
Warrington 16 Johnson; Drummond, Forster
(2t), Peters, Carbert; Woods (2g), Holden;
K. Tamati, Webb (Harmon), Humphries,
Sanderson, Roberts, M. Gregory (1t)
Referee: G.F. Lindop (Wakefield)
1988-89
Wigan 22 Hampson; T. Iro, K. Iro (2t, 3g),
Bell (1t), Lydon (Byrne); Edwards, Gregory;
Lucas (Betts), Dermott, Shelford (1t), Platt,
Goodway, Hanley
Salford 17 Williams (Blease); Evans (1t).
Bentley (1t), Jones, Hadley; Shaw, Cairns;
Herbert (1t), Moran, Brown (2g), Gormley, M.
Worrall (1dg), Horo (McTigue)
Referee: K. Allatt (Southport)

179

MAN OF THE MATCH AWARDS

An award for the adjudged man of the match in the Lancashire Cup final was first presented in 1974-75. For four years the award was sponsored by the *Rugby Leaguer* newspaper. From 1978-85 the trophy was presented by Burtonwood Brewery, then from 1986 by Greenall Whitley, as part of their sponsorship of the Lancashire Cup. Under the auspices of the *Rugby Leaguer*, the choice was made by the Editor, while the breweries invited a panel of the Press to make the decision.

Season	Winner	Team	Position
1974-75	Mike Coulman	Salford (v. Widnes)	Second row
1975-76	Mick George	Widnes (v. Salford)	Centre
1976-77	David Eckersley	Widnes (v. Workington T.)	Stand off
1977-78	Arnold Walker	Workington T. (v. Wigan)	Scrum half
1978-79	Arnold Walker	Workington T. (v. Widnes)	Scrum half
1979-80	Mick Adams	Widnes (v. Workington T.)	Loose forward
1980-81	Tony Waller	Warrington (v. Wigan)	Hooker
1981-82	Ray Tabern	Leigh (v. Widnes)	Hooker
1982-83	Steve Hesford	Warrington (v. St. Helens)	Full back
1983-84	David Cairns	Barrow (v. Widnes)	Scrum half
1984-85	Mal Meninga	St. Helens (v. Wigan)	Centre
1985-86	Steve Ella	Wigan (v. Warrington)	Stand off
1986-87	Mike Ford	Wigan (v. Oldham)	Scrum half
1987-88	Shaun Edwards	Wigan (v. Warrington)	Stand off
1988-89	Paul Shaw	Salford (v. Wigan)	Stand off
1989-90	Bob Jackson	Warrington (v. Oldham)	Second row

LANCASHIRE CUP FINAL RECORDS

TEAM

Most appearances: 34 by Wigan
Most wins: 20 by Wigan
Highest score: Wigan 34 v. Warrington 8 1985
Widest margin: St. Helens 30 v. Oldham 2 1968
Biggest attendance:
42,793 St. Helens v. Wigan (at Swinton) 1953

INDIVIDUAL

Most tries:
4 by Brian Nordgren (Wigan) v. Leigh 1949
Most goals:
7 by Jim Ledgard (Leigh) v. Widnes 1955
    Steve Hesford (Warrington) v. Wigan 1980
    David Stephenson (Wigan) v. Warrington .. 1985
Most points:
17 (7g, 1t) by Steve Hesford (Warrington) v. Wigan
    1980

Warrington celebrate their first trophy haul for more than three years with the 1989 Grunhalle Lager Lancashire Cup.

YORKSHIRE CUP

1989 Final

Scrum half Paul Harkin continued his habit of collecting big game Man of the Match awards by steering Bradford Northern to their second John Smiths Yorkshire Cup triumph in three years.

It was a typically efficient performance by the Odsal number seven who became the first player to win the White Rose Trophy twice, matching his John Player Final Man of the Match double with Hull K.R. in 1985 and 1986.

The action on the field was marred by trouble on the terraces which caused play to be suspended for five minutes in the first half. Police arrested a small number of youths and others were ejected, referee Robin Whitfield having to hold up play when Featherstone fans spilled onto the pitch for safety following a disputed Bradford try.

The isolated troublespot blighted a tense encounter, with Harkin running the show in midfield, sneaking Northern's first two tries to halt Featherstone's momentum. Harkin's first score — a penalty try — in the 26th minute was controversial, putting in a short kick from a play-the-ball to be awarded the touchdown for obstruction. David Hobbs added the goal from under the posts.

Rovers skipper Deryck Fox made it 6-6 with his third penalty goal, having given them an early lead and then Harkin struck again, wriggling through for his second try. It was another close-in effort as he pulled out of a tackle to lunge over.

Although new Welsh winger Gerald Cordle touched down twice, Harkin's main rival for the Man of the Match award was teammate Karl Fairbank, a powerful second rower. The

Colliers had several players who deserved more than a runners-up medal, particularly centre Paul Newlove with his progressive running making big strides through the Northern defence. Better finishing would have changed the course of the game.

The newly-capped Great Britain star, the youngest-ever, produced the best solo run of an enthralling match when he broke through tackles early on and pounded 50 yards only for full back Chris Bibb to miss the pass which would have brought a try.

Another stray pass also cost Rovers dearly. New Zealander Iva Ropati ran well to bring them away from their own line, only for the centre to throw out a pass which fell short and ex-Cardiff RU winger Cordle swooped to kick ahead over 40 yards for Northern's last score on the hour.

Cordle's first touchdown was created by ex-Leeds forward Paul Medley with the sort of break which made him such a favourite at Headingley. The Test packman broke a tackle near halfway and galloped away before the cover closed in just as he slipped out a pass to the unmarked Cordle.

Medley and Keith Mumby came on as substitutes within the opening quarter, Mumby being carried off in the 66th minute, while John Pendlebury was troubled with an arm injury for most of the match. Even so, Northern's winning margin would have been greater but for Featherstone's covering, particularly by Bibb and veteran loose forward Peter Smith.

It was Smith who scored Rovers' first try just before half-time to leave the Colliers trailing 12-10 at the break, their other score coming in the last minute when Ropati crossed at the corner from Gary Price's pass, minutes after a claim for a penalty try by Bibb had been turned down.

JOHN SMITHS YORKSHIRE CUP FINAL

5 November   **Leeds**

BRADFORD NORTHERN 20		FEATHERSTONE ROVERS 14
Ian Wilkinson	1.	Chris Bibb
Gerald Cordle	2.	Barry Drummond
Steve McGowan	3.	Iva Ropati
Roger Simpson	4.	Paul Newlove
Richard Francis	5.	Alan Banks
Ivan Henjak	6.	Ian Smales
Paul Harkin	7.	Deryck Fox, Capt.
Kelvin Skerrett	8.	Jeff Grayshon
Glenn Barraclough	9.	Trevor Clark
Jon Hamer	10.	Glen Bell
David Hobbs, Capt.	11.	Gary Price
Karl Fairbank	12.	Glen Booth
John Pendlebury	13.	Peter Smith
Keith Mumby	14.	Alan Dakin
Paul Medley	15.	Andy Fisher

T: Harkin (2), Cordle (2)
G: Hobbs (2)
Substitutions:
Mumby for Henjak (13 min.)
Medley for Hamer (9 min.)
Half-time: 12-10
Attendance: 12,607

T: Smith, Ropati
G: Fox (3)
Substitutions:
Dakin for Bell (51 min.)
Fisher for Booth (51 min.)
Referee: Robin Whitfield (Widnes)

1989 Round by Round

One of the major shocks of the tournament came in the preliminary round with Second Division Dewsbury beating First Division Wakefield Trinity at Crown Flatt. With the scores level at 16-apiece, Dewsbury having missed five drop goal attempts, Neil Kelly was on target with eight minutes left only for Trinity's Mark Conway to equalise four minutes later. Willie Johnson then dropped a goal at his fourth attempt to give Dewsbury an 18-17 success. Playing their first match at Harvey Hadden Stadium, newly-named Nottingham City, formerly Mansfield Marksman, were hammered 56-6 by Hull, who ran in 10 tries after leading 22-0 at the interval.

In the first round, all three Leeds-based clubs were drawn at home ... and all lost. Leeds entertained arch rivals Bradford Northern, going down 15-8 as caretaker player-coach David Hobbs made a try for ex-Headingley full back Ian Wilkinson and kicked three goals in front of 13,214 fans. At Elland Road, Second Division Hunslet fell 44-0 to a Castleford side inspired by the debut of Australian scrum half Gary French, a tryscorer after only two minutes, winger David Plange contributing four touchdowns. Over at Bramley, visitors Hull K.R. ran out victors 54-12 with Australian centre Greg Austin marking his debut with two classic tries as well as creating scores for Tony Sullivan and Mike Fletcher, who totalled 22 points by adding nine goals. Loose forward Les Holliday was the architect of Halifax's 22-7 success at Dewsbury, who had Don Gregoire sent off in injury time.

Featherstone Rovers crushed Keighley 86-18 in a record breaking performance at Post Office Road, beating their previous best of 66 against Barrow in 1987. Winger

Mark Knapper amassed 30 points from 13 goals and a try — goals and points records for the club — while full back Chris Bibb touched down six times to equal the club record set by Mike Smith in 1968. Australian Jeff Hardy registered a hat-trick of tries in Sheffield Eagles' 36-5 victory at Batley, the first after only five minutes and the other two after returning from a second half spell in the sin bin. Eagles duo Mark Gamson and Mark Fleming were both sent off. Hull powered into a 20-0 half-time lead with two tries each from Australian David Liddiard and hooker Lee Jackson before visitors Ryedale-York staged a comeback with touchdowns from skipper Stuart Horton and winger Paul White, to go down 20-10. New Zealand centre Tony Kemp scored a try and a drop goal in Doncaster's 23-4 home victory over Huddersfield, whose points came from two Simon Kenworthy goals.

The only surprise of the second round was Second Division Halifax disposing of Hull 13-2 at Thrum Hall. Halifax took the lead with a 23rd minute Wilf George try before Holliday dropped a goal and then provided the vital pass for winger Eddie Riddlesden to score in the corner, Hull's sole reply being a 27th minute goal from Rob Nolan. Sheffield Eagles' skipper Daryl Powell scored a try, Mark Aston adding the goal, to give the visitors a 6-4 half-time lead at Bradford Northern before tries from Paul Harkin and Steve McGowan sealed a 19-6 success for the Odsal outfit. Castleford clinched a semi-final spot with a spell of three tries in 10 minutes at the start of the second half, visitors Hull K.R. having led 6-4 at the break before Wheldon Road stand off Graham Steadman completed his hat-trick of tries in a 28-12 win. Featherstone Rovers went through 37-22 after two tries in three minutes from New Zealander Iva Ropati and substitute Andy Fisher demoralised Doncaster at Post Office Road when the

Second Division side had led 18-17 early in the second half.

Both semi-final ties went to replays. Halifax recovered from a 16-4 deficit at home to Bradford Northern to draw level at 16-all, superbly marshalled by player-coach John Dorahy, who added the goal to Steve Smith's late try to force a replay. There was not the same drama at Odsal where Northern won 26-4, Hobbs marking his last match as caretaker coach by creating two tries and kicking five goals. Castleford winger David Plange scored a try five minutes from time to set up an 18-18 draw at Featherstone, the lead having changed hands four times with Deryck Fox and Jeff Grayshon outstanding for the Colliers and Australian full back Steve Larder scoring two Castleford tries. In the Wheldon Road replay, Rovers staged a remarkable comeback to gain a 28-26 victory. Having trailed 26-16 with a quarter of an hour left, a touchline goal from winger Knapper four minutes from time put Featherstone through to deny Castleford their seventh county final appearance of the decade.

Three Yorkshire Cup Final goals for Featherstone Rovers skipper Deryck Fox

1989 RESULTS

Preliminary Round

Dewsbury	18	Wakefield	17
Nottingham City	6	Hull	56

First Round

Batley	5	Sheffield E.	36
Bramley	12	Hull K.R.	54
Dewsbury	7	Halifax	22
Doncaster	23	Huddersfield	4
Featherstone R.	86	Keighley	18
Hull	20	Ryedale-York	10
Hunslet	0	Castleford	44
Leeds	8	Bradford N.	15

Second Round

Bradford N.	19	Sheffield E.	6
Castleford	28	Hull K.R.	12
Featherstone R.	37	Doncaster	22
Halifax	13	Hull	2

Semi-Finals

Featherstone R.	18	Castleford	18
Halifax	16	Bradford N.	16

Replays

Bradford N.	26	Halifax	4
Castleford	26	Featherstone R.	28

Final

Bradford N.	20	Featherstone R.	14
(at Leeds)			

YORKSHIRE CUP ROLL OF HONOUR

Year	Winners		Runners-up		Venue	Attendance	Receipts
1905-06	Hunslet	13	Halifax	3	Bradford P.A.	18,500	£465
1906-07	Bradford	8	Hull K.R.	5	Wakefield	10,500	£286
1907-08	Hunslet	17	Halifax	0	Leeds	15,000	£397
1908-09	Halifax	9	Hunslet	5	Wakefield	13,000	£356
1909-10	Huddersfield	21	Batley	0	Leeds	22,000	£778
1910-11	Wakefield T.	8	Huddersfield	2	Leeds	19,000	£696
1911-12	Huddersfield	22	Hull K.R.	10	Wakefield	20,000	£700
1912-13	Batley	17	Hull	3	Leeds	16,000	£523
1913-14	Huddersfield	19	Bradford N.	3	Halifax	12,000	£430
1914-15	Huddersfield	31	Hull	0	Leeds	12,000	£422
1918-19	Huddersfield	14	Dewsbury	8	Leeds	21,500	£1,309
1919-20	Huddersfield	24	Leeds	5	Halifax	24,935	£2,096
1920-21	Hull K.R.	2	Hull	0	Leeds	20,000	£1,926
1921-22	Leeds	11	Dewsbury	3	Halifax	20,000	£1,650
1922-23	York	5	Batley	0	Leeds	33,719	£2,414
1923-24	Hull	10	Huddersfield	4	Leeds	23,300	£1,728
1924-25	Wakefield T.	9	Batley	8	Leeds	25,546	£1,912
1925-26	Dewsbury	2	Huddersfield	0	Wakefield	12,616	£718
1926-27	Huddersfield	10	Wakefield T.	3	Leeds	11,300	£853
1927-28	Dewsbury	8	Hull	2	Leeds	21,700	£1,466
1928-29	Leeds	5	Featherstone R.	0	Wakefield	13,000	£838
1929-30	Hull K.R.	13	Hunslet	7	Leeds	11,000	£687
1930-31	Leeds	10	Huddersfield	2	Halifax	17,812	£1,405
1931-32	Huddersfield	4	Hunslet	2	Leeds	27,000	£1,764
1932-33	Leeds	8	Wakefield T.	0	Huddersfield	17,685	£1,183
1933-34	York	10	Hull K.R.	4	Leeds	22,000	£1,480
1934-35	Leeds	5	Wakefield T.	5	Dewsbury	22,598	£1,529
Replay	Leeds	2	Wakefield T.	2	Huddersfield	10,300	£745
Replay	Leeds	13	Wakefield T.	0	Hunslet	19,304	£1,327
1935-36	Leeds	3	York	0	Halifax	14,616	£1,113
1936-37	York	9	Wakefield T.	2	Leeds	19,000	£1,294
1937-38	Leeds	14	Huddersfield	8	Wakefield	22,000	£1,508
1938-39	Huddersfield	18	Hull	10	Bradford	28,714	£1,534
1939-40	Featherstone R.	12	Wakefield T.	9	Bradford	7,077	£403
1940-41	Bradford N.	15	Dewsbury	5	Huddersfield	13,316	£939
1941-42	Bradford N.	24	Halifax	0	Huddersfield	5,989	£635

Year	Winners		Runners-up		Venue	Attendance	Receipts
1942-43	Dewsbury	7	Huddersfield	0	Dewsbury	11,000	£680
	Huddersfield	2	Dewsbury	0	Huddersfield	6,252	£618
	Dewsbury won on aggregate 7-2						
1943-44	*Bradford N.*	*5*	*Keighley*	*2*	*Bradford*	*10,251*	*£757*
	Keighley	*5*	*Bradford N.*	*5*	*Keighley*	*8,993*	*£694*
	Bradford N. won on aggregate 10-7						
1944-45	Hunslet	3	Halifax	12	Hunslet	11,213	£744
	Halifax	2	Hunslet	0	Halifax	9,800	£745
	Halifax won on aggregate 14-3						
1945-46	Bradford N.	5	Wakefield T.	2	Halifax	24,292	£1,934
1946-47	Wakefield T.	10	Hull	0	Leeds	34,300	£3,718
1947-48	Wakefield T.	7	Leeds	7	Huddersfield	24,344	£3,461
Replay	Wakefield T.	8	Leeds	7	Bradford	32,000	£3,251
1948-49	Bradford N.	18	Castleford	9	Leeds	31,393	£5,053
1949-50	Bradford N.	11	Huddersfield	4	Leeds	36,000	£6,365
1950-51	Huddersfield	16	Castleford	3	Leeds	28,906	£5,152
1951-52	Wakefield T.	17	Keighley	3	Huddersfield	25,495	£3,347
1952-53	Huddersfield	18	Batley	8	Leeds	14,705	£2,471
1953-54	Bradford N.	7	Hull	2	Leeds	22,147	£3,833
1954-55	Halifax	22	Hull	14	Leeds	25,949	£4,638
1955-56	Halifax	10	Hull	10	Leeds	23,520	£4,385
Replay	Halifax	7	Hull	0	Bradford	14,000	£2,439
1956-57	Wakefield T.	23	Hunslet	5	Leeds	30,942	£5,609
1957-58	Huddersfield	15	York	8	Leeds	22,531	£4,123
1958-59	Leeds	24	Wakefield T.	20	Bradford	26,927	£3,833
1959-60	Featherstone R.	15	Hull	14	Leeds	23,983	£4,156
1960-61	Wakefield T.	16	Huddersfield	10	Leeds	17,456	£2,937
1961-62	Wakefield T.	19	Leeds	9	Bradford	16,329	£2,864
1962-63	Hunslet	12	Hull K.R.	2	Leeds	22,742	£4,514
1963-64	Halifax	10	Featherstone R.	0	Wakefield	13,238	£2,471
1964-65	Wakefield T.	18	Leeds	2	Huddersfield	13,527	£2,707
1965-66	Bradford N.	17	Hunslet	8	Leeds	17,522	£4,359
1966-67	Hull K.R.	25	Featherstone R.	12	Leeds	13,241	£3,482
1967-68	Hull K.R.	8	Hull	7	Leeds	16,729	£5,515
1968-69	Leeds	22	Castleford	11	Wakefield	12,573	£3,746
1969-70	Hull	12	Featherstone R.	9	Leeds	11,089	£3,419
1970-71	Leeds	23	Featherstone R.	7	Bradford	6,753	£1,879
1971-72	Hull K.R.	11	Castleford	7	Wakefield	5,536	£1,589
1972-73	Leeds	36	Dewsbury	9	Bradford	7,806	£2,659
1973-74	Leeds	7	Wakefield T.	2	Leeds	7,621	£3,728
1974-75	Hull K.R.	16	Wakefield T.	13	Leeds	5,823	£3,090
1975-76	Leeds	15	Hull K.R.	11	Leeds	5,743	£3,617
1976-77	Leeds	16	Featherstone R.	12	Leeds	7,645	£5,198
1977-78	Castleford	17	Featherstone R.	7	Leeds	6,318	£4,528
1978-79	Bradford N.	18	York	8	Leeds	10,429	£9,188
1979-80	Leeds	15	Halifax	6	Leeds	9,137	£9,999
1980-81	Leeds	8	Hull K.R.	7	Huddersfield	9,751	£15,578
1981-82	Castleford	10	Bradford N.	5	Leeds	5,852	£10,359
1982-83	Hull	18	Bradford N.	7	Leeds	11,755	£21,950
1983-84	Hull	13	Castleford	2	Elland Rd, Leeds	14,049	£33,572
1984-85	Hull	29	Hull K.R.	12	Hull C. FC	25,237	£68,639
1985-86	Hull K.R.	22	Castleford	18	Leeds	12,686	£36,327
1986-87	Castleford	31	Hull	24	Leeds	11,132	£31,888
1987-88	Bradford N.	12	Castleford	12	Leeds	10,947	£40,283
Replay	Bradford N.	11	Castleford	2	Elland Rd, Leeds	8,175	£30,732
1988-89	Leeds	33	Castleford	12	Elland Rd, Leeds	22,968	£76,658
1989-90	Bradford N.	20	Featherstone R.	14	Leeds	12,607	£50,775

YORKSHIRE CUP FINAL .... A REVIEW

1968-69
Leeds 22 Risman (5g); Alan Smith (1t), Hynes, Watson (1t), Atkinson (1t); Shoebottom, Seabourne; Clark, Crosby, K. Eyre, Ramsey (Hick 1t), A. Eyre, Batten
Castleford 11 Edwards; Howe, Hill (1t, 2g), Thomas, Stephens; Hardisty (2g), Hargrave; Hartley, C. Dickinson, Ward, Small, Lockwood (Redfearn), Reilly
Referee: J. Manley (Warrington)
1969-70
Hull 12 Owbridge; Sullivan (1t), Gemmell, Maloney (2g), A. Macklin; Hancock, Davidson; Harrison, McGlone, J. Macklin (1t), Kirchin, Forster, Brown (1g)
Featherstone R. 9 C. Kellett (3g); Newlove, Jordan, M. Smith, Hartley (T. Hudson); D. Kellett, Nash (1t); Tonks, Farrar, Lyons, A. Morgan, Thompson, Smales
Referee: R.L. Thomas (Oldham)
1970-71
Leeds 23 Holmes; Alan Smith (2t), Hynes (4g), Cowan, Atkinson (1t); Wainwright (Langley), Shoebottom; J. Burke, Dunn (1t), Cookson, Ramsey (1t), Haigh, Batten
Featherstone R. 7 C. Kellett (2g); M. Smith, Cotton, Newlove, Hartley (1t); Harding (Coventry), Hudson; Windmill, D. Morgan, Lyons, Rhodes, Thompson, Farrar
Referee: D.S. Brown (Preston)
1971-72
Hull K.R. 11 Markham; Stephenson, Coupland, Kirkpatrick, Longstaff (1t); Millward (4g), Daley; Wiley, Flanagan, Millington, Wallis, Palmer (Cooper), Brown
Castleford 7 Edwards; Foster (1t), S. Norton, Worsley, Lowndes; Hargrave, Stephens; Hartley, Miller, I. Van Bellen (Ackroyd 2g), A. Dickinson, Lockwood, Blakeway
Referee: A. Givvons (Oldham)
1972-73
Leeds 36 Holmes (3t); Alan Smith, Hynes (1g), Dyl (2t), Atkinson (1t); Hardisty (1t), Hepworth (Langley); Clawson (5g) (Fisher), Ward, Ramsey, Cookson, Eccles (1t), Batten
Dewsbury 9 Rushton; Ashcroft (1t), Childe, Day, Yoward; Agar (3g), A. Bates; Bell (Beverley), M. Stephenson, Lowe, Grayshon, J. Bates (Lee), Hankins
Referee: M.J. Naughton (Widnes)
1973-74
Leeds 7 Holmes; Langley (1t) (Marshall 1g), Hynes (1g), Dyl, Atkinson; Hardisty, Hepworth; Jeanes (Ramsey), Ward, Clarkson, Eccles, Cookson, Batten

Wakefield T. 2 Wraith (Sheard); D. Smith, Crook (1g), Hegarty, B. Parker; Topliss, Bonnar; Valentine, Morgan, Bratt, Knowles (Ballantyne), Endersby, Holmes
Referee: M.J. Naughton (Widnes)
1974-75
Hull K.R. 16 Smithies; Sullivan (Dunn lt), Watson (2t), Coupland, Kirkpatrick (1t); Millward, Stephenson; Millington, Heslop, Rose, Wallis, N. Fox (2g) (Madley), Brown
Wakefield T. 13 Sheard; D. Smith (1t), Crook (2g), Hegarty (1t), Archer; Topliss, Bonnar; Ballantyne, Handscombe, Bratt (1t), Skerrett, A. Tonks (Goodwin), (Holmes), Morgan
Referee: M.J. Naughton (Widnes)
1975-76
Leeds 15 Marshall; Alan Smith, Hague, Dyl (1t), Atkinson; Holmes (4g, 1dg), Hynes; Harrison, Payne, Pitchford, (Dickinson), Eccles, Batten, Cookson (1t)
Hull K.R. 11 Wallace; Dunn, A. Burwell, Watson, Sullivan (1t); Turner, Millward (1dg); Millington, Dickinson, Lyons, Rose, N. Fox (2g, 1t), Hughes (Holdstock)
Referee: J.V. Moss (Manchester)
1976-77
Leeds 16 Marshall (2g); Hague, Hynes, Dyl (2t), D. Smith; Holmes, Banner; Dickinson, Ward, Pitchford, Eccles (1t), Burton, Cookson (1t)
Featherstone R. 12 Box; Bray (1t), Coventry, Quinn (3g), K. Kellett; Newlove, Fennell; Gibbins, Bridges, Farrar, Stone, P. Smith (1t), Bell (Spells)
Referee: M.J. Naughton (Widnes)
1977-78
Castleford 17 Wraith; Richardson, Joyner, P. Johnson, Fenton; Burton (2t, 1dg), Pickerill (Stephens); Fisher (Woodall), Spurr, Weston, Huddlestone, Reilly, Lloyd (5g)
Featherstone R. 7 Marsden; Evans, Gilbert, Quinn (1g) (N. Tuffs), K. Kellett; Newlove, Butler; Townend (1g), Bridges, Farrar, Gibbins, Stone (P. Smith 1t), Bell
Referee: M.J. Naughton (Widnes)
1978-79
Bradford N. 18 Mumby; Barends, Gant (1t), D. Parker (1t), D. Redfearn; Slater (Wolford), A. Redfearn (1t); Thompson, Fisher, Forsyth (Joyce), Fox (3g), Trotter, Haigh (1t)
York 8 G. Smith (1t); T. Morgan, Day (Crossley), Foster, Nicholson; Banks (2g), Harkin; Dunkerley, Wileman, Harris, Rhodes, Hollis (1dg) (Ramshaw), Cooper
Referee: M.J. Naughton (Widnes)

1979-80
Leeds 15 Hague; Alan Smith (2t), D. Smith
(1t), Dyl, Atkinson; Holmes (J. Sanderson),
Dick (3g); Dickinson, Ward, Pitchford, Eccles,
D. Heron (Adams), Cookson
Halifax 6 Birts (3g); Howard (Snee), Garrod,
Cholmondeley, Waites; Blacker, Langton;
Jarvis (Callon), Raistrick, Wood, Scott, Sharp,
Busfield
Referee: M.J. Naughton (Widnes)
1980-81
Leeds 8 Hague; Alan Smith (1t), D. Smith,
Atkinson, Oulton; Holmes, Dick (2g, 1dg);
Harrison, Ward, Pitchford, Eccles, Cookson
(Carroll), D. Heron
Hull K.R. 7 Robinson; McHugh (1t),
M. Smith, Hogan (2g), Youngman; Hall,
Harkin; Holdstock, Price, Crooks (Rose),
Lowe, Casey, Crane
Referee: R. Campbell (Widnes)
1981-82
Castleford 10 Claughton; Richardson, Fenton,
Hyde (1t), Morris; Joyner (1t), R. Beardmore;
Hardy (P. Norton), Spurr, B. Johnson, Finch
(2g), Ward, Timson
Bradford N. 5 Mumby; Barends, Hale,
A. Parker (1t), Gant; Hanley (1g), A. Redfearn;
Grayshon, Noble, Sanderson (D. Redfearn),
G. Van Bellen (Jasiewicz), Idle, Rathbone
Referee: M.R. Whitfield (Widnes)
1982-83
Hull 18 Kemble; S. Evans (1t), Day, Leuluai,
Prendiville (1t); Topliss, Harkin; Skerrett,
Bridges, Stone, Rose (2t), L. Crooks (2g, 2dg),
Crane (Norton)
Bradford N. 7 Mumby; Barends, Gant,
A. Parker, Pullen (Smith); Whiteman (1t),
Carroll (1g, 2dg); Grayshon, Noble, G. Van
Bellen (Sanderson), Idle, Jasiewicz, Hale
Referee: S. Wall (Leigh)
1983-84
Hull 13 Kemble; Solal, Schofield, Leuluai,
O'Hara (1t); Topliss, Dean; Edmonds,
Wileman, Skerrett, Proctor (1t), L. Crooks,
Crane (1t, 1dg)
Castleford 2 Coen; Fenton, Marchant, Hyde
(Orum), Kear; Joyner, R. Beardmore (1g);
Connell, Horton, Reilly, Timson, James,
England
Referee: W.H. Thompson (Huddersfield)
1984-85
Hull 29 Kemble (2t); Leuluai, Schofield (4g,
1dg), S. Evans (1t), O'Hara; Ah Kuoi,
Sterling; Edmonds, Patrick, L. Crooks (1t),
Norton (1t), Proctor, Divorty (Rose)
Hull K.R. 12 Fairbairn (1t); Clark, Robinson
(1t), Prohm, Laws; M. Smith, Harkin (Rudd);

Broadhurst, Watkinson, Ema (Hartley),
Burton, Kelly, Hall (1t)
Referee: G.F. Lindop (Wakefield)
1985-86
Hull K.R. 22 Fairbairn (Lydiat); Clark (1t),
Dorahy (5g), Prohm, Laws; G. Smith, Harkin;
Des Harrison, Watkinson, Ema, Burton, Hogan
(Kelly), Miller (2t)
Castleford 18 Lord; Plange, Marchant (2t),
Hyde, Spears; Diamond (1g), R. Beardmore
(1t, 2g); Ward, K. Beardmore, B. Johnson,
England, Ketteridge, Joyner
Referee: R. Campbell (Widnes)
1986-87
Castleford 31 Scott; Plange, Marchant, Johns,
Hyde (Lord); Joyner, R. Beardmore (1dg);
Ward (1t), K. Beardmore (2t), B. Johnson,
Ketteridge (1t, 5g), Atkins (1t) (Shillito),
England
Hull 24 Kemble; Brand (2t), Schofield, O'Hara
(2t), Eastwood; Ah Kuoi, Windley; Brown
(Puckering), S. Patrick, Dannatt, Norton
(Divorty), L. Crooks (4g), Sharp
Referee: J. McDonald (Wigan)
1987-88
Bradford N. 12 Mercer; Ford, McGowan,
Simpson, Francis; Mumby (2g), Harkin;
Grayshon (Hobbs 2g), Noble, Hill, Skerrett,
Fairbank (1t), Holmes (Roebuck)
Castleford 12 Roockley; Plange (1t), Marchant,
Beattie, Hyde; Joyner, R. Southernwood;
Shillito (R. Beardmore), K. Beardmore
(Sampson), Ward, Ketteridge (2g), Fifita,
Lindner (1t)
Referee: K. Allatt (Southport)
Replay
Bradford N. 11 Mumby; Ford, McGowan,
Mercer, Simpson; Stewart, Harkin; Hobbs (1g,
1dg), Noble, Hill (1t), Skerrett, Fairbank,
Heron (1t)
Castleford 2 Roockley; Plange, Marchant,
Beattie, Hyde; R. Southernwood, R.
Beardmore; Ward, Hill, Fifita (Sampson),
Ketteridge (1g), England (Boothroyd), Joyner
Referee: K. Allatt (Southport)
1988-89
Leeds 33 Spencer; Ettingshausen, Schofield
(2t, 1dg), Stephenson (6g), Gibson (2t);
C. Lyons, Ashton; Crooks, Maskill, Waddell
(Backo), Powell, Brooke-Cowden (Medley, 1t),
Heron
Castleford 12 Belcher; Plange, Marchant,
Boothroyd (1t), Chapman (Roockley)
(Sampson); Anderson, R. Beardmore; Ward,
K. Beardmore, England, Ketteridge (2g),
Gibbs, Joyner (1t)
Referee: R. Whitfield (Widnes)

THE WHITE ROSE TROPHY

First awarded in 1966, the trophy is presented to the adjudged man of the match in the Yorkshire Cup final.

Donated by the late T.E. Smith, of York, the award is organised by the Yorkshire Federation of Rugby League Supporters' Clubs and judged by a panel of the Press.

The trophy is not awarded in replays, although Bradford Northern's Brendan Hill was named Man of the Match in the second game against Castleford in 1987.

Season	Winner	Team	Position
1966-67	Cyril Kellett	Hull K.R. (v. Featherstone R.)	Full back
1967-68	Chris Davidson	Hull (v. Hull K.R.)	Scrum half
1968-69	Barry Seabourne	Leeds (v. Castleford)	Scrum half
1969-70	Joe Brown	Hull (v. Featherstone R.)	Loose forward
1970-71	Syd Hynes	Leeds (v. Featherstone R.)	Centre
1971-72	Ian Markham	Hull K.R. (v. Castleford)	Full back
1972-73	John Holmes	Leeds (v. Dewsbury)	Full back
1973-74	Keith Hepworth	Leeds (v. Wakefield T.)	Scrum half
1974-75	Roger Millward	Hull K.R. (v. Wakefield T.)	Stand off
1975-76	Neil Fox	Hull K.R. (v. Leeds)	Second row
1976-77	Les Dyl	Leeds (v. Featherstone R.)	Centre
1977-78	Bruce Burton	Castleford (v. Featherstone R.)	Stand off
1978-79	Bob Haigh	Bradford N. (v. York)	Loose forward
1979-80	Alan Smith	Leeds (v. Halifax)	Winger
1980-81	Kevin Dick	Leeds (v. Hull K.R.)	Scrum half
1981-82	Barry Johnson	Castleford (v. Bradford N.)	Prop
1982-83	Keith Mumby	Bradford N. (v. Hull)	Full back
1983-84	Mick Crane	Hull (v. Castleford)	Loose forward
1984-85	Peter Sterling	Hull (v. Hull K.R.)	Scrum half
1985-86	Gavin Miller	Hull K.R. (v. Castleford)	Loose forward
1986-87	Kevin Beardmore	Castleford (v. Hull)	Hooker
1987-88	Paul Harkin	Bradford N. (v. Castleford)	Scrum half
1988-89	Cliff Lyons	Leeds (v. Castleford)	Stand Off
1989-90	Paul Harkin	Bradford N. (v Featherstone R.)	Scrum half

YORKSHIRE CUP FINAL RECORDS

TEAM
Most appearances: 21 Leeds
Most wins: 17 Leeds
Highest score: Leeds 36 v. Dewsbury 9............ 1972
Widest margin win: Huddersfield 31 v. Hull 0... 1914
Biggest attendance:
36,000 Bradford N. v. Huddersfield (at Leeds).. 1949

INDIVIDUAL
Most tries:
4 by Stan Moorhouse (Huddersfield) v. Leeds.... 1919
Most goals:
6 by David Stephenson (Leeds) v. Castleford..... 1988
Most points:
14 (5g, 1t) by Martin Ketteridge (Castleford)
    v. Hull 1986

Paul Harkin, 1989 Man of the Match

1989 CHARITY SHIELD

Jonathan Davies produced the most decisive spell of his Rugby League career to date to inspire a dazzling Widnes comeback that swept them to victory in the new-style CIS Insurance Charity Shield.

A controversial switch from the Isle of Man to Liverpool FC's Anfield stadium attracted a gate of 17,263 — three times the Manx record set the previous year — with receipts of £91,287.

The first 13-a-side code encounter to be staged on the world famous soccer ground cast aside once and for all any doubts that this opening fixture of the new campaign was a pre-season friendly. The opening quarter produced blockbusting tackles and a string of penalties, Widnes hooker Paul Hulme enjoying the referee's leniency after a high tackle on Wigan winger Dean Bell who was eventually substituted after 20 minutes.

As the game rapidly developed into a fast flowing contest, Wigan fully deserved a 16-7 interval lead, with Man of the Match Denis Betts leading an enterprising pack and scrum half Andy Gregory, after a summer stint with Australian club Illawara, shining in the back division. It was the Great Britain scrum half who sent Andy Platt over for the opening try in the 14th minute, before sending Joe Lydon over in the corner 25 minutes later after cashing in on a slack Tony Myler pass.

Three minutes after the break, Davies put his seal on the thrilling encounter to set up a repeat of Widnes's triumph in Douglas a year earlier. Half-time substitute Derek Pyke, coming on for New Zealander Joe Grima, sent out a shrewd pass to the Welshman whose surging run set up a touchdown for wing partner Brimah Kebbie.

Six minutes later Davies — a long-time Liverpool fan — scooped up the ball after Andy Goodway lost possession in a crunching Richard Eyres tackle and ran 25 yards unopposed to the line.

The 11-minute scoring blitz was completed with the try of the match from Great Britain winger Martin Offiah, with his blistering pace finishing off an Alan Tait move. It fully justified Offiah's early return from Sydney club duty with Eastern Suburbs where he had scored nine tries.

Six minutes from time, the Stones Bitter Champions crowned a dramatic comeback with scrum half David Hulme producing a juggling act to touch down by the posts, for Davies to add his fifth goal. New Zealand centre Kevin Iro's last minute try for the Riversiders did little more than emphasise the closeness of the game's current top two sides.

Chemics skipper Kurt Sorensen lifted the new CIS Insurance Charity Shield and a prize cheque for £10,000, watched by North-West viewers in Granada Television's first live Rugby League broadcast.

Half-time substitute Derek Pyke, an inspiration for trailing Widnes.

CIS INSURANCE CHARITY SHIELD

27 August   Anfield, Liverpool

WIDNES 27		**WIGAN 22**
Alan Tait	1.	Steve Hampson
Brimah Kebbie	2.	Dean Bell, Capt.
Jonathan Davies	3.	Kevin Iro
Darren Wright	4.	Joe Lydon
Martin Offiah	5.	Mark Preston
Tony Myler	6.	Ged Byrne
David Hulme	7.	Andy Gregory
Kurt Sorensen, Capt.	8.	Ian Lucas
Paul Hulme	9.	Nicky Kiss
Joe Grima	10.	Andy Platt
Mike O'Neill	11.	Denis Betts
Emosi Koloto	12.	Ian Gildart
Richard Eyres	13.	Andy Goodway
David Marsh	14.	John Gilfillan
Derek Pyke	15.	Gerard Stazicker

T: Kebbie, Davies, Offiah,
D. Hulme
G: Davies (5), Tait (dg)
Substitution:
Pyke for Grima (Half-time)
Half-time: 7-16
Referee: John Holdsworth (Kippax)

T: Platt, Lydon, Iro

G: Lydon (5)
Substitutions:
Gilfillan for Bell (20 min.)
Stazicker for Platt (78 min.)
Attendance: 17,263

Wigan's Ian Gildart falls to Widnes forward Mike O'Neill.

CHARITY SHIELD ROLL OF HONOUR

Year	Winners		Runners-up		Venue	Attendance
1985-86	Wigan	34	Hull K.R.	6	Isle of Man	4,066
1986-87	Halifax	9	Castleford	8	Isle of Man	3,276
1987-88	Wigan	44	Halifax	12	Isle of Man	4,804
1988-89	Widnes	20	Wigan	14	Isle of Man	5,044
1989-90	Widnes	27	Wigan	22	Liverpool FC	17,263

CHARITY SHIELD .... A REVIEW

1985-86

Wigan 34 Hampson; P. Ford, Stephenson (7g), Donlan (2t), Gill (2t); Edwards, M. Ford (1t), Courtney (Mayo), Kiss, Campbell, West (Lucas), Du Toit, Wane

Hull K.R. 6 Fairbairn (Lydiat 1g); Clark (1t), Robinson, Prohm, Laws; M. Smith, G. Smith; Des Harrison, Watkinson, Ema, Kelly (Rudd), Burton, Hogan
Referee: R. Campbell (Widnes)

1986-87

Halifax 9 Smith (Wilson); Riddlesden, Whitfield (1t), Hague (1dg), George (1t); C. Anderson, Stephens; Dickinson, McCallion, Juliff, Scott (James), Bell, Dixon

Castleford 8 Roockley; Plange, Lord (1t), Irwin (R. Southernwood), Spears; Joyner (Fletcher), R. Beardmore; Ward, K. Beardmore, Johnson, Ketteridge (2g), Mountain, England
Referee: G. F. Lindop (Wakefield)

1987-88

Wigan 44 Hampson (2t); Stephenson (8g), Byrne (Russell), Bell (2t), Gill (1t); Edwards (2t), Gregory; West, Kiss, Case, Gildart (Wane), Potter, Goodway

Halifax 12 Eadie (2g); Taylor, Wilson, T. Anderson, George; Simpson (Juliff, 1t), Stephens; Dickinson, Pendlebury, Beevers, James, Scott (Bell), Dixon (1t)
Referee: J. Holdsworth (Kippax)

1988-89

Widnes 20 Tait; Thackray, Currier (4g), Wright (1t), Offiah (1t); Dowd, D. Hulme; Sorensen, McKenzie (1t), Grima (Pyke), M. O'Neill, P. Hulme, Eyres

Wigan 14 Hampson; Gill, Lydon (1t, 1g), Bell, Preston (Lucas); Byrne, Gregory; Shelford (Betts), Kiss, Case, T. Iro (2t), Wane, Goodway
Referee: R. Tennant (Castleford)

MAN OF THE MATCH AWARDS

Season	Winner	Team	Position
1985-86	Shaun Edwards	Wigan (v. Hull K.R.)	Stand off
1986-87	Chris Anderson	Halifax (v. Castleford)	Stand off
1987-88	Shaun Edwards	Wigan (v. Halifax)	Stand off
1988-89	Phil McKenzie	Widnes (v. Wigan)	Hooker
1989-90	Denis Betts	Wigan (v. Widnes)	Second row

● From 1987 it became the Jack Bentley Trophy in memory of the former Daily Express Rugby League journalist.

191

1989 WORLD CLUB CHALLENGE

Widnes added the world title to their British and European Championships in front of a 30,000-plus Old Trafford crowd after surviving the trauma of trailing 12-0 to Australian Premiers Canberra after only 11 minutes.

The Chemics scored six tries to three in an epic Foster's £50,000 World Club Challenge, as they transformed from lethargy in the opening quarter to dominance and incision for the next hour.

It was Widnes who started as though they were suffering from jet lag. The Raiders, who arrived in Britain only three days earlier after a week of Sydney Premiership celebrations, started the prestigious Anglo-Aussie challenge with confidence bordering on arrogance.

The giant shadow of Test centre Mal Meninga once again cast itself over the British game when the Canberra skipper touched down in the eighth minute after a scintillating five-man move involving Chris O'Sullivan, Gary Belcher and Laurie Daley.

Within two minutes Meninga was reviving memories of Australian Test massacres on British soil by putting winger Matthew Wood in the clear. After brushing aside centre Darren Wright, he drew Test full back Alan Tait to send former Oldham stand off O'Sullivan between the posts, Wood again adding the goal.

It could have been worse as the high speed Raiders displayed the flowing style which exempted them from the stereotyped Australian club image of defence-orientated football. Wood missed a relatively easy shot at goal, while Daley's touchdown was ruled out by French referee Francis Desplas who judged Bradley Clyde's pass to be forward.

It was nearly half an hour before the Widnes nightmare subsided. Then prop Joe Grima and scrum half David Hulme combined to send in Paul Hulme for a 26th minute touchdown.

Canberra's Test loose forward Bradley Clyde leaves Widnes duo Paul Hulme (left) and Joe Grima in his wake.

Five minutes before the interval left winger Martin Offiah went over in the corner after fine work by Australian hooker Phil McKenzie, Jonathan Davies adding a touch-line goal to leave the Chemics trailing only 12-10 at the break.

The Widnes transition was based on grit and determination as well as skill, typified by a Man of the Match performance by David Hulme and an outstanding contribution by prop forward Derek Pyke.

The turning point came five minutes into the second half with Raiders substitute Paul Martin on for Meninga. Canberra centre Daley was sin-binned for a high, late tackle on Davies which did not prevent the Welsh-man scoring in the corner.

While Daley was off the field, Widnes grabbed two more touchdowns to clinch the match. Wright broke away from Grima's pass to slip the ball to wing partner Offiah for a 30-yard sprint to the line. Then, in the 52nd minute, Offiah turned creator when he linked with ex-Leigh prop Pyke to send loose forward Richard Eyres over, Davies adding the goal to open up a 24-12 lead.

The Chemics were now in full flow and confirmed their superiority nine minutes from time when substitute Barry Dowd put Wright away for a touchdown to which Davies added the goal.

With only two minutes left, Widnes eased off to allow outstanding hooker Steve Walters to force over for a consolation try, O'Sullivan adding the goal.

It was the second Foster's World Club Challenge, the Wigan club having introduced the event in 1987, meeting Manly at Central Park in an unofficial title match. The Widnes-Canberra encounter was staged by the Rugby Football League with the blessing of the International Board, upgrading the promotion by use of a top class neutral venue, double sponsorship money and British television exposure.

The Foster's world title match lived up to its billing, an enthralled Old Trafford crowd paying £207,764 while the contest was tele-vised nationally in highlight form in Britain and live throughout Australia. Both Widnes and Canberra received £68,000 in the final share-out, with the British and Australian League's sharing £34,000 to make the Anglo-Aussie production a huge success both on and off the field.

Widnes centre Darren Wright, scorer of the last of their six tries.

193

FOSTER'S WORLD CLUB CHALLENGE

4 October   **Old Trafford, Manchester**

WIDNES 30   **CANBERRA 18**

Alan Tait	1.	Gary Belcher
Andy Currier	2.	Matthew Wood
Jonathan Davies	3.	Mal Meninga, Capt.
Darren Wright	4.	Laurie Daley
Martin Offiah	5.	John Ferguson
Tony Myler	6.	Chris O'Sullivan
David Hulme	7.	Ricky Stuart
Joe Grima	8.	Steve Jackson
Phil McKenzie	9.	Steve Walters
Derek Pyke	10.	Glen Lazarus
Kurt Sorensen, Capt.	11.	Dean Lance
Paul Hulme	12.	Gary Coyne
Richard Eyres	13.	Bradley Clyde
Barry Dowd	14.	Phil Carey
Paul Moriarty	15.	Paul Martin
Brimah Kebbie	16.	Mark Lowry
David Smith	17.	Craig Bellamy

T: Offiah (2), P. Hulme, Davies
Eyres, Wright
G: Davies (3)
Substitutions:
Dowd for Myler (43 min.)
Moriarty for Grima (61 min.)
Referee: Francis Desplas (France)

T: Meninga, O'Sullivan, Walters
G: Wood (2), O'Sullivan
Substitutions:
Martin for Meninga (Half-time)
Lowry for Jackson (66 min.)
Half-time: 10-12
Attendance: 30,786
Receipts; £207,764

WORLD CLUB CHALLENGE ROLL OF HONOUR

Year	Winners		Runners-up		Venue	Attendance	Receipts
1987	Wigan	8	Manly-Warringah	2	Wigan	36,895	£131,000
1989	Widnes	30	Canberra	18	Old Trafford, Man'r	30,786	£207,764

WORLD CLUB CHALLENGE . . . . A REVIEW
1987-88
Wigan 8 Hampson; Russell, Stephenson (4g), Lydon, Gill; Edwards, Gregory; Case (Lucas), Kiss, Wane, Goodway, Potter, Hanley
Manly 2 Shearer; Ronson, Williams (Ticehurst), O'Connor (1g), Davis; Lyons, Hasler; Daley, Cochrane, Gately (Brokenshire), Gibbs, Cunningham (Shaw), Vautin
Referee: John Holdsworth (Kippax)

MAN OF THE MATCH AWARDS
1987: Shaun Wane
1989: David Hulme (Widnes)

Man of the Match David Hulme.

Australian hooker Phil McKenzie, one of the key figures in the Widnes comeback, kicking past Canberra prop Glen Lazarus.

BBC-2 FLOODLIT TROPHY

The BBC-2 Floodlit Trophy competition was launched in 1965. Eight clubs competed in the first year and the total had grown to 22 by 1980 when the competition was abolished as part of the BBC's financial cut-backs.

For 15 years the matches became a regular television feature on Tuesday evenings throughout the early winter months.

Although the format changed slightly over the years, it was basically a knockout competition on the lines of the Challenge Cup.

In 1966 the Floodlit Competition was used to introduce the limited tackle rule, then four tackles, which proved such a great success it was adopted in all other matches before the end of the year.

BBC-2 FLOODLIT TROPHY FINALS
(Only the 1967, at Leeds, and 1972, at Wigan, finals were played on neutral grounds)

Season	Winners		Runners-up		Venue	Attendance	Receipts
1965-66	Castleford	4	St. Helens	0	St. Helens	11,510	£1,548
1966-67	Castleford	7	Swinton	2	Castleford	8,986	£1,692
1967-68	Castleford	8	Leigh	5	Leeds	9,716	£2,099
1968-69	Wigan	7	St. Helens	4	Wigan	13,479	£3,291
1969-70	Leigh	11	Wigan	6	Wigan	12,312	£2,854
1970-71	Leeds	9	St. Helens	5	Leeds	7,612	£2,189
1971-72	St. Helens	8	Rochdale H.	2	St. Helens	9,300	£2,493
1972-73	Leigh	5	Widnes	0	Wigan	4,691	£1,391
1973-74	Bramley	15	Widnes	7	Widnes	4,422	£1,538
1974-75	Salford	0	Warrington	0	Salford	4,473	£1,913
Replay	Salford	10	Warrington	5	Warrington	5,778	£2,434
1975-76	St. Helens	22	Dewsbury	2	St. Helens	3,858	£1,747
1976-77	Castleford	12	Leigh	4	Leigh	5,402	£2,793
1977-78	Hull K.R.	26	St. Helens	11	Hull K.R.	10,099	£6,586
1978-79	Widnes	13	St. Helens	7	St. Helens	10,250	£7,017
1979-80	Hull	13	Hull K.R.	3	Hull	18,500	£16,605

BBC2 FLOODLIT TROPHY .... A REVIEW

1965-66
Castleford 4 Edwards; C. Battye, M. Battye, Willett (2g), Briggs; Hardisty, Millward; Terry, J. Ward, C. Dickinson, Bryant, Taylor, Small
St. Helens 0 F. Barrow; Vollenhoven, Wood, Benyon, Killeen; Murphy, Prosser; French, Dagnall, Watson, Hicks, Mantle, Laughton
Referee: L. Gant (Wakefield)

1966-67
Castleford 7 Edwards; Howe, Stenton, Willett (1g), Austin (1t); Hardisty, Hepworth (1g); Hartley, C. Dickinson, McCartney, Bryant, Small, Walker
Swinton 2 Gowers; Whitehead (1g), Gomersall, Buckley, Davies; Fleet, G. Williams; Halliwell, D. Clarke, Scott (Cummings), Rees, Simpson, Robinson
Referee: J. Manley (Warrington)

1967-68
Castleford 8 Edwards; Harris, Thomas, Stenton, Willett (4g); Hardisty, Hepworth; Hartley, J. Ward, Walton, Bryant (C. Dickinson), Redfearn, Reilly

Leigh 5 Grainey; Tickle (1t), Lewis, Collins, Walsh; Entwistle, A. Murphy; Whitworth, Ashcroft, Major, Welding, M. Murphy, Gilfedder (1g)
Referee: G.F. Lindop (Wakefield)

1968-69
Wigan 7 Tyrer (2g); Francis, Ashton, Ashurst, Rowe; C. Hill (1t), Jackson; J. Stephens, Clarke, Mills, Fogerty (Lyon), Kevin O'Loughlin, Laughton
St. Helens 4 Williams; Wilson, Benyon, Myler, Wills; Whittle, Bishop; Warlow, Sayer, Watson, Mantle, Hogan, Coslett (2g)
Referee: E. Clay (Leeds)

1969-70
Leigh 11 Ferguson (3g) (Lewis); Tickle (1t), Dorrington, Collins, Walsh; Eckersley, Murphy (1g); D. Chisnall, Ashcroft, Watts, Welding, Grimes, Lyon
Wigan 6 C. Hill; Wright, Francis (2g), Rowe, Kevin O'Loughlin; D. Hill (1g), Jackson; J. Stephens, Clarke, Ashcroft, Ashurst, Mills, Laughton
Referee: W.H. Thompson (Huddersfield)

1970-71
Leeds 9 Holmes (2g); Alan Smith, Hynes (1t, 1g), Cowan, Atkinson; Wainwright, Shoebottom; J. Burke, Fisher, Barnard, Haigh, Ramsey, Batten
St. Helens 5 F. Barrow; L. Jones (1t), Benyon, Walsh, Wilson; Whittle, Heaton; Rees, A. Karalius, E. Chisnall, Mantle, E. Prescott, Coslett (1g)
Referee: E. Lawrinson (Warrington)
1971-72
St. Helens 8 G. Pimblett; L. Jones, Benyon, Walsh, Wilson; Kelly, Heaton; Rees, A. Karalius, E. Chisnall, E. Prescott, Mantle, Coslett (4g)
Rochdale H. 2 Chamberlain (1g); Brelsford, Crellin, Taylor, Glover; Myler, Gartland; Birchall, P. Clarke, Brown, Welding, Sheffield (Hodkinson), Delooze
Referee: E. Clay (Leeds)
1972-73
Leigh 5 Hogan; Lawson (1t) (Lester), Atkin, Collins, Stacey; A. Barrow, Sayer (Ryding); Grimes, D. Clarke, Fletcher, Fiddler (1g), F. Barrow, Martyn
Widnes 0 Dutton; A. Prescott, Aspey, Blackwood, McDonnell; Lowe, Ashton; Mills, Elwell, Warlow, Foran, Sheridan, Nicholls
Referee: G.F. Lindop (Wakefield)
1973-74
Bramley 15 Keegan; Goodchild (1t), Bollon, Hughes, Austin (1t); T. Briggs, Ward (1g) (Ashman); D. Briggs, Firth, Cheshire, D. Sampson (1t), Idle, Wolford (2g)
Widnes 7 Dutton (2g); D. O'Neill, Hughes, Aspey, Macko (1t); Warburton, Bowden; Hogan, Elwell, Nelson, Sheridan, Blackwood (Foran) Laughton
Referee: D. G. Kershaw (York)

1974-75
Salford 0 Charlton; Fielding, Hesketh, Graham, Richards; Brophy (Taylor), Banner; Coulman, Devlin, Grice, Knighton, Dixon, E. Prescott
Warrington 0 Whitehead; Sutton, Cunliffe (Lowe), Whittle, Bevan; Briggs, Gordon; D. Chisnall, Ashcroft, Wright, Gaskell, Conroy, B. Philbin (Jewitt)
Referee: W.H. Thompson (Huddersfield)
Replay
Salford 10 Stead; Fielding (1t), Watkins (2g), Hesketh, Richards (1t); Gill, Banner; Grice, Walker, Mackay, Dixon, Knighton, E. Prescott

Warrington 5 Cunliffe; Whitehead (1g), Pickup, Whittle, Bevan (1t); Noonan (Briggs), Gordon; D. Chisnall, Ashcroft, Wanbon, Conroy, Nicholas (Brady), B. Philbin
Referee: W.H. Thompson (Huddersfield)
1975-76
St. Helens 22 G. Pimblett (2g); L. Jones, Benyon (1t), Hull (1t), Mathias (2t); Wilson (1t), Heaton (1dg); Mantle, A. Karalius, James, Nicholls, E. Chisnall, Coslett (1g)
Dewsbury 2 Langley; Hegarty, Chalkley, Simpson, Mitchell; N. Stephenson (1g) (Lee), A. Bates; Beverley, Price, Hankins, Halloran (Artis), Bell, Grayshon
Referee: W.H. Thompson (Huddersfield)
1976-77
Castleford 12 Wraith; Fenton, Joyner, P. Johnson, Walsh (1t); Burton (1t), Stephens; Khan, Spurr, A. Dickinson, Reilly, Lloyd (3g), S. Norton
Leigh 4 Hogan; A. Prescott, Stacey, Woods, Walsh (1t); Taylor, Sayer; D. Chisnall, Ashcroft (1dg), Fletcher, Macko, Grimes, Boyd
Referee: J.E. Jackson (Pudsey)
1977-78
Hull K.R. 26 Hall (4g); Dunn (2t), M. Smith (1t), Watson, Sullivan (1t); Hartley (1t), Millward; Millington, Watkinson, Cunningham (Hughes), Lowe, Rose (1t), Casey
St. Helens 11 G. Pimblett (Platt); L. Jones (Courtney), Noonan, Cunningham (1t), Glynn (2t, 1g); Francis, K. Gwilliam; D. Chisnall, Liptrot, James, Hope, A. Karalius, Pinner
Referee: M. J. Naughton (Widnes)
1978-79
Widnes 13 Eckersley; Wright (2t), Hughes, Aspey, P. Shaw; Burke (2g, 1t), Bowden; Hogan, Elwell, Mills, Adams, Dearden, Laughton
St. Helens 7 G. Pimblett (2g), L. Jones, Glynn, Cunningham, Mathias; Francis, Holding; D. Chisnall (1t), Liptrot, James, Nicholls, Knighton (E. Chisnall), Pinner
Referee: J. McDonald (Wigan)
1979-80
Hull 13 Woods; Bray, G. Evans (1t), Coupland, Dennison (1t, 2g); Newlove, Hepworth; Tindall, Wileman, Farrar, Stone, Boxall (Birdsall 1t), Norton
Hull K.R. 3 Robinson; Hubbard (1t), M. Smith, Watson, Sullivan; Hall, Agar; Holdstock, Tyreman, Lockwood, Clarkson (Hartley), Lowe, Hogan (Millington)
Referee: W.H. Thompson (Huddersfield)

CAPTAIN MORGAN TROPHY

This sponsored competition, with a winners' prize of £3,000, lasted only one season. Entry was restricted to the 16 clubs who won their Yorkshire and Lancashire Cup first round ties. The Lancashire contingent was made up to eight by including the side which lost their first round county Cup-tie by the narrowest margin. The first round of the Captain Morgan Trophy was zoned with clubs being drawn against those in their own county. The remainder of the competition was integrated. The final was on a neutral ground as follows:

1973-74   Warrington   4   Featherstone R.   0   Salford   5,259   £2,265

1973-74

Warrington 4 Whitehead (2g); M. Philbin, Noonan, Reynolds (Pickup), Bevan; Whittle, Gordon; D. Chisnall, Ashcroft, Brady, Wanbon (Price), Wright, Mather

Featherstone R. 0 Box; Coventry, M. Smith, Hartley, Bray; Mason, Wood; Tonks, Bridges, Harris, Gibbins (Stone), Rhodes, Bell
Referee: G.F. Lindop (Wakefield)

Table-toppers . . . Wigan's Australian coach John Monie and skipper Ellery Hanley hoist aloft the Stones Bitter Championship Trophy after defeating Leigh in the last match of the 1989-90 campaign.

LEAGUE

1989-90 CHAMPIONSHIP

Wigan lifted the Stones Bitter Championship Trophy — and a record prize cheque of £40,000 — for the second time in four seasons, clinching the coveted title on the last day of the league campaign.

Needing only one point from a home clash with neighbours Leigh, the Riversiders ran in six tries in a 34-6 rout which sent the Hilton Park side into the Second Division. More than 20,000 fans witnessed Wigan's title success, with the final try being claimed by club skipper Ellery Hanley, coming on as substitute with a groin injury which had restricted him to 10 full league appearances.

Under new Australian coach John Monie, the Riversiders won 20 of their 26 fixtures, achieving the best defensive record and overcoming a series of long-term injuries to key players including Hanley, Andy Platt and Andy Gregory, plus lengthy suspensions imposed on Steve Hampson, Dean Bell and Ian Lucas.

The title race peeked a week from the end of the league campaign with Wigan at the top of the table, two points ahead of nearest rivals Leeds, each with three matches remaining. Wigan's rearranged midweek meeting with the Loiners at Central Park attracted a crowd of 24,462, with the head-to-head clash being televised by BSB, Granada and Yorkshire Television.

Leading 14-4 at the interval, the Riversiders held off a second half comeback by trophy-hungry Leeds to clinch a vital 16-12 success. Hit by injuries, Wigan went down 35-10 in the Good Friday derby encounter at St. Helens before crushing Alex Murphy's Leigh to take the Stones Bitter prize.

Leeds went on to take the runners-up spot earning a prize cheque of £18,000 — their highest-ever league placing in two-division history. Former skipper and hooker David Ward took over the coaching role from Malcolm Reilly after the Great Britain coach's resignation in September and succeeded in installing much-needed pride and commitment in the Headingley club.

Widnes failed in their bid to become the first club to register a hat-trick of First Division titles, finishing third, level on points with Bradford Northern and St. Helens, who were the top points scorers.

As well as the traditional qualification for the end-of-season Stones Bitter Premiership, the top eight clubs were also rewarded with a fixture against the 1990 Australian tourists, with the exception of Bradford Northern as a punishment for fielding a weakened side against the 1989 New Zealanders. Ninth-placed Wakefield Trinity took their place.

At the lower end of the table, Featherstone Rovers were second from bottom at the start of the new year with two victories from 13 matches, half the full programme. The Colliers refound the form which had earned them sixth place the previous season and finished 10th with 10 wins.

Newly-promoted Sheffield Eagles opened their first-ever Stones Bitter Championship campaign with five victories in their first seven league matches, highlighted by the 31-6 defeat of Widnes only four days after their Foster's World Club Challenge success over Canberra Raiders. Only a couple of weeks before the season, the Eagles found themselves homeless with the unavailability of Owlerton Stadium due to ground safety restrictions.

Tagged The Nomads, Sheffield staged their 'home' matches around Yorkshire, hiring soccer venues, with Sheffield Wednesday's Hillsborough, Sheffield United's Bramall Lane and Chesterfield's Saltergate each being used twice for league fixtures, Barnsley's Oakwell once. The remaining six 'home' fixtures were played on Rugby League grounds, five at Doncaster and one at Wakefield Trinity.

Promoted as Second Division Champions, Leigh made an immediate return to the lower reaches. They sacked coach Billy Benyon at the start of March, days after a 46-0 away defeat to fellow strugglers Sheffield Eagles and Alex Murphy was brought back for his fourth coaching stint at Hilton Park. After a 44-6 success at Barrow, Leigh drew 20-20 at home to Widnes while Murphy was carrying out a television commentary commitment at the France versus Great Britain Test match in Perpignan.

But Leigh lost four of their last six matches to finish third from bottom, level on points with Sheffield Eagles but carrying a scoring deficit of 200 points, compared with the Eagles' 71.

Barrow recorded only one victory in their 26-match programme, at Featherstone Rovers. The Shipbuilders sacked Australian coach Rod Reddy in the November after a two-year reign, appointing Dennis Jackson for a second spell as caretaker coach, before former Test loose forward Steve Norton took over from the end of the season. Barrow conceded a First Division record 1,135 points, scoring only 201. The Cumbrians suffered First Division records in defeat with a 90-0 hammering at Leeds, plus a 66-0 home rout at the hands of Wigan.

A record First Division gate was registered at Central Park when Wigan entertained derby rivals St. Helens on Boxing Day in front of 27,075 fans. Top First Division scorers were Widnes winger Martin Offiah with 28 tries, St. Helens centre Paul Loughlin with 96 goals and Hull winger Paul Eastwood with 238 points from 81 goals and 19 tries.

In the Second Division, Hull K.R. were promoted as champions 12 months after being relegated from bottom position, revitalised Rochdale Hornets and Oldham claiming the two other promotion spots.

Hull K.R. received £18,000 prize money and added to their First Division titles of 1984 and 1985 by recording the Second Division's best scoring and defensive tallies.

Surprise package Rochdale, under new coach Allan Agar and led by Stones Bitter Second Division Player of the Year John Woods, clinched a return to the First Division after an 11-season absence.

Oldham, having reached the final of the Grunhalle Lager Lancashire Cup and the semi-finals of the Silk Cut Challenge Cup, faltered in their title bid with defeats at Workington Town and Swinton in the last fortnight of the league campaign to finish two points adrift of Hull K.R. despite having beaten the Robins home and away.

Newly named and relocated Ryedale-York finished fourth in the table for the second successive season, while Halifax started as 11-8 title favourites and could only manage fifth spot. Halifax reached the final of the Regal Trophy in January but suffered a financial crisis, resulting in end-of-the-season threats of a players' strike.

Having finished 17th the previous season, Fulham responded to the arrival of Australian coach Ross Strudwick, formerly with Halifax, and the concession of being able to field six overseas players by claiming eighth spot and qualifying for a first-ever Second Division Premiership first round tie at Hull K.R.

Adopting a youth policy under new coach Dave Chisnall, Runcorn Highfield became the first club to finish a Second Division campaign without a point, being beaten in all their 28 matches. The fruitless season left Runcorn with a league record of 47 successive matches without a victory extending back to October 1988.

Top scorers in the division were Hull K.R. duo Greg Austin, with 35 tries, and centre partner Mike Fletcher with 167 goals — a Division Two record — and 382 points, including 12 tries.

Jubilant Hull K.R. celebrate their Second Division Championship title success, headed by skipper Mike Smith, fourth from left on the back row.

FINAL TABLES 1988-89

STONES BITTER CHAMPIONSHIP

	P.	W.	D.	L.	Dr.	FOR Gls.	Trs.	Pts.	Dr.	AGAINST Gls.	Trs.	Pts.	Pts.
Wigan	26	20	0	6	3	98	125	699	5	60	56	349	40
Leeds	26	18	0	8	12	108	119	704	5	67	61	383	36
Widnes	26	16	2	8	1	95	117	659	5	73	68	423	34
Bradford N.	26	17	0	9	10	92	105	614	4	68	69	416	34
St. Helens	26	17	0	9	4	121	117	714	10	89	89	544	34
Hull	26	16	1	9	5	92	97	577	6	61	68	400	33
Castleford	26	16	0	10	3	112	119	703	4	74	74	448	32
Warrington	26	13	1	12	12	74	66	424	9	75	73	451	27
Wakefield T.	26	12	1	13	4	83	83	502	6	77	92	528	25
Featherstone R.	26	10	0	16	7	74	81	479	10	97	112	652	20
Sheffield E.	26	9	1	16	9	82	86	517	4	92	100	588	19
Leigh	26	9	1	16	2	72	74	442	6	100	109	642	19
Salford	26	4	1	21	7	63	72	421	5	111	118	699	9
Barrow	26	1	0	25	1	32	34	201	1	154	206	1133	2

Corals pre-season betting for the 1989-90 Championship: 6-4 Widnes, Wigan; 6-1 Leeds; 9-1 St. Helens; 16-1 Castleford, Hull; 20-1 Bradford N.; 33-1 Warrington; 50-1 Featherstone R.; 80-1 Salford; 100-1 Leigh, Sheffield E., Wakefield T.; 250-1 Barrow.

SECOND DIVISION

	P.	W.	D.	L.	Dr.	FOR Gls.	Trs.	Pts.	Dr.	AGAINST Gls.	Trs.	Pts.	Pts.
Hull K.R.	28	25	0	3	2	168	191	1102	2	32	31	190	50
Rochdale H.	28	24	0	4	3	147	170	977	2	74	68	422	48
Oldham	28	24	0	4	3	128	155	879	3	51	55	325	48
Ryedale-York	28	20	1	7	3	97	114	653	4	65	51	338	41
Halifax	28	20	0	8	5	106	131	741	4	66	56	360	40
Swinton	28	20	0	8	7	89	122	673	13	64	66	405	40
Dewsbury	28	19	1	8	13	81	82	503	7	54	74	411	39
Fulham	28	16	2	10	2	75	86	496	2	81	81	488	34
Doncaster	28	15	2	11	7	67	98	533	7	66	65	399	32
Trafford B.	28	15	0	13	11	80	95	551	5	87	93	551	30
Huddersfield	28	14	0	14	7	77	77	469	11	77	69	441	28
Batley	28	13	0	15	6	68	81	466	6	68	84	478	26
Bramley	28	11	0	17	13	74	63	413	7	90	109	623	22
Hunslet	28	10	0	18	7	68	72	431	3	85	103	585	20
Chorley	28	10	0	18	9	67	64	399	6	94	106	618	20
Whitehaven	28	10	0	18	6	63	66	396	6	104	124	710	20
Carlisle	28	9	0	19	1	81	87	511	7	83	113	625	18
Workington T.	28	6	0	22	9	53	49	311	10	105	122	708	12
Keighley	28	6	0	22	8	66	74	436	11	121	146	837	12
Nottingham C.	28	4	0	24	5	57	51	323	8	146	183	1032	8
Runcorn H.	28	0	0	28	4	35	36	218	7	134	165	935	0

Corals pre-season betting for the 1989-90 Championship: 11-8 Halifax; 15-8 Hull K.R.; 3-1 Oldham; 16-1 Swinton; 20-1 Ryedale-York; 33-1 Doncaster, Whitehaven; 50-1 Hunslet; 66-1 Bramley, Dewsbury, Rochdale H.; 100-1 Batley, Carlisle, Chorley, Fulham, Huddersfield, Keighley, Nottingham C., Runcorn H., Trafford B., Workington T.

TWO DIVISION CHAMPIONSHIP ROLL OF HONOUR

	FIRST DIVISION	SECOND DIVISION
1902-03	Halifax	Keighley
1903-04	Bradford	Wakefield Trinity
1904-05	Oldham	Dewsbury
1962-63	Swinton	Hunslet
1963-64	Swinton	Oldham
1973-74	Salford	Bradford Northern
1974-75	St. Helens	Huddersfield
1975-76	Salford	Barrow
1976-77	Featherstone Rovers	Hull
1977-78	Widnes	Leigh
1978-79	Hull Kingston Rovers	Hull
1979-80	Bradford Northern	Featherstone Rovers
1980-81	Bradford Northern	York
1981-82	Leigh	Oldham
1982-83	Hull	Fulham
1983-84	Hull Kingston Rovers	Barrow
1984-85	Hull Kingston Rovers	Swinton
1985-86	Halifax	Leigh
1986-87	Wigan	Hunslet
1987-88	Widnes	Oldham
1988-89	Widnes	Leigh
1989-90	Wigan	Hull Kingston Rovers

THE UPS AND DOWNS OF TWO DIVISION FOOTBALL
Since re-introduction of two divisions in 1973-74.

● Figure in brackets indicates position in division.

	RELEGATED	PROMOTED
1973-74	Oldham (13)	Bradford Northern (1)
	Hull K.R. (14)	York (2)
	Leigh (15)	Keighley (3)
	Whitehaven (16)	Halifax (4)
1974-75	York (13)	Huddersfield (1)
	Bramley (14)	Hull K.R. (2)
	Rochdale Hornets (15)	Oldham (3)
	Halifax (16)	Swinton (4)
1975-76	Dewsbury (13)	Barrow (1)
	Keighley (14)	Rochdale Hornets (2)
	Huddersfield (15)	Workington T. (3)
	Swinton (16)	Leigh (4)
1976-77	Rochdale Hornets (13)	Hull (1)
	Leigh (14)	Dewsbury (2)
	Barrow (15)	Bramley (3)
	Oldham (16)	New Hunslet (4)

1977-78	Hull (13)	Leigh (1)
	New Hunslet (14)	Barrow (2)
	Bramley (15)	Rochdale Hornets (3)
	Dewsbury (16)	Huddersfield (4)
1978-79	Barrow (13)	Hull (1)
	Featherstone Rovers (14)	New Hunslet (2)
	Rochdale Hornets (15)	York (3)
	Huddersfield (16)	Blackpool Borough (4)
1979-80	Wigan (13)	Featherstone Rovers (1)
	Hunslet (14)	Halifax (2)
	York (15)	Oldham (3)
	Blackpool Borough (16)	Barrow (4)
1980-81	Halifax (13)	York (1)
	Salford (14)	Wigan (2)
	Workington T. (15)	Fulham (3)
	Oldham (16)	Whitehaven (4)
1981-82	Fulham (13)	Oldham (1)
	Wakefield T. (14)	Carlisle (2)
	York (15)	Workington T. (3)
	Whitehaven (16)	Halifax (4)
1982-83	Barrow (13)	Fulham (1)
	Workington T. (14)	Wakefield T. (2)
	Halifax (15)	Salford (3)
	Carlisle (16)	Whitehaven (4)
1983-84	Fulham (13)	Barrow (1)
	Wakefield T. (14)	Workington T. (2)
	Salford (15)	Hunslet (3)
	Whitehaven (16)	Halifax (4)
1984-85	Barrow (13)	Swinton (1)
	Leigh (14)	Salford (2)
	Hunslet (15)	York (3)
	Workington T. (16)	Dewsbury (4)
1985-86	York (14)	Leigh (1)
	Swinton (15)	Barrow (2)
	Dewsbury (16)	Wakefield T. (3)
1986-87	Oldham (13)	Hunslet (1)
	Featherstone R. (14)	Swinton (2)
	Barrow (15)	
	Wakefield T. (16)	
1987-88	Leigh (12)	Oldham (1)
	Swinton (13)	Featherstone R. (2)
	Hunslet (14)	Wakefield T. (3)
1988-89	Oldham (12)	Leigh (1)
	Halifax (13)	Barrow (2)
	Hull K.R. (14)	Sheffield E. (3)
1989-90	Leigh (12)	Hull K.R. (1)
	Salford (13)	Rochdale H. (2)
	Barrow (14)	Oldham (3)

FIRST DIVISION RECORDS
Since reintroduction in 1973

INDIVIDUAL

Match records

Most tries:
6 Shane Cooper (St. Helens) v. Hull   Feb 17, 1988

Most goals: 13 Geoff Pimblett (St. Helens) v. Bramley
Mar 5, 1978

Most points: 38 (11g, 4t) Bob Beardmore (Castleford) v.
Barrow   Mar 22, 1987

Season records

Most tries: 44 Ellery Hanley (Wigan)   1986-87
Most goals: 130 Steve Hesford (Warrington)   1978-79
Most points: 295 (101g, 1dg, 23t) John Woods (Leigh)
1983-84

TEAM

Highest score and widest margin: Leeds 90 v. Barrow 0   Feb 11, 1990

Biggest away win and widest margin: Wakefield T. 6 v.
Wigan 72   Mar 29, 1987; Barrow 0 v. Wigan 66
Oct 1, 1989

Most points by losing team: Hunslet 40 v. Barrow 41
Sep 9, 1984

Scoreless draw: Wigan 0 v. Castleford 0   Jan 26, 1974

Highest score draw: Hunslet 32 v. Swinton 32
Sep 20, 1987

Best opening sequence: 13 wins then a draw by Widnes
1981-82

Longest winning run: 25 by St. Helens
Won last 13 of 1985-86 and first 12 of 1986-87.
(Also longest unbeaten run.)

Longest losing run: 20 by Whitehaven   1983-84

Longest run without a win: 23, including 3 draws, by
Whitehaven 1981-82 (Also worst opening sequence)

Biggest attendance: 27,075 Wigan v. St. Helens
Dec 26, 1989

100 Division One tries
183 Ellery Hanley (Bradford N., Wigan)
165 Keith Fielding (Salford)
144 David Smith (Wakefield T., Leeds, Bradford N.)
139 Stuart Wright (Wigan, Widnes)
136 Roy Mathias (St. Helens)
132 John Joyner (Castleford)
130 John Bevan (Warrington)
126 Steve Hartley (Hull K.R.)
126 David Topliss (Wakefield T., Hull, Oldham)
125 John Woods (Leigh, Bradford N., Warrington)
122 Maurice Richards (Salford)
122 Steve Evans (Featherstone R., Hull, Wakefield T.,
Bradford N.)
122 Garry Schofield (Hull, Leeds)
118 Phil Ford (Warrington, Wigan, Bradford N., Leeds)
114 Des Drummond (Leigh, Warrington)
113 David Redfearn (Bradford N.)
107 Henderson Gill (Bradford N., Wigan)
105 Gary Hyde (Castleford, Oldham)

103 Keiron O'Loughlin (Wigan, Workington T.,
Widnes, Salford)
103 Neil Holding (St. Helens)

500 Division One goals
854 John Woods (Leigh, Bradford N., Warrington)
845 Steve Hesford (Warrington)
818 Steve Quinn (Featherstone R.)
811 George Fairbairn (Wigan, Hull K.R.)
586 Sammy Lloyd (Castleford, Hull)
574 Colin Whitfield (Salford, Wigan, Halifax)

1,000 Division One points
2,130 John Woods (Leigh, Bradford N., Warrington)
1,814 George Fairbairn (Wigan, Hull K.R.)
1,768 Steve Quinn (Featherstone R.)
1,756 Steve Hesford (Warrington)
1,396 Colin Whitfield (Salford, Wigan, Halifax)
1,264 Sammy Lloyd (Castleford, Hull)
1,159 Keith Mumby (Bradford N.)
1,151 Bob Beardmore (Castleford, Leigh)
1,127 Mick Burke (Widnes, Oldham)

20 Division One tries in a season
1973-74	36	Keith Fielding (Salford)
	29	Roy Mathias (St. Helens)
	21	David Smith (Wakefield T.)
1974-75	21	Maurice Richards (Salford)
	21	Roy Mathias (St. Helens)
1975-76	26	Maurice Richards (Salford)
	20	David Smith (Wakefield T.)
1976-77	22	David Topliss (Wakefield T.)
	21	Keith Fielding (Salford)
	21	Ged Dunn (Hull K.R.)
	20	David Smith (Leeds)
	20	Stuart Wright (Widnes)
1977-78	26	Keith Fielding (Salford)
	25	Steve Fenton (Castleford)
	24	Stuart Wright (Widnes)
	20	David Smith (Leeds)
	20	Bruce Burton (Castleford)
	20	John Bevan (Warrington)
1978-79	28	Steve Hartley (Hull K.R.)
1979-80	24	Keith Fielding (Salford)
	21	Roy Mathias (St. Helens)
	21	Steve Hubbard (Hull K.R.)
	20	David Smith (Leeds)
1980-81	20	Steve Hubbard (Hull K.R.)
1981-82		David Hobbs (Featherstone R.) was top scorer with 19 tries.
1982-83	22	Bob Eccles (Warrington)
	20	Steve Evans (Hull)
1983-84	28	Garry Schofield (Hull)
	23	John Woods (Leigh)
	20	James Leuluai (Hull)
1984-85	40	Ellery Hanley (Bradford N.)
	34	Gary Prohm (Hull K.R.)
	23	Henderson Gill (Wigan)
	22	Barry Ledger (St. Helens)
	22	Mal Meninga (St. Helens)
1985-86	22	Ellery Hanley (Wigan)
1986-87	44	Ellery Hanley (Wigan)
	24	Phil Ford (Bradford N.)
	24	Henderson Gill (Wigan)
	23	Garry Schofield (Hull)
	21	John Henderson (Leigh)

1987-88 33 Martin Offiah (Widnes)
22 Ellery Hanley (Wigan)
1988-89 37 Martin Offiah (Widnes)
20 Grant Anderson (Castleford)
1989-90 28 Martin Offiah (Widnes)
25 Mark Preston (Wigan)
20 Steve Larder (Castleford)

Top Division One goalscorers
1973-74 126 David Watkins (Salford)
1974-75 96 Sammy Lloyd (Castleford)
1975-76 118 Sammy Lloyd (Castleford)
1976-77 113 Steve Quinn (Featherstone R.)
1977-78 116 Steve Hesford (Warrington)
1978-79 130 Steve Hesford (Warrington)
1979-80 104 Steve Hubbard (Hull K.R.)
1980-81 96 Steve Diamond (Wakefield T.)
1981-82 110 Steve Quinn (Featherstone R.)
           John Woods (Leigh)
1982-83 105 Bob Beardmore (Castleford)
1983-84 106 Steve Hesford (Warrington)
1984-85 114 Sean Day (St. Helens)
1985-86 85 David Stephenson (Wigan)
1986-87 120 Paul Loughlin (St. Helens)
1987-88 95 John Woods (Warrington)
1988-89 95 David Hobbs (Bradford N.)
1989-90 96 Paul Loughlin (St. Helens)

Top Division One pointscorer 1989-90
238 (81g, 19t) Paul Eastwood (Hull)

SECOND DIVISION RECORDS
Since reintroduction in 1973

INDIVIDUAL

Match records
Most tries: 6 Ged Dunn (Hull K.R.) v. New Hunslet
Feb 2, 1975; David Kettlestring (Ryedale-York) at
Keighley Mar 11, 1990
Most goals: 15 Mick Stacey (Leigh) v. Doncaster
Mar 28, 1976
Most points: 38 (13g, 4t) John Woods (Leigh) v.
Blackpool B. Sep 11, 1977

Season records
Most tries: 48 Steve Halliwell (Leigh) 1985-86
Most goals: 167 Mike Fletcher (Hull K.R.) 1989-90
Most points: 395 (163g, 3dg, 22t) Lynn Hopkins
(Workington T.) 1981-82

TEAM

Highest score: Leigh 92 v. Keighley 2 Apr 30, 1986;
Hull K.R. 92 v. Whitehaven 10 Mar 18, 1990;
Rochdale H. 92 v. Runcorn H. 0 Nov 5, 1989
(Also widest margin)
Highest away: Runcorn H. 2 v. Leigh 88 Jan 15, 1989
(Also widest margin)
Most points by losing team:
Dewsbury 36 v. Rochdale H. 34 Oct 9, 1988;
Oldham 50 v. Keighley 34 Nov 12, 1989

Highest score draw: Huddersfield B. 32 v. Keighley 32
Apr 17, 1986
Scoreless draw: Dewsbury 0 v. Rochdale H. 0.
Jan 30, 1983
Longest winning run: 30 by Leigh in 1985-86. Hull won
all 26 matches in 1978-79
Longest losing run: 40 by Doncaster (16 in 1975-76 and
24 in 1976-77)
Longest run without a win: 47, inc 1 draw, Runcorn H.
(19 in 1988-89 and 28 in 1989-90)
Biggest attendance: 12,424 Hull v. New Hunslet
May 18, 1979

1989-90 Top Division Two scorers
Most tries: 35 Greg Austin (Hull K.R.)
Most goals: 167 Mike Fletcher (Hull K.R.)
Most points: 382 (167g, 12t) Mike Fletcher (Hull K.R.)
NB. Division One and Two records do not include scores
in abandoned matches that were replayed.

*John Woods, top Division One goalscorer in 1988 and
holder of Second Division points in a match record.*

TWO DIVISION SCORING

The following tables show the scoring totals for each two-division season:

DIVISION ONE

Season	Matches each club played	Goals	1-Point drop goals	Tries	Pts
1973-74	30	1,508	—	1,295	6,901
1974-75	30	1,334	48	1,261	6,499
1975-76	30	1,498	53	1,331	7,042
1976-77	30[1]	1,435	91	1,423	7,230
1977-78	30[2]	1,402	99	1,443	7,232
1978-79	30	1,367	119	1,448	7,197
1979-80	30	1,389	131	1,349	6,956
1980-81	30	1,439	147	1,342	7,051
1981-82	30	1,486	132	1,354	7,166
1982-83	30	1,369	64	1,386	6,960
1983-84	30	1,472	108	1,479	8,968
1984-85	30	1,464	84	1,595	9,392
1985-86	30	1,296	80	1,435	8,412
1986-87	30	1,412	90	1,607	9,342
1987-88	26	1,070	75	1,170	6,895
1988-89	26	1,107	80	1,154	6,910
1989-90	26	1,198	80	1,295	7,656

[1] Salford & Leeds played 29 matches — their final match was abandoned and not replayed. This match was expunged from league records.
[2] Featherstone R. & Bradford N. played 29 matches — their final match was cancelled following Featherstone's strike.

DIVISION TWO

Season	Matches each club played	Goals	1-Point drop goals	Tries	Pts
1973-74	26	1,054	—	955	4,973
1974-75	26	992	36	919	4,777
1975-76	26	1,034	49	963	5,006
1976-77	26	942	78	1,046	5,100
1977-78	26	976	86	1,020	5,098
1978-79	26	971	114	972	4,972
1979-80	26	1,046	106	1,069	5,405
1980-81	28	1,133	123	1,220	6,049
1981-82	32	1,636	152	1,589	8,189
1982-83	32	1,510	103	1,648	8,067
1983-84	34	1,782	254	1,897	11,406
1984-85	28[1]	1,542	226	1,666	9,974
1985-86	34	1,722	130	2,021	11,658
1986-87	28[1]	1,323	112	1,496	8,742
1987-88	28[2]	1,443	125	1,543	9,183
1988-89	28	1,644	162	1,784	10,586
1989-90	28	1,747	130	1,965	11,484

[1] The 20 clubs played 28 matches each.
[2] The 18 clubs played 28 matches each.

SEVENTEEN-SEASON TABLE

Widnes have been the most successful Division One club since the reintroduction of two divisions in 1973 in terms of most points gained. The three times champions head a 17-season table with 656 points from 498 matches.

St. Helens, however, are the only club to have finished in the top eight in each season although their only championship success was in 1974-75. In addition to St. Helens, only Widnes, Castle-ford, Leeds and Warrington have remained in Division One.

Three clubs have spent the entire 17 seasons in Division Two — Batley, Doncaster and Runcorn Highfield.

Bradford Northern, Hull and Leigh were all Division Two champions who went on to win the Division One title a few seasons after being promoted, while Hull Kingston Rovers, Halifax and Wigan are other former lower grade clubs who later won the major championship.

The highest place gained by a newly-promoted club is third by Hull in 1979-80 after winning the Division Two championship with a 100 per cent record the previous season.

Division One champions who were relegated a few seasons after winning the Division One title were Salford, Featherstone Rovers, Leigh, Halifax and Hull K.R.

The records of the five clubs who have appeared in Division One throughout the 17 seasons are as follows:

	P.	W.	D.	L.	F.	A.	Pts
1. Widnes	498	318	20	160	9,196	6,402	656
2. St. Helens	498	317	19	162	10,362	6,898	653
3. Leeds	497	290	19	188	9,345	7,311	599
4. Warrington	498	273	18	207	8,446	7,185	564
5. Castleford	498	255	25	218	9,357	7,992	535

● Although Wigan and Bradford Northern have had only 16 seasons in Division One their points totals exceed some of the above, having each won the title twice. Wigan have totalled 584 points and Bradford 542.

CHAMPIONSHIP PLAY-OFFS

Following the breakaway from the English Rugby Union, 22 clubs formed the Northern Rugby Football League. Each club played 42 matches and Manningham won the first Championship as league leaders in 1895-96.

This format was then abandoned and replaced by the Yorkshire Senior and Lancashire Senior Combination leagues until 1901-02 when 14 clubs broke away to form the Northern Rugby League with Broughton Rangers winning the first Championship.

The following season two divisions were formed with the Division One title going to Halifax (1902-03), Bradford (1903-04), who won a play-off against Salford 5-0 at Halifax after both teams tied with 52 points, and Oldham (1904-05).

In 1905-06 the two divisions were merged with Leigh taking the Championship as league leaders. They won the title on a percentage basis as the 31 clubs did not play the same number of matches. The following season the top four play-off was introduced as a fairer means of deciding the title.

The top club played the fourth-placed, the second meeting the third, with the higher club having home advantage. The final was staged at a neutral venue.

It was not until 1930-31 that all clubs played the same number of league matches, but not all against each other, the top four play-off being a necessity until the reintroduction of two divisions in 1962-63.

This spell of two division football lasted only two seasons and the restoration of the Championship table brought about the introduction of a top-16 play-off, this format continuing until the reappearance of two divisions in 1973-74.

Since then the Championship Trophy has been awarded to the leaders of the First Division, with the Second Division champions receiving a silver bowl.

Slalom Lager launched a three-year sponsorship deal of the Championship and the Premiership in 1980-81 in a £215,000 package, extending the deal for another three years from 1983-84 for £270,000. From 1986-87, the sponsorship was taken over by brewers Bass, under the Stones Bitter banner, in a new £400,000 three-year deal, renewed for a further three years from 1989-90 for £750,000.

CHAMPIONSHIP PLAY-OFF FINALS

Season	Winners		Runners-up		Venue	Attendance	Receipts
Top Four Play-Offs							
1906-07	Halifax	18	Oldham	3	Huddersfield	13,200	£722
1907-08	Hunslet	7	Oldham	7	Salford	14,000	£690
Replay	Hunslet	12	Oldham	2	Wakefield	14,054	£800
1908-09	Wigan	7	Oldham	3	Salford	12,000	£630
1909-10	Oldham	13	Wigan	7	Broughton	10,850	£520
1910-11	Oldham	20	Wigan	7	Broughton	15,543	£717
1911-12	Huddersfield	13	Wigan	5	Halifax	15,000	£591
1912-13	Huddersfield	29	Wigan	2	Wakefield	17,000	£914
1913-14	Salford	5	Huddersfield	3	Leeds	8,091	£474
1914-15	Huddersfield	35	Leeds	2	Wakefield	14,000	£750
COMPETITION SUSPENDED DURING WAR TIME							
1919-20	Hull	3	Huddersfield	2	Leeds	12,900	£1,615
1920-21	Hull	16	Hull K.R.	14	Leeds	10,000	£1,320
1921-22	Wigan	13	Oldham	2	Broughton	26,000	£1,825
1922-23	Hull K.R.	15	Huddersfield	5	Leeds	14,000	£1,370
1923-24	Batley	13	Wigan	7	Broughton	13,729	£968
1924-25	Hull K.R.	9	Swinton	5	Rochdale	21,580	£1,504
1925-26	Wigan	22	Warrington	10	St. Helens	20,000	£1,100
1926-27	Swinton	13	St. Helens Recs.	8	Warrington	24,432	£1,803
1927-28	Swinton	11	Featherstone R.	0	Oldham	15,451	£1,136
1928-29	Huddersfield	2	Leeds	0	Halifax	25,604	£2,028
1929-30	Huddersfield	2	Leeds	2	Wakefield	32,095	£2,111
Replay	Huddersfield	10	Leeds	0	Halifax	18,563	£1,319
1930-31	Swinton	14	Leeds	7	Wigan	31,000	£2,100
1931-32	St. Helens	9	Huddersfield	5	Wakefield	19,386	£943
1932-33	Salford	15	Swinton	5	Wigan	18,000	£1,053
1933-34	Wigan	15	Salford	3	Warrington	31,564	£2,114
1934-35	Swinton	14	Warrington	3	Wigan	27,700	£1,710
1935-36	Hull	21	Widnes	2	Huddersfield	17,276	£1,208

209

Season	Winners		Runners-up		Venue	Attendance	Receipts
1936-37	Salford	13	Warrington	11	Wigan	31,500	£2,000
1937-38	Hunslet	8	Leeds	2	Elland Rd., Leeds	54,112	£3,572
1938-39	Salford	8	Castleford	6	Man. City FC	69,504	£4,301

WAR-TIME EMERGENCY PLAY-OFFS
For the first two seasons the Yorkshire League and Lancashire League champions met in a two-leg final as follows:

1939-40	Swinton	13	Bradford N.	21	Swinton	4,800	£237
	Bradford N.	16	Swinton	9	Bradford	11,721	£570
	Bradford N. won 37-22 on aggregate						
1940-41	Wigan	6	Bradford N.	17	Wigan	11,245	£640
	Bradford N.	28	Wigan	9	Bradford	20,205	£1,148
	Bradford N. won 45-15 on aggregate						

For the remainder of the War the top four in the War League played-off as follows:

1941-42	Dewsbury	13	Bradford N.	0	Leeds	18,000	£1,121
1942-43	Dewsbury	11	Halifax	3	Dewsbury	7,000	£400
	Halifax	13	Dewsbury	22	Halifax	9,700	£683

Dewsbury won 33-16 on aggregate but the Championship was declared null and void because they had played an ineligible player

1943-44	Wigan	13	Dewsbury	9	Wigan	14,000	£915
	Dewsbury	5	Wigan	12	Dewsbury	9,000	£700
	Wigan won 25-14 on aggregate						
1944-45	Halifax	9	Bradford N.	2	Halifax	9,426	£955
	Bradford N.	24	Halifax	11	Bradford	16,000	£1,850
	Bradford N. won 26-20 on aggregate						
1945-46	Wigan	13	Huddersfield	4	Man. C. FC	67,136	£8,387
1946-47	Wigan	13	Dewsbury	4	Man. C. FC	40,599	£5,895
1947-48	Warrington	15	Bradford N.	5	Man. C. FC	69,143	£9,792
1948-49	Huddersfield	13	Warrington	12	Man. C. FC	75,194	£11,073
1949-50	Wigan	20	Huddersfield	2	Man. C. FC	65,065	£11,500
1950-51	Workington T.	26	Warrington	11	Man. C. FC	61,618	£10,993
1951-52	Wigan	13	Bradford N.	6	Huddersfield Town FC	48,684	£8,215
1952-53	St. Helens	24	Halifax	14	Man. C. FC	51,083	£11,503
1953-54	Warrington	8	Halifax	7	Man. C. FC	36,519	£9,076
1954-55	Warrington	7	Oldham	3	Man. C. FC	49,434	£11,516
1955-56	Hull	10	Halifax	9	Man. C. FC	36,675	£9,179
1956-57	Oldham	15	Hull	14	Bradford	62,199	£12,054
1957-58	Hull	20	Workington T.	3	Bradford	57,699	£11,149
1958-59	St. Helens	44	Hunslet	22	Bradford	52,560	£10,146
1959-60	Wigan	27	Wakefield T.	3	Bradford	83,190	£14,482
1960-61	Leeds	25	Warrington	10	Bradford	52,177	£10,475
1961-62	Huddersfield	14	Wakefield T.	5	Bradford	37,451	£7,979

TWO DIVISIONS 1962-63 and 1963-64

Top Sixteen Play-Offs

1964-65	Halifax	15	St. Helens	7	Swinton	20,786	£6,141
1965-66	St. Helens	35	Halifax	12	Swinton	30,634	£8,750
1966-67	Wakefield T.	7	St. Helens	7	Leeds	20,161	£6,702
Replay	Wakefield T.	21	St. Helens	9	Swinton	33,537	£9,800
1967-68	Wakefield T.	17	Hull K.R.	10	Leeds	22,586	£7,697
1968-69	Leeds	16	Castleford	14	Bradford	28,442	£10,130
1969-70	St. Helens	24	Leeds	12	Bradford	26,358	£9,791
1970-71	St. Helens	16	Wigan	12	Swinton	21,745	£10,200
1971-72	Leeds	9	St. Helens	5	Swinton	24,055	£9,513
1972-73	Dewsbury	22	Leeds	13	Bradford	18,889	£9,479

CHAMPIONSHIP FINAL . . . . A 10-YEAR REVIEW

1961-62 HUDDERSFIELD 14 Dyson (4g); Breen, Deighton, Booth, Wicks (1t); Davies, Smales (1t); Slevin, Close, Noble, Kilroy, Bowman, Ramsden
WAKEFIELD T. 5 Round; F. Smith, Skene, N. Fox (1t, 1g), Hirst; Poynton, Holliday; Wilkinson, Kosanovic, Firth, Briggs, Vines, Turner
Referee: N. T. Railton (Wigan)

TWO DIVISIONS — NO PLAY-OFFS 1963 and 1964

1964-65 HALIFAX 15 James (3g); Jackson (1t), Burnett (2t), Kellett, Freeman; Robinson, Daley; Roberts, Harrison, Scroby, Fogerty, Dixon, Renilson
ST. HELENS 7 F. Barrow; Harvey, Vollenhoven, Northey, Killeen (1t, 2g); Murphy, Smith; Tembey (Warlow), Dagnall, Watson, French, Mantle, Laughton
Referee: D. S. Brown (Dewsbury)

1965-66 ST. HELENS 35 F. Barrow; A. Barrow (1t), Murphy (1g), Benyon, Killeen (3t, 6g); Harvey; Bishop; Halsall (3t), Sayer, Watson, French, Warlow (Hitchen), Mantle
HALIFAX 12 Cooper (3g); Jones, Burnett, Dixon, Freeman; Robinson, Baker (1t); Roberts, Harrison, Scroby, Ramshaw (Duffy), Fogerty (1t), Renilson
Referee: J. Manley (Warrington)

1966-67 WAKEFIELD T. 7 Cooper; Hirst, Brooke, N. Fox (2g), Coetzer; Poynton, Owen (1t); Bath, Prior, Campbell, Clarkson, Haigh, D. Fox
ST. HELENS 7 F. Barrow; Vollenhoven, A. Barrow, Smith, Killeen (2g); Douglas, Bishop; Warlow, Sayer, Watson (1t), French, Hogan (Robinson), Mantle
Referee: G. Philpott (Leeds)

Replay: WAKEFIELD T. 21 Cooper; Hirst (1t), Brooke (2t), N. Fox (3g), Coetzer; Poynton (1t), Owen (1t); Bath, Prior, Campbell, Clarkson, Haigh, D. Fox
ST. HELENS 9 F. Barrow; Vollenhoven (1t), A. Barrow, Smith, Killeen (2g); Douglas, Bishop; Warlow, Sayer, Watson, French, Hogan, Mantle
Referee: J. Manley (Warrington)

1967-68 WAKEFIELD T. 17 G. Cooper; Coetzer, Brooke, N. Fox (1t, 2g), Batty; Poynton (1g), Owen (1t); Jeanes (1t), Shepherd, D. Fox (1g), Haigh, McLeod, Hawley
HULL K.R. 10 Wainwright; C. Young, Moore (1t), A. Burwell, Longstaff (1t); Millward (2g), C. Cooper; L. Foster, Flanagan, Mennell, Lowe, Major, F. Foster
Referee: D. S. Brown (Preston)

1968-69 LEEDS 16 Risman (4g); Cowan (1t), Hynes, Watson, Atkinson (1t); Shoebottom, Seabourne (Langley); Clark (Hick), Crosby, K. Eyre, Joyce, Ramsey (1g), Batten
CASTLEFORD 14 Edwards; Briggs, Howe, Thomas, Lowndes; Hardisty (1t, 1g), Hepworth; Hartley, C. Dickinson (1t), J. Ward, Redfearn (3g), Lockwood, Reilly (Fox)
Referee: W. H. Thompson (Huddersfield)

1969-70 ST. HELENS 24 F. Barrow; L. Jones, Benyon, Walsh (1t, 2g), E. Prescott (2t), Myler, Heaton; Halsall, Sayer (1t), Watson, Mantle, E. Chisnall, Coslett (4g)
LEEDS 12 Holmes (3g); Alan Smith (1t), Hynes, Cowan (1t), Atkinson; Shoebottom, Seabourne; J. Burke, Crosby, A. Eyre, Ramsey (Hick), Eccles, Batten
Referee: W. H. Thompson (Huddersfield)

1970-71 ST. HELENS 16 Pimblett; L. Jones, Benyon (1t), Walsh, Blackwood (1t); Whittle, Heaton; J. Stephens, A. Karalius, Rees (Wanbon), Mantle, E. Chisnall, Coslett (5g)
WIGAN 12 Tyrer (1g); Kevin O'Loughlin; Francis, Rowe, Wright; D. Hill, Ayres; Hogan, Clarke, Fletcher, Ashurst (1t, 2g), Robinson (1t) (Cunningham), Laughton
Referee: E. Lawrinson (Warrington)

1971-72 LEEDS 9 Holmes (Hick); Alan Smith, Langley, Dyl, Atkinson (1t); Hardisty, Barham; Clawson (3g), Ward, Fisher (Pickup), Cookson, Eccles, Batten
ST. HELENS 5 Pimblett; L. Jones (Whittle), Benyon, Walsh (1g), Wilson; Kelly, Heaton; Rees, Greenall (1t), J. Stephens, Mantle, E. Chisnall, Coslett
Referee: S. Shepherd (Oldham)

1972-73 DEWSBURY 22 Rushton; Ashcroft, Clark, N. Stephenson (5g, 1t), Day; Agar (1t), A. Bates; Beverley (Taylor), M. Stephenson (2t), Lowe, Grayshon, J. Bates, Whittington
LEEDS 13 Holmes; Alan Smith, Hynes (1g), Dyl (1t), Atkinson; Hardisty, Hepworth; Clawson (1g), Fisher (Ward), Clarkson (Langley), Cookson (1t), Eccles (1t), Haigh
Referee: H. G. Hunt (Prestbury)

LEAGUE LEADERS TROPHY
While the top 16 play-off decided the Championship between 1964 and 1973 it was decided to honour the top club in the league table with a League Leaders Trophy. The winners were:

1964-65 St. Helens
1965-66 St. Helens
1966-67 Leeds
1967-68 Leeds
1968-69 Leeds
1969-70 Leeds
1970-71 Wigan
1971-72 Leeds
1972-73 Warrington

CLUB CHAMPIONSHIP (Merit Table)
With the reintroduction of two divisions, a complicated merit table and Division Two preliminary rounds system produced a 16 club play-off with the Club Championship finalists as follows:

Season	Winners		Runners-up		Venue	Attendance	Receipts
1973-74	Warrington	13	St. Helens	12	Wigan	18,040	£10,032

This format lasted just one season and was replaced by the Premiership.

CLUB CHAMPIONSHIP FINAL . . . . A REVIEW
1973-74 WARRINGTON 13 Whitehead (2g); M. Philbin (1t), Noonan (1t), Pickup (Lowe), Bevan; Whittle, A. Murphy; D. Chisnall, Ashcroft, Brady (1t), Wanbon (Gaskell), Mather, B. Philbin

ST. HELENS 12 Pimblett; Brown, Wills, Wilson (2t), Mathias; Eckersley, Heaton; Mantle, Liptrot, M. Murphy, E. Chisnall (Warlow), Nicholls, Coslett (3g)

Referee: P. Geraghty (York)

PREMIERSHIP
With the further reintroduction of two divisions in 1973-74, it was declared that the title of Champions would be awarded to the leaders of the First Division.

However, it was also decided to continue the tradition of an end-of-season play-off, the winners to receive the newly instituted Premiership Trophy.

*For full details of the Premiership Trophy see the CUPS section.

John Bevan, Warrington winger in the 1973-74 Club Championship final.

COUNTY LEAGUE
In the early seasons of the code the Lancashire Senior and Yorkshire Senior Competitions, not to be confused with the later reserve leagues, were major leagues. The winners were:

	Lancashire SC	Yorkshire SC
1895-96	Runcorn	Manningham
1896-97	Broughton Rangers	Brighouse Rangers
1897-98	Oldham	Hunslet
1898-99	Broughton Rangers	Batley
1899-00	Runcorn	Bradford
1900-01	Oldham	Bradford
1901-02	Wigan	Leeds

With the introduction of two divisions in 1902-03, the county league competitions were scrapped until they reappeared as the Lancashire League and Yorkshire League in 1907-08. Clubs from the same county played each other home and away to decide the titles. These games were included in the main championship table along with inter-county fixtures. The county leagues continued until 1970, with the exception of war-time interruptions and two seasons when regional leagues with play-offs operated during the 1960s two division era. They were then abolished when a more integrated fixture formula meant clubs did not play all others from the same county, this system later being replaced by the present two division structure.

LEAGUE LEADERS .... A REVIEW

The following is a list of the League leaders since the formation of the Northern Union, with the exception of the three eras of two-division football — 1902-05, 1962-64 and 1973-85 — which are comprehensively featured earlier in this section. From 1896 to 1901, the League was divided into a Lancashire Senior Competition and a Yorkshire Senior Competition, winners of both leagues being listed for those seasons. From 1905 to 1930 not all the clubs played each other, the League being determined on a percentage basis.

LSC — Lancashire Senior Competition
LL — Lancashire League
YSC — Yorkshire Senior Competition
YL — Yorkshire League
WEL — War Emergency League
★ Two points deducted for breach of professional rules
† Decided on a percentage basis after Belle Vue Rangers withdrew shortly before the start of the season.

		P.	W.	D.	L.	F.	A.	Pts.	
1895-96	Manningham	42	33	0	9	367	158	66	
1896-97	Broughton R.	26	19	5	2	201	52	43	LSC
	Brighouse R.	30	22	4	4	213	68	48	YSC
1897-98	Oldham	26	23	1	2	295	94	47	LSC
	Hunslet	30	22	4	4	327	117	48	YSC
1898-99	Broughton R.	26	21	0	5	277	74	42	LSC
	Batley	30	23	2	5	279	75	48	YSC
1899-00	Runcorn	26	22	2	2	232	33	46	LSC
	Bradford	30	24	2	4	324	98	50	YSC
1900-01	Oldham	26	22	1	3	301	67	45	LSC
	Bradford	30	26	1	3	387	100	51★	YSC
1901-02	Broughton R.	26	21	1	4	285	112	43	
1902-05	Two Divisions								
1905-06	Leigh	30	23	2	5	245	130	48	80.00%
1906-07	Halifax	34	27	2	5	649	229	56	82.35%
1907-08	Oldham	32	28	2	2	396	121	58	90.62%
1908-09	Wigan	32	28	0	4	706	207	56	87.50%
1909-10	Oldham	34	29	2	3	604	184	60	88.23%
1910-11	Wigan	34	28	1	5	650	205	57	83.82%
1911-12	Huddersfield	36	31	1	4	996	238	63	87.50%
1912-13	Huddersfield	32	28	0	4	732	217	56	87.50%
1913-14	Huddersfield	34	28	2	4	830	258	58	85.29%
1914-15	Huddersfield	34	28	4	2	888	235	60	88.24%
1915-18	Competitive matches suspended during First World War								
1918-19	Rochdale H.	12	9	0	3	92	52	18	75.00% LL
	Hull	16	13	0	3	392	131	26	81.25% YL
1919-20	Huddersfield	34	29	0	5	759	215	58	85.29%
1920-21	Hull K.R.	32	24	1	7	432	233	49	76.56%
1921-22	Oldham	36	29	1	6	521	201	59	81.94%
1922-23	Hull	36	30	0	6	587	304	60	83.33%
1923-24	Wigan	38	31	0	7	824	228	62	81.57%
1924-25	Swinton	36	30	0	6	499	224	60	83.33%
1925-26	Wigan	38	29	3	6	641	310	61	80.26%
1926-27	St. Helens R.	38	29	3	6	544	235	61	80.26%
1927-28	Swinton	36	27	3	6	439	189	57	79.16%

		P.	W.	D.	L.	F.	A.	Pts.	
1928-29	Huddersfield	38	26	4	8	476	291	56	73.68%
1929-30	St. Helens	40	27	1	12	549	295	55	68.75%
1930-31	Swinton	38	31	2	5	504	156	64	
1931-32	Huddersfield	38	30	1	7	636	368	61	
1932-33	Salford	38	31	2	5	751	165	64	
1933-34	Salford	38	31	1	6	715	281	63	
1934-35	Swinton	38	30	1	7	468	175	61	
1935-36	Hull	38	30	1	7	607	306	61	
1936-37	Salford	38	29	3	6	529	196	61	
1937-38	Hunslet	36	25	3	8	459	301	53	
1938-39	Salford	40	30	3	7	551	191	63	
1939-40	Swinton	22	17	0	5	378	158	34	WEL LL
	Bradford N.	28	21	0	7	574	302	42	WEL YL
1940-41	Wigan	16	15	1	0	297	71	31	WEL LL
	Bradford N.	25	23	1	1	469	126	47	WEL YL
1941-42	Dewsbury	24	19	1	4	431	172	39	81.25% WEL
1942-43	Wigan	16	13	0	3	301	142	26	81.25% WEL
1943-44	Wakefield T.	22	19	0	3	359	97	38	86.36% WEL
1944-45	Bradford N.	20	17	0	3	337	69	34	85.00% WEL
1945-46	Wigan	36	29	2	5	783	219	60	
1946-47	Wigan	36	29	1	6	567	196	59	
1947-48	Wigan	36	31	1	4	776	258	63	
1948-49	Warrington	36	31	0	5	728	247	62	
1949-50	Wigan	36	31	1	4	853	320	63	
1950-51	Warrington	36	30	0	6	738	250	60	
1951-52	Bradford N.	36	28	1	7	758	326	57	
1952-53	St. Helens	36	32	2	2	769	273	66	
1953-54	Halifax	36	30	2	4	538	219	62	
1954-55	Warrington	36	29	2	5	718	321	60	
1955-56	Warrington	34	27	1	6	712	349	55	80.88% †
1956-57	Oldham	38	33	0	5	893	365	66	
1957-58	Oldham	38	33	1	4	803	415	67	
1958-59	St. Helens	38	31	1	6	1,005	450	63	
1959-60	St. Helens	38	34	1	3	947	343	69	
1960-61	Leeds	36	30	0	6	620	258	60	
1961-62	Wigan	36	32	1	3	885	283	65	
1962-64	Two Divisions								
1964-65	St. Helens	34	28	0	6	621	226	56	
1965-66	St. Helens	34	28	1	5	521	275	57	
1966-67	Leeds	34	29	0	5	704	373	58	
1967-68	Leeds	34	28	0	6	720	271	56	
1968-69	Leeds	34	29	2	3	775	358	60	
1969-70	Leeds	34	30	0	4	674	314	60	
1970-71	Wigan	34	30	0	4	662	308	60	
1971-72	Leeds	34	28	2	4	750	325	58	
1972-73	Warrington	34	27	2	5	816	400	56	

*Stones Bitter Coach of the Year, John Monie, with the
Silk Cut Challenge Cup, accompanied by Wigan skipper
Ellery Hanley.*

COACHES

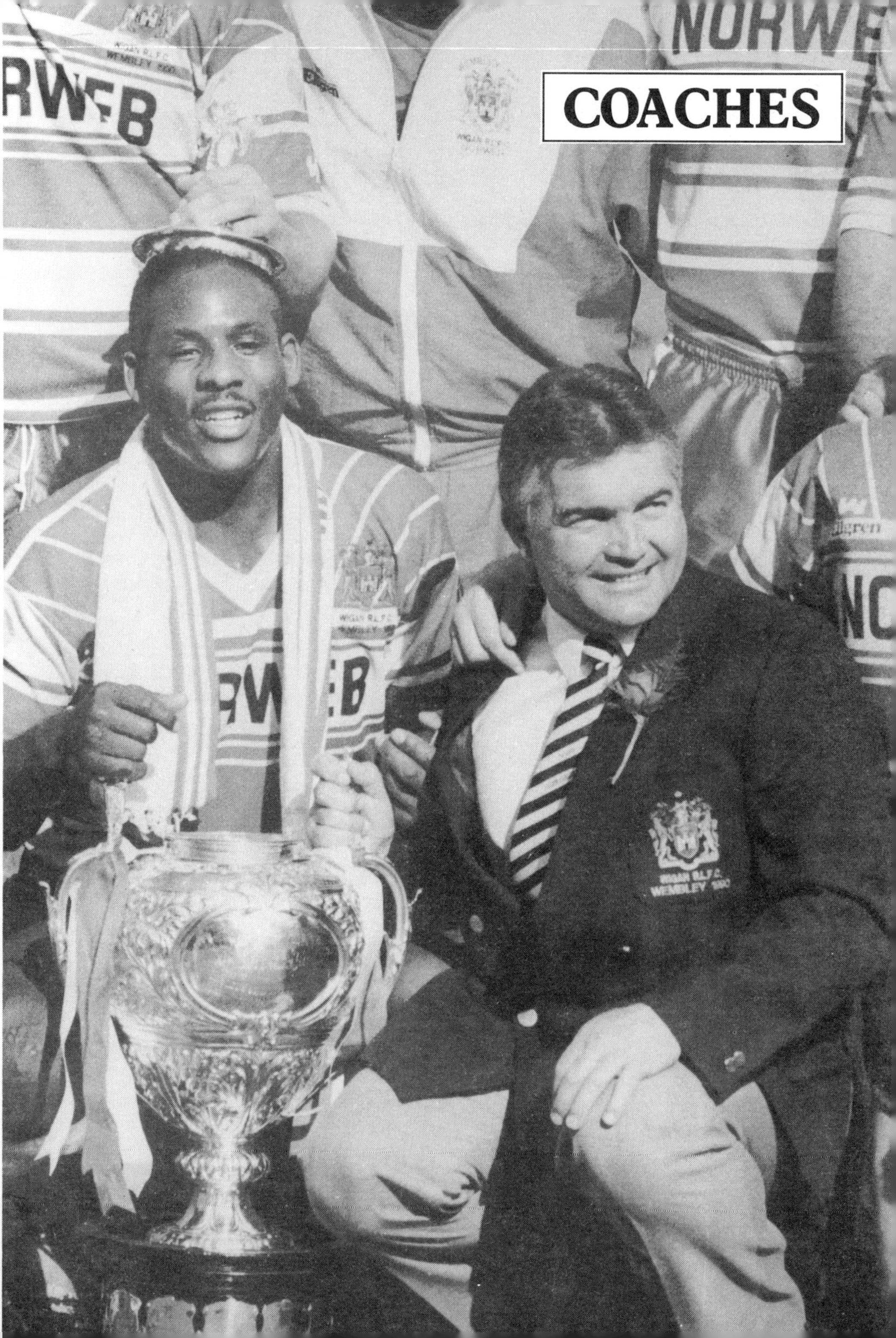

COACHES

Between June 1989 and end of May 1990 a total of 21 clubs made first team coaching changes, some more than once. Thirteen new coaches had their first British senior appointments bringing the total of coaches since the start of the 1974-75 season to 221.

This chapter is a compilation of those appointments, featuring a club-by-club coaches register, an index, plus a detailed dossier of the 1989-90 coaches.

CLUB-BY-CLUB REGISTER

The following is a list of coaches each club has had since the start of the 1974-75 season.

BARROW

Frank Foster	May 73 - Apr. 83
Tommy Dawes	May 83 - Feb. 85
Tommy Bishop	Feb. 85 - Apr. 85
Ivor Kelland	May 85 - Feb. 87
Dennis Jackson	Feb. 87 - Nov. 87
Rod Reddy	Nov. 87 - Nov. 89
Dennis Jackson	Nov. 89 - Apr. 90
Steve Norton	May 90 -

BATLEY

Don Fox	Nov. 72 - Oct. 74
Alan Hepworth	Nov. 74 - Apr. 75
Dave Cox	May 75 - June 75
Trevor Walker	June 75 - June 77
Albert Fearnley	June 77 - Oct. 77
Dave Stockwell	Oct. 77 - June 79
*Tommy Smales	June 79 - Oct. 81
Trevor Lowe	Oct. 81 - May 82
Terry Crook	June 82 - Nov. 84
George Pieniazek	Nov. 84 - Nov. 85
Brian Lockwood	Nov. 85 - May 87
Paul Daley	July 87 - Apr. 90
Keith Rayne	May 90 -

*Ex-forward

BRADFORD NORTHERN

Ian Brooke	Jan. 73 - Sept. 75
Roy Francis	Oct. 75 - Apr. 77
Peter Fox	Apr. 77 - May 85
Barry Seabourne	May 85 - Sep. 89
Ron Willey	Oct. 89 - Mar. 90
David Hobbs	Mar. 90 -

BRAMLEY

Arthur Keegan	May 73 - Sept. 76
Peter Fox	Sept. 76 - Apr. 77
*Tommy Smales	May 77 - Dec. 77
Les Pearce	Jan. 78 - Oct. 78
Don Robinson	Oct. 78 - May 79
Dave Stockwell	June 79 - June 80
Keith Hepworth	June 80 - May 82
Maurice Bamford	May 82 - Oct. 83
Peter Jarvis	Oct. 83 - Apr. 85
Ken Loxton	Apr. 85 - Dec. 85
Allan Agar	Dec. 85 - Apr. 87
Chris Forster	June 87 - Nov. 87
Tony Fisher	Nov. 87 - Feb. 89
Barry Johnson	Mar. 89 -

*Ex-forward

CARLISLE

Allan Agar	May 81 - June 82
Mick Morgan	July 82 - Feb. 83
John Atkinson	Feb. 83 - Feb. 86
Alan Kellett	Feb. 86 - May 86
Roy Lester	June 86 - Nov. 88
Tommy Dawes	Dec. 88 - Jan. 90
Cameron Bell	Feb. 90 -

CASTLEFORD

Dave Cox	Apr. 74 - Nov. 74
*Malcolm Reilly	Dec. 74 - May 87
Dave Sampson	May 87 - Apr. 88
Darryl Van de Velde	July 88 -

*Shortly after his appointment Reilly returned to Australia to fulfil his contract before resuming at Castleford early the next season.

CHORLEY

Stan Gittins	June 89 - Apr. 90
Bob Eccles	May 90 -

DEWSBURY

Maurice Bamford	June 74 - Oct. 74
Alan Hardisty	Oct. 74 - June 75
Dave Cox	June 75 - July 77
Ron Hill	July 77 - Dec. 77
Lewis Jones	Dec. 77 - Apr. 78
Jeff Grayshon	May 78 - Oct. 78
Alan Lockwood	Oct. 78 - Oct. 80
Bernard Watson	Oct. 80 - Oct. 82
Ray Abbey	Nov. 82 - Apr. 83
*Tommy Smales	May 83 - Feb. 84
Jack Addy	Feb. 84 - Jan. 87
Dave Busfield	Jan. 87 - Apr. 87
Terry Crook	Apr. 87 - Dec. 88
Maurice Bamford	Dec. 88 -

Ex-forward

DONCASTER

Ted Strawbridge	Feb. 73 - Apr. 75
Derek Edwards	July 75 - Nov. 76
Don Robson	Nov. 76 - Sept. 77
Trevor Lowe	Sept. 77 - Apr. 79
*Tommy Smales	Feb. 78 - Apr. 79
Billy Yates	Apr. 79 - May 80
Don Vines	Sept. 79 - Jan. 80
Bill Kenny	June 80 - May 81
Alan Rhodes	Aug. 81 - Mar. 83
Clive Sullivan	Mar. 83 - May 84
John Sheridan	June 84 - Nov. 87
Graham Heptinstall	Nov. 87 - Jan. 88
John Sheridan	Jan. 88 - Apr. 89
Dave Sampson	May 89 -

Ex-forward, who shared the coaching post with Trevor Lowe for just over a year.

FEATHERSTONE ROVERS

*Tommy Smales	July 74 - Sept. 74
Keith Goulding	Sept. 74 - Jan. 76
†Tommy Smales	Feb. 76 - May 76
Keith Cotton	June 76 - Dec. 77
Keith Goulding	Dec. 77 - May 78
Terry Clawson	July 78 - Nov. 78
†Tommy Smales	Nov. 78 - Apr. 79
Paul Daley	May 79 - Jan. 81
Vince Farrar	Feb. 81 - Nov. 82
Allan Agar	Dec. 82 - Oct. 85
George Pieniazek	Nov. 85 - Nov. 86
Paul Daley	Nov. 86 - Apr. 87
Peter Fox	May 87 -

Ex-forward
†Ex-scrum half

FULHAM

Reg Bowden	July 80 - June 84
Roy Lester	June 84 - Apr. 86
Bill Goodwin	Apr. 86 - May 88
*Bev Risman	May 88 - Feb. 89
Phil Sullivan	Feb. 89 - Mar. 89
Bill Goodwin	Mar. 89 - Apr 89
Ross Strudwick	June 89 -

Team manager

Maurice Bamford, his second coaching stint at Dewsbury.

HALIFAX

Derek Hallas	Aug. 74 - Oct. 74
Les Pearce	Oct. 74 - Apr. 76
Alan Kellett	May 76 - Apr. 77
Jim Crellin	June 77 - Oct. 77
Harry Fox	Oct. 77 - Feb. 78
Maurice Bamford	Feb. 78 - May 80
Mick Blacker	June 80 - June 82
Ken Roberts	June 82 - Sept. 82
Colin Dixon	Sept. 82 - Nov. 84
Chris Anderson	Nov. 84 - May 88
Graham Eadie	May 88 - Aug 88
Ross Strudwick	Aug. 88 - Feb. 89
Alan Hardisty	Feb. 89 - Apr. 89
John Dorahy	June 89 -

HUDDERSFIELD

Brian Smith	Jan. 73 - Mar. 76
Keith Goulding	Mar. 76 - Dec. 76
Bob Tomlinson	Jan. 77 - May 77
Neil Fox	June 77 - Feb. 78
*Roy Francis	-
Keith Goulding	May 78 - July 79
Ian Brooke	July 79 - Mar. 80
Maurice Bamford	May 80 - May 81
Les Sheard	June 81 - Nov. 82
Dave Mortimer	Nov. 82 - Aug. 83
Mel Bedford	Aug. 83 - Nov. 83
Brian Lockwood	Nov. 83 - Feb. 85
Chris Forster	Feb. 85 - Dec. 86
Jack Addy	Jan. 87 - Mar. 88
Allen Jones Neil Whittaker	Mar. 88 - Nov. 88
Nigel Stephenson	Nov. 88 - Mar. 90
Barry Seabourne	Mar. 90 -

Although Roy Francis was appointed he was unable to take over and Dave Heppleston stood in until the next appointment.

HULL

David Doyle-Davidson	May 74 - Dec. 77
Arthur Bunting	Jan. 78 - Dec. 85
Kenny Foulkes	Dec. 85 - May 86
Len Casey	June 86 - Mar. 88
Tony Dean Keith Hepworth	Mar. 88 - Apr. 88
Brian Smith	July 88 -

HULL KINGSTON ROVERS

Arthur Bunting	Feb. 72 - Nov. 75
Harry Poole	Dec. 75 - Mar. 77
Roger Millward	Mar. 77 -

HUNSLET

Paul Daley	Apr. 74 - Aug. 78
Bill Ramsey	Aug. 78 - Dec. 79
Drew Broatch	Dec. 79 - Apr. 81
Paul Daley	Apr. 81 - Nov. 85
*Peter Jarvis	Nov. 85 - Apr. 88
*David Ward	July 86 - Apr. 88
Nigel Stephenson	Jun. 88 - Oct. 88
Jack Austin John Wolford	Oct. 88 - Jan. 89
David Ward	Jan. 89 - May 89
Graeme Jennings	Sept. 89 - Apr. 90
Paul Daley	May 90 -

Joint coaches from July 1986.

KEIGHLEY

Alan Kellett	Jan. 73 - May 75
Roy Sabine	Aug. 75 - Oct. 77
Barry Seabourne	Nov. 77 - Mar. 79
Albert Fearnley (Mgr)	Apr. 79 - Aug. 79
Alan Kellett	Apr. 79 - Apr. 80
Albert Fearnley	May 80 - Feb. 81
Bakary Diabira	Feb. 81 - Sept. 82
Lee Greenwood	Sept. 82 - Oct. 83
Geoff Peggs	Nov. 83 - Sept. 85
Peter Roe	Sept. 85 - July 86
Colin Dixon	July 86 - June 89
Les Coulter	July 86 - Apr. 90

LEEDS

Roy Francis	June 74 - May 75
Syd Hynes	June 75 - Apr. 81
Robin Dewhurst	June 81 - Oct. 83
Maurice Bamford	Nov. 83 - Feb. 85
Malcolm Clift	Feb. 85 - May 85
Peter Fox	May 85 - Dec. 86
Maurice Bamford	Dec. 86 - Apr. 88
Malcolm Reilly	Aug. 88 - Sept. 89
David Ward	Sept. 89 -

LEIGH

Eddie Cheetham	May 74 - Mar. 75
Kevin Ashcroft	June 75 - Jan. 77
Bill Kindon	Jan. 77 - Apr. 77
John Mantle	Apr. 77 - Nov. 78
Tom Grainey	Nov. 78 - Dec. 80
*Alex Murphy	Nov. 80 - June 82
*Colin Clarke	June 82 - Dec. 82
Peter Smethurst	Dec. 82 - Apr. 83
Tommy Bishop	June 83 - June 84
John Woods	June 84 - May 85
Alex Murphy	Feb. 85 - Nov. 85
Tommy Dickens	Nov. 85 - Dec. 86
Billy Benyon	Dec. 86 - Mar. 90
Alex Murphy	Mar. 90 -

From Dec. 80 to June 82 Clarke was officially appointed coach and Murphy manager

NOTTINGHAM CITY

Mick Blacker	May 84 - Oct. 85
Bill Kirkbride	Nov. 85 - Mar. 86
Steve Dennison	Apr. 86 - Dec. 86
Jim Crellin	Dec. 86 - June 88
Billy Platt	July 88 - Dec. 88
Steve Nash	Dec. 88 - Feb. 89
Lee Greenwood	Feb. 89 - Mar. 90
Mel Wibberley	Mar. 90 -

OLDHAM

Jim Challinor	Aug. 74 - Dec. 76
Terry Ramshaw	Jan. 77 - Feb. 77
Dave Cox	July 77 - Dec. 78
Graham Starkey (Mngr)	Jan. 79 - May 81
Bill Francis	June 79 - Dec. 80
Frank Myler	May 81 - Apr. 83
Peter Smethurst	Apr. 83 - Feb. 84
Frank Barrow	Feb. 84 - Feb. 84
Brian Gartland	Mar. 84 - June 84
Frank Myler	June 84 - Apr. 87
*Eric Fitzsimons	June 87 - Nov. 88
*Mal Graham	June 87 - Apr. 88
Tony Barrow	Nov. 88 -

Joint coaches June 87 - Apr. 88

ROCHDALE HORNETS

Frank Myler	May 71 - Oct. 74
Graham Starkey	Oct. 74 - Nov. 75
Henry Delooze	Nov. 75 - Nov. 76
Kel Coslett	Nov. 76 - Aug. 79
Paul Longstaff	Sept. 79 - May 81
Terry Fogerty	May 81 - Jan. 82
Dick Bonser	Jan. 82 - May 82
Bill Kirkbride	June 82 - Sept. 84
Charlie Birdsall	Sept. 84 - Apr. 86
Eric Fitzsimons	June 86 - June 87
Eric Hughes	June 87 - June 88
Jim Crellin	June 88 - June 89
Allan Agar	July 89 -

RUNCORN HIGHFIELD

Terry Gorman	Aug. 74 - May 77
Geoff Fletcher	Aug. 77 - June 86
Frank Wilson	July 86 - Nov. 86
Arthur Daley Paul Woods	Nov. 86 - Apr. 87
Bill Ashurst	Apr. 87 - Jan. 89
John Cogger	Jan. 89 - Feb. 89
Geoff Fletcher	Feb. 89 - Apr. 89
Dave Chisnall	June 89 -

RYEDALE-YORK

Keith Goulding	Nov. 73 - Sept. 74
Gary Cooper	Dec. 74 - Sept. 76
Mal Dixon	Sept. 76 - Dec. 78
Paul Daley	Jan. 79 - May 79
David Doyle-Davidson	July 79 - July 80
Bill Kirkbride	Aug. 80 - Apr. 82
Alan Hardisty	May 82 - Jan. 83
Phil Lowe	Mar. 83 - Mar. 87
Danny Sheehan	Mar. 87 - Apr. 88
Gary Stephens	Apr. 88 -

ST. HELENS

Eric Ashton	May 74 - May 80
Kel Coslett	June 80 - May 82
Billy Benyon	May 82 - Nov. 85
Alex Murphy	Nov. 85 - Jan. 90
Mike McClennan	Feb. 90 -

SALFORD

Les Bettinson	Dec. 73 - Mar. 77
Colin Dixon	Mar. 77 - Jan. 78
Stan McCormick	Feb. 78 - Mar. 78
Alex Murphy	May 78 - Nov. 80
Kevin Ashcroft	Nov. 80 - Mar. 82
Alan McInnes	Mar. 82 - May 82
Malcolm Aspey	May 82 - Oct. 83
Mike Coulman	Oct. 83 - May 84
Kevin Ashcroft	May 84 - Oct. 89
Kevin Tamati	Oct. 89 -

SHEFFIELD EAGLES

Alan Rhodes	Apr. 84 - May 86
Gary Hetherington	July 86 -

SWINTON

Austin Rhodes	June 74 - Nov. 75
Bob Fleet	Nov. 75 - Nov. 76
John Stopford	Nov. 76 - Apr. 77
Terry Gorman	June 77 - Nov. 78
Ken Halliwell	Nov. 78 - Dec. 79
Frank Myler	Jan. 80 - May 81
Tom Grainey	May 81 - Oct. 83
Jim Crellin	Nov. 83 - May 86
Bill Holliday Mike Peers	June 86 - Oct. 87
Frank Barrow	Oct. 87 - June 89
Jim Crellin	July 89 -

TRAFFORD BOROUGH

Tommy Blakeley	Aug. 74 - Apr. 76
Jim Crellin	May 76 - Mar. 77
Joe Egan Jnr.	Mar. 77 - Oct 77
Albert Fearnley (Mgr)	Nov. 77 - Apr. 79
Bakary Diabira	Nov. 78 - June 79
Graham Rees	June 79 - Mar. 80
Geoff Lyon	July 80 - Aug. 81
Bob Irving	Aug. 81 - Feb. 82
John Mantle	Feb. 82 - Mar. 82
Tommy Dickens	Mar. 82 - Nov. 85
*Stan Gittins	Nov. 85 - June 88
*Mike Peers	June 88 -

*Joint coaches Aug. 87 - June 88

WAKEFIELD TRINITY

Peter Fox	June 74 - May 76
Geoff Gunney	June 76 - Nov. 76
Brian Lockwood	Nov. 76 - Jan. 78
Ian Brooke	Jan. 78 - Jan. 79
Bill Kirkbride	Jan. 79 - Apr. 80
Ray Batten	Apr. 80 - May 81
Bill Ashurst	June 81 - Apr. 82
Ray Batten	May 82 - July 83
Derek Turner	July 83 - Feb. 84
Bob Haigh	Feb. 84 - May 84
Geoff Wraith	May 84 - Oct. 84
David Lamming	Oct. 84 - Apr. 85
Len Casey	Apr. 85 - June 86
Tony Dean	June 86 - Dec. 86
Trevor Bailey	Dec. 86 - Apr. 87
David Topliss	May 87 -

WARRINGTON

Alex Murphy	May 71 - May 78
Billy Benyon	June 78 - Mar. 82
Kevin Ashcroft	Mar. 82 - May 84
Reg Bowden	June 84 - Mar. 86
Tony Barrow	Mar. 86 - Nov. 88
Brian Johnson	Nov. 88 -

WHITEHAVEN

Jeff Bawden	May 72 - May 75
Ike Southward	Aug. 75 - June 76
Bill Smith	Aug. 76 - Oct. 78
Ray Dutton	Oct. 78 - Oct. 79
Phil Kitchin	Oct. 79 - Jan. 82
Arnold Walker	Jan. 82 - May 82
Tommy Dawes	June 82 - May 83
Frank Foster	June 83 - June 85
Phil Kitchin	June 85 - Oct. 87
John McFarlane	Oct. 87 - May 88
Barry Smith	July 88 - Sept 89
Eric Fitzsimons	Oct. 89 - Mar. 90

WIDNES

Vince Karalius	Jan. 72 - May 75
Frank Myler	May 75 - May 78
Doug Laughton	May 78 - Mar. 83
Harry Dawson	Mar. 83 - May 83
Colin Tyrer	
*Vince Karalius	May 83 - May 84
Harry Dawson	
Eric Hughes	June 84 - Jan. 86
Doug Laughton	Jan. 86 -

Dawson quit as coach in March 1984 with Karalius continuing as team manager.

WIGAN

Ted Toohey	May 74 - Jan. 75
Joe Coan	Jan. 75 - Sept. 76
Vince Karalius	Sept. 76 - Sept. 79
Kel Coslett	Oct. 79 - Apr. 80
George Fairbairn	Apr. 80 - May 81
Maurice Bamford	May 81 - May 82
Alex Murphy	June 82 - Aug. 84
Colin Clarke	Aug. 84 - May 86
Alan McInnes	
Graham Lowe	Aug. 86 - June 89
John Monie	Sept. 89 -

WORKINGTON TOWN

Ike Southward	Aug. 73 - June 75
Paul Charlton	June 75 - June 76
Ike Southward	June 76 - Feb. 78
Sol Roper	Feb. 78 - Apr. 80
Keith Irving	Aug. 80 - Oct. 80
Tommy Bishop	Nov. 80 - June 82
Paul Charlton	July 82 - Dec. 82
Dave Cox	Mar. 83 - Mar. 83
Harry Archer/Bill Smith	May 83 - June 84
Bill Smith	June 84 - Apr. 85
Jackie Davidson	Apr. 85 - Jan. 86
Keith Davies	Feb. 86 - Mar. 87
Norman Turley	Mar. 87 - Apr. 88
Maurice Bamford	July 88 - Dec. 88
Phil Kitchin	Dec. 88 - May 90

REPRESENTATIVE REGISTER

The following is a list of international and county coaches since 1974-75.

GREAT BRITAIN

Jim Challinor	Dec. 71 - Aug. 74
	(Inc. tours)
David Watkins	1977 World Championship
Peter Fox	1978
Eric Ashton	1979 tour
Johnny Whiteley	Aug. 80 - Nov. 82
Frank Myler	Dec. 82 - Aug. 84
	(Inc. tour)
Maurice Bamford	Oct. 84 - Dec. 86
Malcolm Reilly	Jan. 87 -
	(Inc. tours)

ENGLAND

Alex Murphy	Jan. 75 - Nov. 75
	(Inc. World Championship tour)
Peter Fox	1976-77
Frank Myler	1977-78
Eric Ashton	1978-79 & 1979-80
Johnny Whiteley	1980-81 & 1981-82
Reg Parker	1984-85
(Mngr)	

WALES

Les Pearce	Jan. 75 - Nov. 75
	(Inc. World Championship tour)
David Watkins	1976-77
Bill Francis	
Kel Coslett	1977-78
Bill Francis	
Kel Coslett	1978-79 to 1981-82
David Watkins	1982-83, 1984-85

GREAT BRITAIN UNDER-24s

Johnny Whiteley	1976-82
Frank Myler	1983-84

GREAT BRITAIN UNDER-21s

Maurice Bamford	Oct. 84 - Dec. 86
Malcolm Reilly	1986-87, 1987-88, 1989-90
David Topliss	1988-89

CUMBRIA

Ike Southward	1975-76
Frank Foster	1976-77 & 1977-78
Sol Roper	1978-79
Frank Foster	1979-80
Phil Kitchin	1980-81 to 1981-82
Frank Foster	1982-83
Jackie Davidson	1985-86
Phil Kitchin	1986-87 to 1989-90

LANCASHIRE

Alex Murphy	1973-74 to 1977-78
Eric Ashton	1978-79 to 1979-80
Tom Grainey	1980-81 to 1981-82
Doug Laughton	1982-83, 1988-89, 1989-90
Alex Murphy	1985-86 to 1987-88

YORKSHIRE

Johnny Whiteley	1970-71 to 1979-80
Arthur Keegan	1980-81
Johnny Whiteley	1981-82 to 1982-83
Peter Fox	1985-86 to 1989-90

OTHER NATIONALITIES

Dave Cox	1974-75 to 1975-76

Johnny Whiteley, coach of Yorkshire throughout the 1970s.

INDEX OF COACHES

The following is an index of the 221 coaches who have held first team coaching posts since the start of the 1974-75 season with the alphabetical listing of British clubs they coached in this period.

Ray Abbey (Dewsbury)
Jack Addy (Dewsbury, Huddersfield B.)
Allan Agar (Bramley, Carlisle, Featherstone R., Rochdale H.)
Dave Alred (Bridgend)
Chris Anderson (Halifax)
Harry Archer (Workington T.)
Kevin Ashcroft (Leigh, Salford, Warrington)
Eric Ashton M.B.E. (St. Helens)
Bill Ashurst (Runcorn H., Wakefield T.)
Mal Aspey (Salford)
Jack Austin (Hunslet)
John Atkinson (Carlisle)

Trevor Bailey (Wakefield T.)
Maurice Bamford (Bramley, Dewsbury, Halifax, Huddersfield, Leeds, Wigan, Workington T.)
Frank Barrow (Oldham, Swinton)
Tony Barrow (Oldham, Warrington)
Ray Batten (Wakefield T.)
Jeff Bawden (Whitehaven)
Mel Bedford (Huddersfield)
Cameron Bell (Carlisle)
Billy Benyon (Leigh, St. Helens, Warrington)
Les Bettinson (Salford)
Charlie Birdsall (Rochdale H.)
Tommy Bishop (Barrow, Leigh, Workington T.)
Mick Blacker (Halifax, Mansfield M.)
Tommy Blakeley (Blackpool B.)
Dick Bonser (Rochdale H.)
Reg Bowden (Fulham, Warrington)
Drew Broatch (Hunslet)
Ian Brooke (Bradford N., Huddersfield, Wakefield T.)
Arthur Bunting (Hull, Hull K.R.)
Dave Busfield (Dewsbury)

Len Casey (Hull, Wakefield T.)
Jim Challinor (Oldham)
Paul Charlton (Workington T.)
Eddie Cheetham (Leigh)
Dave Chisnall (Runcorn H.)
Colin Clarke (Leigh, Wigan)
Terry Clawson (Featherstone R.)
Malcolm Clift (Leeds)

Joe Coan (Wigan)
John Cogger (Runcorn H.)
Gary Cooper (York)
Kel Coslett (Rochdale H., St. Helens, Wigan)
Keith Cotton (Featherstone R.)
Mike Coulman (Salford)
Les Coulter (Keighley)
Dave Cox (Batley, Castleford, Dewsbury, Huyton, Oldham, Workington T.)
Jim Crellin (Blackpool B., Halifax, Mansfield M., Rochdale H., Swinton)
Terry Crook (Batley, Dewsbury)
Arthur Daley (Runcorn H.)
Paul Daley (Batley, Featherstone R., Hunslet, York)
Jackie Davidson (Workington T.)
Keith Davies (Workington T.)
Tommy Dawes (Barrow, Carlisle, Whitehaven)
Harry Dawson (Widnes)
Tony Dean (Wakefield T., Hull)
Henry Delooze (Rochdale H.)
Steve Dennison (Mansfield M.)
Robin Dewhurst (Leeds)
Bakary Diabira (Blackpool B., Keighley)
Tommy Dickens (Blackpool B., Leigh)
Colin Dixon (Halifax, Keighley, Salford)
Mal Dixon (York)
John Dorahy (Halifax)
David Doyle-Davidson (Hull, York)
Ray Dutton (Whitehaven)

Graham Eadie (Halifax)
Bob Eccles (Chorley)
Derek Edwards (Doncaster)
Joe Egan Jnr. (Blackpool B.)

George Fairbairn (Wigan)
Vince Farrar (Featherstone R.)
Albert Fearnley (Batley, Blackpool B., Keighley)
Tony Fisher (Bramley)
Eric Fitzsimons (Rochdale H., Oldham, Whitehaven)
Bob Fleet (Swinton)
Geoff Fletcher (Huyton, Runcorn H.)
Terry Fogerty (Rochdale H.)
Chris Forster (Huddersfield B., Bramley)
Frank Foster (Barrow, Whitehaven)
Kenny Foulkes (Hull)
Don Fox (Batley)
Harry Fox (Halifax)
Neil Fox (Huddersfield)
Peter Fox (Bradford N., Bramley, Featherstone R., Leeds, Wakefield T.)

Bill Francis (Oldham)
Roy Francis (Bradford N., Huddersfield, Leeds)

Brian Gartland (Oldham)
Stan Gittins (Blackpool B./Springfield B., Chorley)
Bill Goodwin (Fulham, Kent Invicta)
Terry Gorman (Huyton, Swinton)
Keith Goulding (Featherstone R., Huddersfield, York)
Mal Graham (Oldham)
Tom Grainey (Leigh, Swinton)
Jeff Grayshon (Dewsbury)
Lee Greenwood (Keighley, Mansfield M./Nottingham C.)
Geoff Gunney M.B.E. (Wakefield T.)

Bob Haigh (Wakefield T.)
Derek Hallas (Halifax)
Ken Halliwell (Swinton)
Alan Hardisty (Dewsbury, Halifax, York)
Graham Heptinstall (Doncaster)
Alan Hepworth (Batley)
Keith Hepworth (Bramley, Hull)
Gary Hetherington (Sheffield E.)
Ron Hill (Dewsbury)
David Hobbs (Bradford N.)
Bill Holliday (Swinton)
Eric Hughes (Widnes, Rochdale H.)
Syd Hynes (Leeds)

Bob Irving (Blackpool B.)
Keith Irving (Workington T.)

Dennis Jackson (Barrow)
Peter Jarvis (Bramley, Hunslet)
Graeme Jennings (Hunslet)
Barry Johnson (Bramley)
Brian Johnson (Warrington)
Allen Jones (Huddersfield B.)
Lewis Jones (Dewsbury)

Vince Karalius (Widnes, Wigan)
Arthur Keegan (Bramley)
Ivor Kelland (Barrow)
Alan Kellett (Carlisle, Halifax, Keighley)
Bill Kenny (Doncaster)
Bill Kindon (Leigh)
Bill Kirkbride (Mansfield M., Rochdale H., Wakefield T., York)
Phil Kitchin (Whitehaven, Workington T.)

Dave Lamming (Wakefield T.)
Steve Lane (Kent Invicta)

Doug Laughton (Widnes)
Roy Lester (Carlisle, Fulham)
Alan Lockwood (Dewsbury)
Brian Lockwood (Batley, Huddersfield, Wakefield T.)
Paul Longstaff (Rochdale H.)
Graham Lowe (Wigan)
Phil Lowe (York)
Trevor Lowe (Batley, Doncaster)
Ken Loxton (Bramley)
Geoff Lyon (Blackpool B.)

John Mantle (Blackpool B., Cardiff C., Leigh)
Stan McCormick (Salford)
John McFarlane (Whitehaven)
Alan McInnes (Salford, Wigan)
Mike McClennan (St. Helens)
Roger Millward M.B.E. (Hull K.R.)
John Monie (Wigan)
Mick Morgan (Carlisle)
David Mortimer (Huddersfield)
Alex Murphy (Leigh, St. Helens, Salford, Warrington, Wigan)
Frank Myler (Oldham, Rochdale H., Swinton, Widnes)

Steve Nash (Mansfield M.)
Steve Norton (Barrow)

Les Pearce (Bramley, Halifax)
Mike Peers (Chorley B./Trafford B., Swinton)
Geoff Peggs (Keighley)
George Pieniazek (Batley, Featherstone R.)
Billy Platt (Mansfield M.)
Harry Poole (Hull K.R.)

Bill Ramsey (Hunslet)
Terry Ramshaw (Oldham)
Keith Rayne (Batley)
Rod Reddy (Barrow)
Graham Rees (Blackpool B.)
Malcolm Reilly (Castleford)
Alan Rhodes (Doncaster, Sheffield E.)
Austin Rhodes (Swinton)
Bev Risman (Fulham)
Ken Roberts (Halifax)
Don Robinson (Bramley)
Don Robson (Doncaster)
Peter Roe (Keighley)
Sol Roper (Workington T.)

Roy Sabine (Keighley)
Dave Sampson (Castleford, Doncaster)

Barry Seabourne (Bradford N., Huddersfield, Keighley)
Les Sheard (Huddersfield)
Danny Sheehan (York)
John Sheridan (Doncaster)
Tommy Smales [*Scrum-half*] (Featherstone R.)
Tommy Smales [*Forward*] (Batley, Bramley, Dewsbury, Doncaster, Featherstone R.)
Peter Smethurst (Leigh, Oldham)
Barry Smith (Whitehaven)
Bill Smith (Whitehaven, Workington T.)
Brian Smith (Huddersfield)
Brian Smith (Hull)
Ike Southward (Whitehaven, Workington T.)
Graham Starkey (Oldham, Rochdale H.)
Gary Stephens (York)
Nigel Stephenson (Hunslet, Huddersfield)
Dave Stockwell (Bramley, Batley)
John Stopford (Swinton)
Ted Strawbridge (Doncaster)
Ross Strudwick (Fulham, Halifax)
Clive Sullivan (Doncaster, Hull)
Phil Sullivan (Fulham)

Kevin Tamati (Salford)
Bob Tomlinson (Huddersfield)
Ted Toohey (Wigan)
David Topliss (Wakefield T.)
Norman Turley (Workington T.)
Derek Turner (Wakefield T.)
Colin Tyrer (Widnes)

Darryl Van de Velde (Castleford)
Don Vines (Doncaster)

Arnold Walker (Whitehaven)
Trevor Walker (Batley)
David Ward (Hunslet, Leeds)
John Warlow (Bridgend)
David Watkins (Cardiff C.)
Bernard Watson (Dewsbury)
Neil Whittaker (Huddersfield B.)
Mel Wibberley (Nottingham C.)
Ron Willey (Bradford N.)
Frank Wilson (Runcorn H.)
John Wolford (Hunslet)
Jeff Woods (Bridgend)
John Woods (Leigh)
Paul Woods (Runcorn H.)
Geoff Wraith (Wakefield T.)

Billy Yates (Doncaster)

DOSSIER OF 1989-90 COACHES

The following is a dossier of the coaching and playing careers of coaches holding first team posts from June 1989 to the end of May 1990. Overseas details are not included.
● BF — beaten finalist.

ALLAN AGAR
Carlisle: May 81 - June 82 (Promotion)
Featherstone R: Dec 82 - Oct 85
                    (RL Cup winners)
Bramley: Dec. 85 - Apr. 87
Rochdale H: July 89 - (Promotion)
Played for: Featherstone R., Dewsbury, New Hunslet, Hull K.R., Wakefield T., Carlisle, Bramley

KEVIN ASHCROFT
Leigh: June 75 - Jan. 77 (Promotion, Floodlit Trophy BF)
Salford: Nov. 80 - Mar. 82
Warrington: Mar. 82 - May 84
                    (Lancs. Cup winners, BF)
Salford: May 84 - Oct. 89 (Promotion)
Played for: Dewsbury, Rochdale H., Leigh, Warrington, Salford

MAURICE BAMFORD
Dewsbury: Aug. - Oct. 74
Halifax: Feb. 78 - May 80
                    (Yorks. Cup BF., Promotion)
Huddersfield: May 80 - May 81
Wigan: May 81 - May 82
Bramley: May 82 - Oct. 83
Leeds: Nov. 83 - Feb. 85
                    (John Player winners)
Leeds: Dec. 86 - Apr. 88
                    (John Player BF)
Workington T: July 88 - Dec. 88
Dewsbury: Dec. 88 -
Great Britain &
    Under-21s: Oct. 84 - Dec. 86
Played for: Dewsbury, Hull, Batley

FRANK BARROW
Oldham: Feb. 84 - Feb. 84
Swinton: Oct. 87 - June 89
                    (Div 2 Premier BF)
Played for: St. Helens, Leigh

TONY BARROW
Warrington: Mar. 86 - Nov. 88 (Premier winners and BF, John Player BF., Lancs. Cup BF)
Oldham: Nov. 88 - (Promotion, Lancs. Cup BF, Div. 2 Premier winners)
Played for: St. Helens, Leigh

CAMERON BELL (New Zealander)
Carlisle: Feb. 90 -

BILLY BENYON
Warrington: June 78 - Mar. 82
                    (Lancs. Cup winners, John Player winners and BF)
St. Helens: May 82 - Nov. 85
                    (Lancs. Cup winners and BF, Premier winners)
Leigh: Dec. 86 - Mar. 90
                    (Div. 2 champs)
Played for: St. Helens, Warrington

LES COULTER
Keighley: July 86 - Apr. 90
Played for: Blackpool B., Doncaster

DAVE CHISNALL
Runcorn H.:   June 89 -
Played for: Leigh, Warrington, Swinton, St. Helens, Barrow, Keighley, Mansfield M., Rochdale H.

JIM CRELLIN
Blackpool B.:   May 76 - Mar. 77
                    (John Player BF)
Halifax: June 77 - Oct. 77
Swinton: Nov. 83 - May 86 (Div. 2 champs)
Mansfield M.:   Dec. 86 - June 88
Rochdale H: June 88 - June 89
Played for: Workington T., Oldham, Rochdale H.

PAUL DALEY
New Hunslet: Apr. 74 - Aug. 78 (Promotion)
York: Jan. 79 - May 79 (Promotion)
Featherstone R.:   May 79 - Jan. 81 (Div. 2 champs)
Hunslet: Apr. 81 - Nov. 85 (Promotion)
Featherstone R.:   Nov. 86 - Apr. 87
Batley: July 87 - Apr. 90
Hunslet: May 90 -
Played for: Halifax, Bradford N., Hull K.R., Hunslet

TOMMY DAWES
Whitehaven: June 82 - May 83 (Promotion)
Barrow: May 83 - Feb. 85 (Lancs. Cup
               Winners, Div. 2 champs)
Carlisle: Dec. 88 - Jan. 90
Played for: Barrow

COLIN DIXON
Salford: Mar. 77 - Jan. 78
Halifax: Sep. 82 - Nov. 84 (Promotion)
Keighley: July 86 - June 89
Played for: Halifax, Salford, Hull KR

JOHN DORAHY (Australian)
Halifax: June 89 - (Regal BF)
Played for: Leigh, Hull K.R., Halifax

BOB ECCLES
Chorley: May 90 -
Played for: Warrington, Springfield B./Chorley B./ Trafford B.

ERIC FITZSIMONS
Rochdale H.:   June 86 - June 87
Oldham: June 87 - Nov. 88
               (Div. 2 champs, Div. 2 Premier
               winners)
Whitehaven: Oct. 89 - Mar. 90
Played for: Oldham, Hunslet, Rochdale H.

PETER FOX
Featherstone R.:   Jan. 71 - May 74
               (RL Cup winners & BF)
Wakefield T.:   June 74 - May 76
               (Yorks. Cup BF)
Bramley: Sep. 76 - Apr. 77 (Promotion)
Bradford N.:   Apr. 77 - May 85 (Div. 1
               champs (2), Yorks. Cup winners
               and BF (2), Premier winners
               and BF (2), John Player winners)
Leeds: May 85 - Dec. 86
Featherstone R.:   May 87 - (Promotion, Div. 2
               Premier BF, Yorks Cup BF)
England: 1977 (2 matches)
Great Britain: 1978 (3 Tests v. Australia)
Yorkshire: 1985-86 to 1989-90
Played for: Featherstone R., Batley, Hull K.R., Wakefield T.

STAN GITTINS
Blackpool B./
Springfield B.:   Nov. 85 - June 88
Chorley: June 89 - Apr. 90
Played for: Batley, Swinton

LEE GREENWOOD
Keighley: Sep. 82 - Oct. 83
Mansfield M./
Nottingham C.   Feb. 89 - Mar. 90
Played for: Halifax, Keighley

GARY HETHERINGTON
Sheffield E.:   July 86 - (Promotion, Div. 2
               Premier winners)
Played for: York, Leeds, Kent I., Sheffield E.

DAVID HOBBS
Bradford N.:   Mar. 90 - (Premier BF)
Played for: Featherstone R., Oldham, Bradford N.

DENNIS JACKSON
Barrow: Feb. 87 - Nov. 87
Barrow: Nov. 89 - Apr. 90
Played for: Barrow, Blackpool B., Whitehaven, Workington T.

GRAEME JENNINGS (Australian)
Hunslet: Sep. 89 - Apr. 90
Played for: Hunslet

BARRY JOHNSON
Bramley: Mar. 89 -
Played for: Castleford, Bramley

BRIAN JOHNSON (Australian)
Warrington: Nov. 88 - (Lancs. Cup
               Winners, RL Cup BF)
Played for: Warrington

PHIL KITCHIN
Whitehaven: Oct. 79 - Jan. 82 (Promotion)
Whitehaven: June 85 - Oct. 87
Workington T: Dec. 88 - May 90
Cumbria: 1980-81, 1981-82, 1986-87,
               1987-88, 1989-90
Played for: Whitehaven, Workington T.

DOUG LAUGHTON
Widnes: May 78 - Mar. 83
               (RL Cup winners (2) and BF,
               Lancs. Cup winners (2) and
               BF, John Player winners and
               BF, Premier winners (2),
               Floodlit Trophy Winners
Widnes: Jan. 86 - (Div. 1 champs (2),
               Premier winners (3), Charity
               Shield winners (2), John Player
               BF)
Lancashire: 1982-83 & 1988-89
Played for: Wigan, St. Helens, Widnes

MIKE McCLENNAN (New Zealander)
St. Helens   Feb. 90 -

ROGER MILLWARD
Hull K.R.:   Mar. 77 - (Div. 1 champs (3),
                  RL Cup winners and BF (2),
                  John Player winners and BF (2),
                  Premier winners (2) and BF,
                  Yorks. Cup winners and BF (2),
                  Floodlit Trophy winners and BF,
                  Charity Shield BF, Div. 2
                  champs, Div. 2 Premier BF
Played for: Castleford, Hull K.R.

JOHN MONIE (Australian)
Wigan: Sep. 89 - (Div 1 champs, RL
                  Cup winners, Regal winners)

ALEX MURPHY
Leigh: Nov. 66 - May 71
                  (RL Cup winners, Lancs. Cup
                  winners and BF, Floodlit
                  Trophy winners and BF)
Warrington: May 71 - May 78 (League
                  Leaders, Club Merit winners,
                  RL Cup winners and BF,
                  John Player winners (2),
                  Floodlit Trophy BF,
                  Capt. Morgan winners,
                  Premier BF)
Salford: May 78 - Nov. 80
Leigh: Nov. 80 - June 82 (Div. 1
                  champs, Lancs. Cup winners)
Wigan: June 82 - Aug. 84 (John Player
                  winners, RL Cup BF)
Leigh: Feb. 85 - Nov. 85
St. Helens: Nov. 85 - Jan. 90 (RL Cup BF
                  (2), John Player winners,
                  Premier BF)
Leigh: Mar. 90 -
Lancashire: 1973-74 to 1977-78 Champions
                  (2); 1985-86 to 1987-88
England: 1975 (including World
                  Championship (European
                  Champions))
Played for: St. Helens, Leigh, Warrington

STEVE NORTON
Barrow: May 90 -
Played for: Castleford, Hull, Wakefield T.

MIKE PEERS
Swinton: June 86 - Oct. 87 (Promotion,
                  Div. 2 Premier winners)
Springfield B./
Chorley B./
Trafford B.:   Aug. 87 -
Played for: Warrington, Swinton

KEITH RAYNE
Batley: May 90 -
Played for: Wakefield T., Leeds.

ROD REDDY (Australian)
Barrow: Nov. 87 - Nov. 89 (Promotion)
Played for: Barrow

MALCOLM REILLY
Castleford: Dec. 74 - May 87 (Yorks. Cup
                  winners (3) and BF (2), Floodlit
                  Trophy winners, John Player
                  winners, Premier BF, RL Cup
                  winners, Charity Shield BF)
Leeds: Aug. 88 - Sep. 89 (Yorks. Cup
                  winners)
Great Britain: Jan. 87 -
Under-21s: 1986-87, 1987-88, 1989-90
Played for: Castleford

Malcolm Reilly, coach of Great Britain since January 1987.

227

BARRY SEABOURNE
Keighley: Nov. 77 - Mar. 79
Bradford N.:   May 85 - Sep. 89 (Yorks. Cup
                      winners)
Huddersfield: Mar. 90 -
Played for: Leeds, Bradford N., Keighley

BARRY SMITH
Whitehaven: July 88 - Sep. 89
Played for: Whitehaven

BRIAN SMITH (Australian)
Hull: July 88 - (Premier BF)

GARY STEPHENS
York: Apr. 88 -
Played for: Castleford, Wigan, Leigh, Halifax,
Leeds, York

NIGEL STEPHENSON
Hunslet: June - Oct 88
Huddersfield: Nov. 88 - Mar. 90
Played for: Dewsbury, Bradford N., Carlisle,
Wakefield T., York, Huddersfield

ROSS STRUDWICK (Australian)
Halifax: Aug. 88 - Feb. 89
Fulham: June 89 -

KEVIN TAMATI (New Zealander)
Salford: Oct. 89 -
Played for: Widnes, Warrington

DAVID TOPLISS
Wakefield T.:   May 87 - (Promotion)
Under-21s: 1988-89
Played for: Wakefield T., Hull, Oldham

DARRYL VAN DE VELDE (Australian)
Castleford: July 88 - (Yorks. Cup BF)

DAVID WARD
Hunslet: July 86 - Apr. 88 (Div. 2
                champs, Div. 2 Premier BF)
Hunslet: Jan. 89 - May 89
Leeds: Sep. 89 -
Played for: Leeds, Workington T.

MEL WIBBERLEY
Nottingham C: Mar. 90 -
Non-professional player

RON WILLEY (Australian)
Bradford N: Oct. 89 - Mar. 90 (Yorks Cup
                Winners)

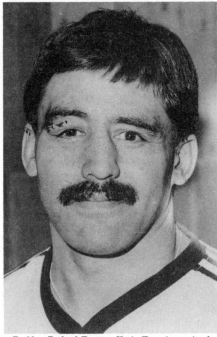

Ex-New Zealand Test star Kevin Tamati, appointed coach of Salford in October 1989.

Australian Test scrum half Peter Sterling, first capped on the 1982 Kangaroo tour of Britain.

AUSTRALIA

AUSTRALIA

The following is a list of international matches involving Australia. For Tests versus Great Britain see the GREAT BRITAIN section.

Australia v. France Tests

2 Jan. 1938	W	35-6	Paris
16 Jan. 1938	W	16-11	Marseilles
9 Jan. 1949	W	29-10	Marseilles
23 Jan. 1949	W	10-0	Bordeaux
11 Jun. 1951	L	15-26	Sydney
30 Jun. 1951	W	23-11	Brisbane
21 Jul. 1951	L	14-35	Sydney
27 Dec. 1952	W	16-12	Paris
11 Jan. 1953	L	0-5	Bordeaux
25 Jan. 1953	L	5-13	Lyons
11 Jun. 1955	W	20-8	Sydney
2 Jul. 1955	L	28-29	Brisbane
27 Jul. 1955	L	5-8	Sydney
1 Nov. 1956	W	15-8	Paris
23 Dec. 1956	W	10-6	Bordeaux
13 Jan. 1957	W	25-21	Lyons
31 Oct. 1959	W	20-19	Paris
20 Dec. 1959	W	17-2	Bordeaux
20 Jan. 1960	W	16-8	Roanne
11 Jun. 1960	D	8-8	Sydney
2 Jul. 1960	W	56-6	Brisbane
16 Jul. 1960	L	5-7	Sydney
8 Dec. 1963	L	5-8	Bordeaux
22 Dec. 1963	W	21-9	Toulouse
18 Jan. 1964	W	16-8	Paris
13 Jun. 1964	W	20-6	Sydney
4 Jul. 1964	W	27-2	Brisbane
18 Jul. 1964	W	35-9	Sydney
17 Dec. 1967	D	7-7	Marseilles
24 Dec. 1967	L	3-10	Carcassone
7 Jan. 1968	L	13-16	Toulouse
9 Dec. 1973	W	21-9	Perpignan
16 Dec. 1973	W	14-3	Toulouse
26 Nov. 1978	L	10-13	Carcassone
10 Dec. 1978	L	10-11	Toulouse
4 Jul. 1981	W	43-3	Sydney
18 Jul. 1981	W	17-2	Brisbane
5 Dec. 1982	W	15-4	Avignon
18 Dec. 1982	W	23-9	Narbonne
30 Nov. 1986	W	44-2	Perpignan
*13 Dec. 1986	W	52-0	Carcassonne

*Also World Cup

	P	W	D	L	F	A
TOTALS	41	27	2	12	784	390

Australia v. France World Cup

11 Nov. 1954	L	5-15	Nantes
22 Jun. 1957	W	26-9	Sydney
24 Sep. 1960	W	13-12	Wigan
8 Jun. 1968	W	37-4	Brisbane
10 Jun. 1968	W	20-2	Sydney
1 Nov. 1970	L	15-17	Bradford
5 Nov. 1972	W	31-9	Toulouse
22 Jun. 1975	W	26-6	Brisbane
26 Oct. 1975	W	41-2	Perpignan
11 Jun. 1977	W	21-9	Sydney

● Second Test in 1986 also World Cup.

Australia v. France other matches

1960	W	37-12	Toulouse
11 Nov. 1970	W	7-4	Perpignan

Australia v. Great Britain Tests
see GREAT BRITAIN section.

Australia v. Great Britain World Cup

31 Oct. 1954	L	13-28	Lyons
17 Jun. 1957	W	31-6	Sydney
8 Oct. 1960	L	3-10	Bradford
25 May. 1968	W	25-10	Sydney
24 Oct. 1970	L	4-11	Leeds
7 Nov. 1970	W	12-7	Leeds
29 Oct. 1972	L	21-27	Perpignan
11 Nov. 1972	D	10-10	Lyon
18 Jun. 1977	W	19-5	Brisbane
25 Jun. 1977	W	13-12	Sydney

● Third Tests in 1986 and 1988 were also World Cup matches.

Australia v. New Zealand Tests

9 May 1908	L	10-11	Sydney
30 May 1908	L	12-24	Brisbane
6 Jun. 1908	W	14-9	Sydney
12 Jun. 1909	L	11-19	Sydney
26 Jun. 1909	W	10-5	Brisbane
3 Jul. 1909	W	25-5	Sydney
23 Aug. 1919	W	44-21	Wellington
30 Aug. 1919	L	10-26	Christchurch
6 Sep. 1919	W	34-23	Auckland
13 Sep. 1919	W	32-2	Auckland
28 Sep. 1935	L	14-22	Auckland
2 Oct. 1935	W	29-8	Auckland
5 Oct. 1935	W	31-8	Auckland
7 Aug. 1937	W	12-8	Auckland
14 Aug. 1937	L	15-16	Auckland
29 May 1948	L	19-21	Sydney
12 Jun. 1948	W	13-4	Brisbane
17 Sep. 1949	L	21-26	Wellington
8 Oct. 1949	W	13-10	Auckland
9 Jun. 1952	W	25-13	Sydney
28 Jun. 1952	L	25-49	Brisbane
2 Jul. 1952	L	9-19	Sydney
27 Jun. 1953	L	5-25	Christchurch
4 Jul. 1953	L	11-12	Wellington
18 Jul. 1953	W	18-16	Auckland
9 Jun. 1956	W	12-9	Sydney
23 Jun. 1956	W	8-2	Brisbane
30 Jun. 1956	W	31-14	Sydney
13 Jun. 1959	W	9-8	Sydney
27 Jun. 1959	W	38-10	Brisbane
4 Jul. 1959	L	12-28	Sydney
1 Jul. 1961	L	10-12	Auckland
8 Jul. 1961	W	10-8	Auckland
8 Jun. 1963	W	7-3	Sydney
22 Jun. 1963	L	13-16	Brisbane
29 Jun. 1963	W	14-0	Sydney
19 Jun. 1965	W	13-8	Auckland
26 Jun. 1965	L	5-7	Auckland
10 Jun. 1967	W	22-13	Sydney
1 Jul. 1967	W	35-22	Brisbane
8 Jul. 1967	W	13-9	Sydney
1 Jun. 1969	W	20-10	Auckland
7 Jun. 1969	L	14-18	Auckland
26 Jun. 1971	L	3-24	Auckland
8 Jul. 1972	W	36-11	Sydney
15 Jul. 1972	W	31-7	Brisbane
24 Jun. 1978	W	24-2	Sydney
15 Jul. 1978	W	38-7	Brisbane
22 Jul. 1978	W	33-16	Sydney
1 Jun. 1980	W	27-6	Auckland
15 Jun. 1980	W	15-6	Auckland
3 Jul. 1982	W	11-8	Brisbane
17 Jul. 1982	W	20-2	Sydney
12 Jun. 1983	W	16-4	Auckland
9 Jul. 1983	L	12-19	Brisbane
18 Jun. 1985	W	26-20	Brisbane
30 Jun. 1985	W	10-6	Auckland
*7 Jul. 1985	L	0-18	Auckland
6 Jul. 1986	W	22-8	Auckland
19 Jul. 1986	W	29-12	Sydney
*29 Jul. 1986	W	32-12	Brisbane
21 Jul. 1987	L	6-13	Brisbane
9 Jul. 1989	W	26-6	Christchurch
16 Jul. 1989	W	8-0	Rotorua
23 Jul. 1989	W	22-14	Auckland

*Also World Cup

	P	W	D	L	F	A
TOTALS	65	44	0	21	1,195	820

Australia v. New Zealand World Cup

7 Nov. 1954	W	34-15	Marseilles
15 Jun. 1957	W	25-5	Brisbane
1 Oct. 1960	W	21-15	Leeds
1 Jun. 1968	W	31-12	Brisbane
21 Oct. 1970	W	47-11	Wigan
1 Nov. 1972	W	9-5	Paris
1 Jun. 1975	W	36-8	Brisbane
27 Sep. 1975	W	24-8	Auckland
29 May. 1977	W	27-12	Auckland
9 Oct. 1988	W	25-12	Auckland

● Tests on 7 July 1985 and 29 July 1986 also World Cup matches.

Australia v. New Zealand other matches

19 Nov. 1954	W	18-5	Leigh
27 Nov. 1954	W	30-13	California
Nov. 1954	W	28-18	Los Angeles

Australia v. Papua New Guinea Tests
2 Oct. 1982   W   38-2   Port Moresby
*4 Oct. 1986   W   62-12   Port Moresby
*20 Jul. 1988   W   70-8   Wagga
*Also World Cup

Australia v. South Africa Tests
20 Jul. 1963   W   34-6   Brisbane
27 Jul. 1963   W   54-21   Sydney

Australia v. England World Cup
28 Jun. 1975   D   10-10   Sydney
1 Nov. 1975   L   13-16   Wigan

Australia v. England other matches
2 Jan. 1909   L   9-14   Huddersfield
3 Feb. 1909   D   17-17   Glasgow
3 Mar. 1909   L   7-14   Everton
18 Oct. 1911   W   11-6   Fulham
6 Dec. 1911   L   3-5   Nottingham
10 Oct. 1921   L   4-5   Arsenal
31 Dec. 1933   W   63-13   Paris
13 Jan. 1934   L   14-19   Gateshead
12 Nov. 1975   W   25-0   Leeds

Australia v. Wales World Cup
14 Jun. 1975   W   30-13   Sydney
19 Oct. 1975   W   18-6   Swansea

Australian prop forward Sam Backo.

Australia v. Wales other matches
7 Oct. 1911   W   28-20   Ebbw Vale
10 Dec. 1921   W   21-16   Pontypridd
18 Jan. 1930   W   26-10   Wembley
30 Dec. 1933   W   51-19   Wembley
20 Nov. 1948   W   12-5   Swansea
15 Oct. 1978   W   8-3   Swansea
24 Oct. 1982   W   37-7   Cardiff

Australia v. other international sides
18 Nov. 1908   Northern RL   W   10-9   Everton
16 Jan. 1909   Welsh League   L   13-14   Merthyr Tydfil
25 Oct. 1911   Northern RL   W   16-3   Everton
20 Dec. 1911   Wales & West England   W   23-3   Bristol
31 Jan. 1912   Northern RL   W   20-12   Wigan
4 Dec. 1929   Northern RL   W   5-18   Wigan
18 Dec. 1929   Northern RL   W   32-22   Newcastle
1 Nov. 1933   Northern RL   L   5-7   York
29 Oct. 1956   Northern RL   W   19-15   Leigh
4 Oct. 1978   Britain Under-24   W   30-8   Hull Kingston Rovers
27 Jul. 1988   Rest of the World   W   22-10   Sydney

AUSTRALIA TEAMS . . .
A 25-year review

The following is a compendium of Australia Test and World Cup teams since 1965. Only playing substitutes are included on the teamsheet.

Key: *: Captain (WC): World Cup t: try g:goal dg: drop goal

1965 New Zealand
Auckland: 19 June
Won 13-8
Johns 2g
Cleary
Gasnier
Langlands
Irvine 2t
Lisle
Smith
Quinn
*Walsh
Weier 1t
Veivers, M.
Morgan, John
Hambly

1965 New Zealand
Auckland: 26 June
Lost 5-7
Johns 1g
Cleary
Gasnier
Langlands
Irvine 1t
Lisle
Smith
Weier
*Walsh
Quinn
Morgan, John
Veivers, M.
Hambly

1966 Great Britain
Sydney: 25 June
Lost 13-17
Barnes 5g
Irvine
Langlands
McDonald
King
Banks 1t
Smith
Weier
*Walsh
Crowe
Bradstreet
Crema
Raper

1966 Great Britain
Brisbane: 16 July
Won 6-4
Barnes 3g
Irvine
Langlands
Greaves
King
Gleeson
Smith
Wittenberg
*Walsh
Kelly
Veivers, M.
Thornett, R.
Lynch

1966 Great Britain
Sydney: 23 July
Won 19-14
Johns 2g
Irvine 3t
Dimond
Greaves
King 1t
Gleeson
Smith
Wittenberg
*Walsh
Kelly
Veivers, M.
Beetson
Lynch 1t
Sub: Thornett, R.

1967 New Zealand
Sydney: 10 June
Won 22-13
Langlands 1t, 2g
Irvine 1t
*Gasnier 1t
Greaves
Hanigan 2t
Gleeson 1t
Smith
Kelly
Fitzsimmons
Gallagher, P.
Thomson, A.
Tutty
Raper

1967 New Zealand
Brisbane: 1 July
Won 35-22
Langlands 1t, 1g
Irvine 2t
*Gasnier
McDonald 2t, 6g
Hanigan 1t
Gleeson
Smith
Kelly
Buman
Gallagher, P.
Lynch
Thomson, A.
Raper 1t

1967 New Zealand
Sydney: 8 July
Won 13-9
Langlands
Irvine 1t
*Gasnier
McDonald 2t, 2g
King
Gleeson
Smith
Gallagher, P.
Buman
Kelly
Connell
Lynch
Raper

1967 Great Britain
Leeds: 21 Oct.
Lost 11-16
Johns
McDonald
Langlands 1t, 4g
*Gasnier
King
Gleeson
Smith
Manteit
Kelly
Gallagher, P.
Lynch
Rasmussen
Raper

1967 Great Britain
White City, London: 3 Nov.
Won 17-11
Johns
Greaves
Langlands 1t, 4g
McDonald
King 1t
Branson
Gleeson
Gallagher, N.
Kelly
*Gallagher, P.
Lynch
Rasmussen
Coote 1t

1967 Great Britain
Swinton: 9 Dec.
Won 11-3
Johns
King 1t
Langlands 1g
Greaves
McDonald
Gleeson
Smith
Gallagher, P.
Kelly
Manteit
Rasmussen
Coote 1t
*Raper
Sub: Branson 1t

1967 France
Marseilles: 17 Dec.
Drew 7-7
Johns 1t, 1g
King
Langlands 1g
Greaves
Irvine
Branson
Smith
Manteit
Kelly
Gallagher, P.
Rasmussen
Coote
*Raper
Sub: Lynch

1967 France
Carcassonne: 24 Dec.
Lost 3-10
Johns
King
Greaves 1t
Langlands
McDonald
Branson
Smith
Rasmussen
Gallagher, N.
Gallagher, P.
Lynch
Coote
*Raper

1968 France
Toulouse: 7 Jan.
Lost 13-16
Johns 1g
King
Greaves 2t
Langlands 1t, 1g
McDonald
Branson
Smith
Gallagher, P.
Kelly
Rasmussen
Thomson, A.
Coote
*Raper

1968 Great Britain (WC)
Sydney: 25 May
Won 25-10
Simms 8g
Rhodes
Greaves
Langlands
King
Branson
Smith 1t
Wittenberg
Jones
Beetson
Thornett, R.
Coote 1t
*Raper 1t

1968 New Zealand (WC)
Brisbane: 1 June
Won 31-12
Simms 8g
Rhodes 1t
Greaves
Langlands
King 2t
Branson
Smith
Wittenberg
Jones 1t
Rasmussen
Thornett, R.
Coote 1t
*Raper
Sub: Fulton

1968 France (WC)
Brisbane: 8 June
Won 37-4
Simms 5g
James
Rhodes
Greaves 1t
Williamson 2t
Fulton 2t
Smith 1t, 3g
Wittenberg
Fitzsimmons
Beetson
Manteit
Coote 1t
*Raper

1968 France (WC)
Sydney: 10 June
Won 20-2
Simms 4g
Williamson 2t
Langlands
Greaves 1t
Rhodes
Fulton
Smith
Wittenberg
Jones
Beetson
Thornett, R.
Coote 1t
*Raper
Sub: Rasmussen

1969 New Zealand
Auckland: 1 June
Won 20-10
Johns 4g
Cootes 1t
Langlands
McDonald
Honan
Pittard 1t
Ward
Wittenberg
Walters
*Sattler
Costello
McCarthy
Coote 2t

1969 New Zealand
Auckland: 7 June
Lost 14-18
Johns 4g
Cootes
Langlands
McDonald
Honan
Pittard
Ward
Wittenberg
Walters
*Sattler
Weiss
McCarthy 1t
Coote 1t

1970 Great Britain
Brisbane: 6 June
Won 37-15
*Langlands 9g
King 2t
McDonald 1t
Brass
Cootes
Hawthorne 2g
Smith
Morgan, Jim 2t
Walters
Wittenberg
Lynch
Beetson
Coote
Sub: Weiss

1970 Great Britain
Sydney: 20 June
Lost 7-28
Laird
Cootes
Brass
McDonald 1g
King 1t
Hawthorne 1g
Smith
*Sattler
Fitzsimmons
Wittenberg
Beetson
Weiss
Coote

1970 Great Britain
Sydney: 4 July
Lost 17-21
McKean 7g
McDonald
Brass
Fulton
King
*Hawthorne
Grant, R.
Beetson
Walters
Morgan, Jim
Costello
McCarthy 1t
Coote

1970 New Zealand (WC)
Wigan: 21 Oct.
Won 47-11
Simms 10g, 1t
Branighan 1t
Cootes 2t
Fulton 1t
Williamson
Pittard
Smith 1t
O'Neill
Walters
O'Reilly
McCarthy 1t
Sait
*Coote 1t
Sub: Turner 1t

1970 Great Britain (WC)
Leeds: 24 Oct.
Lost 4-11
Simms 1g
Williamson
Branighan
Fulton 1g
Harris
Pittard
*Smith
O'Neill
Walters
O'Reilly
McCarthy
Sait
Sullivan

1970 France (WC)
Bradford: 1 Nov.
Lost 15-17
Simms 3g
Branighan
Cootes 2t
Fulton 1t
Williamson
Pittard
Smith
McTaggart
Walters
O'Reilly
McCarthy
Sait
*Coote
Subs: Turner
      Sullivan

1970 Great Britain (WC)
Leeds: 7 Nov.
Won 12-7
Simms 3g
Williamson 1t
Cootes 1t
Sait
Harris
Fulton
Smith
O'Neill
Turner
O'Reilly
Costello
McCarthy
*Coote
Subs: Branighan
      Walters

1971 New Zealand
Auckland: 26 June
Lost 3-24
*Langlands
Branighan
Fulton
Sait
Williamson
Branson
Grant, R.
Sattler
Fitzsimmons
O'Reilly
Costello
McCarthy
Campbell 1t

1972 New Zealand
Sydney: 8 July
Won 36-11
*Langlands 6g
Harris
Starling 1t
Fulton 1t
Ambrum 2t
Pickup
Raudonikis
Beetson
Walters
O'Reilly
McCarthy 2t
Elford
Sullivan 2t

1972 New Zealand
Brisbane: 15 July
Won 31-7
*Langlands
Stewart 5g
Starling 2t
Fulton 2t
Ambrum
Pickup
Raudonikis 1t
Beetson
Walters
O'Reilly
McCarthy
Elford 2t
Sullivan
Subs: Murphy
      Goodwin

1972 Great Britain (WC)
Perpignan: 29 Oct.
Lost 21-27
*Langlands 4g
Harris
Branighan
Starling
Knight
Fulton 3t
Raudonikis 1t
Beetson
Walters
O'Neill
Elford
McCarthy 1dg
Sullivan
Subs: Ward
     Sait

1972 New Zealand (WC)
Paris: 1 Nov.
Won 9-5
*Langlands
Grant, J.
Branighan 1g
Starling
Knight
Fulton 1t, 1dg
Ward 1t
O'Reilly
Walters
O'Neill
Sullivan
Elford
Sait
Sub: Stevens

1972 France (WC)
Toulouse: 5 Nov.
Won 31-9
*Langlands
Grant, J.
Harris 2t
Starling
Branighan 5g
Fulton 1t
Ward
O'Neill 1t
Walters 1t
O'Reilly
Stevens
Beetson
Sait 2t

1972 Great Britain (WC)
Lyon: 11 Nov.
Drew 10-10
*Langlands
Branighan 2g
Starling
Harris
Grant, J.
Fulton
Ward
O'Neill 1t
Walters
O'Reilly
Beetson 1t
Stevens
Sullivan

1973 Great Britain
Wembley: 3 Nov.
Lost 12-21
*Langlands 3g
Goodwin
Fulton 1t
Starling
Branighan 1t
Pickup
Raudonikis
O'Reilly
Walters
Beetson
McCarthy
Maddison
Sait

1973 Great Britain
Leeds: 24 Nov.
Won 14-6
Eadie 5g
Williamson
Starling
Branighan
Waite
Fulton 1dg
Raudonikis
O'Reilly
Walters
Beetson
*McCarthy 1t
Stevens
Sait
Sub: Maddison

236

1973 Great Britain
Warrington: 1 Dec.
Won 15-5
Eadie
Williamson
Starling 1t
Branighan
Waite
Fulton 1t
*Raudonikis
O'Reilly
Walters 1t
Beetson
Maddison 2t
Stevens
Sait
Sub: Pickup

1973 France
Perpignan: 9 Dec.
Won 21-9
Branighan 2g
Williamson
Fulton 2t
Cronin 1g
Waite
Pickup
*Raudonikis
Beetson
Lang
O'Neill
Pierce
Walters
Starling 1t
Sub: Goodwin 2t

1973 France
Toulouse: 16 Dec.
Won 14-3
Branighan 1t
Goodwin
Cronin 1t, 1g
Starling
Waite
Fulton 1t
Pickup
*Beetson
Walters
O'Reilly
Maddison 1t
Stevens
Sait

1974 Great Britain
Brisbane: 15 June
Won 12-6
*Langlands 4g
Orr 1t
Fulton 1dg
Cronin
Waite
Richardson
Raudonikis
Beetson
Walters
O'Reilly
Sait
Higgs
Coote

1974 Great Britain
Sydney: 6 July
Lost 11-16
Eadie
Orr
Fulton 1t
Cronin 1g
Waite
Richardson
Raudonikis
*Beetson
Lang 1t
O'Reilly
Stevens
Sait
Coote 1t
Subs: Branighan
        McCarthy

1974 Great Britain
Sydney: 20 July
Won 22-18
*Langlands 1t, 5g
Williamson 1t
Fulton
Cronin
Branighan
Pickup
Raudonikis
Beetson
Turner
O'Neill
Stevens
McCarthy 1t
Coote 1t

1975 New Zealand (WC)
Brisbane: 1 June
Won 36-8
*Langlands 2t
Anderson
Fulton 1t
Cronin 2t, 6g
Fahey
Pickup
Strudwick
Randall 1t
Lang
Wright
Stevens
Platz, L. 1t
Coote
Subs: Branighan 1t
        Sait

1975 Wales (WC)
Sydney: 14 June
Won 30-13
*Langlands 1t
Harris 1t
Fulton 1t
Cronin 9g
Rhodes
Pickup
Raudonikis 1t
O'Neill
Lang
Randall
Stevens
Platz, L.
Sait
Sub: Donnelly

1975 France (WC)
Brisbane: 22 June
Won 26-6
*Langlands
Harris 2t
Cronin 1t, 4g
Fulton 2t
Rhodes
Pickup 1t
Raudonikis
Donnelly
Lang
Beetson
Randall
Platz, L.
Coote

1975 England (WC)
Sydney: 28 June
Drew 10-10
*Langlands
Rhodes
Fulton
Cronin 2g
Harris
Pickup
Raudonikis
Beetson
Lang
Randall
Stevens
Platz, L.
Coote 1t
Subs: Anderson 1t
     Donnelly

1975 New Zealand (WC)
Auckland: 27 Sept.
Won 24-8
Eadie
Rhodes
Cronin 1t, 6g
*Brass
Schubert 1t
Peard
Mayes
Veivers, G.
Piggins
Mackay
Platz, L.
Higgs 1t
Quayle 1t
Subs: Raudonikis
     Fitzgerald

1975 Wales (WC)
Swansea: 19 Oct.
Won 18-6
Eadie
McMahon
Cronin 3g
Rogers
Schubert 3t
Peard 1t
Mayes
*G. Beetson
Piggins
Veivers, G.
Randall
Higgs
Quayle
Subs: Porter
     Mackay

1975 France (WC)
Perpignan: 26 Oct
Won 41-2
Eadie 7g, 1t
Rhodes 1t
Rogers 2t
Brass
Porter
Peard 1t
Raudonikis 1t
*Beetson
Lang
Randall 1t
Platz, L. 1t
Higgs 1t
Pierce
Sub: Schubert

1975 England (WC)
Wigan: 1 Nov.
Lost 13-16
Eadie
Schubert 3t
Brass
Cronin 2g
Rhodes
Peard
Mayes
*Beetson
Piggins
Mackay
Higgs
Randall
Pierce
Sub: Rogers

1977 New Zealand (WC)
Auckland: 29 May
Won 27-12
Eadie
Harris 1t
Cronin 6g
Thomas 1t
McMahon 2t
Peard 1t
Raudonikis
*Veivers, G.
Geiger
Fitzgerald
Randall
Higgs
Pierce

1977 France (WC)
Sydney: 11 June
Won 21-9
Eadie 2t
McMahon 1t
Cronin 3g
Thomas
Fahey
Peard
Raudonikis
Veivers, G. 1t
Geiger
Fitzgerald 1t
Randall
*Beetson
Reddy
Subs: Gartner
     Higgs

1977 Great Britain (WC)
Brisbane: 18 June
Won 19-5
Eadie 2t
McMahon
Cronin 5g
Thomas
Fahey
Peard
Raudonikis
Fitzgerald
Geiger
Veivers, G.
*Beetson
Randall 1t
Pierce
Sub: Higgs

1977 Great Britain (WC)
Sydney: 25 June
Won 13-12
Eadie
McMahon 1t
Cronin 2g
Gartner 1t
Harris
Peard
Kolc 1t
Veivers, G.
Geiger
Randall
*Beetson
Higgs
Pierce
Sub: Fitzgerald

1978 New Zealand
Sydney: 24 June
Won 24-2
Eadie
Fahey 1t
Cronin 6g
Rogers 1t
Boustead 1t
*Fulton
Morris, S.
Olling
Peponis 1t
Thomson, I.
Pierce
Reddy
Price
Sub: Oliphant

1978 New Zealand
Brisbane: 15 July
Won 38-7
Dorahy
Boustead 2t
Cronin 7g
Rogers 1t
Glover 2t
*Fulton
Oliphant
Donnelly
Lang
Olling
Platz, G.
Reddy 1t
Price 2t
Sub: R. Morris

1978 New Zealand
Sydney: 22 July
Won 33-16
Dorahy 1t
Glover
Cronin 9g
Rogers
Boustead 1t
*Fulton 2t
Raudonikis
Morris, R.
Krilich
Young
Pierce 1t
Reddy
Price

1978 Great Britain
Wigan: 21 Oct.
Won 15-9
Eadie
Boustead 1t
Rogers
Cronin 4g
Anderson
*Fulton 1t, 1dg
Raudonikis
Young
Krilich
Olling
Gerard
Reddy
Price

1978 Great Britain
Bradford: 5 Nov.
Lost 14-18
Eadie
Boustead
Rogers 1t, 2g
Cronin 2g
Anderson
*Fulton
Raudonikis
Olling
Krilich
Young
Gerard
Reddy
Price 1t
Subs: Thompson
Boyd

1978 Great Britain
Leeds: 18 Nov.
Won 23-6
Eadie
Boustead
Rogers
Cronin 5g
Anderson
*Fulton 1dg
Raudonikis 1t
Young
Peponis 1t
Morris, R.
Gerard 1t
Boyd 1t
Price
Subs: Thompson
Thomson, I.

1978 France
Carcassonne: 26 Nov.
Lost 10-13
Eadie 1t
Boustead
Cronin 1t, 2g
Martin
Anderson
*Fulton
Raudonikis
Morris, R.
Peponis
Young
Gerard
Boyd
Price

1978 France
Toulouse: 10 Dec.
Lost 10-11
Eadie
Boustead 1t
Rogers 1t
Cronin 2g
Anderson
*Fulton
Raudonikis
Thomson, I.
Hilditch
Young
Gerard
Reddy
Price

1979 Great Britain
Brisbane: 16 June
Won 35-0
Eadie
Corowa 1t
Rogers
Cronin 10g
Boustead 2t
Thompson
Raudonikis
Young
*Peponis
Morris, R.
Reddy
Boyd
Price 2t

1979 Great Britain
Sydney: 30 June
Won 24-16
Eadie
Corowa
Rogers 1t
Cronin 2t, 6g
Boustead
Thompson
Raudonikis
Young
*Peponis
Morris, R.
Reddy 1t
Boyd
Price

1979 Great Britain
Sydney: 14 July.
Won 28-2
Eadie 1t
Anderson
Cronin 8g
Rogers
Fahey
Thompson
Raudonikis
Young
*Peponis
Morris, R.
Reddy 1t
Boyd 1t
Price 1t

1980 New Zealand
Auckland: 1 June
Won 27-6
Dowling, Gary
Boustead 1t
Cronin 6g
Brentnall
Anderson
Thompson 2t
Raudonikis
Morris, R.
*Peponis
Young 1t
Reddy 1t
Boyd
Price

1980 New Zealand
Auckland: 15 June
Won 15-6
Dowling, Gary
Quinn, G.
Cronin 1t, 3g
Brentnall
Anderson
Thompson
Raudonikis
Young
*Peponis
Morris, R.
Boyd 1t
Reddy 1t
Price

1981 France
Sydney: 4 July
Won 43-3
Brentnall 1t
Ribot 1t
Cronin 8g
*Rogers 1t
Boustead 1t
Lewis
Mortimer, S. 2t
Hilditch
Masterman 1t
Young
Boyd
McCabe 2t
Price
Subs: Sigsworth
    Morris, R.

1981 France
Brisbane: 18 July
Won 17-2
Brentnall
Ribot
*Rogers
Cronin 4g
Fahey 2t
Lewis
Mortimer, S.
Hilditch
Masterman
Morris, R. 1t
McCabe
Boyd
Price
Sub: Ayliffe

1982 New Zealand
Brisbane: 3 July
Won 11-8
Brentnall
Ribot
Cronin 4g
Rogers
Boustead
Lewis
Mortimer, S.
Young
*Krilich
Morris, R.
Hancock
Boyd
Vautin
Sub: Muggleton 1t

1982 New Zealand
Sydney: 17 July
Won 20-2
Brentnall 1t
Boustead 1t
Cronin 4g
Meninga
Ribot
Lewis 1t
Mortimer, S.
Young
*Krilich
Hancock
Muggleton
Boyd
Price 1t
Subs: Rogers
    Morris, R.

1982 Papua-New Guinea
Port Moresby: 2 Oct.
Won 38-2
Brentnall 2t
Boustead 1t
Rogers 1t
Meninga 1t, 4g
Ribot 4t
Kenny 1t
Mortimer, S.
Young
*Krilich
Hancock
Muggleton
Reddy
Price
Subs: Murray
    Brown, R.

1982 Great Britain
Hull City FC: 30 Oct.
Won 40-4
Brentnall
Boustead 1t
Meninga 1t, 8g
Rogers
Grothe 1t
Kenny 1t
Sterling
Young
*Krilich
Boyd 1t
Pearce 1t
Reddy 1t
Price 1t

1982 Great Britain
Wigan: 20 Nov.
Won 27-6
Brentnall
Boustead
Meninga 1t, 6g
Rogers 1t
Grothe 1t
Kenny
Sterling 1t
Young
*Krilich
Boyd
Pearce
Reddy
Price 1t
Subs: Lewis
        Brown, R.

1982 Great Britain
Leeds: 28 Nov.
Won 32-8
Brentnall
Boustead 1t
Meninga 7g
Rogers 1t
Ribot 1t
Kenny 1t
Sterling
Boyd
*Krilich 1t
Morris, R.
McCabe
Reddy
Pearce 1t
Subs: Lewis
        Brown, R.

1982 France
Avignon: 5 Dec.
Won 15-4
Brentnall
Boustead
Rogers
Kenny
Meninga 3g
Lewis
Sterling
Young
*Krilich
Morris, R.
McCabe
Boyd
Pearce 1t
Subs: Grothe 2t
        Brown, R.

1982 France
Narbonne: 18 Dec.
Won 23-9
Brentnall
Boustead
Rogers
Meninga 1t, 4g
Grothe 2t
Kenny 1t
Sterling
Young
*Krilich
Boyd
McCabe
Reddy 1t
Pearce

1983 New Zealand
Auckland: 12 June
Won 16-4
Brentnall
Boustead
Meninga 4g
Rogers 1t
Grothe 1t
Lewis
Sterling
Brown, D.
*Krilich
Gerard
Fullerton-Smith
McCabe
Vautin
Subs: Murray
        Jarvis

1983 New Zealand
Brisbane: 9 July
Lost 12-19
Scott
Boustead
Meninga 2g
Miles
Grothe 1t
Lewis
Mortimer
Tessman
*Krilich
Brown, D.
Fullerton-Smith
Vautin
Price
Subs: Ella 1t
        Brown, R.

1984 Great Britain
Sydney: 9 June
Won 25-8
Jack
Boustead 1t
Miles
Kenny
Conlon 4g
*Lewis 1t, 1dg
Murray 1t
Brown, D.
Conescu
Dowling, Greg
Niebling
Pearce
Price 1t
Sub: Young

1984 Great Britain
Brisbane: 26 June
Won 18-6
Jack
Boustead
Meninga 1t, 3g
Miles
Grothe 1t
*Lewis
Murray
Brown, D.
Conescu
Dowling, Greg
Niebling
Vautin
Pearce 1t
Subs: Mortimer, S.
        Fullerton-Smith

1984 Great Britain
Sydney: 7 July
Won 20-7
Jack 1t
Boustead
Meninga 4g
Miles
Grothe 1t
*Lewis
Mortimer, S.
Niebling
Conescu 1t
Dowling, Greg
Fullerton-Smith
Pearce
Price
Subs: Kenny
     Brown, D.

1985 New Zealand
Brisbane: 18 June
Won 26-20
Jack
Ribot 2t, 1g
Close 1t
Meninga 2g
Ferguson
*Lewis
Murray
Dowling, Greg
Conescu
Roach 1t
Cleal 1t
Wynn, P.
Pearce
Sub: Tunks

1985 New Zealand
Auckland: 30 June
Won 10-6
Jack
Ribot 1t, 1g
Close
Meninga 2g
Ferguson
*Lewis
Murray
Dowling, Greg
Conescu
Roach
Vautin
Wynn, P.
Pearce
Subs: Ella
     Cleal

1985 New Zealand
Auckland: 7 July
Lost 0-18
Jack
Ribot
Meninga
Ella
Ferguson
*Lewis
Hasler
Tunks
Elias
Roach
Vautin
Wynn, P.
Pearce
Subs: Close
     Dowling

1986 New Zealand
Auckland: 6 July
Won 22-8
Jack
O'Connor 3g
Kenny 2t
Miles
Shearer 1t
*Lewis
Sterling
Roach
Simmons
Tunks
Cleal
Folkes 1t
Pearce
Subs: Lamb
     Niebling

1986 New Zealand
Sydney: 19 July
Won 29-12
Jack 1t
O'Connor 4g
Kenny 1t
Miles 1t
Kiss
*Lewis 1t
Sterling 1dg
Roach
Simmons
Tunks
Cleal
Folkes
Pearce 1t
Sub: Niebling

1986 New Zealand (Also WC)
Brisbane: 29 July
Won 32-12
Jack
O'Connor 1t, 4g
Kenny 2t
Miles 1t
Kiss
*Lewis 1t
Sterling 1t
Roach
Simmons
Tunks
Cleal
Folkes
Pearce
Subs: Lamb
     Niebling

1986 Papua New Guinea (Also WC)
Port Moresby: 4 Oct.
Won 62-12
Jack 1t
Kiss 2t
Mortimer, C. 1t
Miles
O'Connor 2t, 7g
*Lewis 1t
Hasler 1t
Roach 1t
Simmons
Niebling
Dunn
Cleal 2t
Lindner 1t
Subs: Meninga
     Sironen

1986 Great Britain
Old Trafford: 25 Oct.
Won 38-16
Jack 1t
Kiss
Kenny
Miles 3t
O'Connor 3t, 5g
*Lewis
Sterling
Dowling
Simmons
Roach
Cleal
Niebling
Lindner
Subs: Lamb
     Meninga

1986 Great Britain
Elland Rd, Leeds: 8 Nov.

Won 34-4

Jack 2t
Shearer
Kenny 1t
Miles
O'Connor 1t, 5g
*Lewis 1t
Sterling
Dowling
Simmons
Dunn
Cleal
Niebling
Lindner 1t
Subs: Lamb
Meninga

1986 Great Britain (Also WC)
Wigan: 22 Nov.

Won 24-15

Jack
Shearer 1t
Kenny
Miles 1t
O'Connor 4g
*Lewis 1t
Sterling
Dowling
Simmons
Dunn
Meninga
Niebling
Lindner 1t
Subs: Lamb
Davidson

1986 France
Perpignan: 30 Nov.

Won 44-2

Jack 1t
Shearer
Kenny
Miles 2t
O'Connor 3t, 4g
*Lewis
Sterling 1t
Dowling
Simmons
Dunn
Davidson
Niebling
Lindner 2t
Subs: Lamb
Sironen

1986 France
Carcassonne: 13 Dec.

Won 52-0

Jack 3t
Shearer 4t
Kenny
Miles
O'Connor 1t, 6g
*Lewis
Sterling
Dowling
Simmons
Dunn
Folkes 1t
Niebling 1t
Lindner
Subs: Lamb
Davidson

1987 New Zealand
Brisbane: 21 July

Lost 6-13

Jack
Shearer
Miles
Kenny
O'Connor 1g
*Lewis
Sterling 1t
Dowling
Simmons
Tunks
Pearce
Niebling
Lindner
Subs: B. Johnston
Davidson

1988 Great Britain
Sydney: 11 June

Won 17-6

Jack
Ettingshausen
O'Connor 2g
Jackson 2t
Currie
*Lewis 1dg
Sterling
Daley
Conescu
Backo 1t
Fullerton-Smith
Vautin
Lindner
Subs: Belcher
Folkes

1988 Great Britain
Brisbane: 28 June

Won 34-14

Jack
Ettingshausen 1t
O'Connor 1t, 5g
Jackson 1t
Currie
*Lewis 1t
Sterling
Daley
Conescu
Backo 1t
Fullerton-Smith
Vautin
Pearce 1t
Subs: Belcher
Lindner

1988 Great Britain (Also WC)
Sydney: 9 July

Lost 12-26

Jack
Ettingshausen
O'Connor 2g
Jackson
Currie
*Lewis 1t
Sterling
Bella
Conescu
Backo 1t
Fullerton-Smith
Vautin
Pearce
Subs: Belcher
Lindner

Wally Fullerton-Smith.

243

1988 Papua New Guinea

Wagga: 20 July

Won 70-8

Jack 1t
O'Connor 4t, 7g
Meninga 2t
Jackson
Currie 1t
*Lewis 1t
Langer 2t
Dunn
Conescu 1t
Daley
Fullerton-Smith 1t
Miller 1t
Pearce
Subs: Hasler
      Vautin

1989 New Zealand

Rotorua: 16 July

Won 8-0

Belcher
Shearer
Meninga 2g
Currie
Hancock 1t
*Lewis
Alexander
Backo
Walters, K.
Roach
Sironen
Clyde
Vautin
Sub: Hasler

1989 New Zealand

Auckland: 23 July

Won 22-14

Belcher
Hancock
Shearer 1t
Currie
O'Connor 1t, 2g
*Lewis
Hasler
Backo
Walters, K.
Roach
Meninga 1t, 1g
Clyde 1t
Vautin
Sub: McGuire

1988 New Zealand (WC)

Auckland: 9 Oct.

Won 25-12

Jack
O'Connor 4g
Farrar
McGaw
Shearer 1t
*Lewis
Langer 2t
Dunn
Elias 1dg
Roach
Sironen
Miller 1t
Pearce
Subs: Lamb
      Gillespie

1989 New Zealand

Christchurch: 9 July

Won 26-6

Belcher
Shearer
Meninga 5g
Currie 1t
Hancock
*Lewis 1t
Alexander
Backo
Walters, K. 1t
Roach
Sironen 1t
Clyde
Vautin
Subs: O'Connor
      McGuire

Balmain's Garry Jack, Australia's full back in the 1988 World Cup final in Auckland.

AUSTRALIA REGISTER . . .
1965-89

The following is an index of players who have appeared for Australia, toured or been members of a World Cup squad since 1965. Where a player began his international career before 1965 his preceding record is also given.

Appearances refer to Test and World Cup matches only. For matches in France the year given is for the first half of the season.

World Cup matches are in bold letters in the list of *Appearances*. Substitute appearances are in lower case letters. In 1975 the World Cup was in two sections — 1 refers to the first part in Australasia, 2 refers to the second part in Britain and France.

Key: B - Britain, E - England, F - France, NSW - New South Wales, NZ - New Zealand, PNG - Papua-New Guinea, SA - South Africa, W - Wales.

ALEXANDER, Greg (NSW)
Tours: Britain 1986; NZ 1989
Appearances: 1989 NZ2
AMBRUM, George (NSW)
Appearances: 1972 NZ2
ANDERSON, Chris (NSW)
Tours: Britain 1978,1982; NZ 1980
World Cup: 1975 (1)
Appearances: **1975 NZ,e**; 1978 B3,F2; 1979 B; 1980 NZ2
AYLIFFE, Royce (NSW)
Appearances: 1981 f

BACKO, Sam (Queensland)
Tours: NZ 1989
Appearances: 1988 B3; 1989 NZ3
BANKS, Gary (NSW)
Appearances: 1966 B
BARNES, Keith (NSW)
Tours: Britain 1959
World Cup: 1957,1960
Appearances: **1957 NZ**; 1959 NZ2,B3,F3; 1960 F3, **NZ,B**; 1962 B; 1966 B2
BEATH, Barry (NSW)
Tours: NZ 1965,1971
BEETSON, Arthur (NSW)
Tours: Britain 1973
World Cup: 1968,1972,1975(1&2),1977
Appearances: 1966 B; **1968 B,F2**; 1970 B3; 1972 NZ2, **B2,F**; 1973 B3,F2; 1974 B3; **1975 F2,E2,W; 1977 F,B2**

BELCHER, Gary (Queensland)
Tours: Britain 1986; NZ 1989
Appearances: 1988 b3; 1989 NZ3
BELLA, Martin (Queensland)
Tours: Britain 1986; NZ 1989
Appearances: 1988 B
BENNETT, Wayne (Queensland)
Tours: NZ 1971
BOUSTEAD, Kerry (Queensland)
Tours: Britain 1978,1982; NZ 1980
Appearances: 1978 NZ3,B3,F2; 1979 B2; 1980 NZ; 1981 F; 1982 NZ2,PNG,B3,F2; 1983 NZ2; 1984 B3
BOYD, Les (NSW)
Tours: Britain 1978,1982; NZ 1980
Appearances: 1978 Bb,F; 1979 B3; 1980 NZ2; 1981 F2; 1982 NZ2,B3,F2
BRADSTREET, Bill (NSW)
Appearances: 1966 B
BRANIGHAN, Ray (NSW)
Tours: Britain 1973; NZ 1971
World Cup: 1970,1972,1975(1)
Appearances: **1970 NZ,Bb,F**; 1971 NZ; **1972 B2,NZ,F**; 1973 B3,F2; 1974 Bb; **1975 nz**
BRANSON, Tony (NSW)
Tours: Britain 1967; NZ 1971
World Cup: 1968
Appearances: 1967 Bb,F3; **1968 B,NZ**; 1971 NZ
BRASS, John (NSW)
World Cup: 1975(2)
Appearances: 1970 B3; **1975 NZ,F,E**
BRENTNALL, Greg (NSW)
Tours: Britain 1982; NZ 1980
Appearances: 1980 NZ2; 1981 F2; 1982 NZ2,PNG,B3,F2; 1983 NZ
BROWN, Dave (NSW)
Appearances: 1983 NZ2; 1984 B2b
BROWN, Johnny (Queensland)
World Cup: 1970
BROWN, Ray (NSW)
Tours: Britain 1982
Appearances: 1982 png,b2, f; 1983 nz
BUMAN, Allan (NSW)
Tours: NZ 1965
Appearances: 1967 NZ2

CAMPBELL, Keith (NSW)
Tours: Britain 1971
Appearances: 1971 NZ
CAVANAGH, Noel (Queensland)
Tours: NZ 1965
CLEAL, Noel (NSW)
Tours: NZ 1985; Britain 1986
Appearances: 1985 NZnz, 1986 NZ3, PNG, B2
CLEARY, Michael (NSW)
Tours: Britain 1963; NZ 1965,1969
Appearances: 1962 B; 1963 NZ F; 1964 F3; 1965 NZ2

CLOSE, Chris (Queensland)
Tours: NZ 1980,1985
Appearances: 1985 NZ2nz
CLYDE, Bradley (NSW)
Tours: NZ 1989
Appearances: 1989 NZ3
CONESCU, Greg (Queensland)
Tours: Britain 1982; NZ 1985
Appearances: 1984 B3; 1985 NZ2; 1988 B3, PNG
CONLON, Ross (NSW)
Appearances: 1984 B
CONNELL, Geoff (Queensland)
Appearances: 1967 NZ
COOTE, Ron (NSW)
Tours: Britain 1967; NZ 1969
World Cup: 1968,1970,1975(1)
Appearances: 1967 B2,F3; **1968 B,NZ,F2;** 1969 NZ2;
   1970 B3; **1970 NZ,F,B;** 1974 B3; **1975 NZ,F,E**
COOTES, John (NSW)
Tours: NZ 1969
World Cup: 1970
Appearances: 1969 NZ2; 1970 B2; **1970 NZ,F,B**
COROWA, Larry (NSW)
Tours: Britain 1978
Appearances: 1979 B2
COSTELLO, Ron (NSW)
Tours: NZ 1969,1971
World Cup: 1970
Appearances: 1969 NZ; 1970 B; **1970 B;** 1971 NZ
CREAR, Steve (Queensland)
World Cup: 1977
CREMA, Angelo (Queensland)
Appearances: 1966 B
CRONIN, Michael (NSW)
Tours: Britain 1973,1978; NZ 1980
World Cup: 1975(1&2),1977
Appearances: 1973 F2; 1974 B3; **1975 NZ2,W2,E2,F;**
   1977 NZ,F,B2; 1978 NZ3,B3,F2; 1979 B3;
   1980 NZ2; 1981 F2; 1982 NZ2
CROWE, Ron (NSW)
Tours: NZ 1961
Appearances: 1961 NZ2; 1964 F2; 1966 B
CURRIE, Tony (Queensland)
Tours: NZ 1989
Appearances: 1988 B3, PNG; 1989 NZ3

DALEY, Phil (NSW)
Tours: Britain 1986
Appearances: 1988 B2, PNG
DAVIDSON, Les (NSW)
Tours: Britain 1986
Appearances: 1986 b, Ff; 1987 nz
DENMAN, Jeff (Queensland)
Tours: NZ 1969
DIMOND, Peter (NSW)
Tours: Britain 1963
Appearances: 1958 B2; 1962 B; 1963 B3,F3; 1966 B

DONNELLY, John (NSW)
World Cup: 1975(1)
Appearances: **1975 F,e,w;** 1978 NZ
DORAHY, John (NSW)
Appearances: 1978 NZ2
DOWLING, Gary (NSW)
Tours: NZ 1980
Appearances: 1980 NZ2
DOWLING, Greg (Queensland)
Tours: NZ 1985; Britain 1986
Appearances: 1984 B3; 1985 NZ2 nz; 1986 B3, F2;
   1987 NZ
DUNN, Paul (NSW)
Tours: Britain 1986
Appearances: 1986 PNG, B2, F2; 1988 PNG, **NZ**

EADIE, Graham (NSW)
Tours: Britain 1973,1978
World Cup: 1975(2),1977
Appearances: 1973 B2; 1974 B; **1975 NZ,W,F,E;**
   1977 B2,NZ,F; 1978 NZ,B3,F2; 1979 B3
ELFORD, John (NSW)
World Cup: 1972
Appearances: 1972 NZ2; **1972 B,NZ**
ELIAS, Ben (NSW)
Tours: NZ 1985; Britain 1986
Appearances: 1985 NZ; 1988 NZ
ELLA, Steve (NSW)
Tours: Britain 1982; NZ 1985
Appearances: 1983 nz; 1985 NZ nz
ETTINGSHAUSEN, Andrew (NSW)
Appearances: 1988 B3

FAHEY, Terry (NSW)
World Cup: 1975(1),1977
Appearances: **1975 NZ; 1977 F,B;** 1978 NZ; 1979 B;
   1981 F
FARRAR, Andrew (NSW)
Appearances: **1988 NZ**
FERGUSON, John (NSW)
Tours: NZ 1985
Appearances: 1985 NZ3
FITZGERALD, Denis (NSW)
World Cup: 1975(1),1977
Appearances: **1975 NZ; 1977 NZ,F,Bb**
FITZSIMMONS, Brian (Queensland)
Tours: NZ 1969,1971
World Cup: 1968
Appearances: 1967 NZ; **1968 F;** 1970 B; 1971 NZ
FOLKES, Steve (NSW)
Tours: Britain 1986
Appearances: 1986 NZ3, F; 1988 b
FULLERTON-SMITH, Wally (Queensland)
Tours: NZ 1985
Appearances: 1983 NZ2; 1984 Bb; 1988 B3, PNG
FULTON, Bobby (NSW)
Tours: Britain 1973,1978; NZ 1971
World Cup: 1968,1970,1972,1975(1)

Appearances: **1968 nz,F2;** 1970 B; **1970 B2,NZ,F;**
1971 NZ; 1972 NZ2; **1972 B2,NZ,F;** 1973 B3,F2;
1974 B3; **1975 NZ,W,F,E;** 1978 NZ3,B3,F2

GALLAGHER, Noel (Queensland)
Tours: Britain 1967
Appearances: 1967 B,F
GALLAGHER, Peter (Queensland)
Tours: Britain 1963,1967
Appearances: 1963 NZ3,SA2,B,F2; 1967 NZ3,B3,F3
GARTNER, Russel (NSW)
World Cup: 1977
Appearances: **1977 B,f**
GASNIER, Reg (NSW)
Tours: Britain 1959,1963,1967; NZ 1961,1965
World Cup: 1960
Appearances: 1959 NZ3,B3,F3; **1960 F,NZ,B;** 1960 F3;
1961 NZ2; 1962 B2; 1963 NZ3,SA2,B3,F3; 1964 F3;
1965 NZ2; 1967 NZ3,B
GEIGER, Nick (Queensland)
World Cup: 1977
Appearances: **1977 B2,NZ,F**
GERARD, Geoff (NSW)
Tours: Britain 1978
Appearances: 1978 B3,F2; 1983 NZ
GIBBS, Johnny (NSW)
Tours: Britain 1978
GILLESPIE, David (NSW)
Appearances: **1988 nz**
GLEESON, John (Queensland)
Tours: Britain 1963,1967; NZ 1965
Appearances: 1964 F2; 1966 B2; 1967 NZ3,B3
GLOVER, Neville (NSW)
Appearances: 1978 NZ2
GOLDSPINK, Kevin (NSW)
Tours: Britain 1967
GOODWIN, Ted (NSW)
Tours: Britain 1973
Appearances: 1972 nz; 1973 B,Ff
GRANT, Bob (NSW)
Tours: NZ 1971
Appearances: 1970 B; 1971 NZ
GRANT, John (Queensland)
World Cup: 1972
Appearances: **1972 NZ,F,B**
GREAVES, Johnny (NSW)
Tours: Britain 1967
World Cup: 1968
Appearances: 1966 B2; 1967 NZ,B2,F3; **1968 B,NZ,F2**
GROTHE, Eric (NSW)
Tours: Britain 1982
Appearances: 1982 B2,Ff; 1983 NZ2; 1984 B2

HAMBLY, Brian (NSW)
Tours: Britain 1959,1963; NZ 1965
World Cup: 1960

Appearances: 1959 B3,F3; 1960 F2; **1960 F,NZ,B;**
1963 NZ2,B2,F3; 1964 F; 1965 NZ2
HAMILTON, Bill (NSW)
Tours: Britain 1973
HANCOCK, Michael (Queensland)
Tours: NZ 1989
Appearances: 1989 NZ3
HANCOCK, Rohan (Queensland)
Tours: Britain 1982; NZ 1980
Appearances: 1982 NZ2 PNG
HANIGAN, Les (NSW)
Tours: Britain 1967
Appearances: 1967 NZ2
HARRIS, Mark (NSW)
World Cup: 1970,1972,1975(1),1977
Appearances: **1970 B2;** 1972 NZ; **1972 B2,F; 1975 W,F,E;**
1977 NZ,B
HASLER, Des (NSW)
Tours: NZ 1985, 1989; Britain 1986
Appearances: 1985 NZ; 1986 PNG; 1988 png; 1989 NZnz
HAWTHORNE, Phil (NSW)
Appearances: 1970 B3
HIGGS, Ray (Queensland-NSW)
World Cup: 1975(2),1977
Appearances; 1974 B; **1975 NZ,W,F,E; 1977 NZ,f,bB**
HILDITCH, Ron (NSW)
Tours: Britain 1978
Appearances: 1978 F; 1981 F2
HONAN, Bob (NSW)
Tours: NZ 1969
Appearances: 1969 NZ2

IRVINE, Ken (NSW)
Tours: Britain 1959,1963,1967; NZ 1961,1965
World Cup: 1960
Appearances: 1959 F; 1960 F3; **1960 F,NZ;** 1961 NZ2;
1962 B3; 1963 NZ3,SA2,B3,F2; 1964 F3; 1965 NZ2;
1966 B3; 1967 NZ3,F

JACK, Garry (NSW)
Tours: NZ 1985; Britain 1986
Appearances: 1984 B3; 1985 NZ3; 1986 NZ3,PNG,B3,
F2; 1987 NZ; 1988 B3, PNG, **NZ**
JACKSON, Peter (Queensland)
Tours: NZ 1989
Appearances: 1988 B3, PNG
JAMES, Brian (NSW)
World Cup: 1968
Appearances: **1968 F**
JARVIS, Pat (NSW)
Appearances: 1983 nz
JOHNS, Les (NSW)
Tours: Britain 1963, 1967; NZ 1965, 1969
Appearances: 1963 SA2; 1964 F; 1965 NZ2; 1966 B;
1967 B3,F3; 1969 NZ2
JOHNSTON, Brian (NSW)
Appearances: 1987 nz

JONES, Fred (NSW)
World Cup: 1968,1972
Appearances: **1968 B,NZ,F**
JUNEE, Kevin (NSW)
Tours: Britain 1967

KELLY, Noel (NSW)
Tours: Britain 1959,1963,1967
World Cup: 1960
Appearances: 1959 NZ3; 1960 F; **1960 F,NZ,B**;
   1963 NZ,SA2,B3,F3; 1964 F2; 1966 B2;
   1967 NZ3,B3,F2
KENNY, Brett (NSW)
Tours: Britain 1982, 1986
Appearances: 1982 PNG,B3,F2; 1984 Bb; 1986 NZ3,
   B3,F2; 1987 NZ
KING, Johnny (NSW)
Tours: Britain 1967
World Cup: 1968
Appearances: 1966 B3; 1967 NZ,B3,F3; **1968 B,NZ**;
   1970 B3
KISS, Les (Queensland)
Tours: Britain 1986
Appearances: 1986 NZ2,PNG,B
KNEEN, Steve (NSW)
Tours: Britain 1978
KNIGHT, Stephen (NSW)
World Cup: 1972
Appearances: **1972 B,NZ**
KOLC, John (NSW)
World Cup: 1977
Appearances: **1977 B**
KRILICH, Max (NSW)
Tours: Britain 1978,1982
Appearances: 1978 NZ,B2; 1982 NZ2,PNG,B3,F2;
   1983 NZ2

LAIRD, Ray (Queensland)
Appearances: 1970 B
LAMB, Terry (NSW)
Tours: Britain 1986
Appearances: 1986 nz2,b3,f2; **1988 nz**
LANG, John (Queensland, NSW)
Tours: Britain 1973; NZ 1980
World Cup: 1975 (1&2)
Appearances: 1973 F; 1974 B; **1975 NZ,W,F2,E**; 1978 NZ
LANGER, Allan (Queensland)
Appearances: 1988 PNG,**NZ**
LANGLANDS, Graeme (NSW)
Tours: Britain 1963,1967,1973; NZ 1965,1969,1971
World Cup: 1968,1972,1975(1)
Appearances: 1963 NZ3,SA2,B3,F2; 1964 F2; 1965 NZ2;
   1966 B2; 1967 NZ3,B3,F3; **1968 F,B,NZ**; 1969 NZ2;
   1970 B; 1971 NZ; 1972 NZ2; **1972 B2,NZ,F**; 1973 B;
   1974 B2; **1975 NZ,W,F,E**
LANGMACK, Paul (NSW)
Tours: Britain 1986

LEIS, Jim (NSW)
Tours: NZ 1980
LEWIS, Wally (Queensland)
Tours: Britain 1982, 1986; NZ 1985, 1989
Appearances: 1981 F2; 1982 NZ2,b2,F; 1983 NZ2;
   1984 B3; 1985 NZ3; 1986, NZ3,PNG,B3,F2; 1987
   NZ; 1988 B3, PNG, **NZ**; 1989 NZ 3
LINDNER, Bob (Queensland)
Tours: Britain 1986
Appearances: 1986 PNG, B3, F2; 1987 NZ; 1988 Bb2
LISLE, Jimmy (NSW)
Tours: Britain 1963; NZ 1965
Appearances: 1962 B; 1964 F3; 1965 NZ2
LYE, Graeme (NSW)
Tours: NZ 1969
LYNCH, Ron (NSW)
Tours: Britain 1967; NZ 1961
Appearances: 1961 NZ2; 1962 B; 1966 B2;
   1967 NZ2,B2,Ff; 1970 B

MACKAY, Ian (NSW)
World Cup: 1975(2)
Appearances: **1975 NZ,E,w**
McCABE, Paul (NSW)
Tours: Britain 1982
Appearances: 1981 F2; 1982 B,F2; 1983 NZ
McCARTHY, Bob (NSW)
Tours: Britain 1973; NZ 1969,1971
World Cup: 1970,1972
Appearances: 1969 NZ2; 1970 B; **1970 NZ,B2,F**;
   1971 NZ; 1972 NZ2; **1972 B**; 1973 B2; 1974 Bb
McDONALD, John (Queensland, NSW)
Tours: Britain 1967; NZ 1969
Appearances: 1966 B; 1967 NZ2,B3,F2; 1969 NZ2;
   1970 B3
McGAW, Mark (NSW)
Appearances: 1988 **NZ**
McGUIRE, Bruce (NSW)
Tours: NZ 1989
Appearances: 1989 nz2
McKEAN, Allan (NSW)
Appearances: 1970 B
McKINNON, Don (NSW)
Tours: Britain 1982
McMAHON, Allan (NSW)
Tours: Britain 1978
World Cup: 1975(2),1977
Appearances: **1975 W; 1977 NZ,F,B2**
McTAGGART, Barry (NSW)
World Cup: 1970
Appearances: **1970 F**
MADDISON, Ken (NSW)
Tours: Britain 1973
Appearances: 1973 B2b,F
MANTEIT, Dennis (Queensland)
Tours: Britain 1967; NZ 1969

World Cup: 1968
Appearances: 1967 B2,F; **1968 F**
MARTIN, Steve (NSW)
Tours: Britain 1978; NZ 1980
Appearances: 1978 F
MASTERMAN, Jeff (NSW)
Appearances: 1981 F2
MAYES, Johnny (NSW)
World Cup: 1975(2)
Appearances: **1975 NZ,W,E**
MENINGA, Mal (Queensland)
Tours: Britain 1982, 1986; NZ 1985, 1989
Appearances: 1982 NZ,PNG,B3,F2; 1983 NZ2; 1984 B2;
 1985 NZ3; 1986 png,Bb2; 1988 PNG; 1989 NZ3
MILES, Gene (Queensland)
Tours: Britain 1982, 1986
Appearances: 1983 NZ; 1984 B3; 1986 NZ3,PNG,
 B3,F2; 1987 NZ
MILLER, Gavin (NSW)
Appearances: 1988 PNG,**NZ**
MOORE, Brian (NSW)
Tours: Britain 1967
MORGAN, Jim (NSW)
Appearances: 1970 B2
MORGAN, John (NSW)
Tours: NZ 1965
Appearances: 1965 NZ2
MORRIS, Rod (Queensland, NSW)
Tours: Britain 1978,1982; NZ 1980
Appearances: 1978 NZnz,B,F; 1979 B3; 1980 NZ2;
 1981 Ff; 1982 NZnz,B,F
MORRIS, Steve (NSW)
Appearances: 1978 NZ
MORTIMER, Chris (NSW)
Tours: Britain 1986
Appearances: 1986 PNG
MORTIMER, Steve (NSW)
Tours: Britain 1982
Appearances: 1981 F2; 1982 NZ2 PNG; 1983 NZ; 1984 Bb
MUGGLETON, John (NSW)
Tours: Britain 1982
Appearances: 1982 NZnz PNG
MURPHY, Jim (Queensland)
Tours: NZ 1971
Appearances: 1972 nz
MURRAY, Mark (Queensland)
Tours: Britain 1982; NZ 1985
Appearances: 1982 png; 1983 nz; 1984 B2; 1985 NZ2

NIEBLING, Bryan (Queensland)
Tours: Britain 1986
Appearances: 1984 B3; 1986 nz3,PNG,B3,F2;
 1987 NZ

O'CONNOR, Michael (NSW)
Tours: NZ 1985, 1989; Britain 1986

Appearances: 1986 NZ3,PNG,B3,F2; 1987 NZ;
 1988 B3,PNG,**NZ;** 1989 nzNZ
OLIPHANT, Greg (Queensland)
Tours: Britain 1978
Appearances: 1978 NZnz
OLLING, Graeme (NSW)
Tours: Britain 1978
Appearances: 1978 NZ2,B2
O'NEILL, John (NSW)
Tours: Britain 1973
World Cup: 1970,1972,1975(1)
Appearances: **1970 NZ,B2; 1972 B2,NZ,F**; 1973 F;
 1974 B; **1975 W**
O'REILLY, Bob (NSW)
Tours: Britain 1973; NZ 1971
World Cup: 1970,1972
Appearances: **1970 NZ,B2,F**; 1971 NZ; 1972 NZ2;
 1972 NZ,F,B; 1973 B3,F; 1974 B2
ORR, Warren (Queensland)
Tours: Britain 1973
Appearances: 1974 B2

PANNOWITZ, Terry (NSW)
Tours: NZ 1965
PEARCE, Wayne (NSW)
Tours: Britain 1982; NZ 1985
Appearances: 1982 B3,F2; 1984 B3; 1985 NZ3;
 1986 NZ3; 1987 NZ; 1988 B2,PNG,**NZ**
PEARD, John (NSW)
World Cup: 1975(2),1977
Appearances: **1975 NZ,W,F,E; 1977 NZ,F,B2**
PEPONIS, George (NSW)
Tours: Britain 1978; NZ 1980
Appearances: 1978 NZ,B,F; 1979 B3; 1980 NZ2
PICKUP, Tim (NSW)
Tours: Britain 1973
World Cup: 1975(1)
Appearances: 1972 NZ2; 1973 Bb,F2; 1974 B;
 1975 NZ,W,F,E
PIERCE, Greg (NSW)
Tours: Britain 1973,1978
World Cup: 1975(2),1977
Appearances: 1973 F; **1975 F,E; 1977 NZ,B2**; 1978 NZ2
PIGGINS, George (NSW)
World Cup: 1975(2)
Appearances: **1975 NZ,W,E**
PITTARD, Denis (NSW)
Tours: NZ 1969
World Cup: 1970
Appearances: 1969 NZ2; **1970 NZ,B,F**
PLATZ, Greg (Queensland)
Appearances: 1978 NZ
PLATZ, Lew (Queensland)
World Cup: 1975(1&2)
Appearances: **1975 NZ2,F2,W,E**
PORTER, Jim (NSW)
World Cup: 1975(2)
Appearances: **1975 F,w**

249

PRICE, Ray (NSW)
Tours: Britain 1978,1982; NZ 1980
Appearances: 1978 NZ3,B3,F2; 1979 B3; 1980 NZ2;
  1981 F2; 1982 NZ,PNG,B2; 1983 NZ; 1984 B2

QUAYLE, John (NSW)
World Cup: 1975(2)
Appearances: **1975 NZ,W**
QUINN, Graham (NSW)
Tours: NZ 1980
Appearances; 1980 NZ
QUINN, Paul (NSW)
Tours; Britain 1963; NZ 1965
Appearances: 1963 SA,B2,F; 1964 F; 1965 NZ2

RANDALL, Terry (NSW)
Tours: Britain 1973
World Cup: 1975(1&2),1977
Appearances: **1975 NZ,W2,F2,E2; 1977 NZ,F,B2**
RAPER, Johnny (NSW)
Tours: Britain 1959,1963,1967
World Cup: 1960,1968
Appearances: 1959 NZ3,B,F2; 1960 F3; **1960 F,NZ;**
  1962 B2; 1963 NZ3,SA2,B3,F2; 1964 F3; 1966 B;
  1967 NZ3,B2,F3; **1968 B,NZ,F2**
RASMUSSEN, Elton (Queensland)
Tours: Britain 1959, 1967; NZ 1961
World Cup: 1960,1968
Appearances: 1959 B,F; 1960 F3; **1960 B;** 1961 NZ2;
  1962 B2; 1967 B3,F3; **1968 NZ,f**
RAUDONIKIS, Tom (NSW)
Tours: Britain 1973,1978; NZ 1971,1980
World Cup: 1972,1975(1&2),1977
Appearances: 1972 NZ2; **1972 B;** 1973 B3F; 1974 B3;
  1975 W,F2,E,nz; 1977 NZ,F,B; 1978 NZ,B3,F2;
  1979 B3; 1980 NZ2
REDDY, Rod (NSW)
Tours: Britain 1978,1982; NZ 1980
World Cup: 1977
Appearances: **1977 F;** 1978 NZ3,B2,F; 1979 B3;
  1980 NZ2; 1982 PNG,B3,F
RHODES, Johnny (Queensland)
World Cup: 1968,1975(1&2)
Appearances: **1968 B,NZ,F2; 1975 W,F2,E2,NZ**
RIBOT, John (Queensland)
Tours: Britain 1982; NZ 1985
Appearances: 1981 F2; 1982 NZ2,PNG,B; 1985 NZ3
RICHARDSON, Geoff (Queensland)
Appearances: 1974 B2
ROACH, Steve (NSW)
Tours: NZ 1985, 1989; Britain 1986
Appearances: 1985 NZ3; 1986 NZ3,PNG,B;
  1988 **NZ;** 1989 NZ3
ROBSON, Ian (Queensland)
Tours: NZ 1969
ROGERS, Steve (NSW)
Tours: Britain 1973,1978,1982

World Cup: 1975(2)
Appearances: **1975 NZ,F,e;** 1978 NZ3,B3,F; 1979 B3;
  1981 F2; 1982 NZnz,PNG,B3,F2; 1983 NZ

SADDLER, Ron (NSW)
Tour: Britain 1967
SAIT, Paul (NSW)
Tours: Britain 1973; NZ 1971
World Cup: 1970,1972,1975(1)
Appearances: **1970 NZ,B2, F;** 1971 NZ; **1972 b,NZ,F;**
  1973 B3,F; 1974 B2; **1975 nz,W**
SATTLER, John (NSW)
Tours: Britain 1967; NZ 1969,1971
Appearances: 1969 NZ2; 1970 B; 1971 NZ
SCHUBERT, Ian (NSW)
Tours: Britain 1978,1982
World Cup: 1975(2)
Appearances: **1975 NZ,W,f,E**
SCOTT, Colin (Queensland)
Appearances; 1983 NZ
SHEARER, Dale (Queensland)
Tours: Britain 1986; NZ 1989
Appearances: 1986 NZ,GB2,F2; 1987 NZ; 1988 **NZ;**
  1989 NZ3
SIGSWORTH, Phil (NSW)
Appearances: 1981 f
SIMMONS, Royce (NSW)
Tour: Britain 1986
Appearances: 1986 NZ3,PNG,B3,F2; 1987 NZ
SIMMS, Eric (NSW)
World Cup: 1968,1970
Appearances: **1968 B,NZ,F2; 1970 NZ,B2,F**
SIRONEN, Paul (NSW)
Tours: Britain 1986; NZ 1989
Appearances: 1986 png,f; 1988 **NZ;** 1989 NZ2
SMITH, Billy (NSW)
Tours: Britain 1967; NZ 1965
World Cup: 1968,1970
Appearances: 1964 F3; 1965 NZ2; 1966 B3;
  1967 NZ3,B2,F3; **1968 F2,B,NZ;** 1970 B2;
  1970 NZ,B2,F
STAINS, Danny (Queensland)
Tours: NZ 1989
STARLING, Geoff (NSW)
Tours: Britain 1973; NZ 1971
World Cup: 1972
Appearances: 1972 NZ2; **1972 B2,NZ,F;** 1973 B3,F2
STERLING, Peter (NSW)
Tours: Britain 1982, 1986
Appearances: 1982 B3,F2; 1983 NZ; 1986 NZ3,B3,F2;
  1987 NZ; 1988 B3
STEVENS, Gary (NSW)
Tours: Britain 1973
World Cup: 1972,1975(1)
Appearances: **1972 nz,F,B;** 1973 B2,F; 1974 B2;
  1975 NZ,W,E

STEWART, Wayne (Queensland)
Appearances: 1972 NZ
STRUDWICK, Ross (Queensland)
World Cup: 1975(1)
Appearances: **1975 NZ**
SULLIVAN, Gary (NSW)
World Cup: 1970,1972
Appearances: **1970 B,f**; 1972 NZ2; **1972 B2,NZ**

TESSMAN, Brad (Queensland)
Appearances: 1983 NZ
THOMAS, Mark (Queensland)
World Cup: 1977
Appearances: **1977 NZ,F,B**
THOMPSON, Alan (NSW)
Tours: Britain 1978; NZ 1980
Appearances: 1978 b2; 1979 B3; 1980 NZ2
THOMSON, Alan (NSW)
Tours: Britain 1967
Appearances: 1967 NZ2,F
THOMSON, Ian (NSW)
Tours: Britain 1978
Appearances: 1978 NZ,b,F
THORNETT, Dick (NSW)
Tours: Britain 1963
World Cup: 1968
Appearances: 1963 SA2, B3,F; 1964 F3; 1966 Bb;
   1968 B,NZ,F
TREWHELLA, David (NSW)
Tours: NZ 1989
TUNKS, Peter (NSW)
Tours: NZ 1985
Appearances: 1985 NZ nz; 1986 NZ3; 1987 NZ
TURNER, Ron (NSW)
World Cup: 1970
Appearances: **1970 nz,f,B**; 1974 B
TUTTY, Dennis (NSW)
Appearances: 1967 NZ

VAUTIN, Paul (NSW)
Tours: NZ 1985, 1989
Appearances: 1982 NZ; 1983 NZ2; 1984 B; 1985 NZ2;
   1988 B3,PNG; 1989 NZ3
VEIVERS, Greg (Queensland)
World Cup: 1975(2), 1977
Appearances: **1975 NZ,W; 1977 NZ,F,B2**
VEIVERS, Mick (Queensland)
Tours: NZ 1965
Appearances: 1962 B2; 1965 NZ2; 1966 B2

WAITE, David (NSW)
Tours: Britain 1973
Appearances: 1973 B2,F2; 1974 B2

WALKER, Bruce (NSW)
Tours: Britain 1978
WALSH, Ian (NSW)
Tours: Britain 1959,1963; NZ 1961,1965
Appearances: 1959 B3,F3; 1961 NZ2; 1962 B3;
   1963 NZ3,SA,B3,F; 1964 F; 1965 NZ2; 1966 B3
WALTERS, Elwyn (NSW)
Tours: Britain 1967,1973; NZ 1969
World Cup: 1970,1972
Appearances: 1969 NZ2; 1970 B2; **1970 NZ, Bb, F**;
   1972 NZ2; **1972 B2,NZ,F**; 1973 B3,F2; 1974 B
WALTERS, Kerrod (Queensland)
Tours: NZ 1989
Appearances: 1989 NZ3
WARD, Dennis (NSW)
Tours: Britain 1973; NZ 1969
World Cup: 1972
Appearances: 1969 NZ2; **1972 Bb,NZ,F**
WEIER, Lloyd (NSW)
Tours: NZ 1965
Appearances: 1965 NZ2; 1966 B
WEISS, Col (Queensland)
Tours: NZ 1969
Appearances: 1969 NZ; 1970 Bb
WELLINGTON, Gary (Queensland)
Tours: NZ 1965
WILLIAMSON, Lionel (Queensland, NSW)
Tours: Britain 1973. NZ 1971
World Cup: 1968,1970
Appearances: **1968 F2; 1970 NZ,B2,F**; 1971 NZ;
   1973 B2,F; 1974 B
WITTENBERG, John (Queensland, NSW)
Tours: NZ 1969
World Cup: 1968
Appearances: 1966 B2; **1968 B,NZ,F2**; 1969 NZ2; 1970 B2
WRIGHT, David (Queensland)
World Cup: 1975(1)
Appearances: **1975 NZ**
WYNN, Graeme (NSW)
Tours: NZ 1980
WYNN, Peter (NSW)
Tours: NZ 1985
Appearances: 1985 NZ3

YAKICH, Nick (NSW)
Tours: NZ 1965
YOUNG, Craig (NSW)
Tours: Britain 1978,1982; NZ 1980
Appearances: 1978 NZ,B3,F2; 1979 B3; 1980 NZ2;
   1981 F; 1982 NZ2,PNG,B2,F2; 1984 b

AUSTRALIA TOURS OF BRITAIN

1908-09 TOUR

MATCH RESULTS

Mid-Rhondda	won	20-6	7,500
Bradford N.	won	12-11	4,000
Rochdale H	won	5-0	3,000
York	drew	5-5	3,000
Salford	drew	9-9	6,100
Runcorn	won	9-7	3,000
Cumberland League (W'haven)	**won**	**52-10**	**4,000**
Leigh	lost	11-14	6,000
Dewsbury	lost	0-15	2,000
Yorkshire (Hull)	**won**	**24-11**	**3,500**
Hunslet	won	12-11	6,000
Aberdare	won	37-10	5,000
Warrington	lost	3-10	5,000
Northern RL (Everton)	**won**	**10-9**	**6,000**
Hull KR	lost	16-21	7,000
Lancashire (Wigan)	**won**	**20-6**	**4,000**
Barrow	won	21-5	6,500
Halifax	lost	8-12	6,000
Swinton	won	10-9	1,500
BRITAIN (QPR, London)	**drew**	**22-22**	**2,000**
Treherbert	won	6-3	4,000
Wakefield T	lost	13-20	3,000
Leeds	won	14-10	12,000
Oldham	lost	5-11	12,000
England (Huddersfield)	**lost**	**9-14**	**7,000**
Widnes	won	13-2	1,000
†Wigan	lost	7-10	4,000
Batley	lost	5-12	2,000
Welsh League (Merthyr Tydfil)	**lost**	**13-14**	**6,000**
Ebbw Vale	won	9-8	5,000
†Wigan	lost	8-16	8,000
BRITAIN (Newcastle)	**lost**	**5-15**	**22,000**
Keighley	drew	8-8	1,000
Hull	lost	8-9	10,000
England (Glasgow)	**drew**	**17-17**	**3,000**
Cumberland (Carlisle)	**lost**	**2-11**	**2,000**
Broughton R	lost	12-14	12,000
St. Helens	lost	0-9	1,500
Warrington	drew	8-8	7,000
BRITAIN (Birmingham)	**lost**	**5-6**	**9,000**
Huddersfield	lost	3-5	9,677
Barrow	lost	3-11	6,000
Merthyr Tydfil	lost	13-15	4,000
England (Everton)	**lost**	**7-14**	**4,500**
Lancashire (Leigh)	**won**	**14-9**	**4,000**

●The tourists also played an exhibition match against Widnes at Southport on January 1, winning 55-3, but this is not included in tour records.

†There were two matches against Wigan because the first was marred by fog.

SUMMARY

Played 45   Won 17   Drew 6   Lost 22
For
Tries 113   Goals 87   Points 513
Against
Tries 106   Goals 78   Points 474
Lost Test series 2-0 with one drawn
Attendance total: 250,777

TOUR PARTY

Manager: J. Giltinan   Captain: D. Lutge

	App	Tries	Gls	Pts
J. Abercrombie	31	2	6	18
T. Anderson	5	0	0	0
E. Anlezark	17	1	0	3
W. Bailey	3	3	0	9
M. Bolewski	33	2	0	6
A. Burdon	25	3	0	9
A. Butler	23	4	1	14
W. Cann	8	0	0	0
F. Cheadle	7	0	0	0
A. Conlon	7	3	2	13
E. Courtney	27	8	0	24
J. Davis	6	0	0	0
S. Deane	27	6	0	18
J. Devereux	30	17	3	57
A. Dobbs	5	0	0	0
D. Frawley	22	10	0	30
R. Graves	21	2	0	6
A. Halloway	29	5	0	15
W. Hardcastle	6	1	0	3
C. Hedley	17	1	1	5
W. Heidke	25	3	0	9
A. Hennessy	7	0	0	0
L. Jones	5	1	0	3
D. Lutge	5	0	0	0
T. McCabe	20	4	0	12
H. Messenger	32	10	65	160
P. Moir	4	2	0	6
A. Morton	23	4	9	30
W. Noble	3	0	0	0
L. O'Malley	35	5	0	15
S. Pearce	32	2	0	6
A. Rosenfeld	15	5	0	15
J. Rosewall	1	0	0	0
P. Walsh	29	9	0	27

MEMO

First match on October 3, last match March 8.

All three Test matches were played on soccer grounds outside the Northern Union area in a move to expand the game, but it was not a success.

The party included Herbert "Dally" Messenger who had toured the previous season with New Zealand.

Among the players who were to sign for English clubs was Albert Rosenfeld who scored a record 80 tries in a season while with Huddersfield.

1911-12 TOUR

MATCH RESULTS

Midlands — South (Coventry)	**won**	**20-11**	**3,000**
Yorkshire (Sheffield)	**won**	**33-13**	**4,000**
Broughton R	won	18-8	12,000
Lancashire (Blackburn)	**won**	**25-12**	**5,000**
Wales (Ebbw Vale)	**won**	**28-20**	**7,000**
Widnes	won	23-0	5,000
St. Helens	won	16-5	12,000
England (Fulham)	**won**	**11-6**	**6,000**
Hunslet	drew	3-3	4,000
Northern RL (Everton)	**won**	**16-3**	**6,000**
Wigan	lost	2-7	25,000
Swinton	won	28-9	4,000
Hull	won	26-7	6,000
BRITAIN (Newcastle)	**won**	**19-10**	**6,500**
Oldham	lost	8-14	10,000
Leigh	won	13-12	6,000
Wakefield T	won	24-10	5,000
Cumberland (Maryport)	**won**	**5-2**	**6,000**
Barrow	won	44-8	6,500
Runcorn	won	23-7	2,000
Huddersfield	lost	7-21	17,000
England (Nottingham)	**lost**	**3-5**	**3,000**
Salford	won	6-3	4,000
York	won	16-8	1,500
BRITAIN (Edinburgh)	**drew**	**11-11**	**6,000**
Wales and West of England (Bristol)	**won**	**23-3**	**1,000**
Rochdale H	won	18-6	4,500
Halifax	won	23-5	10,000
Warrington	won	34-6	8,500
BRITAIN (Birmingham)	**won**	**33-8**	**4,000**
Leeds	won	8-6	1,000
Hull K.R.	won	5-2	7,000
Barrow	won	22-5	1,500
Batley	lost	5-13	4,000
Northern RL (Wigan)	**won**	**20-12**	**2,000**

SUMMARY

Played 35   Won 28   Drew 2   Lost 5

For
Tries 149   Goals 86   Points 619

Against
Tries 63   Goals 46   Points 281

Won Test series 2-0 with one drawn

Attendance total: 216,000

The Australians also played an exhibition match against Runcorn at Southport on December 25, winning 54-6 but this is not included in tour records.

TOUR PARTY

Managers: J. Quinlan and C. Ford
Captain: C. McKivat

	App	Tries	Gls	Pts
T. Berecry	12	12	0	36
A. Broomham	19	5	0	15
P. Burge	4	1	0	3
W. Cann	21	10	3	36
E. Courtney	25	4	0	12
R. Craig	30	8	2	28
S. Darmody	6	0	9	18
V. Farnsworth	28	18	0	54
W. Farnsworth	14	1	0	3
A. Francis (NZ)	24	9	49	125
C. Fraser	20	0	12	24
D. Frawley	11	13	3	45
H. Gilbert	29	20	2	64
G. Gillett (NZ)	4	0	0	0
H. Hallett	29	12	1	38
A. Halloway	12	0	0	0
P. McCue	22	6	0	18
C. McKivat	31	10	0	30
C. McMurtie	8	3	0	9
J. Murray	7	1	0	3
W. Neill	7	0	0	0
W. Noble	21	1	0	3
C. Russell	24	9	5	37
C. Savory (NZ)	4	1	0	3
R. Stuart	2	0	0	0
C. Sullivan	16	1	0	3
R. Williams	19	3	0	9
F. Woodward (NZ)	6	1	0	3

MEMO

First match on September 23, last match on January 31.

The tour party included the following New Zealanders: Francis, Gillett, Savory and Woodward.

A star of the party was Gilbert who later signed for Hull and became the first overseas player to captain an RL Challenge Cup-winning side, in 1914.

Often regarded as the best-ever touring party, they were the first Australian squad to remain unbeaten in a Test series in this country.

The Tests were again played on soccer grounds outside the Northern Union area, again without success.

1921-22 **TOUR**

MATCH RESULTS

Salford	won	48-3	9,000
Keighley	won	29-0	5,500
Hull KR	won	26-6	13,000
Bradford N	won	53-3	3,000
BRITAIN (Leeds)	**lost**	**5-6**	**32,000**
Widnes	won	28-4	11,000
Broughton R	won	18-6	17,000
England (Arsenal)	**lost**	**4-5**	**12,000**
Wigan	won	14-6	24,308
Leeds	won	11-5	14,000
Wakefield T	won	29-3	6,000
Batley	won	33-7	6,000
Warrington	lost	5-8	16,000
York	lost	3-9	5,000
BRITAIN (Hull)	**won**	**16-2**	**21,504**
Bramley	won	92-7	1,500
Rochdale H	won	16-2	12,000
Swinton	lost	0-9	6,000
Huddersfield	won	36-2	12,000
St. Helens	won	16-8	6,000
Oldham	won	16-5	15,000
Lancashire League (Everton)	**won**	**29-6**	**17,000**
Barrow	won	24-15	8,000
Yorkshire (Wakefield)	**won**	**24-8**	**6,000**
Wales (Pontypridd)	**won**	**21-16**	**13,000**
Lancashire (Warrington)	**lost**	**6-8**	**6,000**
Dewsbury	lost	6-13	6,000
Leigh	won	17-4	5,000
Hull	won	21-10	12,000
Widnes	won	17-8	12,000
Halifax	won	35-6	12,000
Hunslet	won	19-10	3,174
Cumberland (Workington)	**won**	**25-12**	**5,000**
BRITAIN (Salford)	**lost**	**0-6**	**21,000**
Oldham	lost	5-15	6,000
St. Helens Recs	won	16-5	5,000

SUMMARY

Played 36 Won 27 Lost 9

For
Tries 187 Goals 101 Points 763

Against
Tries 44 Goals 58 Points 248

Lost Test series 2-1

Attendance total: 384,986

TOUR PARTY

Managers: S. Ball and W. Cann
Captain: L. Cubitt

	App	Tries	Gls	Pts
C. Blinkhorn	29	39	0	117
N. Broadfoot	4	2	0	6
E. Brown	4	1	0	3
F. Burge	23	33	6	111
H. Caples	24	7	0	21
G. Carstairs	17	7	2	25
J. Craig	24	10	14	58
L. Cubitt	4	1	0	3
C. Fraser	23	2	1	8
B. Gray	5	2	0	6
H. Horder	25	35	11	127
J. Ives	6	1	0	3
A. Johnston	12	3	1	11
B. Laing (NZ)	10	4	0	12
R. Latta	22	7	0	21
E. McGrath	16	1	2	7
R. Norman	21	2	13	32
S. Pearce	21	0	0	0
H. Peters	4	2	0	6
N. Potter	10	1	0	3
C. Prentice	25	3	2	13
W. Richards	15	4	0	12
F. Ryan	24	6	0	18
W. Schultz	24	1	0	3
D. Thompson	26	3	49	107
R. Townsend	13	2	0	6
R. Vest	26	7	0	21
J. Watkins	11	1	0	3

MEMO

First match on September 17, last match on January 21.

Three players dominated the tryscoring on this tour. Blinkhorn, a winger, scored a tour record 39 tries and Burge's 33 tries were the most by a forward on tour. Horder, another winger, scored 35 tries.

Blinkhorn's total included a tour record nine against Bramley, who were beaten 92-7 — another tour record. Horder also got five as the tourists ran in 24 tries despite being penalised 18 times to Bramley's three. The half-time score was 43-5.

"Sandy" Pearce, a hooker, who was in the first tour party of 1908, returned at 41 years of age, to play 21 matches including two Tests.

1929-30 TOUR

MATCH RESULTS

Rochdale H	won	36-3	6,521
York	won	32-11	4,729
Batley	won	27-5	6,000
Widnes	won	37-13	6,400
Broughton R	won	21-8	6,514
Lancashire (Warrington)	**won**	**29-14**	**24,000**
Wakefield T	lost	3-14	9,786
Keighley	won	15-9	3,000
BRITAIN (Hull KR)	**won**	**31-8**	**20,000**
Castleford	won	53-2	4,000
Huddersfield	won	18-8	18,560
Leigh	won	19-16	8,000
Barrow	won	13-10	10,000
Leeds	lost	7-8	10,000
Hull	won	35-2	10,000
Oldham	won	18-10	18,000
BRITAIN (Leeds)	**lost**	**3-9**	**31,402**
Bradford N	won	26-17	7,000
St. Helens	drew	18-18	9,500
Yorkshire (Wakefield)	**won**	**25-12**	**7,011**
Halifax	won	58-9	8,440
Swinton	lost	5-9	9,000
Northern League (Wigan)	**lost**	**5-18**	**9,987**
Cumberland (Workington)	**lost**	**5-8**	**3,500**
Glamorgan and Monmouth-shire (White City, Cardiff)	**won**	**39-9**	**3,000**
St. Helens Recs	won	22-8	9,000
Northern League (Newcastle)	**won**	**32-22**	**9,690**
Warrington	lost	8-17	12,826
Hunslet	lost	3-18	12,000
Hull KR	won	10-5	12,000
Wigan	won	10-9	8,000
(Abandoned after 65 min — waterlogged)			
BRITAIN (Swinton)	**drew**	**0-0**	**34,709**
Salford	won	21-5	8,000
BRITAIN (Rochdale)	**lost**	**0-3**	**16,743**
Wales (Wembley)	**won**	**26-10**	**16,000**

SUMMARY

Played 35   Won 24   Drew 2   Lost 9

For
Tries 164   Goals 109   Points 710

Against
Tries 67   Goals 73   Points 347

Lost Test series 2-1, and one drawn

Attendance total: 393,318

TOUR PARTY

Managers: J. Dargan and H. Sunderland
Captain: T. Gorman   Coach: A. Hennessy

	App	Tries	Gls	Pts
V. Armbruster	19	6	0	18
G. Bishop	15	4	0	12
W. Brogan	20	2	0	6
J. Busch	19	2	0	6
D. Dempsey	10	0	0	0
A. Edwards	9	3	0	9
C. Fifield	22	8	0	24
H. Finch	10	16	18	84
T. Gorman	22	2	0	6
A. Henderson	7	0	0	0
J. Holmes	12	5	0	15
A. Justice	13	2	0	6
H. Kadwell	8	2	5	16
J. Kingston	26	18	0	54
F. Laws	15	2	5	16
P. Madsen	17	1	0	3
P. Maher	12	4	0	12
F. McMillan	26	0	4	8
W. Prigg	16	4	0	12
A. Ridley	7	11	0	33
E. Root	15	3	0	9
L. Sellars	8	1	0	3
W. Shankland	23	24	17	106
W. Spencer	22	23	0	69
W. Steinohrt	21	0	0	0
G. Treweeke	22	6	0	18
J. Upton	19	10	4	38
E. Weissel	20	5	56	127

MEMO

First match on September 7, last match on January 18. This was the tour that featured a fourth Test match. The unique extra Test followed a 0-0 draw in the third match after Britain had lost the first and won the second.

Demands for a deciding Test match were answered with a Wednesday afternoon fixture at Rochdale on January 15. A late try by Stan Smith snatched Britain a 3-0 victory.

This was also the first tour in which Australia appointed an official coach to join the party, the position going to Arthur Hennessy.

1933-34 TOUR

MATCH RESULTS

St. Helens Recs	won	13-9	8,880
Leigh	won	16-7	4,600
Hull K.R.	won	20-0	7,831
Bramley	won	53-6	1,902
Oldham	won	38-6	15,281
Yorkshire (Leeds)	**won**	**13-0**	**10,309**
Barrow	won	24-5	12,221
Lancashire (Warrington)	**won**	**33-7**	**16,576**
Wigan	won	10-4	15,712
Castleford	won	39-6	4,250
Halifax	won	16-5	10,358
BRITAIN (Belle Vue, Man'r)	**lost**	**0-4**	**34,000**
Bradford N	lost	5-7	3,328
Warrington	lost	12-15	16,431
Hunslet	won	22-18	6,227
Salford	lost	9-16	15,761
Widnes	won	31-0	6,691
Wakefield T	won	17-6	5,596
Bradford N	won	10-7	9,937
Northern League (York)	lost	5-7	3,158
Swinton	lost	4-10	13,341
BRITAIN (Leeds)	**lost**	**5-7**	**29,618**
Keighley	won	14-7	3,800
Huddersfield	won	13-5	7,522
London Highfield	won	20-5	10,541
Broughton R	won	19-0	5,527
Leeds	won	15-7	5,295
St. Helens	won	20-11	5,735
Rochdale H	won	26-4	3,603
Cumberland (Whitehaven)	**lost**	**16-17**	**5,800**
BRITAIN (Swinton)	**lost**	**16-19**	**10,990**
York	won	15-7	6,500
Hull	won	19-5	16,341
Wales (Wembley)	**won**	**51-19**	**10,000**
England (Paris)	**won**	**63-13**	**5,000**
Oldham	won	38-5	4,000
England (Gateshead)	**lost**	**14-19**	**15,576**

SUMMARY

Played 37   Won 27   Lost 10

For
Tries 162   Goals 134   Points 754

Against
Tries 47   Goals 77   Points 295

Lost Test series 3-0

Attendance total: 368,238

TOUR PARTY

Managers: H. Sunderland and W. Webb
Captain: F. McMillan

	App	Tries	Gls	Pts
D. Brown	32	19	114	285
F. Curran	12	0	0	0
D. Dempsey	12	1	0	3
H. Denny	8	0	0	0
F. Doonar	11	2	0	6
J. Doyle	21	7	0	21
A. Folwell	21	2	0	6
F. Gardner	20	13	2	43
J. Gibbs	19	10	0	30
F. Gilbert	4	2	0	6
M. Glasheen	2	1	0	3
V. Hey	26	14	0	42
F. Laws	15	1	5	13
J. Little	4	0	0	0
M. Madsen	25	2	0	6
F. McMillan	21	1	3	9
L. Mead	15	2	5	16
F. Neumann	9	1	0	3
F. O'Connor	16	7	0	21
C. Pearce	27	6	1	20
S. Pearce	24	12	4	44
W. Prigg	32	16	0	48
A. Ridley	27	25	0	75
W. Smith	16	3	0	9
R. Stehr	26	4	0	12
V. Thicknesse	18	3	0	9
J. Why	17	8	0	24

● R. Morris was taken ill en route to England and died in hospital in Malta.

MEMO

First match on August 26, last match on January 13.

Dave Brown scored 114 goals and 285 points on this tour, two records which still stand. The centre's points total, which included 19 tries, came from 32 matches.

The tourists helped launch the game in France by playing England in Paris on December 31, winning 63-13.

Vic Hey was one of the tour's biggest successes, later returning to England and becoming a great favourite at Leeds.

An extra fixture to the official programme of matches was a seven-a-side match against England at Roundhay Park, Leeds.

1937 TOUR

MATCH RESULTS

Leigh	won	11-9	5,000
York	won	15-6	5,000
Newcastle	won	37-0	4,000
Lancashire (Warrington)	**lost**	**5-7**	**16,250**
Halifax	lost	2-12	14,500
Yorkshire (Bradford)	**won**	**8-4**	**7,570**
Wakefield T	won	17-10	8,696
Rochdale H	won	6-0	2,400
BRITAIN (Leeds)	**lost**	**4-5**	**31,949**
Widnes	drew	13-13	4,201
Hull	won	22-12	15,000
Bradford N	won	19-6	5,748
Salford	lost	8-11	12,000
Wigan	won	25-23	9,800
Oldham	won	10-6	15,000
BRITAIN (Swinton)	**lost**	**3-13**	**31,724**
Liverpool S	won	28-9	1,500
Huddersfield	lost	7-17	9,383
Swinton	lost	3-5	4,113
Warrington	lost	6-8	12,637
Leeds	lost	8-21	5,000
St. Helens XIII	won	15-7	2,000
Barrow	lost	8-12	8,153
BRITAIN (Huddersfield)	**won**	**13-3**	**9,093**
Broughton R	lost	0-13	3,000

SUMMARY

Played 25   Won 13   Drew 1   Lost 11

For
Tries 67   Goals 46   Points 293

Against
Tries 40   Goals 56   Points 232

Lost Test series 2-1

Attendance total: 243,717

TOUR PARTY

Managers: H. Sunderland and R. Savage
Captain: W. Prigg

	App	Tries	Gls	Pts
J. Beaton	18	3	28	65
E. Collins	2	1	0	3
F. Curran	11	4	0	12
L. Dawson	17	6	0	18
P. Fairall	8	0	0	0
J. Gibbs	12	0	0	0
F. Gilbert	13	2	4	14
F. Griffiths	6	0	0	0
C. Hazelton	8	3	0	9
L. Heidke	14	1	0	3
E. Lewis	12	2	0	6
G. McLennan	11	1	0	3
R. McKinnon	19	3	6	21
D. McLean	5	1	0	3
H. Narvo	15	5	0	15
F. Nolan	5	0	0	0
E. Norman	16	3	0	9
A. Norval	10	6	0	18
H. Pierce	15	3	0	9
W Prigg	18	8	0	24
J. Reardon	19	7	0	21
H. Robison	9	2	0	6
R. Stehr	12	0	0	0
R. Thompson	5	1	2	7
L. Ward	18	1	0	3
G. Whittle	7	0	0	0
B. Williams	11	4	0	12
P. Williams	9	0	6	12

● J. Pearce was injured in New Zealand and although he continued the trip did not play in England. H. Narvo replaced him.

MEMO

First match on September 18, last match on December 25.

This was Harry Sunderland's third trip as manager and Wally Prigg completed his hat-trick as a player, this time captaining the squad.

For the first time Australia made a brief tour of France, including two Tests which they won.

A reduced number of matches and a less adventurous style resulted in a drop in tryscoring with no player scoring more than 10 on the tour.

1948 TOUR

MATCH RESULTS

Huddersfield	lost	3-22	26,017
Belle Vue Rangers	won	14-9	7,535
Hull	won	13-3	16,616
Wakefield T	won	26-19	20,040
Leigh	won	24-12	12,968
Salford	won	13-2	16,627
Castleford	won	10-8	14,004
BRITAIN (Leeds)	**lost**	**21-23**	**36,529**
Cumberland (Whitehaven)	**lost**	**4-5**	**8,818**
St. Helens	lost	8-10	20,175
Dewsbury	won	14-4	13,614
Hull K.R.	lost	12-17	7,614
Wigan	lost	11-16	28,554
Barrow	won	11-5	13,143
Leeds	won	15-2	13,542
Warrington	lost	7-16	26,879
BRITAIN (Swinton)	**lost**	**7-16**	**36,354**
Bradford N	won	21-7	13,287
Workington T	lost	7-10	13,253
Swinton	won	21-0	5,849
Wales (Swansea)	**won**	**12-5**	**9,161**
Yorkshire (Leeds)	**lost**	**2-5**	**5,310**
Halifax	won	10-8	6,520
Oldham	won	27-7	14,798
Lancashire (Wigan)	**lost**	**8-13**	**11,788**
Widnes	won	18-8	10,761
BRITAIN (Bradford)	**lost**	**9-23**	**42,000**

SUMMARY

Played 27 Won 15 Lost 12

For
Tries 76 Goals 60 Points 348

Against
Tries 57 Goals 52 Points 275

Lost Test series 3-0

Attendance total: 451,756

TOUR PARTY

Managers: W. Buckley and E. Simmonds
Captain: C. Maxwell

	App	Tries	Gls	Pts
F. de Belin	10	1	0	3
I. Benton	6	0	0	0
E. Brosnan	12	0	0	0
V. Bulgin	11	0	1	2
C. Churchill	16	0	1	2
L. Cowie	15	5	0	15
R. Dimond	9	2	0	6
K. Froome	12	2	21	48
A. Gibbs	13	1	0	3
J. Graves	15	6	24	66
D. Hall	15	5	0	15
N. Hand	11	1	0	3
J. Hawke	17	7	0	21
J. Holland	17	3	0	9
B. Hopkins	9	0	8	16
J. Horrigan	16	13	5	49
F. Johnson	3	0	0	0
R. Lulham	13	8	0	24
P. McMahon	18	10	0	30
D. McRitchie	8	1	0	3
C. Maxwell	9	2	0	6
N. Mulligan	15	1	0	3
W. O'Connell	15	1	0	3
L. Pegg	10	1	0	3
J. Rayner	19	2	0	6
K. Schubert	17	1	0	3
W. Thompson	11	1	0	3
W. Tyquin	9	2	0	6

MEMO

First match on September 18, last match on January 29.

The final match was to have been the third Test at Bradford on December 18 but fog caused a postponement and the party left to tour France.

They lost only one of 10 matches in France and returned for the third Test against Britain on January 29. Although Britain had already retained the Ashes there was a record crowd for a Test against Australia in this country of 42,000.

Britain won the Test series 3-0, but several of Australia's best players were playing for English clubs. Three different captains were used in the Tests, Wally O'Connell, Col Maxwell and Bill Tyquin.

A surprise omission from the party was Len Smith who had led Australia in the previous Test series against New Zealand. He was expected to be an automatic choice as centre and captain.

This was the first tour by Clive Churchill who was to become one of Australia's greatest full-backs. He was on tour again as a player in 1952 and 1956, and also coached the 1959 squad.

1952 TOUR

MATCH RESULTS

Keighley	won	54-4	7,431
Hull	won	28-0	15,364
Barrow	won	26-2	16,045
Whitehaven	won	15-5	9,253
Oldham	drew	7-7	19,370
Halifax	won	39-7	18,773
Wigan	won	23-13	16,223
St. Helens	lost	8-26	17,205
Featherstone R	won	50-15	3,700
BRITAIN (Leeds)	**lost**	**6-19**	**34,505**
Bradford N	won	20-6	29,287
Warrington	won	34-10	21,478
Leigh	won	34-5	8,409
Swinton	won	31-8	10,269
Hunslet	won	49-2	3,273
Workington T	won	27-15	11,341
Doncaster	won	41-13	2,452
Huddersfield	won	27-9	25,494
BRITAIN (Swinton)	**lost**	**5-21**	**32,421**
Wakefield T	won	58-8	7,239
Hull K.R.	won	31-6	5,817
Lancashire (Warrington)	**won**	**36-11**	**5,863**
Leeds	won	45-4	20,335
Yorkshire (Huddersfield)	**won**	**55-11**	**3,737**
Dewsbury	won	22-7	2,485
Widnes	won	18-7	7,411
BRITAIN (Bradford)	**won**	**27-7**	**30,509**

SUMMARY

Played 27   Won 23   Drew 1   Lost 3

For
Tries 176   Goals 144   Points 816

Against
Tries 42   Goals 61   Points 248

Lost Test series 2-1

Attendance total: 385,689

TOUR PARTY

Managers: D. McLean and N. Robinson
Captain: C. Churchill

	App	Tries	Gls	Pts
F. Ashton	14	7	0	21
R. Bull	9	1	0	3
B. Carlson	14	19	2	61
C. Churchill	17	2	17	40
A. Collinson	17	9	0	27
H. Crocker	11	2	0	6
B. Davies	16	7	0	21
C. Donohoe	11	4	0	12
R. Duncan	12	8	0	24
D. Flannery	11	15	0	45
C. Geelan	15	8	0	24
C. Gill	14	1	0	3
D. Hall	17	2	0	6
G. Hawick	9	4	0	12
N. Hazzard	16	5	0	15
K. Holman	10	8	7	38
K. Kearney	12	0	0	0
K. McCaffery	8	8	0	24
D. McGovern	6	10	0	30
A. Paul	13	8	4	32
N. Pidding	15	17	79	209
J. Rooney	12	1	0	3
T. Ryan	13	16	0	48
K. Schubert	14	0	0	0
F. Stanmore	15	3	0	9
T. Tyrrell	13	7	0	21
H. Wells	7	2	0	6
R. Willey	10	2	35	76

MEMO

First match on September 6, last match on December 13.

This was the most free-scoring tour squad of all time. They opened with a 54-4 defeat of Keighley and went on to score a record 816 points from 27 matches.

They also scored half centuries against Featherstone Rovers, Wakefield Trinity and Yorkshire.

The only club side to beat them was St. Helens, Oldham forcing a draw.

After losing the first two Tests, Australia finished with a third Test victory in a brawling match which gained notoriety as "The Battle of Odsal".

For the first time an Australian tour match was televised, when BBC covered the opening match at Keighley. The whole of the first Test match was also televised.

Australia used 23 players in the Test matches with only Clive Churchill, Brian Davies, Noel Hazzard and Duncan Hall playing in all three.

Captained by Willie Horne, Britain used 17 players in the Tests with nine playing in all three.

1956 TOUR

MATCH RESULTS

Liverpool C	won	40-12	4,712
Leeds	lost	13-18	24,459
Hull-Hull KR	won	37-14	17,172
Barrow	won	25-11	9,988
Whitehaven	lost	11-14	10,840
Bradford N	won	23-11	2,743
Warrington	lost	17-21	15,613
League XIII (Leigh)	**won**	**19-15**	**7,811**
York	won	20-18	6,842
Oldham	lost	2-21	8,458
Huddersfield	won	20-10	12,127
BRITAIN (Wigan)	**lost**	**10-21**	**22,473**
Hunslet	won	27-11	4,451
St. Helens	lost	2-44	15,579
BRITAIN (Bradford)	**won**	**22-9**	**23,634**
Halifax	lost	3-6	2,254
Wigan	won	32-4	15,854
Wakefield T	lost	12-17	3,381
BRITAIN (Swinton)	**lost**	**0-19**	**17,542**

SUMMARY

Played 19 Won 10 Lost 9

For
Tries 69 Goals 64 Points 335

Against
Tries 58 Goals 61 Points 296

Lost Test series 2-1

Attendance total: 225,933

TOUR PARTY

Managers: C. Fahy and C. Connell
Captain: K. Kearney

	App	Tries	Gls	Pts
D. Adams	8	6	0	18
R. Banks	13	3	0	9
R. Bull	14	2	0	6
C. Churchill	9	0	11	22
G. Clifford	9	1	34	71
G. Connell	9	6	1	20
B. Davies	10	5	1	17
L. Doyle	10	2	0	6
D. Flannery	11	8	0	24
D. Furner	10	0	3	6
E. Hammerton	8	0	0	0
K. Holman	10	5	2	19
I. Johnston	6	3	0	9
K. Kearney	11	0	0	0
W. Marsh	12	3	0	9
D. McGovern	8	5	0	15
I. Moir	10	7	0	21
K. O'Brien	7	2	0	6
B. Orrock	3	0	0	0
K. O'Shea	11	2	0	6
T. Payne	8	0	0	0
R. Poole	12	6	0	18
N. Provan	9	0	0	0
B. Purcell	6	0	12	24
T. Tyquin	10	2	0	6
A. Watson	13	1	0	3

MEMO

First match on October 10, last match on December 15.

A disappointing tour with no player totalling more than 10 tries during a programme reduced to fewer than 20 matches for the first time.

They were badly hit by a series of injuries to Norman Provan, one of their greatest ever forwards, which caused him to miss all three Test matches.

Alan Prescott led Britain and was one of nine players to appear in all three Tests.

Clive Churchill, regarded as one of the legendary figures of Australian rugby, ended an illustrious international career against Britain after the first Test.

Ken Kearney returned as captain of the tour squad after having played for Leeds.

Ernie Hammerton, eight tour appearances.

1959 TOUR

MATCH RESULTS

Leeds	won	44-20	14,629
Rochdale H	won	27-14	10,155
Warrington	won	30-24	17,112
Lancashire (St. Helens)	**lost**	**22-30**	**15,743**
Salford	won	22-20	11,008
Yorkshire (York)	**lost**	**15-47**	**7,338**
Widnes	won	45-15	9,381
Oldham	won	25-14	17,630
Leigh	lost	17-18	11,932
St. Helens	won	15-2	29,156
BRITAIN (Swinton)	**won**	**22-14**	**35,224**
Whitehaven-Workington T	won	13-8	7,463
Barrow	lost	9-12	8,488
Hull-Hull KR	won	29-9	15,944
Bradford N	won	29-8	4,126
Halifax	won	17-5	8,274
Featherstone R	lost	15-23	7,671
Wigan	lost	9-16	24,466
BRITAIN (Leeds)	**lost**	**10-11**	**30,184**
Swinton	won	25-24	5,021
Wakefield T	lost	10-20	17,615
Huddersfield	won	21-7	2,349
Hunslet	won	12-11	8,061
BRITAIN (Wigan)	**lost**	**12-18**	**26,089**

SUMMARY

Played 24   Won 15   Lost 9

For
Tries 93   Goals 108   Points 495

Against
Tries 68   Goals 93   Points 390

Lost Test series 2-1

Attendance total: 345,059

TOUR PARTY:

Managers: J. Argent and E. Keefer
Captain: K. Barnes   Coach: C. Churchill

	App	Tries	Gls	Pts
K. Barnes	12	0	52	104
D. Beattie	15	0	0	0
R. Boden	11	4	0	12
A. Brown	6	2	0	6
R. Budgen	5	4	0	12
P. Burke	8	4	0	12
B. Carlson	15	10	39	108
D. Chapman	12	1	0	3
B. Clay	14	2	0	6
W. Delamere	11	2	0	6
R. Gasnier	12	14	0	42
B. Hambly	12	5	0	15
K. Irvine	13	7	0	21
N. Kelly	9	2	0	6
E. Lumsden	16	8	0	24
R. Mossop	19	0	0	0
B. Muir	13	1	0	3
G. Parcell	12	1	0	3
D. Parish	9	3	16	41
J. Paterson	12	2	0	6
J. Raper	8	7	0	21
E. Rasmussen	13	3	1	11
J. Riley	11	2	0	6
I. Walsh	15	1	0	3
H. Wells	16	6	0	18
W. Wilson	13	2	0	6

MEMO
First match September 12, last match December 12.
Australia again flattered to deceive. After winning the first Test they went down in the other two, but only a late try and goal robbed them of the Ashes in the second Test.
Reg Gasnier made a sensational first tour and went on to become probably Australia's greatest centre of all time.
Gasnier scored three tries on his Test match debut and was a prominent figure in the other two.
Australia used only 15 players for the three Test matches, led each time by Keith Barnes.
The second Test saw the start of Neil Fox's long career for Britain. In the third Test the big centre scored 15 of Britain's 18 points with six goals and a try.

Harry Wells, six tries in 16 matches.

261

1963 TOUR

MATCH RESULTS

Warrington	won	28-20	20,090
Huddersfield	won	6-5	13,398
Yorkshire (Hull KR)	**lost**	**5-11**	**10,324**
Leeds	won	13-10	16,641
Lancashire (Wigan)	**lost**	**11-13**	**15,068**
St. Helens	won	8-2	21,284
Featherstone R	lost	17-23	7,898
Oldham	won	12-4	11,338
Leigh	won	33-7	9,625
Hull-Hull KR XIII	won	23-10	10,481
BRITAIN (Wembley)	**won**	**28-2**	**13,946**
Rochdale H	won	3-0	8,637
Hunslet	won	17-13	4,400
Wakefield T	won	29-14	15,821
Cumberland (Workington)	**won**	**21-0**	**8,229**
Barrow	won	18-5	10,130
BRITAIN (Swinton)	**won**	**50-12**	**30,833**
Castleford	lost	12-13	7,887
Wigan	won	18-10	11,746
Widnes	won	20-9	6,509
Swinton	drew	2-2	11,947
BRITAIN (Leeds)	**lost**	**5-16**	**20,497**

SUMMARY

Played 22   Won 16   Drew 1   Lost 5

For
Tries 75   Goals 77   Points 379

Against
Tries 31   Goals 54   Points 201

Won Test series 2-1

Attendance total: 286,729

Johnny Raper, two tries in 13 appearances.

TOUR PARTY

Managers: J. Lynch and A. Sparkes
Captain: A. Summons

	App	Tries	Gls	Pts
J. Cleary	6+1	0	0	0
M. Cleary	13	6	0	18
K. Day	9	0	0	0
P. Dimond	15	6	0	18
P. Gallagher	12	0	0	0
R. Gasnier	10	11	0	33
J. Gleeson	5	0	0	0
R. Hambly	13	1	0	3
E. Harrison	11+1	3	0	9
K. Irvine	17	17	2	55
L. Johns	10	2	24	54
N. Kelly	14	1	0	3
G. Langlands	15	11	51	135
J. Lisle	8	0	0	0
B. Muir	13	1	0	3
P. Quinn	15	1	0	3
J. Raper	13	2	0	6
B. Rushworth	10+1	5	0	15
K. Ryan	4	0	0	0
K. Smyth	8	1	0	3
F. Stanton	9+1	1	0	3
A. Summons	7	0	0	0
K. Thornett	11	1	0	3
R. Thornett	15	4	0	12
I. Walsh	16	1	0	3
G. Wilson	7	0	0	0

MEMO

First match September 14, last match November 30.

One of the most successful of all touring teams to Britain, the Australians returned home with the Ashes for the first time since 1911-12.

They clinched the series in the second Test with a record victory over Britain of 50-12. Britain were reduced to 11 men during the match because of injuries, but Australia had already displayed their superiority.

In the first Test at Wembley Australia won 28-2 with Reg Gasnier scoring another hat-trick of tries, the match watched by the Duke of Edinburgh.

Britain made several changes for the third Test which they won 16-5. This was a brawling affair at Headingley with referee Eric Clay sending off Australia's Brian Hambly and Barry Muir, plus Britain's Cliff Watson.

Although Arthur Summons was captain and coach of the squad, he did not play against Britain, Ian Walsh leading Australia in all three Tests.

The only club teams to beat Australia were Castleford and Featherstone Rovers but the Kangaroos also lost to Lancashire and Yorkshire.

1967 TOUR

MATCH RESULTS

Warrington	won	16-7	11,642
Yorkshire (Wakefield)	**lost**	**14-15**	**19,370**
Hull K.R.	lost	15-27	11,252
Lancashire (Salford)	**won**	**14-2**	**9,369**
Wigan	lost	6-12	22,770
Rochdale H	won	25-2	2,676
BRITAIN (Leeds)	**lost**	**11-16**	**22,293**
St. Helens	lost	4-8	17,275
Wakefield T	won	33-7	10,056
BRITAIN, (W'City, London)	**won**	**17-11**	**17,445**
Castleford	lost	3-22	6,137
Oldham	won	18-8	3,174
Widnes	won	33-11	9,828
Barrow	drew	10-10	8,418
Cumberland (Workington)	**lost**	**15-17**	**7,545**
Swinton	won	12-9	5,640
Leeds	won	7-4	5,522
Halifax	won	22-2	5,285
Bradford N	won	7-3	14,173
BRITAIN (Swinton)	**won**	**11-3**	**13,615**

SUMMARY

Played 20   Won 12   Drew 1   Lost 7

For
Tries 57   Goals 61   Points 293

Against
Tries 30   Goals 53   Points 196

Won Test series 2-1

Attendance total: 223,485

TOUR PARTY

Managers: J. Drewes and H. Schmidt
Captain: R. Gasnier

	App	Tries	Gls	Pts
A. Branson	11 + 1	3	0	9
R. Coote	13	5	0	15
N. Gallagher	10	0	0	0
P. Gallagher	11 + 1	1	0	3
R. Gasnier	5	1	0	3
J. Gleeson	11	2	1	8
J. Greaves	10	2	0	6
K. Goldspink	9	0	0	0
L. Hanigan	8	2	0	6
K. Irvine	13	8	5	34
L. Johns	9 + 1	1	5	13
K. Junee	6	2	1	8
N. Kelly	12	0	0	0
J. King	13	8	0	24
G. Langlands	14	3	36	81
R. Lynch	12	2	0	6
J. McDonald	11	4	10	32
D. Manteit	10 + 1	2	0	6
B. Moore	7	4	0	12
J. Raper	9	0	0	0
E. Rasmussen	13	0	0	0
R. Saddler	8	0	0	0
J. Sattler	9 + 1	0	0	0
W. Smith	11	3	3	15
A. Thomson	8 + 1	2	0	6
E. Walters	5	2	0	6

*Including substitute appearances

MEMO

First match September 30, last match December 9.

Australia retained the Ashes with victory in the third Test at a frostbound Swinton. Heavy snow fell during the match in which Arthur Keegan's tackling at full back kept Australia's winning margin down to 11-3.

Britain had won the first Test at Headingley, but lost the second at White City, London.

Reg Gasnier's great international career ended in the first Test when he received a broken leg, a match which was Roger Millward's first Test against Australia.

In Gasnier's absence, Peter Gallagher captained Australia in the second Test and Johnny Raper took over for the third.

Australia recovered after losing five of their first eight matches although they later crashed 22-3 at Castleford.

Tour skipper Reg Gasnier.

1973 TOUR

MATCH RESULTS

Salford	won	15-12	11,064
Wakefield T	won	13-9	5,863
Dewsbury	won	17-3	5,685
Castleford	won	*18-10	2,419
Widnes	won	25-10	5,185
Oldham	won	44-10	2,895
Cumbria (Whitehaven)	**won**	**28-2**	**3,666**
Bradford N	won	50-14	5,667
BRITAIN (Wembley)	**lost**	**12-21**	**9,874**
Hull K.R.	won	25-9	5,150
Huddersfield	won	32-2	1,333
Leigh	won	31-4	2,607
St. Helens	lost	7-11	10,013
Featherstone R	won	18-13	5,659
BRITAIN (Leeds)	**won**	**14-6**	**16,674**
BRITAIN (Warrington)	**won**	**15-5**	**10,019**

*Australia's score includes penalty under 7-point try rule although this was not within International Rules.

SUMMARY

Played 16   Won 14   Lost 2

For
Tries 81   Goals 60   Drop goals 1   Points 364

Against
Tries 18   Goals 42   Drop goals 3   Points 141

Won Test series 2-1

Attendance total: 103,773

TOUR PARTY

Managers: C. Gibson and A. Bishop
Captain-coach: Graeme Langlands

	App	Tries	Gls	Pts
A. Beetson	13	3	0	9
R. Branighan	10+1	6	0	18
M. Cronin	8+1	6	23	64
G. Eadie	10	4	10	32
R. Fulton	10+1	16	0(1)	49
E. Goodwin	6+1	5	0	15
W. Hamilton	5+2	1	0	3
J. Lang	6	1	0	3
G. Langlands	8	4	27	66
R. McCarthy	8	4	0	12
K. Maddison	11+1	5	0	15
J. O'Neill	3+1	0	0	0
R. O'Reilly	11+1	0	0	0
W. Orr	5+1	2	0	6
T. Pickup	8+1	2	0	6
G. Pierce	6	0	0	0
T. Randall	5	1	0	3
T. Raudonikis	9	3	0	9
S. Rogers	5+1	2	0	6
P. Sait	10+1	2	0	6
G. Starling	10+1	7	0	21
G. Stevens	7	1	0	3
D. Waite	9+1	4	0	12
E. Walters	11+1	2	0	6
D. Ward	7	0	0	0
L. Williamson	7+1	0	0	0

( )One point drop goal

MEMO

First match September 30, last match December 1.

After losing the series Down Under in 1970, Australia returned to power despite being convincingly beaten in the first Test at Wembley.

They won the second Test at Headingley and regained the Ashes with a 15-5 victory at Warrington on a frostbound pitch. Australia scored five tries to one to win much more easily than the score suggests.

St. Helens were the only club side to beat the tourists, with Bradford Northern suffering the biggest defeat by 50-14.

A serious hand injury ruled out tour captain Graeme Langlands for the second and third Tests, giving the chance for Graham Eadie to emerge as a new Test star at full back.

Other stars of the tour were Bobby Fulton and Arthur Beetson, while centres Steve Rogers and Mick Cronin were to gain valuable experience as stars of the future.

Bobby Fulton, 16 tries in 11 appearances.

1978 TOUR

MATCH RESULTS

Blackpool B	won	39-1	2,700
Cumbria (Barrow)	**won**	**47-4**	**5,964**
Britain Under-24 (Hull KR)	**won**	**30-8**	**6,418**
Bradford N	won	21-11	15,755
Warrington	lost	12-15	10,143
Wales (Swansea)	**won**	**8-3**	**4,250**
Leeds	won	25-19	9,781
BRITAIN (Wigan)	**won**	**15-9**	**17,644**
Widnes	lost	10-11	12,202
Hull	won	34-2	10,723
Salford	won	14-2	6,155
BRITAIN (Bradford)	**lost**	**14-18**	**26,447**
Wigan	won	28-2	10,645
St. Helens	won	26-4	16,352
York	won	29-2	5,155
BRITAIN (Leeds)	**won**	**23-6**	**29,627**

SUMMARY

Played 16   Won 13   Lost 3

For
Tries 79   Goals 68   Drop goals 2   Points 375

Against
Tries 12   Goals 39   Drop goals 3   Points 117

Won Test series 2-1

Attendance total: 189,961

TOUR PARTY

Managers: P. Moore and J. Caldwell
Captain: R. Fulton   Coach: F. Stanton

	App	Tries	Gls	Pts
C. Anderson	9	3	0	9
K. Boustead	10	2	0	6
L. Boyd	7+1	3	0	9
L. Corowa	5	4	0	12
M. Cronin	10+1	2	46	98
G. Eadie	9+1	4	0	12
R. Fulton	12	9	0(2)	29
G. Gerard	8+2	3	0	9
J. Gibbs	2	1	0	3
R. Hilditch	5	1	0	3
S. Kneen	5	2	0	6
M. Krilich	6	0	0	0
A. McMahon	8	6	1	20
S. Martin	4+3	1	0	3
R. Morris	7+2	2	0	6
G. Oliphant	3	0	0	0
G. Olling	7	2	0	6
G. Peponis	6	6	0	18
G. Pierce	4	0	0	0
R. Price	9+1	2	0	6
T. Raudonikis	11	4	0	12
R. Reddy	10	3	0	9
S. Rogers	12	8	21	66
I. Schubert	8	3	0	9
A. Thompson	9+4	4	0	12
I. Thomson	8+2	0	0	0
B. Walker	5	2	0	6
C. Young	9+2	2	0	6

( )One point drop goal

MEMO

First match September 30, last match November 18.

Australia's dominance continued despite going down to Britain's "Dad's Army" pack in the second Test at Odsal.

The Kangaroos had a narrow first Test win but retained the Ashes with a runaway success in the third Test at Headingley.

The only club teams to beat the tourists were Warrington and Widnes.

Defence was the tourists' strong point. They did not concede a try until their fourth match and finished with only 12 against them in 16 matches.

The tourists did much to revive interest in international rugby with attendances showing a big increase over the previous tour.

It was a magnificent farewell to touring for Australia's captain Bobby Fulton, but a sad end to the wonderful Test career of Britain's captain Roger Millward.

Prop Craig Young, two tries in 11 appearances.

265

1982 TOUR

MATCH RESULTS

Hull KR	won	30-10	10,742
Wigan	won	13-9	12,158
Barrow	won	29-2	6,282
St. Helens	won	32-0	8,190
Leeds	won	31-4	11,570
Wales (Cardiff)	**won**	**37-7**	**5,617**
BRITAIN (Hull C FC)	**won**	**40-4**	**26,771**
Leigh	won	44-4	7,680
Bradford N	won	13-6	10,506
Cumbria (Carlisle)	**won**	**41-2**	**5,748**
Fulham	won	22-5	10,432
Hull	won	13-7	16,049
BRITAIN (Wigan)	**won**	**27-6**	**23,216**
Widnes	won	19-6	9,790
BRITAIN (Leeds)	**won**	**32-8**	**17,318**

SUMMARY

Played 15   Won 15   Lost 0

For
Tries 97   Goals 66   Points 423

Against
Tries 7   Goals 29   Drop goals 1   Points 80

Won Test series 3-0

Attendance total: 182,069

Manly hooker Max Krilich, 1982 Kangaroo skipper.

TOUR PARTY

Managers: F. Farrington and T. Drysdale
Captain: M. Krilich   Coach: F. Stanton

	App	Tries	Gls	Pts
C. Anderson	7	3	0	9
K. Boustead	8 + 1	8	0	24
L. Boyd	10	3	0	9
G. Brentnall	9	1	0	3
R. Brown	5 + 4	0	0	0
G. Conescu	2 + 2	1	0	3
S. Ella	7 + 1	9	3	33
E. Grothe	7	7	0	21
R. Hancock	4	0	0	0
B. Kenny	8	2	0	6
M. Krilich	8	1	0	3
W. Lewis	7 + 5	3	9	27
P. McCabe	8	7	0	21
D. McKinnon	5	3	1	11
M. Meninga	10	6	50	118
G. Miles	6	1	0	3
R. Morris	6 + 2	0	0	0
S. Mortimer	5	2	0	6
J. Muggleton	6 + 2	4	0	12
M. Murray	4 + 1	3	0	9
W. Pearce	9	4	0	12
R. Price	6 + 2	2	0	6
R. Reddy	8	1	0	3
J. Ribot	8	10	0	30
S. Rogers	9 + 3	8	3	30
I. Schubert	7	2	0	6
P. Sterling	8	5	0	15
C. Young	8	1	0	3

MEMO

First match October 10, last match November 28.

The young 28-man squad — only two players were over 30 — rewrote the record books by displaying a showcase of skill, strength and speed that was to thrill millions worldwide and set alarm bells ringing throughout the British game.

The 1982 Kangaroos became the first touring party from any country to win all their matches in Britain and the first tourists to win all three Tests in Britain, their total of 99 points being the most scored in an Anglo-Aussie Test series in either country.

The tourists amassed 97 tries and conceded only seven in their 15-match programme in which they piled up 27 points or more on 10 occasions.

Tour stars such as triple record breaker Mal Meninga, inspiring captain Max Krilich, mercurial Peter Sterling, artistic Brett Kenny and rampaging Wayne Pearce captivated the British public, the average tour gate of 12,138 being the best for 20 years.

1986 TOUR

MATCH RESULTS

Wigan	won	26-18	30,622
Hull KR	won	46-10	6,868
Leeds	won	40-0	11,389
Cumbria (Barrow)	**won**	**48-12**	**4,233**
BRITAIN (Man U FC)	**won**	**38-16**	**50,583**
Halifax	won	36-2	7,193
St. Helens	won	32-8	15,381
Oldham	won	22-16	5,678
BRITAIN (Elland Rd, Leeds)	**won**	**34-4**	**30,808**
Widnes	won	20-4	10,268
Hull	won	48-0	8,213
Bradford N.	won	38-0	10,663
BRITAIN (Wigan)	**won**	**24-15**	**20,169**

SUMMARY

Played 13   Won 13   Lost 0

For
Tries 85   Goals 56   Points 452

Against
Tries 14   Goals 24   Drop goals 1   Points 105

Won Test series 3-0

Attendance total: 212,068

MEMO

First match October 12, last match November 22.

The Kangaroos arrived with the added pressure of being compared with the 1982 *Invincibles* who won all their matches. They responded by equalling that feat and earning the tag of *Invincibles II.*

Their 13-match tour was the shortest ever but they again made a lasting impression with the average attendance of 16,313, second only to the 16,732 of 1948.

It opened with an all-time record crowd for a club tour game of 30,622 at Wigan and the first Test attracted the biggest-ever attendance for an international match in this country of 50,583 at Old Trafford, Manchester.

Captain Wally Lewis was elected the outstanding player, while Terry Lamb emerged as the busiest after playing in all 13 matches including seven as substitute.

The Kangaroos' 100 per cent success record meant they had not lost in Britain since the second Test of 1978, giving them a winning run of 32 matches.

They also went on to win all seven matches in France for the second successive trip.

TOUR PARTY

Managers: J. Fleming and G. Treichel
Captain: W. Lewis   Coach: D. Furner

	App	Tries	Gls	Pts
G. Alexander	5 + 1	8	5	42
G. Belcher	6	2	0	8
M. Bella	6	1	0	4
N. Cleal	7	3	0	12
P. Daley	3 + 1	0	0	0
L. Davidson	5 + 4	0	0	0
G. Dowling	6 + 1	1	0	4
P. Dunn	6 + 1	0	0	0
B. Elias	6	3	0	12
S. Folkes	3	0	0	0
D. Hasler	2 + 1	2	0	8
G. Jack	7	5	0	20
B. Kenny	8 + 1	4	0	16
L. Kiss	4	1	0	4
T. Lamb	6 + 7	15	13	86
P. Langmack	6	1	0	4
W. Lewis	7	6	0	24
R. Lindner	7	3	0	12
M. Meninga	8 + 3	5	7	34
G. Miles	8	6	0	24
C. Mortimer	6	3	0	12
B. Niebling	7	1	0	4
M. O'Connor	8 + 1	7	31	90
S. Roach	4	0	0	0
D. Shearer	9	6	0	24
R. Simmons	7	0	0	0
P. Sironen	5 + 2	0	0	0
P. Sterling	7	2	0	8

AUSTRALIA APPENDIX

In addition to full tours, World Cup parties made occasional appearances as follows, Australia score first:

1960	St. Helens	lost	12-15	12,750
1970	St. Helens	lost	10-37	15,570
1972	St. Helens	won	24-9	10,000
	Wigan	drew	18-18	6,000
	Bradford N	won	29-16	2,820
1975	Salford	won	44-6	5,357
	St. Helens	won	32-7	10,170
	Oldham	won	20-10	3,575
	York	won	45-4	4,082
	England (Leeds)	won	25-0	7,680

(cont)

RECORDS AGAINST CLUB SIDES

Highest score: 92-7 v. Bramley in 1921-22
(Also widest margin win)
Biggest defeat: 2-44 v. St. Helens in 1956. Also lost
55-11 to Yorkshire in 1952, their biggest defeat in any
match on tour
Biggest attendance: 30,622 v. Wigan in 1986

INDIVIDUAL RECORDS

Club and representative matches
Most tries on tour: 39 by C. Blinkhorn in 1921-22
Most goals and points on tour: 114g-285pts (19t) by
  D. Brown in 1933-34
Most appearances on tour: 35 by L. O'Malley in 1908-09

AUSTRALIA TOURS OF FRANCE

Each tour immediately
followed trip to Britain

	P	W	D	L	F	A
1937-38 Won Test series 2-0	10	9	—	1	267	80
1948-49 Won Test series 2-0	10	9	—	1	279	71
1952-53 Lost Test series 2-1	13	10	—	3	301	125
1956-57 Won Test series 3-0	9	8	1	—	207	110
1959-60 Won Test series 3-0	11	9	—	2	277	120
1963-64 Won Test series 2-1	14	12	—	2	328	111
1967-68 Lost Test series 2-0, one drawn	7	4	1	2	105	53
1973-74 Won Test series 2-0	3	3	—	—	59	24
1978-79 Lost Test series 2-0	6	3	—	3	116	73
1982-83 Won Test series 2-0	7	7	—	—	291	20
1986-87 Won Test series 2-0	7	7	—	—	286	21

● During their tour of Britain in 1933-34 Australia beat
England 63-13 in Paris in an exhibition game.

● The 1960 World Cup squad played an extra game
against France, winning 37-12. The 1970 squad beat
France 7-4 and France B 36-8. In 1975, Rouergue were
beaten 35-4.

AUSTRALIA TOURS OF NEW ZEALAND

	P	W	D	L	F	A
1919 Won Test series 3-1	9	8	—	1	443	101
1935 Won Test series 2-1	6	5	—	1	173	95
1937	3	1	—	2	32	40

En route to Britain, the Australians played two Test
matches against New Zealand recording a win and a loss.
They also lost against the Maoris.

	P	W	D	L	F	A
1949 Drew Test series 1-1	10	9	—	1	299	123
1953 Lost Test series 2-1	9	7	—	2	366	98
1961 Drew Test series 1-1	9	7	—	2	215	68
1965 Drew Test series 1-1	8	7	—	1	159	58
1969 Drew Test series 1-1	6	4	—	2	137	78
1971 Lost Test series 1-0	3	1	—	2	52	53
1980 Won Test series 2-0	7	5	1	1	158	48
1985 Won Test series 2-1 including one Test win in Australia	6	5	—	1	192	44
1989 Won Test series 3-0	6	5	—	1	158	74

● World Cup squads also played extra games as follows:

1975 Beat Auckland 17-6.

1977 Beat South Island 68-5 and lost 19-15 to Auckland.

1988 Beat Wellington Invitation 24-12.

AUSTRALIA TOUR SQUADS TO NEW ZEALAND
Captains in bold

1919

A. Halloway

F. Burge
L. Cubitt
C. Fraser
H. Gilbert
A. Halloway
H. Horder
A. Johnston
J. Kerwick
R. Latta
R. Norman
C. O'Donnell
A. Oxford
B. Paten
N. Potter
C. Prentice
J. Robinson
F. Ryan
W. Schultz
T. Sweeney
D. Thompson
C. Thorogood
R. Townsend
R. Vest
J. Watkins

Managers: C. Upton
W. Webb

1935

D. Brown

H. Bichel
D. Brown
E. Collins
F. Curran
P. Fairall
J. Gibbs
F. Gilbert
S. Goodwin
R. Hines
E. Lewis
W. Mahon
R. McKinnon
E. Norman
S. Pearce
W. Prigg
M. Shields
R. Stehr
V. Thicknesse
L. Ward
J. Whittle

Managers: W. Chareling
H. Sunderland

1949

K. Froome

V. Bulgin
R. Bull
C. Churchill
L. Cowie
F. de Belin
K. Froome
J. Graves
R. Griffiths
K. Hansen
J. Hawke
J. Holland
I. Johnston
M. McCoy
P. McMahon
N. Mulligan
W. O'Connell
J. Rayner
R. Roberts
K. Schubert
F. Stanmore
A. Thompson
W. Thompson

Managers: A. Thompson
F. Moynihan

1953

C. Churchill

F. Ashton
R. Banks
R. Bull
B. Carlson
C. Churchill
L. Cowie
H. Crocker
B. Davies
B. Drew
C. Gill
G. Hawick
K. Holman
A. Hornery
K. Kearney
K. McCaffery
D. McGovern
A. Paul
N. Pidding
A. Watson
H. Wells

Managers: D. Locke
G. McLeod

1961

B. Carlson

D. Beattie
R. Beaven
B. Carlson
R. Crowe
K. Day
F. Drake
R. Gasnier
R. Gehrke
A. Gill
K. Irvine
E. Lumsden
R. Lynch
B. Muir
W. Owen
D. Parish
J. Paterson
E. Rasmussen
J. Sinclair
A. Summons
I. Walsh

Managers: J. Kessey
J. Allen

1965

I. Walsh

B. Beath
A. Buman
N. Cavanagh
M. Cleary
R. Gasnier
J. Gleeson
B. Hambly
K. Irvine
L. Johns
G. Langlands
J. Lisle
J. Morgan
T. Pannowitz
P. Quinn
W. Smith
M. Veivers
I. Walsh
L. Weier
G. Wellington
N. Yakich

Managers: A. Stehr
D. Green

1969

J. Sattler

M. Cleary
R. Coote
J. Cootes
R. Costello
J. Denman
B. Fitzsimmons
R. Honan
L. Johns
G. Langlands
G. Lye
D. Manteit
R. McCarthy
J. McDonald
D. Pittard
I. Robson
J. Sattler
E. Walters
D. Ward
C. Weiss
J. Wittenberg

Managers: E. Burns
J. Lynch
Coach: H. Bath

1971

G. Langlands

B. Beath
W. Bennett
R. Branighan
A. Branson
K. Campbell
R. Costello
B. Fitzsimmons
R. Fulton
R. Grant
G. Langlands
R. McCarthy
J. Murphy
R. O'Reilly
T. Raudonikis
P. Sait
J. Sattler
G. Starling
L. Williamson

Managers: R. Dunn
R. Stafford
Coach: H. Bath

1980

G. Peponis

C. Anderson
K. Boustead
L. Boyd
G. Brentnall
C. Close
M. Cronin
G. Dowling
R. Hancock
J. Lang
J. Leis
S. Martin
R. Morris
G. Peponis
R. Price
G. Quinn
T. Raudonikis
R. Reddy
A. Thompson
G. Wynn
C. Young

Managers: T. Bellow
J. Caldwell
Coach: F. Stanton

1985

W. Lewis

N. Cleal
C. Close
G. Conescu
G. Dowling
B. Elias
S. Ella
J. Ferguson
W. Fullerton-Smith
D. Hasler
G. Jack
W. Lewis
M. Meninga
M. Murray
M. O'Connor
W. Pearce
J. Ribot
S. Roach
P. Tunks
P. Vautin
P. Wynn

Managers: J. Garrahy
D. Barnhill
Coach: T. Fearnley

1989

W. Lewis

G. Alexander
S. Backo
G. Belcher
M. Bella
B. Clyde
A. Currie
M. Hancock
D. Hasler
P. Jackson
W. Lewis
B. McGuire
M. Meninga
M. O'Connor
S. Roach
D. Shearer
P. Sironen
D. Stains
D. Trewhella
P. Vautin
Kerrod Walters

Managers: K. Brasch
P. Moore
Coach: R. Fulton

Wally Lewis, captain of the 1985 and 1989 Australian tour squads to New Zealand.

AUSTRALIA WORLD CUP SQUADS

1954 in France	1957 in Australia	1960 in Britain
C. Churchill	**R. Poole**	**K. Barnes**
R. Banks	K. Barnes	K. Barnes
R. Bull	B. Carlson	D. Beattie
C. Churchill	B. Clay	R. Boden
M. Crocker	B. Davies	A. Brown
B. Davies	G. Hawick	R. Budgen
P. Diversi	K. Holman	B. Carlson
D. Flannery	K. Kearney	R. Gasnier
D. Hall	W. Marsh	B. Hambly
G. Hawick	K. McCaffery	K. Irvine
K. Holman	I. Moir	N. Kelly
K. Kearney	K. O'Shea	L. Morgan
K. McCaffery	R. Poole	R. Mossop
I. Moir	N. Provan	B. Muir
K. O'Shea	R. Ritchie	G. Parcell
N. Pidding	D. Schofield	J. Raper
N. Provan	T. Tyquin	E. Rasmussen
A. Watson	A. Watson	W. Rayner
H. Wells	H. Wells	H. Wells

Managers: J. McMahon
          S. O'Neill
Coach: V. Hey

Manager: N. C. Robinson
Coach: R. Poole

Managers: J. O'Toole
          P. Duggan
Coach: K. Barnes

1968 in Australia and New Zealand	1970 in Britain	1972 in France
J. Raper	**R. Coote**	**G. Langlands**
A. Beetson	R. Branighan	A. Beetson
A. Branson	J. Brown	E. Branighan
R. Coote	R. Coote	J. Elford
B. Fitzsimmons	J. Cootes	R. Fulton
R. Fulton	R. Costello	J. Grant
J. Greaves	R. Fulton	M. Harris
B. James	M. Harris	F. Jones
F. Jones	R. McCarthy	S. Knight
J. King	B. McTaggart	G. Langlands
G. Langlands	J. O'Neill	R. McCarthy
D. Manteit	R. O'Reilly	J. O'Neill
J. Raper	D. Pittard	R. O'Reilly
E. Rasmussen	P. Sait	T. Raudonikis
J. Rhodes	E. Simms	P. Sait
E. Simms	W. Smith	G. Starling
W. Smith	G. Sullivan	G. Stevens
R. Thornett	R. Turner	G. Sullivan
L. Williamson	E. Walters	E. Walters
J. Wittenberg	L. Williamson	D. Ward

Managers: A. M. Kingston
Coach: H. Bath

Managers: K. Arthurson
          J. B. Quinn
Coach: H. Bath

Managers: A. M. Kingston
          J. Clark
Coach: H. Bath

1975 First phase In Australia	1975 Second phase in New Zealand, Britain and France	1977 in Australia and New Zealand
G. Langlands	**A. Beetson**	**A. Beetson**
C. Anderson	A. Beetson	A. Beetson
A. Beetson	J. Brass	S. Crear
R. Branighan	M. Cronin	M. Cronin
R. Coote	G. Eadie	G. Eadie
M. Cronin	D. Fitzgerald	T. Fahey
J. Donnelly	R. Higgs	D. Fitzgerald
T. Fahey	J. Lang	R. Gartner
R. Fulton	I. Mackay	E. Geiger
M. Harris	A. McMahon	M. Harris
J. Lang	J. Mayes	R. Higgs
G. Langlands	J. Peard	J. Kolc
J. O'Neill	G. Pierce	A. McMahon
T. Pickup	G. Piggins	J. Peard
L. Platz	L. Platz	G. Pierce
T. Randall	J. Porter	T. Randall
T. Raudonikis	J. Quayle	T. Raudonikis
J. Rhodes	T. Randall	R. Reddy
P. Sait	T. Raudonikis	M. Thomas
G. Stevens	J. Rhodes	G. Veivers
R. Strudwick	S. Rogers	
D. Wright	I. Schubert	Manager: C. Brown
	G. Veivers	D. Hall
Manager: R. Stafford		Coach: T. Fearnley
Coach: G. Langlands	Manager: R. Abbott	
	J. Cairns	
	Coach: G. Langlands	

RECORDS IN TEST AND WORLD CUP MATCHES

For Australia

Highest score: 70-8 v. Papua New Guinea at Wagga 20 July, 1988 (also widest margin)

Most tries in a match: 4 by J. Ribot v. Papua New Guinea at Port Moresby 2 Oct., 1982
    4 by D. Shearer v. France, Second Test at Carcassonne 13 Dec., 1986
    4 by M. O'Connor v. Papua New Guinea at Wagga 20 July, 1988

Most goals in a match: 10 by K. Barnes v. France, Second Test at Brisbane 2 July, 1960
    10 by E. Simms v. New Zealand, World Cup at Wigan 10 Oct., 1970
    10 by M. Cronin v. Britain, First Test at Brisbane 16 June, 1979

Most points in a match: 30(7g,4t) by M. O'Connor v. Papua New Guinea at Wagga 20 July, 1988

Most appearances: 45 by G. Langlands (1963-1975)

Most career tries: 34 by K. Irvine (1959-1967)

Most career goals: 141 by M. Cronin (1973-1982)

Most career points: 309(141g,9t) by M. Cronin (1973-1982)

Biggest attendance: 70,204 v. Britain, First Test at Sydney 6 June, 1932

Against Australia

Highest score: 49-25 v. New Zealand, Second Test at Brisbane 28 June, 1952 (also widest margin)

Most tries in a match: 4 by J. Leytham (Britain) Second Test at Brisbane 2 July, 1910

Most goals in a match: 11 by D. White (New Zealand) Second Test at Brisbane 28 June, 1952

Most points in a match: 22 by D. White (as above).

Kiwi threequarter Mark Elia, scorer of four tries in four games on the British leg of the 1989 tour.

1989 KIWIS

1989 KIWIS

1989 TOUR REVIEW

The 1989 Kiwis came within a try — a disallowed one at that — of maintaining their 24-year unbeaten Test series record on British soil.

Australian referee Greg McCallum rejected claims for a Gary Mercer touchdown in the closing minutes of the third British Coal Test at Wigan to send the New Zealanders tumbling to a 10-6 defeat, earning Great Britain their first home series success since 1965 by two Tests to one.

A draw at Central Park, having won comfortably at Old Trafford in the first encounter before being hammered at Elland Road, would have been a replica of the 1985 and 1980 tour tallies.

The 12th party of Kiwis, although losing the Test series, achieved a 66 per cent success rate in their 12 tour fixtures, which was on par with the best-ever success ratio. The midweek side, led by hooker Wayne Wallace and calling on only a few established Test stars, remained unbeaten while running up the tour's highest score — 44-8 at Hull and 44-20 at Featherstone — the former also being the widest margin.

The New Zealanders also produced the highest crowd aggregate since 1965, when 23 games were fulfilled, and the best for a Kiwi Test series since 1961.

A total of 115,423 saw the dozen tour matches compared with 107,347 at the same number of games on the last trip in 1985. The three-match British Coal Test series pulled in a total of 51,692 against 50,306 in 1985.

Yet there was a lack of excitement surrounding the seven-week visit. Against local advice, the New Zealanders elected to be based at York, isolating themselves from the media and the heartland of the 13-a-side code. In an era of public relations and promotions, Kiwi coach Tony Gordon proved to be taciturn, especially when compared with his 1985 predecessor Graham Lowe and recent Australian tour counterparts Don Furner and Frank Stanton.

On the playing front, the Kiwis failed to hit the headlines as crowd pleasers, particularly in the build-up to the first Test at Manchester United's Old Trafford. A dramatic defeat of their Test line-up in the opening game against an injury-hit St. Helens was followed by a late two-point victory over a Castleford side lacking half a dozen regulars. Defeat at Wigan preceded a comfortable victory at Bradford Northern, who were subsequently banned by the League from hosting a Kangaroo tour fixture in 1990 for playing a weakened side.

In the week of the opening Test, the Kiwis moved up a gear by hammering Leeds and Cumbria, the Headingley encounter producing a personality performance for the first time in the shape of scrum half Gary Freeman, a hat-trick hero.

With Great Britain's absentees through injury including crowdpullers Ellery Hanley, Joe Lydon, Garry Schofield and Kevin Ward, the Old Trafford encounter provided a disappointing attendance. Although a repeat of the 50,000-plus crowd for the first Test against the 1986 Australians was never anticipated, the 18,000 turnout was well below expectations.

The surprise 24-16 victory for the Kiwis was a well-earned success and yet only just over 13,000 passed through the turnstiles at Elland Road, Leeds, a week later to see Great Britain pull off one of the most memorable Test victories after being reduced to 12 men inside two minutes. A more satisfactory crowd of over 20,000 witnessed the tense decider at Wigan, Britain's first home series success over the Kiwis for 24 years.

The 1989 Kiwis were a combination of the fading, the familiar and the future. Skipper Hugh McGahan, while the perfect ambassador, was not the commanding figure of the past. With British clubs investing heavily in the world transfer market, many of the tourists were regulars on the domestic scene, particularly Kevin Iro and Adrian Shelford, who were released by Wigan for the tour, while top scorer Phil Bancroft, Morven Edwards, Mark Elia, Gary Freeman, Tony Kemp, Mike Kuiti, Gary Mercer, Kelly Shelford, Brent Todd and David Watson had all served British clubs. Experienced Dean Bell, of Wigan, and Widnes skipper Kurt Sorensen were also called up for the three British Coal Tests.

The refreshing new faces brightened up the midweek side and augered well for the development of international Rugby League in New Zealand. Esene Faimalo, Francis Leota and Tawera Nikau were among the newcomers to make an impact.

Following the French leg of the European trip, the following tourists joined British clubs on varying lengths of contracts: Kemp (Doncaster), Kuiti (Leeds), Leota and Nikau (Sheffield Eagles), Tea Ropati (St. Helens), Kelly Shelford (Whitehaven), Duane Mann and Mercer (Warrington), and Watson (Ryedale-York).

Second row man Nikau was the only player to be sent off, for dissent and later found not guilty, while 10 players were sent to the sin bin, Duane Mann and Darrell Williams twice.

Prop James Goulding, with a broken wrist, and centre Ropati were both sent home injured to be replaced by George Mann and David Ewe respectively. Ropati's knee injury subsequently prevented him from fulfilling a contract with St. Helens as he broke down after only half a match.

Great Britain's new sponsors, British Coal, provided Man of the Match awards in each of the three Tests. The inspirational Freeman was the winner in the first encounter, British stand off Shaun Edwards taking the honours at Elland Road with home winger Martin Offiah claiming the Wigan award. The British Coal Men of the Series, judged by the respective team managements, went to Edwards and Mercer.

New Zealand hooker Duane Mann faces British stand off Shaun Edwards in the second British Coal Test at Elland Road, Leeds.

BRITISH TOUR RESULTS

Date		Result	Score	Opposition	Venue	Attendance
Oct	1	L	26-27	St. Helens	St. Helens	7,040
	3	W	22-20	Castleford	Castleford	5,993
	8	L	14-24	Wigan	Wigan	15,013
	11	W	26-8	Bradford N.	Bradford	3,498
	15	W	34-4	Leeds	Leeds	9,632
	17	W	28-2	Cumbria	Whitehaven	3,983
	21	W	24-16	GREAT BRITAIN	Old Trafford, Man'r	18,273
	28	L	6-26	GREAT BRITAIN	Elland Road, Leeds	13,073
Nov	1	W	44-8	Hull	Hull	5,894
	5	W	26-18	Widnes	Widnes	9,905
	7	W	44-20	Featherstone R.	Featherstone	2,773
	11	L	6-10	GREAT BRITAIN	Wigan	20,346

BRITISH TOUR SUMMARY

				FOR					AGAINST			
P	W	D	L	T	G	Dr	Pts	T	G	Dr	Pts
12	8	0	4	50	49	2	300	30	31	1	183

BRITISH TEST SUMMARY

				FOR					AGAINST			
P	W	D	L	T	G	Dr	Pts	T	G	Dr	Pts
3	1	0	2	7	4	0	36	9	8	0	52

BRITISH TOUR RECORDS

Biggest attendance: 20,346, third Test at Wigan

Highest score: 44-8 v. Hull; 44-20 v. Featherstone R.

Widest margin: 44-8 v. Hull

Highest score against: Lost to St. Helens 27-26

Widest margin defeat: Lost to Great Britain 26-6

Most tries in a match: 3 by Gary Freeman v. Leeds

Most goals in a match:
      6 by Phil Bancroft v. Cumbria
                   v. Hull
                   v. Featherstone R.

Most points in match: 14 by Kelly Shelford (1 try and 5 goals) v. St. Helens

Most tries on tour: 6 by David Watson

Most goals on tour: 29 by Phil Bancroft

Most points on tour: 58 by Phil Bancroft

Most appearances: 9 (including two as substitute) by Sam Stewart

Most full appearances: 8 by Gary Mercer

Sent off: Tawera Nikau v. Hull

Sin bin: James Goulding v. St. Helens; Mark Elia v. Bradford N.; Duane Mann and Darrell Williams v. Leeds; Kelly Shelford v. Great Britain, first Test; Duane Mann and Gary Freeman v. Great Britain, second Test; Darrell Williams v. Widnes; Dean Clark v. Featherstone R.; Kurt Sorensen v. Great Britain, third Test

Opponent sent off: Steve Hampson (Great Britain, second Test)

Opponents' sin bin: David Croft (Bradford N.); Andy Goodway (Great Britain, first Test); John Devereux (Widnes)

FRENCH TOUR RESULTS

Date	Result	Score	Opposition	Venue	Attendance
Nov 15	W	36-12	**Midi-Pyrenees**	Toulouse	1,000

T: Watson (2), Leota (2), Elia, K. Shelford
G: Bancroft (6)

19	W	16-14	**FRANCE**	Carcassonne	4,830

France: Pougeau; Ratier (capt), Fourquet, Fraisse
(1t), Pons (1t); Dumas (3g), Entat; Rabot, Khedemi,
Buttignol, Divet, Cabestany, Bernabe. Subs:
Saumitou, Chamorin (both played).
New Zealand: Kemp; Iro (1t), Bell, Williams,
Mercer; K. Shelford (1t, 2g), Freeman (1t); Todd,
D. Mann, Faimalo, Sorensen, Stewart, McGahan
(capt). Subs: Leota, Kuiti (both played).
Referee: Robin Whitfield (England)

22	W	70-0	**Selection De L'aude**	Carcassone	500

T: Watson (4), Elia (2), Kemp (2), McGahan (2),
Taewa, Kuiti
G: Bancroft (11)

25	W	62-2	**France B**	Albi	1,126

T: Freeman (2), McGahan (2), Watson (2), G. Mann,
D. Mann, Nikau, Taewa, Clark
G: Edwards (5), Bancroft (4)

Dec 3	W	34-0	**FRANCE** (Also World Cup)	Carcassonne	4,208

France: Pougeau; Chiron, Fourquet, Fraisse, Pons;
Dumas (capt), Entat; Rabot, Khedemi, Storer,
Cabestany, Divet, Bernabe. Subs: Courty, Biennes
(both played).
New Zealand: Kemp (1t); Watson (3t), Bell (1t),
Williams (1t), Mercer; Clark, Freeman; Todd, D.
Mann, G. Mann, Kuiti (1t), Stewart, McGahan
(capt). Subs: Sherlock (3g), K. Shelford (both
played).
Referee: Robin Whitfield (England)

● A match against Provence-Cote D'Azur at Avignon was cancelled because of the tourists'
late arrival at the ground caused by a traffic hold-up.

FRENCH TOUR SUMMARY

				FOR			AGAINST		
P	W	L	T	G	Pts		T	G	Pts
5	5	0	39	31	218		4	6	28

TOUR PARTY

Managers: Ian Jenkins and Tom McKeown
Coach: Tony Gordon
Physiotherapist: Peter Boyle
Doctor: Wayne Morris

Player	Club	IN BRITAIN					IN FRANCE					TOUR TOTALS				
		App	Sub	T	G	Pts	App	Sub	T	G	Pts	App	Sub	T	G	Pts
BANCROFT, Phil	Auckland (NZ)	5	1	–	29	58	2	1	1	21	42	7	2	–	50	100
CLARK, Dean	Auckland (NZ)	5	1	1	–	4	3	–	1	–	4	8	1	2	–	8
EDWARDS, Morven	Wellington (NZ)	5	–	2	–	8	2	–	–	5	10	7	–	2	5	18
ELIA, Mark	Canterbury-Bankstown (Aus)	3	1	4	–	16	2	–	3	–	12	5	1	7	–	28
FAIMALO, Esene	Canterbury (NZ)	6	1	1	–	4	2	–	–	–	–	8	1	1	–	4
FREEMAN, Gary	Balmain (Aus)	7	1	5	–	20	3	–	3	–	12	10	1	8	–	32
GOULDING, James	Newcastle Knights (Aus)	4	1	1	–	4	Did not tour, injured					4	1	1	–	4
IRO, Kevin	Wigan (GB)	7	–	4	–	16	1	–	1	–	4	8	–	5	–	20
KEMP, Tony	Newcastle Knights (Aus)	6	2	1	–	4	3	1	3	–	12	9	2	4	–	16
KUITI, Mike	Wellington (NZ)	6	1	4	–	16	3	1	2	–	8	9	2	6	–	24
LEOTA, Francis	Auckland (NZ)	5	3	2	–	8	2	1	2	–	8	7	4	4	–	16
MANN, Duane	Auckland (NZ)	7	–	–	–	–	2	1	1	–	4	9	1	1	–	4
McGAHAN, Hugh	Eastern Suburbs (Aus)	7	–	3	(1)	13	4	–	4	–	16	11	–	7	(1)	29
MERCER, Gary	Bay of Plenty (NZ)	8	–	2	–	8	3	–	–	–	–	11	–	2	–	8
NIKAU, Tawera	Auckland (NZ)	5	1	2	–	8	2	1	1	–	4	7	1	3	–	12
ROPATI, Tea	Auckland (NZ)	2	–	–	–	–	Did not tour, injured					2	–	–	–	–
SHELFORD, Adrian	Wigan (GB)	4	–	–	–	–	Did not tour, injured					4	–	–	–	–
SHELFORD, Kelly	Auckland (NZ)	7	1	3	12(1)	37	2	1	2	2	12	9	1	5	14(1)	49
SHERLOCK, Kurt	Eastern Suburbs (Aus)	6	1	1	7	18	2	1	1	3	6	8	2	1	10	24
STEWART, Sam	Newcastle Knights (Aus)	7	2	1	–	4	2	1	–	–	–	9	3	1	–	4
TAEWA, Whetu	Canterbury (NZ)	5	–	3	–	12	3	–	2	–	8	8	–	5	–	20
TODD, Brent	Canberra (Aus)	7	–	–	–	–	2	–	–	–	–	9	–	–	–	–
TUUTA, Brendon	Canterbury (NZ)	5	1	1	–	4	3	–	–	–	–	8	1	1	–	4
WALLACE, Wayne	Canterbury (NZ)	5	1	1	–	4	3	–	–	–	–	8	1	1	–	4
WATSON, Dave	Auckland (NZ)	6	1	6	–	24	4	1	11	–	44	10	1	17	–	68
WILLIAMS, Darrell	Manly (Aus)	7	1	2	–	8	3	–	1	–	4	10	1	3	–	12
*EWE, David	Wellington (NZ)	2	1	–	1	2	Sent home without playing					2	1	–	1	2
†MANN, George	Mangere East (NZ)	1	1	–	–	–	4	–	1	–	4	5	1	1	–	4

( ) indicates drop goal.
* Replaced injured Tea Ropati.
† Replaced injured James Goulding.
(Aus) Australia (GB) Great Britain (NZ) New Zealand.
● Not in tour squad, Dean Bell (Wigan) played in five Tests, scoring one try, and Kurt Sorensen (Widnes) played in four Tests without scoring.

1989 Kiwis, left to right, Back Row: Kemp, Elia, Mercer, Nikau, Iro, Leota, Kuiti, Williams, Adrian Shelford. Middle Row: Peter Boyle (Physio), Stewart, Wallace, Ropati, Taewa, Sherlock, Faimalo, Edwards, Kelly Shelford, Clark, Wayne Morris (Doctor). Front Row: Watson, Duane Mann, Tony Gordon (Coach), Ian Jenkins (Manager), McGahan (Captain), Tom McKeown (Business Manager), Tuuta, Goulding, Bancroft.

MATCH BY MATCH

1 October

ST. HELENS	27
NEW ZEALAND	26

1. Williams
2. Mercer
3. Watson
4. Iro
5. Elia
6. K. Shelford
7. Freeman
8. A. Shelford (Nikau)
9. D. Mann
10. Goulding
11. Stewart
12. Faimalo
13. McGahan, Capt.

T: Elia (2), K. Shelford, Iro
G: K. Shelford (5)

St. Helens:
Veivers; Large, Haggerty, Hunte, Tanner; Bailey, Holding; Evans, Groves (Jones), Bateman, Forber, Cosgrove, Cooper

T: Hunte, Evans, Tanner, Forber
G: Tanner (5), Holding (dg)

Half-time: 7-14

Referee: Ray Tennant (Castleford)
Attendance: 7,040

Makeshift St. Helens entered the last quarter trailing 26-15 to New Zealand's virtual Test side. In a dramatic finish to a thrilling encounter, the Saints staged a magnificent comeback to snatch victory with a Forber try two minutes from time.

There was still enough time for the Kiwis to gain a morale boosting victory but stand off Kelly Shelford failed with a last minute penalty which drifted wide after prop forward Bateman, signed from Hunslet for £60,000 before the match, had strayed offside.

Having been in control for most of the game, New Zealand were left deflated by the defeat, also showing concern for a lack of discipline including conceding 15 penalties, mainly for offside, and having Goulding sent to the sin bin for a high tackle.

Injury-hit Saints took an early 7-0 lead before the visitors found their rhythm with tries from Kelly Shelford and Elia to lead 14-7 at the break. The Kiwis then appeared to clinch victory in the second half with touchdowns from Iro and Elia, while Kelly Shelford added his fifth goal.

3 October

CASTLEFORD	20
NEW ZEALAND	22

1. Edwards
2. Taewa
3. Iro
4. Sherlock
5. Ropati
6. Clark (Freeman)
7. Bancroft
8. Leota
9. Wallace, Capt.
10. Todd (Goulding)
11. Kuiti
12. Nikau
13. Tuuta

T: Iro, Wallace, Sherlock
G: Bancroft (5)

Castleford:
Gibson (Price); Ellis, Irwin, McAllister, Marchant; Smith, French; Clarke, Beardmore, Sampson, Ketteridge, Crabtree, Joyner (Whitehead)

T: French, Clarke, Crabtree
G: Ellis (4)

Half-time: 20-8

Referee: Robin Whitfield (Widnes)
Attendance: 5,993

Former Castleford player Freeman came on as a 38th minute substitute to inspire New Zealand to their first victory, sealed with a Sherlock try five minutes for time.

Castleford, despite lacking several regulars, were leading 20-8 when Freeman replaced Clark at stand off, his experience providing a settling influence as the Kiwis prevented any further home score in the second half.

Aided by Bancroft's top class goalkicking, hitting the target five times, the Kiwis pulled back with a rampaging break by Iro creating a touchdown for skipper Wallace, before Leeds-bound Kuiti laid on Sherlock's face-saving try.

The majority of the Kiwis had not played a game for several weeks and their rustiness showed in a first half plagued by basic errors. With centre Iro the only established Test star in the starting line-up, the visitors conceded three first half tries to injury-hit Castleford, winger Ellis kicking four goals on his debut after signing from Ryedale-York.

Former Castleford half back Gary Freeman, an inspirational substitute in the tour game at Wheldon Road.

Prop forward Esene Faimalo, seven appearances in Britain.

8 October

| **WIGAN** | **24** |
| **NEW ZEALAND** | **14** |

1. Williams
2. Mercer
3. Watson
4. Sherlock
5. Elia
6. K. Shelford (Bancroft)
7. Freeman
8. Goulding
9. D. Mann
10. Todd
11. Stewart
12. Kuiti (Leota)
13. McGahan, Capt.

T: Freeman, Elia
G: K. Shelford (2), Bancroft

Wigan:
Hampson: Gill, Bell, Blake, Lydon (Byrne); Edwards, Goulding; Davidson, Dermott, Lucas (Stazicker), Platt, Gildart, Goodway

T: Lydon, Platt, Davidson, Byrne
G: Blake (4)

Half-time: 12-8

Referee: Dave Carter (Widnes)
Attendance: 15,013

Defensively vulnerable and laboured on attack, the New Zealanders had only one really convincing period, the 10 minutes before half-time when pulling back to 12-8. They were again only four points adrift at 18-14 in the 66th minute but at no time did the Kiwis suggest they might win.

Their second defeat in three outings again damaged the tourists' credibility with the first British Coal Test two weeks away, especially against an uninspired Wigan whose best player was half-time substitute back Byrne, who scored a try.

The classy McGahan struggled in a pack lacking pace and ideas, while only Test half backs Kelly Shelford and Freeman shone in the backs where full back Williams was again fragile on defence.

11 October

| **BRADFORD N.** | **8** |
| **NEW ZEALAND** | **26** |

1. Edwards
2. Taewa
3. Kemp
4. Iro
5. Ropati (Elia)
6. Clark
7. Bancroft
8. A. Shelford (Kuiti)
9. Wallace, Capt.
10. Faimalo
11. Nikau
12. Leota
13. Tuuta

T: Kemp, Iro, Edwards, Clark
G: Bancroft (5)

Bradford N:
Mumby; Mackay, Johnson, Simpson (Hellewell), Francis; Wilson (Cooper), Stewart; Richards, Barraclough, Croft, Snee, Rhodes, Roebuck

T: Mackay (2)

Half-time: 4-10

Referee: John Kendrew (Castleford)
Attendance: 3,498

Bradford Northern lined up a Rugby League fine by fielding a much-weakened side which featured an all-reserve pack and a well below strength back division. Pleading a long injury list, the Odsal club were also preparing for a Yorkshire Cup replay with Halifax four days later, their seventh match in 21 days.

Despite the under-strength opposition, the Kiwis were still not convincing, although prop Faimalo made a strong claim for a Test spot.

Northern opened the scoring with a spectacular 40-yard try for Australian winger Mackay before New Zealand took a 10-4 interval lead through touchdowns from British-based centres Kemp and Iro.

Further tries came from Clark and Edwards, but Bradford's Mackay finished with the best as he swerved through and powered 75 yards to the line. New Zealand's Elia and Odsal prop forward Croft were sent to the sin bin in separate incidents.

15 October

LEEDS 4
NEW ZEALAND 34

1. Williams
2. Mercer
3. Sherlock
4. Kemp
5. Elia (Watson)
6. K. Shelford
7. Freeman
8. Faimalo
9. D. Mann
10. Todd (Tuuta)
11. Goulding
12. Stewart
13. McGahan, Capt.

T: Freeman (3), Elia, Williams, McGahan
G: Sherlock (4), K. Shelford

Leeds:
Spencer; Fawcett, Lord, Gibson (Bentley), Francis; Delaney, Coleman; Izzard, Maskill (Gunn), Dixon, Powell, Divorty, Heron

G: Maskill (2)

Half-time: 4-20

Referee: Alan Burke (Oldham)
Attendance: 9,632

Kiwi morale was lifted by a six-try performance at Headingley, inspired by skipper McGahan — who had turned down a short-term contract from Leeds — and hat-trick hero Freeman. With the first British Coal Test only six days away, the tourists improved their support play and defence as they grew in confidence.

The result was never in doubt after Elia scored the first try in the 15th minute following good work by Sherlock and Williams, Freeman sending over McGahan 10 minutes later.

The Kiwis were equally satisfied with keeping their line intact for the first time on the tour, Leeds being restricted to two Maskill penalty goals.

Blackspots for the relieved New Zealanders were a pulled hamstring for Elia, the sin-binning of Duane Mann and Williams and the conceding of 15 penalties.

17 October

Whitehaven

CUMBRIA 2
NEW ZEALAND 28

1. Edwards
2. Taewa
3. Watson
4. Kemp
5. Iro
6. Clark
7. Bancroft
8. A. Shelford (Stewart)
9. Wallace, Capt.
10. Leota
11. Kuiti
12. Nikau
13. Tuuta

T: Taewa, Watson, Kuiti, Nikau
G: Bancroft (6)

Cumbria:
Lightfoot (Hull K.R.); Lofthouse (Whitehaven), Penrice (Workington T.), Beckwith (Barrow), Trainor (Barrow); Cameron (Whitehaven), Murdock (Carlisle); Armstrong (Hull K.R.), Falcon (Workington T.), Herbert (Salford), G. Kendall (Barrow), D. Kendall (Carlisle), Walker (Barrow). Substitutions: Smith (Workington T.) for Penrice, Brierley (Carlisle) for Herbert

G: Armstrong

Half-time: 2-2

Referee: Gerry Kershaw (Easingwold)
Attendance: 3,983

The New Zealanders registered four tries without reply, the comprehensive victory being marred by the loss of Test prop Adrian Shelford in the sixth minute with a recurrence of a troublesome calf injury.

Cumbria, lacking a host of first choice selections, held the Kiwis 2-2 at the break, being denied the lead through lack of accuracy by goalkickers Armstrong and Cameron.

The Kiwis broke the deadlock with a 54th minute Kuiti try and never looked back, well served by packman Leota and six-goal Bancroft.

FIRST TEST

New Zealand tore up their tour form book to outclass a disjointed Great Britain seeking to record their first home Test series success against the Kiwis for 24 years.

Sorely missing the individual brillance of the injured Ellery Hanley, Joe Lydon, Garry Schofield and Kevin Ward, the Lions contributed to their downfall with poor tackling, woeful handling and failure to follow the gameplan. Meanwhile, the Kiwis cast aside their dismal tour performances and served up a display of top-class support play, kicking and defence.

The much-maligned tourists were superbly directed by the British Coal Man of the Match, scrum half Gary Freeman, who tormented the ragged British defence throughout.

Only one British player shone in the gloom, left winger Martin Offiah, yet his team mates continually refused to spread the ball wide. On the right flank, Phil Ford received only four passes, taking a high one to score in the 19th minute, while Offiah received seven passes. To neglect Ford's unorthodox talent was folly, to ignore the Widnes winger's exceptional ability was criminal.

Only two of Offiah's passes gave him a running chance, brilliantly setting up a try for clubmate Alan Tait from one. To score one of the greatest Test tries of all time, Offiah had to get the ball himself, going to acting half back inside his own 25-yard zone. He slipped easily between the first two Kiwi defenders, high stepped out of a tackle and then turned Gary Mercer inside out on a bewildering run of perfect poise to turn the 18,000-plus crowd's dejected boos to cheers in the 66th minute.

Paul Loughlin's goal suddenly put Britain back in the game at 20-16, although a snatched success would have been unjust to the vastly superior Kiwis. As it was, hero Offiah was cast as the villain of a 71st minute touchdown by opposite number Kevin Iro as the Wigan winger brushed him aside, though he also evaded covering forwards Andy Goodway and David Hobbs.

The 72nd Anglo-Kiwi Test opened in dramatic fashion when Australian referee Greg McCallum sent Britain's Goodway and visiting stand off Kelly Shelford to the sin bin after only four minutes, Kiwi centre Kurt Sherlock kicking the resultant penalty goal. Ten minutes later prop forward James Goulding forced his way over at the corner to herald an outstanding performance despite breaking a wrist which caused his early return home.

Ford's 19th minute try was wiped out by further New Zealand scores from Hugh McGahan and Kelly Shelford, Sherlock adding a goal to put the visitors 16-4 ahead on the half hour, a Paul Loughlin penalty goal reducing the arrears before the interval.

Freeman's 53rd minute touchdown made the British bench spring into action, Wigan's Shaun Edwards being brought on to replace Widnes debutant centre Andy Currier, whose defence had been paper thin. With scrum half Andy Gregory struggling to find Test pace and form in his second game after a lengthy injury lay off, Edwards provided the spark which ignited Britain's comeback bid.

With Freeman ruling the centre of the field, the Kiwis fully exploited their tactic of giving wingmen Iro and Mercer a roving role, while with the possible exception of new British cap Kelvin Skerrett, the Kiwi pack dominated their counterparts man for man.

Reilly brought Featherstone Rovers three-quarter Paul Newlove on as a 76th minute substitute for Ford, the son of the former Featherstone and Hull back, John, becoming the youngest-ever Great Britain debutant at 18 years 72 days.

FIRST BRITISH COAL TEST

21 October   **Old Trafford, Manchester**

GREAT BRITAIN 16   NEW ZEALAND 24

Alan Tait (Widnes)	1.	Darrell Williams
Phil Ford (Leeds)	2.	Kevin Iro
Andy Currier (Widnes)	3.	Dean Bell
Paul Loughlin (St. Helens)	4.	Kurt Sherlock
Martin Offiah (Widnes)	5.	Gary Mercer
David Hulme (Widnes)	6.	Kelly Shelford
Andy Gregory (Wigan)	7.	Gary Freeman
Kelvin Skerrett (Bradford N.)	8.	James Goulding
Kevin Beardmore (Castleford)	9.	Duane Mann
David Hobbs (Bradford N.)	10.	Brent Todd
Andy Goodway (Wigan)	11.	Kurt Sorensen
Andy Platt (Wigan)	12.	Sam Stewart
Mike Gregory (Warrington) Capt.	13.	Hugh McGahan, Capt.
Paul Newlove (Featherstone R.)	14.	Tony Kemp
Roy Powell (Leeds)	15.	Phil Bancroft
Shaun Edwards (Wigan)	16.	Mike Kuiti
Paul Hulme (Widnes)	17.	Francis Leota

T: Ford, Tait, Offiah
G: Loughlin (2)
Substitutions:
Edwards for Currier (54 min.)
Newlove for Ford (76 min.)
Half-time: 6-16
Referee: Greg McCallum (Australia)

T: Goulding, McGahan,
K. Shelford, Freeman, Iro
G: Sherlock (2)
Substitution:
Kemp for Williams (77 min.)
Attendance: 18,273

Scorechart

Minute	Score	GB	NZ
4:	Sherlock (PG)	0	2
14:	Goulding (T)	0	6
19:	Ford (T)	4	6
24:	McGahan (T)	4	10
29:	K. Shelford (T)		
	Sherlock (G)	4	16
31:	Loughlin (PG)	6	16
53:	Freeman (T)	6	20
57:	Tait (T)	10	20
66:	Offiah (T)		
	Loughlin (G)	16	20
71:	Iro (T)	16	24
	Scrums	14	4
	Penalties	6	5

Kiwi centre Kurt Sherlock, scorer of two goals.

285

SECOND TEST

What a difference a week makes . . . a transformed Great Britain overwhelmed New Zealand with a text book display despite being reduced to 12 men after only 95 seconds when stand-in full back Steve Hampson was sent off for butting.

Called up in mid-week when Alan Tait strained a hamstring in training, Hampson caught a high ball in the dead ball area and was physically hampered by Kiwi scrum half Gary Freeman as he ran to the 25-yard line to resume play. Australian referee Greg McCallum did not hesitate to point to the dressing room when a frustrated Hampson butted Freeman in the face in a bid to free himself from the half back's attentions.

Against the odds, Britain set about answering all the questions which were asked after the Old Trafford debacle a week earlier. The Lions' tackling and handling were first class as pride and passion formed a firm resolve to overcome the loss of Hampson, who subsequently received a two-match ban for the offence.

The emphatic and thoroughly deserved victory, featuring the scoring of four tries to one, was one to savour for coach Malcolm Reilly. Surrounded by pre-match speculation about the renewal of his contract if the series was lost, Reilly stayed loyal to his squad system. Although he had made seven changes from the first Test, two were because of injury, two positional, and all from within his original 20-man squad except for new substitute forward Keith England.

Hampson's dismissal pushed St. Helens centre Paul Loughlin to full back, with Wigan second row man Andy Goodway moving to the centre. Britain's five-man pack rose to the occasion with Roy Powell working himself to a standstill.

Proving a point on his recall to the stand off role, Wigan's Shaun Edwards took the British Coal Man of the Match award ahead of clubmate Goodway, scorer of two tries, by the odd vote in 31 pressmen. While the two Riversiders were the pick of the side, there were no shirkers in a display of resilience and character. Edwards and half back partner David Hulme also fully utilised a kicking game which had been so evidently absent at Old Trafford seven days earlier.

There was no shortage of needle in such a vital game, especially in the first half, and Kiwi duo Duane Mann and Freeman were despatched to the sin bin in separate incidents before the interval.

Loughlin opened the scoring with a penalty goal after 15 minutes before Edwards touched down seven minutes later. The try was created by Widnes winger Martin Offiah whose rapidly growing maturity in the 13-a-side code was confirmed by his palming a high pass into the hands of Edwards to slice through the disorganised Kiwi defence.

Offiah returned to the accustomed role of tryscorer in the 33rd minute, Loughlin adding the goal to give 12-man Britain a 12-point lead at half-time. With props Kelvin Skerrett and Andy Platt constant threats in a well-organised, albeit depleted, pack, the home side continued to affirm their superiority.

Four minutes after the break, Goodway touched down, Loughlin obliging with the goal and a 60th penalty to stretch Britain's lead to 20-0. The tiring dozen relaxed to allow Freeman to put Hugh McGahan in for a try, Kurt Sherlock adding the goal, before Goodway charged down a Darrell Williams kick to score his second try, Loughlin rounding off the scoring with his sixth goal.

New Zealand, confronted by such determined opponents, showed hardly a bright attacking idea all afternoon, failing to capitalise on their numerical advantage mainly because of Britain's exemplary tackling stint with two and three men driving into every tackle.

SECOND BRITISH COAL TEST

28 October   **Elland Road, Leeds**

GREAT BRITAIN 26   NEW ZEALAND 6

Steve Hampson (Wigan)	1.	Darrell Williams
Phil Ford (Leeds)	2.	Kevin Iro
Paul Newlove (Featherstone R.)	3.	Dean Bell
Paul Loughlin (St. Helens)	4.	Kurt Sherlock
Martin Offiah (Widnes)	5.	Gary Mercer
Shaun Edwards (Wigan)	6.	Kelly Shelford
David Hulme (Widnes)	7.	Gary Freeman
Kelvin Skerrett (Bradford N.)	8.	Adrian Shelford
Paul Hulme (Widnes)	9.	Duane Mann
Andy Platt (Wigan)	10.	Brent Todd
Andy Goodway (Wigan)	11.	Kurt Sorensen
Roy Powell (Leeds)	12.	Sam Stewart
Mike Gregory (Warrington) Capt.	13.	Hugh McGahan, Capt.
Daryl Powell (Sheffield E.)	14.	Tony Kemp
David Hobbs (Bradford N.)	15.	Phil Bancroft
Deryck Fox (Featherstone R.)	16.	Mike Kuiti
Keith England (Castleford)	17.	Esene Faimalo

T: Goodway (2), Edwards, Offiah
G: Loughlin (5)
Substitutions:
Hobbs for Skerrett (65 min.)
Fox for D. Hulme (74 min.)
Half-time: 12-0
Attendance: 13,073

T: McGahan
G: Sherlock
Substitutions:
Faimalo for A. Shelford (36 min.)
Kemp for Sherlock (65 min.)
Referee: Greg McCallum
(Australia)

Scorechart

Minute	Score	GB	NZ
15:	Loughlin (PG)	2	0
22:	Edwards (T)	6	0
33:	Offiah (T)		
	Loughlin (G)	12	0
44:	Goodway (T)		
	Loughlin (G)	18	0
60:	Loughlin (PG)	20	0
64:	McGahan (T)		
	Sherlock (G)	20	6
69:	Goodway (T)		
	Loughlin (G)	26	6
	Scrums	7	11
	Penalties	12	3

Skipper Hugh McGahan, sole Kiwi tryscorer.

1 November

HULL	8
NEW ZEALAND	**44**

1. Edwards
2. Taewa
3. Watson
4. Kemp (Williams)
5. Mercer
6. Clark
7. Bancroft
8. Leota
9. Wallace, Capt.
10. Faimalo (G. Mann)
11. Kuiti
12. Nikau
13. Tuuta

T: Watson (2), Kuiti (2), Mercer, Leota, Tuuta, Williams
G: Bancroft (6)

Hull:
Nolan; O'Hara, Cleal, Blacker, Eastwood; Gay, Doherty; Crooks (Puckering), Patrick, Harrison (L. Jackson), Welham, Sharp, McNamara

T: Eastwood
G: Eastwood (2)

Half-time: 8-8

Referee: Colin Morris (Huddersfield)
Attendance: 5,894

5 November

WIDNES	18
NEW ZEALAND	**26**

1. Kemp
2. Ewe
3. Watson (Sherlock)
4. Williams
5. Mercer
6. K. Shelford
7. Freeman
8. Todd
9. D. Mann
10. Faimalo
11. Kuiti (Leota)
12. Stewart
13. McGahan, Capt.

T: Faimalo, Watson, Mercer, Stewart
G: K. Shelford (3, 1dg), Ewe, McGahan (dg)

Widnes:
Tait; Kebbie, Currier, Wright (Devereux), Offiah; Davies, D. Hulme; Grima (Moriarty), McKenzie, Pyke, Sorensen, O'Neill, P. Hulme

T: Tait, D. Hulme, O'Neill, Kebbie
G: Davies

Half-time: 14-12

Referee: Paul Crashley (Wakefield)
Attendance: 9,905

New Zealand's second string were reduced to 12 men after 36 minutes but still ran up their highest score of the tour to send Hull down to their biggest defeat against a Kiwi side.

The tourists suffered their first full dismissal of the tour when second row man Nikau was sent off for dissent. Five minutes earlier there had been a novel sending off when the Kiwi physiotherapist was ordered to the dressing room for taking a water bottle onto the field against the referee's instructions.

The Kiwis had just drawn level at 8-8 when Nikau departed, wingman Eastwood having given the Airlie Birds the lead with a try and two goals.

The visitors cut loose in the second half with six tries carved out in spectacular fashion, aided by some weak Hull tackling. Centre Watson gave his best performance with two tries and creating one for substitute Williams, while two-try Kuiti took their Man of the Match award, only Welham coming off with any credit to claim the Hull prize.

New Zealand gained the ideal boost for the forthcoming British Coal Test decider by defeating World Club Challenge title holders Widnes in convincing fashion.

The tourists dominated a bad tempered contest, opposing centres Watson and Welshman Devereux sent to the sin bin. However, the Kiwis also appreciated the impact of their own Test packman Sorensen who provided a meaty mixture of brawn and brain to carve out Widnes tries for Tait and O'Neill.

Trailing 14-12 at the break, the Kiwis shut down Widnes in the second half while turning possession into points with tries from Stewart and Watson opening up a 24-12 lead.

The Chemics struck back with a try from Kebbie, engineered by Sorensen and Currier, before the New Zealanders assured themselves of victory with drop goals from McGahan and Kelly Shelford in the dying minutes.

7 November

FEATHERSTONE R.   **20**
NEW ZEALAND   **44**

1. Edwards
2. Taewa
3. Watson
4. Sherlock
5. Ewe
6. Clark
7. Bancroft
8. Leota
9. Wallace, Capt.
10. G. Mann
11. Kuiti
12. Nikau
13. Tuuta (Stewart)

T: Taewa (2), Watson (2), Edwards, Leota, Kuiti, Nikau
G: Bancroft (6)

Featherstone R.:
Bibb (S. Newlove); Drummond, Ropati, Manning, Banks; Smales, Sharp; Bell, Clark, Dakin (Grayshon), Price, Smith, Fisher

T: Clark, Manning, Fisher
G: Smales (4)

Half-time: 4-22

Referee: Alex Bowman (Whitehaven)
Attendance: 2,773

Centre Dave Watson, double touchdown hero in the eight-try rout at Featherstone.

The Kiwis equalled their highest score of the tour in their final club game, running in eight tries. Had Bancroft added the goal to the last touchdown, it would have equalled the highest-ever score by a New Zealand side in England.

The tourists' backs showed plenty of pace and power, threequarters Taewa and Watson each collecting two tries, and they had a pair of strong-running props in Leota and George Mann. Leota showed rare pace for a front row forward when he broke through from the halfway line for the best solo try of the night.

Featherstone, who began without four of the previous Sunday's beaten Yorkshire Cup final side, lost another when full back Bibb went off in the 18th minute, the Kiwis already leading 10-2, going on to build up a 22-4 half-time supremacy.

With veteran prop Grayshon on as substitute forward, the Colliers made a big effort to get back into the game after the break and soon narrowed the gap to eight points. As a grandstand finish looked likely, the New Zealanders stepped up a gear and finished with four tries in the last 18 minutes.

THIRD TEST

It would have been no miscarriage of justice if this British Coal Test series had finished all-square, as did the last two Anglo-Kiwi contests of 1980 and 1985.

Great Britain built a defensive wall in a scoreless second half to uphold a 10-6 interval lead and clinch a home series success against the New Zealanders for the first time in 24 years.

Wigan's Central Park was no place for the faint-hearted as the Kiwis were forced to abandon caution at the end of the first half and throughout the second when they were the more threatening side.

The enthralling encounter was full of imponderables, mainly centred around the decisions of Australian referee Greg McCallum.

The Kiwi camp claimed that the superb support play in the build-up to Alan Tait's 20th minute try contained a forward pass; and that Gary Mercer's disallowed touchdown in the final minutes should have been granted because full back Tait played the ball on. A counter claim from Britain alleged that Phil Ford should been awarded an obstruction try 10 minutes from time when crudely halted by Wigan's Dean Bell. It was that close a contest!

To suggest that New Zealand were unlucky to lose is not to say that Great Britain were fortunate to win. Adopting a safety first approach in the tense second half, a devoted tackling stint saved them. But this was a performance that deserved the ovation it received from a 20,000 crowd as skipper Mike Gregory received the British Coal Trophy.

There was a time when Great Britain used to score great tries and lose Test matches. This time, the Lions had the satisfaction of scoring an exceptional touchdown and celebrating victory. It was Tait's try at the end of the first quarter, a move which unfolded over 80 yards involving a representative from every department, notably young Paul Newlove and scrum half David Hulme.

Britain's opening try after nine minutes was also a classy production, Shaun Edwards making an incisive midfield break before timing his pass to perfection for Martin Offiah to include a try in his most impressive all-round performance to date. He became only the third British player to touchdown in each of a home Test against New Zealand. Had Paul Loughlin's place kicking been accurate, Britain could have been 18 points in credit by the interval, but in wet conditions the St. Helens centre missed four attempts.

Offiah was again under-used as a lethal striking force, but despite limited opportunities he took the British Coal Man of the Match award, partly as a reflection of his unaccustomed role of defender. On attack, the Widnes flier scored his try as a result of intelligent support play and was an important link in the magnificent eight-man move for Tait's try. Offiah's pace and alertness almost brought him two other touchdowns as he chased kicks.

In the second half Offiah had to take difficult kicks on his own line three times with the Kiwis striving desperately to save the game and the series.

New Zealand were hampered by Kurt Sorensen being sent to the sin bin after only three minutes for a tackle on Andy Goodway, during which time Offiah scored his try. They came back into the game four minutes before the break when back row forward Sam Stewart made light of a two-man tackle to send stand off Kelly Shelford curving around Tait, before adding the goal.

Scrum half Gary Freeman was also back to his menacing best, while the Kiwis paid the price for ignoring the explosive talents of Kevin Iro, isolated on the wing when Britain were showing signs of tiring.

THIRD BRITISH COAL TEST

11 November   **Wigan**

GREAT BRITAIN 10		NEW ZEALAND 6
Alan Tait (Widnes)	1.	Tony Kemp
Phil Ford (Leeds)	2.	Kevin Iro
Paul Newlove (Featherstone R.)	3.	Dean Bell
Paul Loughlin (St. Helens)	4.	Darrell Williams
Martin Offiah (Widnes)	5.	Gary Mercer
Shaun Edwards (Wigan)	6.	Kelly Shelford
David Hulme (Widnes)	7.	Gary Freeman
Kelvin Skerrett (Bradford N.)	8.	Brent Todd
Paul Hulme (Widnes)	9.	Duane Mann
Andy Platt (Wigan)	10.	Esene Faimalo
Andy Goodway (Wigan)	11.	Kurt Sorensen
Roy Powell (Leeds)	12.	Sam Stewart
Mike Gregory (Warrington) Capt.	13.	Hugh McGahan, Capt.
Joe Lydon (Wigan)	14.	Kurt Sherlock
David Hobbs (Bradford N.)	15.	Dean Clark
Deryck Fox (Featherstone R.)	16.	Francis Leota
Keith England (Castleford)	17.	Mike Kuiti

T: Offiah, Tait
G: Loughlin
Substitutions:
Lydon for Newlove (33 min.)
England for Skerrett (52 min.)
Half-time: 10-6
Attendance: 20,346

T: K. Shelford
G: K. Shelford
Substitutions:
Leota for Faimalo (52 min.)
Clark for K. Shelford (61 min.)
Referee: Greg McCallum (Australia)

Scorechart

Minute	Score	GB	NZ
9:	Offiah (T)		
	Loughlin (G)	6	0
20:	Tait (T)	10	0
36:	K. Shelford (T)		
	K. Shelford (G)	10	6
	Scrums	7	5
	Penalties	10	8

Stand off Kelly Shelford, scorer of the tourists' six points.

291

Gary Mercer, chosen by the New Zealand management as their British Coal Man of the Series.

Laurie Daley, centre for Canberra Raiders, winners of the 1989 Sydney Grand Final, comes up against Tony Myler of Widnes in the 1989 Foster's World Club Challenge.

DOWN UNDER

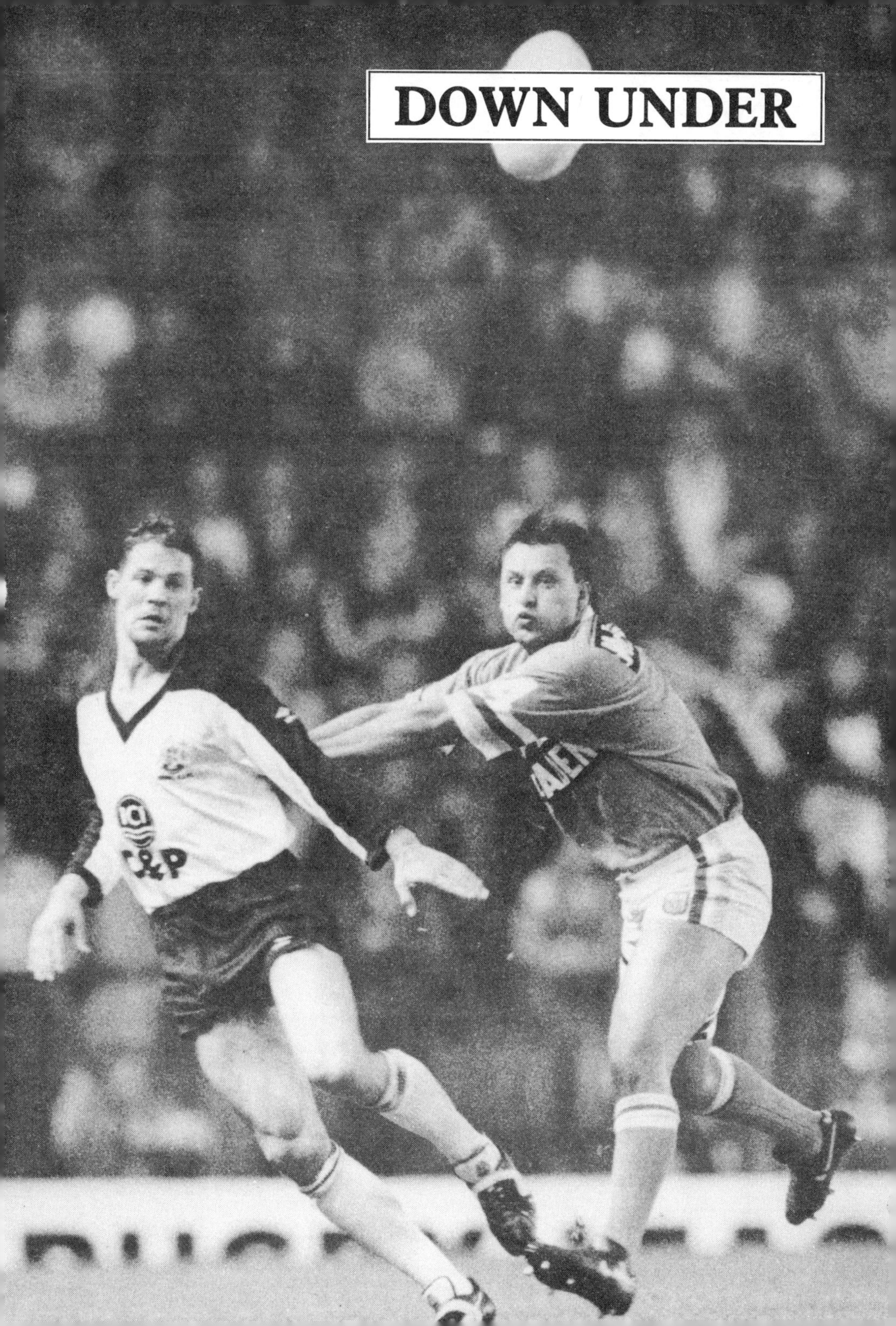

DOWN UNDER

THE SYDNEY PREMIERSHIP
1989 Grand Final

England had a player in the Sydney Grand Final for the third successive year when Canberra beat Balmain 19-14 after a thrilling game which went into extra time.

Andy Currier of Widnes was in the centre for Balmain, who also sent on Wigan's Shaun Edwards as a substitute in the 11th minute of extra time.

Although Currier kicked three goals he had an indifferent game and was blamed for the error which led to Canberra clinching victory with a try three minutes from the end. It was a disappointing finish to a season in which Currier had made a big impact on the Sydney scene.

Canberra became the first team to win the trophy from fourth position since the five-club play-off system was introduced in 1973. They did it after trailing 12-2 at half-time and not equalising at 14-14 until two minutes from the end of normal time. The vital late try went to John Ferguson, who scored two tries for Wigan when they beat Hull in the 1985 Challenge Cup final at Wembley.

The capacity crowd of 40,500 was slightly up on the previous year's full house at the new Sydney Football Stadium's inaugural staging of the final.

SYDNEY GRAND FINAL
Sydney Football Stadium

24 September 1989

CANBERRA 19 **BALMAIN 14**

● After extra time of 20 minutes; score after 80 min., 14-14

Canberra	No.	Balmain
Gary Belcher	1.	Garry Jack
Matthew Wood	2.	James Grant
Mal Meninga, Capt.	3.	Tim Brasher
Laurie Daley	4.	Andy Currier
John Ferguson	5.	Steve O'Brien
Chris O'Sullivan	6.	Michael Neil
Ricky Stuart	7.	Gary Freeman
Brent Todd	8.	Steve Roach
Steve Walters	9.	Ben Elias
Glenn Lazarus	10.	Steve Edmed
Gary Coyne	11.	Paul Sironen
Dean Lance	12.	Bruce McGuire
Bradley Clyde	13.	Wayne Pearce, Capt.

T: Belcher, Ferguson, Jackson
G: Meninga (3), O'Sullivan (dg)
Substitutions:
Paul Martin for Wood (54 min.)
Steve Jackson for Todd (63 min.)
*Head bin: Kevin Walters for Daley (69 min.)
Coach: Tim Sheens
Half-time: 2-12
Referee: Bill Harrigan
Clive Churchill Medal for Man of the Match: Bradley Clyde (Canberra).
*Temporary substitution for a player with head injury.

T: Grant, Sironen
G: Currier (3)
Substitutions:
Kevin Hardwick for Roach (65 min.)
Michael Pobjie for Sironen (79 min.)
Shaun Edwards for Pobjie (91 min.)
Coach: Warren Ryan
Scrums: 11-16
Penalties: 8-2
Attendance: 40,500

1989 WINFIELD CUP

	P.	W.	D.	L.	F.	A.	Pts
South Sydney	22	18	1	3	390	207	37
Penrith	22	16	0	6	438	241	32
Balmain	22	14	1	7	380	236	29
Canberra	22	14	0	8	457	287	28
Brisbane Broncos	22	14	0	8	398	290	28
Cronulla-Sutherland	22	14	0	8	368	281	28
Newcastle	22	11	0	11	281	281	22
Parramatta	22	11	0	11	346	366	22
Canterbury-Bankstown	22	10	2	10	280	337	22
St. George	22	10	0	12	330	356	20
Eastern Suburbs	22	9	1	12	348	346	19
Manly-Warringah	22	9	1	12	334	343	19
Gold Coast	22	7	1	14	223	383	15
Western Suburbs	22	7	1	14	229	389	15
North Sydney	22	5	1	16	194	406	11
Illawarra	22	2	1	19	256	503	5

WINFIELD CUP PLAY-OFF
Fifth place play off
Cronulla 38 v. Brisbane 14
Minor preliminary semi-final
Canberra 31 v. Cronulla 10
Major preliminary semi-final
Balmain 24 v. Penrith 12
Minor semi-final
Canberra 27 v. Penrith 18
Major semi-final
Balmain 20 v. Souths 10
Preliminary final
Canberra 32 v. Souths 16
Grand Final
Canberra 19 v. Balmain 14 (After extra time)

● All matches played at the Sydney Football Stadium except for the fifth place play-off at the Parramatta Stadium.

LEADING SCORERS
● Not including play-offs

Tries
Greg Alexander (Penrith) 15
Goals (incl. drop goals)
Neil Baker (Penrith) 50
Points
Ricky Walford (St. George) 146

Winfield Cup winning Canberra skipper Mal Meninga.

BRITISH PLAYERS IN GRAND FINALS

British players who have appeared in the Sydney Grand Final are:

Dick Huddart (St. George) 1966 winners, 1 try
Dave Bolton (Balmain) 1966 losers; 1969 winners, 2 drop goals
Mervyn Hicks (Canterbury) 1967 losers
Ken Batty (St. George) 1971 losers
Malcolm Reilly (Manly) 1972 winners, 1973 winners
Tommy Bishop (Cronulla) 1973 losers
Bob Wear (Cronulla) 1973 losers
Cliff Watson (Cronulla) 1973 losers
Brian Lockwood (Canterbury) 1974 losers
Gary Stephens (Manly) 1976 winners
Steve Norton (Manly) 1976 winners
Phil Lowe (Manly) 1976 winners, 1 try
Kevin Ward (Manly) 1987 winners
Ellery Hanley (Balmain) 1988 losers
Andy Currier (Balmain) 1989 losers, 3 goals
Shaun Edwards (Balmain) 1989 losers, sub

Apart from Hicks, Wear and Currier, all the above also appeared in a Challenge Cup final at Wembley. In addition Len Killeen, the South African winger who began his league career with St. Helens, also played at Wembley and got a Grand Final winners' medal with Balmain in 1969 when he kicked two goals.

Australians who have achieved the big double since the Grand Final became mandatory in 1954 are: Chris Anderson, Harry Bath, Graham Eadie, John Ferguson, Kerry Hemsley, Brett Kenny, John Muggleton, Peter Sterling, Michael O'Connor and Paul Vautin.

There were a record four British players in the 1973 Grand Final. Reilly got a winners' medal with Manly, while Bishop, Watson and Wear were in the beaten Cronulla side.

Three British players — Stephens, Norton and Lowe — were also in the Manly side which won the final in 1976.

Ellery Hanley was the first player to appear in both major finals in the same year. In 1988 he led Wigan to success at Wembley and four months later was in Balmain's beaten Grand Final team.

Shaun Edwards is the only other player to play in both finals in the same year. He was stand off when Wigan beat St. Helens at Wembley in 1989 and made a late substitute appearance for Balmain when they were beaten by Canberra at Sydney.

BRITISH PLAYERS IN 1989 SYDNEY PREMIERSHIP

A record total of 14 British players appeared in the Sydney Premiership during the 1989 season compared with only four the previous year.

The most successful was Andy Currier of Widnes who made 17 appearances, including one as substitute, and scored 146 points from 10 tries plus 53 goals.

Western Suburbs had the biggest contingent of British players with the signing of Ellery Hanley (Wigan), Garry Schofield (Leeds) and Kelvin Skerrett (Bradford Northern).

Hanley was reported to have been paid a world record £80,000 to play for Wests, who had finished bottom the previous year. His arrival created tremendous interest but they were able to improve by only two places.

British players records in the 1989 Sydney Premiership, including play-off matches:

	App	T	G	Pts
Andy Currier (Widnes-Balmain)	16 + 1	10	53	146
Bernard Dwyer (St. Helens-Manly)	1 + 4	—	—	—
Shaun Edwards (Wigan-Balmain)	5 + 7	1	—	4
Andy Gregory (Wigan-Illawarra)	8 + 1	3	—	12
Steve Hampson (Wigan-Illawarra)	11	1	—	4
Ellery Hanley (Wigan-Wests)	13	4	—	16
Tracy Lazenby (Wakefield T.-Penrith)	1 + 3	—	—	—
Joe Lydon (Wigan-Easts)	9 + 1	2	9	26
Martin Offiah (Widnes-Easts)	12	9	—	36
Garry Schofield (Leeds-Wests)	8 + 1	5	+ 1	21
Kelvin Skerrett (Bradford N.-Wests)	3 + 2	—	—	—
Graham Steadman (Featherstone R.-Gold Coast)	3 + 2	1	—	4
Paul Vannet (Workington T.-Cronulla)	0 ÷ 1	—	—	—
Hugh Waddell (Leeds-Manly)	10 + 2	1	—	4

STATE OF ORIGIN

The State of Origin matches between New South Wales and Queensland began in 1980 and are now established as a major part of the Australian Rugby League scene.

Their introduction revived interest in the inter-state matches which had been dominated by New South Wales, who had won the last 15 matches by mainly wide margins.

Under the old system players appeared for the state in which they were playing club rugby at the time and this gave a big advantage to New South Wales because many of Queensland's best players were with Sydney clubs.

But in State of Origin matches players appear for the state in which they first played senior rugby and this has resulted in the matches becoming more fiercely and evenly fought before increased attendances.

NEW SOUTH WALES v. QUEENSLAND RESULTS
State of Origin only.

Date	Winner	Score	Venue	Attendance
8 July 1980	Queensland	20 - 10	Brisbane	31,000
28 July 1981	Queensland	22 - 15	Brisbane	25,613
1 June 1982	New South Wales	20 - 16	Brisbane	27,326
8 June 1982	Queensland	11 - 7	Brisbane	19,435
22 June 1982	Queensland	10 - 5	Sydney	20,242
7 June 1983	Queensland	24 - 12	Brisbane	29,412
21 June 1983	New South Wales	10 - 6	Sydney	21,620
28 June 1983	Queensland	43 - 22	Brisbane	26,084
29 May 1984	Queensland	29 - 12	Brisbane	33,662
19 June 1984	Queensland	14 - 2	Sydney	29,088
17 July 1984	New South Wales	22 - 12	Brisbane	16,599
28 May 1985	New South Wales	18 - 2	Brisbane	33,011
11 June 1985	New South Wales	21 - 14	Sydney	39,068
23 July 1985	Queensland	20 - 6	Brisbane	18,825
27 May 1986	New South Wales	22 - 16	Brisbane	33,000
10 June 1986	New South Wales	24 - 20	Sydney	40,707
1 July 1986	New South Wales	18 - 16	Brisbane	21,097
2 June 1987	New South Wales	20 - 16	Brisbane	33,411
16 June 1987	Queensland	12 - 6	Sydney	42,048
15 July 1987	Queensland	10 - 8	Brisbane	33,000
*6 Aug. 1987	New South Wales	30 - 18	California	12,349
17 May 1988	Queensland	26 - 18	Sydney	26,441
31 May 1988	Queensland	16 - 6	Brisbane	31,817
21 June 1988	Queensland	38 - 22	Sydney	16,910
23 May 1989	Queensland	36 - 6	Brisbane	33,000
14 June 1989	Queensland	16 - 12	Sydney	40,000
28 June 1989	Queensland	36 - 16	Brisbane	33,000

SUMMARY
New South Wales won 10; Queensland won 17.
Since it became a three-match series in 1982 Queensland have won six series to New South Wales' two.
*Not part of 1987 series.

English referees
English referees who have taken charge of State of Origin matches are: Billy Thompson on 8 July 1980 and Robin Whitfield on 28 June 1983.

1989 STATE OF ORIGIN MATCHES

*Denotes captain

23 May
Brisbane
New South Wales 6

Jack (Balmain)
Johns (Brisbane B.)
Farrar (Canterbury)
L. Daley (Canberra) 1g
Ferguson (Canberra)
Lamb (Canterbury)
Hasler (Manly)
Dunn (Canterbury)
Fenech (Souths)
Cartwright (Penrith)
Sironen (Balmain)
*Miller (Cronulla)
Clyde (Canberra)

Subs: Lazarus (Canberra)
    Alexander (Penrith)
    Ettingshausen (Cronulla) 1t
    C. Mortimer (Penrith)

14 June
Sydney
New South Wales 12

Jack (Balmain)
Johns (Brisbane B.) 1t
Ettingshausen (Cronulla)
L. Daley (Canberra) 1t
Ferguson (Canberra)
C. Mortimer (Penrith)
Alexander (Penrith) 2g
Dunn (Canterbury)
Fenech (Souths)
Kelly (Penrith)
McGuire (Balmain)
*Miller (Cronulla)
Clyde (Canberra)

Subs: Hasler (Manly)
    Cartwright (Penrith)
    Wilson (Cronulla)
    Mackay (St. George)

28 June
Brisbane
New South Wales 16

Jack (Balmain)
O'Connor (Manly) 2g
Johns (Brisbane B.)
Johnston (St. George)
Ferguson (Canberra)
Hasler (Manly) 1t
Alexander (Penrith)
Kelly (Penrith)
Trewhella (Easts) 1t
McGuire (Balmain) 1t
Geyer (Penrith)
*Miller (Cronulla)
Mackay (St. George)

Subs: Matterson (Brisbane B.)
    Cartwright (Penrith)
    Blake (Souths)
    Wilson (Cronulla)

Queensland 36

Belcher (Canberra)
Hancock (Brisbane B.) 2t
Currie (Brisbane B.)
Meninga (Canberra) 2t, 4g
McIndoe (Penrith) 1t
*Lewis (Brisbane B.)
Langer (Brisbane B.) 1t
Stains (Cronulla)
Kerrod Walters (Brisbane B.)
Bella (Norths)
Miles (Brisbane B.)
Vautin (Manly)
Lindner (Gold Coast) 1t

Subs: Shearer (Manly)
    Coyne (Canberra)
    Hagan (Newcastle)
    Gillmeister (Easts)
Referee: Michael Stone
Man of the Match: Bella

Queensland 16

Belcher (Canberra) 1g
Hancock (Brisbane B.) 1t
Currie (Brisbane B.)
Meninga (Canberra) 1g
McIndoe (Penrith)
*Lewis (Brisbane B.) 1t
Langer (Brisbane B.)
Bella (Norths)
Kerrod Walters (Brisbane B.) 1t
Backo (Brisbane B.)
Miles (Brisbane B.)
Vautin (Manly)
Lindner (Gold Coast)

Subs: Hagan (Newcastle)
    Shearer (Manly)
    Gillmeister (Easts)
    Coyne (Canberra)
Referee: David Manson
Man of the Match: Lewis

Queensland 36

Belcher (Canberra) 1t
Hancock (Brisbane B.) 1t
Currie (Brisbane B.) 1t
Shearer (Manly) 2t, 4g
McIndoe (Penrith) 1t
*Lewis (Brisbane B.)
Hagan (Newcastle)
Backo (Brisbane B.)
Kerrod Walters (Brisbane B.) 1t
Bella (Norths)
Stains (Cronulla)
Miles (Brisbane B.)
Vautin (Manly)

Subs: Jackson (Brisbane B.)
    Coyne (Canberra)
    Gillmeister (Easts)
    Kevin Walters (Canberra)
Referee: Greg McCallum
Man of the Match: Kerrod Walters

NEW SOUTH WALES v. QUEENSLAND RECORDS
State of Origin only

NEW SOUTH WALES

Highest score:	30-18 at California, 6 August 1987
Widest margin:	18-2 at Brisbane, 28 May 1985
Most appearances:	17 by Garry Jack (Balmain)
Most tries in a match:	3 by Chris Anderson (Canterbury), 28 June 1983
Most goals in a match:	No player has kicked more than five
Most points in a match:	18 (2t, 5g) Michael O'Connor (Manly), 28 May 1985
Biggest home attendance:	42,048, 16 June 1987

QUEENSLAND

Highest score:	43-22 at Brisbane, 28 June 1983
Widest Margin:	36-6 at Brisbane, 23 May 1989
Most appearances:	26 by Wally Lewis (Fortitude Valley, Wynum Manly, Brisbane Broncos)
Most tries in a match:	3 by Kerry Boustead (Manly), 29 May 1984
Most goals in a match:	7 by Mal Meninga (Souths, B), 8 July 1980
Most points in a match:	16 (2t, 4g) by Mal Meninga (Canberra), 23 May 1989 and Dale Shearer (Manly), 28 June 1989
Biggest home attendance:	33,662, 29 May 1984

Coaches:

New South Wales:	Ted Glossop (1980, 1981, 1983); Frank Stanton (1982, 1984); Terry Fearnley (1985); Ron Willey (1986, 1987); John Peard (1988); Jack Gibson (1989)
Queensland:	John McDonald (1980); Arthur Beetson (1981, 1982, 1983, 1984, 1989); Des Morris (1985); Wayne Bennett (1986, 1987, 1988)

QUEENSLAND REGISTER

The following is a register of players who have appeared for Queensland in the State of Origin series plus the match against New South Wales in the United States of America, up to and including 1989. + indicates number of matches played as a substitute. B-Brisbane, S-Sydney.

BACKER, Brad (3) Easts, B
BACKO, Sam (5) Canberra 3; Brisbane Broncos 2
BEETSON, Arthur (1) Parramatta
BELCHER, Gary (12) Canberra
BELLA, Martin (8) North, S
BOUSTEAD, Kerry (6) Easts, S 3; Manly 3
BRENNAN, Mitch (4) Souths, S 3; Redcliffe 1
BROHMAN, Darryl (2) Penrith
BROWN, Dave (10) Manly 6; Easts, S 4
BUTLER, Terry (1) Wynnum Manly

CARR, Norm (2) Wests, B
CLOSE, Chris (9) Manly 7; Redcliffe 2
CONESCU, Greg (20) Norths, B 4; Redcliffe 10; Gladstone Brothers 3; Brisbane Broncos 3
COYNE, Gary (+3) Canberra
CURRIE, Tony (8+3) Wests, B +1; Redcliffe +1; Canterbury 5+1; Brisbane Broncos 3

DOWLING, Greg (11) Wynnum Manly 7; Norths, B 4
DOWLING, John (3) St. George

FRENCH, Brett (1+3) Wynnum Manly; Norths S +3
FRENCH, Ian (3+6) Wynnum Manly 2+3; Norths, S 1+3
FULLERTON-SMITH, Wally (10) Redcliffe 7; St. George 3

GILLMEISTER, Trevor (4+3) Easts, S

HAGAN, Michael (1+2) Newcastle
HANCOCK, Michael (3) Brisbane Broncos
HANCOCK, Rohan (5) Easts, B 1; Toowoomba 1; Wattles 4
HENRICK, Ross (2) Norths, B 1; Fortitude Valley 1
HEUGH, Cavill (2+1) Easts, B

JACKSON, Peter (7+2) Canberra 7; Souths, B +1; Brisbane Broncos +1
JONES, Gavin (3) Norths, S

KELLAWAY, Bob (+1) Souths, B
KHAN, Paul (4) Easts, B 3; Cronulla 1
KILROY, Joe (2) Brisbane Broncos

KISS, Les (2) Norths, S

LANG, John (1) Easts, S
LANGER, Allan (9) Ipswich 4, Brisbane Broncos 5
LEWIS, Wally (26) Wynnum Manly 13; Fortitude Valley 8; Brisbane Broncos 5
LINDNER, Bob (14) Souths, B 1; Wynnum Manly 5; Parramatta 6; Gold Coast 2

McCABE, Paul (5) Easts, S 1; Manly 4
McINDOE, Alan (6) Illawarra 3; Penrith 3
MENINGA, Mal (18) Souths, B 13; Canberra 5
MILES, Gene (19) Wynnum Manly 14; Brisbane Broncos 5
MORRIS, Rod (4) Balmain 2; Wynnum Manly 2
MURRAY, Mark (14) Fortitude Valley 3, Redcliffe 11

NIEBLING, Bryan (9) Fortitude Valley 3; Redcliffe 6

OLIPHANT, Greg (1) Balmain

PHELAN, Chris (2) Souths, B 1; Parramatta 1

QUINN, Graham (1) St. George

REDDY, Rod (1) St. George
RIBOT, John (8) Manly 5; Redcliffe 3

SCOTT, Colin (16+1) Wynnum Manly 15+1; Easts, B 1
SHEARER, Dale (11+2) Manly
SMITH, Allan (1) Norths, S
SMITH, Gary (+1) Brothers
STACEY, Steve (2) Easts, B
STAINS, Danny (2) Cronulla

TESSMAN, Brad (4+1) Souths, B 3; Easts, S 1+1
TRONC, Scott (+1) Wests, S

VAUTIN, Paul (19+1) Manly

WALKER, Bruce (1) Manly
WALTERS, Kerrod (3) Brisbane Broncos
WALTERS, Kevin (+1) Canberra

NEW SOUTH WALES REGISTER

The following is a register of players who have appeared for New South Wales in the State of Origin series plus the match against Queensland in the United States of America, up to and including 1989. + indicates number of matches played as a substitute. B-Brisbane, S-Sydney.

ALEXANDER, Greg (2 + 1) Penrith
ANDERSON, Chris (4) Canterbury
AYLIFFE, Royce (1 + 2) Easts, S

BLAKE, Phil (+1) Souths, S
BOWDEN, Steve (1) Newtown
BOYD, Les (3) Manly
BOYLE, David (2 + 2) Souths, S
BRENTNALL, Greg (4) Canterbury
BROOKS, David (1) Balmain
BROWN, Ray (1 + 2) Manly
BUGDEN, Geoff (2) Parramatta

CARTWRIGHT, John (1 + 2) Penrith
CLEAL, Noel (11 + 1) Manly
CLYDE, Bradley (2) Canberra
CONLON, Ross (3) Canterbury
COOPER, Bob (1) Wests, S
COVENEY, John (2) Canterbury
CRONIN, Mick (6) Parramatta

DALEY, Laurie (2) Canberra
DALEY, Phil (3) Manly
DAVIDSON, Les (5) Souths, S
DOCKING, Jonathan (2) Cronulla
DUKES, Phillip (1) Moree
DUNN, Paul (2 + 1) Canterbury

EADIE, Graham (1) Manly
EDGE, Steve (1) Parramatta
ELIAS, Ben (5) Balmain
ELLA, Steve (3 + 4) Parramatta
ETTINGSHAUSEN, Andrew (7 + 1) Cronulla

FAHEY, Terry (2) Easts, S
FARRAR, Andrew (5) Canterbury
FENECH, Mario (2) Souths, S
FERGUSON, John (8) Easts, S 3; Canberra 5
FIELD, Paul (2) Cootamundra
FLORIMO, Greg (+1) Norths, S
FOLKES, Steve (8 + 1) Canterbury

GERARD, Geoff (2) Manly
GEYER, Mark (1) Penrith
GILLESPIE, David (+3) Canterbury
GROTHE, Eric (9) Parramatta
GURR, Marty (2) Easts, S

HAMBLY, Gary (1) Souths, S
HANSON, Steve (1) Norths, S
HASLER, Des (4 + 4) Manly
HASTINGS, Kevin (+1) Easts, S
HETHERINGTON, Brian (1 + 1) Illawarra
HILDITCH, Ron (1) Parramatta
HUNT, Neil (2) Parramatta

IZZARD, Brad (2 + 1) Penrith

JACK, Garry (13) Balmain
JARVIS, Pat (6 + 2) St. George (4 + 2), Canterbury 2

JENSEN, Barry (1) Newtown
JOHNS, Chris (3) Brisbane Broncos
JOHNSTON, Brian (8) St. George
JOHNSTON, Lindsey (2) Norths, S
JURD, Stan (1 + 1) Parramatta

KELLY, Peter (2) Penrith
KENNY, Brett (16 + 1) Parramatta
KRILICH, Max (5) Manly

LAMB, Terry (4 + 3) Canterbury 3 + 3, Wests, S 1
LANGMACK, Paul (3 + 1) Canterbury
LAZARUS, Glen (+1) Canberra
LEIS, Jim (1) Wests, S
LYONS, Cliff (4) Manly

MACKAY, Brad (1) St. George
MATTERSON, Terry, (+1) Brisbane Broncos
McGAW, Mark (6 + 1) Cronulla
McGUIRE, Bruce (2) Balmain
McKINNON, Don (1) Norths, S
MERLO, Paul (1) Wests, S
MELROSE, Tony (1) Souths, S
MILLER, Gavin (5) Cronulla
MORRIS, Steve (2) St. George
MORTIMER, Chris (8 + 1) Canterbury 7, Penrith 1 + 1
MORTIMER, Steve (8) Canterbury
MUGGLETON, John (2) Parramatta

NISZCOTT, Ziggy (2) Souths, S

O'CONNOR, Michael (14) St. George 6, Manly 8

PEARCE, Wayne (15) Balmain
POTTER, Michael (+1) Canterbury
PRICE, Ray (8) Parramatta

RAMPLING, Tony (2 + 1) Souths, S
RAUDONIKIS, Tom (1) Newtown
ROACH, Steve (12) Balmain
ROGERS, Steve (4) Cronulla

SIGSWORTH, Phil (3) Newtown 2, Manly 1
SIMMONS, Royce (10) Penrith
SIRONEN, Paul (1) Balmain
STERLING, Peter (13) Parramatta
STONE, Robert (+1) St. George

THOMPSON, Alan (5 + 1) Manly
TREWHELLA, David (1 + 1) Easts, S
TUNKS, Peter (7 + 1), Souths 1, Canterbury 6 + 1

WALSH, Chris (1) St. George
WILSON, Alan (+2) Cronulla
WRIGHT, Rex (1) N. Newcastle
WYNN, Graeme (1) St. George
WYNN, Peter (4) Parramatta

YOUNG, Craig (4 + 1) St. George

AUSTRALIA TOUR OF NEW ZEALAND 1989

Date	Result	Score	Opposition	Venue	Attendance
4 July	W	50-18	**President's XIII** T: Belcher 3, Alexander 3, Backo, Hasler, O'Connor G: O'Connor 7	Palmerston North	5,000

| 9 July | W | 26-6 | **NEW ZEALAND** | Christchurch | 17,000 |

New Zealand:
Williams; T. Iro, K. Iro (1g), Kemp, Elia (1t); Cooper,
Friend; Todd, Harvey, Goulding, McGahan (Capt), Stewart,
Tuuta. Sub: Freeman (played).
Australia:
Belcher; Shearer, Meninga (5g), Currie (1t), Hancock;
Lewis (Capt, 1t), Alexander; Backo, Walters (1t), Roach,
Sironen (1t), Clyde, Vautin. Subs: O'Connor, McGuire (both
played).
Referee: Ray Tennant (England)

| 12 July | L | 24-26 | **Auckland**
T: Shearer (2), Currie,
Hancock, Alexander,
G: O'Connor 2 | Auckland | 9,000 |

| 16 July | W | 8-0 | **NEW ZEALAND** | Rotorua | 26,000 |

New Zealand:
Williams; T. Iro, K. Iro, Kemp, Mercer; Cooper, Freeman;
Todd, D. Mann, Goulding, McGahan (Capt), Stewart, Tuuta.
Subs: Bancoft, M. Horo (both played).
Australia:
Belcher, Shearer, Meninga (2g), Currie, Hancock (1t);
Lewis (Capt), Alexander; Backo, Walters, Roach, Sironen,
Clyde, Vautin. Sub: Hasler (played).
Referee: Ray Tennant (England)

| 19 July | W | 28-10 | **Wellington**
T: Shearer 2, Hancock,
Alexander, O'Connor
G: O'Connor 4 | Wellington | 6,000 |

| 23 July | W | 22-14 | **NEW ZEALAND** | Auckland | 15,000 |

New Zealand:
Williams; Mercer (1t), K. Iro, Kemp, Elia (1t);
K. Shelford (3g), Freeman; Todd, D. Mann, Goulding,
Stewart, M. Horo, McGahan (Capt). Subs: Sherlock, Tuuta
(both played).
Australia:
Belcher; Hancock, Shearer (1t), Currie, O'Connor (1t,2g);
Lewis (Capt), Hasler; Backo, Walters, Roach, Meninga (1t,1g),
Clyde (1t), Vautin. Subs: McGuire (played).
Referee: Ray Tennant (England)

TOUR SUMMARY

P	W	L	F	A
6	5	1	158	74

TOUR REGISTER

Captain: Wally Lewis
Coach: Bobby Fulton

Player	Club and State	App	Sub	T	G	Pts
ALEXANDER, Greg	Penrith (NSW)	5	—	5	—	20
BACKO, Sam	Brisbane Broncos (Q)	5	1	1	—	4
BELCHER, Gary	Canberra (Q)	5	—	3	—	12
BELLA, Martin	North Sydney (Q)	2	1	—	—	—
CLYDE, Bradley	Canberra (NSW)	3	1	1	—	4
CURRIE, Tony	Brisbane Broncos (Q)	5	—	2	—	8
HANCOCK, Michael	Brisbane Broncos (Q)	6	—	3	—	12
HASLER, Des	Manly (NSW)	3	1	1	—	4
JACKSON, Peter	Brisbane Broncos (Q)	3	—	—	—	—
LEWIS, Wally	Brisbane Broncos (Q)	3	—	1	—	4
McGUIRE, Bruce	Balmain (NSW)	3	2	—	—	—
MENINGA, Mal	Canberra (Q)	3	—	1	8	20
O'CONNOR, Michael	Manly (NSW)	4	1	3	15	42
ROACH, Steve	Balmain (NSW)	5	—	—	—	—
SHEARER, Dale	Manly (Q)	5	—	5	—	20
SIRONEN, Paul	Balmain (NSW)	3	—	1	—	4
STAINS, Danny	Cronulla (Q)	3	—	—	—	—
TREWHELLA, David	Eastern Suburbs (NSW)	3	—	—	—	—
VAUTIN, Paul	Manly (Q)	6	—	—	—	—
WALTERS, Kerrod	Brisbane Broncos (Q)	3	2	1	—	4

Managers: Peter Moore
         Kevin Brash

Garry Schofield, back in action for Great Britain in Perpignan in March 1990 after an eight-Test absence through injury, going on to make a record-equalling third tour Down Under.

GREAT BRITAIN

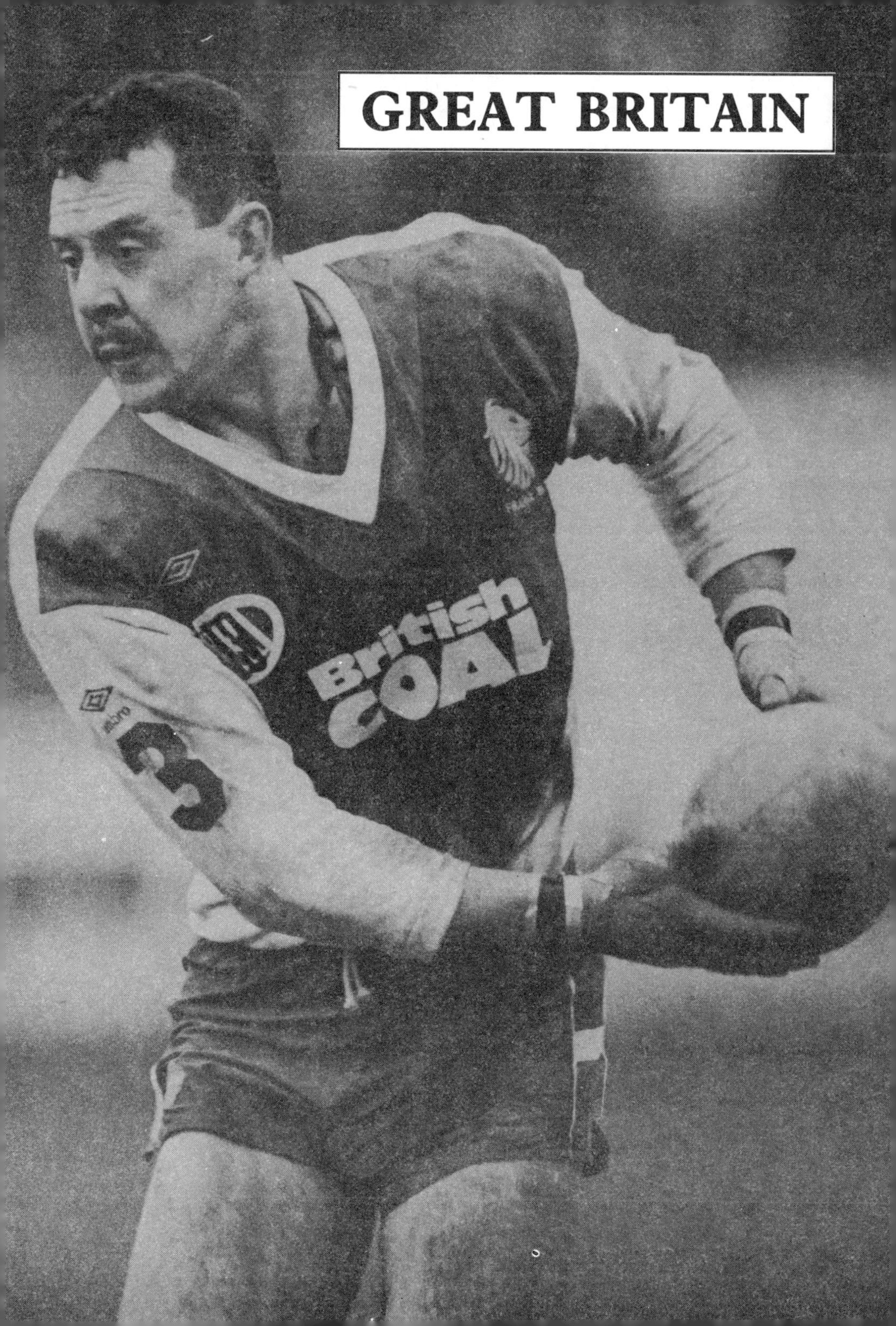

GREAT BRITAIN

1989-90 TEST REVIEW

In the autumn, Great Britain recorded their first home series success since 1965 with a 2-1 triumph over New Zealand. In the spring, the Lions were on the receiving end as the revitalised French registered their first Test success on British soil for 23 years and ran up their highest-ever score against them of 25-18.

The swing reflected Britain's five-Test season which opened with a shock 24-16 defeat at the hands of the previously uninspired touring Kiwis. Malcolm Reilly's charges re-established their credibility a week later with a memorable 26-6 success despite being reduced to 12 men inside only two minutes, before clinching the series with a hard-earned 10-6 success in the final encounter at Wigan. A chronicle of the Anglo-Kiwi Tests, plus the remaining nine tour fixtures, is featured in the chapter 1989 KIWIS.

Building for the forthcoming tour to Papua New Guinea and New Zealand, the Lions' form deteriorated in a low-key performance at Perpignan in March. Britain extended their record to eight successive victories over France, but only after a tremendous struggle against a well-prepared Gallic unit, themselves working towards a summer trip Down Under to Australia.

There was little indication of the battle to follow when Britain split the home defence in great style after only four minutes for winger Martin Offiah to claim his 42nd try of the season in typical lethal style. Centre partner Paul Loughlin suffered a leg injury in a cover tackle while releasing his winger and was carried off for X-rays, to be followed to hospital 16 minutes later by prop forward Andy Platt.

Britain's performance was reflected in their British Coal Man of the Match award which went to Bradford Northern prop forward Kelvin Skerrett, who drove in harder and more often than anyone but made little impression on a well-drilled French pack.

Skipper Ellery Hanley, featuring in his first Test of the season after being ruled out of the New Zealand series through injury, was hampered by a painful pelvis which was aggravated by an early bruising tackle. But the battling captain rallied his troops to produce tackling that rivalled the French in precision and ferocity.

Despite Kevin Beardmore's 10-7 pull in the scrums, little was seen of the British backs although debutant substitute Daryl Powell — Sheffield Eagles' first Test player — did well after replacing Loughlin. Offiah was again left to spend much of his time in isolation after opening the scoring in such blistering fashion, Britain's only other scores coming from two penalty goals from deputy goalkicker Garry Schofield in the 14th and 50th minutes.

The vital goals came after French left winger Cyrille Pons had equalised with an 11th minute touchdown, created by a long pass from their best player, stand off Gilles Dumas. The adventurous French failed to apply maximum pressure when Dumas, twice, and centre David Fraisse, three times, missed kicks at goal.

France's pre-tour programme of regular weekend camps and trial matches paid full dividend three weeks later with a well-deserved 25-18 triumph at Headingley, Leeds.

Classed as the best result for international football since Britain's triumph over Australia in 1988, the shock success was their first in Britain since a 23-13 victory at Wigan in 1967. The winning margin of three goals and a drop goal ended the Lions' record sequence of eight successive wins; was the basis of only their second victory in the previous 15 Anglo-French matches; and represented the first French Test win at Headingley in seven contests since the first-ever official Anglo-French meeting in 1957.

The Tricolours tally of 25 points was a record score against the British in their 52nd encounter, topping the 24 scored at Grenoble in 1959 and at Perpignan in 1985.

Britain took the field at Headingley without six injured regulars who had taken part in the unimpressive success at Perpignan — skipper Ellery Hanley, Wigan clubmates Joe Lydon Andy Gregory, Platt and Andy Goodway, plus Loughlin. Yet it would have been unfair to put all the blame on the newcomers, although some cast their tour chances in jeopardy.

Debuts were given to Bradford Northern's Welsh winger Gerald Cordle, Castleford stand off Graham Steadman plus substitutes Shaun Irwin, of Castleford, and Hull K.R.'s ex-Wales RU scrum half David Bishop. First full appearances were made by Carl Gibson, Karl Fairbank and Denis Betts, all of whom had previously made only one substitute appearance.

The shock setback came only four days before the announcement of Britain's 28-man touring squad and anticipated confirmation became unexpected reassessment.

Despite losing the scrums 18-9, the French half backs dominated the midfield with Dumas taking the British Coal Man of the Match award for a masterful all-round display which included a touchline goal and a drop goal. In contrast, new boy Steadman hardly justified his upgraded £170,000 record price tag, while Edwards, leading Britain for the first time, was uninspiring at scrum half, losing his self control in the dying minutes when sent to the sin bin for dissent.

Full back Alan Tait was a constant danger for the hapless Lions, while Cordle's well taken debut try was counter balanced by two defensive lapses which led to tries before being replaced by Irwin. On the opposite flank, Offiah was again left wandering in the wilderness, having to roam inside in the final minutes to touch down on the far side from his left wing touchline and complete a record of scoring a try in all five Tests in the season.

1990 TOURING SQUAD

A 28-man British Lions squad to tour Papua New Guinea and New Zealand was named on 11 April. Included in the party for the 15-match trip were a record number of 10 Wigan players, topping the previous best of eight, again from Wigan, in 1950.

The original squad was: Denis Betts, Phil Clarke, Martin Dermott, Shaun Edwards, Bobby Goulding, Steve Hampson, Ellery Hanley, Ian Lucas, Joe Lydon and Andy Platt (all Wigan); Jonathan Davies, Les Holliday, Martin Offiah and Alan Tait (Widnes); Keith England, Shaun Irwin and Graham Steadman (Castleford); Carl Gibson, Roy Powell and Garry Schofield (Leeds); Deryck Fox and Ian Smales (Featherstone R.); Paul Eastwood and Lee Jackson (Hull); David Bishop (Hull K.R.); Mike Gregory (Warrington); Paul Loughlin (St. Helens); and Kelvin Skerrett (Bradford N.).

Days after the announcement skipper Hanley withdrew through injury, Hampson and Holliday for personal reasons, their replacements being Chris Bibb (Featherstone R.), Karl Fairbank (Bradford N.) and Gary Price (Wakefield T.).

Then Edwards and Platt pulled out with injuries, Daryl Powell (Sheffield E.) and Paul Dixon (Leeds) taking their place.

Loughlin was then forced to withdraw with a groin injury, Roger Simpson (Bradford N.) standing in, while Anthony Sullivan (Hull K.R.) was drafted in to replace Offiah, whose arrival was being delayed by a toe injury.

Five days before departure, Lydon's troublesome ankle was operated on, putting back his out-going until the New Zealand section of the trip, Wigan's final tally of tourists being six. Sullivan was sent home without playing a game due to a torn hamstring suffered in training. He was replaced by John Devereux (Widnes). The tour will be chronicled in the 1991-92 *Rothmans Rugby League Yearbook*.

FIRST BRITISH COAL TEST

18 March   Perpignan

GREAT BRITAIN 8		**FRANCE 4**
Alan Tait (Widnes)	1.	Jean-Philippe Pougeau (St. Esteve)
Joe Lydon (Wigan)	2.	Hugues Ratier (Lezignan) Capt.
Garry Schofield (Leeds)	3.	David Fraisse (Carcassonne)
Paul Loughlin (St. Helens)	4.	Guy Delaunay (XIII Catalan)
Martin Offiah (Widnes)	5.	Cyrille Pons (St. Gaudens)
Shaun Edwards (Wigan)	6.	Gilles Dumas (St. Gaudens)
Andy Gregory (Wigan)	7.	Patrick Entat (Avignon)
Kelvin Skerrett (Bradford N.)	8.	Jean-Luc Rabot (Villeneuve)
Kevin Beardmore (Castleford)	9.	Thierry Valero (Lezignan)
Andy Platt (Wigan)	10.	Thierry Buttignol (Avignon)
Mike Gregory (Warrington)	11.	Daniel Divet (Carcassonne)
Andy Goodway (Wigan)	12.	Didier Cabestany (St. Esteve)
Ellery Hanley (Wigan) Capt.	13.	Jacques Moliner (Pamiers)
Graham Steadman (Castleford)	14.	Pierre Ailleres (Toulouse)
Denis Betts (Wigan)	15.	Jean Ruiz (St. Esteve)
Daryl Powell (Sheffield E.)	16.	Denis Bienes (St. Gaudens)
Keith England (Castleford)	17.	Philippe Sokolow (Carcassonne)

T: Offiah
G: Schofield (2)
Substitutions:
Powell for Loughlin (5 min.)
Betts for Platt (23 min.)
Manager: Maurice Lindsay
Coach: Malcolm Reilly

T: Pons
Substitution:
·Ailleres for Buttignol (72 min.)
Half-time: 6-4
Referee: Jim Stokes (New Zealand)
Attendance: 6,000

Scorechart

Minute	Score	GB	France
4:	Offiah (T)	4	0
11:	Pons (T)	4	4
14:	Schofield (P)	6	4
50:	Schofield (P)	8	4
	Scrums	10	7
	Penalties	16	12

Debutant substitute forward Denis Betts.

SECOND BRITISH COAL TEST

7 April   **Leeds**

GREAT BRITAIN 18   FRANCE 25

Alan Tait (Widnes)	1.	David Fraisse (Carcassonne)
Gerald Cordle (Bradford N.)	2.	Hugues Ratier (Lezignan) Capt.
Garry Schofield (Leeds)	3.	Guy Delaunay (XIII Catalan)
Carl Gibson (Leeds)	4.	Denis Bienes (St. Gaudens)
Martin Offiah (Widnes)	5.	Cyrille Pons (St. Gaudens)
Graham Steadman (Castleford)	6.	Gilles Dumas (St. Gaudens)
Shaun Edwards (Wigan) Capt.	7.	Patrick Entat (Avignon)
Kelvin Skerrett (Bradford N.)	8.	Thierry Buttignol (Avignon)
Kevin Beardmore (Castleford)	9.	Thierry Valero (Lezignan)
Keith England (Castleford)	10.	Jean-Luc Rabot (Villeneuve)
Denis Betts (Wigan)	11.	Daniel Divet (Carcassonne)
Karl Fairbank (Bradford N.)	12.	Didier Cabestany (St. Esteve)
Mike Gregory (Warrington)	13.	Jacques Moliner (Pamiers)
Deryck Fox (Featherstone R.)	14.	Marc Tisseyre (Pamiers)
Shaun Irwin (Castleford)	15.	Charles Frison (Toulouse)
David Bishop (Hull K.R.)	16.	Jean-Paul Marquet (Limoux)
Roy Powell (Leeds)	17.	Philippe Sokolow (Carcassonne)

T: Cordle, Tait, Offiah

G: Steadman (3)

Substitutions:

Irwin for Cordle (55 min.)

Bishop for Skerrett (61 min.)

Manager: Maurice Lindsay

Coach: Malcolm Reilly

T: Pons, Rabot, Divet

G: Fraisse (5), Dumas (1,1dg)

Substitution:

Frison for Cabestany (77 min.)

Half-time: 12-8

Referee: Jim Stokes (New Zealand)

Attendance: 6,554

Scorechart

Minute	Score	GB	France	Minute	Score	GB	France
5:	Steadman (P)	2	0	66:	Steadman (P)	14	16
18:	Cordle (T)	6	0	68:	Dumas (dg)	14	17
22:	Tait (T)			71:	Divet (T)		
	Steadman (G)	12	0		Fraisse (G)	14	23
28:	Pons (T)			77:	Offiah (T)	18	23
	Dumas (G)	12	6	79:	Fraisse (P)	18	25
37:	Fraisse (P)	12	8		Scrums	18	9
51:	Fraisse (P)	12	10		Penalties	6	8
53:	Rabot (T)						
	Fraisse (G)	12	16				

Bradford Northern's Gerald Cordle during his 55-minute Test debut against France in Leeds.

An uplifting experience for Wigan half back Shaun Edwards in Perpignan.

TESTS

● Although early Tests were played under the titles of Northern Union or England, it is acceptable to regard them as Great Britain.

W-Won, D-Drawn, L-Lost refer to Great Britain.

GREAT BRITAIN v. AUSTRALIA

12 Dec. 1908	D	22-22	QPR, London	2,000
23 Jan. 1909	W	15-5	Newcastle	22,000
15 Feb. 1909	W	6-5	Birmingham	9,000
18 Jun. 1910	W	27-20	Sydney	42,000
2 Jul. 1910	W	22-17	Brisbane	18,000
8 Nov. 1911	L	10-19	Newcastle	6,500
16 Dec. 1911	D	11-11	Edinburgh	6,000
1 Jan. 1912	L	8-33	Birmingham	4,000
27 Jun. 1914	W	23-5	Sydney	40,000
29 Jun. 1914	L	7-12	Sydney	55,000
4 Jul. 1914	W	14-6	Sydney	34,420
26 Jun. 1920	L	4-8	Brisbane	28,000
3 Jul. 1920	L	8-21	Sydney	40,000
10 Jul. 1920	W	23-13	Sydney	32,000
1 Oct. 1921	W	6-5	Leeds	32,000
5 Nov. 1921	L	2-16	Hull	21,504
14 Jan. 1922	W	6-0	Salford	21,000
23 Jun. 1924	W	22-3	Sydney	50,000
28 Jun. 1924	W	5-3	Sydney	33,842
12 Jul. 1924	L	11-21	Brisbane	36,000
23 Jun. 1928	W	15-12	Brisbane	39,200
14 Jul. 1928	W	8-0	Sydney	44,548
21 Jul. 1928	L	14-21	Sydney	37,000
5 Oct. 1929	L	8-31	Hull K.R.	20,000
9 Nov. 1929	W	9-3	Leeds	31,402
4 Jan. 1930	D	0-0	Swinton	34,709
15 Jan. 1930	W	3-0	Rochdale	16,743
6 Jun. 1932	W	8-6	Sydney	70,204
18 Jun. 1932	L	6-15	Brisbane	26,500
16 Jul. 1932	W	18-13	Sydney	50,053
7 Oct. 1933	W	4-0	Belle Vue, Manchester	34,000
11 Nov. 1933	W	7-5	Leeds	29,618
16 Dec. 1933	W	19-16	Swinton	10,990
29 Jun. 1936	L	8-24	Sydney	63,920
4 Jul. 1936	W	12-7	Brisbane	29,486
18 Jul. 1936	W	12-7	Sydney	53,546
16 Oct. 1937	W	5-4	Leeds	31,949
13 Nov. 1937	W	13-3	Swinton	31,724
18 Dec. 1937	L	3-13	Huddersfield	9,093
17 Jun. 1946	D	8-8	Sydney	64,527
6 Jul. 1946	W	14-5	Brisbane	40,500
20 Jul. 1946	W	20-7	Sydney	35,294
9 Oct. 1948	W	23-21	Leeds	36,529
6 Nov. 1948	W	16-7	Swinton	36,354
29 Jan. 1949	W	23-9	Bradford	42,000
12 Jun. 1950	W	6-4	Sydney	47,215
1 Jul. 1950	L	3-15	Brisbane	35,000
22 Jul. 1950	L	2-5	Sydney	47,178
4 Oct. 1952	W	19-6	Leeds	34,505
8 Nov. 1952	W	21-5	Swinton	32,421
13 Dec. 1952	L	7-27	Bradford	30,509
12 Jun. 1954	L	12-37	Sydney	65,884
3 Jul. 1954	W	38-21	Brisbane	46,355
17 Jul. 1954	L	16-20	Sydney	67,577
17 Nov. 1956	W	21-10	Wigan	22,473
1 Dec. 1956	L	9-22	Bradford	23,634
15 Dec. 1956	W	19-0	Swinton	17,542
14 Jun. 1958	L	8-25	Sydney	68,777
5 Jul. 1958	W	25-18	Brisbane	32,965
19 Jul. 1958	W	40-17	Sydney	68,720
17 Oct. 1959	L	14-22	Swinton	35,224
21 Nov. 1959	W	11-10	Leeds	30,184
12 Dec. 1959	W	18-12	Wigan	26,089
9 Jun. 1962	W	31-12	Sydney	70,174
30 Jun. 1962	W	17-10	Brisbane	34,766
14 Jul. 1962	L	17-18	Sydney	42,104
16 Oct. 1963	L	2-28	Wembley	13,946
9 Nov. 1963	L	12-50	Swinton	30,833
30 Nov. 1963	W	16-5	Leeds	20,497
25 Jun. 1966	W	17-13	Sydney	57,962
16 Jul. 1966	L	4-6	Brisbane	45,057
23 Jul. 1966	L	14-19	Sydney	63,503
21 Oct. 1967	W	16-11	Leeds	22,293
3 Nov. 1967	L	11-17	White City, London	17,445
9 Dec. 1967	L	3-11	Swinton	13,615
6 Jun. 1970	L	15-37	Brisbane	42,807
20 Jun. 1970	W	28-7	Sydney	60,962
4 Jul. 1970	W	21-17	Sydney	61,258
3 Nov. 1973	W	21-12	Wembley	9,874
24 Nov. 1973	L	6-14	Leeds	16,674
1 Dec. 1973	L	5-15	Warrington	10,019
15 Jun. 1974	L	6-12	Brisbane	30,280
6 Jul. 1974	W	16-11	Sydney	48,006
20 Jul. 1974	L	18-22	Sydney	55,505
21 Oct. 1978	L	9-15	Wigan	17,644
5 Nov. 1978	W	18-14	Bradford	26,447
18 Nov. 1978	L	6-23	Leeds	29,627
16 Jun. 1979	L	0-35	Brisbane	23,051

30 Jun. 1979	L	16-24	Sydney	26,837	
14 Jul. 1979	L	2-28	Sydney	16,844	
30 Oct. 1982	L	4-40	Hull C. FC	26,771	
20 Nov. 1982	L	6-27	Wigan	23,216	
28 Nov. 1982	L	8-32	Leeds	17,318	
9 Jun. 1984	L	8-25	Sydney	30,190	
26 Jun. 1984	L	6-18	Brisbane	26,534	
7 Jul. 1984	L	7-20	Sydney	18,756	

25 Oct. 1986	L	16-38	Man U. FC	50,583
8 Nov. 1986	L	4-34	Elland Rd, Leeds	30,808
*22 Nov. 1986	L	15-24	Wigan	20,169
11 Jun. 1988	L	6-17	Sydney	24,202
28 Jun. 1988	L	14-34	Brisbane	27,103
*9 Jul. 1988	W	26-12	Sydney	15,994

* Also World Cup match.

	Played	Won	Drawn	Lost	Tries	Goals	Dr	Pts for
Great Britain	102	50	4	48	250	256	5	1284
Australia	102	48	4	50	293	321	6	1565

GREAT BRITAIN-AUSTRALIA TEST MATCH RECORDS

Britain

Highest score: 40-17 Third Test at Sydney 19 July 1958 (Also widest margin win)

Most tries in a match: 4 by J. Leytham (Wigan) Second Test at Brisbane 2 July 1910

Most goals in a match: 10 by B. L. Jones (Leeds) Second Test at Brisbane 3 July 1954

Most points in a match: 20 by B. L. Jones (as above)
20 (7g,2t) by R. Millward (Hull K.R.) Second Test at Sydney 20 June 1970.

Biggest attendance: 50,583 First Test at Old Trafford, Manchester, 25 Oct 1986

Australia

Highest score: 50-12 Second Test at Swinton, 9 Nov 1963 (Also widest margin win)

Most tries in a match: 3 by J. Devereux, First Test at QPR, London, 12 Dec 1908
3 by R. Gasnier, First Test at Swinton, 17 Oct 1959
3 by R. Gasnier, First Test at Wembley, 16 Oct 1963
3 by K. Irvine, Second Test at Swinton, 9 Nov 1963
3 by K. Irvine, Third Test at Sydney, 23 July 1966
3 by G. Miles, First Test at Old Trafford, Manchester, 25 Oct 1986
3 by M. O'Connor, First Test at Old Trafford, Manchester, 25 Oct 1986

Most goals in a match: 10 by M. Cronin, First Test at Brisbane, 16 June 1979

Most points in a match: 22 (5g,3t) by M. O'Connor First Test at Old Trafford, Manchester, 25 Oct 1986

Biggest attendance: 70,204 First Test at Sydney, 6 June 1932

● In a World Cup match at Perpignan, France, on 29 October 1972, R. Fulton scored 3 tries.

GREAT BRITAIN v. NEW ZEALAND

25 Jan. 1908	W	14-6	Leeds	8,182	30 Sept. 1961	L	11-29	Leeds	16,540
8 Feb. 1908	L	6-18	Chelsea	14,000	21 Oct. 1961	W	23-10	Bradford	19,980
15 Feb. 1908	L	5-8	Cheltenham	4,000	4 Nov. 1961	W	35-19	Swinton	22,536
30 Jul. 1910	W	52-20	Auckland	16,000	28 Jul. 1962	L	0-19	Auckland	14,976
1 Aug. 1914	W	16-13	Auckland	15,000	11 Aug. 1962	L	8-27	Auckland	16,411
31 Jul. 1920	W	31-7	Auckland	34,000	25 Sept. 1965	W	7-2	Swinton	8,541
7 Aug. 1920	W	19-3	Christchurch	10,000	23 Oct. 1965	W	15-9	Bradford	15,740
14 Aug. 1920	W	11-10	Wellington	4,000	6 Nov. 1965	D	9-9	Wigan	7,919
2 Aug. 1924	L	8-16	Auckland	22,000	6 Aug. 1966	W	25-8	Auckland	14,494
6 Aug. 1924	L	11-13	Wellington	6,000	20 Aug. 1966	W	22-14	Auckland	10,657
9 Aug. 1924	W	31-18	Dunedin	14,000	11 Jul. 1970	W	19-15	Auckland	15,948
2 Oct. 1926	W	28-20	Wigan	14,500	19 Jul. 1970	W	23-9	Christchurch	8,600
13 Nov. 1926	W	21-11	Hull	7,000	25 Jul. 1970	W	33-16	Auckland	13,137
15 Jan. 1927	W	32-17	Leeds	6,000	25 Sept. 1971	L	13-18	Salford	3,764
4 Aug. 1928	L	13-17	Auckland	28,000	16 Oct. 1971	L	14-17	Castleford	4,108
18 Aug. 1928	W	13-5	Dunedin	12,000	6 Nov. 1971	W	12-3	Leeds	5,479
25 Aug. 1928	W	6-5	Christchurch	21,000	27 Jul. 1974	L	8-13	Auckland	10,466
30 Jul. 1932	W	24-9	Auckland	25,000	4 Aug. 1974	W	17-8	Christchurch	6,316
13 Aug. 1932	W	25-14	Christchurch	5,000	10 Aug. 1974	W	20-0	Auckland	11,574
20 Aug. 1932	W	20-18	Auckland	6,500	21 Jul. 1979	W	16-8	Auckland	9,000
8 Aug. 1936	W	10-8	Auckland	25,000	5 Aug. 1979	W	22-7	Christchurch	8,500
15 Aug. 1936	W	23-11	Auckland	17,000	11 Aug. 1979	L	11-18	Auckland	7,000
10 Aug. 1946	L	8-13	Auckland	10,000	18 Oct. 1980	D	14-14	Wigan	7,031
4 Oct. 1947	W	11-10	Leeds	28,445	2 Nov. 1980	L	8-12	Bradford	10,946
8 Nov. 1947	L	7-10	Swinton	29,031	15 Nov. 1980	W	10-2	Leeds	8,210
20 Dec. 1947	W	25-9	Bradford	42,680	14 Jul. 1984	L	0-12	Auckland	10,238
29 Jul. 1950	L	10-16	Christchurch	10,000	22 Jul. 1984	L	12-28	Christchurch	3,824
12 Aug. 1950	L	13-20	Auckland	20,000	28 Jul. 1984	L	16-32	Auckland	7,967
6 Oct. 1951	W	21-15	Bradford	37,475	19 Oct. 1985	L	22-24	Leeds	12,591
10 Nov. 1951	W	20-19	Swinton	29,938	2 Nov. 1985	W	25-8	Wigan	15,506
15 Dec. 1951	W	16-12	Leeds	18,649	*9 Nov. 1985	D	6-6	Elland Rd, Leeds	22,209
24 Jul. 1954	W	27-7	Auckland	22,097					
31 Jul. 1954	L	14-20	Greymouth	4,240	*17 Jul. 1988	L	10-12	Christchurch	8,525
14 Aug. 1954	W	12-6	Auckland	6,186	21 Oct. 1989	L	16-24	Man U. FC	18,273
8 Oct. 1955	W	25-6	Swinton	21,937	28 Oct. 1989	W	26-6	Elland Rd, Leeds	13,073
12 Nov. 1955	W	27-12	Bradford	24,443					
17 Dec. 1955	L	13-28	Leeds	10,438	*11 Nov. 1989	W	10-6	Wigan	20,346
26 Jul. 1958	L	10-15	Auckland	25,000					
9 Aug. 1958	W	32-15	Auckland	25,000	* Also World Cup match				

	Played	Won	Lost	Drawn	Tries	Goals	Dr	Pts for
Great Britain	74	45	26	3	265	214	3	1248
New Zealand	74	26	45	3	172	210	0	964

GREAT BRITAIN-NEW ZEALAND TEST MATCH RECORDS

Britain

Highest score:	52-20 First Test at Auckland, 30 July 1910 (Also widest margin win)
Most tries in a match:	4 by W. Boston (Wigan) First Test at Auckland, 24 July 1954
	4 by G. Schofield (Hull) Second Test at Wigan, 2 Nov 1985

Most goals in a match: 7 by N. Fox (Wakefield T.) Third Test at Swinton, 4 Nov 1961
                         7 by E. Fraser (Warrington) Second Test at Auckland, 9 Aug 1958
Most points in a match: 16 (4t) by G. Schofield (Hull) Second Test at Wigan, 2 Nov 1985
Biggest attendance: 42,680 Third Test at Bradford, 20 Dec 1947

● In a World Cup match at Pau, France, on 4 November 1972, Britain won 53-19 with J. Holmes (Leeds) scoring 26 points from 10 goals and two tries.
In a World Cup match at Sydney on 8 June 1968, Bev Risman scored 7 goals.

New Zealand
Highest score: 32-16 Third Test at Auckland, 28 July 1984
Widest margin win: 19-0 First Test at Auckland, 28 July 1962
                         27-8 Second Test at Auckland, 11 Aug 1962
No player has scored three tries or more in a Test.
Most goals and points: 7g-14pts by D. White, Second Test at Greymouth, 31 July 1954
                         J. Fagan, First Test at Headingley, 30 Sep 1961
                         E. Wiggs, Second Test at Auckland, 20 Aug 1966
Biggest attendance: 34,000 First Test at Auckland, 31 July 1920
● In a World Cup match at Sydney, Australia, on 25 June 1957, W. Sorensen also scored 7 goals, 14 points.

GREAT BRITAIN v. FRANCE
● **Results since France were given Test match status.**

Date	Result	Venue	Attendance	Date	Result	Venue	Attendance
26 Jan. 1957	W 45-12	Leeds	20,221	2 Feb. 1969	L 9-13	Toulouse	10,000
3 Mar. 1957	D 19-19	Toulouse	16,000	7 Feb. 1971	L 8-16	Toulouse	14,960
10 Apr. 1957	W 29-14	St. Helens	23,250	17 Mar. 1971	W 24-2	St. Helens	7,783
3 Nov. 1957	W 25-14	Toulouse	15,000	6 Feb. 1972	W 10-9	Toulouse	11,508
23 Nov. 1957	W 44-15	Wigan	19,152	12 Mar. 1972	W 45-10	Bradford	7,313
2 Mar. 1958	W 23-9	Grenoble	20,000	20 Jan. 1974	W 24-5	Grenoble	5,500
14 Mar. 1959	W 50-15	Leeds	22,000	17 Feb. 1974	W 29-0	Wigan	10,105
5 Apr. 1959	L 15-24	Grenoble	8,500	6 Dec. 1981	W 37-0	Hull	13,173
6 Mar. 1960	L 18-20	Toulouse	15,308	20 Dec. 1981	L 2-19	Marseilles	6,500
26 Mar. 1960	D 17-17	St. Helens	14,000	20 Feb. 1983	W 20-5	Carcassonne	3,826
11 Dec. 1960	W 21-10	Bordeaux	8,000	6 Mar. 1983	W 17-5	Hull	6,055
28 Jan. 1961	W 27-8	St. Helens	18,000	29 Jan. 1984	W 12-0	Avignon	4,000
17 Feb. 1962	L 15-20	Wigan	17,277	17 Feb. 1984	W 10-0	Leeds	7,646
11 Mar. 1962	L 13-23	Perpignan	14,000	1 Mar. 1985	W 50-4	Leeds	6,491
2 Dec. 1962	L 12-17	Perpignan	5,000	17 Mar. 1985	L 16-24	Perpignan	5,000
3 Apr. 1963	W 42-4	Wigan	19,487	*16 Feb. 1986	D 10-10	Avignon	4,000
8 Mar. 1964	W 11-5	Perpignan	4,326	1 Mar. 1986	W 24-10	Wigan	8,112
18 Mar. 1964	W 39-0	Leigh	4,750	*24 Jan. 1987	W 52-4	Leeds	6,567
6 Dec. 1964	L 8-18	Perpignan	15,000	8 Feb. 1987	W 20-10	Carcassonne	2,000
23 Jan. 1965	W 17-7	Swinton	9,959	24 Jan. 1988	W 28-14	Avignon	6,500
16 Jan. 1966	L 13-18	Perpignan	6,000	6 Feb. 1988	W 30-12	Leeds	7,007
5 Mar. 1966	L 4-8	Wigan	14,004	21 Jan. 1989	W 26-10	Wigan	8,266
22 Jan. 1967	W 16-13	Carcassonne	10,650	5 Feb. 1989	W 30-8	Avignon	6,500
4 Mar. 1967	L 13-23	Wigan	7,448	18 Mar. 1990	W 8-4	Perpignan	6,000
11 Feb. 1968	W 22-13	Paris	8,000	7 Apr. 1990	L 18-25	Leeds	6,554
2 Mar. 1968	W 19-8	Bradford	14,196				
30 Nov. 1968	W 34-10	St. Helens	6,080				

* Also World Cup match.

	Played	Won	Drawn	Lost	Tries	Goals	Dr	Pts for
Great Britain	52	35	3	14	227	217	0	1170
France	52	14	3	35	98	132	4	583

GREAT BRITAIN-FRANCE TEST MATCH RECORDS

Britain
Highest score: 52-4 at Leeds, 24 January 1987
(Also widest margin win)
Most tries in a match: 4 by A. Murphy (St. Helens) at Leeds, 14 March 1959
Most goals in a match: 10 by B. Ganley (Oldham) at Wigan, 23 November 1957
Most points in a match: 21 (9g,1t) by B.L. Jones (Leeds) at Leeds, 26 January 1957
        21 (9g,1t) by N. Fox (Wakefield T.) at Wigan, 3 April 1963
        21 (9g,1t) by N. Fox (Wakefield T.) at Leigh, 18 March 1964
Biggest attendance: 23,250 at St. Helens, 10 April 1957

France
Highest score: 25-18 at Leeds, 7 April 1990
Widest margin win: 19-2 at Marseilles, 20 December 1981
Most tries in a match: 3 by D. Couston at Perpignan, 17 March 1985
Most goals in a match: 7 by P. Lacaze at Wigan, 4 March 1967
Most points in a match: 14 by P. Lacaze (as above).
        14 (4g,2t) by G. Benausse at Wigan, 17 February 1962
Biggest attendance: 20,000 at Grenoble, 2 March 1958
●In a World Cup match at Toulouse on 7 November 1954, there were 37,471

Additional Great Britain v. France

Pre-Test status
22 May 1952	L	12-22	Paris	16,466
24 May 1953	L	17-28	Lyons	
27 Apr. 1954	W	17-8	Bradford	14,153
11 Dec. 1955	L	5-17	Paris	18,000
11 Apr. 1956	W	18-10	Bradford	10,453

Other match
31 July 1982	L	7-8	Venice	1,500

GREAT BRITAIN v PAPUA NEW GUINEA
5 Aug. 1984	W	38-20	Mt. Hagen	7,510
* 24 Oct. 1987	W	42-0	Wigan	9,121
* 22 May 1988	W	42-22	Port Moresby	12,107

* Also World Cup

Mike Gregory halted by French centre Denis Bienes at Leeds.

GREAT BRITAIN REPRESENTATION CLUB-BY-CLUB

Wigan beat their own record by fielding eight players in the Great Britain side which met Papua New Guinea at Wigan on 24 October 1987. The octet was backs Steve Hampson, David Stephenson, Joe Lydon, Shaun Edwards and Andy Gregory, plus forwards Brian Case, Andy Goodway and Ellery Hanley. The previous best of seven were backs Martin Ryan, Gordon Ratcliffe, Ernie Ashcroft, Jack Hilton and Tommy Bradshaw; plus forwards Ken Gee and Joe Egan in the 6-4 victory over Australia at Sydney on 12 June, 1950. Wigan also hold the record for the total of players selected with a remarkable 74.

Mick Sullivan gained Test honours with four clubs — Huddersfield (16), Wigan (19), St. Helens (10) and York (1). Billy Boston gained the most Test honours with a single club, making all 31 of his appearances for Britain while with Wigan.

Only six of last season's clubs have not had a player selected for Great Britain in Test or World Cup matches — Chorley, Bramley, Doncaster, Carlisle, Nottingham City and Trafford Borough. Of the extinct clubs only Broughton Rangers (later Belle Vue Rangers), Merthyr Tydfil, St. Helens Recs and the old Runcorn had players selected for Britain.

The following is a club-by-club register of Great Britain players. The figure in brackets after a player's name is the number of Great Britain appearances he made while serving the club under whose entry he is listed, and the number after the + sign indicates playing substitute. This is followed by the time span between his first and last British cap while at that club.

BARROW (19 players)
W. Burgess (16) 1924-29
W. Burgess (13) 1962-68
D. Cairns (2) 1984
C. Camilleri (2) 1980
C. Carr (7) 1924-26
F. Castle (4) 1952-54
R. Francis (1) 1947
H. Gifford (2) 1908
D. Goodwin (5) 1957-58
J. Grundy (12) 1955-57
P. Hogan (4 + 1) 1977-78
W. Horne (8) 1946-52
P. Jackson (27) 1954-58
J. Jones (1) 1946
B. Knowelden (1) 1946
E. Szymala (1 + 1) 1981
E. Toohey (3) 1952
L. A. Troup (2) 1936
J. Woods (1) 1933

BATLEY (4 players)
N. Field (1) 1963
F. Gallagher (8) 1924-26
C. Gibson (+ 1) 1985
J. Oliver (4) 1928

BRADFORD NORTHERN (31 players)
D. Barends (2) 1979
E. Batten (4) 1946-47
I. Brooke (5) 1966
L. Casey (5) 1979
G. Cordle (1) 1990
W. T. H. Davies (3) 1946-47
K. Fairbank (1 + 1) 1987-90
A. Fisher (8) 1970-78
P. Ford (7) 1987-88
T. Foster (3) 1946-48
J. Grayshon (11) 1979-82
E. Hanley (10 + 1) 1984-85
D. Hobbs (1 + 1) 1989
R. Jasiewicz (1) 1984
J. Kitching (1) 1946
A. Mann (2) 1908
K. Mumby (11) 1982-84
B. Noble (11) 1982-84
T. Price (1) 1970

J. Rae (1) 1965
W. Ramsey (+ 1) 1974
A. Rathbone (4 + 1) 1982-85
A. Redfearn (1) 1979
D. Redfearn (6 + 1) 1972-74
K. Skerrett (5) 1989-90
T. Smales (3) 1965
H. Smith (2) 1926
J. Thompson (1) 1978
K. Traill (8) 1950-54
E. Ward (20) 1946-52
F. Whitcombe (2) 1946

BROUGHTON/BELLE VUE RANGERS (8 players)
W. Bentham (2) 1924
L. Clampitt (3) 1907-14
E. Gwyther (6) 1947-51
A. Hogg (1) 1907
S. McCormick (2) 1948
D. Phillips (1) 1950
J. Price (2) 1921
J. Ruddick (3) 1907-10

CASTLEFORD (25 players)
A. Atkinson (11) 1929-36
K. Beardmore (13 + 1) 1984-90
W. Bryant (4 + 1) 1964-67
A. Croston (1) 1937
B. Cunniffe (1) 1937
W. J. Davies (1) 1933
D. Edwards (3 + 2) 1968-71
K. England (2 + 3) 1987-90
A. Hardisty (12) 1964-70
D. Hartley (9) 1968-70
K. Hepworth (11) 1967-70
S. Irwin (+ 1) 1990
J. Joyner (14 + 2) 1978-84
B. Lockwood (7) 1972-74
A. Marchant (3) 1986
R. Millward (1) 1966
S. Norton (2 + 1) 1974
D. Plange (1) 1988
M. Reilly (9) 1970
P. Small (1) 1962
G. Steadman (1) 1990
G. Stephens (5) 1979
D. Walton (1) 1965
J. Ward (3) 1963-64
K. Ward (14) 1984-89

DEWSBURY (6 players)
A. Bates (2 + 2) 1974
F. Gallagher (4) 1920-21
J. Ledgard (2) 1947
R. Pollard (1) 1950
M. Stephenson (5 + 1) 1971-72
H. Street (4) 1950

**FEATHERSTONE ROVERS
(14 players)**
T. Askin (6) 1928
K. Bridges (3) 1974
T. Clawson (2) 1962
M. Dixon (2) 1962-64
S. Evans (5 + 3) 1979-80
Deryck Fox (9 + 1) 1985-89
Don Fox (1) 1963
D. Hobbs (7 + 1) 1984
G. Jordan (2) 1964-67
A. Morgan (4) 1968
S. Nash (16) 1971-74
P. Newlove (2 + 1) 1989
P. Smith (1 + 5) 1977-84
J. Thompson (19 + 1) 1970-77

FULHAM (1 player)
J. Dalgreen (1) 1982

HALIFAX (29 players)
A. Ackerley (2) 1952-58
A. Bassett (2) 1946
J. Beames (2) 1921
N. Bentham (2) 1929
H. Beverley (2) 1937
O. Burgham (1) 1911
A. Daniels (3) 1952-55
W. T. Davies (1) 1911
C. Dixon (1) 1968
P. Dixon (3 + 3) 1987-88
P. Eccles (1) 1907
T. Fogerty (+ 1) 1966
A. Halmshaw (1) 1971
N. James (1) 1986
R. Lloyd (1) 1920
A. Milnes (2) 1920
S. Prosser (1) 1914
D. Rees (1) 1926
C. Renilson (7 + 1) 1965-68
J. Riley (1) 1910
K. Roberts (10) 1963-66
A. Robinson (3) 1907-08
D. Schofield (1) 1955
J. Shaw (5) 1960-62
J. C. Stacey (1) 1920
J. Thorley (4) 1954
J. Wilkinson (6) 1954-55
F. Williams (2) 1914
D. Willicombe (1) 1974

HUDDERSFIELD (24 players)
J. Bowden (3) 1954
K. Bowman (3) 1962-63
B. Briggs (1) 1954
S. Brogden (9) 1929-33
J. Chilcott (3) 1914
D. Clark (11) 1911-20
D. Close (1) 1967
R. Cracknell (2) 1951
J. Davies (2) 1911
F. Dyson (1) 1959
B. Gronow (7) 1911-20
F. Longstaff (2) 1914
K. Loxton (1) 1971
S. Moorhouse (2) 1914
R. Nicholson (3) 1946-48
J. Rogers (7) 1914-21
K. Senior (2) 1965-67
T. Smales (5) 1962-64
M. Sullivan (16) 1954-57
G. Thomas (8) 1920-21
D. Valentine (15) 1948-54
R. Valentine (1) 1967
H. Wagstaff (12) 1911-21
H. Young (1) 1929

HULL (30 players)
W. Batten (1) 1921
H. Bowman (8) 1924-29
F. Boylen (1) 1908
R. Coverdale (4) 1954
M. Crane (1) 1982
L. Crooks (11 + 2) 1982-87
A. Dannatt (2) 1985
G. Divorty (2) 1985
J. Drake (1) 1960
W. Drake (1) 1962
S. Evans (2) 1982
V. Farrar (1) 1978
R. Gemmell (2) 1968-69
T. E. Gwynne (3) 1928-29
T. Harris (25) 1954-60
M. Harrison (7) 1967-73
W. Holder (1) 1907
A. Keegan (9) 1966-69
E. Morgan (2) 1921
S. Norton (9) 1978-82
W. Proctor (+ 1) 1984
P. Rose (1) 1982
G. Schofield (15) 1984-87
T. Skerrett (6) 1980-82
W. Stone (8) 1920-21
C. Sullivan (17) 1967-73
H. Taylor (3) 1907
R. Taylor (2) 1921-26
D. Topliss (1) 1982
J. Whiteley (15) 1957-62

**HULL KINGSTON ROVERS
(26 players)**
D. Bishop (+ 1) 1990
C. Burton (8 + 1) 1982-87
A. Burwell (7 + 1) 1967-69
L. Casey (7 + 2) 1977-83
G. Clark (3) 1984-85
A. Dockar (1) 1947
G. Fairbairn (3) 1981-82
J. Feetham (1) 1929
P. Flanagan (14) 1962-70
F. Foster (1) 1967
D. Hall (2) 1984
P. Harkin (+ 1) 1985
S. Hartley (2) 1980-81
P. Hogan (2 + 2) 1979
R. Holdstock (2) 1980
W. Holliday (8 + 1) 1964-67
D. Laws (1) 1986
B. Lockwood (1 + 1) 1978-79
P. Lowe (12) 1970-78
R. Millward (27 + 1) 1967-78
H. Poole (1) 1964
P. Rose (1 + 3) 1974-78
M. Smith (10 + 1) 1979-84
B. Tyson (3) 1963-67
D. Watkinson (12 + 1) 1979-86
C. Young (5) 1967-68

315

HUNSLET (23 players)
W. Batten (9) 1907-11
H. Beverley (4) 1936-37
A. Burnell (3) 1951-54
H. Crowther (1) 1929
J. Evans (4) 1951-52
K. Eyre (1) 1965
B. Gabbitas (1) 1959
G. Gunney (11) 1954-65
D. Hartley (2) 1964
J. Higson (2) 1908
D. Jenkins (1) 1929
A. Jenkinson (2) 1911
W. Jukes (6) 1908-10
B. Prior (1) 1966
W. Ramsey (7) 1965-66
B. Shaw (5) 1956-60
G. Shelton (7) 1964-66
F. Smith (9) 1910-14
S. Smith (4) 1954
C. Thompson (2) 1951
L. White (7) 1932-33
R. Williams (3) 1954
H. Wilson (3) 1907

KEIGHLEY (1 player)
T. Hollindrake (1) 1955

LEEDS (67 players)
L. Adams (1) 1932
J. Atkinson (26) 1968-80
J. Bacon (11) 1920-26
R. Batten (3) 1969-73
J. Birch (1) 1907
S. Brogden (7) 1936-37
J. Brough (5) 1928-36
G. Brown (6) 1954-55
M. Clark (5) 1968
T. Clawson (3) 1972
D. Creasser (2 + 2) 1985-88
L. Crooks (1) 1989
W. A. Davies (2) 1914
K. Dick (2) 1980
R. Dickinson (2) 1985
L. Dyl (11) 1974-82
A. Fisher (3) 1970-71
P. Ford (5) 1989
R. Gemmell (1) 1964
C. Gibson (1) 1990
J. Grayshon (2) 1985
R. Haigh (3 + 1) 1970-71
D. Hallas (2) 1961
F. Harrison (3) 1911
D. Heron (1 + 1) 1982
J. Holmes (14 + 6) 1971-82
S. Hynes (12 + 1) 1970-73
J. W. Jarman (2) 1914
D. Jeanes (3) 1972

D. Jenkins (1) 1947
B. L. Jones (15) 1954-57
K. Jubb (2) 1937
J. Lowe (1) 1932
P. Medley (3 + 1) 1987-88
I. Owens (4) 1946
S. Pitchford (4) 1977
H. Poole (2) 1966
R. Powell (9 + 2) 1985-89
D. Prosser (1) 1937
Keith Rayne (4) 1984
Kevin Rayne (1) 1986
B. Risman (5) 1968
D. Robinson (5) 1956-60
D. Rose (4) 1954
G. Schofield (6) 1988-90
B. Seabourne (1) 1970
B. Shaw (1) 1961
M. Shoebottom (10 + 2) 1968-71
B. Simms (1) 1962
A. Smith (10) 1970-73
S. Smith (10) 1929-33
D. Stephenson (4 + 1) 1988
J. Stevenson (15) 1955-58
S. Stockwell (3) 1920-21
A. Terry (1) 1962
A. Thomas (4) 1926-29
P. Thomas (1) 1907
J. Thompson (12) 1924-32
A. Turnbull (1) 1951
H. Waddell (1) 1989
D. Ward (12) 1977-82
W. Ward (1) 1910
F. Webster (3) 1910
R. Williams (9) 1948-51
H. Woods (1) 1937
G. Wriglesworth (5) 1965-66
F. Young (1) 1908

LEIGH (19 players)
K. Ashcroft (5) 1968-70
J. Cartwright (7) 1920-21
D. Chisnall (2) 1970
J. Darwell (5) 1924
S. Donlan (+ 2) 1984
D. Drummond (22) 1980-86
P. Foster (3) 1955
C. Johnson (1) 1985
F. Kitchen (2) 1954
J. Ledgard (9) 1948-54
G. Lewis (1) 1965
M. Martyn (2) 1958-59
W. Mooney (2) 1924
S. Owen (1) 1958
C. Pawsey (7) 1952-54
W. Robinson (2) 1963
Joe Walsh (1) 1971
W. Winstanley (2) 1910
J. Woods (7 + 3) 1979-83

MERTHYR TYDFIL (1 player)
D. Jones (2) 1907

OLDHAM (40 players)
A. Avery (4) 1910-11
C. Bott (1) 1966
A. Brough (2) 1924
T. Clawson (9) 1973-74
A. Davies (20) 1955-60
E. Davies (3) 1920
T. Flanagan (4) 1983-84
D. Foy (3) 1984-85
B. Ganley (3) 1957-58
A. Goodway (11) 1983-85
W. Hall (4) 1914
H. Hilton (7) 1920-21
D. Hobbs (2) 1987
D. Holland (4) 1914
R. Irving (8 + 3) 1967-72
K. Jackson (2) 1957
E. Knapman (1) 1924
S. Little (10) 1956-58
T. Llewellyn (2) 1907
J. Lomas (2) 1911
W. Longworth (3) 1908
L. McIntyre (1) 1963
T. O'Grady (5) 1954
J. Oster (1) 1929
D. Parker (2) 1964
D. Phillips (3) 1946
F. Pitchford (2) 1958-62
T. Rees (1) 1929
S. Rix (9) 1924-26
R. Sloman (5) 1928
A. Smith (6) 1907-08
I. Southward (7) 1959-62
L. Thomas (1) 1947
D. Turner (11) 1956-58
G. Tyson (4) 1907-08
H. Waddell (4) 1988
T. White (1) 1907
C. Winslade (1) 1959
A. Wood (4) 1911-14
M. Worrall (3) 1984

**ROCHDALE HORNETS
(8 players)**
J. Baxter (1) 1907
J. Bennett (6) 1924
J. Bowers (1) 1920
T. Fogerty (1) 1974
E. Jones (4) 1920
M. Price (2) 1967
J. Robinson (2) 1914
T. Woods (2) 1911

RUNCORN (2 players)
J. Jolley (3) 1907
R. Padbury (1) 1908

**RUNCORN HIGHFIELD/
HUYTON/LIVERPOOL/WIGAN
HIGHFIELD (4 players)**
R. Ashby (1) 1964
W. Belshaw (6) 1936-37
N. Bentham (6) 1928
H. Woods (5) 1936

ST. HELENS (46 players)
C. Arkwright (+2) 1985
L. Aston (3) 1947
W. Benyon (5+1) 1971-72
T. Bishop (15) 1966-69
F. Carlton (1) 1958
E. Chisnall (4) 1974
E. Cunningham (1) 1978
R. Dagnall (4) 1961-65
D. Eckersley (2+2) 1973-74
A. Ellaby (13) 1928-33
L. Fairclough (6) 1926-29
J. Fieldhouse (1) 1986
A. Fildes (4) 1932
A. Frodsham (3) 1928-29
P. Gorley (2+1) 1980-81
D. Greenall (6) 1951-54
P. Groves (1) 1987
R. Haggerty (2) 1987
M. Hicks (1) 1965
N. Holding (4) 1984
R. Huddart (12) 1959-63
L. Jones (1) 1971
A. Karalius (4+1) 1971-72
V. Karalius (10) 1958-61
K. Kelly (2) 1972
B. Ledger (2) 1985-86
P. Loughlin (11) 1988-90
J. Mantle (13) 1966-73
S. McCormick (1) 1948
T. McKinney (1) 1957
R. Mathias (1) 1979
G. Moses (9) 1955-57
A. Murphy (26) 1958-66
F. Myler (9) 1970
G. Nicholls (22) 1973-79
H. Pinner (5+1) 1980-86
A. Platt (4+3) 1985-88
A. Prescott (28) 1951-58
A. Rhodes (4) 1957-61
J. Stott (1) 1947
M. Sullivan (10) 1961-62
J. Tembey (2) 1963-64
A. Terry (10) 1958-61
John Walsh (4+1) 1972
J. Warlow (3+1) 1964-68
C. Watson (29+1) 1963-71

ST. HELENS RECS (5 players)
F. Bowen (3) 1928
A. Fildes (11) 1926-29
J. Greenall (1) 1921
J. Owen (1) 1921
J. Wallace (1) 1926

SALFORD (28 players)
W. Burgess (1) 1969
P. Charlton (17+1) 1970-74
M. Coulman (2+1) 1971
G. Curran (6) 1946-48
E. Curzon (1) 1910
T. Danby (3) 1950
C. Dixon (11+2) 1969-74
A. Edwards (7) 1936-37
J. Feetham (7) 1932-33
K. Fielding (3) 1974-77
K. Gill (5+2) 1974-77
J. Gore (1) 1926
C. Hesketh (21+2) 1970-74
B. Hudson (8) 1932-37
E. Jenkins (9) 1933-37
J. Lomas (5) 1910-10
T. McKinney (7) 1951-54
A. Middleton (1) 1929
S. Nash (8) 1977-82
M. Richards (2) 1974
A. Risman (17) 1932-46
J. Spencer (1) 1907
J. Ward (1) 1970
S. Warwick (2) 1907
D. Watkins (2+4) 1971-74
W. Watkins (7) 1933-37
P. Williams (1+1) 1989
W. Williams (2) 1929-32

SHEFFIELD EAGLES (1 player)
D. Powell (+1) 1990

SWINTON (15 players)
T. Armitt (8) 1933-37
A. Buckley (7) 1963-66
F. Butters (2) 1929
W. Davies (1) 1968
B. Evans (10) 1926-33
F. Evans (4) 1924
J. Evans (3) 1926
K. Gowers (14) 1962-66
H. Halsall (1) 1929
M. Hodgson (16) 1929-37
R. Morgan (2) 1963
W. Rees (11) 1926-29
D. Robinson (12) 1965-67
J. Stopford (12) 1961-66
J. Wright (1) 1932

**WAKEFIELD TRINITY
(22 players)**
I. Brooke (8) 1967-68
N. Fox (29) 1959-69
R. Haigh (2) 1968-70
W. Horton (14) 1928-33
D. Jeanes (5) 1971-72
B. Jones (3) 1964-66
H. Kershaw (2) 1910
F. Mortimer (2) 1956
H. Murphy (1) 1950
H. Newbould (1) 1910
J. Parkin (17) 1920-29
C. Pollard (1) 1924
E. Pollard (2) 1932
H. Poynton (3) 1962
D. Robinson (5) 1954-55
G. Round (8) 1959-62
T. Skerrett (4) 1979
S. Smith (1) 1929
D. Topliss (3) 1973-79
D. Turner (13) 1959-62
D. Vines (3) 1959
J. Wilkinson (7) 1959-62

WARRINGTON (43 players)
J. Arkwright (6) 1936-37
K. Ashcroft (+1) 1974
W. Aspinall (1) 1966
W. Belshaw (2) 1937
N. Bentham (2) 1929
J. Bevan (6) 1974-78
T. Blinkhorn (1) 1929
E. Brooks (3) 1908
J. Challinor (3) 1958-60
N. Courtney (+1) 1982
W. Cunliffe (11) 1920-26
G. Dickenson (1) 1908
W. Dingsdale (3) 1929-33
D. Drummond (2) 1987-88
R. Duane (3) 1983-84
R. Eccles (1) 1982
J. Featherstone (6) 1948-52
M. Forster (2) 1987
E. Fraser (16) 1958-61
L. Gilfedder (5) 1962-63
R. Greenough (1) 1960
A. Gregory (1) 1986
M. Gregory (14) 1987-90
G. Helme (12) 1948-54
K. Holden (1) 1963
A. Johnson (6) 1946-47
K. Kelly (2) 1980-82
T. McKinney (3) 1955
J. Miller (6) 1933-36
A. Murphy (1) 1971
A. Naughton (2) 1954
T. O'Grady (1) 1961

H. Palin (2) 1947
K. Parr (1) 1968
A. Pimblett (3) 1948
R. Price (9) 1954-57
R. Ryan (5) 1950-52
R. Ryder (1) 1952
F. Shugars (1) 1910
G. Skelhorne (7) 1920-21
G. Thomas (1) 1907
D. Whitehead (3) 1971
J. Woods (+1) 1987

WHITEHAVEN (5 players)
V. Gribbin (1) 1985
W. Holliday (1) 1964
R. Huddart (4) 1958
P. Kitchin (1) 1965
A. Walker (1) 1980

WIDNES (40 players)
M. Adams (11+2) 1979-84
J. Basnett (2) 1984-86
K. Bentley (1) 1980
M. Burke (14+1) 1980-86
F. Collier (1) 1964
A. Currier (1) 1989
R. Dutton (6) 1970
K. Elwell (3) 1977-80
R. Eyres (+1) 1989
J. Fieldhouse (6) 1985-86
R. French (4) 1968
L. Gorley (4+1) 1980-82
A. Gregory (8+1) 1981-84
I. Hare (1) 1967
F. Higgins (6) 1950-51
H. Higgins (2) 1937
E. Hughes (8) 1978-82
D. Hulme (7+1) 1988-89
P. Hulme (3+2) 1988-89
A. Johnson (4) 1914-20
V. Karalius (2) 1963
G. Kemel (2) 1965
D. Laughton (4) 1973-79
J. Lydon (9+1) 1983-85
T. McCue (6) 1936-46
J. Measures (2) 1963
J. Mills (6) 1974-79
A. Myler (14) 1983-86
F. Myler (14+1) 1960-67
G. Nicholls (7) 1971-72
M. Offiah (12) 1988-90
D. O'Neill (2+1) 1971-72
M. O'Neill (3) 1982-83
H. Pinner (1) 1986
G. Shaw (1) 1980
N. Silcock (12) 1932-37
A. Tait (6) 1989-90
J. Warlow (3) 1971
D. Wright (+1) 1988
S. Wright (7) 1977-78

WIGAN (74 players)
R. Ashby (1) 1965
E. Ashcroft (11) 1947-54
E. Ashton (26) 1957-63
W. Ashurst (3) 1971-72
F. Barton (1) 1951
J. Barton (2) 1960-61
J. Bennett (1) 1926
D. Betts (1+1) 1990
D. Bevan (1) 1952
W. Blan (3) 1951
D. Bolton (23) 1957-63
W. Boston (31) 1954-63
T. Bradshaw (6) 1947-50
F. Carlton (1) 1962
B. Case (6+1) 1984-88
N. Cherrington (1) 1960
C. Clarke (7) 1965-73
A. Coldrick (4) 1914
F. Collier (1) 1963
J. Cunliffe (4) 1950-54
S. Edwards (14+3) 1985-90
J. Egan (14) 1946-50
R. Evans (4) 1961-62
G. Fairbairn (14) 1977-80
T. Fogerty (1) 1967
P. Ford (1) 1985
W. Francis (4) 1967-77
D. Gardiner (1) 1965
K. Gee (17) 1946-51
H. Gill (14+1) 1981-88
A. Goodway (12) 1985-90
J. Gray (5+3) 1974
A. Gregory (12) 1987-90
S. Hampson (4+1) 1987-89
E. Hanley (18) 1985-90
C. Hill (1) 1966
D. Hill (1) 1971
J. Hilton (4) 1950
T. Howley (6) 1924
W. Hudson (1) 1948
D. Hurcombe (8) 1920-24
B. Jenkins (12) 1907-14
K. Jones (2) 1970
R. Kinnear (1) 1929
N. Kiss (1) 1985
D. Laughton (11) 1970-71
J. Lawrenson (3) 1948
J. Leytham (5) 1907-10
J. Lydon (10+1) 1986-90
B. McTigue (25) 1958-63
J. Miller (1) 1911
J. Morley (2) 1936-37
A. Platt (4) 1989-90
I. Potter (7+1) 1985-86
J. Price (4) 1924
R. Ramsdale (8) 1910-14
G. Ratcliffe (3) 1947-50
J. Ring (2) 1924-26
D. Robinson (1) 1970

M. Ryan (4) 1947-50
W. Sayer (7) 1961-63
J. Sharrock (4) 1910-11
N. Silcock (3) 1954
R. Silcock (1) 1908
D. Stephenson (5) 1982-87
J. Sullivan (25) 1924-33
M. Sullivan (19) 1957-60
G. Thomas (1) 1914
J. Thomas (8) 1907-11
S. Wane (2) 1985-86
E. Ward (3) 1946-47
L. White (2) 1947
D. Willicombe (2) 1974
W. Winstanley (3) 1911

**WORKINGTON TOWN
(9 players)**
E. Bowman (4) 1977
P. Charlton (1) 1965
B. Edgar (11) 1958-66
N. Herbert (6) 1961-62
W. Martin (1) 1962
V. McKeating (2) 1951
A. Pepperell (2) 1950-51
I. Southward (4) 1958
G. Wilson (3) 1951

YORK (7 players)
E. Dawson (1) 1956
H. Field (3) 1936
G. Smith (3) 1963-64
J. Stevenson (4) 1959-60
M. Sullivan (1) 1963
B. Watts (5) 1954-55
L. White (4) 1946

Wigan's Ellery Hanley, the fifth most capped Great Britain player with 29 appearances.

318

GREAT BRITAIN TEAMS
...A 20-year review

The following is a compendium of Great Britain Test and World Cup teams since the start of the 1970-71 season.

Initials are included where more than one celebrated player shared a surname in the same era. Only playing substitutes are included on the teamsheet.

(WC): World Cup t: try g: goal dg: drop goal * captain

Prop forward John Warlow, who gained the last of his seven Test caps in 1971.

1970 Australia (WC)
Leeds: 24 Oct
Won 11-4

Dutton (Widnes) 3g
Smith, A (Leeds)
Hynes (Leeds) 1t,1g
*Myler (St. Helens)
Atkinson, J (Leeds)
Shoebottom (Leeds)
Hepworth (Castleford)
Hartley, D (Castleford)
Fisher (Bradford)
Watson (St. Helens)
Laughton (Wigan)
Thompson, J (Featherstone)
Reilly (Castleford)

1970 France (WC)
Castleford: 28 Oct
Won 6-0

Dutton (Widnes) 3g
Jones, K (Wigan)
Hynes (Leeds)
*Myler (St. Helens)
Atkinson, J (Leeds)
Shoebottom (Leeds)
Hepworth (Castleford)
Hartley, D (Castleford)
Ashcroft, K (Leigh)
Watson (St. Helens)
Laughton (Wigan)
Thompson, J (Featherstone)
Reilly (Castleford)

1970 New Zealand (WC)
Swinton: 31 Oct
Won 27-17

Dutton (Widnes) 6g
Jones, K (Wigan)
Hynes (Leeds)
Hesketh (Salford) 1t
Atkinson, J (Leeds) 1t
Shoebottom (Leeds)
Hepworth (Castleford)
Chisnall, D (Leigh)
Ashcroft, K (Leigh)
Watson (St. Helens) 1t
Haigh (Leeds)
Thompson, J (Featherstone)
*Laughton (Wigan) 1t
Sub: Charlton (Salford)

1970 Australia (WC)
Leeds: 7 Nov
Lost 7-12

Dutton (Widnes) 1g
Smith, A (Leeds)
Hynes (Leeds) 1g
*Myler (St. Helens)
Atkinson, J (Leeds) 1t
Shoebottom (Leeds)
Hepworth (Castleford)
Hartley, D (Castleford)
Fisher (Leeds)
Watson (St. Helens)
Laughton (Wigan)
Thompson, J (Featherstone)
Reilly (Castleford)
Sub: Hesketh (Salford)
     Haigh (Leeds)

1971 France
Toulouse: 7 Feb
Lost 8-16

Whitehead (Warrington) 1g
Smith, A (Leeds) 1t
*Hynes (Leeds)
Benyon (St. Helens)
Atkinson, J (Leeds)
Hill, D (Wigan)
Shoebottom (Leeds)
Jeanes (Wakefield) 1t
Fisher (Leeds)
Warlow (Widnes)
Mantle (St. Helens)
Haigh (Leeds)
Laughton (Wigan)
Sub: Hesketh (Salford)
     Thompson, J (Featherstone)

1971 France
St. Helens: 17 March
Won 24-2

Whitehead (Warrington) 1t,3g
Smith, A (Leeds) 1t
Hesketh (Salford)
Benyon (St. Helens) 1t
Atkinson, J (Leeds)
Millward (Hull KR) 2t
Nash (Featherstone)
Warlow (Widnes)
Fisher (Leeds)
Watson (St. Helens)
Mantle (St. Helens)
Thompson, J (Featherstone) 1t
*Laughton (Wigan)
Sub: Watkins, D (Salford)
     Coulman (Salford)

1971 New Zealand
Salford: 25 Sep
Lost 13-18
Whitehead (Warrington) 2g
Jones, L (St. Helens)
Benyon (St. Helens) 1t
Hesketh (Salford) 1t
Sullivan, C (Hull)
*Millward (Hull KR)
Nash (Featherstone)
Warlow (Widnes)
Karalius, A (St. Helens)
Jeanes (Wakefield)
Ashurst (Wigan) 1t
Coulman (Salford)
Mantle (St. Helens)
Sub: Edwards, D (Castleford)

1971 New Zealand
Castleford: 16 Oct
Lost 14-17
Edwards, D (Castleford)
Sullivan, C (Hull) 1t
Watkins, D (Salford) 1g
Hesketh (Salford)
Walsh, Joe (Leigh) 1t
*Millward (Hull KR) 1t
Murphy, A (Warrington)
Harrison, M (Hull)
Karalius, A (St. Helens)
Coulman (Salford) 1t
Dixon, C (Salford)
Mantle (St. Helens)
Haigh (Leeds)
Sub: Benyon (St. Helens)
    Stephenson, M (Dewsbury)

1971 New Zealand
Leeds: 6 Nov
Won 12-3
Edwards, D (Castleford)
Sullivan, C (Hull)
Hesketh (Salford)
Holmes (Leeds) 2g,2dg
Atkinson, J (Leeds) 2t
*Millward (Hull KR)
Loxton (Huddersfield)
Harrison, M (Hull)
Karalius, A (St. Helens)
Jeanes (Wakefield)
Irving (Oldham)
Nicholls (Widnes)
Halmshaw (Halifax)
Sub: O'Neill, D (Widnes)

1972 France
Toulouse: 6 Feb
Won 10-9
Charlton (Salford)
*Sullivan, C (Hull) 1t
Holmes (Leeds) 2g
Benyon (St. Helens) 1t
Atkinson, J (Leeds)
Kelly (St. Helens)
Nash (Featherstone)
Harrison, M (Hull)
Karalius, A (St. Helens)
Jeanes (Wakefield)
Ashurst (Wigan)
Lowe, P (Hull KR)
Nicholls (Widnes)

1972 France
Bradford: 12 March
Won 45-10
Charlton (Salford) 1t
*Sullivan, C (Hull) 1t
Holmes (Leeds) 1t,6g
Benyon (St. Helens) 1t
Atkinson, J (Leeds) 1t
Kelly (St. Helens)
Nash (Featherstone)
Harrison, M (Hull)
Stephenson, M (Dewsbury) 1t
Jeanes (Wakefield) 1t
Ashurst (Wigan) 2t
Lowe, P (Hull KR) 1t
Nicholls (Widnes)
Sub: Walsh, John (St. Helens) 1t
    Irving (Oldham)

1972 Australia (WC)
Perpignan: 29 Oct
Won 27-21
Charlton (Salford)
*Sullivan, C (Hull) 1t
Hesketh (Salford)
Walsh, John (St. Helens)
Atkinson, J (Leeds) 1t
O'Neill, D (Widnes) 1t
Nash (Featherstone)
Clawson (Leeds) 6g
Stephenson, M (Dewsbury) 1t
Jeanes (Leeds)
Lockwood (Castleford)
Lowe, P (Hull KR) 1t
Nicholls (Widnes)
Sub: Holmes (Leeds)

1972 France (WC)
Grenoble: 1 Nov
Won 13-4
Charlton (Salford)
*Sullivan, C (Hull) 1t
Hesketh (Salford)
Walsh, John (St. Helens)
Atkinson, J (Leeds)
O'Neill, D (Widnes)
Nash (Featherstone)
Clawson (Leeds) 2g
Stephenson, M (Dewsbury)
Lockwood, B (Castleford)
Dixon, C (Salford)
Lowe, P (Hull KR) 2t
Nicholls (Widnes)

1972 New Zealand (WC)
Pau: 4 Nov
Won 53-19
Charlton (Salford) 1t
*Sullivan, C (Hull) 1t
Hesketh (Salford) 1t
Walsh, John (St. Helens)
Atkinson, J (Leeds) 2t
Holmes (Leeds) 10g,2t
Nash (Featherstone) 1t
Jeanes (Leeds) 1t
Stephenson, M (Dewsbury) 1t
Lockwood (Castleford)
Irving (Oldham)
Lowe, P (Hull KR)
Nicholls (Widnes) 1t
Sub: Redfearn, D (Bradford)
    Karalius, A (St. Helens)

1972 Australia (WC)
Lyon: 11 Nov
Drew 10-10
Charlton (Salford)
*Sullivan, C (Hull) 1t
Hesketh (Salford)
Walsh, John (St. Helens)
Atkinson, J (Leeds)
Holmes (Leeds)
Nash (Featherstone)
Clawson (Leeds) 2g
Stephenson, M (Dewsbury) 1t
Jeanes (Leeds)
Lockwood, B (Castleford)
Lowe, P (Hull KR)
Nicholls (Widnes)
Sub: Irving (Oldham)

1973 Australia
Wembley: 3 Nov
Won 21-12
Charlton (Salford)
*Sullivan (Hull)
Hynes (Leeds)
Hesketh (Salford)
Atkinson, J (Leeds)
Topliss (Wakefield)
Nash (Featherstone) 1dg
Clawson (Oldham) 4g '
Clarke (Wigan) 1t
Lockwood (Castleford) 1t
Nicholls (St. Helens)
Lowe, P (Hull KR) 2t
Batten (Leeds)

1973 Australia
Leeds: 24 Nov
Lost 6-14
Charlton (Salford)
*Sullivan (Hull)
Hynes (Leeds)
Hesketh (Salford)
Atkinson, J (Leeds)
Topliss (Wakefield)
Nash (Featherstone)
Clawson (Oldham) 3g
Clarke (Wigan)
Lockwood (Castleford)
Mantle (St. Helens)
Lowe, P (Hull KR)
Batten, R (Leeds)
Sub: Eckersley (St. Helens)
 Dixon, C (Salford)

1973 Australia
Warrington: 1 Dec
Lost 5-15
Charlton (Salford)
Smith, A (Leeds)
Hynes (Leeds)
Hesketh (Salford)
*Sullivan, C (Hull)
Eckersley (St. Helens)
Millward (Hull KR) 1t,1g
Clawson (Oldham)
Clarke (Wigan)
Harrison, M (Hull)
Nicholls (St. Helens)
Lowe, P (Hull KR)
Laughton (Widnes)
Sub: Watkins, D (Salford)
 Dixon, C (Salford)

1974 France
Grenoble: 20 Jan
Won 24-5
Charlton (Salford)
Fielding (Salford) 3t
Willicombe (Halifax) 1t
Hesketh (Salford)
Redfearn, D (Bradford)
Gill, K (Salford) 1t
Bates, A (Dewsbury)
Clawson (Oldham) 3g
Bridges (Featherstone)
Lockwood (Castleford)
Dixon, C (Salford)
Nicholls (St. Helens)
*Laughton (Widnes) 1t
Sub: Watkins, D (Salford)
 Gray (Wigan)

1974 France
Wigan: 17 Feb
Won 29-0
Charlton (Salford) 2t
Fielding (Salford)
Willicombe (Wigan) 1t
Hesketh (Salford)
Redfearn, D (Bradford) 2t
Gill, K (Salford)
Bates, A (Dewsbury)
Clawson (Oldham) 2g
Bridges (Featherstone)
Fogerty (Rochdale)
Dixon, C (Salford)
Nicholls (St. Helens)
*Laughton (Widnes) 1t
Sub: Watkins, D (Salford) 1g
 Gray (Wigan) 1t,1g

1974 Australia
Brisbane: 15 June
Lost 6-12
Charlton (Salford)
Redfearn, D (Bradford)
Watkins, D (Salford) 1g
*Hesketh (Salford)
Bevan, J (Warrington)
Millward (Hull KR)
Nash (Featherstone)
Clawson (Oldham) 2g
Bridges (Featherstone)
Mills (Widnes)
Dixon, C (Salford)
Thompson, J (Featherstone)
Nicholls (St. Helens)
Sub: Eckersley (St. Helens)
 Gray (Wigan)

1974 Australia
Sydney: 6 July
Won 16-11
Charlton (Salford)
Dyl (Leeds)
Eckersley (St. Helens)
*Hesketh (Salford)
Millward (Hull KR)
Gill, K (Salford) 1t
Nash (Featherstone)
Mills (Widnes)
Gray (Wigan) 3g,1dg
Thompson, J (Featherstone)
Dixon, C (Salford) 1t
Chisnall, E (St. Helens) 1t
Nicholls (St. Helens)
Sub: Norton (Castleford)

1974 Australia
Sydney: 20 July
Lost 18-22
Charlton (Salford)
Richards (Salford) 1t
Dyl (Leeds) 1t
*Hesketh (Salford)
Bevan, J (Warrington)
Gill, K (Salford)
Nash (Featherstone)
Clawson (Oldham)
Gray (Wigan) 6g
Thompson, J (Featherstone)
Dixon, C (Salford)
Chisnall, E (St. Helens)
Nicholls (St. Helens)
Sub: Millward (Hull KR)
 Rose, P (Hull KR)

1974 New Zealand
Auckland: 27 July
Lost 8-13
Charlton (Salford)
Redfearn, D (Bradford)
Dyl (Leeds)
*Hesketh (Salford)
Bevan, J (Warrington) 1t
Gill, K (Salford)
Nash (Featherstone) 1t
Clawson (Oldham) 1g
Gray (Wigan)
Thompson, J (Featherstone)
Dixon, C (Salford)
Norton (Castleford)
Nicholls (St. Helens)
Sub: Ashcroft (Warrington)

1974 New Zealand

Christchurch: 4 Aug

Won 17-8

Charlton (Salford)
Redfearn, D (Bradford) 1t
Dyl (Leeds) 1t
Dixon, C (Salford)
Richards (Salford)
*Hesketh (Salford) 1t
Nash (Featherstone)
Mills (Widnes)
Gray (Wigan) 4g
Thompson, J (Featherstone)
Chisnall, E (St. Helens)
Norton (Castleford)
Nicholls (St. Helens)
Sub: Bates, A (Dewsbury)

1974 New Zealand

Auckland: 10 Aug

Won 20-0

Charlton (Salford)
Redfearn, D (Bradford)
Willicombe (Wigan)
Dyl (Leeds) 1t
Bevan, J (Warrington) 2t
*Hesketh (Salford) 1t
Nash (Featherstone)
Clawson (Oldham)
Gray (Wigan) 4g
Thompson, J (Featherstone)
Chisnall, E (St. Helens)
Dixon, C (Salford)
Nicholls (St. Helens)
Sub: Bates, A (Dewsbury)
    Ramsey (Bradford)

1977 France (WC)

Auckland: 5 June

Won 23-4

Fairbairn (Wigan) 7g
Fielding (Salford)
Holmes (Leeds)
Dyl (Leeds) 1t
Wright, S (Widnes) 1t
*Millward (Hull KR) 1t
Nash (Salford)
Thompson, J (Featherstone)
Ward, D (Leeds)
Pitchford, S (Leeds)
Bowman, E (Workington)
Nicholls (St. Helens)
Hogan (Barrow)
Sub: Gill, K (Salford)
    Casey (Hull KR)

1977 New Zealand (WC)

Christchurch: 12 June

Won 30-12

Fairbairn (Wigan) 6g
Wright, S (Widnes) 2t
Holmes (Leeds)
Dyl (Leeds)
Francis, W (Wigan)
*Millward (Hull KR) 1t
Nash (Salford)
Thompson, J (Featherstone)
Ward, D (Leeds)
Pitchford, S (Leeds)
Bowman, E (Workington) 1t
Nicholls (St. Helens) 1t
Hogan (Barrow) 1t
Sub: Casey (Hull KR)

1977 Australia (WC)

Brisbane: 18 June

Lost 5-19

Fairbairn (Wigan) 1g
Wright, S (Widnes)
Francis, W (Wigan)
Dyl (Leeds)
Fielding (Salford)
*Millward (Hull KR) 1t
Nash (Salford)
Thompson, J (Featherstone)
Ward, D (Leeds)
Pitchford, S (Leeds)
Bowman, E (Workington)
Nicholls (St. Helens)
Hogan (Barrow)
Sub: Holmes (Leeds)
    Smith, P (Featherstone)

1977 Australia (WC)

Sydney: 25 June

Lost 12-13

Fairbairn (Wigan) 3g
Wright, S (Widnes)
Holmes (Leeds)
Dyl (Leeds)
Francis, W (Wigan)
*Millward (Hull KR)
Nash (Salford)
Thompson, J (Featherstone)
Elwell (Widnes)
Pitchford, S (Leeds) 1t
Bowman, E (Workington)
Casey (Hull KR)
Hogan (Barrow)
Sub: Gill, K (Salford) 1t
    Smith, P (Featherstone)

1978 Australia

Wigan: 21 Oct

Lost 9-15

Fairbairn (Wigan) 3g
Wright, S (Widnes)
Hughes (Widnes)
Cunningham (St. Helens)
Bevan, J (Warrington) 1t
*Millward (Hull KR)
Nash (Salford)
Thompson, J (Bradford)
Ward, D (Leeds)
Rose, P (Hull KR)
Nicholls (St. Helens)
Casey (Hull KR)
Norton (Hull)
Sub: Holmes (Leeds)
    Hogan (Barrow)

1978 Australia

Bradford: 5 Nov

Won 18-14

Fairbairn (Wigan) 6g
Wright, S (Widnes) 2t
Joyner (Castleford)
Dyl (Leeds)
Atkinson, J (Leeds)
*Millward (Hull KR)
Nash (Salford)
Mills (Widnes)
Fisher (Bradford)
Lockwood (Hull KR)
Nicholls (St. Helens)
Lowe, P (Hull KR)
Norton (Hull)
Sub: Holmes (Leeds)
    Rose, P (Hull KR)

1978 Australia

Leeds: 18 Nov

Lost 6-23

Fairbairn (Wigan)
Wright, S (Widnes)
Joyner (Castleford)
Bevan, J (Warrington) 1t
Atkinson, J (Leeds)
*Millward (Hull KR) 1t
Nash (Salford)
Mills (Widnes)
Fisher (Bradford)
Farrar (Hull)
Nicholls (St. Helens)
Lowe, P (Hull KR)
Norton (Hull)
Sub: Holmes (Leeds)
    Rose, P (Hull KR)

1979 Australia
Brisbane: 16 June
Lost 0-35
Woods, J (Leigh)
Barends (Bradford)
Joyner (Castleford)
Hughes (Widnes)
Mathias (St. Helens)
Holmes (Leeds)
Stephens (Castleford)
Mills (Widnes)
Ward, D (Leeds)
Skerrett (Wakefield)
Nicholls (St. Helens)
*Laughton (Widnes)
Norton (Hull)
Sub: Evans, S (Featherstone)
     Hogan (Hull KR)

1979 Australia
Sydney: 30 June
Lost 16-24
Fairbairn (Wigan)
Barends (Bradford)
Joyner (Castleford) 1t
Woods, J (Leigh) 5g
Hughes (Widnes) 1t
Holmes (Leeds)
Stephens (Castleford)
*Nicholls (St. Helens)
Ward, D (Leeds)
Skerrett (Wakefield)
Casey (Bradford)
Grayshon (Bradford)
Adams, M (Widnes)
Sub: Evans, S (Featherstone)
     Watkinson (Hull KR)

1979 Australia
Sydney: 14 July
Lost 2-28
Fairbairn (Wigan) 1g
Evans, S (Featherstone)
Joyner (Castleford)
Woods, J (Leigh)
Hughes (Widnes)
Topliss (Wakefield)
Redfearn, A (Bradford)
*Nicholls (St. Helens)
Ward, D (Leeds)
Casey (Bradford)
Hogan (Hull KR)
Grayshon (Bradford)
Norton (Hull)
Sub: Holmes (Leeds)
     Adams, M (Widnes)

1979 New Zealand
Auckland: 21 July
Won 16-8
Fairbairn (Wigan) 1t,2g
Evans, S (Featherstone) 1t
Joyner (Castleford)
Smith, M (Hull KR) 1t
Hughes (Widnes) 1t
Holmes (Leeds)
Stephens (Castleford)
Casey (Bradford)
Ward, D (Leeds)
*Nicholls (St. Helens)
Hogan (Hull KR)
Grayshon (Bradford)
Adams, M (Widnes)
Sub: Lockwood (Hull KR)

1979 New Zealand
Christchurch: 5 Aug
Won 22-7
Fairbairn (Wigan) 5g
Evans, S (Featherstone) 1t
Joyner (Castleford)
Smith, M (Hull KR)
Hughes (Widnes) 1t
Holmes (Leeds)
Stephens (Castleford)
*Nicholls (St. Helens)
Ward, D (Leeds)
Skerrett (Wakefield)
Casey (Bradford) 1t
Grayshon (Bradford) 1t
Adams, M (Widnes)

1979 New Zealand
Auckland: 11 Aug
Lost 11-18
Fairbairn (Wigan) 1g
Evans, S (Featherstone)
Joyner (Castleford)
Smith, M (Hull KR) 1t
Hughes (Widnes) 1t
Holmes (Leeds)
Stephens (Castleford) 1t
Skerrett (Wakefield)
Ward, D (Leeds)
*Nicholls (St. Helens)
Casey (Bradford)
Grayshon (Bradford)
Adams, M (Widnes)
Sub: Woods, J (Leigh)
     Hogan (Hull KR)

1980 New Zealand
Wigan: 18 Oct
Drew 14-14
*Fairbairn (Wigan) 4g
Camilleri (Barrow) 1t
Joyner (Castleford)
Smith, M (Hull KR) 1t
Bentley (Widnes)
Hartley, S (Hull KR)
Dick (Leeds)
Holdstock (Hull KR)
Watkinson (Hull KR)
Skerrett (Hull)
Gorley, L (Widnes)
Grayshon (Bradford)
Casey (Hull KR)
Sub: Pinner (St. Helens)

1980 New Zealand
Bradford: 2 Nov
Lost 8-12
*Fairbairn (Wigan) 4g
Drummond (Leigh)
Joyner (Castleford)
Smith, M (Hull KR)
Camilleri (Barrow)
Kelly (Warrington)
Dick (Leeds)
Holdstock (Hull KR)
Elwell (Widnes)
Shaw, G (Widnes)
Casey (Hull KR)
Grayshon (Bradford)
Pinner (St. Helens)
Sub: Evans, S (Featherstone)
     Gorley, L (Widnes)

1980 New Zealand
Leeds: 15 Nov
Won 10-2
Burke (Widnes) 2g
Drummond (Leigh) 2t
Joyner (Castleford)
Evans, S (Featherstone)
Atkinson, J (Leeds)
Woods, J (Leigh)
Walker (Whitehaven)
Skerrett (Hull)
Elwell (Widnes)
*Casey (Hull KR)
Gorley, P (St. Helens)
Adams, M (Widnes)
Norton (Hull)

323

1981 France
Hull: 6 Dec
Won 37-0
Fairbairn (Hull KR) 1g
Drummond (Leigh) 2t
Smith, M (Hull KR)
Woods, J (Leigh) 1t,7g
Gill (Wigan) 3t
Hartley (Hull KR) 1t
Gregory, A (Widnes)
Grayshon (Bradford)
*Ward, D (Leeds)
Skerrett (Hull)
Gorley, L (Widnes)
Gorley, P (St. Helens)
Norton (Hull)
Sub: Burke (Widnes)
      Szymala (Barrow)

1981 France
Marseilles: 20 Dec
Lost 2-19
Burke (Widnes)
Drummond (Leigh)
Smith, M (Hull KR)
Woods, J (Leigh) 1g
Gill (Wigan)
Hartley (Hull KR)
Gregory, A (Widnes)
*Grayshon (Bradford)
Watkinson (Hull KR)
Skerrett (Hull)
Gorley, L (Widnes)
Szymala (Barrow)
Norton (Hull)
Sub: Gorley, P (St. Helens)

1982 Australia
Hull City FC: 30 Oct
Lost 4-40
Fairbairn (Hull KR)
Drummond (Leigh)
Hughes (Widnes)
Dyl (Leeds)
Evans, S (Hull)
Woods, J (Leigh)
*Nash (Salford)
Grayshon (Bradford)
Ward, D (Leeds)
Skerrett (Hull)
Gorley, L (Widnes)
Crooks, L (Hull) 2g
Norton (Hull)
Sub: D. Heron (Leeds)

1982 Australia
Wigan: 20 Nov
Lost 6-27
Mumby (Bradford) 3g
Drummond (Leigh)
Smith, M (Hull KR)
Stephenson, D (Wigan)
Gill (Wigan)
Holmes (Leeds)
Kelly, K (Warrington)
*Grayshon (Bradford)
Dalgreen (Fulham)
Skerrett (Hull)
Eccles (Warrington)
Burton (Hull KR)
Heron, D (Leeds)
Sub: Woods, J (Leigh)
      Rathbone (Bradford)

1982 Australia
Leeds: 28 Nov
Lost 8-32
Fairbairn (Hull KR)
Drummond (Leigh)
Stephenson, D (Wigan)
Smith, M (Hull KR)
Evans (Hull) 1t
*Topliss (Hull)
Gregory, A (Widnes)
O'Neill, M (Widnes)
Noble (Bradford)
Rose (Hull)
Smith, P (Featherstone)
Crooks, L (Hull) 2g,1dg
Crane (Hull)
Sub: Courtney (Warrington)

1983 France
Carcassonne: 20 Feb
Won 20-5
Burke (Widnes) 1g
Drummond (Leigh)
Joyner (Castleford) 1t
Duane, R (Warrington)
Lydon (Widnes) 1t,3g
Myler, A (Widnes)
Gregory, A (Widnes)
O'Neill, M (Widnes)
Noble (Bradford) 1t
Goodway (Oldham) 1t
*Casey (Hull KR)
Rathbone (Bradford)
Flanagan (Oldham)
Sub: Woods, J (Leigh)
      Smith, P (Featherstone)

1983 France
Hull: 6 March
Won 17-5
Mumby (Bradford) 4g
Drummond (Leigh)
Joyner (Castleford)
Duane, R (Warrington) 1t
Lydon (Widnes)
Myler, A (Widnes)
Gregory, A (Widnes) 1t
O'Neill, M (Widnes)
Noble (Bradford)
Goodway (Oldham)
*Casey (Hull KR)
Rathbone (Bradford)
Flanagan (Oldham)
Sub: Smith, P (Featherstone) 1t

1984 France
Avignon: 29 Jan
Won 12-0
*Mumby (Bradford)
Drummond (Leigh)
Duane, R (Warrington)
Foy, D (Oldham) 1t
Clark (Hull KR)
Lydon (Widnes)
Cairns (Barrow)
Rayne, Keith (Leeds)
Watkinson (Hull KR)
Goodway (Oldham) 1t
Worrall, M (Oldham)
Hobbs, D (Featherstone)
Hall (Hull KR)
Sub: Hanley (Bradford)
      Crooks, L (Hull) 2g

1984 France
Leeds: 17 Feb
Won 10-0
Mumby (Bradford)
Clark (Hull KR)
Joyner (Castleford)
Schofield (Hull)
Basnett (Widnes)
Hanley (Bradford)
Cairns (Barrow)
Rayne, Keith (Leeds)
*Noble (Bradford)
Ward, K (Castleford)
Jasiewicz (Bradford)
Hobbs, D (Featherstone) 5g
Hall (Hull KR)
Sub: Smith, M (Hull KR)
      Smith, P (Featherstone)

1984 Australia
Sydney: 9 June
Lost 8-25
Burke (Widnes) 2g
Drummond (Leigh)
Schofield (Hull) 1t
Mumby (Bradford)
Hanley (Bradford)
Foy, D (Oldham)
Holding (St. Helens)
Crooks, L (Hull)
*Noble (Bradford)
Goodway (Oldham)
Burton (Hull KR)
Worrall, M (Oldham)
Adams (Widnes)
Sub: Lydon (Widnes)
 Hobbs, D (Featherstone)

1984 Australia
Brisbane: 26 June
Lost 6-18
Burke (Widnes) 1g
Drummond (Leigh)
Schofield (Hull) 1t
Mumby (Bradford)
Hanley (Bradford)
Myler, A (Widnes)
Holding (St. Helens)
Rayne, Keith (Leeds)
*Noble (Bradford)
Crooks, L (Hull)
Burton (Hull KR)
Goodway (Oldham)
Worrall (Oldham)
Sub: Gregory, A (Widnes)
 Adams (Widnes)

1984 Australia
Sydney: 7 July
Lost 7-20
Burke (Widnes) 1g
Drummond (Leigh)
Schofield (Hull)
Mumby (Bradford)
Hanley (Bradford) 1t
Myler, A (Widnes)
Holding (St. Helens) 1dg
Hobbs, D (Featherstone)
*Noble (Bradford)
Case (Wigan)
Burton (Hull KR)
Goodway (Oldham)
Adams (Widnes)

1984 New Zealand
Auckland: 14 July
Lost 0-12
Burke (Widnes)
Drummond (Leigh)
Schofield (Hull)
Mumby (Bradford)
Hanley (Bradford)
Smith, M (Hull KR)
Holding (St. Helens)
Hobbs, D (Featherstone)
*Noble (Bradford)
Case (Wigan)
Burton (Hull KR)
Goodway (Oldham)
Adams (Widnes)

1984 New Zealand
Christchurch: 22 July
Lost 12-28
Burke (Widnes) 2g
Drummond (Leigh)
Hanley (Bradford) 1t
Mumby (Bradford)
Lydon (Widnes)
Myler, A (Widnes) 1t
Gregory, A (Widnes)
Hobbs, D (Featherstone)
*Noble (Bradford)
Case (Wigan)
Burton (Hull KR)
Goodway (Oldham)
Adams (Widnes)
Sub: Joyner (Castleford)
 Beardmore, K (Castleford)

1984 New Zealand
Auckland: 28 July
Lost 16-32
Burke (Widnes) 4g
Drummond (Leigh)
Hanley (Bradford) 1t
Mumby (Bradford) 1t
Lydon (Widnes)
Myler, A (Widnes)
Gregory, A (Widnes)
Hobbs, D (Featherstone)
*Noble (Bradford)
Case (Wigan)
Adams (Widnes)
Goodway (Oldham)
Flanagan (Oldham)
Sub: Donlan (Leigh)
 Joyner (Castleford)

1984 Papua New Guinea
Mount Hagen: 5 Aug
Won 38-20
Burke (Widnes) 1t,5g
Drummond (Leigh) 2t
Hanley (Bradford) 1t
Mumby (Bradford) 1t
Lydon (Widnes)
Myler, A (Widnes)
Gregory, A (Widnes)
Rayne, Keith (Leeds) 1t
*Noble (Bradford)
Goodway (Oldham)
Flanagan (Oldham)
Hobbs, D (Featherstone) 1t
Adams (Widnes)
Sub: Donlan (Leigh)
 Proctor (Hull)

1985 France
Leeds: 1 March
Won 50-4
Edwards (Wigan)
Ledger (St. Helens)
Creasser (Leeds) 8g
Gribbin (Whitehaven) 1t
Gill (Wigan) 1t
Hanley (Bradford) 2t
Fox (Featherstone) 2t,1g
Dickinson (Leeds)
Watkinson (Hull KR) 1t
Dannatt (Hull)
*Goodway (Oldham)
Rathbone (Bradford)
Divorty (Hull) 1t
Sub: Gibson (Batley)
 Platt (St. Helens)

1985 France
Perpignan: 17 March
Lost 16-24
Johnson, C (Leigh)
Clark (Hull KR)
Creasser (Leeds) 1g
Foy, D (Oldham) 1t
Ford, P (Wigan) 2t
*Hanley (Bradford)
Fox (Featherstone)
Dickinson (Leeds)
Kiss (Wigan)
Wane (Wigan)
Dannatt (Hull)
Rathbone (Bradford)
Divorty (Hull) 1g
Sub: Harkin (Hull KR)
 Powell, R (Leeds)

1985 New Zealand
Leeds: 19 Oct
Lost 22-24
Burke (Widnes) 3g
Drummond (Leigh)
Schofield (Hull)
Hanley (Wigan) 1t
Lydon (Widnes) 1t,2g
Myler, A (Widnes)
Fox (Featherstone)
Crooks, L (Hull)
Watkinson (Hull KR)
Fieldhouse (Widnes)
Goodway (Wigan) 1t
Potter (Wigan)
*Pinner (St. Helens)
Sub: Arkwright (St. Helens)

1985 New Zealand
Wigan: 2 Nov
Won 25-8
Burke (Widnes)
Drummond (Leigh)
Schofield (Hull) 4t
Hanley (Wigan)
Lydon (Widnes) 4g
Myler, A (Widnes)
Fox (Featherstone)
Grayshon (Leeds)
Watkinson (Hull KR)
Fieldhouse (Widnes)
Goodway (Wigan)
Potter (Wigan)
*Pinner (St. Helens) 1dg
Sub: Edwards (Wigan)
 Burton (Hull KR)

1985 New Zealand (Also WC)
Elland Rd, Leeds: 9 Nov
Drew 6-6
Burke (Widnes)
Drummond (Leigh)
Schofield (Hull)
Edwards (Wigan)
Lydon (Widnes)
Hanley (Wigan)
Fox (Featherstone)
Grayshon (Leeds)
Watkinson (Hull KR)
Fieldhouse (Widnes)
Goodway (Wigan)
Potter (Wigan)
*Pinner (St. Helens)
Sub: Arkwright (St. Helens)
 Crooks, L (Hull) 3g

1986 France (Also WC)
Avignon: 16 Feb
Drew 10-10
Burke (Widnes)
Drummond (Leigh)
Schofield (Hull)
Hanley (Wigan) 1t
Gill (Wigan)
Myler, A (Widnes)
Fox (Featherstone)
Crooks, L (Hull) 3g
Watkinson (Hull KR)
Wane (Wigan)
Potter (Wigan)
Fieldhouse (Widnes)
*Pinner (St. Helens)
Sub: Platt (St. Helens)

1986 France
Wigan: 1 March
Won 24-10
Lydon (Wigan)
Drummond (Leigh) 1t
Schofield (Hull) 1t,2g
Marchant (Castleford) 1t
Laws (Hull KR)
Myler, A (Widnes)
Fox (Featherstone)
Crooks, L (Hull) 2g
*Watkinson (Hull KR)
Fieldhouse (Widnes)
Rayne, Kevin (Leeds)
James (Halifax) 1t
Potter (Wigan)
Sub: Platt (St. Helens)

1986 Australia
Man. U. FC. 25 Oct
Lost 16-38
Lydon (Wigan) 1t
Marchant (Castleford)
Schofield (Hull) 2t
Hanley (Wigan)
Gill (Wigan) 1g
Myler, A (Widnes)
Fox (Featherstone)
Ward (Castleford)
*Watkinson (Hull KR)
Fieldhouse (Widnes)
Crooks, L (Hull) 1g
Potter (Wigan)
Goodway (Wigan)

1986 Australia
Elland Rd, Leeds: 8 Nov
Lost 4-34
Lydon (Wigan)
Ledger (St. Helens)
Schofield (Hull) 1t
Marchant (Castleford)
Gill (Wigan)
Myler, A (Widnes)
Fox (Featherstone)
Ward (Castleford)
*Watkinson (Hull KR)
Fieldhouse (St. Helens)
Crooks, L (Hull)
Potter (Wigan)
Goodway (Wigan)
Sub: Edwards (Wigan)
 Platt (St. Helens)

1986 Australia (Also WC)
Wigan: 22 Nov
Lost 15-24
Lydon (Wigan) 2g
Gill (Wigan) 1g
Schofield (Hull) 2t,1dg
Stephenson (Wigan)
Basnett (Widnes)
Myler, A (Widnes)
Gregory, A (Warrington)
Ward (Castleford)
*Watkinson (Hull KR)
Crooks, L (Hull)
Burton (Hull KR)
Goodway (Wigan)
Pinner (Widnes)
Sub: Potter (Wigan)

1987 France (Also WC)
Leeds: 24 Jan
Won 52-4
Lydon (Wigan) 1t,8g
Forster (Warrington) 1t
Schofield (Hull)
Stephenson (Wigan)
Gill (Wigan)
*Hanley (Wigan) 2t
Edwards (Wigan) 2t
Hobbs (Oldham)
Beardmore, K (Castleford)
Crooks, L (Hull)
Goodway (Wigan) 1t
Haggerty (St. Helens)
Gregory, M (Warrington) 2t
Sub: Creasser (Leeds)
 England (Castleford)

1987 France

Carcassonne: 8 Feb

Won 20-10

Lydon (Wigan) 4g
Forster (Warrington)
Schofield (Hull)
*Hanley (Wigan) 1t
Gill (Wigan) 1t
Edwards (Wigan)
Gregory, A (Wigan)
Hobbs (Oldham)
Beardmore, K (Castleford) 1t
England (Castleford)
Burton (Hull KR)
Haggerty (St. Helens)
Gregory, M (Warrington)
Sub: Dixon (Halifax)

1987 Papua New Guinea (Also WC)

Wigan: 24 Oct

Won 42-0

Hampson (Wigan)
Drummond (Warrington)
Stephenson (Wigan) 7g
Lydon (Wigan) 1t
Ford (Bradford) 1t
Edwards (Wigan) 2t
Gregory, A (Wigan) 1t
Ward (Castleford)
Groves (St. Helens)
Case (Wigan)
Medley (Leeds) 1t
Goodway (Wigan)
*Hanley (Wigan) 1t
Sub: Woods (Warrington)
Fairbank (Bradford)

1988 France

Avignon: 24 Jan

Won 28-14

Hampson (Wigan)
Drummond (Warrington) 1t
Schofield (Leeds) 2t
Loughlin (St. Helens) 3g
Offiah (Widnes) 1t
*Hanley (Wigan) 1t
Edwards (Wigan)
Ward (Castleford)
Beardmore, K (Castleford)
Waddell (Oldham)
Powell, R (Leeds)
Medley (Leeds)
Platt (St. Helens)
Sub: Creasser (Leeds) 1g
Dixon (Halifax)

1988 France

Leeds: 6 Feb

Won 30-12

Hampson (Wigan)
Plange (Castleford) 1t
Schofield (Leeds) 1t,5g
*Hanley (Wigan) 2t
Ford (Bradford)
Edwards (Wigan)
Gregory, A (Wigan) 1t
Ward (Castleford)
Beardmore, K (Castleford)
Waddell (Oldham)
Powell, R (Leeds)
Dixon (Halifax)
Platt (St. Helens)
Sub: Stephenson (Leeds)
Medley (Leeds)

1988 Papua New Guinea (Also WC)

Port Moresby: 22 May

Won 42-22

Loughlin (St. Helens) 7g
Ford (Bradford)
Schofield (Leeds) 2t
Stephenson (Leeds) 1t
Gill (Wigan) 2t
Edwards (Wigan)
Gregory, A (Wigan)
Ward (Castleford)
Beardmore, K (Castleford)
Case (Wigan)
Medley (Leeds) 1t
Gregory, M (Warrington) 1t
*Hanley (Wigan)
Sub: Hulme, D (Widnes)
Dixon (Halifax)

1988 Australia

Sydney: 11 June

Lost 6-17

Loughlin (St. Helens) 1g
Ford (Bradford)
Schofield (Leeds)
Stephenson (Leeds)
Offiah (Widnes)
Hulme, D (Widnes)
Gregory, A (Wigan)
Ward (Castleford)
Beardmore, K (Castleford)
Dixon (Halifax)
Gregory, M (Warrington)
Platt (St. Helens)
*Hanley (Wigan) 1t
Sub: Gill (Wigan)
Powell, R (Leeds)

1988 Australia

Brisbane: 28 June

Lost 14-34

Loughlin (St. Helens) 3g
Gill (Wigan)
Ford (Bradford) 1t
*Hanley (Wigan)
Offiah (Widnes) 1t
Hulme, D (Widnes)
Gregory, A (Wigan)
Ward (Castleford)
Beardmore, K (Castleford)
Powell, R (Leeds)
Dixon (Halifax)
Platt (St. Helens)
Gregory, M (Warrington)
Sub: Wright (Widnes)
Hulme, P (Widnes)

1988 Australia (Also WC)

Sydney: 9 July

Won 26-12

Ford (Bradford) 1t
Gill (Wigan) 2t
Stephenson (Leeds)
Loughlin (St. Helens) 3g
Offiah (Widnes) 1t
Hulme, D (Widnes)
Gregory, A (Wigan)
Ward (Castleford)
Hulme, P (Widnes)
Waddell (Oldham)
Gregory, M (Warrington) 1t
Powell, R (Leeds)
*Hanley (Wigan)
Sub: Case (Wigan)

Wingman Henderson Gill, a two-try hero at Sydney in July 1988.

1988 New Zealand (Also WC)
Christchurch: 17 July
Lost 10-12
Ford (Bradford)
Gill (Wigan)
Stephenson (Leeds)
Loughlin (St. Helens) 1t,1g
Offiah (Widnes)
Hulme, D (Widnes) 1t
Gregory, A (Wigan)
Ward (Castleford)
Beardmore, K (Castleford)
Waddell (Oldham)
Gregory, M (Warrington)
Powell, R (Leeds)
*Hanley (Wigan)
Sub: Hulme, P (Widnes)

1989 France
Wigan: 21 Jan
Won 26-10
Tait (Widnes)
Ford (Leeds) 1t
Loughlin (St. Helens) 3g
Lydon (Wigan) 1t
Offiah (Widnes) 1t
Edwards (Wigan) 1t
Gregory, A (Wigan)
Ward (Castleford)
Beardmore, K (Castleford)
Waddell (Leeds)
Gregory, M (Warrington)
Powell, R (Leeds)
*Hanley (Wigan) 1t
Sub: Williams (Salford)
Eyres (Widnes)

1989 France
Avignon: 5 Feb
Won 30-8
Tait (Widnes) 1t
Ford (Leeds) 2t
Williams (Salford) 1t
Lydon (Wigan) 3g
Offiah (Widnes)
Edwards (Wigan) 1t
Gregory, A (Wigan)
Ward (Castleford)
Beardmore, K (Castleford)
Crooks, L (Leeds)
Gregory, M (Warrington)
Powell, R (Leeds)
*Hanley (Wigan) 1t
Sub: Hampson (Wigan)
England (Castleford)

1989 New Zealand
Man. U. FC: 21 Oct
Lost 16-24
Tait (Widnes) 1t
Ford (Leeds) 1t
Currier (Widnes)
Loughlin (St. Helens) 2g
Offiah (Widnes) 1t
Hulme, D (Widnes)
Gregory, A (Wigan)
Skerrett (Bradford)
Beardmore, K (Castleford)
Hobbs (Bradford)
Goodway (Wigan)
Platt (Wigan)
*Gregory, M (Warrington)
Sub: Edwards (Wigan)
Newlove, P (Featherstone)

1989 New Zealand
Elland Rd, Leeds: 28 Oct
Won 26-6
Hampson (Wigan)
Ford (Leeds)
Newlove, P (Featherstone)
Loughlin (St. Helens) 5g
Offiah (Widnes) 1t
Edwards (Wigan) 1t
Hulme, D (Widnes)
Skerrett (Bradford)
Hulme, P (Widnes)
Platt (Wigan)
Goodway (Wigan) 2t
Powell, R (Leeds)
*Gregory, M (Warrington)
Sub: Hobbs (Bradford)
Fox (Featherstone)

1989 New Zealand (Also WC)
Wigan: 11 Nov
Won 10-6
Tait (Widnes) 1t
Ford (Leeds)
Newlove, P (Featherstone)
Loughlin (St. Helens) 1g
Offiah (Widnes) 1t
Edwards (Wigan)
Hulme, D (Widnes)
Skerrett (Bradford)
Hulme, P (Widnes)
Platt (Wigan)
Goodway (Wigan)
Powell, R (Leeds)
*Gregory, M (Warrington)
Sub: Lydon (Wigan)
England (Castleford)

1990 France
Perpignan: 18 Mar
Won 8-4
Tait (Widnes)
Lydon (Wigan)
Schofield (Leeds) 2g
Loughlin (St. Helens)
Offiah (Widnes) 1t
Edwards (Wigan)
Gregory, A (Wigan)
Skerrett (Bradford)
Beardmore, K (Castleford)
Platt (Wigan)
Gregory, M (Warrington)
Goodway (Wigan)
*Hanley (Wigan)
Sub: Powell, D (Sheffield)
Betts (Wigan)

1990 France
Leeds: 7 Apr
Lost 18-25
Tait (Widnes) 1t
Cordle (Bradford) 1t
Schofield (Leeds)
Gibson (Leeds)
Offiah (Widnes) 1t
Steadman (Castleford) 3g
*Edwards (Wigan)
Skerrett (Bradford)
Beardmore, K (Castleford)
England (Castleford)
Betts (Wigan)
Fairbank, K (Bradford)
Gregory, M (Warrington)
Sub: Irwin (Castleford)
Bishop (Hull KR)

Castleford's Shaun Irwin, a Test debutant at Leeds in April 1990.

GREAT BRITAIN RECORDS

Most appearances

46	Mick Sullivan*
31	Billy Boston
29 + 1	Cliff Watson
29	George Nicholls
29	Neil Fox
28 + 1	Roger Millward
28 + 1	Ellery Hanley
28	Alan Prescott
27	Phil Jackson
27	Alex Murphy
26	Eric Ashton
26	John Atkinson
25	Brian McTigue
25	Jim Sullivan
25	Tommy Harris

*Mick Sullivan's record number of appearances include a record run of 36 successive matches. In addition he played in two matches against France before they were given Test status.

Most tries

41, Mick Sullivan, also scoring two against France before they were given Test status.

Most goals and points

93 goals, (14 tries), 228 points, Neil Fox.

Longest Test careers

14 years   — Gus Risman
1932 to 1946 (17 appearances)

13 years 9 months — Billy Batten
1908 to 1921 (10 appearances)

13 years 6 months — Alex Murphy
1958 to 1971 (27 appearances)

12 years 9 months — Roger Millward
1966 to 1978 (28 + 1 appearances)

12 years 6 months — John Atkinson
1968 to 1980 (26 appearances)

12 years 6 months — Terry Clawson
1962 to 1974 (14 appearances)

Youngest Test player

Paul Newlove was 18 years 72 days old when he made his Great Britain Test debut as a 76th minute substitute in the first Test against New Zealand at Old Trafford, Manchester on 21 October 1989, making his full debut a week later. Born on 10 August 1971, he beat the previous record held by Shaun Edwards (born 17 October 1966) who was 18 years 135 days old when capped against France at Leeds on 1 March 1985.

Roger Millward (born 16 September 1947) was 18 years 37 days old when he was a non-playing substitute for the second Test against New Zealand at Bradford on 23 October 1965.

Oldest Test player

Jeff Grayshon (born 4 March 1949), was 36 years 8 months when he played in his last Test for Britain, against New Zealand at Elland Road, Leeds, on 9 November 1985.

Record team changes

The record number of team changes made by the Great Britain selectors is 10. This has happened on three occasions, all against Australia.

In 1929, Britain crashed 31-8 to Australia in the first Test at Hull KR and retained only three players for the second Test at Leeds where they won 9-3.

After their biggest ever defeat of 50-12 in the 1963 second Test at Swinton, Britain dropped nine players and were forced to make another change when Vince Karalius was injured and replaced by Don Fox. Britain stopped Australia making a clean sweep of the series by winning 16-5 at Leeds in the last Test.

Following the 40-4 first Test defeat at Hull City's soccer ground in 1982, the selectors again made 10 changes, not including substitutes, Britain going down 27-6 in the second Test at Wigan.

Britain have never fielded the same team for three or more successive Tests.

GREAT BRITAIN REGISTER

The following is a record of the 570 players who have appeared for Great Britain in 256 Test and World Cup matches.

It does not include matches against France before 1957, the year they were given official Test match status.

Figures in brackets are the total of appearances, with the plus sign indicating substitute appearances, e.g. (7 + 3).

For matches against touring teams, the year given is for the first half of the season.

World Cup matches are in bold letters except when also classified as Test matches. Substitute appearances are in lower case letters.

A - Australia, F - France, NZ - New Zealand, P - Papua New Guinea.

ACKERLEY, A (2) Halifax: 1952 A; 1958 NZ
ADAMS, L (1) Leeds: 1932 A
ADAMS, M (11 + 2) Widnes: 1979 Aa, NZ3; 1980 NZ; 1984 A2a, NZ3, P
ARKWRIGHT, C (+2) St. Helens: 1985 nz2
ARKWRIGHT, J (6) Warrington: 1936 A2, NZ; 1937 A3
ARMITT, T (8) Swinton: 1933 A; 1936 A2, NZ2; 1937 A3
ASHBY, R (2) Liverpool: 1964 F; Wigan: 1965 F
ASHCROFT, E (11) Wigan: 1947 NZ2; 1950 A3, NZ; 1954 A3, NZ2
ASHCROFT, K (5 + 1) Leigh: **1968 A**; 1968 F; 1969 F; **1970 F,NZ**; Warrington: 1974 nz
ASHTON, E (26) Wigan: **1957 A,NZ**; 1958 A2,NZ2; 1959 F, A3; 1960 F2; **1960 NZ,A**; 1961 NZ3; 1962 F3,A3; 1963 F,A2
ASHURST, W (3) Wigan: 1971 NZ; 1972 F2
ASKIN, T (6) Featherstone R: 1928 A3,NZ3
ASPINALL, W (1) Warrington: 1966 NZ
ASTON, L (3) St. Helens: 1947 NZ3
ATKINSON, A (11) Castleford: 1929 A3; 1932 A3,NZ3; 1933 A; 1936 A
ATKINSON, J (26) Leeds: **1968 F,NZ**; 1970 A3,NZ3; **1970 A2,F,NZ**; 1971 F2,NZ; 1972 F2; **1972 A2,F,NZ**; 1973 A2; 1978 A2; 1980 NZ
AVERY, A (4) Oldham: 1910 A,NZ; 1911 A2

BACON, J (11) Leeds: 1920 A3,NZ3; 1921 A3; 1924 A; 1926 NZ
BARENDS, D (2) Bradford N: 1979 A2
BARTON, F (1) Wigan: 1951 NZ
BARTON, J (2) Wigan: 1960 F; 1961 NZ
BASNETT, J (2) Widnes: 1984 F; 1986 A
BASSETT, A (2) Halifax: 1946 A2
BATES, A (2 + 2) Dewsbury: 1974 F2,nz2
BATTEN, E (4) Bradford N: 1946 A2,NZ; 1947 NZ
BATTEN, R (3) Leeds: 1969 F; 1973 A2
BATTEN, W (10) Hunslet: 1907 NZ; 1908 A3; 1910 A2,NZ; 1911 A2; Hull: 1921 A

BAXTER, J (1) Rochdale H: 1907 NZ
BEAMES, J (2) Halifax: 1921 A2
BEARDMORE, K (13 + 1) Castleford: 1984 nz; 1987 F2; 1988 F2, P, A2, NZ; 1989 F2, NZ; 1990 F2
BELSHAW, W (8) Liverpool S: 1936 A3,NZ2; 1937 A; Warrington: A2
BENNETT, J (7) Rochdale H: 1924 A3,NZ3; Wigan: 1926 NZ
BENTHAM, N (10) Wigan H: 1928 A3,NZ3; Halifax: 1929 A2; Warrington: 1929(cont) A2
BENTHAM, W (2) Broughton R: 1924 NZ2
BENTLEY, K (1) Widnes: 1980 NZ
BENYON, W (5 + 1) St. Helens: 1971 F2,NZ,nz; 1972 F2
BETTS, D (1 + 1) Wigan: 1990 fF
BEVAN, D (1) Wigan: 1952 A
BEVAN, J (6) Warrington: 1974 A2,NZ2; 1978 A2
BEVERLEY, H (6) Hunslet: 1936 A3; 1937 A; Halifax: A2
BIRCH, J (1) Leeds: 1907 NZ
BISHOP, D (+1) Hull KR: 1990 f
BISHOP, T (15) St. Helens: 1966 A3,NZ2; 1967 A3; 1968 F3; **1968 A,F,NZ**; 1969 F
BLAN, W (3) Wigan: 1951 NZ3
BLINKHORN, T (1) Warrington: 1929 A
BOLTON, D (23) Wigan: 1957 F3; 1958 F,A2; 1959 F,A3; 1960 F2; 1961 NZ3; 1962 F2,A,NZ2; 1963 F,A2
BOSTON, W (31) Wigan: 1954 A2,NZ3; 1955 NZ; 1956 A3; 1957 F5; **1957 F,A**; 1958 F; 1959 A; 1960 F; **1960 A**; 1961 F,NZ3; 1962 F2,A3,NZ; 1963 F
BOTT, C (1) Oldham: 1966 F
BOWDEN, J (3) Huddersfield: 1954 A2,NZ
BOWEN, F (3) St. Helens Rec: 1928 NZ3
BOWERS, J (1) Rochdale H: 1920 NZ
BOWMAN, E (4) Workington T: **1977 F, NZ, A2**
BOWMAN, H (8) Hull: 1924 NZ2; 1926 NZ2; 1928 A2,NZ; 1929 A
BOWMAN, K (3) Huddersfield: 1962 F; 1963 F,A

BOYLEN, F (1) Hull: 1908 A
BRADSHAW, T (6) Wigan: 1947 NZ2; 1950 A3,NZ
BRIDGES, K (3) Featherstone R: 1974 F2,A
BRIGGS, B (1) Huddersfield: 1954 NZ
BROGDEN, S (16) Huddersfield: 1929 A; 1932 A3, NZ3; 1933 A2; Leeds: 1936 A3,NZ2; 1937 A2
BROOKE, I (13) Bradford N: 1966 A3,NZ2; Wakefield: 1967 A3; 1968 F2; **1968 A,F,NZ**
BROOKS, E (3) Warrington: 1908 A3
BROUGH, A (2) Oldham: 1924 A,NZ
BROUGH, J (5) Leeds: 1928 A2,NZ2; 1936 A
BROWN, G (6) Leeds: **1954 F2,NZ,A**; 1955 NZ2
BRYANT, W (4+1) Castleford: 1964 F2; 1966 Aa; 1967 F
BUCKLEY, A (7) Swinton: 1963 A; 1964 F; 1965 NZ; 1966 F,A2,NZ
BURGESS, W (16) Barrow: 1924 A3,NZ3; 1926 NZ3; 1928 A3,NZ2; 1929 A2
BURGESS, W (14) Barrow: 1962 F; 1963 A; 1965 NZ2; 1966 F,A3,NZ2; 1967 F,A; 1968 F; Salford: 1969 F
BURGHAM, O (1) Halifax: 1911 A
BURKE, M (14+1) Widnes: 1980 NZ; 1981 fF; 1983 F; 1984 A3, NZ3, P; 1985 NZ3; 1986 F
BURNELL, A (3) Hunslet: 1951 NZ2; 1954 NZ
BURTON, C (8+1) Hull KR: 1982 A; 1984 A3, NZ2; 1985 nz; 1986 A; 1987 F
BURWELL, A (7+1) Hull KR: 1967 a; 1968 F3; **1968 A,F,NZ**; 1969 F
BUTTERS, F (2) Swinton: 1929 A2

CAIRNS, D (2) Barrow: 1984 F2
CAMILLERI, C (2) Barrow: 1980 NZ2
CARLTON, F (2) St. Helens: 1958 NZ; Wigan: 1962 NZ
CARR, C (7) Barrow: 1924 A2,NZ2; 1926 NZ3
CARTWRIGHT, J (7) Leigh: 1920 A,NZ3; 1921 A3
CASE, B (6+1) Wigan: 1984 A, NZ3; 1987 P; 1988 P, a
CASEY, L (12+2) Hull KR: **1977 f,nz,A**; 1978 A; Bradford N: 1979 A2,NZ3; Hull KR: 1980 NZ3; 1983 F2
CASTLE, F (4) Barrow: 1952 A3; 1954 A
CHALLINOR, J (3) Warrington: 1958 A,NZ; **1960 F**
CHARLTON, P (18+1) Workington T: 1965 NZ; Salford: **1970 nz**; 1972 F2; **1972 A2,F,NZ**; 1973 A3; 1974 F2,A3,NZ3
CHERRINGTON, N (1) Wigan: 1960 F
CHILCOTT, J (3) Huddersfield: 1914 A3
CHISNALL, D (2) Leigh: 1970 A; **1970 NZ**
CHISNALL, E (4) St. Helens: 1974 A2,NZ2
CLAMPITT, L (3) Broughton R: 1907 NZ; 1911 A; 1914 NZ
CLARK, D (11) Huddersfield: 1911 A2; 1914 A3; 1920 A3,NZ3
CLARK, G (3) Hull KR: 1984 F2; 1985 F
CLARK, M (5) Leeds: 1968 F2; **1968 A,F,NZ**
CLARKE, C (7) Wigan: 1965 NZ; 1966 F,NZ; 1967 F; 1973 A3

CLAWSON, T (14) Featherstone R: 1962 F2; Leeds: **1972 A2,F**; Oldham: 1973 A3; 1974 F2,A2,NZ2
CLOSE, D (1) Huddersfield: 1967 F
COLDRICK, A (4) Wigan: 1914 A3,NZ
COLLIER, F (2) Wigan: 1963 A; Widnes: 1964 F
CORDLE, G (1) Bradford N: 1990 F
COULMAN, M (2+1) Salford: 1971 f,NZ2
COURTNEY, N (+1) Warrington: 1982 a
COVERDALE, R (4) Hull: **1954 F2,NZ,A**
CRACKNELL, R (2) Huddersfield: 1951 NZ2
CRANE, M (1) Hull: 1982 A
CREASSER, D (2+2) Leeds: 1985 F2; 1987 f; 1988 f
CROOKS, L (12+2) Hull: 1982 A2; 1984 f, A2; 1985 NZ, nz; 1986 F2, A3; 1987 F; Leeds: 1989 F
CROSTON, A (1) Castleford: 1937 A
CROWTHER, H (1) Hunslet: 1929 A
CUNLIFFE, J (4) Wigan: 1950 A,NZ; 1951 NZ; 1954 A
CUNLIFFE, W (11) Warrington: 1920 A,NZ2; 1921 A3; 1924 A3,NZ; 1926 NZ
CUNNIFFE, B (1) Castleford: 1937 A
CUNNINGHAM, E (1) St. Helens: 1978 A
CURRAN, G (6) Salford: 1946 A,NZ; 1947 NZ; 1948 A3
CURRIER, A (1) Widnes: 1989 NZ
CURZON, E (1) Salford: 1910 A

DAGNALL, R (4) St.Helens: 1961 NZ2; 1964 F; 1965 F
DALGREEN, J (1) Fulham: 1982 A
DANBY, T (3) Salford: 1950 A2,NZ
DANIELS, A (3) Halifax: 1952 A2; 1955 NZ
DANNATT, A (2) Hull: 1985 F2
DARWELL, J (5) Leigh: 1924 A3,NZ2
DAVIES, A (20) Oldham: 1955 NZ; 1956 A3; **1957 F,A**; 1957 F2; 1958 F,A2,NZ2; 1959 F2,A; **1960 NZ,F,A**; 1960 F
DAVIES, E (3) Oldham: 1920 NZ3
DAVIES, J (2) Huddersfield: 1911 A2
DAVIES, W (1) Swinton: 1968 F
DAVIES, W.A (2) Leeds: 1914 A,NZ
DAVIES, W.J (1) Castleford: 1933 A
DAVIES, W.T (1) Halifax: 1911 A
DAVIES, W.T.H (3) Bradford N: 1946 NZ; 1947 NZ2
DAWSON, E (1) York: 1956 A
DICK, K (2) Leeds: 1980 NZ2
DICKENSON, G (1) Warrington: 1908 A
DICKINSON, R (2) Leeds: 1985 F2
DINGSDALE, W (3) Warrington: 1929 A2; 1933 A
DIVORTY, G (2) Hull: 1985 F2
DIXON, C (12+2) Halifax: 1968 F; Salford: 1969 F; 1971 NZ; **1972 F**; 1973 a2; 1974 F2,A3,NZ3
DIXON, M (2) Featherstone R: 1962 F; 1964 F
DIXON, P (3+3) Halifax: 1987 f; 1988 f, F, p, A2
DOCKAR, A (1) Hull KR: 1947 NZ
DONLAN, S (+2) Leigh: 1984 nz, p

GRAYSHON, J (13) Bradford N: 1979 A2,NZ3; 1980 NZ2; 1981 F2; 1982 A2; Leeds: 1985 NZ2

GREENALL, D (6) St.Helens: 1951 NZ3; 1952 A2; 1954 NZ

GREENALL, J (1) St.Helens Rec: 1921 A

GREENOUGH, R (1) Warrington: **1960 NZ**

GREGORY, A (21 + 1) Widnes: 1981 F2; 1982 A; 1983 F2; 1984 a, NZ2, P; Warrington: 1986 A; Wigan: 1987 F, P; 1988 F, P, A3, NZ; 1989 F2, NZ; 1990 F

GREGORY, M (14) Warrington: 1987 F2; 1988 P, A3, NZ; 1989 F2, NZ3; 1990 F2

GRIBBIN, V (1) Whitehaven: 1985 F

GRONOW, B (7) Huddersfield: 1911 A2, 1920 A2, NZ3

GROVES, P (1) St. Helens: 1987 P

GRUNDY, J (12) Barrow: 1955 NZ3; 1956 A3; 1957 F3; **1957 F,A,NZ**

GUNNEY, G (11) Hunslet: 1954 NZ3; 1956 A; 1957 F3; **1957 F,NZ**; 1964 F; 1965 F

GWYNNE, T. E (3) Hull: 1928 A,NZ; 1929 A

GWYTHER, E (6) Belle Vue R: 1947 NZ2; 1950 A3; 1951 NZ

HAGGERTY, R (2) St. Helens: 1987 F2

HAIGH, R (5 + 1) Wakefield T: **1968 A,F**; Leeds: **1970 NZ,a**; 1971 F,NZ

HALL, D (2) Hull KR: 1984 F2

HALL, W (4) Oldham: 1914 A3,NZ

HALLAS, D (2) Leeds: 1961 F,NZ

HALMSHAW, A (1) Halifax: 1971 NZ

HALSALL, H (1) Swinton: 1929 A

HAMPSON, S (4 + 1) Wigan: 1987 P; 1988 F2; 1989 f, NZ

HANLEY, E (28 + 1) Bradford N: 1984 fF, A3, NZ3, P; 1985 F2; Wigan: 1985 NZ3; 1986 F, A; 1987 F2, P; 1988 F2, P, A3, NZ; 1989 F2; 1990 F

HARDISTY, A (12) Castleford: 1964 F3; 1965 F,NZ; 1966 A3,NZ; 1967 F2; 1970 A

HARE, I (1) Widnes: 1967 F

HARKIN, P (+ 1) Hull KR: 1985 f

HARRIS, T (25) Hull: 1954 NZ2; 1956 A3; 1957 F5; **1957 F,A**; 1958 A3,NZ,F; 1959 F2,A3; 1960 F2; **1960 NZ**

HARRISON, F (3) Leeds: 1911 A3

HARRISON, M (7) Hull: 1967 F2; 1971 NZ2; 1972 F2; 1973 A

HARTLEY, D (11) Hunslet: 1964 F2; Castleford: 1968 F; 1969 F; 1970 A2,NZ2; **1970 A2,F**

HARTLEY, S (3) Hull KR: 1980 NZ; 1981 F2

HELME, G (12) Warrington: 1948 A3; 1954 A3,NZ2; **1954 F2,A,NZ**

HEPWORTH, K (11) Castleford: 1967 F2; 1970 A3,NZ2; **1970 A2,F,NZ**

HERBERT, N (6) Workington T: 1961 NZ; 1962 F,A3,NZ

HERON, D (1 + 1) Leeds: 1982 aA

HESKETH, C (21 + 2) Salford: 1970 NZ; **1970 NZ,a**; 1971 Ff,NZ3; **1972 A2,F,NZ**; 1973 A3; 1974 F2,A3,NZ3

HICKS, M (1) St.Helens: 1965 NZ

HIGGINS, F (6) Widnes: 1950 A3,NZ2; 1951 NZ

HIGGINS, H (2) Widnes: 1937 A2

HIGSON, J (2) Hunslet: 1908 A2

HILL, C (1) Wigan: 1966 F

HILL, D (1) Wigan: 1971 F

HILTON, H (7) Oldham: 1920 A3,NZ3; 1921 A

HILTON, J (4) Wigan: 1950 A2,NZ2

HOBBS, D (10 + 2) Featherstone R: 1984 F2, Aa, NZ3, P; Oldham: 1987 F2; Bradford N: 1989 NZnz

HODGSON, M (16) Swinton: 1929 A2; 1932 A3,NZ3; 1933 A3; 1936 A3,NZ; 1937 A

HOGAN, P (6 + 3) Salford: **1977 F,NZ,A2**; 1978 a; Hull KR: 1979 Aa,NZ,nz

HOGG, A (1) Broughton R: 1907 NZ

HOLDEN, K (1) Warrington: 1963 A

HOLDER, W (1) Hull: 1907 NZ

HOLDING, N (4) St. Helens: 1984 A3, NZ

HOLDSTOCK, R (2) Hull KR: 1980 NZ2

HOLLAND, D (4) Oldham: 1914 A3,NZ

HOLLIDAY, W (9 + 1) Whitehaven: 1964 F; Hull KR: 1965 F,NZ3; 1966 Ff; 1967 A3

HOLLINDRAKE, T (1) Keighley: 1955 NZ

HOLMES, J (14 + 6) Leeds: 1971 NZ; 1972 F2; **1972 Aa,NZ**; **1977 F,NZ,Aa**; 1978 a3; 1979 A2a,NZ3; 1982 A

HORNE, W (8) Barrow: 1946 A3; 1947 NZ; 1948 A; 1952 A3

HORTON, W (14) Wakefield T: 1928 A3,NZ3; 1929 A; 1932 A3,NZ; 1933 A3

HOWLEY, T (6) Wigan: 1924 A3,NZ3

HUDDART, R (16) Whitehaven: 1958 A2,NZ2; St.Helens: 1959 A; 1961 NZ3; 1962 F2,A3,NZ2; 1963 A

HUDSON, B (8) Salford: 1932 NZ; 1933 A2; 1936 A,NZ2; 1937 A2

HUDSON, W (1) Wigan: 1948 A

HUGHES, E (8) Widnes: 1978 A; 1979 A3,NZ3; 1982 A

HULME, D (7 + 1) Widnes: 1988 p, A3, NZ; 1989 NZ3

HULME, P (3 + 2) Widnes: 1988 Aa, nz; 1989 NZ2

HURCOMBE, D (8) Wigan: 1920 A2,NZ; 1921 A; 1924 A2,NZ2

HYNES, S (12 + 1) Leeds: 1970 A2,NZ2nz; **1970 A2,F,NZ**; 1971 F; 1973 A3

IRVING, R (8 + 3) Oldham: 1967 F2,A3; 1970 a,NZ; 1971 NZ; 1972 f; **1972 NZ,a**

IRWIN, S (+ 1) Castleford: 1990 f

JACKSON, K (2) Oldham: 1957 F2

JACKSON, P (27) Barrow: 1954 A3,NZ3; **1954 F2,A,NZ**; 1955 NZ3; 1956 A3; **1957 F,NZ**; 1957 F5; 1958 F,A2,NZ

JAMES, N (1) Halifax: 1986 F

JARMAN, J W (2) Leeds: 1914 A2
JASIEWICZ, R (1) Bradford N: 1984 F
JEANES, D (8) Wakefield T: 1971 F,NZ2; 1972 F2;
   Leeds: **1972 A2,NZ**
JENKINS, B (12) Wigan: 1907 NZ3; 1908 A3; 1910
   A,NZ; 1911 A2, 1914 A,NZ
JENKINS, D (1) Hunslet: 1929 A
JENKINS, D (1) Leeds: 1947 NZ
JENKINS, E (9) Salford: 1933 A; 1936 A3,NZ2;
   1937 A3
JENKINSON, A (2) Hunslet: 1911 A2
JOHNSON, A (4) Widnes: 1914 A,NZ; 1920 A2
JOHNSON, A (6) Warrington: 1946 A2,NZ;
   1947 NZ3
JOHNSON, C (1) Leigh: 1985 F
JOLLEY, J (3) Runcorn: 1907 NZ3
JONES, B (3) Wakefield T: 1964 F; 1965 F; 1966 F
JONES, B.L (15) Leeds: 1954 A3,NZ3; 1955 NZ3;
   1957 F3; **1957 F,A,NZ**
JONES, D (2) Merthyr: 1907 NZ2
JONES, E (4) Rochdale H: 1920 A,NZ3
JONES, J (1) Barrow: 1946 NZ
JONES, K (2) Wigan: **1970 F,NZ**
JONES, L (1) St.Helens: 1971 NZ
JORDAN, G (2) Featherstone R: 1964 F; 1967 A
JOYNER, J (14+2) Castleford: 1978 A2; 1979
   A3,NZ3; 1980 NZ3; 1983 F2; 1984 F, nz2
JUBB, K (2) Leeds: 1937 A2
JUKES, W (6) Hunslet: 1908 A3; 1910 A2,NZ

KARALIUS, A (4+1) St.Helens: 1971 NZ3; 1972 F;
   1972 nz
KARALIUS, V (12) St.Helens: 1958 A2,NZ2; 1959
   F; **1960 NZ,F,A**; 1960 F; 1961 F; Widnes:
   1963 A2
KEEGAN, A (9) Hull: 1966 A2; 1967 F2,A3; 1968 F;
   1969 F
KELLY, K (4) St.Helens: 1972 F2; Warrington: 1980
   NZ; 1982 A
KEMEL, G (2) Widnes: 1965 NZ2
KERSHAW, H (2) Wakefield T: 1910 A,NZ
KINNEAR, R (1) Wigan: 1929 A
KISS, N (1) Wigan: 1985 F
KITCHEN, F (2) Leigh: **1954 A,NZ**
KITCHIN, P (1) Whitehaven: 1965 NZ
KITCHING, J (1) Bradford N: 1946 A
KNAPMAN, E (1) Oldham: 1924 NZ
KNOWELDEN, B (1) Barrow: 1946 NZ

LAUGHTON, D (15) Wigan: 1970 A3,NZ2; **1970
   A2,F,NZ**; 1971 F2; Widnes: 1973 A; 1974 F2;
   1979 A
LAWRENSON, J (3) Wigan: 1948 A3
LAWS, D (1) Hull K.R: 1986 F
LEDGARD, J (11) Dewsbury: 1947 NZ2; Leigh:
   1948 A; 1950 A2,NZ; 1951 NZ; **1954 F2,A,NZ**
LEDGER, B (2) St. Helens: 1985 F; 1986 A

LEWIS, G (1) Leigh: 1965 NZ
LEYTHAM, J (5) Wigan: 1907 NZ2; 1910 A2,NZ
LITTLE, S (10) Oldham: 1956 A; 1957 F5; **1957
   F,A,NZ**; 1958 F
LLEWELLYN, T (2) Oldham: 1907 NZ2
LLOYD, R (1) Halifax: 1920 A
LOCKWOOD, B (8+1) Castleford: **1972 A2,F,NZ**;
   1973 A2; 1974 F; Hull KR: 1978 A; 1979 nz
LOMAS, J (7) Salford: 1908 A2; 1910 A2,NZ;
   Oldham: 1911 A2
LONGSTAFF, F (2) Huddersfield: 1914 A,NZ
LONGWORTH, W (3) Oldham: 1908 A3
LOUGHLIN, P (11) St.Helens: 1988 F, P, A3, NZ;
   1989 F, NZ3; 1990 F
LOWE, J (1) Leeds: 1932 NZ
LOWE, P (12) Hull KR: 1970 NZ; 1972 F2; **1972
   A2,F,NZ**; 1973 A3, 1978 A2
LOXTON, K (1) Huddersfield: 1971 NZ
LYDON, J (19+2) Widnes: 1983 F2; 1984 F, a,
   NZ2, P; 1985 NZ3; Wigan: 1986 F, A3; 1987
   F2, P; 1989 F2, nz; 1990 F

MANN, A (2) Bradford N: 1908 A2
MANTLE, J (13) St.Helens: 1966 F2,A3; 1967 A2;
   1969 F; 1971 F2,NZ2; 1973 A
MARCHANT, A (3) Castleford: 1986 F, A2
MARTIN, W (1) Workington T: 1962 F
MARTYN, M (2) Leigh: 1958 A; 1959 A
McCORMICK, S (3) Belle Vue R: 1948 A2;
   St.Helens: A
McCUE, T (6) Widnes: 1936 A; 1937 A; 1946 A3,NZ
McINTYRE, L (1) Oldham: 1963 A
McKEATING, V (2) Workington T: 1951 NZ2
McKINNEY, T (11) Salford: 1951 NZ; 1952 A2;
   1954 A3,NZ; Warrington: 1955 NZ3; St.Helens:
   1957 NZ
McTIGUE, B (25) Wigan: 1958 A2,NZ2; 1959 F2,A3;
   1960 F2; **1960 NZ,F,A**; 1961 F,NZ3; 1962
   F,A3,NZ2; 1963 F
MATHIAS, R (1) St.Helens: 1979 A
MEASURES, J (2) Widnes: 1963 A2
MEDLEY, P (3+1) Leeds: 1987 P; 1988 Ff, P
MIDDLETON, A (1) Salford: 1929 A
MILLER, J (1) Wigan: 1911 A
MILLER, J (6) Warrington: 1933 A3; 1936 A,NZ2
MILLS, J (6) Widnes: 1974 A2,NZ; 1978 A2; 1979 A
MILLWARD, R (28+1) Castleford: 1966 F; Hull
   KR: 1967 A3; 1968 F2; **1968 A,F,NZ**; 1970
   A2,NZ3; 1971 F,NZ3; 1973 A; 1974 A2a; **1977
   F,NZ,A2**; 1978 A3
MILNES, A (2) Halifax: 1920 A2
MOONEY, W (2) Leigh: 1924 NZ2
MOORHOUSE, S (2) Huddersfield: 1914 A,NZ
MORGAN, A (4) Featherstone R: 1968 F2;
   1968 F,NZ
MORGAN, E (2) Hull: 1921 A2
MORGAN, R (2) Swinton: 1963 F,A

MORLEY, J (2) Wigan: 1936 A; 1937 A
MORTIMER, F (2) Wakefield T: 1956 A2
MOSES, G (9) St.Helens: 1955 NZ2; 1956 A; 1957
F3; **1957 F,A,NZ**
MUMBY, K (11) Bradford N: 1982 A; 1983 F; 1984
F2, A3, NZ3, P
MURPHY, A (27) St.Helens: 1958 A3,NZ; 1959
F2,A; **1960 NZ,F,A**; 1960 F; 1961 F,NZ3; 1962
F,A3; 1963 A2; 1964 F; 1965 F,NZ; 1966 F2;
Warrington: 1971 NZ
MURPHY, H (1) Wakefield T: 1950 A
MYLER, A (14) Widnes: 1983 F2; 1984 A2, NZ2, P;
1985 NZ2; 1986 F2, A3
MYLER, F (23 + 1) Widnes: **1960 NZ,F,A**; 1960 F;
1961 F; 1962 F; 1963 A; 1964 F; 1965 F,NZ;
1966 A,NZnz; 1967 F2; St.Helens: 1970
A3,NZ3; **1970 A2,F**

NASH, S (24) Featherstone R: 1971 F,NZ; 1972 F2;
1972 A2,F,NZ; 1973 A2; 1974 A3,NZ3; Salford:
1977 F,NZ,A2; 1978 A3; 1982 A
NAUGHTON, A (2) Warrington: **1954 F2**
NEWBOULD, H (1) Wakefield T: 1910 A
NEWLOVE, P (2 + 1) Featherstone R: 1989 nzNZ2
NICHOLLS, G (29) Widnes: 1971 NZ; 1972 F2;
1972 A2,F,NZ; St.Helens: 1973 A2; 1974
F2,A3,NZ3; **1977 F,NZ,A**; 1978 A3; 1979
A3,NZ3
NICHOLSON, R (3) Huddersfield: 1946 NZ;
1948 A2
NOBLE, B (11) Bradford N: 1982 A; 1983 F2; 1984
F, A3, NZ3, P
NORTON, S (11 + 1) Castleford: 1974 a,NZ2; Hull:
1978 A3; 1979 A2; 1980 NZ; 1981 F2; 1982 A

OFFIAH, M (12) Widnes: 1988 F, A3, NZ; 1989 F2,
NZ3; 1990 F2
O'GRADY, T (6) Oldham: 1954 A2,NZ3;
Warrington: 1961 NZ
OLIVER, J (4) Batley: 1928 A3,NZ
O'NEILL, D (2 + 1) Widnes: 1971 nz; **1972 A,F**
O'NEILL, M (3) Widnes: 1982 A; 1983 F2
OSTER, J (1) Oldham: 1929 A
OWEN, J (1) St.Helens Recs: 1921 A
OWEN, S (1) Leigh: 1958 F
OWENS, I (4) Leeds: 1946 A3,NZ

PADBURY, R (1) Runcorn: 1908 A
PALIN, H (2) Warrington: 1947 NZ2
PARKER, D (2) Oldham: 1964 F2
PARKIN, J (17) Wakefield T: 1920 A2,NZ3; 1921
A2;1924 A3,NZ; 1926 NZ2; 1928 A,NZ; 1929 A2
PARR, K (1) Warrington: 1968 F
PAWSEY, C (7) Leigh: 1952 A3; 1954 A2,NZ2
PEPPERELL, A (2) Workington T: 1950 NZ; 1951
NZ

PHILLIPS, D (4) Oldham: 1946 A3, Belle Vue R:
1950 A
PIMBLETT, A (3) Warrington: 1948 A3
PINNER, H (6 + 1) St.Helens: 1980 nzNZ; 1985
NZ3; 1986 F; Widnes: 1986 A
PITCHFORD, F (2) Oldham: 1958 NZ; 1962 F
PITCHFORD, S (4) Leeds: **1977 F,NZ,A2**
PLANGE, D (1) Castleford: 1988 F
PLATT, A (8 + 3) St. Helens: 1985 f; 1986 f, a;
1988 F2, A2; 1989 NZ3; 1990 F
POLLARD, C (1) Wakefield T: 1924 NZ
POLLARD, E (2) Wakefield T: 1932 A2
POLLARD, R (1) Dewsbury: 1950 NZ
POOLE, H (3) Hull KR: 1964 F; Leeds: 1966 NZ2
POTTER, I (7 + 1) Wigan: 1985 NZ3; 1986 F2, A2a
POWELL, D (+ 1) Sheffield E: 1990 f
POWELL, R (9 + 2) Leeds: 1985 f; 1988 F2, A2a,
NZ; 1989 F2, NZ2
POYNTON, H (3) Wakefield T: 1962 A2,NZ
PRESCOTT, A (28) St.Helens: 1951 NZ2; 1952 A3;
1954 A3,NZ3; 1955 NZ3; 1956 A3; 1957 F5;
1957 F,A,NZ; 1958 F,A2
PRICE, J (6) Broughton R: 1921 A2; Wigan: 1924
A2,NZ2
PRICE, M (2) Rochdale H: 1967 A2
PRICE, R (9) Warrington: 1954 A,NZ2; 1955 NZ;
1956 A3; 1957 F2
PRICE, T (1) Bradford N: 1970 A
PRIOR, B (1) Hunslet: 1966 F
PROCTOR, W (+ 1) Hull: 1984 p
PROSSER, D (1) Leeds: 1937 A
PROSSER, S (1) Halifax: 1914 A

RAE, J (1) Bradford N: 1965 NZ
RAMSDALE, R (8) Wigan: 1910 A2; 1911 A2; 1914
A3,NZ
RAMSEY, W (7 + 1) Hunslet: 1965 NZ2; 1966
F,A2,NZ2; Bradford N; 1974 nz
RATCLIFFE, G (3) Wigan: 1947 NZ; 1950 A2
RATHBONE, A (4 + 1) Bradford N: 1982 a; 1983 F2;
1985 F2
RAYNE, KEITH (4) Leeds: 1984 F2, A, P
RAYNE, KEVIN (1) Leeds: 1986 F
REDFEARN, A (1) Bradford N: 1979 A
REDFEARN, D (6 + 1) Bradford N: **1972 nz**; 1974
F2,A,NZ3
REES, D (1) Halifax: 1926 NZ
REES, T (1) Oldham: 1929 A
REES, W (11) Swinton: 1926 NZ2; 1928 A3,NZ3;
1929 A3
REILLY, M (9) Castleford: 1970 A3,NZ3; **1970 A2,F**
RENILSON, C (7 + 1) Halifax: 1965 NZ; 1967 a;
1968 F3; **1968 A,F,NZ**
RHODES, A (4) St.Helens: **1957 NZ**; **1960 F,A**;
1961 NZ
RICHARDS, M (2) Salford: 1974 A,NZ
RILEY, J (1) Halifax: 1910 A

335

RING, J (2) Wigan: 1924 A; 1926 NZ
RISMAN, A (17) Salford: 1932 A,NZ3; 1933 A3; 1936 A2,NZ2; 1937 A3; 1946 A3
RISMAN, B (5) Leeds: 1968 F2; **1968 A,F,NZ**
RIX, S (9) Oldham: 1924 A3,NZ3; 1926 NZ3
ROBERTS, K (10) Halifax: 1963 A; 1964 F2; 1965 F,NZ3; 1966 F,NZ2
ROBINSON, A (3) Halifax: 1907 NZ; 1908 A2
ROBINSON, Dave (13) Swinton: 1965 NZ; 1966 F2,A3,NZ2; 1967 F2,A2; Wigan: 1970 A
ROBINSON, Don (10) Wakefield T: **1954 F2,NZ,A**; 1955 NZ; Leeds: 1956 A2; 1959 A2; 1960 F
ROBINSON, J (2) Rochdale H: 1914 A2
ROBINSON, W (2) Leigh: 1963 F,A
ROGERS, J (7) Huddersfield: 1914 A; 1920 A3; 1921 A3
ROSE, D (4) Leeds: **1954 F2,A,NZ**
ROSE, P (2+3) Hull KR: 1974 a; 1978 Aa2; Hull: 1982 A
ROUND, G (8) Wakefield T: 1959 A; 1962 F2,A3,NZ2
RUDDICK, J (3) Broughton R: 1907 NZ2; 1910 A
RYAN, M (4) Wigan: 1947 NZ; 1948 A2; 1950 A
RYAN, R (5) Warrington: 1950 A,NZ2; 1951 NZ; 1952 A
RYDER, R (1) Warrington: 1952 A

SAYER, W (7) Wigan: 1961 NZ; 1962 F,A3,NZ; 1963 A
SCHOFIELD, D (1) Halifax: 1955 NZ
SCHOFIELD, G (21) Hull: 1984 F, A3, NZ; 1985 NZ3; 1986 F2, A3; 1987 F2; Leeds: 1988 F2,P,A; 1990 F2
SEABOURNE, B (1) Leeds: 1970 NZ
SENIOR, K (2) Huddersfield: 1965 NZ; 1967 F
SHARROCK, J (4) Wigan: 1910 A2,NZ; 1911 A
SHAW, B (6) Hunslet: 1956 A2; **1960 F,A**; 1960 F; Leeds: 1961 F
SHAW, G (1) Widnes: 1980 NZ
SHAW, J (5) Halifax: **1960 F,A**; 1960 F; 1961 F; 1962 NZ
SHELTON, G (7) Hunslet: 1964 F2; 1965 NZ3; 1966 F2
SHOEBOTTOM, M (10+2) Leeds: **1968 A,nz**; 1969 F; 1970 A2a,NZ; **1970 A2,F,NZ**; 1971 F
SHUGARS, F (1) Warrington: 1910 NZ
SILCOCK, N (12) Widnes: 1932 A2,NZ2; 1933 A3; 1936 A3; 1937 A2
SILCOCK, N (3) Wigan: 1954 A3
SILCOCK, R (1) Wigan: 1908 A
SIMMS, B (1) Leeds: 1962 F
SKELHORNE, G (7) Warrington: 1920 A,NZ3; 1921 A3
SKERRETT, K (5) Bradford N: 1989 NZ3; 1990 F2
SKERRETT, T (10) Wakefield T: 1979 A2,NZ2; Hull: 1980 NZ2; 1981 F2; 1982 A2

SLOMAN, R (5) Oldham: 1928 A3,NZ2
SMALES, T (8) Huddersfield: 1962 F; 1963 F,A; 1964 F2; Bradford N: 1965 NZ3
SMALL, P (1) Castleford: 1962 NZ
SMITH, A (6) Oldham: 1907 NZ3; 1908 A3
SMITH, A (10) Leeds: 1970 A2,NZ3; **1970 A2**; 1971 F2; 1973 A
SMITH, F (9) Hunslet: 1910 A,NZ; 1911 A3; 1914 A3,NZ
SMITH, G (3) York: 1963 A; 1964 F2
SMITH, H (2) Bradford N: 1926 NZ2
SMITH, M (10+1) Hull KR: 1979 NZ3; 1980 NZ2; 1981 F2; 1982 A2; 1984 f,NZ
SMITH, P (1+5) Featherstone R: **1977 a2**; 1982 A; 1983 f2; 1984 f
SMITH, S (11) Wakefield T: 1929 A; Leeds: A2; 1932 A3,NZ3; 1933 A2
SMITH, S (4) Hunslet: **1954 A,NZ,F2**
SOUTHWARD, I (11) Workington T: 1958 A3,NZ; Oldham: 1959 F2,A2; 1960 F2; 1962 NZ
SPENCER, J (1) Salford: 1907 NZ
STACEY, J.C (1) Halifax: 1920 NZ
STEADMAN, G (1) Castleford: 1990 F
STEPHENS, G (5) Castleford: 1979 A2,NZ3
STEPHENSON, D (9+1) Wigan: 1982 A2; 1986 A; 1987 F, P; Leeds: 1988 f, P, A2, NZ
STEPHENSON, M (5+1) Dewsbury: 1971 nz; 1972 F; **1972 A2,F,NZ**
STEVENSON, J (19) Leeds: 1955 NZ3; 1956 A3; 1957 F5; **1957 F,A,NZ**; 1958 F; York: 1959 A2; 1960 F2
STOCKWELL, S (3) Leeds: 1920 A; 1921 A2
STONE, W (8) Hull: 1920 A3,NZ3; 1921 A2
STOPFORD, J (12) Swinton: 1961 F; 1963 F,A2; 1964 F2; 1965 F,NZ2; 1966 F2,A
STOTT, J (1) St.Helens: 1947 NZ
STREET, H (4) Dewsbury: 1950 A3,NZ
SULLIVAN, C (17) Hull: 1967 F; **1968 A,F,NZ**; 1970 A; 1971 NZ3; 1972 F2; **1972 A2,F,NZ**; 1973 A3
SULLIVAN, J (25) Wigan: 1924 A3,NZ; 1926 NZ3; 1928 A3,NZ3; 1929 A3; 1932 A3,NZ3; 1933 A3
SULLIVAN, M (46) Huddersfield: **1954 F2,NZ,A**; 1955 NZ3; 1956 A3; 1957 F3; **1957 F,A,NZ**; Wigan: 1957 F2; 1958 F,A3,NZ2; 1959 F2,A3; 1960 F3; **1960 F,NZ,A**; St.Helens: 1961 F,NZ2; 1962 F3,A3,NZ; York: 1963 A
SZYMALA, E (1+1) Barrow: 1981 fF

TAIT, A (6) Widnes: 1989 F2, NZ2; 1990 F2
TAYLOR, H (3) Hull: 1907 NZ3
TAYLOR, R (2) Hull: 1921 A; 1926 NZ
TEMBEY, J (2) St.Helens: 1963 A; 1964 F
TERRY, A (11) St.Helens: 1958 A2; 1959 F2,A3; 1960 F; 1961 F,NZ; Leeds: 1962 F
THOMAS, A (4) Leeds: 1926 NZ2; 1929 A2

THOMAS, G (1) Warrington: 1907 NZ
THOMAS, G (9) Wigan: 1914 A; Huddersfield: 1920 A3,NZ2; 1921 A3
THOMAS, J (8) Wigan: 1907'NZ; 1908 A3; 1910 A2,NZ; 1911 A
THOMAS, L (1) Oldham: 1947 NZ
THOMAS, P (1) Leeds: 1907 NZ
THOMPSON, C (2) Hunslet: 1951 NZ2
THOMPSON, J (12) Leeds: 1924 A,NZ2; 1928 A,NZ; 1929 A; 1932 A3,NZ3
THOMPSON, J (20+1) Featherstone R: 1970 A2,NZ2; **1970 A2,F,NZ**; 1971 Ff; 1974 A3,NZ3 **1977 F,NZ,A2**; Bradford N: 1978 A
THORLEY, J (4) Halifax: **1954 F2,NZ,A**
TOOHEY, E (3) Barrow: 1952 A3
TOPLISS, D (4) Wakefield T: 1973 A2; 1979 A; Hull: 1982 A
TRAILL, K (8) Bradford N: 1950 NZ2; 1951 NZ; 1952 A3; 1954 A,NZ
TROUP, L A (2) Barrow: 1936 NZ2
TURNBULL, A (1) Leeds: 1951 NZ
TURNER, D (24) Oldham: 1956 A2; 1957 F5; **1957 F,A,NZ**; 1958 F; Wakefield: 1959 A; 1960 F3; **1960 NZ,A**; 1961 F,NZ; 1962 A2,NZ2,F
TYSON, B (3) Hull KR: 1963 A; 1965 F; 1967 F
TYSON, G (4) Oldham: 1907 NZ; 1908 A3

VALENTINE, D (15) Huddersfield: 1948 A3; 1951 NZ; 1952 A2; 1954 A3,NZ2; **1954 F2,NZ,A**
VALENTINE, R (1) Huddersfield: 1967 A
VINES, D (3) Wakefield T: 1959 F2,A

WADDELL, H (5) Oldham: 1988 F2, A, NZ; Leeds: 1989 F
WAGSTAFF, H (12) Huddersfield: 1911 A2; 1914 A3,NZ; 1920 A2,NZ2; 1921 A2
WALKER, A (1) Whitehaven: 1980 NZ
WALLACE, J (1) St.Helens Recs: 1926 NZ
WALSH, Joe (1) Leigh: 1971 NZ
WALSH, John (4+1) St.Helens: 1972 f; **1972 A2,F,NZ**
WALTON, D (1) Castleford: 1965 F
WANE, S (2) Wigan: 1985 F; 1986 F
WARD, D (12) Leeds: **1977 F,NZ,A**; 1978 A; 1979 A3,NZ3;1981 F; 1982 A
WARD, Edward (3) Wigan: 1946 A2; 1947 NZ
WARD, Ernest (20) Bradford N: 1946 A3,NZ; 1947 NZ2; 1948 A3; 1950 A3,NZ2; 1951 NZ3; 1952 A3
WARD, J (4) Castleford: 1963 A; 1964 F2; Salford: 1970 NZ
WARD, K (14) Castleford: 1984 F; 1986 A3; 1987 P; 1988 F2, P, A3, NZ; 1989 F2

WARD, W (1) Leeds: 1910 A
WARLOW, J (6+1) St.Helens: 1964 F; **1968 f,NZ**; 1968 F; Widnes: 1971 F2,NZ
WARWICK, S (2) Salford: 1907 NZ2
WATKINS, D (2+4) Salford: 1971 f,NZ; 1973 a; 1974 f2,A
WATKINS, W (7) Salford: 1933 A; 1936 A2,NZ2; 1937 A2
WATKINSON, D (12+1) Hull KR: 1979 a; 1980 NZ; 1981 F; 1984 F; 1985 F, NZ3; 1986 F2, A3
WATSON, C (29+1) St.Helens: 1963 A2; 1966 F2,A3,NZ2; 1967 F,A3; 1968 F2; **1968 A,F,nz**; 1969 F; 1970 A3,NZ3; **1970 A2,F,NZ**; 1971 F
WATTS, B (5) York: **1954 F2,NZ,A**; 1955 NZ
WEBSTER, F (3) Leeds: 1910 A2,NZ
WHITCOMBE, F (2) Bradford N: 1946 A2
WHITE, L (7) Hunslet: 1932 A3,NZ2; 1933 A2
WHITE, L (6) York: 1946 A3,NZ; Wigan: 1947 NZ2
WHITE, T (1) Oldham: 1907 NZ
WHITEHEAD, D (3) Warrington: 1971 F2,NZ
WHITELEY, J (15) Hull: **1957 A**; 1958 A3,NZ; 1959 F2,A2; 1960 F; **1960 NZ,F**; 1961 NZ2; 1962 F
WILKINSON, J (13) Halifax: 1954 A,NZ2; 1955 NZ3; Wakefield T: 1959 A; 1960 F2; **1960 NZ,F,A**; 1962 NZ
WILLIAMS, F (2) Halifax: 1914 A2
WILLIAMS, P (1+1) Salford: 1989 fF
WILLIAMS, R (12) Leeds: 1948 A3; 1950 A2,NZ2; 1951 NZ3; Hunslet: 1954 A2,NZ
WILLIAMS, W (2) Salford: 1929 A; 1932 A
WILLICOMBE, D (3) Halifax: 1974 F; Wigan: F,NZ
WILSON, G (3) Workington T: 1951 NZ3
WILSON, H (3) Hunslet: 1907 NZ3
WINSLADE, C (1) Oldham: 1959 F
WINSTANLEY, W (5) Leigh: 1910 A,NZ; Wigan: 1911 A3
WOOD, A (4) Oldham: 1911 A2; 1914 A,NZ
WOODS, H (6) Liverpool S: 1936 A3,NZ2; Leeds: 1937 A
WOODS, J (1) Barrow: 1933 A
WOODS, J (7+4) Leigh: 1979 A3,nz; 1980 NZ; 1981 F2; 1982 Aa; 1983 f; Warrington: 1987 p
WOODS, T (2) Rochdale H: 1911 A2
WORRALL, M (3) Oldham: 1984 F, A2
WRIGHT, D (+1) Widnes: 1988 a
WRIGHT, J (1) Swinton: 1932 NZ
WRIGHT, S (7) Widnes: **1977 F,NZ,A2**; 1978 A3
WRIGLESWORTH, G (5) Leeds: 1965 NZ; 1966 A2,NZ2

YOUNG, C (5) Hull KR: 1967 A3; 1968 F2
YOUNG, F (1) Leeds: 1908 A
YOUNG, H (1) Huddersfield: 1929 A

GREAT BRITAIN TOUR SUMMARIES

1910	P	W	D	L	T	For G	Pts	T	Against G	Pts
In Australia	14	9	1	4	76	56	340	51	47	247
In New Zealand	4	4	0	0	43	29	187	11	7	47
TOTAL	18	13	1	4	119	85	527	62	54	294

1914	P	W	D	L	T	G	Pts	T	G	Pts
In Australia	12	9	0	3	77	55	341	24	31	134
In New Zealand	6	6	0	0	46	28	194	12	13	62
TOTAL	18	15	0	3	123	83	535	36	44	196

1920	P	W	D	L	T	G	Pts	T	G	Pts
In Australia	15	12	0	3	83	64	377	48	42	228
In New Zealand	10	9	0	1	89	47	361	24	16	104
TOTAL	25	21	0	4	172	111	738	72	58	332

1924	P	W	D	L	T	G	Pts	T	G	Pts
In Australia	18	14	0	4	104	77	466	56	45	258
In New Zealand	9	7	0	2	64	40	272	25	21	117
TOTAL	27	21	0	6	168	117	738	81	66	375

1928	P	W	D	L	T	G	Pts	T	G	Pts
In Australia	16	11	1	4	67	60	321	43	45	219
In New Zealand	8	7	0	1	55	36	237	16	12	72
TOTAL	24	18	1	5	122	96	558	59	57	291

1932	P	W	D	L	T	G	Pts	T	G	Pts
In Australia	18	15	1	2	105	84	483	32	38	172
In New Zealand	8	8	0	0	65	52	299	17	18	87
TOTAL	26	23	1	2	170	136	782	49	56	259

1936	P	W	D	L	T	G	Pts	T	G	Pts
In Australia	17	14	0	3	79	82	401	38	45	204
In New Zealand	8	8	0	0	52	27	210	8	16	56
TOTAL	25	22	0	3	131	109	611	46	61	260

1946	P	W	D	L	T	G	Pts	T	G	Pts
In Australia	20	16	1	3	146	100	638	36	45	198
In New Zealand	7	5	0	2	35	20	145	12	21	78
TOTAL	27	21	1	5	181	120	783	48	66	276

1950	P	W	D	L	T	G	Pts	T	G	Pts
In Australia	19	15	0	4	133	102	603	22	56	178
In New Zealand	6	4	0	2	37	25	161	16	20	88
TOTAL	25	19	0	6	170	127	764	38	76	266

							For				**Against**
1954		P	W	D	L	T	G	Pts	T	G	Pts
In Australia		*22	13	1	7	133	114	627	78	96	426
In New Zealand		10	8	0	2	60	56	292	14	32	106
TOTAL		*32	21	1	9	193	170	919	92	128	532

*One match abandoned. Scores included in points total.

							For				**Against**
1958		P	W	D	L	T	G	Pts	T	G	Pts
In Australia		21	19	1	1	184	129	810	64	93	378
In New Zealand		9	8	0	1	88	61	386	18	27	108
TOTAL		30	27	1	2	272	190	1,196	82	120	486
1962		P	W	D	L	T	G	Pts	T	G	Pts
In Australia		21	18	0	3	151	113	679	61	60	303
In New Zealand		9	6	0	3	73	50	319	35	28	161
TOTAL		30	24	0	6	224	163	998	96	88	464
1966		P	W	D	L	T	G	Pts	T	G	Pts
In Australia		22	13	0	9	112	85	506	47	83	307
In New Zealand		8	8	0	0	57	47	265	10	24	78
TOTAL		30	21	0	9	169	132	771	57	107	385
1970		P	W	D	L	T	G	Pts	T	G	Pts
In Australia		17	15	1	1	104	92	496	27	66	213
In New Zealand		7	7	0	0	61	37	257	9	24	75
TOTAL		24	22	1	1	165	129	753	36	90	288

								For				**Against**
1974	P	W	D	L	T	G	DG	Pts	T	G	DG	Pts
In Australia	20	15	0	5	104	93	2	500	38	59	3	235
In New Zealand	8	6	0	2	37	32	0	175	8	27	0	78
TOTAL	28	21	0	7	141	125	2	675	46	86	3	313

								For				**Against**
1979		P	W	D	L	T	G	DG	Pts	T	G	Pts
In Australia		18	13	1	4	66	73	3	347	39	68	253
In New Zealand		9	8	0	1	48	34	0	212	15	12	69
TOTAL		27	21	1	5	114	107	3	559	54	80	332

								For				**Against**
1984	P	W	D	L	T	G	DG	Pts	T	G	DG	Pts
In Australia	15	11	0	4	70	59	1	399	40	46	2	254
In New Zealand	8	4	0	4	32	25	1	179	21	21	0	126
In Papua New Guinea	1	1	0	0	7	5	0	38	4	2	0	20
TOTAL	24	16	0	8	109	89	2	616	65	69	2	400

								For				**Against**
1988	P	W	D	L	T	G	DG	Pts	T	G	DG	Pts
In Papua New Guinea	2	2	0	0	13	13	0	78	7	6	0	40
In Australia	13	8	0	5	59	47	0	330	42	36	1	241
In New Zealand	3	1	0	2	8	8	0	48	10	10	0	60
TOTAL	18	11	0	7	80	68	0	456	59	52	1	341

GREAT BRITAIN TOUR SQUADS
Captains in bold

1910 Tour

J. Lomas (Salford)
A. Avery (Oldham)
J. Bartholomew (Huddersfield)
W. Batten (Hunslet)
F. Boylen (Hull)
E. Curzon (Salford)
J. Davies (Huddersfield)
F. Farrar (Hunslet)
T. Helm (Oldham)
B. Jenkins (Wigan)
T. Jenkins (Ebbw Vale)
W. Jukes (Hunslet)
H. Kershaw (Wakefield T.)
J. Leytham (Wigan)
T. Newbould (Wakefield T.)
R. Ramsdale (Wigan)
J. Riley (Halifax)
G. Ruddick (Broughton R.)
J. Sharrock (Wigan)
F. Shugars (Warrington)
F. Smith (Hunslet)
J. Thomas (Wigan)
W. Ward (Leeds)
F. Webster (Leeds)
W. Winstanley (Leigh)
F. Young (Leeds)

Managers: J. Clifford
(Huddersfield) and J.
Houghton (St. Helens)

1924 Tour

J. Parkin (Wakefield T.)
J. Bacon (Leeds)
J. Bennett (Rochdale H.)
W. Bentham (Broughton R.)
H. Bowman (Hull)
A. Brough (Oldham)
W. Burgess (Barrow)
C. Carr (Barrow)
W. Cunliffe (Warrington)
J. Darwell (Leigh)
F. Evans (Swinton)
F. Gallagher (Batley)
B. Gronow (Huddersfield)
T. Howley (Wigan)

1914 Tour

H. Wagstaff (Huddersfield)
J. Chilcott (Huddersfield)
J. Clampitt (Broughton R.)
D. Clark (Huddersfield)
A. Coldrick (Wigan)
W. Davies (Leeds)
A. Francis (Hull)
J. Guerin (Hunslet)
W. Hall (Oldham)
D. Holland (Oldham)
J. Jarman (Leeds)
B. Jenkins (Wigan)
A. Johnson (Widnes)
F. Longstaff (Huddersfield)
S. Moorhouse (Huddersfield)
J. O'Garra (Widnes)
W. Prosser (Halifax)
R. Ramsdale (Wigan)
J. Robinson (Rochdale H.)
J. Rogers (Huddersfield)
W. Roman (Rochdale H.)
J. Smales (Hunslet)
F. Smith (Hunslet)
G. Thomas (Wigan)
F. Williams (Halifax)
A. Wood (Oldham)

Managers: J. Clifford
(Huddersfield) and J.
Houghton (St. Helens)

D. Hurcombe (Wigan)
E. Knapman (Oldham)
W. Mooney (Leigh)
C. Pollard (Wakefield T.)
J. Price (Wigan)
D. Rees (Halifax)
J. Ring (Wigan)
S. Rix (Oldham)
R. Sloman (Oldham)
J. Sullivan (Wigan)
J. Thompson (Leeds)
S. Whitty (Hull)

Managers: J.H. Dannatt
(Hull) and E. Osborne
(Warrington)

1920 Tour

H. Wagstaff (Huddersfield)
J. Bacon (Leeds)
J. Bowers (Rochdale H.)
J. Cartwright (Leigh)
D. Clark (Huddersfield)
W. Cunliffe (Warrington)
E. Davies (Oldham)
J. Doyle (Barrow)
F. Gallagher (Dewsbury)
B. Gronow (Huddersfield)
H. Hilton (Oldham)
D. Hurcombe (Wigan)
A. Johnson (Widnes)
E. Jones (Rochdale H.)
R. Lloyd (Halifax)
A. Milnes (Halifax)
J. Parkin (Wakefield T.)
G. Rees (Leeds)
W. Reid (Widnes)
J. Rogers (Huddersfield)
G. Skelhorne (Warrington)
J. Stacey (Halifax)
S. Stockwell (Leeds)
W. Stone (Hull)
G. Thomas (Huddersfield)
A. Wood (Oldham)

Managers: S. Foster (Halifax)
and J. Wilson (Hull K.R.)

1928 Tour

J. Parkin (Wakefield T.)
T. Askin (Featherstone R.)
N. Bentham (Wigan Highfield)
F. Bowen (St. Helens Recs)
H. Bowman (Hull)
J. Brough (Leeds)
W. Burgess (Barrow)
O. Dolan (St. Helens Recs)
A. Ellaby (St. Helens)
B. Evans (Swinton)
J. Evans (Swinton)
L. Fairclough (St. Helens)
A. Fildes (St. Helens Recs)
A. Frodsham (St. Helens)

W. Gowers (Rochdale H.)
T. Gwynne (Hull)
B. Halfpenny (St. Helens)
W. Horton (Wakefield T.)
J. Oliver (Batley)
W. Rees (Swinton)
M. Rosser (Leeds)
R. Sloman (Oldham)
J. Sullivan (Wigan)
J. Thompson (Leeds)
W. Williams (Salford)
H. Young (Bradford N.)

Managers: G. Hutchins
(Oldham) and E. Osborne
(Warrington)

1932 Tour

J. Sullivan (Wigan)
A. Atkinson (Castleford)
L. Adams (Leeds)
S. Brogden (Huddersfield)
F. Butters (Swinton)
I. Davies (Halifax)
W. Dingsdale (Warrington)
A. Ellaby (St. Helens)
B. Evans (Swinton)
J. Feetham (Salford)
N. Fender (York)
A. Fildes (St. Helens)
M. Hodgson (Swinton)
W. Horton (Wakefield T.)
B. Hudson (Salford)
J. Lowe (Leeds)
E. Pollard (Wakefield T.)
A. Risman (Salford)
G. Robinson (Wakefield T.)
N. Silcock (Widnes)
S. Smith (Leeds)
J. Thompson (Leeds)
L. White (Hunslet)
W. Williams (Salford)
J. Woods (Barrow)
J. Wright (Swinton)

Managers: R. Anderton
(Warrington) and G. Hutchins
(Oldham)

1936 Tour

J. Brough (Leeds)
J. Arkwright (Warrington)
T. Armitt (Swinton)
A. Atkinson (Castleford)
W. Belshaw (Liverpool S.)
H. Beverley (Hunslet)
S. Brogden (Leeds)
E. Davies (Wigan)
A. Edwards (Salford)
H. Ellerington (Hull)
G. Exley (Wakefield T.)
H. Field (York)
F. Harris (Leeds)
M. Hodgson (Swinton)
B. Hudson (Salford)
E. Jenkins (Salford)
H. Jones (Keighley)
T. McCue (Widnes)
J. Miller (Warrington)
J. Morley (Wigan)
A. Risman (Salford)
N. Silcock (Widnes)
S. Smith (Leeds)
L. Troup (Barrow)
W. Watkins (Salford)
H. Woods (Liverpool S.)

Managers: R. Anderton
(Warrington) and
W. Popplewell (Bramley)

1946 Tour

A. Risman (Salford)
A. Bassett (Halifax)
E. Batten (Bradford N.)
G. Curran (Salford)
W. Davies (Bradford N.)
J. Egan (Wigan)
T. Foster (Bradford N.)
K. Gee (Wigan)
W. Horne (Barrow)
F. Hughes (Workington T.)
D. Jenkins (Leeds)
A. Johnson (Warrington)
J. Jones (Barrow)
J. Kitching (Bradford N.)

B. Knowelden (Barrow)
J. Lewthwaite (Barrow)
T. McCue (Widnes)
H. Murphy (Wakefield T.)
R. Nicholson (Huddersfield)
I. Owens (Leeds)
D. Phillips (Oldham)
M. Ryan (Wigan)
Edward Ward (Wigan)
Ernest Ward (Bradford N.)
F. Whitcombe (Bradford N.)
L. White (York)

Managers: W. Popplewell
(Bramley) and W. Gabbatt
(Barrow)

1950 Tour

E. Ward (Bradford N.)
E. Ashcroft (Wigan)
T. Bradshaw (Wigan)
J. Cunliffe (Wigan)
T. Danby (Salford)
A. Daniels (Halifax)
J. Egan (Wigan)
J. Featherstone (Warrington)
K. Gee (Wigan)
E. Gwyther (Belle Vue R.)
F. Higgins (Widnes)
J. Hilton (Wigan)
W. Horne (Barrow)
J. Ledgard (Leigh)
H. Murphy (Wakefield T.)
D. Naughton (Widnes)
F. Osmond (Swinton)
A. Pepperell (Workington T.)
D. Phillips (Belle Vue R.)
R. Pollard (Dewsbury)
G. Ratcliffe (Wigan)
M. Ryan (Wigan)
R. Ryan (Warrington)
H. Street (Dewsbury)
K. Traill (Bradford N.)
R. Williams (Leeds)

Managers: G. Oldroyd
(Dewsbury) and T. Spedding
(Belle Vue R.)

1954 Tour

R. Williams (Hunslet)
E. Ashcroft (Wigan)
W. Boston (Wigan)
J. Bowden (Huddersfield)
B. Briggs (Huddersfield)
A. Burnell (Hunslet)
E. Cahill (Rochdale H.)
F. Castle (Barrow)
J. Cunliffe (Wigan)
D. Greenall (St. Helens)
G. Gunney (Hunslet)
T. Harris (Hull)
G. Helme (Warrington)
J. Henderson (Workington T.)
P. Jackson (Barrow)
B. L. Jones (Leeds)
T. McKinney (Salford)
T. O'Grady (Oldham)
C. Pawsey (Leigh)
A. Prescott (St. Helens)
R. Price (Warrington)
N. Silcock (Wigan)
K. Traill (Bradford N.)
A. Turnbull (Leeds)
D. Valentine (Huddersfield)
J. Wilkinson (Halifax)

Managers: T. Hesketh
(Wigan) and H. Rawson
(Hunslet)

1958 Tour

A. Prescott (St. Helens)
A. Ackerley (Halifax)
H. Archer (Workington T.)
E. Ashton (Wigan)
D. Bolton (Wigan)
F. Carlton (St. Helens)
J. Challinor (Warrington)
A. Davies (Oldham)
B. Edgar (Workington T.)
E. Fraser (Warrington)
D. Goodwin (Barrow)
T. Harris (Hull)
R. Huddart (Whitehaven)
K. Jackson (Oldham)
P. Jackson (Barrow)
V. Karalius (St. Helens)

M. Martyn (Leigh)
B. McTigue (Wigan)
G. Moses (St. Helens)
A. Murphy (St. Helens)
F. Pitchford (Oldham)
I. Southward (Workington T.)
M. Sullivan (Wigan)
A. Terry (St. Helens)
J. Whiteley (Hull)
W. Wookey (Workington T.)

Managers: B. Manson
(Swinton) and T. Mitchell
(Workington T.)
Coach: J. Brough
(Workington T.)

1962 Tour

E. Ashton (Wigan)
D. Bolton (Wigan)
W. Boston (Wigan)
F. Carlton (Wigan)
G. Cooper (Featherstone R.)
B. Edgar (Workington T.)
R. Evans (Wigan)
N. Fox (Wakefield T.)
D. Fox (Featherstone R.)
E. Fraser (Warrington)
L. Gilfedder (Warrington)
N. Herbert (Workington T.)
R. Huddart (St. Helens)
B. McTigue (Wigan)
A. Murphy (St. Helens)
K. Noble (Huddersfield)
H. Poynton (Wakefield T.)
G. Round (Wakefield T.)
W. Sayer (Wigan)
J. Shaw (Halifax)
P. Small (Castleford)
I. Southward (Workington T.)
M. Sullivan (St. Helens)
J. Taylor (Hull K.R.)
D. Turner (Wakefield T.)
J. Wilkinson (Wakefield T.)

Managers: S. Hadfield
(Wakefield T.) and A. Walker
(Rochdale H.)
Coach: C. Hutton (Hull K.R.)

1966 Tour

H. Poole (Leeds)
W. Aspinall (Warrington)
T. Bishop (St. Helens)
I. Brooke (Bradford N.)
W. Bryant (Castleford)
A. Buckley (Swinton)
W. Burgess (Barrow)
C. Clarke (Wigan)
G. Crewdson (Keighley)
C. Dooler (Featherstone R.)
B. Edgar (Workington T.)
P. Flanagan (Hull K.R.)
T. Fogerty (Halifax)
K. Gowers (Swinton)
A. Hardisty (Castleford)
B. Jones (Wakefield T.)
A. Keegan (Hull)
J. Mantle (St. Helens)
F. Myler (Widnes)
W. Ramsey (Hunslet)
K. Roberts (Halifax)
D. Robinson (Swinton)
G. Shelton (Hunslet)
J. Stopford (Swinton)
C. Watson (St. Helens)
G. Wriglesworth (Leeds)

Managers: W. Spaven (Hull
K.R.) and J. Errock (Oldham)

1970 Tour

F. Myler (St. Helens)
J. Atkinson (Leeds)
D. Chisnall (Leigh)
R. Dutton (Widnes)
D. Edwards (Castleford)
A. Fisher (Bradford N.)
P. Flanagan (Hull K.R.)
A. Hardisty (Castleford)
D. Hartley (Castleford)
K. Hepworth (Castleford)
C. Hesketh (Salford)
S. Hynes (Leeds)
R. Irving (Oldham)
D. Laughton (Wigan)
P. Lowe (Hull K.R.)
R. Millward (Hull K.R.)
T. Price (Bradford N.)

M. Reilly (Castleford)
D. Robinson (Wigan)
B. Seabourne (Leeds)
M. Shoebottom (Leeds)
A. Smith (Leeds)
C. Sullivan (Hull)
J. Thompson (Featherstone R.)
J. Ward (Salford)
C. Watson (St. Helens)

Manager: J. Harding (Leigh)
Coach: J. Whiteley (Hull)

1974 Tour

C. Hesketh (Salford)
K. Ashcroft (Warrington)
J. Atkinson (Leeds)
A. Bates (Dewsbury)
J. Bates (Dewsbury)
J. Bevan (Warrington)
J. Bridges (Featherstone R.)
J. Butler (Rochdale H.)
P. Charlton (Salford)
E. Chisnall (St. Helens)
T. Clawson (Oldham)
C. Dixon (Salford)
L. Dyl (Leeds)
D. Eckersley (St. Helens)
K. Gill (Salford)
J. Gray (Wigan)
J. Mills (Widnes)
R. Millward (Hull K.R.)
S. Nash (Featherstone R.)
G. Nicholls (St. Helens)
S. Norton (Castleford)
D. Redfearn (Bradford N.)
P. Rose (Hull K.R.)
J. Thompson (Featherstone R.)
D. Watkins (Salford)
D. Willicombe (Wigan)

Replacements during tour
W. Ramsey (Bradford N.) for
J. Bates; M. Richards
(Salford) for Atkinson

Manager: R. Parker
(Blackpool B.)
Coach: J. Challinor
(St. Helens)

1979 Tour

D. Laughton (Widnes)
M. Adams (Widnes)
D. Barends (Bradford N.)
L. Casey (Bradford N.)
S. Evans (Featherstone R.)
P. Glynn (St. Helens)
J. Grayshon (Bradford N.)
P. Hogan (Hull K.R.)
J. Holmes (Leeds)
E. Hughes (Widnes)
M. James (St. Helens)
J. Joyner (Castleford)
G. Liptrot (St. Helens)
B. Lockwood (Hull K.R.)
T. Martyn (Warrington)
R. Mathias (St. Helens)
J. Mills (Widnes)
R. Millward (Hull K.R.)
K. Mumby (Bradford N.)
S. Nash (Salford)
G. Nicholls (St. Helens)
S. Norton (Hull)
A. Redfearn (Bradford N.)
T. Skerrett (Wakefield T.)
M. Smith (Hull K.R.)
G. Stephens (Castleford)
C. Stone (Hull)
D. Ward (Leeds)
D. Watkinson (Hull K.R.)
J. Woods (Leigh)

Replacements during tour
J. Burke (Wakefield T.) for
Mills; G. Fairbairn (Wigan)
for Martyn; D. Topliss
(Wakefield T.) for Millward

Managers: H. Womersley
(Bradford N.) and
R. Gemmell (Hull)
Coach E. Ashton (St. Helens)

1984 Tour

B. Noble (Bradford N.)
M. Adams (Widnes)
R. Ashton (Oldham)
K. Beardmore (Castleford)
M. Burke (Widnes)

C. Burton (Hull K.R.)
B. Case (Wigan)
G. Clark (Hull K.R.)
L. Crooks (Hull)
S. Donlan (Leigh)
D. Drummond (Leigh)
R. Duane (Warrington)
T. Flanagan (Oldham)
D. Foy (Oldham)
A. Goodway (Oldham)
A. Gregory (Widnes)
E. Hanley (Bradford N.)
D. Hobbs (Featherstone R.)
N. Holding (St. Helens)
J. Joyner (Castleford)
J. Lydon (Widnes)
K. Mumby (Bradford N.)
A. Myler (Widnes)
M. O'Neill (Widnes)
H. Pinner (St. Helens)
W. Proctor (Hull)
Keith Rayne (Leeds)
G. Schofield (Hull)
M. Smith (Hull K.R.)
M. Worrall (Oldham)

Replacement during tour
J. Basnett (Widnes) for Duane

Managers: R. Gemmell (Hull)
and R. Davis (RLHQ)
Coach: Frank Myler (Oldham)

1988 Tour

E. Hanley (Wigan)
K. Beardmore (Castleford)
B. Case (Wigan)
L. Crooks (Leeds)
P. Dixon (Halifax)
S. Edwards (Wigan)
K. Fairbank (Bradford N.)
M. Ford (Oldham)
P. Ford (Bradford N.)
C. Gibson (Leeds)
H. Gill (Wigan)
A. Gregory (Wigan)
M. Gregory (Warrington)
P. Groves (St. Helens)
R. Haggerty (St. Helens)
D. Hulme (Widnes)

P. Loughlin (St. Helens)
P. Medley (Leeds)
M. Offiah (Widnes)
A. Platt (St. Helens)
R. Powell (Leeds)
G. Schofield (Leeds)
D. Stephenson (Leeds)
H. Waddell (Oldham)

K. Ward (Castleford)
I. Wilkinson (Halifax)

Replacements during tour
D. Wright (Widnes) for
Edwards; A. Currier (Widnes)
and P. Hulme (Widnes) for
Schofield and Medley; R.

Eyres (Widnes) and J. Joyner
(Castleford) for Crooks, Dixon
and Platt

Managers: L. Bettinson
(Salford) and D. Howes
(RLHQ)
Coach: M. Reilly

ALL TIME TOUR RECORDS

IN AUSTRALIA
Highest score: 101-0 v. South Australia in 1914

Biggest defeat: 42-6 v. New South Wales in 1920
(Also *widest margin*)

Fewest defeats: 1 (and 1 draw) from 21 matches in
1958 and from 17 matches in 1970

Most defeats: 9 from 22 matches in 1966

Biggest attendances: 70,419 v. New South Wales
(Sydney) in 1950

IN NEW ZEALAND
Highest score: 81-14 v. Bay of Plenty in 1962

Widest margin win: 72-3 v. Buller in 1928
72-3 v. North Island in 1958

Biggest defeat: 46-13 v. Auckland in 1962 (Also *widest margin*)

Fewest defeats: The tourists have won all their matches
in the following years: 1910 (4 matches), 1914 (6),
1932 (8), 1936 (8), 1966 (8), 1970 (7).

Most defeats: 4 from 8 matches in 1984

Biggest attendance: 35,000 v. Auckland in 1920

PLAYERS' FULL TOUR RECORDS
Most full appearances: 24 by Dick Huddart in 1958

Most tries: 38 by Mick Sullivan in 1958

Most goals and points: 127g, 278 pts by Lewis Jones in
1954

Most tours: 3 by Jonathan Parkin (1920, 1924, 1928)
Jim Sullivan (1924, 1928, 1932)
Joe Thompson (1924, 1928, 1932)
Augustus Risman (1932, 1936, 1946)
Brian Edgar (1958, 1962, 1966)
Roger Millward (1970, 1974, 1979)
John Joyner (1979, 1984, 1988 as
replacement)
Garry Schofield (1984, 1988, 1990)

Biggest club representation: 8 by Wigan in 1950 —
Ernie Ashcroft, Tommy Bradshaw, Jack Cunliffe, Joe
Egan, Ken Gee, Jack Hilton, Gordon Ratcliffe, Martin
Ryan

Brothers touring together: Bryn and Jack Evans (1928),
Don and Neil Fox (1962), Alan and John Bates
(1974), David and Paul Hulme (1988, Paul as
replacement)

GREAT BRITAIN IN THE WORLD CUP
A — Australia, Fr — France, GB — Great Britain, NZ — New Zealand, PNG — Papua New Guinea

1954 in France   *Winners:* Great Britain

30 Oct.	Fr	22	NZ	13	Paris	13,240
31 Oct.	GB	28	A	13	Lyons	10,250
7 Nov.	GB	13	Fr	13	Toulouse	37,471
7 Nov.	A	34	NZ	15	Marseilles	20,000
11 Nov.	GB	26	NZ	6	Bordeaux	14,000
11 Nov.	A	5	Fr	15	Nantes	13,000

Play off

13 Nov.	GB	16	Fr	12	Paris	30,368

Final Table

	P.	W.	D.	L.	F.	A.	Pts.
Great Britain	3	2	1	0	67	32	5
France	3	2	1	0	50	31	5
Australia	3	1	0	2	52	58	2
New Zealand	3	0	0	3	34	82	0

1957 in Australia   *Winners:* Australia

15 June	GB	23	Fr	5	Sydney	50,007
15 June	A	25	NZ	5	Brisbane	29,636
17 June	GB	6	A	31	Sydney	57,955
17 June	NZ	10	Fr	14	Brisbane	28,000
22 June	A	26	Fr	9	Sydney	35,158
25 June	GB	21	NZ	29	Sydney	14,263

Final Table

	P.	W.	D.	L.	F.	A.	Pts.
Australia	3	3	0	0	82	20	6
Great Britain	3	1	0	2	50	65	2
New Zealand	3	1	0	2	44	60	2
France	3	1	0	2	28	59	2

1960 in England   *Winners:* Great Britain

24 Sept.	GB	23	NZ	8	Bradford	20,577
24 Sept.	A	13	Fr	12	Wigan	20,278
1 Oct.	A	21	NZ	15	Leeds	10,773
1 Oct.	GB	33	Fr	7	Swinton	22,923
8 Oct.	A	3	GB	10	Bradford	32,773
8 Oct.	NZ	9	Fr	0	Wigan	2,876

Final Table

	P.	W.	D.	L.	F.	A.	Pts.
Great Britain	3	3	0	0	66	18	6
Australia	3	2	0	1	37	37	4
New Zealand	3	1	0	2	32	44	2
France	3	0	0	3	19	55	0

1968 in Australia   *Winners:* Australia
and New Zealand

25 May	A	25	GB	10	Sydney	62,256
25 May	Fr	15	NZ	10	Auckland	18,000
1 June	A	31	NZ	12	Brisbane	23,608
2 June	Fr	7	GB	2	Auckland	15,760
8 June	A	37	Fr	4	Brisbane	32,600
8 June	GB	38	NZ	14	Sydney	14,105

Final Table

	P.	W.	D.	L.	F.	A.	Pts.
Australia	3	3	0	0	93	26	6
France	3	2	0	1	26	49	4
Great Britain	3	1	0	2	50	46	2
New Zealand	3	0	0	3	36	84	0

Play off final

| 10 June | A | 20 | Fr | 2 | Sydney | 54,290 |

1970 in England   *Winners:* Australia

21 Oct.	A	47	NZ	11	Wigan	9,586
24 Oct.	GB	11	A	4	Leeds	15,084
25 Oct.	NZ	16	Fr	15	Hull	3,824
28 Oct.	GB	6	Fr	0	Castleford	8,958
31 Oct.	GB	27	NZ	17	Swinton	5,609
1 Nov.	Fr	17	A	15	Bradford	6,215

Final Table

	P.	W.	D.	L.	F.	A.	Pts.
Great Britain	3	3	0	0	44	21	6
Australia	3	1	0	2	66	39	2
France	3	1	0	2	32	37	2
New Zealand	3	1	0	2	44	89	2

Play off final

| 7 Nov. | A | 12 | GB | 7 | Leeds | 18,776 |

1972 in France   *Winners:* Great Britain

28 Oct.	Fr	20	NZ	9	Marseilles	20,748
29 Oct.	GB	27	A	21	Perpignan	6,324
1 Nov.	A	9	NZ	5	Paris	8,000
1 Nov.	GB	13	Fr	4	Grenoble	5,321
4 Nov.	GB	53	NZ	19	Pau	7,500
5 Nov.	A	31	Fr	9	Toulouse	10,332

Final Table

	P.	W.	D.	L.	F.	A.	Pts.
Great Britain	3	3	0	0	93	44	6
Australia	3	2	0	1	61	41	4
France	3	1	0	2	33	53	2
New Zealand	3	0	0	3	33	82	0

Play off final

| 11 Nov. | GB | 10 | A | 10 | Lyons | 4,231 |

No further score after extra-time so Great Britain took the championship because they had scored the greatest number of points in the qualifying League table.

1977 in Australia   *Winners:* Australia
and New Zealand

29 May	A	27	NZ	12	Auckland	18,000
5 June	GB	23	Fr	4	Auckland	10,000
11 June	A	21	Fr	9	Sydney	13,231
12 June	GB	30	NZ	12	C'church	7,000
18 June	A	19	GB	5	Brisbane	27,000
19 June	NZ	28	Fr	20	Auckland	8,000

Final Table

	P.	W.	D.	L.	F.	A.	Pts.
Australia	3	3	0	0	67	26	6
Great Britain	3	2	0	1	58	35	4
New Zealand	3	1	0	2	52	77	2
France	3	0	0	3	33	72	0

Play off final

25 June A	13 GB	12 Sydney	24,457

1985-88 Series   *Winners:* Australia

1985

7 July	NZ	18 A	0 Auckland	19,000
9 Nov.	GB	6 NZ	6 Leeds	22,209
7 Dec.	Fr	0 NZ	22 Perpignan	5,000

1986

16 Feb.	Fr	10 GB	10 Avignon	4,000
29 July	A	32 NZ	12 Brisbane	22,811
17 Aug.	PNG	24 NZ	22 Port Moresby	15,000
4 Oct.	PNG	12 A	62 Port Moresby	17,000
22 Nov.	GB	15 A	24 Wigan	20,169
13 Dec.	Fr	0 A	52 Carcassonne	3,000

1987

24 Jan.	GB	52 Fr	4 Leeds	6,567
24 Oct.	GB	42 PNG	0 Wigan	9,121
15 Nov.	Fr	21 PNG	4 Carcassonne	5,000

1988

22 May	PNG	22 GB	42 Port Moresby	12,077
9 July	A	12 GB	26 Sydney	15,994
10 July	NZ	66 PNG	14 Auckland	8,392
17 July	NZ	12 GB	10 Christchurch	8,525
20 July	A	70 PNG	8 Wagga Wagga	11,685

Final Table

	P.	W.	D.	L.	F.	A.	Pts.
Australia	7	5	0	2	252	91	12*
New Zealand	7	4	1	2	158	86	11*
Great Britain	8	4	2	2	203	90	10
P. N. Guinea	7	1	0	6	84	325	4*
France	5	1	1	3	35	140	3

*Awarded two points in lieu of France's non-fulfilment of fixtures Down Under.

Play off final

1988

9 Oct.	A	25 NZ	12 Auckland	47,363

GREAT BRITAIN WORLD CUP SQUADS

Captains in bold

1954 IN FRANCE

D. Valentine (Huddersfield)
W. Banks (Huddersfield)
H. Bradshaw (Huddersfield)
G. Brown (Leeds)
R. Coverdale (Hull)
G. Helme (Warrington)
P. Jackson (Barrow)
F. Kitchen (Leigh)
J. Ledgard (Leigh)

A. Naughton (Warrington)
D. Robinson (Wakefield T)
D. Rose (Leeds)
R. Rylance (Huddersfield)
S. Smith (Hunslet)
M. Sullivan (Huddersfield)
J. Thorley (Halifax)
B. Watts (York)
J. Whiteley (Hull)

Manager: G. Shaw (Castleford)

1957 IN AUSTRALIA

A. Prescott (St. Helens)
E. Ashton (Wigan)
W. Boston (Wigan)
A. Davies (Oldham)
J. Grundy (Barrow)
G. Gunney (Hunslet)
T. Harris (Hull)
P. Jackson (Barrow)
L. Jones (Leeds)

S. Little (Oldham)
T. McKinney (St. Helens)
G. Moses (St. Helens)
R. Price (Warrington)
A. Rhodes (St. Helens)
J. Stevenson (Leeds)
M. Sullivan (Huddersfield)
D. Turner (Oldham)
J. Whiteley (Hull)

Managers: W. Fallowfield (RL Secretary) and H. Rawson (Hunslet)

1960 IN ENGLAND

E. Ashton (Wigan)
W. Boston (Wigan)
J. Challinor (Warrington)
A. Davies (Oldham)
E. Fraser (Warrington)
R. Greenough (Warrington)
T. Harris (Hull)
V. Karalius (St. Helens)
B. McTigue (Wigan)

A. Murphy (St. Helens)
F. Myler (Widnes)
A. Rhodes (St. Helens)
B. Shaw (Hunslet)
J. Shaw (Halifax)
M. Sullivan (Wigan)
D. Turner (Wakefield T)
J. Whiteley (Hull)
J. Wilkinson (Wakefield T)

Manager: W. Fallowfield (RL Secretary)

1968 IN AUSTRALIA AND NEW ZEALAND

B. Risman (Leeds)
K. Ashcroft (Leigh)
J. Atkinson (Leeds)
T. Bishop (St. Helens)
I. Brooke (Wakefield T)
A. Burwell (Hull KR)
M. Clark (Leeds)

D. Edwards (Castleford)
P. Flanagan (Hull KR)
R. French (Widnes)
R. Haigh (Wakefield T)
R. Millward (Hull KR)
A. Morgan (Featherstone R)
C. Renilson (Halifax)

M. Shoebottom (Leeds)
C. Sullivan (Hull)
J. Warlow (St. Helens)
C. Watson (St. Helens)
C. Young (Hull KR)

Manager: W. Fallowfield (RL Secretary)   Coach: C. Hutton (Hull KR)

1970 IN ENGLAND

F. Myler (St. Helens)
K. Ashcroft (Leigh)
J. Atkinson (Leeds)
P. Charlton (Salford)
D. Chisnall (Leigh)
R. Dutton (Widnes)
A. Fisher (Bradford N & Leeds)

R. Haigh (Leeds)
D. Hartley (Castleford)
K. Hepworth (Castleford)
C. Hesketh (Salford)
S. Hynes (Leeds)
K. Jones (Wigan)
D. Laughton (Wigan)

M. Reilly (Castleford)
M. Shoebottom (Leeds)
A. Smith (Leeds)
J. Thompson (Featherstone R)
C. Watson (St. Helens)

Manager: J. Harding (Leigh)   Coach: J. Whiteley (Hull KR)

1972 IN FRANCE

C. Sullivan (Hull)
J. Atkinson (Leeds)
P. Charlton (Salford)
T. Clawson (Leeds)
C. Dixon (Salford)
C. Hesketh (Salford)
J. Holmes (Leeds)

R. Irving (Oldham)
D. Jeanes (Leeds)
A. Karalius (St. Helens)
B. Lockwood (Castleford)
P. Lowe (Hull KR)
S. Nash (Featherstone R)
G. Nicholls (Widnes)

D. O'Neill (Widnes)
D. Redfearn (Bradford N)
M. Stephenson (Dewsbury)
D. Topliss (Wakefield T)
John Walsh (St. Helens)

Manager: W. Spaven (Hull KR)   Coach: J. Challinor (St. Helens)

347

1977 IN AUSTRALIA AND NEW ZEALAND

R. Millward (Hull KR)
E. Bowman (Workington T)
L. Casey (Hull KR)
L. Dyl (Leeds)
K. Elwell (Widnes)
G. Fairbairn (Wigan)
K. Fielding (Salford)

W. Francis (Wigan)
K. Gill (Salford)
A. Hodkinson (Rochdale H)
P. Hogan (Barrow)
J. Holmes (Leeds)
S. Lloyd (Castleford)
S. Nash (Salford)

G. Nicholls (St. Helens)
S. Pitchford (Leeds)
P. Smith (Featherstone R)
J. Thompson (Featherstone R)
D. Ward (Leeds)
S. Wright (Widnes)

Manager: R. Parker (Blackpool B)   Coach: D. Watkins (Salford)

French hooker Christophe Fontaine stands over British
winger Vince Fawcett in the British Coal Under-21
international at Doncaster.

UNDER-21s

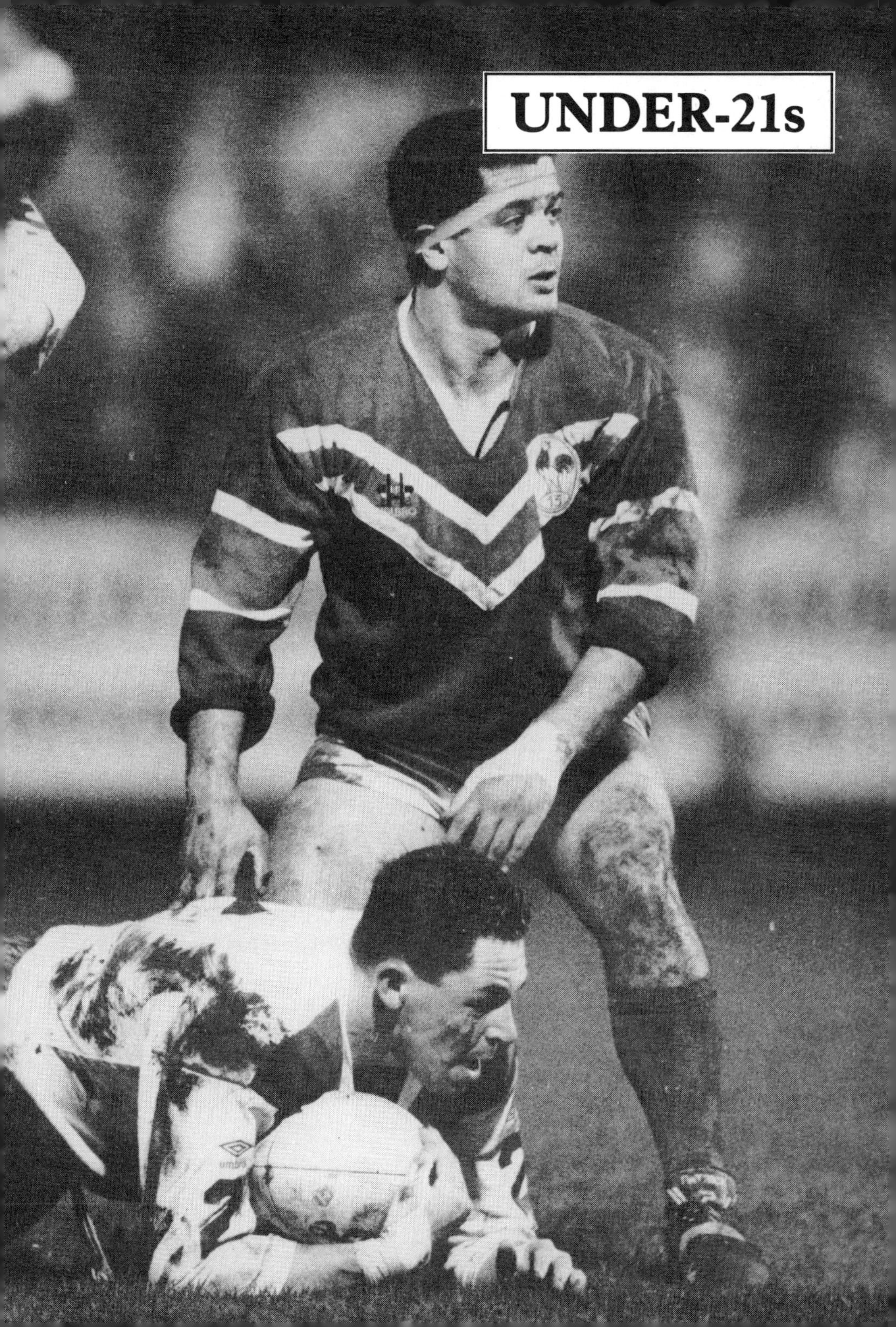

UNDER-21s

Britain's highly-acclaimed Under-21s fulfilled their promise by gaining the first home-and-away double over their French counterparts for three years, the young Gauls being kept scoreless on home soil for the first time in the 25-year history of Under-21 and Under-24 football.

Coach Malcolm Reilly, back in charge of the side, declared that the squad travelling to Villeneuve for the opening encounter was the best-ever selection, bringing in a further five new faces for the return fixture at Doncaster to emphasise the strength in depth of youth talent in the British game.

The Young Lions' 22-0 defeat of the French in Villeneuve, featuring five tries, was followed by a 20-6 success on home territory. An Under-21 record crowd of 4,596 packed Tattersfield for Doncaster's first floodlit match, the latest in a series of improvements to the Bentley Road ground.

The opening encounter was an evening kick off, staged in freezing conditions, although the match itself threatened to boil over on the hour with Britain holding a decisive 18-0 lead. But Reilly's charges obeyed pre-match instructions to keep calm as the French turned the clock back to the dark days of undisciplined mayhem with a sending off and two sin bins. Huddersfield referee Colin Morris experienced a tough international debut. As the football became more scrappy in the second half, he sent prop Remi Riverola to the sin bin in the 57th minute for fighting, followed a minute later by hooker Christophe Fontaine for butting. Only three more minutes passed before British second row man Sonny Nickle was sent to the sidelines for 10 minutes as fighting broke out again. Almost on the whistle, French stand off Pascal Fages was dismissed for a high tackle on British Coal Man of the Match Phil Clarke, son of former Great Britain and Wigan hooker Colin.

Fielding eight new caps, Britain opened the scoring after only six minutes, debutant hooker Graham Southernwood plunging over from close range. Strong-running Vince Fawcett scored two tries in a 17-minute spell before half-time to give the visitors a 12-0 interval lead.

Six minutes after the break, rangy back row forward Denis Betts burst through two tackles on a 20-yard dash to the line, Wigan team-mate Bobby Goulding adding the goal. Britain's final score came in the 58th minute — in between the two French sin bins — with Alan Hunte finishing off a crossfield passing movement.

The highly successful staging of a first international at Doncaster was crowned by a four tries to one home success. Two of the four new caps figured on the scoresheet, Hull K.R. winger Anthony Sullivan — following in the footsteps of his late father, Clive — opening the scoring with a seventh minute try, Warrington stand off Robert Turner contributing two goals. A third debutant, St. Helens full back Gary Connolly, took the British Coal Man of the Match award.

Powerful prop Molloy added a try as Britain built a 10-2 interval lead, centres Grant Anderson and Paul Newlove touching down in the second half. With skipper Shaun Irwin having withdrawn with a thigh injury on the morning of the match, Wigan scrum half Goulding led the side only days after his 18th birthday.

The French provided stiffer opposition, with only one flare-up late in the second half and Britain's Betts being sent to the sin bin, a consolation try coming in the dying minutes when skipper Didier Cabestany drove over to add to a first half penalty goal from scrum half Sylvain Crismanovich.

20 January **Villeneuve**

GREAT BRITAIN 22

David Mycoe (Sheffield E.)	1.	Jean-Marc Garcia (St. Esteve)
Vince Fawcett (Leeds)	2.	Patrick Costes (Lezignan)
Paul Newlove (Featherstone R.)	3.	Eric Bonnet (Carcassonne)
Shaun Irwin (Castleford), Capt.	4.	David Despin (Villeneuve)
Alan Hunte (St. Helens)	5.	Luc Durand (Avignon)
Grant Anderson (Castleford)	6.	Pascal Fages (Pia)
Bobby Goulding (Wigan)	7.	Christophe Delbert (Villeneuve)
Steve Molloy (Warrington)	8.	Remi Riverola (Carcassonne)
Graham Southernwood (Castleford)	9.	Christophe Fontaine (Villeurbanne)
Ian Gildart (Wigan)	10.	Bruno Lucchese (Carcassonne)
Denis Betts (Wigan)	11.	Patrick Jammes (Limoux)
Sonny Nickle (Sheffield E.)	12.	Didier Cabestany (St. Esteve), Capt.
Philip Clarke (Wigan)	13.	David Amat (Lezignan)
Paul Delaney (Leeds)	14.	Frederick Jacquet (Avignon)
Jason Critchley (Widnes)	15.	Christophe Grandjean (Lezignan)
Anthony Farrell (Sheffield E.)	16.	Sylvain Crismanovich (Chatillon)
Neil Roebuck (Castleford)	17.	Ahmed Djebarni (Villeneuve)

FRANCE 0

T: Fawcett (2), Southernwood,
Betts, Hunte. G: Goulding
Subs: Delaney for Mycoe (47 min.)
Critchley for Nickle (72 min.)

Subs: Grandjean for Riverola (66 min.)
Crismanovich for Despin (66 min.)
Half-time: 12-0. Attendance: 1,500
Referee: Colin Morris (Huddersfield)

---

16 February **Doncaster**

GREAT BRITAIN 20

Gary Connolly (St. Helens)	1.	Jean-Marc Garcia (St. Esteve)
Vince Fawcett (Leeds)	2.	Luc Durand (Avignon)
Grant Anderson (Castleford)	3.	Eric Bonnet (Carcassonne)
Paul Newlove (Featherstone R.)	4.	Adolphe Alesina (Pamier)
Anthony Sullivan (Hull K.R.)	5.	Patrick Costes (Lezignan)
Robert Turner (Warrington)	6.	Pascal Fages (Pia)
Bobby Goulding (Wigan), Capt.	7.	Sylvain Crismanovich (Chatillon)
Steve Molloy (Warrington)	8.	Remi Riverola (Carcassonne)
Graham Southernwood (Castleford)	9.	Christophe Fontaine (Villeurbanne)
Phil Sumner (Warrington)	10.	Bruno Lucchese (Carcassonne)
Denis Betts (Wigan)	11.	Patrick Jammes (Limoux)
Ian Gildart (Wigan)	12.	Didier Cabestany (St. Esteve), Capt.
Gary Price (Wakefield T.)	13.	David Amat (Lezignan)
Paul Delaney (Leeds)	14.	Christophe Grandjean (Lezignan)
Neil Roebuck (Castleford)	15.	Lilian Hebert (Vernajoul)
Sonny Nickle (Sheffield E.)	16.	Philippe Ricard (Limoux)
	17.	Frederic Abadie (Lezignan)

FRANCE 6

T: Sullivan, Molloy, Anderson, Newlove
G: Turner (2)
Subs: Roebuck for Sumner (Half-time)
Delaney for Newlove (60 min.)
Manager: Maurice Lindsay ⎱ both games
Coach: Malcolm Reilly ⎰

T: Cabestany
G: Crismanovich
Subs: Abadie for Garcia (31 min.)
Grandjean for Jammes (61 min.)
Half-time:10-2. Attendance: 4,596
Referee: Guy Legueziec (France)

GREAT BRITAIN
UNDER-21s RESULTS

25 Nov.	1984	W 24-8	v.	F	Castleford
16 Dec.	1984	W 8-2	v.	F	Albi
9 Oct.	1985	L 12-16	v.	NZ	Bradford
19 Jan.	1986	L 6-19	v.	F	St. Esteve
2 Feb.	1986	W 6-2	v.	F	Whitehaven
8 Mar.	1987	W 40-7	v.	F	St. Jean de Luz
21 Mar.	1987	W 54-6	v.	F	St. Helens
6 Mar.	1988	L 13-14	v.	F	Ausillon
19 Mar.	1988	L 4-8	v.	F	St. Helens
20 Jan.	1989	W 30-0	v.	F	Leeds
4 Feb.	1989	L 8-16	v.	F	Carpentras
20 Jan.	1990	W 22-0	v.	F	Villeneuve
16 Feb.	1990	W 20-6	v.	F	Doncaster

Key: F - France,
NZ - New Zealand

GREAT BRITAIN
UNDER-21s REGISTER

The following is a register of appearances for Great Britain Under-21s since this classification of match was introduced in 1984.

Figures in brackets are the total appearances, with the plus sign indicating substitute appearances, e.g. (3 + 1).

Away matches are in bold letters. Substitute appearances are in lower case letters.

ALLEN, S. (1) St. Helens: 1984 F
ANDERSON, G. (4) Castleford: 1989 F, **F**; 1990 **F**, F

BECKWITH, M. (1 + 1) Whitehaven: 1986 f, **F**
BETTS, D. (4) Wigan: 1989 F, **F**; 1990 **F**, F
BIBB, C. (5) Featherstone R.: 1987 **F**, F; 1988 **F**; 1989 F, **F**
BISHOP, P. (1 + 1) Warrington: 1987 **F**, f
BOOTHROYD G. (1) Castleford: 1989 F
CARBERT, B. (3) Warrington: 1985 NZ; 1986 **F**, F
CASSIDY, F. (1 + 1) Swinton: 1988 f, F
CLARK, G. (2) Hull K.R.: 1984 F, **F**
CLARKE, P. (1) Wigan: 1990 **F**
CONNOLLY, G. (1) St. Helens: 1990 F
CONWAY, M. (1) Leeds: 1984 F

CREASSER, D. (5) Leeds: 1984 F, **F**; 1985 NZ; 1986 **F**, F
CRITCHLEY, J. (+ 1) Widnes: 1990 f
CROOKS, L. (2) Hull: 1984 F, **F**
CURRIER, A. (2) Widnes: 1984 F, **F**

DALTON, J. (3) Whitehaven: 1985 NZ; 1986 **F**, F
DANNATT, A. (6) Hull: 1984 F, **F**; 1985 NZ; 1986 **F**; 1987 **F**, F
DELANEY, P. (+ 2) Leeds: 1990 f, f
DERMOTT, M. (5) Wigan: 1987 **F**, F; 1988 **F**, **F**; 1989 F
DISLEY, G. (+ 1) Salford: 1987 f
DIVORTY, G. (6) Hull: 1984 F; 1985 NZ; 1986 **F**, F; 1987 **F**, F

EASTWOOD, P. (2) Hull: 1987 **F**, F
EDWARDS, S. (4) Wigan: 1984 F; 1985 NZ; 1987 **F**, F

FARRELL, A. (1 + 1) Huddersfield: 1989 f, **F**
FAWCETT, V. (2) Leeds: 1990 **F**, F
FLETCHER, M. (2) Hull K.R.: 1988 **F**, F
FORD, M. (3 + 1) Wigan: 1985 NZ; 1986 **F**; Leigh: 1987 f, F
FORSTER, M. (3) Warrington: 1985 NZ; 1986 **F**, F
FOX, D. (1) Featherstone R.: 1984 **F**

GILDART, I. (6) Wigan: 1988 **F**, F; 1989 F, **F**; 1990 **F**, F
GOULDING, B. (2) Wigan: 1990 **F**, F
GREGORY, M. (1) Warrington: 1984 F
GRIBBIN, V. (1 + 1) Whitehaven: 1984 f, **F**
GROVES, P. (3) Salford: 1984 F, **F**; 1985 NZ

HARCOMBE, K. (1) Rochdale H.: 1986 F
HARMON, N. (1 + 3) Warrington: 1988 f, **F**; 1989 f, f
HILL, B. (+ 1) Leeds: 1986 f
HILL, K. (3) Castleford: 1988 **F**, F; 1989 **F**
HUGHES, G. (1) Leigh: 1986 F
HULME, D. (2 + 1) Widnes: 1985 nz; 1986 **F**, F
HUNTE, A. (1) St. Helens: 1990 **F**

IRWIN, S. (4) Castleford: 1988 **F**; 1989 F, **F**; 1990 **F**

JOHNSON, E. (2) Leeds: 1988 **F**, F

LAY, S. (+ 1) Hunslet: 1989 f
LORD, G. (1) Castleford: 1988 **F**
LOUGHLIN, P. (2) St. Helens: 1987 **F**, F
LUCAS, I. (4) Wigan: 1988 **F**, F; 1989 F, **F**
LYMAN, P. (3) Featherstone R.: 1985 NZ; 1986 **F**, F
LYON, D. (2) Widnes: 1985 NZ; 1986 **F**

McCORMACK, K. (2) St. Helens: 1987 **F**, F
MEDLEY, P. (2) Leeds: 1987 **F**, F
MOLLOY, S. (2) Warrington: 1990 **F**, F

MOUNTAIN, D. (+1) Castleford: 1987 f
MYCOE, D. (1) Sheffield E.: 1990 **F**

NEWLOVE, P. (4) Featherstone R: 1989 F, **F**;
1990 **F**, **F**
NICKLE, S. (1) Sheffield E.: 1990 **F**

PARKER, W. (2) Hull K.R.: 1988 **F**, F
POWELL, R. (5) Leeds: 1984 F, **F**; 1985 NZ;
1986 **F**, F
PRATT, R. (2) Leeds: 1988 **F**, F
PRICE, G. (3+1) Wakefield T.: 1988 f; 1989 F, **F**;
1990 F
PRICE, R. (2) Hull: 1989 F, **F**
PROCTOR, W. (+1) Hull: 1984 f
PUCKERING, N. (4) Hull: 1986 **F**, F; 1987 **F**, F

RIPPON, A. (1) Swinton: 1984 **F**
ROBINSON, S. (1) Halifax: 1988 **F**
ROEBUCK, N. (+1) Castleford: 1990 f
ROUND, P. (1+1) St. Helens: 1984 F, f
RUSSELL, R. (1+1) Wigan: 1987 **F**; 1988 f

SAMPSON, D. (1) Castleford: 1988 **F**
SANDERSON, G. (4) Warrington: 1987 **F**, F;
1988 **F**, F
SCHOFIELD, G. (2) Hull: 1984 **F**, F
SOUTHERNWOOD, G. (2) Castleford: 1990 **F**, F
SOUTHERNWOOD, R. (2) Castleford: 1989 F, **F**
STREET, T. (2) Leigh: 1989 F, **F**
SULLIVAN, A. (1) Hull K.R.: 1990 F
SUMNER, P. (1) Warrington: 1990 F

TURNER, R. (1) Warrington: 1990 F

WANE, S. (3) Wigan: 1984 **F**; 1985 NZ; 1986 **F**
WESTHEAD, J. (1+2) Leigh: 1985 nz; 1986 f, F
WRIGHT, D. (2) Widnes: 1987 **F**; 1988 **F**

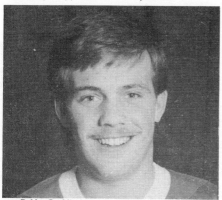
Bobby Goulding, youngest-ever under-21 skipper.

GREAT BRITAIN UNDER-24s RESULTS

3 Apr. 1965	W	17-9	v.	F	Toulouse
20 Oct. 1965	W	12-5	v.	F	Oldham
26 Nov. 1966	L	4-7	v.	F	Bayonne
17 Apr. 1969	W	42-2	v.	F	Castleford
14 Nov. 1976	W	19-2	v.	F	Hull K.R.
5 Dec. 1976	W	11-9	v.	F	Albi
12 Nov. 1977	W	27-9	v.	F	Hull
18 Dec. 1977	W	8-4	v.	F	Tonneins
4 Oct. 1978	L	8-30	v.	A	Hull K.R.
14 Jan. 1979	W	15-3	v.	F	Limoux
24 Nov. 1979	W	14-2	v.	F	Leigh
13 Jan. 1980	W	11-7	v.	F	Carcassonne
5 Nov. 1980	L	14-18	v.	NZ	Fulham
10 Jan. 1981	W	9-2	v.	F	Villeneuve
16 Jan. 1982	W	19-16	v.	F	Leeds
21 Feb. 1982	W	24-12	v.	F	Tonneins
16 Jan. 1983	W	19-5	v.	F	Carpentras
11 Nov. 1983	W	28-23	v.	F	Villeneuve
4 Dec. 1983	W	48-1	v.	F	Oldham

GREAT BRITAIN UNDER-24s REGISTER
Since reintroduction in 1976

The following is a register of appearances for Great Britain Under-24s since this classification of match was reintroduced in 1976, until it was replaced by the new Under-21 level in 1984.

Figures in brackets are the total appearances, with the plus sign indicating substitute appearances, e.g. (7+3).

Away matches are in bold letters. Substitute appearances are in lower case letters.

ARKWRIGHT, C. (1) St. Helens: 1982 F
ASHTON, R. (3) Oldham: 1983 **F**, **F**, F

BANKS, B. (1) York: 1979 **F**
BELL, K. (2) Featherstone R.: 1977 F, **F**
BENTLEY, K. (+1) Widnes: 1980 nz
BURKE, M. (5) Widnes: 1979 F; 1980 **F**, NZ;
1982 F; 1983 **F**
BURTON, B. (2) Castleford: 1976 F, **F**

CAIRNS, D. (2) Barrow: 1979 F; 1982 **F**
CASE, B. (3+1) Warrington: 1979 **F**; 1980 NZ: 1981 F; 1982 f
CLARK, G. (3) Hull K.R.: 1983 **F, F,** F
CRAMPTON, J. (4) Hull: 1976 F, **F**; 1977 F, **F**
CROOKS, L. (1) Hull: 1983 F

DICKINSON, R. (5) Leeds: 1976 F, **F**; 1977 F, **F**; 1978 A
DRUMMOND, D. (5) Leigh: 1979 F; 1980 **F**; 1981 **F**; 1982 F, **F**
DUANE, R. (2) Warrington: 1983 **F, F**
DUNN, B. (2) Wigan: 1983 **F,** F

ECCLES, R. (2) Warrington: 1978 A; 1979 F
ENGLAND, K. (+1) Castleford: 1983 f
EVANS, S. (3) Featherstone R.: 1980 NZ; 1981 F; Hull: 1982 **F**

FENNELL, D. (1) Featherstone R.: 1978 A
FENTON, S. (6) Castleford: 1977 F, **F**; 1979 F; 1980 **F**, NZ; 1981 **F**
FIELDHOUSE, J. (1+1) Warrington: 1983 **F,** f
FLANAGAN, T. (5) Oldham: 1980 NZ; 1981 **F**; 1983 **F, F,** F
FORD, Phil (1) Warrington: 1982 **F**
FOX, V. (1) Whitehaven: 1980 NZ
FOY, D. (2) Oldham: 1983 **F,** F

GIBBINS, M. (2) Featherstone R.: 1977 F, **F**
GILBERT, J. (2+1) Featherstone R.: 1977 F; 1977 f; 1981 **F**
GILL, H. (1) Wigan: 1982 **F**
GOODWAY, A. (2) Oldham: 1983 **F,** F
GREGORY, A. (1) Widnes: 1982 F

HALL, D. (+1) Hull K.R.: 1976 f
HANLEY, E. (2) Bradford N.: 1982 F; 1983 F
HARKIN, P. (1) Hull K.R.: 1981 **F**
HARTLEY, I. (1) Workington T.: 1979 **F**
HOBBS, D. (2) Featherstone R.: 1982 F, **F**
HOGAN, P. (2) Barrow: 1978 A; Hull K.R.: 1979 **F**
HOLDING, N. (4) St. Helens: 1979 F; 1980 **F**, NZ; 1983 **F**
HOLDSTOCK, R. (3) Hull K.R.: 1978 A; 1979 F; 1980 **F**
HORNBY, J. (2) Wigan: 1978 A; 1979 **F**
HYDE, G. (1+1) Castleford: 1980 NZ; 1982 f

JAMES, K. (1) Bramley: 1980 **F**
JOHNSON, B. (2) Castleford: 1982 F, **F**

JOYNER, J. (4+1) Castleford: 1976 f; 1977 F, **F**; 1978 A; 1979 **F**

LEDGER, B. (2) St. Helens: 1983 **F,** F
LIPTROT, G. (4) St. Helens: 1977 F, **F**; 1978 A; 1979 **F**
LYDON, J. (3) Widnes: 1983 **F, F,** F

MASKILL, C. (1) Wakefield T.: 1983 **F**
MOLL, D. (1) Keighley: 1983 **F**
MUMBY, K. (6) Bradford N.: 1976 F, **F**; 1977 F, **F**; 1978 A; 1981 **F**
MUSCROFT, P. (3) New Hunslet: 1976 F, **F**; 1978 A
MYLER, A. (3) Widnes: 1982 **F**; 1983 **F,** F
MYLER, J. (1+1) Widnes: 1982 f; **F**

NOBLE, B. (4) Bradford N.: 1982 F, **F**; 1983 F, F
NULTY, J. (2) Wigan: 1976 F, **F**

O'NEILL, M. (3+2) Widnes: 1980 nz; 1982 F, f; 1983 **F, F**
O'NEILL, P. (3) Salford: 1980 **F**, NZ; 1981 **F**
O'NEILL, S. (2) Wigan: 1979 **F**; 1981 **F**

PINNER, H. (4+4) St. Helens: 1976 F, **F**; 1977 f, f; 1978 a; 1979 f, **F**, 1980 **F**
POTTER, I. (4) Warrington: 1979 **F**; 1981 **F**; Leigh: 1982 F, **F**
PROCTOR, W. (1) Hull: 1983 **F**

RATHBONE, A. (+1) Leigh: 1979 f
RAYNE, Keith (2) Wakefield T.: 1979 F; 1980 **F**
RICHARDSON, T. (1) Castleford: 1979 **F**
ROE, P. (4) Bradford N.: 1976 F, **F**; 1977 F, **F**
RUDD, I. (1+1) Workington T.: 1979 f; 1980 **F**

SCHOFIELD, G. (+2) Hull: 1983 f, f
SHEPHERD, M. (2) Huddersfield: 1977 F, **F**
SKERRETT, T. (1) Wakefield T.: 1977 F
SMITH, D. (2) Leeds: 1976 F, **F**
SMITH, Malcolm (1) Wigan: 1979 F
SMITH, Mike (7) Hull K.R.: 1976 F, **F**; 1977 F; 1978 A; 1979 **F**, F; 1980 **F**
SMITH, P. (1) Featherstone R.: 1978 A
SMITH, R. (+1) Salford: 1983 f
STEPHENSON, D. (5) Salford: 1979 F; 1980 **F**, NZ; 1982 F; Wigan: 1982 **F**
SWANN, M. (1) Leigh: 1979 F
SYZMALA, E. (2) Barrow: 1976 F, **F**

THACKRAY, R. (1) Warrington: 1980 NZ
TIMSON, A. (2) Castleford: 1982 F, **F**
TURNBULL, S. (2) Salford: 1976 F, **F**

VAN BELLEN, G. (2) Bradford N.: 1980 NZ; 1982 **F**

WARD, D. (+2) Leeds: 1976 f, f
WARD, K. (3) Castleford: 1980 **F**, NZ; 1981 **F**
WHITFIELD, C. (1) Salford: 1981 **F**
WILKINSON, A. (1) Leigh: 1977 **F**
WOOD, J. (2) Widnes: 1977 F, **F**
WOODS, J. (5) Leigh: 1977 F, **F**; 1978 A; 1979 **F,** F
WORRALL, M. (3) Oldham: 1983 **F, F,** F

Outstanding Yorkshire forward Andy Goodway is halted by Lancashire's Mike Gregory and Richard Eyres (right).

WAR OF THE ROSES

WAR OF THE ROSES

1989 RODSTOCK WAR OF THE ROSES
Proud Yorkshire stormed to their fifth successive Rodstock Trophy success over arch rivals Lancashire, running up the biggest score and widest margin in the 94-year history of inter-county clashes.

The 86th Roses encounter produced a landslide 56-12 victory for Peter Fox's inspired charges at Wigan, Lancashire contributing only embarrassment, even taking into account their pre-match withdrawals through injury.

A crowd of 10,182 — the best Roses turnout for 23 years — paid a record £34,000 to witness the White Rose rout, the contest being over within half an hour as the visitors bagged half a dozen tries on the way to a 32-0 half-time lead.

The final tally of 56 points topped the previous best of 45 set by Lancashire in 1963, while the 48-point winning margin far outstripped the record 27 margin established in Yorkshire's 30-3 success at Wakefield in 1932.

Yorkshire maintained Peter Fox's 100 per cent success record with the county by producing a now traditional brand of commitment and passion, the coach's namesake and club captain, Deryck, serving up a Man of the Match performance ahead of a handful of close candidates.

Lancashire's woe began within days of the side being announced, threequarters Darren Wright, of Widnes, then Wigan's Joe Lydon withdrawing through injury, to be followed by Widnes half back pairing Tony Myler and David Hulme. On the day itself, Wigan second row man Denis Betts, hoping to impress the Great Britain management, pulled a hamstring in training only hours before the kick off. Yorkshire's only withdrawal was the injured Kevin Ward.

The Red Rose gloom was deepened within two minutes of the start when Yorkshire centre Garry Schofield strode through for the first of the visitors' 10 tries, skipper David Hobbs and stand off Graham Steadman sharing eight goals.

Within six minutes Featherstone Rovers winger Paul Newlove had celebrated his Yorkshire debut by ghosting past Billy McGinty and Steve Hampson in high stepping fashion for a try, Steadman breaking through for the first of his two touchdowns in the 14th minute as Yorkshire swept into a 16-0 lead.

Ill luck struck Lancashire again when skipper Andy Gregory had to be stretchered off with knee ligament trouble in the 16th minute, though the contest was out of reach even at that early stage. Fellow Test star Schofield followed him to hospital on the stroke of half-time with a suspected broken ankle, but his departure did not deter Yorkshire from adding 24 second half points.

It was only fleetingly early in the second half that Doug Laughton's side moved with any fluency. Loose forward Mike Gregory claimed their first touchdown after 53 minutes before winger Mark Preston intercepted a pass from Yorkshire's 50th minute substitute Paul Medley to sprint 50 yards for a touchdown, Medley soon making amends by snapping up a loose ball and crashing through from close range.

Yorkshire's pack laid the foundations for a victory which broke the Roses deadlock of 41 victories each. Loose forward Andy Goodway bagged a brace of tries, while props Kelvin Skerrett and Paul Dixon outpowered their Red Rose counterparts. Fittingly, the try of the match went to scrum half Fox, who created so many of the Yorkshire moves.

As a Test trial a month before Great Britain's first meeting with New Zealand, the Rodstock encounter provided a stage for a handful of Test candidates, particularly Newlove, Fox, Hobbs and Goodway.

RODSTOCK WAR OF THE ROSES

20 September   **Wigan**

YORKSHIRE 56

Chris Bibb (Featherstone R.)	1.	Steve Hampson (Wigan)
Carl Gibson (Leeds)	2.	Mark Forster (Warrington)
Garry Schofield (Leeds)	3.	Paul Loughlin (St. Helens)
Daryl Powell (Sheffield E.)	4.	Paul Cullen (Warrington)
Paul Newlove (Featherstone R.)	5.	Mark Preston (Wigan)
Graham Steadman (Castleford)	6.	Ged Byrne (Wigan)
Deryck Fox (Featherstone R.)	7.	Andy Gregory (Wigan) Capt.
Kelvin Skerrett (Bradford N.)	8.	Mike O'Neill (Widnes)
Kevin Beardmore (Castleford)	9.	Paul Hulme (Widnes)
Paul Dixon (Leeds)	10.	Andy Platt (Wigan)
David Hobbs (Bradford N.) Capt.	11.	Billy McGinty (Warrington)
Roy Powell (Leeds)	12.	Richard Eyres (Widnes)
Andy Goodway (Wigan)	13.	Mike Gregory (Warrington)
Andy Mason (Wakefield T.)	14.	Peter Williams (Salford)
Paul Medley (Bradford N.)	15.	Ian Gildart (Wigan)

LANCASHIRE 12

T: Goodway (2), Newlove (2), Steadman (2), Schofield, Fox, Medley, Hobbs
G: Hobbs (4), Steadman (4)
Substitutions:
Mason for Schofield (Half-time)
Medley for Skerrett (50 min.)
Coach: Peter Fox
Attendance: 10,182

T: M. Gregory, Preston
G: Loughlin (2)
Substitutions:
Williams for A. Gregory (16 min.)
Gildart for Hampson (71 min.)
Coach: Doug Laughton
Half-time: 32-0
Referee: Gerry Kershaw (Easingwold)

Yorkshire winger Carl Gibson off loads, watched by teammate Graham Steadman.

LANCASHIRE v. YORKSHIRE RESULTS

All county championship matches except where stated.

Date	Result		Score	Venue	Attendance
7 Dec. 1895	Yorkshire	won	8 - 0	Oldham	9,059
29 Feb. 1896	Lancashire	won	8 - 3	Huddersfield	5,300
21 Nov. 1896	Lancashire	won	7 - 3	Oldham	15,000
20 Nov. 1897	Yorkshire	won	7 - 6	Bradford P.A.	11,000
5 Nov. 1898	Yorkshire	won	20 - 9	Salford	8,000
4 Nov. 1899	Lancashire	won	16 - 13	Halifax	9,000
3 Nov. 1900	Lancashire	won	24 - 5	Rochdale	18,000
15 Feb. 1902	Yorkshire	won	13 - 8	Hull	15,000
15 Nov. 1902	Lancashire	won	13 - 0	Salford	14,000
14 Nov. 1903	Lancashire	won	8 - 0	Leeds	11,000
12 Nov. 1904	Yorkshire	won	14 - 5	Oldham	8,500
4 Nov. 1905	Lancashire	won	8 - 0	Hull	8,000
3 Nov. 1906	Lancashire	won	19 - 0	Salford	5,000
2 Nov. 1907	Yorkshire	won	15 - 11	Halifax	7,000
31 Oct. 1908	Lancashire	won	13 - 0	Salford	5,000
4 Nov. 1909	Yorkshire	won	27 - 14	Hull	6,000
7 Nov. 1910	Lancashire	won	17 - 3	Wigan	2,000
25 Jan. 1912	Lancashire	won	13 - 12	Halifax	3,199
16 Dec. 1912	Yorkshire	won	20 - 8	Oldham	4,000
10 Dec. 1913	Yorkshire	won	19 - 11	Huddersfield	3,500
24 Sept. 1919	Lancashire	won	15 - 5	Broughton	5,000
21 Oct. 1920	Yorkshire	won	18 - 3	Hull	7,000
4 Oct. 1921	Yorkshire	won	5 - 2	Rochdale	4,000
7 Dec. 1922	Match drawn	—	11 - 11	Hull K.R.	8,000
8 Dec. 1923	Lancashire	won	6 - 5	Oldham	8,000
29 Nov. 1924	Lancashire	won	28 - 9	Halifax	6,000
12 Dec. 1925	Lancashire	won	26 - 10	St. Helens	13,000
30 Oct. 1926	Lancashire	won	18 - 13	Wakefield	9,000
29 Oct. 1927	Lancashire	won	35 - 19	Warrington	12,000
3 Nov. 1928	Lancashire	won	33 - 10	Halifax	6,520
22 Mar. 1930	Lancashire	won	18 - 3	Rochdale	4,000
18 Oct. 1930	Yorkshire	won	25 - 15	Wakefield	9,000
17 Oct. 1931	Lancashire	won	11 - 8	Warrington	10,049
*29 Oct. 1932	Yorkshire	won	30 - 3	Wakefield	4,000
25 Sept. 1933	Yorkshire	won	15 - 12	Oldham	2,000
*9 Jan. 1935	Match drawn	—	5 - 5	Leeds	1,500
12 Oct. 1935	Lancashire	won	16 - 5	Widnes	6,700
21 Oct. 1936	Lancashire	won	28 - 6	Castleford	7,648
12 Feb. 1938	Lancashire	won	10 - 9	Rochdale	3,653
*26 Oct. 1938	Match drawn	—	10 - 10	Leeds	3,000
10 Nov. 1945	Lancashire	won	17 - 16	Swinton	11,059
9 Nov. 1946	Yorkshire	won	13 - 10	Hunslet	5,000
12 Nov. 1947	Lancashire	won	22 - 10	Wigan	6,270
3 May 1949	Lancashire	won	12 - 3	Halifax	7,000
5 Oct. 1949	Lancashire	won	22 - 13	Warrington	15,000

Date	Result		Score	Venue	Attendance
18 Oct. 1950	Yorkshire	won	23 - 15	Huddersfield	6,547
10 Oct. 1951	Yorkshire	won	15 - 5	Leigh	11,573
28 Apr. 1953	Yorkshire	won	16 - 8	Hull	8,400
14 Oct. 1953	Lancashire	won	18 - 10	Leigh	12,870
6 Oct. 1954	Yorkshire	won	20 - 10	Bradford	8,500
26 Sept. 1955	Lancashire	won	26 - 10	Oldham	8,000
26 Sept. 1956	Lancashire	won	35 - 21	Hull	8,500
23 Sept. 1957	Yorkshire	won	25 - 11	Widnes	6,200
24 Sept. 1958	Yorkshire	won	35 - 19	Hull K.R.	5,000
29 Oct. 1958	Yorkshire	won	16 - 15	Leigh	8,500
11 Nov. 1959	Yorkshire	won	38 - 28	Leigh	6,417
31 Aug. 1960	Lancashire	won	21 - 20	Wakefield	15,045
9 Oct. 1961	Lancashire	won	14 - 12	Leigh	4,970
26 Sept. 1962	Yorkshire	won	22 - 8	Wakefield	7,956
11 Sept. 1963	Lancashire	won	45 - 20	St. Helens	11,200
23 Sept. 1964	Yorkshire	won	33 - 10	Hull	7,100
10 Nov. 1965	Yorkshire	won	16 - 13	Swinton	5,847
21 Sept. 1966	Lancashire	won	22 - 17	Leeds	10,528
24 Jan. 1968	Lancashire	won	23 - 7	Widnes	8,322
25 Sept. 1968	Yorkshire	won	10 - 5	Hull K.R.	6,656
3 Sept. 1969	Lancashire	won	14 - 12	Salford	4,652
13 Jan. 1971	Yorkshire	won	32 - 12	Castleford	2,000
24 Feb. 1971	Yorkshire	won	34 - 8	Castleford	4,400
29 Sept. 1971	Yorkshire	won	42 - 22	Leigh	4,987
11 Oct. 1972	Yorkshire	won	32 - 18	Castleford	2,474
19 Sept. 1973	Lancashire	won	17 - 15	Widnes	3,357
25 Sept. 1974	Yorkshire	won	20 - 14	Keighley	1,219
16 Oct. 1974	Lancashire	won	29 - 11	Widnes	3,114
20 Dec. 1975	Yorkshire	won	17 - 7	Wigan	700
1 Mar. 1977	Yorkshire	won	18 - 13	Castleford	2,730
††19 Oct. 1977	Lancashire	won	33 - 8	Widnes	5,056
27 Sept. 1978	Lancashire	won	23 - 7	Widnes	4,283
12 Sept. 1979	Yorkshire	won	19 - 16	Castleford	2,738
24 Sept. 1980	Lancashire	won	17 - 9	Widnes	1,593
9 Sept. 1981	Yorkshire	won	21 - 15	Castleford	1,222
26 May 1982	Yorkshire	won	22 - 21	Leigh	1,738
WR11 Sept. 1985	Yorkshire	won	26 - 10	Wigan	6,743
WR17 Sept. 1986	Yorkshire	won	26 - 14	Leeds	5,983
WR16 Sept. 1987	Yorkshire	won	16 - 10	Wigan	9,748
WR21 Sept. 1988	Yorkshire	won	24 - 14	Leeds	8,244
WR20 Sept. 1989	Yorkshire	won	56 - 12	Wigan	10,182

* Match abandoned but result stands   †† Queen's Jubilee match   WR War of the Roses

● There were also a few Lancashire-Yorkshire matches played during the war years but not of a competitive nature.

SUMMARY

Yorkshire won 42   Lancashire won 41   Drawn 3

LANCASHIRE v. YORKSHIRE RECORDS

LANCASHIRE

Highest score:	45-20 at St. Helens, 11 Sept. 1963
Widest margin win:	As above and 33-8 at Widnes, 19 Oct. 1977
Most tries in a match:	No player has scored more than 3
Most goals in a match:	9 by L. Gilfedder (Wigan) at St. Helens, 11 Sept. 1963
Most points in a match:	18 by L. Gilfedder (Wigan) as above
Biggest home attendance:	18,000 at Rochdale, 3 Nov. 1900

OTHER RECORDS (not involving Yorkshire)

Highest score and widest margin:	60-12 v. Cumberland at Wigan, 10 Sept. 1958
Most tries in a match:	4 by T. O'Grady (Oldham) v. Cumberland at Wigan, 6 Sept. 1956
	4 by W. Burgess (Barrow) v. Cumberland at Widnes, 12 Sept. 1962
Most goals in a match:	12 by E. Fraser (Warrington) v. Cumberland at Wigan, 10 Sept. 1958
Most points in a match:	24 by E. Fraser (Warrington) as above
Biggest home attendance:	24,000 v. Australia at Warrington, 26 Sept. 1929

YORKSHIRE

Highest score and widest margin win:	56-12 at Wigan, 20 Sept. 1989
Most tries in a match:	No player has scored more than 3
Most goals in a match:	10 by V. Yorke (York) at Hull K.R., 24 Sept. 1958
Most points in a match:	20 by V. Yorke (York) as above
Biggest home attendance:	15,045 at Wakefield, 31 Aug. 1960

OTHER RECORDS (not involving Lancashire)

Highest score:	51-12 v. Cumberland at Hunslet, 17 Oct. 1923
Highest against:	55-11 v. Australia at Huddersfield, 26 Nov. 1952
Most tries in a match:	5 by J. Parkin (Wakefield T.) v. Cumberland at Halifax, 14 Nov. 1921
Most goals in a match:	10 also by N. Fox (Wakefield T.) v. Australia at York, 28 Sept. 1959
Most points in a match:	23 by N. Fox (Wakefield T.) as above
Biggest home attendance:	19,376 v. Australia at Wakefield, 4 Oct. 1967

LANCASHIRE REGISTER

The following is a register of current players who have appeared for Lancashire. Each played at least one first team game last season.

ARKWRIGHT, C. (4) St. Helens

BENTLEY, K. (4) Widnes
BYRNE, G. (1) Wigan

CASE, B. (3) Warrington 2, Wigan
COTTRELL, A. (+1) Leigh
CULLEN, P. (2) Warrington
CURRIER, A. (1) Widnes

DERMOTT, M. (1) Wigan
DONLAN, S. (1+1) Leigh
DOWD, B. (+1) Widnes
DRUMMOND, D. (4) Leigh 3, Warrington
DUANE, R. (1) Warrington

ECCLES, R. (3) Warrington
EDWARDS, S. (2+1) Wigan
EYRES, R. (1+1) Widnes

FAIRBAIRN, G. (2) Wigan
FIELDHOUSE, J. (2+2) Warrington +2, Widnes 2
FLANAGAN, T. (2+1) Oldham
FORBER, P. (1) St. Helens
FORSTER, M. (2) Warrington

GILDART, I. (+1) Wigan
GITTINS, T. (1+1) Leigh
GLYNN, P. (4+2) St. Helens
GREGORY, A. (9) Widnes 3, Warrington 2, Wigan 4
GREGORY, M. (4) Warrington
GROVES, P. (1) St. Helens

HAGGERTY, R. (+1) St. Helens
HAMPSON, S. (3) Wigan
HENDERSON, J. (1+1) Leigh
HOLDING, N. (2) St. Helens
HULME, D. (1+1) Widnes

HULME, P. (2) Widnes
HUMPHRIES, A. (1) Warrington

KELLY, K. (6) St. Helens, Warrington 5
KISS, N. (5) Wigan

LEDGER, B. (1) St. Helens
LOUGHLIN, P. (2) St. Helens
LYDON, J. (4) Widnes, Wigan 3

McCORMACK, K. (1) St. Helens
McCULLOCH, N. (+1) Leigh
McGINTY, W. (1+1) Warrington
MEADOWS, K. (1) St. Helens
MYLER, A. (2) Widnes

OFFIAH, M. (1) Widnes
O'LOUGHLIN, Keiron (4+1) Wigan 2+1, Widnes, Salford
O'NEILL, M. (9) Widnes
O'NEILL, S. (3) Wigan

PENDLEBURY, J. (1) Salford
PINNER, H. (4+3) St. Helens
PLATT, A. (2) St. Helens, Wigan
POTTER, I. (5) Warrington 2, Leigh 2, Wigan
PRESTON, M. (2) Wigan
PYKE, D. (3) Leigh 2, Widnes

ROBERTS, M. (2) Warrington
ROUND, P. (2) Oldham

STEPHENSON, D. (6) Salford 2, Wigan 4

THACKRAY, R. (1) Widnes

WANE, S. (1+1) Wigan
WHITFIELD, C. (4+1) Salford 3, Wigan +1, Halifax
WILLIAMS, P. (+1) Salford
WOODS, J. (6) Leigh 5, Warrington
WRIGHT, D. (1) Widnes

YORKSHIRE REGISTER

The following is a register of current players who have appeared for Yorkshire. Each played at least one first team game last season.

BEARDMORE, K. (3) Castleford
BELL, K. (4) Featherstone R.
BIBB, C. (1) Featherstone R.
BURTON, C. (3) Hull K.R.

CREASSER, D. (1+1) Leeds
CROOKS, L. (2) Hull, Leeds

DANNATT, A (+1) Hull
DICK, K. (3) Leeds
DICKINSON, R. (3+1) Leeds
DIXON, P. (3+1) Halifax 2+1, Leeds

EASTWOOD, P. (1) Hull

FAIRBANK, K. (1) Bradford N.
FLETCHER, A. (4) Wakefield T.
FOX, D. (7) Featherstone R.

GIBSON, C. (7) Batley 2, Leeds 5
GILL, H. (3) Wigan
GOODWAY, A. (4) Wigan
GRAYSHON, J. (14) Dewsbury 9, Bradford N. 5

HANLEY, E. (4) Wigan
HERON, D. (2+4) Leeds
HILL, B. (1) Leeds
HOBBS, D. (6+1) Featherstone R. +1, Oldham 2, Bradford N. 4
HOLMES, J. (8) Leeds
HYDE, G. (1) Castleford

IDLE, G. (1+1) Bramley +1, Bradford N.

JOYNER, J. (12) Castleford

KAY, A. (1) Hunslet
KELLY, A. (1) Hull K.R.

LAWS, D. (1) Hull K.R.
LYMAN, P. (1+2) Featherstone R.

McCALLION, S. (1) Halifax
MARCHANT, A. (4) Castleford
MASON, A. (4+2) Bramley (2+1), Wakefield T. 2+1
MEDLEY, P. (+2) Leeds, Bradford N.
MUMBY, K. (9) Bradford N.

NASH, S. (10) Featherstone R. 5, Salford 5
NEWLOVE, P. (1) Featherstone R.
NOBLE, B. (2) Bradford N.

POWELL, D. (1) Sheffield E.
POWELL, R. (3) Leeds
PRICE, G. (1) York
PRYCE, G. (1) York

RAYNE, Keith (+1) Leeds
RAYNE, Kevin (2) Wakefield T.
ROOCKLEY, D. (1) Castleford

SCHOFIELD, G. (3) Hull, Leeds 2
SKERRETT, K. (2) Bradford N.
SMITH, G. (+1) York
SMITH, M. (1) Hull K.R.
SMITH, P. (4) Featherstone R.
STEADMAN, G. (1+2) York, Featherstone R. 1+1
STEPHENS, G. (6) Castleford
STEPHENSON, N. (7+3) Dewsbury

VAN BELLEN, G. (2) Bradford N.

WARD, K. (2) Castleford
WATKINSON, D. (2) Hull K.R.
WHITE, B. (+1) York
WILKINSON, I. (2) Leeds, Halifax

COUNTY CHAMPIONSHIP TITLES
(including joint titles)

Lancashire 34
Yorkshire 24
Cumbria....................................... 16
Cheshire....................................... 1

1895-96	Lancashire	1937-38	Lancashire
1896-97	Lancashire	1938-39	Lancashire
1897-98	Yorkshire	1945-46	Lancashire
1898-99	Yorkshire	1946-47	Yorkshire
1899-1900	Lancashire	1947-48	Lancashire
1900-01	Lancashire	1948-49	Cumberland
1901-02	Cheshire	1949-50	Undecided
1902-03	Lancashire	1950-51	Undecided
1903-04	Lancashire	1951-52	Yorkshire
1904-05	Yorkshire	1952-53	Lancashire
1905-06	Lancashire Cumberland	1953-54	Yorkshire
		1954-55	Yorkshire
1906-07	Lancashire	1955-56	Lancashire
1907-08	Cumberland	1956-57	Lancashire
1908-09	Lancashire	1957-58	Yorkshire
1909-10	Cumberland Yorkshire	1958-59	Yorkshire
		1959-60	Cumberland
1910-11	Lancashire	1960-61	Lancashire
1911-12	Cumberland	1961-62	Cumberland
1912-13	Yorkshire	1962-63	Yorkshire
1913-14	Undecided	1963-64	Cumberland
1919-20	Undecided	1964-65	Yorkshire
1920-21	Yorkshire	1965-66	Cumberland
1921-22	Yorkshire	1966-67	Cumberland
1922-23	Lancashire Yorkshire	1967-68	Lancashire
		1968-69	Yorkshire
1923-24	Lancashire	1969-70	Lancashire
1924-25	Lancashire	1970-71	Yorkshire
1925-26	Lancashire	1971-72	Yorkshire
1926-27	Lancashire	1972-73	Yorkshire
1927-28	Cumberland	1973-74	Lancashire
1928-29	Lancashire	1974-75	Lancashire
1929-30	Lancashire	1975-76	Yorkshire
1930-31	Yorkshire	1976-77	Yorkshire
1931-32	Lancashire	1977-78	Not Held
1932-33	Cumberland	1978-79	Lancashire
1933-34	Cumberland	1979-80	Lancashire
1934-35	Cumberland	1980-81	Cumbria
1935-36	Lancashire	1981-82	Cumbria
1936-37	Lancashire	1982-83	Yorkshire

*Ten-cap Wales RU wingman John Bevan, a September
1973 debutant for Warrington.*

RU TO RL

RU to RL

HOME INTERNATIONAL RUGBY UNION SIGNINGS ... A 20-YEAR REVIEW

Between 1970 and 1990 a total of 33 home international Rugby Union players switched to the 13-a-side code: 21 from Wales, 10 from England, one Irishman and one Scotsman. Ten of the converts also toured as British RU Lions.

Of those switching codes, 13 were forwards, the remaining 20 being backs from every position.

Welshman Glyn Shaw was the only forward to graduate to Great Britain Test honours, making just one appearance, while six backs earned British caps: Roy Mathias, Keith Fielding, John Bevan, Peter Williams, Alan Tait and David Bishop.

Rugby Union exiles also gained selection for Great Britain tours Down Under. Record recruit Jonathan Davies was chosen for the 1990 trip to Papua New Guinea and New Zealand, along with Bishop and Tait, plus John Devereux as a replacement; Bevan and Mathias toured in the 1970s. Fielding made World Cup trips with England in 1975 and Britain in 1977, having turned down a full tour invitation in 1974.

The following are career summaries of the Rugby Union internationals who have turned professional in the past 20 years.

The country and figures in brackets refer to total Rugby Union international appearances, while + indicates the number of British Lions appearances where appropriate.

1970

STUART GALLACHER (Wales, 1)
Signed for Bradford Northern from Llanelli. Age 24. Substitute debut v. St. Helens (h) 22 August, lost 3-42. Full debut v. Widnes (a) 9 September, lost 6-22. Toured South Africa with the Barbarians in 1969 and was being sought by several other clubs when Bradford moved in. Rated in Union circles as an outstanding back row forward prospect and good leader, but did not fulfil Bradford's highest hopes. Later moved to Keighley. Played four times for Wales including one as substitute, also for Other Nationalities in the county championship.

KEN GOODALL (Ireland, 19)
Signed for Workington Town from Derry. Age 23. Debut v. Blackpool Borough (h) 22 August, won 30-0, scoring two tries. Toured South Africa with the 1968 RU British Lions and regarded as one of the best running forwards in Union. Workington paid an undisclosed club record fee to sign him ahead of several other clubs. It looked like money well spent as the loose forward made one of the best-ever starts by a Union convert, scoring tries in his first seven matches and finishing with 20 touchdowns for the season. He added only seven more tries in the next injury-hampered seasons before being forced to retire in 1973.

BRYAN WEST (England, 8)
Signed for Wakefield Trinity from Northampton. Age 22. Debut v. Workington Town (a) 5 September, won 22-12. An outstanding Union forward who toured South Africa with the 1968 British RU Lions. Regarded as having plenty of potential but failed to make any impact. Made only 30 appearances for Wakefield.

Welshman Stuart Gallacher.

1972

ROY MATHIAS (Wales, 1)

Signed for St. Helens from Llanelli. Age 23. Debut v. Warrington (h) 22 August, won 15-11, scoring one try. Looked set for a long international Union career as Wales winger, but became one of the most successful players to switch codes in the last 20 years. In a 12-year career with St. Helens he shared in many final triumphs, including the 1976 success at Wembley where he gained a loser's medal two years later. Toured Australasia with Great Britain in 1979, making his one Test appearance after being a late replacement for fellow countryman John Bevan before the squad set off. Also toured Australasia with the 1975 Wales World Cup squad. His total of 20 appearances for Wales is second only to the great Jim Sullivan and included seven at loose forward. Also moved into the pack for St. Helens towards the end of his career. Seven times he finished among the top 10 tryscorers with his best season 1973-74 when he was second with 40. Career total of 240 tries.

Roy Mathias, from Llanelli RU to St. Helens.

RAY HOPKINS (Wales, 1 + British Lions, 1)

Signed for Swinton from Llanelli. Age 24. Debut v. Huyton (h) 3 December, drew 19-19, scoring one try. A top class Union scrum half who toured Australia and New Zealand with the 1971 British Lions. As Welsh understudy to the great Gareth Edwards, *Chico* Hopkins was regarded as a major capture when he signed for Swinton in a then substantial £8,000 deal, but he flopped as a League player. Scrum half is regarded as the most difficult of positions for Union converts to master and Hopkins never looked like succeeding. He was dropped to the reserves after a few matches and made only 29 first team appearances before returning to Wales.

1973

KEITH FIELDING (England, 10)

Signed for Salford from Moseley. Age 24. Debut v. Leigh (h) 17 August, won 31-4. A major Union capture, Fielding had been a regular England winger and was selected to tour Argentina when Salford stepped in with a reported £8,500 offer. Fielding was an immediate success, topping the tryscoring list in his first season with 49, including a club record 46. Finished in the top 10 in each of his first seven seasons, heading the list again with 30 in 1979-80. Made his Great Britain debut after only six months and marked it with a hat-trick against France. Declined an invitation to tour Australasia in 1974 but went with the 1975 England and 1977 Great Britain World Cup squads. Totalled three appearances for Britain and seven for England. Helped Salford to two First Division titles and later became captain. In 10 marvellous seasons he totalled 253 tries for Salford, including 165 Division One touchdowns — a record until beaten recently by Ellery Hanley.

JOHN BEVAN (Wales, 10+ British Lions, 1)
Signed for Warrington from Cardiff. Age 23. Debut v. Castleford (h) 23 September, won 22-5, scoring one try. At about £12,000, a major wing signing. After touring Australia and New Zealand with the British RU Lions in 1971, became one of the few to tour in both codes when going Down Under three years later. Totalled six appearances in a four-year Test career. Also played 17 times for Wales — at wing, centre and second row — captaining them four times. Picked up a winner's medal at Wembley in his first season and scored a try when on the losing side in 1975. Finished among the top 10 tryscorers five times, including third twice. Had his best figures with 31 tries in 1974-75. Totalled 224 tries in a 13-year career at Warrington.

1974

MIKE LEADBETTER (England, 1)
Signed for Rochdale Hornets from Broughton Park. Age 27. Substitute debut v. Halifax (a) 22 September, won 8-5. Full debut v. Bradford Northern (h) 6 October, lost 5-11. Despite having played for England, Lancashire and the Barbarians, the 6ft 3in, 15st forward was an unheralded signing at 27. Made even less impact as a player with a mere two full appearances in the second row for Rochdale, plus five as substitute.

1975

KEITH FAIRBROTHER (England, 12)
Signed for Leigh from Coventry. Age 30. Debut v. Workington Town (h) 12 January, lost 7-18. Turned to Rugby League four years after his last international appearance and having just been dropped by Coventry. Signed for £1,000 down, plus £1,000 a season, but did not stay around to collect more than one fee. Leigh struck the forward off their register within a year, after playing only eight matches.

1977

MIKE LAMPKOWSKI (England, 4)
Signed for Wakefield Trinity from Headingley, Leeds. Age 24. Substitute debut v. Wigan (a) 20 February, scoring one try. Full debut v. Rochdale Hornets (h) 6 March, won 15-9, scoring one try. A then club record capture for more than £9,000. A hefty and battling scrum half who eventually moved to loose forward. Was number seven at Wembley in 1979 when Wakefield lost to Widnes. Hampered by knee injuries and finally forced to quit in 1985.

GLYN SHAW (Wales, 12)
Signed for Widnes from Neath. Age 26. Debut v. New Hunslet (a) 13 November, won 23-0, scoring one try. Full debut v. Dewsbury (a) 27 November, won 17-2. A member of a mighty Wales RU pack, made one of the quickest and most effective code switches by a forward. In his first season he helped Widnes to the First Division title and made the first of seven appearances for Wales. His one Test appearance, in 1980, was the last time a former RU international forward played for Great Britain. At prop when Widnes won at Wembley in 1979 and made a winning substitute appearance two years later. Moved to Wigan in 1981 for £30,000, still a record transfer fee for a former RU international forward. Later moved to Warrington and had a couple of games for the ill-fated Bridgend before finishing his career with Rochdale Hornets in 1986.

KEITH SMITH (England, 4)
Signed for Wakefield Trinity from Roundhay, Leeds. Age 25. Debut v. Salford (h) 13 November, won 14-7. A classic centre with a League background, having played the game at school. Had a key role in Trinity's 1979 march to Wembley where they lost to Widnes. The same year he played for England but never completely fulfilled his potential. Not a robust player, took some bad knocks and after a series of injuries, retired in 1981.

1979

CLIVE GRIFFITHS (Wales, 1)
Signed for St. Helens from Llanelli. Age 25. Debut v. Widnes (h) 19 August, lost 16-28, scoring two goals. A great RU future was forecast for Griffiths after he replaced the legendary J.P.R. Williams as Wales full back, but St. Helens stepped in with a then record £27,500 bid, beating the £15,000 deal David Watkins received from Salford in 1967. Broke an arm in only his second match and was out for three months. Had only moderate success on his return, finishing the season with 44 goals and two tries. Made 98 appearances for St. Helens, including four as substitute and scored 280 goals, including eight drop, 11 tries for 590 points. Moved into the Second Division with Salford and playing on the wing scored 302 points from 18 tries and 118 goals, including six drop, in 1984-85. Played another 16 matches for Salford, including one as substitute, and scored two tries and 39 goals before retiring and returning to St. Helens as fitness coach, moving to Warrington in the same role in 1988. Made two substitute appearances for Wales.

BOB MORDELL (England, 1)
Signed for Oldham from Rosslyn Park. Age 28. Debut v. Bramley (h) 21 October, won 22-9. Four days after his trial match debut the big second row forward played for London Division against New Zealand before deciding to sign for Oldham for about £14,000. Had also played for Barrow A-team earlier in the season. Helped Oldham to promotion in his first season but made little impact and joined ill-fated Kent Invicta for £13,500 at the start of their brief existence in 1983 assisting with coaching. Played a few games for Fulham in 1985-86 before fading out.

1981

TOMMY DAVID (Wales, 4)
Signed for Cardiff City from Pontypridd. Age 32. Debut v. Salford (h) 30 August, lost 21-26 scoring one try. Toured South Africa with the 1974 British RU Lions becoming one of Cardiff City's first convert signings. In his three-season League career, David showed he would have been an even bigger success had he turned professional much earlier. His 26 tries in 1982-83 are still a record for a prop, although one was scored playing second row, and his fourth place the highest for a front row forward. Totalled 55 tries in 82 appearances for Cardiff, including three as substitute. Played twice for Wales.

STEVE FENWICK (Wales, 30 + British Lions, 4)
Signed for Cardiff City from Bridgend. Age 30. Debut v. Salford (h) 30 August. The most capped Union player to switch codes, a 1977 British RU Lions in New Zealand. The £20,000 fee was the highest Cardiff paid for a Union player. But at 30 the centre was another who switched codes too late to make a lasting impact. In three seasons with Cardiff made 85 appearances, including one as substitute, and scored 548 points from 235 goals, including three drop goals, and 25 tries. Twice kicked a century of goals in a season, his 111 in 1982-83 putting him sixth in the chart. Played twice for Wales.

PAUL RINGER (Wales, 8)
Signed for Cardiff City from Llanelli. Age 30. Substitute debut v. Salford (h) 30 August, lost 21-26. Full debut v. Hunslet (h) 13 September, won 32-19, scoring one try. A back row forward who gained some notoriety for being sent off against England at Twickenham in 1980. Became Cardiff's first Rugby Union signing, but came into League too late and made little impact in his three-season career. Played twice for Wales.

1982

BRYNMOR WILLIAMS (Wales, 3 + British Lions, 3)

Signed for Cardiff City from Swansea. Age 30. Substitute debut v. Rochdale Hornets (h) 29 August, won 15-10. Full debut v. Hunslet (a) 12 September, drew 17-17. A scrum half who switched codes for £15,000 after a long Union career including a British Lions tour to New Zealand in 1977. Made his one international League appearance for Wales after only five matches, plus one as substitute, when he scored Wales' only try in a 37-7 defeat by Australia at Cardiff in 1982. Made only 25 appearances for Cardiff, including five as substitute.

Injury-prone Terry Holmes, a 1985 Bradford Northern capture from Welsh RU.

1984

STEVE REDFERN (England, 1)

Signed for Sheffield Eagles from Leicester. Age 26. Debut v. Doncaster (h) 30 December, won 24-12. Sheffield's only Union international signing never looked like making the grade. At 6ft 3in and 17st, was a tremendous scrummager in Union but the prop had little else to offer League. Hampered by injury, retired the following season after only nine appearances, including two as substitute.

1985

TERRY HOLMES (Wales, 25 + British Lions, 1)

Signed for Bradford Northern from Cardiff. Age 28. Debut v. Swinton (a) 8 December, lost 8-0. A 1980 British Lions scrum half in South Africa (1980) and New Zealand (1983). One of the most publicised signings of all time with his £80,000 fee for a three-year contract, a record and the last major one-payment figure before long-term deals became the norm. A great Union scrum half, it was always odds against him making a successful conversion at almost 29 and with a history of injuries. Made a disastrous start when dislocating a shoulder before a 5,247 crowd — treble Swinton's average. Disaster struck again when he attempted a comeback with the reserves and dislocated the same shoulder on 21 January 1986, ruling out the rest of the season. Returned after a strengthening operation and played in 32 matches the following season. Exceptionally big for a scrum half, the almost inevitable move into the pack became permanent when Bradford signed experienced number seven Paul Harkin from Hull K.R. Showing some progress at loose forward, a knee injury finally forced him to quit after being taken off in the drawn Yorkshire Cup final against Castleford at Headingley on 17 October 1987. Played only 37 matches, scoring nine tries.

Hull's 1986 signing from Llanelli, three-cap Wales RU stand off Gary Pearce.

1986

ROB ACKERMAN (Wales, 22 + British Lions, 2)

Signed for Whitehaven from Cardiff. Age 25. Debut v. Huddersfield (h) 13 April, won 38-12, scoring two tries. A 1983 British Lion in New Zealand who never quite became the great RU centre forecast after a memorable debut as a 19-year-old for Wales against New Zealand in 1980. Second Division Whitehaven had the help of British Nuclear Fuels sponsorship to sign Ackerman for £60,000 over three years. Made no great Second Division impact in 107 appearances, including five as substitute, scoring 32 tries. Moved to First Division Leeds in February 1990, being on the list at £48,000 after seeking a move at the end of his contract.

GARY PEARCE (Wales, 3)

Signed for Hull from Llanelli. Age 25. Debut v. Leigh (h) 21 September, won 31-26, scoring three goals. A classy stand off, reported to have signed a four-year contract for around £80,000. Form fluctuated from brilliant to ordinary but retained a regular place until last season. A good tactical kicker, his total of 277 goals includes 30 drop goals. In addition he has crossed for 33 tries in four seasons. Pearce finished fifth in the 1987-88 goal chart with 111.

1987

STUART EVANS (Wales, 9)

Signed for St. Helens from Neath. Age 24. Debut v. Leigh (a) 13 September, lost 27-21. The Neath captain was regarded as one of the top forwards in Britain when he turned professional in a deal reported as high as £80,000 which would be a then record for a Union forward. Weighing in at 18st the prop was put on a crash diet but has yet to acquire the mobility of top League forwards. Made a substitute appearance at Wembley in 1989 when St. Helens crashed 27-0 to Wigan. Hampered by injuries, failed to maintain a regular first team place last season.

1988

PETER WILLIAMS (England, 3)

Signed for Salford from Orrell. Age 29. Debut v. Leigh (h) 23 March, won 28-21, scoring one try. A utility back, Williams withdrew from the England RU squad to Australia to sign for Salford and after only three matches was named in the standby squad for Britain's tour of Australasia. Although he did not tour, Williams' rapid progress was confirmed when he twice played for Britain again France early in 1989. He made his Test debut as a substitute and then scored a try at centre in the return game, his only representative honours. Totalled 19 tries in 49 matches for Salford.

ALAN TAIT (Scotland, 8)
Signed for Widnes from Kelso. Age 23. Substitute debut v. Halifax (h) 24 April, won 36-26. Full debut v. Wigan 21 August, Charity Shield, won 20-14. Son of former Workington Town player picked up first medal before playing a full game of Rugby League, having been a substitute in all three Premiership matches, including the final when he scored a try in the defeat of St. Helens. Switched from centre to full back, became an instant success in his first full season which included two appearances for Great Britain. Selected for Britain's 1990 tour of Papua New Guinea and New Zealand after having already made a total of six Test appearances. The only player to have twice won the Harry Sunderland Trophy as Man of the Match in the Premiership final.

DAVID BISHOP (Wales, 1)
Signed for Hull Kingston Rovers from Pontypool. Age 26. Debut v. Salford (a) 28 August, lost 24-14. One of Union's most controversial players. Had received a long ban and suspended jail sentence for injuring a player. The rugged scrum half was poised to sign for St. Helens at a Press conference in September 1987 when the club withdrew their reported £100,000 offer on medical advice. A fitness check suggested that a broken neck injury received six years earlier had not healed sufficiently. Bishop's move to Hull K.R. followed growing resentment at being overlooked for further international honours though many regarded him as the best half back in Wales. Played his first two League matches at stand off before switching to scrum half. Has won the Rovers Player of the Season award in his first two years. Had the occasional game at loose forward where he made his Test debut as a late substitute against France in April 1990, being named among the forwards for Great Britain's tour of Papua New Guinea and New Zealand.

ADRIAN HADLEY (Wales, 27)
Signed for Salford from Cardiff. Age 25 . Debut v. Warrington (h) 11 September, won 25-18. A regular member for Wales RU with a total of 12 tries, switched codes in a four-year £100,000 deal. Has yet to make anything like the same impact on League with only 16 tries in 42 appearances, including one as substitute. Missed the latter half of last season through injury.

JOHN BENTLEY (England, 2)
Signed for Leeds from Sale. Age 22. Debut v. Salford (a) 27 November, won 24-6. Despite playing most of his club rugby in the centre, both of Bentley's RU international appearances were on the wing where he played on England's tour of Australia in 1988. A long-standing Leeds supporter, had also played League as a schoolboy and his return to the game was almost inevitable. Signed a five-year contract believed to be worth up to £100,000. Used mainly as a winger by Leeds, some spectacular tries towards the end of last season made him a late, but unsuccessful, contender for Britain's tour to Papua New Guinea and New Zealand.

1989

JONATHAN DAVIES (Wales, 23)
Signed for Widnes from Llanelli. Age 26. Substitute debut v. Salford (h) 15 January, won 50-8. Full debut v. Oldham (h) 5 February, won 38-14, scoring a try and five goals. Davies' signing of a four-year £150,000 deal received the biggest nationwide publicity for any event in League's history. The stand off's switching of codes stunned Union followers in Wales where he was idolised. One of the few Union international captains to turn professional. A crowd of 11,871 — almost double the Widnes average at the time — saw his debut as a substitute. Coach Doug Laughton brought him along steadily and caused some criticism by playing him at stand off, centre, wing and full

back. Made 16 appearances, including four as substitute, in his first half season and scored 123 points from seven tries and 48 goals including a drop. Injuries and repeated positional changes gave Davies little chance to settle and he was a controversial choice for Britain's tour of Papua New Guinea and New Zealand, especially as he had just missed three matches with hamstring trouble. Finished ninth in the 1989-90 goals chart with 98, and fifth points scorer with a tally of 260.

PAUL MORIARTY (Wales, 21)

Signed for Widnes from Swansea. Age 25. Substitute debut v. Castleford (h) 30 March, won 36-4. Full debut v. Wakefield Trinity (h) 15 October, won 30-12. The most capped home international forward to switch codes and at about £100,000 one of the costliest. Joined Widnes after being overlooked for the British RU Lions tour of Australia. Made nine substitute appearances for Widnes before making his full debut. Had just gained a regular first team second row place and received a surprise call up for Great Britain fitness checks when a knee injury ruled him out for several months.

Publicity magnet Jonathan Davies, a sensational 1989 recruit by Widnes.

JONATHAN GRIFFITHS (Wales, 2)
Signed for St. Helens from Llanelli. Age 24. Debut v. Sheffield Eagles (a) 3 September, won 36-20, scoring two tries. After an impressive two-try debut, Griffiths looked set to make one of the quickest impacts by a Union scrum half until injuries spoiled his first season and restricted him to 14 appearances, including three as substitute.

JOHN DEVEREUX (Wales, 21)
Signed for Widnes from Bridgend. Age 23. Substitute debut v. Warrington (a) 10 October, lost 28-6. Full debut v. Leigh (h) 12 November, lost 16-18. The powerful centre looked set to add to his long list of international appearances before switching codes for a reported £150,000 over six years. Made several reserve team appearances before being given his senior chance. Continued to be brought along steadily until he settled in on the right wing and was called up as a wing replacement on Great Britain's 1990 tour of Papua New Guinea and New Zealand.

1990

DAVID YOUNG (Wales, 14)
Signed for Leeds from Cardiff. Age 22. Substitute debut v. Barrow (h) 11 February, won 90-0. Full debut v. Featherstone Rovers (h) 13 April, won 25-14. Made three Test appearances for the 1989 RU British Lions in Australia and was regarded as the cornerstone of the Welsh pack for years to come. His five and a half year contract with Leeds was reported to be worth £165,000, putting him in the record bracket, though club officials said he would have to gain top honours to receive anything like that amount. After making a quick debut as substitute, played several reserve team matches before making two full first team appearances near the end of the season.

All Black Rugby Union full back John Gallagher, a record signing by Leeds in May 1990.

TRANSFERS

TRANSFERS

TRANSFER REVIEW
1 June 1989 to 31 May 1990

A unique transfer tribunal valuation resulted in a world record fee of £170,000 being paid by Castleford for Featherstone Rovers stand off Graham Steadman.

The tribunal ruled in June 1989 that Castleford should pay Rovers £145,000, plus £25,000 if Steadman played in a Test match for Great Britain. Steadman pushed the total fee to £170,000 when he made his Test debut against France in April 1990. Featherstone had listed Steadman at £185,000 in May 1989 after learning that he had already agreed terms with Castleford, who offered Rovers about £100,000.

The previous record transfer fee was £155,000 when Leeds signed Test centre Garry Schofield from Hull in October 1987.

Castleford were also involved in the period's second highest transfer fee of £150,000 which they paid to Leeds for Test forward Lee Crooks just before the Silk Cut Challenge Cup register deadline on 8 January. The fee was the same as Leeds had paid Hull for Crooks in June 1987, thus equalling the world record for a forward. Just before Castleford clinched the deal Featherstone had bid £170,000 for Crooks, but the forward rejected the move.

Crooks had been listed at a world record £250,000 in October 1989 when he asked for a move, but after staying away for a spell he was taken off the list about a month later.

Another major deal involving the transfer tribunal resulted in them fixing a fee of £120,000 on Test loose forward Gary Divorty's move from Hull to Leeds. Divorty had been listed at £180,000 in June 1989 after he rejected Hull's new terms. He signed for Leeds on 23 September and had played four matches for them when the tribunal fixed the fee at £120,000. Leeds had offered £70,000 after Hull reduced their valuation to £160,000.

Two Halifax Test forwards were also transferred for six-figure fees — Paul Medley to Bradford Northern for £110,000 and Les Holliday to Widnes for £100,000.

The total of five £100,000 or more transfers reflected the massive rise in fees over the past decade. The first issue of *Rothmans Rugby League Yearbook* for 1981-82 reported a 'staggering' world record £72,500 fee for Test full back George Fairbairn's move from Wigan to Hull K.R. It also felt worth noting that nine players had been transferred for £20,000 or more.

During the present period under review there was a total of 187 transfers between clubs, plus another 26 on loan, including those who returned to their original club. Fees were determined by the tribunal in 15 transfers during 1989-90.

RUGBY UNION SIGNINGS

Leeds stunned the Rugby Union world when they signed New Zealand All Black full back John Gallagher. Their sudden swoop made worldwide headline news on 21 May and days later he attended a much publicised Headingley Press conference.

Although no official figure was put on the deal it was certainly a record, generally reported as being £350,000 for a five-year contract. The previous record was reckoned to be the £150,000 four-year contract Wales international stand off Jonathan Davies received from Widnes in January 1989.

London-born Gallagher, aged 26, played 18 times for New Zealand and had just been named the 1990 International RU Player.

Wigan followed up Leeds' coup by signing another All Black, stand off Frano Botica on 31 May for an estimated £150,000 over three years. Botica, aged 26, had played in seven Tests for New Zealand.

His move completed a devastating month for New Zealand Rugby Union with the loss of four All Blacks to League as full back Matthew Ridge and centre John Schuster had joined Sydney Premiership clubs in

Australia.

Two home international Rugby Union players also switched codes during the period. Bridgend centre John Devereux joined Widnes after playing 21 times for Wales and Cardiff prop David Young went to Leeds with 14 caps for Wales.

Two England B internationals from Headingley to move were centre Simon Irving to nearby Leeds and scrum half Neil Summers to Bradford Northern.

But the total of 16 Rugby Union players to join professional Rugby League clubs was down on the 24 of the previous year.

AMATEUR SIGNINGS

A total of 249 amateur Rugby League players joined the professional ranks compared with 211 the previous year. In addition there were 46 unattached players who signed for clubs, most of whom were also amateurs.

OVERSEAS SIGNINGS

The number of overseas players making first team appearances last season soared to a record 156 — despite it being the first in which there was supposedly stricter control of the quota system which limited clubs to three overseas players at any one time.

The only exemption from that rule was Fulham, who were allowed to play up to six overseas players in any one match because of their London location being deemed a development area. By releasing some players and signing others, a total of 15 overseas players appeared in the Fulham first team over the season.

Every club had at least one overseas player and nearly all manipulated the rule to expand their quota usage, Barrow stretching it to nine, while Leeds, Whitehaven and Nottingham City managed seven.

A total of 90 Australians played first team rugby last season compared with 73 the year before and the record of 95 in 1986-87. They included seven Test players although Bruce McGuire of Sheffield Eagles was the only one who had played for Australia last year.

Wakefield Trinity caused a major surprise when they brought all-time Test great loose forward Ray Price out of a three-year retirement to have one final season.

In addition to Price and McGuire, the other Australian Test players to make their English club debuts were forwards Bryan Niebling at Hull K.R. and Steve Folkes at Hull.

New Zealand supplied a record total of 62 players to English clubs, 12 more than the top figure of a year earlier. They included 19 Test players, which was another record.

One Frenchman played first team rugby, but only briefly as B international scrum half Ronel Zenon made a substitute appearance for Swinton, returning home after being injured.

Hull K.R. signed France Test forward Daniel Divet just before the end of the season and were then told he would be included in their overseas quota of three. As Rovers already had three overseas players lined up for the new season they protested on the grounds that there was a free movement of employment between the European Common Market countries. The case then went to arbitration during the close season.

From the start of the 1990-91 season Carlisle and Nottingham City join Fulham as clubs allowed an increased quota of five overseas players having been granted development status in May 1990. Overseas players who have played five successive seasons in England are also exempt from the quota.

The following is a list of all overseas players who made first team appearances during the 1989-90 season:

OVERSEAS REGISTER 1989-90

*Test players as at 1 June 1990

AUSTRALIA (90)

John Adams	(Hunslet)
Tony Anderson	(Halifax, Oldham)
Greg Austin	(Hull K.R.)
Warwick Badger	(Keighley)
Phil Blake	(Wigan)
Steve Bleakley	(Ryedale-York)
Greg Brake	(Workington T.)
Russell Browning	(Fulham)
Tim Butler	(Dewsbury, Whitehaven)
Brett Clark	(Oldham)
*Noel Cleal	(Hull)
John Cogger	(Oldham)
Keith Cole	(Trafford B.)
Craig Coleman	(Leeds)
Terry Cook	(Bramley)
Glen Coughlan	(Dewsbury)
Jeffrey Coutts	(Fulham)
David Cruickshank	(Leeds)
Mark Cudmore	(Keighley)
Robert Cummings	(Barrow)
Jeremy Cussack	(Barrow)
Brett Daunt	(Fulham)
*Les Davidson	(Wigan)
*John Dorahy	(Halifax)
*Steve Folkes	(Hull)
Ian Freeman	(Barrow)
Gary French	(Castleford)
Ron Gibbs	(Castleford)
Steve Gibson	(Salford)
Wally Gibson	(Huddersfield)
William Greentree	(Bramley)
John Gutherson	(Bramley)
Steve Hall	(Bradford N.)
Jeff Hardy	(Sheffield E., Castleford)
Ivan Henjak	(Bradford N.)
Brian Hetherington	(Halifax)
Cavill Heugh	(Barrow, Leeds)
Craig Izzard	(Leeds)
Bob Jackson	(Warrington)
Brian Jackson	(Wakefield T.)
Graeme Jennings	(Hunslet)
Chris Johns	(Barrow)
Lindsey Johnston	(Halifax)
Eric Kennedy	(Fulham)
David King	(Whitehaven)
Stephen Korn	(Bramley)
Steve Larder	(Castleford)
Mark Laurie	(Leeds)
David Liddiard	(Hull)
Dean Longville	(Nottingham C.)
Brett Love	(Featherstone R.)
Gary Mackay	(Batley)
Graham Mackay	(Bradford N.)
Greg Mackey	(Warrington, Hull)
Peter Marsden	(Runcorn H.)
Michael Matache	(Workington T.)
*Bruce McGuire	(Sheffield E.)
Phil McKenzie	(Widnes)
Ian Mellors	(Fulham)
Darren Morris	(Trafford B.)
Paul Mulherin	(Ryedale-York)
Lex Neal	(Bramley)
*Bryan Niebling	(Hull K.R.)
Greg Pearce	(Fulham)
Chris Perry	(Wakefield T.)
David Perry	(Batley)
Steve Petrie	(Whitehaven)
Joe Phillips	(Barrow, Whitehaven)
Darryl Pitt	(Fulham)
*Ray Price	(Wakefield T.)
Tony Rampling	(Salford)
Darren Robinson	(Chorley)
Lachlan Ross	(Barrow)
Brad Rushton	(Whitehaven)
Wayne Sanchez	(Fulham)
Colin Schofield	(Chorley)
Gary Schubert	(Carlisle)
Greg Shuttleworth	(Huddersfield)
Warren Smiles	(Sheffield E.)
Adam Spicer	(Trafford B.)
Paul Taylor	(Wakefield T.)
Rex Terp	(Leeds)
Brian Torpy	(Chorley)
Phil Veivers	(St. Helens)
James Ward	(Whitehaven)
Brett Welch	(Hunslet)
Ian Wightman	(Fulham)
Sean Willey	(Sheffield E., Ryedale-York)
Brett Williams	(Fulham)
Andrew Zillman	(Fulham)

NEW ZEALAND (62)

Basil Ake	(Ryedale-York)
*Dean Bell	(Wigan)
Glen Bell	(Featherstone R.)
Tony Best	(Fulham)
Tony Botica	(Hull K.R.)
Mark Bourneville	(St. Helens)
Mark Brooke-Cowden	(Salford)
*Peter Brown	(Leigh)
Kurt Burnette	(Chorley)
Trevor Clark	(Featherstone R.)
John Collis	(Keighley)
*Shane Cooper	(St. Helens)
Shane Cummins	(Nottingham C.)
Maurice Davis	(Nottingham C.)
Darryl Dockery	(Workington T.)
Logan Edwards	(Swinton, Rochdale H.)
Mark Faumina	(Ryedale-York, Nottingham C)
Tony Feasey	(Trafford B.)
Stuart Galbraith	(Trafford B., Chorley)
Joe Grima	(Widnes)
Carl Hall	(Doncaster)
Arnold Hema	(Nottingham C.)
Bradley Hemi	(Carlisle)
Terry Hermannson	(Doncaster)
*Kevin Iro	(Wigan)
*Tony Kemp	(Doncaster)
*Mike Kuiti	(Leeds)
*Francis Leota	(Sheffield E.)
*James Leuluai	(Wakefield T.)
*Dean Lonergan	(Rochdale H.)
*Duane Mann	(Warrington)
*George Mann	(St. Helens)
Charlie McAlister	(Oldham)
Vince McHugh	(Swinton)
*Gary Mercer	(Warrington)
Robert Moimoi	(Leigh)
Roby Muller	(Warrington)
Tawera Nikau	(Sheffield E.)
Mark Nixon	(Rochdale H.)
*Dane O'Hara	(Hull)
Hitro Okesene	(Carlisle)
Paul Okesene	(Keighley)
Aaron Palelei	(Nottingham C., Featherstone R.)
Terry Perenara	(Trafford B.)
Karl Robertson	(Fulham)
Iva Ropati	(Featherstone R.)
*Joe Ropati	(Swinton, Warrington)
Peter Ropati	(Leigh)

Warrington's Kiwi Test hooker Duane Mann.

Tea Ropati	(St. Helens)
*Adrian Shelford	(Wigan)
*Kelly Shelford	(Whitehaven)
*Kurt Sorensen	(Widnes)
Russell Stewart	(Bradford N.)
Dean Subritzky	(Batley, Nottingham C.)
Peter Subritzky	(Huddersfield)
Michael Thompson	(Wakefield T.)
Dennis Trembath	(Dewsbury)
Shane Tupaea	(Swinton)
Andrew Vincent	(Doncaster)
*David Watson	(Ryedale-York)
*Graeme West	(Wigan)
Aaron Whittaker	(Chorley)

FRANCE (1)

Ronel Zenon	(Swinton)

MOROCCO (1)

Hussein M'Barki	(Fulham)

TONGA (4)

Lawrence Johansson	(Fulham)
Emosi Koloto	(Widnes)
Boblin Tuavao	(Barrow, Widnes)
Hami Tuavao	(Barrow)

RECORD TRANSFERS

The first £1,000 transfer came in 1921 when Harold Buck joined Leeds from Hunslet, although there were reports at the time that another player was involved in the deal to make up the four-figure transfer. Other claims for the first £1,000 transfer are attached to Stan Brogden's move from Bradford Northern to Huddersfield in 1929. The following list shows how transfer fees have grown this century in straight cash deals only:

Season	Player	Position	From	To	Fee
1901-02	Jim Lomas	Centre	Bramley	Salford	£100
1910-11	Jim Lomas	Centre	Salford	Oldham	£300
1912-13	Billy Batten	Centre	Hunslet	Hull	£600
1921-22	Harold Buck	Wing	Hunslet	Leeds	£1,000
1929-30	Stanley Smith	Wing	Wakefield T.	Leeds	£1,075
1933-34	Stanley Brogden	Wing/centre	Huddersfield	Leeds	£1,200
1937-38	Billy Belshaw	Full back	Liverpool S.	Warrington	£1,450
1946-47	Bill Davies	Full back/centre	Huddersfield	Dewsbury	£1,650
1947-48	Bill Hudson	Forward	Batley	Wigan	£2,000
1947-48	Jim Ledgard	Full back	Dewsbury	Leigh	£2,650
1948-49	Ike Owens	Forward	Leeds	Castleford	£2,750
1948-49	Ike Owens	Forward	Castleford	Huddersfield	£2,750
1948-49	Stan McCormick	Wing	Belle Vue R.	St. Helens	£4,000
1949-50	Albert Naughton	Centre	Widnes	Warrington	£4,600
1950-51	Bruce Ryan	Wing	Hull	Leeds	£4,750
1950-51	Joe Egan	Hooker	Wigan	Leigh	£5,000
1950-51	Harry Street	Forward	Dewsbury	Wigan	£5,000
1957-58	Mick Sullivan	Wing	Huddersfield	Wigan	£9,500
1958-59	Ike Southward	Wing	Workington T.	Oldham	£10,650
1960-61	Mick Sullivan	Wing	Wigan	St. Helens	£11,000
1960-61	Ike Southward	Wing	Oldham	Workington T.	£11,002 10s
1968-69	Colin Dixon	Forward	Halifax	Salford	£12,000
1969-70	Paul Charlton	Full back	Workington T.	Salford	£12,500
1972-73	Eric Prescott	Forward	St. Helens	Salford	£13,500
1975-76	Steve Nash	Scrum half	Featherstone R.	Salford	£15,000
1977-78	Bill Ashurst	Forward	Wigan	Wakefield T.	£18,000
1978-79	Clive Pickerill	Scrum half	Castleford	Hull	£20,000
1978-79	Phil Hogan	Forward	Barrow	Hull K.R.	£35,000
1979-80	Len Casey	Forward	Bradford N.	Hull K.R.	£38,000
1980-81	Trevor Skerrett	Forward	Wakefield T.	Hull	£40,000
1980-81	George Fairbairn	Full back	Wigan	Hull K.R.	£72,500
1985-86	Ellery Hanley	Centre/stand off	Bradford N.	Wigan	£85,000
1985-86	Joe Lydon	Centre	Widnes	Wigan	£100,000
1986-87	Andy Gregory	Scrum half	Warrington	Wigan	£130,000
1987-88	Lee Crooks	Forward	Hull	Leeds	£150,000
1987-88	Garry Schofield	Centre	Hull	Leeds	£155,000
1989-90	Graham Steadman	Stand off	Featherstone R.	Castleford	£170,000

MOST MOVES

Geoff Clarkson extended his record number of transfers to 12 when he left Leigh for Featherstone Rovers on 27 October 1983. He played for 10 different English clubs and had a brief spell in Australia.

Clarkson, born on 12 August 1943 was 40 years old when he finished playing regular first team rugby in 1983-84. He turned professional with Wakefield Trinity in 1966 after gaining Yorkshire County forward honours with Wakefield Rugby Union Club.

Clarkson's club career in England is as follows:

1966 — Wakefield T.
1968 — Bradford N.
1970 — Leigh
1971 — Warrington
1972 — Leeds
1975 — York
1976 — Bramley
1978 — Wakefield T. and Hull K.R.
1980 — Bradford N. and Oldham
1981 — Leigh
1983 — Featherstone R.

1989-90 SIGNINGS

The following is a register of signings by clubs from 1 June 1989 to 31 May 1990. The right-hand column lists the club from which the player was recruited (ARL Amateur Rugby League, RU — Rugby Union).

In some instances a player who wishes to retain his amateur status is not registered although he may be named in the club's list of appearances.

Although this is a register of signings, it is possible to trace a club's transfers by scrutinising the right hand column.

Indicates where clubs have agreed to a player being signed 'on loan', a temporary transfer, the Rugby Football League prohibiting a subsequent transfer within 28 days. Where a player on loan has not been retained his return to his original club is also marked.

BARROW

Signed	Player	Club From
26.6.89	Riley, Stephen	Wath Brow ARL
22.9.89	Phillips, Joe	Beerwah, Aus
1.10.89	Thurbu, Jason	Walney Central ARL
6.10.89	Johns, Chris	Brisbane Broncos, Aus
17.11.89	*Cussack, Jeremy	Bradford N.
29.12.89	Godfrey, Heath	Bradford N.
29.12.89	Rhodes, Paul	Bradford N.
12.1.90	O'Neill, Kevin	Walker Pioneer ARL
12.1.90	Cummings, Robert	Woder Valley, Aus
12.1.90	Lachlan, Ross	Woder Valley, Aus
1.2.90	Tuavao, Boblin	Widnes
2.2.90	McGlynn, Tom	Woder Valley, Aus
2.3.90	Tuavao, Hamoni	Tonga
16.3.90	Barnes, Stephen	Redhill ARL
16.3.90	Gascoigne, Andrew	Redhill ARL
16.3.90	Parker, Russell	Redhill ARL
16.3.90	Thalor, Peter	Lock Lane ARL
16.3.90	Taylor, Wayne	Redhill ARL
23.3.90	Roper, Kevin	Barrow Island ARL

BATLEY

Signed	Player	Club From
23.9.89	*Langton, Steve	Carlisle
23.9.89	*Sanderson, Mark	Nottingham C.
5.10.89	Perry, David	Emerald, Aus
5.10.89	Mackay, Gary	Emerald, Aus
6.10.89	Wilkinson, Mark	Bison ARL
19.10.89	Williamson, Len	Emerald, Aus
22.12.89	Parkinson, Andrew	Halifax
4.2.90	Subritzky, Dean	Carlisle
22.2.90	Heron, Wayne	Bradford N.
31.5.90	Tempest, Andrew	Middleton ARL
31.5.90	Hamill, James	Dewsbury Moor ARL

BRADFORD NORTHERN

Signed	Player	Club From
12.6.89	Green, Alex	Dudley Hill ARL
27.6.89	Henjak, Ivan	Canberra, Aus
1.7.89	Potts, Martin	Doncaster
1.7.89	Tuffs, Simon	Nottingham C.
12.7.89	Cordle, Gerald	Cardiff RU
14.7.89	Mackay, Graham	Western Suburbs, Aus
22.8.89	Adams, Craig	Middleton ARL
31.8.89	Medley, Paul	Halifax
30.11.89	Meehan, Gary	Huddersfield
18.12.89	Marchant, Tony	Castleford
27.12.89	Gill, Henderson	Wigan
26.1.90	Lee, Darren	Middleton ARL
30.1.90	*Cussack, Jeremy	Barrow
30.1.90	Hall, Steve	Aus
30.5.90	Summers, Neil	Headingley RU

379

BRAMLEY

Signed	Player	Club From
31.7.89	Ellis, Andrew	Stanningley ARL
1.8.89	Neal, Lex	Redcliffe, Aus
7.8.89	Kear, John	Castleford
7.8.89	Barnett, Gary	Stanningley ARL
13.10.89	Cook, Terry	Gatton ARL
26.10.89	Greentree, William	Parramatta, Aus
3.11.89	Kain, John	Ryedale-York
22.11.89	Gutherson, John	Forther, Aus
7.12.89	Hemingway, Neil	Batley
16.12.89	Bowie, Iain	Dewsbury
12.1.90	*Thornton, Wayne	Castleford
17.1.90	*Hart, Alan	Castleford
1.2.90	Korn, Stephen	Applecross, Aus
15.2.90	Butterill, Mark	Stanningley ARL
15.2.90	Pitts, David	Stanningley ARL
8.3.90	Clawson, Neil	Oldham
8.3.90	Lidbury, Steve	Sheffield E.
20.3.90	Atkins, Kenneth	—
3.4.90	Harwood, Dean	Eastmoor ARL
23.5.90	Burnell, Steve	East Leeds ARL
23.5.90	Connell, Philip	East Leeds ARL
23.5.90	Welbourne, Stewart	East Leeds ARL

CARLISLE

Signed	Player	Club From
19.6.89	Nicholson, Jeremy	Newcastle-upon-Tyne
17.7.89	Pinner, Harry	Bradford N.
10.8.89	Cubiss, George	Dalston ARL
31.8.89	Williams, Barry	Broughton Red Rose ARL
31.8.89	McNicol, Antony	Barrow
5.10.89	Okesene, Hitro	Manukai, NZ
5.10.89	Hepi, Bradley	Waitemata RU, NZ
20.10.89	Kavanagh, Michael	Askam ARL

CASTLEFORD

Signed	Player	Club From
21.8.89	Steadman, Graham	Featherstone R.
30.8.89	French, Gary	Brisbane Broncos, Aus
1.9.89	Gibbs, Ronnie	Gold Coast, Aus
1.9.89	Larder, Steve	Illawara, Aus
7.9.89	Price, Darren	Pointer Panthers ARL
15.9.89	Ellis, St. John	Ryedale-York
9.11.89	Bragger, Ian	Salford
15.12.89	Roebuck, Neil	Bradford N.
8.1.90	Crooks, Lee	Leeds
8.1.90	Hardy, Jeff	Sheffield E.
16.3.90	*Thornton, Wayne	Bramley
16.3.90	*Hart, Alan	Bramley
27.3.90	Pagdin, Wayne	Heworth ARL

CHORLEY

Signed	Player	Club From
13.7.89	Briscoe, Carl	Trafford B.
14.7.89	Bacon, David	Trafford B.
17.7.89	Duffey, John	St. Cuthberts ARL
17.7.89	Meyrick, Martin	St. Judes ARL
17.7.89	Newton, Gary	St. Cuthberts ARL
17.7.89	Saunders, Peter	St. Cuthberts ARL
17.7.89	Smith, Mike	Trafford B.
17.7.89	Broxton, Paul	Trafford B.
17.7.89	Price, Bill	Trafford B.
17.7.89	Bimson, Jeff	Trafford B.
17.7.89	Mayo, John	Trafford B.
24.7.89	Jones, David	Wigan St Patricks ARL
24.7.89	White, Michael	—
31.7.89	Edwards, Mark	Rose Bridge ARL
16.8.89	Knight, Mark	Warrington
16.8.89	Gittins, Tommy	Barrow
19.8.89	McGuigan, Paul	Chorley RU
19.8.89	Torpy, Brian	Brothers, Aus
23.8.89	Ellis, Jeff	Thatto Heath ARL
1.10.89	Burnette, Kurt	Brisbane Broncos, Aus
26.6.89	Whittaker, Aaron	Halsual, NZ
3.11.89	Cheetham, Michael	Irlam Hornets ARL
7.11.89	Massey, Peter	Irlam Hornets ARL
17.11.89	Williams, Stewart	Barrow
17.11.89	Marshall, Ken	Barrow
29.11.89	O'Hara, Michael	Blackpool Stanley ARL
29.11.89	Grundy, Tracy	Trafford B.
29.11.89	Nanyn, Michael	Trafford B.
28.12.89	Grimmanand, Stanley	—
3.1.90	Wood, David	Rochdale H.
16.1.90	*Chisnall, Chris	Oldham
2.3.90	Evans, Alan	Eccles ARL
15.3.90	Copeland, Anthony	Oldham
29.3.90	Smith, Dave	Blackool Stanley ARL

DEWSBURY

Signed	Player	Club From
1.6.89	Trembath, Denis	Fulham
14.7.89	Bloor, Andrew	—
21.7.89	Haigh, Mark	Hanging Heaton ARL
21.7.89	Tong, Michael	Hanging Heaton ARL
28.7.89	Ellis, Kevin	Doncaster
28.7.89	Charles, Marquis	Westgate Redcourt ARL
28.7.89	Kelly, Richard	Wakefield T.
28.7.89	Garnett, Paul	Oldham St. Annes ARL
24.8.89	Haigh, Chris	Thornhill ARL
25.8.89	Bailey, Howard	Shaws ARL
28.8.89	Hughes, Lee	—
14.9.89	Watkinson, David	Hull K. R.
4.10.89	*Parkinson, Andrew	Halifax
23.11.89	Graham, Nathan	Hanging Heaton ARL
28.11.89	Elsey, Richard	—
1.12.89	Chapman, Mark	Fox Hounds ARL
10.12.89	Coughlan, Glen	Dewsbury Moor ARL
10.1.90	Jones, Kevin	Doncaster
21.2.89	Hall, John	Bradford N.
27.2.90	Whitehead, Craig	Nottingham C.

DONCASTER

Signed	Player	Club From
4.7.89	Idle, Graham	Sheffield E.
3.8.89	Walker, Mark	Jubilee ARL
3.8.89	Hepinstall, Jason	—
3.8.89	Geoghegan, David	—
3.8.89	Barnes, Stephen	Redhill ARL
3.8.89	Thackray, Russell	—
28.8.89	Kemp, Tony	Newcastle Knights, Aus
4.9.89	Jasiewicz, Dick	Wakefield T.
7.9.89	Hall, Carl	Linwood ARL
7.9.89	Vincent, Andrew	Papanui, NZ
12.10.89	Sygrove, Andy	Wakefield T.
12.12.89	Proctor, Wayne	Hull
12.12.89	Puckering, Neil	Hull
12.12.89	Hermansson, Terry	NZ
5.1.90	Brown, Paul	Walnut Warriors ARL
5.1.90	Carroll, Dean	Nottingham C
17.1.90	Bowes, Antony	Walnut Warriors ARL
17.1.70	Sheaton, Terry	Stellows Grange ARL
22.1.90	Vincent, Andrew	NZ
26.1.90	Wilkinson, Neil	Stellows Grange ARL
26.1.90	Barnes, John	Eastmoor ARL
5.2.90	Wright, Andrew	Westgate Reds ARL
6.2.90	McCone, Steve	Jubilee ARL
9.2.90	Linley, Andrew	Upton ARL
9.2.90	Ellis, Mark	Walnut Warriors ARL
16.2.90	Hill, Kenny	Castleford
23.3.90	Sheldon, Ian	Wakefield T.
23.3.90	Zelei, Tony	Wakefield T.

FEATHERSTONE ROVERS

Signed	Player	Club From
21.7.89	Busby, David	Hull
4.8.89	Price, Gary	Leeds
15.9.89	Jepson, John	Travellers ARL
26.9.89	Smith, Michael	Travellers ARL
5.10.89	Drummond, Barry	Thornhill Gate ARL
5.10.89	Ramskill, Jason	Travellers ARL
13.10.89	Manning, Terry	Keighley
29.10.89	Davies, Richard	Normanton ARL
9.11.89	Booth, Craig	Travellers ARL
12.11.89	Dickinson, Robert	Travellers ARL
12.11.89	Minter, Steve	Travellers ARL
28.12.89	Rose, Gary	Keighley
6.1.90	Moules, Robert	Wakefield T.
16.1.90	Wood, Jason	Travellers ARL
6.2.90	Longstaff, Spencer	Travellers ARL
6.2.90	Palelei, Aaron	Nottingham C.
16.2.90	Gibbon, Mark	Doncaster
2.3.90	Powell, Paul	Nottingham C
8.3.90	Beamont, Jonathan	Lock Lane ARL

FULHAM

Signed	Player	Club From
8.8.89	Noble, Michael	—
8.8.89	Render, Andrew	St. Mary's College ARL
8.8.89	Yeoman, Paul	Hemel Hempstead ARL

8.8.89	Taylor, Michael	Halifax
8.8.89	Mellors, Ian	Aus
8.8.89	Sanchez, Wayne	Nottingham C.
13.8.89	Wright, Robert	—
1.9.89	Pearce, Greg	Wyong, Aus
1.9.89	Workman, Glen	—
1.9.89	Robertson, Karl	Glenora, NZ
1.9.89	Best, Anthony	South Invicta ARL
14.9.89	Browning, Russell	Gold Coast, Aus
23.9.89	Kennedy, Eric	Gold Coast, Aus
23.9.89	Williams, Brett	Gold Coast, Aus
1.10.89	Daunt, Brett	Fortitude Valley, Aus
14.10.89	Callow, Steve	West London Institute ARL
15.10.89	Roberts, Steve	—
18.10.89	Look, Timothy	—
25.10.89	Pitt, Darryl	Valleys, Aus
4.11.89	Scott, Conrad	St. Mary's College ARL
1.2.90	Rotheram, David	West London Institute ARL

HALIFAX

Signed	Player	Club From
5.6.89	Parry, Mark	Birkenshaw ARL
31.8.89	Hetherington, Brian	Illawara, Aus
1.9.89	Dorahy, John	North Sydney, Aus
1.9.89	Johnston, Lindsey	South Sydney, Aus
16.9.89	Scott, Mick	Ryedale-York
22.9.89	Carroll, Jason	Ovenden ARL
22.9.89	Syme, Stuart	Siddall ARL
5.10.89	Parkinson, George	Park Amateurs ARL
16.10.89	Walsh, Chris	Knottingley ARL
19.10.89	Atkins, Gary	Ryedale-York
1.11.89	Meades, Richard	Bristol RU
7.1.90	Needham, David	Salford
8.1.90	Rawlinson, Scott	Dudley Hill ARL
8.2.90	Bond, Gary	Swinton

HUDDERSFIELD

Signed	Player	Club From
26.7.89	Ventola, Roy	Paddock ARL
28.7.89	Sewell, Andrew	Moldgreen ARL
28.7.89	Southern, Nigel	Sharlston ARL
28.7.89	Blacker, John	Nottingham C.
28.7.89	Simpson, Andy	Earlsheaton ARL
28.7.89	Totten, Steve	Crofton ARL
2.8.89	Jowett, Chris	Halifax
8.8.89	Diskin, Anthony	Dewsbury Celtic ARL
14.8.89	Cocker, Stuart	BRK ARL
25.8.89	Zee, James	Huddersfield ARL
1.9.89	Gibson, Walter	Forster Tunnicliffe, Aus
14.9.89	Power, Anthony	Underbank ARL
24.9.89	Siddall, Gary	Featherstone R.
29.11.89	Wiltshire, Roy	Trafford B.
1.12.89	Sanderson, Mark	Nottingham C.
5.1.90	Whitehead, Craig	Nottingham C.
7.1.90	Simpson, Andy	Halifax

7.1.90	Chatterton, Ian	—
7.1.90	Naidole, Joseph	Deighton Woolpack ARL
7.1.90	Smith, Sam	—
7.1.90	Smith, Reg	—
7.1.90	Shrewsbury, Ian	—
7.1.90	Want, James	—
7.1.90	Toder, James	—
7.1.90	Mattison, Neil	—
16.1.90	Mountain, Dean	Ryedale-York
16.1.90	Toole, Tim	Dewsbury
25.1.90	Bannister, Andy	Featherstone R.
6.2.90	Malcolm, Trevor	—
6.2.90	Smith, Barry	—
8.3.90	Frankland, Nick	Nottingham C.
15.3.90	Wardle, Chris	Park Amateurs ARL
23.3.90	Staniforth, Tony	Featherstone R.
26.3.90	O'Donnell, Damien	Castleford

HULL

Signed	Player	Club From
24.7.89	Folkes, Steve	Canterbury, Aus
7.8.89	Harrison, Karl	Featherstone R.
14.8.89	Cleal, Noel	Manly, Aus
20.8.89	Mighty, Andrew	Fulham
20.8.89	Dixon, Michael	East Park Juniors ARL
31.8.89	Liddiard, David	Parramatta, Aus
8.9.89	Gay, Richard	Hull Boys Club ARL
27.10.89	Mackey, Greg	Warrington
12.12.89	Turner, Neil	Doncaster
7.1.90	Charles, Marquis	Dewsbury
8.1.90	Walker, Russ	Barrow
1.2.90	Busby, Dean	Bransholme Youth Club ARL

HULL KINGSTON ROVERS

Signed	Player	Club From
27.6.89	Wildridge, Mark	West Hull ARL
2.8.89	Robson, Stephen	East Park ARL
9.8.89	Austin, Greg	Manly, Aus
9.8.89	Niebling, Bryan	Brisbane B., Aus
30.8.89	Botica, Tony	Mount Albert, NZ
4.9.89	Vannett, Paul	Workington T.
15.9.89	Lightfoot, David	Whitehaven
26.3.90	Martin, Peter	Parramatta, Aus

HUNSLET

Signed	Player	Club From
31.7.89	Brook, Richard	Dewsbury Moor ARL
3.8.89	Petan, Andrew	Hunslet Trafalgar ARL
29.8.89	Adams, John	Oberon, Aus
14.9.89	Jennings, Graeme	Nambucca, Aus
14.9.89	Welch, Brett	Nambucca, Aus
3.10.89	Langton, Steve	Batley
22.1.90	Marsh, Richard	Featherstone R.
28.2.90	Liles, Richard	Oulton ARL
15.3.90	Petan, Richard	—

Hull K.R. recruit, Australian Test prop Bryan Niebling.

KEIGHLEY

Signed	Player	Club From
5.6.89	Simpson, Owen	Army RU
8.8.89	Coulter, Garry	Elland ARL
8.8.89	Davis, Maurice	NZ
24.8.89	Thompson, Julian	—
24.8.89	Cox, David	Worth Village ARL
24.8.89	Ambler, Andrew	Brighouse Clayton ARL
24.8.89	Sheffield, Michael	—
24.8.89	Smith, Philip	Birkenshaw ARL
24.8.89	Harrison, Mark	Birkinshaw ARL
24.8.89	Fairbank, Andy	Elland ARL
25.8.89	Johnson, David	Elland ARL
25.8.89	Rodney, Paul	Queensbury ARL
29.8.89	Walton, Darren	Worth Village ARL
29.8.89	Wooler, Mark	Silsden ARL
29.8.89	Coop, Chris	Mayfield ARL
29.8.89	St. Hilaire, Darren	Ryedale-York
19.9.89	Wilson, Shaun	Birkenshaw ARL
19.9.89	Okesere, Paul	Sheffield E.
19.9.89	Collis, John	Mankukau, NZ
27.9.89	Cudmore, Mark	Belrose Eagles, Aus
27.9.89	Badger, Warwick	Silsden ARL
16.11.89	Bardgett, Paul	Bradford N.
16.1.90	Kemp, Martin	Halifax

LEEDS

Signed	Player	Club From
26.7.89	Wilson, Warren	Hunslet
27.7.89	Laurie, Mark	Parramatta, Aus
1.9.89	*James, Neil	Halifax
8.9.89	Izzard, Craig	Parramatta, Aus
14.9.89	Middleton, Graham	East Leeds ARL
15.9.89	Coleman, Craig	South Sydney, Aus
22.9.89	Terp, Rex	Wauchope, Aus
23.9.89	Divorty, Gary	Hull
15.10.89	Mitchell, Pat	Nottingham C.
25.10.89	Hill, Simon	Black Dog ARL
13.12.89	Heugh, Cavill	Barrow
3.1.90	Cruickshank, David	South Sydney, Aus
5.1.90	Ackerman, Robert	Whitehaven
8.1.90	Kuiti, Mike	Upper Hutt, NZ
29.1.90	Irving, Simon	Headingley RU
2.2.90	Maloney, Francis	St. John Fisher ARL
5.2.90	Young, David	Cardiff RU
28.3.90	Tees, Gary	Barrow
29.3.90	*Chick, Stuart	Salford
20.4.90	James, Neil	Halifax
28.5.90	Gallagher, John	New Zealand RU

LEIGH

Signed	Player	Club From
16.8.89	O'Loughlin, Kieron	Salford
29.8.89	Potter, Ian	Wigan
17.9.89	Stephenson, David	Leeds
22.9.89	Brown, Peter	Teatutu, NZ
22.9.89	Ropati, Peter	Teatutu, NZ
9.11.89	Valentine, Peter	Rose Bridge ARL
7.1.90	Gore, Michael	Crown Springs ARL
9.2.90	*Doherty, Paul	Hull
9.5.90	Sheals, Mark	Swinton
9.5.90	Topping, Paul	Swinton

Loose forward Gary Divorty, a £120,000 signing by Leeds from Hull.

NOTTINGHAM CITY

Signed	Player	Club From
2.6.89	Oates, David	Firths ARL
5.6.89	Kay, Paul	Oldham St. Annes ARL
3.8.89	Roberts, Carl	—
4.8.89	Frankland, Nicholas	Featherstone Travellers ARL
9.8.89	Wrigley, James	Ovenden ARL
21.8.89	Sidebottom, Gary	Bradford N.
22.8.89	Carroll, Dean	Carlisle
26.8.89	Hema, Arnold	Petore, NZ
12.11.89	Pritchard, Neil	Normanton ARL
2.2.90	Chrimes, David	Mayfield ARL
10.2.90	*Lidbury, Steve	Sheffield E.
12.2.90	*Bowie, Ian	Dewsbury
12.2.90	*Garforth, David	Dewsbury

OLDHAM

Signed	Player	Club From
1.7.89	Blackman, Richard	Dewsbury Moor ARL
1.7.89	Mort, Craig	Saddleworth Rangers ARL
19.7.89	Russell, Richard	Wigan
1.8.89	Martyn, Tommy	Leigh Miners ARL
1.8.89	Entwistle, Steve	Waterhead ARL
1.8.89	Flanagan, Neil	St. Annes ARL
23.8.89	Fieldhouse, John	St. Helens
1.9.89	McDermott, Chris	Sheffield E.
15.9.89	Clark, Brett	St. George, Aus
21.9.89	Mort, Craig	Saddleworth Rangers ARL
31.10.89	Kelly, Ken	Warrington
15.11.89	*Rutter, Phil	Widnes
14.12.89	Maxwell, John	Leigh Miners ARL
4.1.90	Bate, Derek	Swinton
22.1.90	Mitchell, Pat	Saddleworth Rangers ARL
14.2.90	*Hale, Chris	Featherstone R.
22.2.90	*Chisnall, Chris	Chorley
28.2.90	Lewis, Peter	Bramley
14.3.90	Anderson, Tony	Halifax
22.3.90	Gaskell, Paul	Leigh
24.5.90	Donegan, Austin	St. Helens

ROCHDALE HORNETS

Signed	Player	Club From
27.6.89	Hall, Martin	Oldham
29.7.89	Lord, Mark	Leeds
31.7.89	Woods, John	Warrington
11.8.89	Marriott, Karl	Mayfield ARL
17.8.89	Marsden, Robert	Oldham
21.8.89	Sullivan, Andy	Widnes
25.8.89	Humphries, Tony	Warrington
30.8.89	Malloy, John	Folly Lane ARL
30.8.89	Barrett, David	Langworthy ARL
30.8.89	McDermott, Paul	Sheffield E.
30.8.89	Nixon, Mark	NZ
2.9.89	Lonergan, Dean	NZ
14.9.89	Viller, Paul	—
14.9.89	Sutton, Kent	Newhey
14.9.89	Hilton, Mark	—
19.9.89	Hulmes, Mike	Folly Lane ARL
30.9.89	Hall, Robert	—
15.10.89	Webb, Vincent	—
8.12.89	Bamber, Simon	Chorley
9.1.90	Villers, Mark	Swinton
18.1.90	Myler, John	Swinton
8.3.90	Fox, Phil	Wakefield T.
22.3.90	Juliff, Brian	Castleford
22.3.90	Blackburn, John	Castleford

RUNCORN HIGHFIELD

Signed	Player	Club From
25.7.89	Fenney, Paul	Ruskin Park ARL
25.7.89	Beckett, Peter	Blackbrook ARL
25.7.89	Ashcroft, Simon	Blackbrook ARL
25.7.89	Dolan, Shaun	Blackbrook ARL
1.8.89	Hoey, Robert	Leigh East ARL
1.8.89	O'Garra, Kevin	Blackbrook ARL
8.8.89	Southward, Phil	St. Helens
8.8.89	Barrow, Shaun	St. Helens
29.8.89	Hine, David	Ruskin Park ARL
19.11.89	Platt, Brian	Nutgrove ARL
31.12.89	Goodier, Frank	Keighley
1.1.90	Platt, Billy	Nottingham C.

RYEDALE-YORK

Signed	Player	Club From
1.6.89	Ake, Basil	Bradford N.
12.9.89	Mountain, Dean	Castleford
20.9.89	Wilby, Andrew	Lock Lane ARL
14.11.89	Fagan, Gary	Stanningley ARL
14.11.89	Render, Nick	Lock Lane ARL
17.11.89	Greenwood, Brendan	Ovenden ARL
17.11.89	Shaw, Matthew	Travellers ARL
30.11.89	Smith, Peter	Heworth ARL
30.11.89	Pinkney, Nick	Greatford ARL
8.12.89	Watson, David	Auckland, NZ
4.1.90	Kettlestring, David	York All Blacks ARL
2.2.90	Faumuina, Mark	Nottingham C.
8.3.90	*Doherty, Paul	Hull
8.3.90	*Fletcher, Paul	Hull
20.3.90	Laws, Mark	Newland ARL
29.5.90	Leuluai, James	Wakefield T.
29.5.90	Nikau, Tawera	Auckland, NZ

ST. HELENS

Signed	Player	Club From
8.6.89	Atherton, Peter	Widnes Tigers ARL
31.7.89	Mann, George	Mangere East, NZ
13.8.89	Hodgkinson, Tom	Blackbrook ARL
30.8.89	Frodsham, Tommy	Swinton
13.9.89	Connor, Ian	Swinton
25.9.89	O'Brien, Darren	Widnes Tigers ARL
29.9.89	Bateman, Andy	Hunslet
14.11.89	Riley, Michael	Widnes Tigers ARL
29.12.89	Tonstall, Kevin	—
29.12.89	Bates, David	—
18.1.90	Greenall, Lee	Blackbrook ARL
23.2.90	Bourneville, Mark	Mount Albert, NZ
1.3.90	O'Keefe, Paul	Golborne ARL
7.3.89	Wallwork, Jason	—
18.3.90	Kebbie, Brimah	Widnes

SALFORD

Signed	Player	Club From
12.6.89	Bradshaw, Thomas	Thatto Heath ARL
1.8.89	Brown, Shaun	Leigh East ARL
21.8.89	Brooke-Cowden, Mark	Leeds
23.8.89	Sherratt, Ian	Oldham
4.10.89	Rampling, Tony	South Sydney, Aus
12.10.89	O'Neill, Paul	Leigh Miners ARL
13.11.89	Havard, Joe	Wigan St. Patricks ARL
13.11.89	Cassidy, Frank	Swinton
6.12.89	Birkett, Martin	Frizington ARL
4.1.90	O'Neill, Steve	Swinton
7.1.90	Bloor, Darren	Swinton
7.1.90	Lee, Mark	St. Helens
8.1.90	Clare, Jeff	Wigan
13.1.90	Howard, Anthony	Army RU
6.2.90	Conroy, Anthony	Wigan St. Patricks ARL
23.2.90	*Chick, Stuart	Leeds
23.3.90	Huyte, Patrick	Combined Services RU
5.4.90	Betts, Darren	Langworthy ARL

1989 Kiwi tourist Tawera Nikau, who served Sheffield Eagles before signing for Ryedale-York in May 1990.

SHEFFIELD EAGLES

Signed	Player	Club From
5.6.89	Hall, Stephen	Keighley Albion ARL
10.7.89	Laughton, Dale	Dodworm ARL
10.7.89	Beddis, Chris	Jubilee ARL
10.7.89	Stainforth, Lee	West Hull ARL
10.7.89	Oakley, Graham	—
28.7.89	McGuire, Bruce	Balmain, Aus
31.7.89	Mycoe, David	Crigglestone ARL
31.7.89	Hall, Stephen	Keighley Albion ARL
31.7.89	Picksley, Richard	Lock Lane ARL
8.8.89	Hardy, Jeff	Illawara, Aus
25.8.89	Johnson, Dean	Middleton ARL
25.8.89	Green, Mark	Crigglestone ARL
31.8.89	Cator, Lance	Hull White Star ARL
1.9.89	Wilders, Peter	—
1.10.89	Rowley, Andrew	Pontefract ARL
6.12.89	Leota, Francis	Otahuha, NZ
6.12.89	Nikau, Tawera	Otahuha, NZ
6.1.90	Dobson, Steve	Ryedale-York
6.1.90	Willey, Shaun	Ryedale-York
15.1.90	Branton, Richard	Cottingham ARL
12.3.90	Waddell, Hugh	Leeds
26.3.90	*Ketteridge, Martin	Castleford

SWINTON

Signed	Player	Club From
11.7.89	Tupaea, Shane	Rochdale H.
18.7.89	Pucill, Andrew	Crosfields ARL
26.7.89	Redmond, Michael	Crosfields ARL
3.8.89	Sheals, Mark	Trafford B.
14.8.89	Morrison, Tony	Oldham
30.8.89	Bloor, Darren	St. Helens
5.9.89	Topping, Steve	Orrell St. James ARL
7.9.89	Graziano, Joseph	Mayfield ARL
14.9.89	Hudson, Julian	Salford Juniors ARL
14.9.89	Hancock, Michael	Wigan St. Patricks ARL
19.9.89	Linton, Ralph	Widnes
22.9.89	Chadwick, Les	Rochdale H.
24.9.89	Sutton, Gary	Crosfields ARL
28.9.89	Capewell, Phil	Warrington
28.9.89	Edge, Phil	Nottingham C.
1.10.89	Rourke, Neil	Crosfields ARL
7.10.89	Knowles, Michael	Illawara, Aus
17.10.89	Lamb, Derek	The Oaks ARL
17.10.89	McHugh, Vincent	Addington ARL, NZ
9.11.89	Rabbitt, Jason	Latchford Albion ARL
17.11.89	Ropati, Joe	Warrington
5.1.90	Zenon, Ronel	Toulouse, France
5.1.90	Flanagan, Terry	Oldham
8.1.90	Holden, Keith	Warrington
9.1.90	Peters, Barry	Warrington
17.1.90	Peacham, Gary	Carlisle
28.1.90	Partingham, Carl	Folly Lane ARL
9.2.90	Edwards, Logan	Rochdale H.
9.5.90	Street, Tim	Leigh
9.5.90	Johnson, Chris	Leigh
9.5.90	Kerr, John	Leigh

TRAFFORD BOROUGH

Signed	Player	Club From
1.8.89	Smith, Graham	—
1.8.89	Mellor, Terry	—
20.8.89	Green, Andrew	Woolston ARL
20.8.89	Reynolds, Paul	Crosfields ARL
20.8.89	Hewitt, David	Salford
20.8.89	Smith, Ronnie	Salford
28.8.89	Pugsley, Stuart	Leigh East ARL
28.8.89	Litz, Terry	Crosfields ARL
28.8.89	O'Rourke, Michael	Crosfields ARL
28.8.89	Pendlebury, Gary	Wigan
29.8.89	Rippon, Andy	Swinton
15.9.89	Karalius, Graham	—
23.9.89	Horrocks, John	Swinton
6.10.89	Iddon, Tim	—
6.10.89	Smith, Graham	—
6.10.89	Turley, Norman	Workington T.
6.10.89	Wainwright, Mark	—
16.10.89	Connor, Stephen	Farnworth ARL
24.10.89	Feasey, Tony	NZ
24.10.89	Perenara, Tony	NZ
24.10.89	Gailbraith, Stuart	NZ
15.11.89	Herbert, Steve	Salford
1.12.89	Brewer, Stephen	Irlam Town ARL
1.12.89	*Durnin, Paul	Runcorn H.
12.1.90	Harris, Edward	Crosfields ARL
12.1.90	Spicer, Adam	Applecross, Aus
12.1.90	Wilson, Danny	Swinton
15.1.90	Jones, Ken	Salford
15.1.90	Railton, Paul	—
22.2.90	Meadows, Kevin	Oldham
2.3.90	Massey, Neil	Warrington
2.3.90	Harris, Darren	Warrington
23.3.90	Hodgkiss, Michael	Leigh

WAKEFIELD TRINITY

Signed	Player	Club From
29.6.89	Morris, Lynton	Wakefield ARL
14.8.89	Hirst, John	Wakefield ARL
14.8.89	McElhatton, Craig	Wakefield ARL
29.9.89	Jackson, Brian	Parramatta, Aus
29.9.89	Price, Ray	Parramatta, Aus
5.10.89	Reeves, Mark	Sharlston ARL
23.10.89	Perry, Chris	Grafton Ghosts RU, Aus
23.3.90	Taylor, Paul	Parramatta, Aus
31.5.90	Flannery, Robert	Leigh Miners ARL
31.5.90	Gregory, Paul	Leigh Miners ARL

WARRINGTON

Signed	Player	Club From
1.6.89	Darbyshire, Paul	Wigan St. Patricks ARL
29.6.89	Knight, Mark	Leigh
3.7.89	Myers, David	Widnes
27.7.89	Bennett, Andrew	Woolston Rovers ARL
28.7.89	Savage, Andrew	Woolston Rovers ARL
1.8.89	Rudd, Chris	Kells ARL
1.8.89	Chambers, Gary	Kells ARL
15.8.89	Jackson, Bob	Aus
30.8.89	Mackey, Greg	Canterbury, Aus
12.9.89	Wernham, Michael	Lymm RU

13.9.89	Barber, Thomas	Crosfields ARL
2.10.89	Myler, Robert	Widnes St. Maries ARL
7.10.89	Savage, Andrew	Woolston Rovers ARL
12.11.89	Mercer, Gary	Bay of Plenty, NZ
12.11.89	Mann, Duane	Auckland, NZ
30.5.90	Ellis, Kevin	Bridgend RU

WHITEHAVEN

Signed	Player	Club From
20.6.89	Symes, Geoff	Seaton ARL
5.7.89	Blaney, Gerard	Morehouses ARL
12.9.89	Charlton, Gary	Gold Coast, Aus
21.9.89	Burns, William	Kells ARL
21.9.89	Seager, Stewart	Kells ARL
29.9.89	Milburn, Ray	Kells ARL
11.10.89	Bell, Paul	Broughton Red Rose ARL
25.10.89	Ward, James	Nambour, Aus
25.10.89	Butler, Tim	South Newcastle, Aus
31.12.89	Petrie, Steve	Nambour, Aus
31.12.89	Sparks, Brian	Kells ARL
5.1.90	Shelford, Kelly	Auckland, NZ
16.2.90	Quayle, Barry	Hensingham ARL
27.2.90	Tunstall, Lyn	Carlisle

WIDNES

Signed	Player	Club From
1.8.89	Critchley, Jason	Blackbrook ARL
26.9.89	Devereux, John	Bridgend RU
3.10.89	Harvey, Lee	Widnes Tigers ARL
20.11.89	Spruce, Stuart	Widnes Tigers ARL
20.11.89	Ashton, Lee	Blackbrook ARL
28.11.89	Sarsfield, Mark	Leigh Miners ARL
28.11.89	Bowles, John	Simms Cross ARL
28.11.89	Fazackerly, Adrian	St. Bedes ARL
28.12.89	McCurrie, Stephen	Hensingham ARL
28.12.89	Harrison, Eddie	Simms Cross ARL
28.12.89	Worthington, Peter	Simms Cross ARL
2.1.90	Edwards, David	—
4.1.90	Halliwell, Aiden	Wigan St. Patricks ARL
7.1.90	Atcheson, Paul	Blackbrook ARL
7.1.90	*Rutter, Phil	Oldham
21.3.90	Howard, Harvey	Waterloo RU
23.3.90	Holliday, Les	Halifax

WIGAN

Signed	Player	Club From
1.6.89	*Clare, Jeff	St. Helens
15.8.89	Gartland, Paul	Blackbrook ARL
15.8.89	Blakeley, Steve	Leigh Rangers ARL
27.9.89	Blake, Phil	South Sydney, Aus
27.9.89	Davidson, Les	South Sydney, Aus
5.12.89	Neale, Michael	Parkside ARL
4.1.90	Barr, Brendan	St. Judes ARL
8.5.90	Bridge, Russell	Fulham
30.5.90	Botica, Frano	New Zealand RU
30.5.90	Bardsley, Steve	Leigh Miners ARL

Cumbria county back row forward Les Holliday, subject of a £100,000 move from Halifax to Widnes.

WORKINGTON TOWN

Signed	Player	Club From
1.7.89	McQuirk, Gary	British Steel ARL
20.7.89	Brake, Greg	—
31.8.89	Pickering, Brendan	Westfield ARL
31.8.89	Henney, Russell	—
7.9.89	Kitchin, Wayne	Kells ARL
7.9.89	Wear, Stephen	Kells ARL
9.9.89	Little, Andrew	Great Clifton ARL
21.9.89	Dockery, Darryl	Waitemata, Aus
12.10.89	Matache, Michael	Runaway Bay, Aus
6.1.90	O'Loughlin, Kiernon	Leigh
9.1.90	Penman, Daniel	Ellenborough ARL
10.190	Armstrong, Malcolm	Ellenborough ARL
21.1.90	Ainsworth, Gary	Swinton
6.2.90	Steele, John	Ellenborough ARL

Shaun Edwards, Stones Bitter Man of Steel 1990.

AWARDS

AWARDS

THE 1990 MAN OF STEEL AWARDS

Launched in the 1976-77 season, the Rugby Football League's official awards are presented to the Man of Steel, the personality judged to have made the most impact on the season; the First and Second Division Players of the Year, decided by a ballot of the players; the Young Player of the Year, under-21 at the start of the season; the Coach of the Year and Referee of the Year, all chosen by a panel of judges.

The official award scheme was sponsored by Trumanns Steel from inception in 1977 to 1983, brewers Greenall Whitley taking over in 1984 until 1989. Stones Bitter introduced a three-year £50,000 sponsorship in 1990.

Stones Bitter Man of Steel

A record prize of £4,000 and a £300 silver champagne goblet were presented to Wigan stand off **Shaun Edwards**. Man of the Match in the second British Coal Test against New Zealand, he went on to be named Man of the Series, later receiving the Ernest Ward Memorial Trophy as British International Player of the Year. Eighth in the try chart with 26 touchdowns. During the Silk Cut Challenge Cup Final with Warrington he sustained a double fracture of the eye socket and a depressed cheekbone after 10 minutes but played on, the injury robbing him of captaincy of the British Lions tour to Papua New Guinea and New Zealand.

Stones Bitter First Division Player of the Year

Wigan second row man **Andy Goodway** topped the poll of fellow Stones Bitter Championship players, votes being cast in January and April. The game's top try scoring forward with 26 touchdowns, he played four times for Great Britain and was a key figure in Wigan's hat-trick of trophies.

Stones Bitter Second Division Player of the Year

His fellow players' choice in the twin ballot was Rochdale Hornets skipper **John Woods**, a £50,000 recruit from Warrington during the close season. The inspiration behind the revitalised Hornets clinching runners-up spot in the Second Division title race, he won the same award with Leigh in 1978, making him the only player to achieve this double.

Stones Bitter Young Player of the Year

Teenage Wigan scrum half **Bobby Goulding** took the award to crown a memorable season which included 25 appearances for the Riversiders, including 11 as substitute; two caps for Great Britain Under-21s — the second as stand-in captain; plus selection for the British Lions trip to Papua New Guinea and New Zealand as the youngest-ever tourist at 18 years, three months.

Stones Bitter Referee of the Year

Widnes official **Robin Whitfield** received the award for the second time, having topped the referees' ratings all season. Honours included the John Smiths Yorkshire Cup final, the two France versus New Zealand Tests and the Stones Bitter Second Division Premiership final.

Stones Bitter Coach of the Year

Wigan's new Australian coach **John Monie** was given top rating having masterminded the Riversiders' haul of the Stones Bitter Championship, the Silk Cut Challenge Cup and the Regal Trophy, plus winners' cheques totalling £98,000. The triple success was achieved against a backcloth of long-term injuries to key players, particularly skipper Ellery Hanley.

● Each of the above category winners received £1,000 and a £250 silver wine goblet.

THE MAN OF STEEL AWARDS ROLL OF HONOUR

	Man of Steel	1st Division Player	2nd Division Player	Young Player	Coach	Referee
1977	David Ward (Leeds)	Malcolm Reilly (Castleford)	Ged Marsh (Blackpool B.)	David Ward (Leeds)	Eric Ashton MBE (St. Helens)	Billy Thompson (Huddersfield)
1978	George Nicholls (St. Helens)	George Nicholls (St. Helens)	John Woods (Leigh)	John Woods (Leigh)	Frank Myler (Widnes)	Billy Thompson (Huddersfield)
1979	Doug Laughton (Widnes)	Mick Adams (Widnes)	Steve Norton (Hull)	Steve Evans (Featherstone R.)	Doug Laughton (Widnes)	Mick Naughton (Widnes)
1980	George Fairbairn (Wigan)	Mick Adams (Widnes)	Steve Quinn (Featherstone R.)	Roy Holdstock (Hull K.R.)	Peter Fox (Bradford N.)	Fred Lindop (Wakefield)
1981	Ken Kelly (Warrington)	Ken Kelly (Warrington)	John Crossley (York)	Des Drummond (Leigh)	Billy Benyon (Warrington)	John Holdsworth (Kippax)
1982	Mick Morgan (Carlisle)	Steve Norton (Hull)	Mick Morgan (Carlisle)	Des Drummond (Leigh)	Arthur Bunting (Hull)	Fred Lindop (Wakefield)
1983	Allan Agar (Featherstone R.)	Keith Mumby (Bradford N.)	Steve Nash (Salford)	Brian Noble (Bradford N.)	Arthur Bunting (Hull)	Robin Whitfield (Widnes)
1984	Joe Lydon (Widnes)	Joe Lydon (Widnes)	David Cairns (Barrow)	Joe Lydon (Widnes)	Tommy Dawes (Barrow)	Billy Thompson (Huddersfield)
1985	Ellery Hanley (Bradford N.)	Ellery Hanley (Bradford N.)	Graham Steadman (York)	Lee Crooks (Hull)	Roger Millward MBE (Hull K.R.)	Ron Campbell (Widnes)
1986	Gavin Miller (Hull K.R.)	Gavin Miller (Hull K.R.)	Derek Pyke (Leigh)	Shaun Edwards (Wigan)	Chris Anderson (Halifax)	Fred Lindop (Wakefield)
1987	Ellery Hanley (Wigan)	Andy Gregory (Wigan)	John Cogger (Runcorn H.)	Shaun Edwards (Wigan)	Graham Lowe (Wigan)	John Holdsworth (Kippax)
1988	Martin Offiah (Widnes)	Steve Hampson (Wigan)	Peter Smith (Featherstone R.)	Shaun Edwards (Wigan)	Doug Laughton (Widnes)	Fred Lindop (Wakefield)
1989	Ellery Hanley (Wigan)	David Hulme (Widnes)	Darryl Powell (Sheffield E.)	Paul Newlove (Featherstone R.)	Graham Lowe (Wigan)	John Holdsworth (Kippax)
1990	Shaun Edwards (Wigan)	Andy Goodway (Wigan)	John Woods (Rochdale H.)	Bobby Goulding (Wigan)	John Monie (Wigan)	Robin Whitfield (Widnes)

NOMINEES:

1977 *1st Division Player:* Bruce Burton (Castleford), Vince Farrar (Featherstone R.). *2nd Division Player:* Jeff Grayshon (Hull). *Young Player:* Jimmy Crampton (Hull), Harry Pinner (St. Helens). *Coach:* Keith Cotton (Featherstone R.), Mal Reilly (Castleford). *Referee:* Joe Jackson (Pudsey), Mick Naughton (Widnes).

1978 *1st Division Player:* Roger Millward (Hull K.R.), Harry Pinner (St. Helens). *2nd Division Player:* Phil Hogan (Barrow), Mick Morgan (York). *Young Player:* Neil Hague (Leeds), Keith Mumby (Bradford N.). *Coach:* Eric Ashton MBE (St. Helens), John Mantle (Leigh). *Referee:* Ron Campbell (Widnes), Fred Lindop (Wakefield).

1979 *1st Division Player:* Brian Lockwood (Hull K.R.), Tommy Martyn (Warrington). *2nd Division Player:* Barry Banks (York), John Wolford (Dewsbury). *Young Player:* Mick Burke (Widnes), John Woods (Leigh). *Coach:* Billy Benyon (Warrington), Arthur Bunting (Hull). *Referee:* Fred Lindop (Wakefield), Billy Thompson (Huddersfield).

1980 *1st Division Player:* Len Casey (Hull K.R.), George Fairbairn (Wigan). *2nd Division Player:* Mick Blacker (Halifax), John Wolford (Dewsbury). *Young Player:* Steve Hubbard (Hull K.R.), Harry Pinner (St. Helens). *Coach:* Maurice Bamford (Halifax), Arthur Bunting (Hull). *Referee:* Ron Campbell (Widnes), Billy Thompson (Huddersfield).

1981 *1st Division Player:* Mick Adams (Widnes), Tommy Martyn (Warrington). *2nd Division Player:* Arnie Walker (Whitehaven), Danny Wilson (Swinton). *Young Player:* Paul Harkin (Hull K.R.), Keith Mumby (Bradford N.). *Coach:* Reg Bowden (Fulham), Peter Fox (Bradford N.) *Referee:* Ron Campbell (Widnes), Fred Lindop (Wakefield).

1982 *1st Division Player:* Jeff Grayshon (Bradford N.), Andy Gregory (Widnes). *2nd Division Player:* Denis Boyd (Carlisle), Alan Fairhurst (Swinton). *Young Player:* Lee Crooks (Hull), Andy Gregory (Widnes). *Coach:* Doug Laughton (Widnes), Alex Murphy/Colin Clarke (Leigh). *Referee:* Gerry Kershaw (York), Billy Thompson (Huddersfield).

1983 *1st Division Player:* Bob Eccles (Warrington), David Topliss (Hull). *2nd Division Player:* Tommy David (Cardiff C.), Mike Lampkowski (Wakefield T.). *Young Player:* Ronnie Duane (Warrington), Andy Goodway (Oldham). *Coach:* Alex Murphy (Wigan), Frank Myler (Oldham). *Referee:* John Holdsworth (Leeds), Fred Lindop (Wakefield).

1984 *1st Division Player:* Garry Schofield (Hull), John Woods (Leigh). *2nd Division Player:* Lynn Hopkins (Workington T.), John Wolford (Hunslet). *Young Player:* Gary Divorty (Hull), Garry Schofield (Hull). *Coach:* Arthur Bunting (Hull), Roger Millward (Hull K.R.). *Referee:* Derek Fox (Wakefield), Fred Lindop (Wakefield).

1985 *1st Division Player:* Harry Pinner (St. Helens), Gary Prohm (Hull K.R.). *2nd Division Player:* Terry Langton (Mansfield M.), Peter Wood (Runcorn H.). *Young Player:* Deryck Fox (Featherstone R.), Andy Platt (St. Helens). *Coach:* Arthur Bunting (Hull), Colin Clarke/Alan McInnes (Wigan). *Referee:* Fred Lindop (Wakefield), Stan Wall (Leigh).

1986 *1st Division Player:* Steve Ella (Wigan), John Fieldhouse (Widnes). *2nd Division Player:* John Henderson (Leigh), Graham King (Hunslet). *Young Player:* Paul Lyman (Featherstone R.), Roy Powell (Leeds). *Coach:* Roger Millward (Hull K.R.), John Sheridan (Doncaster). *Referee:* John Holdsworth (Kippax), Robin Whitfield (Widnes).

1987 *1st Division Player:* Lee Crooks (Hull), Ellery Hanley (Wigan). *2nd Division Player:* Andy Bateman (Hunslet), Les Holliday (Swinton). *Young Player:* Paul Loughlin (St. Helens), Kevin McCormack (St. Helens). *Coach:* Chris Anderson (Halifax), Alex Murphy (St. Helens). *Referee:* Kevin Allatt (Southport), Fred Lindop (Wakefield).

1988 *1st Division Player:* Martin Offiah (Widnes), Kurt Sorensen (Widnes). *2nd Division Player:* Deryck Fox (Featherstone R.), Hugh Waddell (Oldham). *Young Player:* Paul Medley (Leeds), Steve Robinson (Halifax). *Coach:* Alex Murphy (St. Helens), Barry Seabourne (Bradford N.). *Referee:* John Holdsworth (Kippax), Ray Tennant (Castleford).

1989 *1st Division Player:* Andy Gregory (Wigan), Kelvin Skerrett (Bradford N.). *2nd Division Player:* Cavill Heugh (Barrow), Chris Johnson (Leigh). *Young Player:* Grant Anderson (Castleford), Denis Betts (Wigan). *Coach:* Peter Fox (Featherstone R.), Brian Smith (Hull). *Referee:* Ray Tennant (Castleford), Robin Whitfield (Widnes).

1990 *1st Division Player:* Deryck Fox (Featherstone R.), Andy Platt (Wigan). *2nd Division Player:* David Bishop (Hull K.R.), John Cogger (Oldham). *Young Player:* Denis Betts (Wigan), Anthony Sullivan (Hull K.R.). *Coach:* Tony Barrow (Oldham), Brian Johnson (Warrington). *Referee:* John Holdsworth (Kippax), Colin Morris (Huddersfield).

STONES BITTER TEAM OF THE MONTH AWARDS 1989-90

Introduced in the 1979-80 season, the scheme acknowledges the adjudged Team of the Month in both Division One and Two.

A panel of judges representing Stones Bitter and the Rugby League selected the two monthly winners, the First Division winners receiving £500, the Second Division £350, plus a framed citation.

The awards were sponsored for the first four seasons by Shopacheck before Lada Cars took over in the 1983-84 season and introduced the first-ever Team of the Year title. Stones Bitter took over the sponsorship in 1987-88, the 1990 Team of the Year, **Wigan,** receiving £1,500.

	First Division	Second Division
Aug./Sept.	Widnes	Fulham
Oct.	Warrington	Oldham
Nov.	St. Helens	Hull K. R.
Dec.	Wigan	Halifax
Jan.	Wakefield T.	Rochdale H.
Feb.	St. Helens	Oldham
Mar.	Castleford	Ryedale-York
Apr./May	Widnes	Dewsbury

Team of the Year
1983-84: Widnes
1984-85: Hull K.R.
1985-86: Halifax
1986-87: Wigan
1987-88: Widnes
1988-89: Wigan
1989-90: Wigan

Stones Bitter Team of the Year, Wigan, celebrating the lifting of the Stones Bitter Championship, one of three trophy successes in 1989-90.

391

WALLACE ARNOLD – SUNDAY MIRROR ENTERTAINER AWARDS 1988-89

Introduced in 1986-87, the scheme was sponsored by Wallace Arnold and promoted by the *Sunday Mirror.*

Each month an adjudged player was chosen as Entertainer of the Month to receive a Wallace Arnold holiday voucher for £300. The Entertainer of the Year was awarded a £1,000 holiday voucher, the 1990 winner being Featherstone Rovers skipper **Deryck Fox,** a 1990 Great Britain tourist.

Mirror Entertainer of the Month

Sept.	David Hobbs
Oct.	Paul Newlove
Nov.	David Heron
Dec.	Shaun Edwards
Jan.	Mark Conway
Feb.	Paul Gearey
Mar.	Anthony Sullivan
Apr./May	Garry Schofield

Entertainer of the Year

1987:	Ellery Hanley (Wigan)
1988:	Martin Offiah (Widnes)
1989:	Martin Offiah (Widnes)
1990:	Deryck Fox (Featherstone R.)

TRAVELEADS TOP FAN 1990

Bradford Northern fan Graham Clay (22) won the 1990 Traveleads awards as official Supporter of the Year, with a prize of a £4,000 holiday for two coinciding with the second and third Tests in New Zealand against the touring Great Britain side.

Wallace Arnold-Sunday Mirror Entertainer of the Year 1990, Featherstone Rovers skipper Deryck Fox.

STONES BITTER TOP SCORERS AWARDS 1989-90

Launched in the 1976-77 season, the scheme was designed to reward the top try and goal scorers in the League. Sponsored by Stones Bitter, the 1990 awards were worth £25 a try and £5 a goal.

For the third successive season, the top try merchant was Widnes winger **Martin Offiah** who touched down 45 times to earn a prize cheque for £1,125.

The top marksman was Hull K. R.'s record breaking centre **Mike Fletcher** who hit the target 199 times to qualify for a prize pay out of £995.

REFEREES

REFEREES' HONOURS 1989-90

Silk Cut Challenge Cup final:
John Holdsworth

Regal Trophy final:
Gerry Kershaw

Stones Bitter Premiership final:
Colin Morris

Second Division Premiership final:
Robin Whitfield

Grunhalle Lager Lancashire Cup final:
Ray Tennant

John Smiths Yorkshire Cup final:
Robin Whitfield

New Zealand v Australia (3):
Ray Tennant

France v New Zealand (2):
Robin Whitfield

Under-21 France v Great Britain:
Colin Morris

Rodstock War of the Roses:
Gerry Kershaw

CIS Insurance Charity Shield:
John Holdsworth

SENIOR REFEREES 1990-91

KEVIN ALLATT (Southport)
Date of birth: 29.12.42
Grade Two: 1970-71
Grade One: 1972-73
Premiership Trophy 1986-87
Lancashire Cup 1983-84, 1988-89
Yorkshire Cup 1987-88 (+replay)
Lancashire v Yorkshire 1975-76

DAVID ASQUITH (York)
Date of birth: 20.6.53
Grade One: 1989-90

GEOFF BERRY (Batley)
Date of birth: 26.4.54
Grade Two: 1981-82
Grade One: 1983-84

ALAN BURKE (Oldham)
Date of birth: 21.1.57
Grade One: 1987-88

DAVID CAMPBELL (St. Helens)
Date of birth: 9.10.54
Grade One: 1989-90

DAVE CARTER (Widnes)
Date of birth: 29.11.55
Grade One: 1984-85
France v Great Britain Under-21s 1988-89

JOHN CONNOLLY (Wigan)
Date of birth: 30.9.59
Grade One: 1990-91

ROBERT CONNOLLY (Wigan)
Date of birth: 30.9.59
Grade One: 1990-91

PAUL CRASHLEY (Wakefield)
Date of birth: 1.8.50
Grade One: 1989-90

STEVE CROSS (Hull)
Date of birth: 23.3.50
Grade One: 1986-87

BRIAN GALTRESS (Bradford)
Date of birth: 9.8.60
Grade One: 1988-89

STEPHEN HAIGH (Ossett)
Date of birth: 5.4.45
Grade Two: 1980-81
Grade One: 1983-84

JOHN HOLDSWORTH (Kippax)
Date of birth: 25.1.47
Grade Two: 1979-80
Grade One: 1980-81
Challenge Cup 1986-87,1989-90
John Player Trophy 1985-86, 1986-87, 1988-89
Premiership Trophy 1980-81, 1987-88, 1988-89
Lancashire Cup 1982-83, 1985-86
World Club Challenge 1987-88
Wales v England 1980-81
Great Britain v Rest of World 1988-89
RL Chairman's XIII v Papua New Guinea 1987-88
Cumbria v Yorkshire 1981-82
France v Great Britain Under-24s 1982-83
War of the Roses 1987-88
Charity Shield 1987-88, 1989-90

GARY HOLGATE (Barrow)
Date of birth: 26.4.48
Grade One: 1987-88

JOHN KENDREW (Castleford)
Date of birth: 22.4.50
Grade Two: 1982-83
Grade One: 1983-84
Lancashire v Papua New Guinea 1987-88

GERRY KERSHAW (Easingwold)
Date of birth: 24.10.43
Grade Two: 1969-70
Grade One: 1970-71
Challenge Cup 1980-81
Lancashire Cup 1980-81
Floodlit Trophy 1973-74
Regal Trophy 1973-74, 1989-90
Wales v England 1981-82
Wales v Australia 1982-83
France v Great Britain Under-24s 1981-82
Lancashire v Yorkshire 1971-72
Lancashire v Cumbria 1972-73
Cumbria v Other Nationalities 1974-75
Cumbria v Lancashire 1978-79, 1980-81
War of the Roses 1989-90

COLIN MORRIS (Huddersfield)
Date of birth: 14.3.57
Grade One: 1989-90
Premiership Trophy 1989-90
France v Great Britain Under-21s 1989-90

KEIRON MORRIS (Widnes)
Date of birth: 29.9.48
Grade One: 1988-89

IAN OLLERTON (Wigan)
Date of birth: 31.3.53
Grade One: 1990-91

JIM SMITH (Halifax)
Date of birth: 2.3.44
Grade Two: 1977-78
Grade One: 1983-84
Lancashire Cup 1986-87

COLIN STEELE (Dalton-in-Furness)
Date of birth: 11.9.60
Grade One: 1987-88
Cumbria v France 1988-89

RAY TENNANT (Castleford)
Date of birth: 7.4.49
Grade One: 1985-86
Challenge Cup 1988-89
New Zealand v Australia (3) 1989
European Club Championship 1988-89
Lancashire Cup 1989-90
Charity Shield 1988-89
Cumbria v Papua New Guinea 1987-88

CHARLIE TIDBALL (Wakefield)
Date of birth: 25.12.48
Grade One: 1987-88

JOHN WHITELAM (Hull)
Date of birth: 11.5.53
Grade One: 1988-89

ROBIN WHITFIELD (Widnes)
Date of birth: 26.11.43
Grade Two: 1979-80
Grade One: 1980-81
Challenge Cup 1982-83, 1985-86
Yorkshire Cup 1981-82, 1988-89
Second Division Premiership 1987-88, 1988-89, 1989-90
France v Australia (2) 1982-83
France v New Zealand (2) 1989-90
New Zealand v Australia 1983
Australia v New Zealand (3) 1986
Yorkshire v Lancashire 1981-82
War of the Roses 1988-89

Kippax referee John Holdsworth, the 1990 Wembley man in the middle.

THE ALLIANCE

SLALOM LAGER ALLIANCE
FINAL TABLES 1989-90

FIRST DIVISION

	P.	W.	D.	L.	FOR	AGAINST	Pts.
Hull	28	23	1	4	847	325	47
Leeds	28	22	1	5	826	422	45
Castleford	28	18	0	10	763	561	36
Hull K.R.	28	17	0	11	600	420	34
St. Helens	28	16	0	12	671	582	32
Wigan	28	16	0	12	644	562	32
Oldham	28	15	1	12	586	495	31
Warrington W.	28	15	1	12	652	669	31
Halifax	28	13	0	15	517	630	26
Featherstone R.	28	11	0	17	635	636	22
Widnes	28	11	0	17	450	685	22
Salford	28	9	2	17	623	600	20
Swinton C.	28	10	0	18	441	802	20
Hunslet	28	7	0	21	425	780	14
Carlisle	28	4	0	24	449	960	8

● Bottom two clubs relegated

SECOND DIVISION

	P.	W.	D.	L.	FOR	AGAINST	Pts.
Wakefield T.	28	24	0	4	656	329	48
Leigh	28	22	0	6	652	386	44
Ryedale-York	28	20	1	7	735	404	41
Bradford N.	28	19	1	8	767	435	39
Rochdale H.	28	16	2	10	568	428	34
Dewsbury	28	15	2	11	454	383	32
Doncaster	28	13	3	12	458	526	29
Sheffield E.	28	13	0	15	503	589	26
Barrow	28	11	0	17	483	519	22
Trafford B.	28	9	2	17	501	616	20
Whitehaven	28	10	0	18	476	609	20
Huddersfield	28	9	2	17	371	646	20
Workington T.	28	7	4	17	408	591	18
Keighley	28	6	4	18	457	689	16
Bramley	28	5	1	22	338	677	11

● Top two clubs promoted

SLALOM LAGER ALLIANCE CHALLENGE CUP 1990

First Round

Barrow	12	Trafford B.	16
Carlisle	46	Whitehaven	2
Doncaster	11	Hull K.R.	22
Featherstone R.	10	Leeds	34
Fulham	28	Sheffield E.	6
Halifax	36	Keighley	10
Hull	64	Bramley	12
Rochdale H.	8	Castleford	24
Ryedale-York	11	St. Helens	6
Salford	30	Oldham	12
Swinton	6	Bradford N.	26
Wakefield T.	38	Huddersfield	16
Widnes	26	Warrington	12
Wigan	10	Hunslet	28
Workington T.	21	Dewsbury	16
Bye: Leigh			

Second Round

Bradford N.	40	Leeds	2
Castleford	8	Wakefield T.	28
Hull	19	Carlisle	6
Hull K.R.	13	Ryedale-York	0
Leigh	6	Hunslet	10
Salford	42	Fulham	10
Widnes	16	Trafford B.	14
Workington T.	4	Halifax	23

Third Round

Bradford N.	46	Widnes	12
Halifax	35	Wakefield T.	6
Hull	34	Salford	22
Hunslet	40	Hull K.R.	34

Semi-Finals

Hull	40	Halifax	4
Hunslet	10	Bradford N.	17

Final

Bradford N.	10	Hull	33

SLALOM LAGER ALLIANCE PLAYER OF THE YEAR

1986: Steve Gill (Castleford)
1987: Shaun Fairhurst (Leigh)
1988: Mike O'Hara (Blackpool S.)
1989: Alan Moses (Barrow)
1990: Tim Lumb (Hunslet)

LANCASHIRE COUNTY CHALLENGE SHIELD 1989-90

First Round

Parkside	10	St. Helens	32
Rochdale H.	12	Workington T.	14
Salford	6	Oldham	0
Swinton C.	42	Barrow	16
Thatto Heath	18	Warrington	30
Trafford B.	10	Carlisle	20
Widnes	18	Leigh	14
Wigan	29	Whitehaven	6

Second Round

Carlisle		Widnes	
● Tie awarded to Carlisle			
Salford	26	Wigan	16
Swinton C.	6	Warrington	11
Workington T.	4	St. Helens	54

Semi-Finals

St. Helens	28	Warrington	10
Salford	24	Carlisle	12

Final

Salford	14	St. Helens	11

YORKSHIRE SENIOR COMPETITION CHALLENGE CUP 1989-90

First Round

Bradford N.	60	Huddersfield	18
Bramley	9	Hull	6
Castleford	34	Halifax	6
Dewsbury	12	Featherstone R.	34
Hunslet	0	Keighley	20
Ryedale-York	28	Doncaster	12
Sheffield E.	12	Leeds	34
Wakefield T.	10	Hull K.R.	13

Second Round

Castleford	32	Bramley	10
Hull K.R.	20	Ryedale-York	4
Keighley	12	Featherstone R.	10
Leeds	26	Bradford N.	12

Semi-Finals

Castleford	9	Leeds	6
Hull K.R.	30	Keighley	4

Final

Castleford	8	Hull K.R.	29

POT POURRI

DIARY OF LANDMARKS

1895 August 29... the beginning. The Northern Rugby Football Union formed at The George Hotel, Huddersfield, following the breakaway from the English RU by 21 clubs who wanted to pay players for taking time off work to play.

September 7... season opens with 22 clubs.

Joseph Platt appointed Rugby League Secretary.

1897 April 24... Batley won the first Northern Union — later Rugby League — Challenge Cup final.

Line-out abolished and replaced by punt from touch.

All goals to be worth two points.

1898 Professionalism allowed but players must be in full-time employment.

1899 Scrum if player cannot release the ball after a tackle.

1901 Punt from touch replaced by 10-yard scrum when ball is carried into touch.

1902 Two divisions introduced.

Punt from touch abolished completely. Touch-finding rule introduced with the ball having to bounce before entering touch.

1905 Two divisions scrapped.

Lancashire and Yorkshire County Cup competitions inaugurated.

1906 Thirteen-a-side introduced, from traditional 15.

Play-the-ball introduced.

1907 First tour — New Zealand to England. The tour party were RU 'rebels'.

First Top Four play-off for championship.

1908 Australia and New Zealand launch Rugby League.

First Australian tour of England.

1910 First British tour of Australia and New Zealand.

1915 Competitive rugby suspended for duration of First World War.

1919 Competitive rugby resumed in January.

1920 John Wilson appointed Rugby League Secretary.

1922 Title of Northern Rugby Football Union changed to Rugby Football League.

Goal from a mark abolished.

1927 First radio broadcast of Challenge Cup Final — Oldham v. Swinton at Wigan.

1929 Wembley staged its first RL Challenge Cup final — Wigan v. Dewsbury.

1932 London exhibition match under floodlights at White City — Leeds v. Wigan.

1933 France staged its first Rugby League match — an exhibition between England and Australia in Paris.

London Highfield, formerly Wigan Highfield, became capital's first Rugby League team, also first to play regularly under floodlights.

1934 A French squad made a short tour of England before Rugby League was officially launched in France.

1935 European Championship introduced, contested by England, France and Wales.

1939 Second World War. Emergency war-time competitions introduced.

1945 War-time emergencies over.

Bill Fallowfield appointed Rugby League Secretary.

1946 First all-ticket match — Hull v. Hull K.R.

1948 King George VI became first reigning monarch to attend Rugby League match — Wigan v. Bradford Northern Cup final at Wembley.

First televised match — at Wembley — but shown only in London area.

Wembley's first all-ticket final.

International Board formed.

1949 Welsh League formed.

1950 Italian squad made brief tour of England.

1951 First televised match in the North — Britain v. New Zealand at Swinton.

First floodlights installation by Northern club, Bradford Northern.

1952 First nationally televised Challenge Cup final — Workington Town v. Featherstone Rovers.

1954 First World Cup, staged in France.

1955	London staged series of televised floodlit matches for the Independent Television Association Trophy.
	Welsh League disbanded.
1956	Sunday rugby for amateurs permitted by the Rugby Football League.
1962	Two divisions reintroduced, with Eastern and Western Divisions also formed.
1964	Substitutes allowed for injuries, but only up to half-time.
	Two division and regional leagues scrapped. One league system with Top-16 play-off for championship.
1965	BBC-2 Floodlit Trophy competition began with regular Tuesday night series.
	Substitutes allowed for any reason up to and including half-time.
	English Schools Rugby League formed.
1966	Four-tackle rule introduced for Floodlit Trophy competition in October, then for all games from December.
1967	First Sunday fixtures played, two matches on December 17th.
1969	Substitutes allowed at any time.
	University Rugby League Association formed.
1971	John Player Trophy competition launched.
1972	Six-tackle rule introduced.
	Timekeepers with hooter system to signal end of match introduced.
	Colts League formed.
1973	Two divisions re-introduced.
	March 4... British Amateur Rugby League Association formed.
1974	Drop goal value halved to one point. Had been reduced earlier in international matches.
	David Oxley appointed Rugby League Secretary.
	David Howes appointed first full-time Public Relations Officer to the Rugby Football League.
	National Coaching Scheme launched.

1975	Premiership Trophy competition launched.
1976	Differential penalty introduced for technical scrum offences.
1977	County Championship not held for first time since 1895, excluding war years.
	Anglo-Australian transfer ban agreed.
1978	Papua New Guinea admitted as full members of International Board.
1981	Rugby League Professional Players' Association formed.
1982	County Championship scrapped.
1983	January 1... Sin bin introduced.
	Try value increased to four points.
	Handover after sixth tackle introduced, among several other new or amended laws following meeting of International Board.
	Anglo-Australian transfer ban lifted.
1984	Alliance League introduced in reserve grade reorganisation.
1985	First Charity Shield match played in Isle of Man.
	War of the Roses launched on Lancashire v. Yorkshire county of origin basis.
	Relegation-promotion reduced to three down, three up.
1986	Relegation-promotion altered for one year only to four down, two up to provide a 14-strong First Division for the 1987-88 season.
1987	Division Two Premiership Trophy competition launched.
	New players' contracts system introduced.
1988	Colts scrapped for new youth scheme.
	Six-man League Board of Directors appointed, plus first-ever Controller of Referees, ex-match official Fred Lindop.
1989	First-ever Sales Marketing Executive, Mike Turner, appointed by the League.
1990	Russia introduced Rugby League and sent 90-man squad of players and officials on three-match tour to Britain.

DISCIPLINARY RECORDS

This sub-section is a compilation of sendings off and disciplinary verdicts for first team players.

The following information is based on the workings of the League's Disciplinary Committee which meets weekly during a season.

Warrington centre Paul Cullen, ruled out of the 1990 Silk Cut Challenge Cup final at Wembley by an eight-match ban.

DISMISSALS .... A five-year review

The following is a review of the number of first team dismissals in each season since 1985-86.
— indicates where a club was not in existence.

	1989-90	1988-89	1987-88	1986-87	1985-86
Barrow	5	4	4	4	3
Batley	1	2	1	7	3
Bradford N.	5	2	2	2	4
Bramley	4	2	4	3	3
Carlisle	0	4	9	3	2
Castleford	6	4	3	1	3
Chorley	3	—	—	—	—
Dewsbury	3	3	5	3	4
Doncaster	2	1	3	2	4
Featherstone R.	4	1	2	0	0
Fulham	4	0	0	6	5
Halifax	8	1	1	2	1
Huddersfield	7	3	0	4	4
Hull	3	1	2	5	5
Hull K.R.	3	3	1	4	8
Hunslet	6	5	2	1	2
Keighley	10	3	5	7	8
Leeds	3	0	2	1	2
Leigh	7	3	6	2	1
Nottingham C.	5	7	2	6	3
Oldham	6	3	4	3	6
Rochdale H.	3	3	5	1	3
Runcorn H.	3	6	3	3	12
Ryedale-York	7	3	4	3	2
St. Helens	6	3	1	3	0
Salford	4	2	2	5	6
Sheffield E.	3	4	0	3	6
Swinton	4	2	3	3	2
Trafford B.	9	2	2	4	5
Wakefield T.	6	1	5	5	6
Warrington	4	2	3	6	6
Whitehaven	6	3	3	2	3
Widnes	6	2	2	4	5
Wigan	8	3	5	3	3
Workington T.	8	3	5	5	9
Totals	**172**	**91**	**101**	**116**	**139**

DISCIPLINARY ANALYSIS 1989-90

The following is a club-by-club disciplinary record for last season, showing the players sent off in first team matches and the findings of the League's Disciplinary Committee.

The committee's verdict is featured in the brackets after the player's name, each number indicating the match ban imposed. SOS stands for sending off sufficient and NG for not guilty. A suspension reduced or increased on appeal is shown as follows, 6 to 4.

During 1988-89 the totting-up system for sin-bin suspensions was abandoned. Previously two points were issued for a 10-minute temporary dismissal, a one-match ban being imposed when the total reached six. Instead, the sin bins were recorded and taken into account when considering a full dismissal.

The 1984-85 season was the first time video action other than official BBC or ITV tapes could be offered in evidence. Seven cases were considered by the committee after viewing a video, the player not having been dismissed.

Club	Total sent off	Dismissed Player	Number of Sin Bins
Barrow	5	P. Stott (2), S. Clayton (2, NG), G. Tees (2), S. McGuire (10)	6
Batley	1	M. Scott (NG)	9
Bradford N.	5	K. Fairbank (8), K. Skerrett (2, SOS), D. Moxon (1), G. Barraclough (8)	9
Bramley	4	N. Hemingway (2), G. Barnett (2), S. Edmondson (8), R. Sharpe (8)	4
Carlisle	0		5
Castleford	6	A. Clark (2), K. England (2), S. Irwin (NG), S. Ellis (3), L. Crooks (8), J. Joyner (NG)	7
Chorley	3	J. Mayo (2), C. Briscoe (NG), J. Duffy (8)	9
Dewsbury	3	D. Gregoire (2), M. Charles (SOS), P. Shuttleworth (NG)	4
Doncaster	2	T. Hermanson (1), K. Rayne (8)	12
Featherstone R.	4	G. Bell (SOS), C. Burton (5), L. Whiteley (4), G. Rose (NG)	9
Fulham	4	H. M'Barki (8), E. Kennedy (1), R. Bridge (NG, NG)	12
Halifax	8	J. Lyons (2), R. Fairbank (5, NG, 2), L. Johnson (3), J. Ramshaw (NG), S. Longstaff (8), E. Riddlesden (SOS)	16
Huddersfield	7	L. St. Hilaire (NG), A. Farrell (NG, 5, 1), P. Grayshon (6), F. Simpson (8), W. Gibson (8 to NG)	10
Hull	3	A. Dannatt (2), K. Harrison, T. Wilby (SOS)	4
Hull K.R.	3	J. Irvine (3), M. Fletcher (NG, SOS)	12
Hunslet	6	J. Lowes (4), S. Langton (NG, NG), M. Jackson (NG), G. Jennings (NG), K. Mason (SOS)	6

Keighley	10	B. White (3, 8), G. Rose (2), M. Fairbank (SOS, 10, 1), P. Moses (1), G. Coulter (4), G. Moorby (4), P. Richardson (8)	8
Leeds	3	D. Heron (4, 8), D. Cruickshank (8)	12
Leigh	7	P. Johnson (SOS), M. Dean (2, 1), D. Stephenson (SOS), A. Collier (8), B. Dunn (NG), J. Westhead (2)	12
Nottingham C.	5	C. Whitehead (8), G. Sidebottom (SOS), N. Rudd (6), P. Kay (SOS), B. Andrews (NG)	5
Oldham	6	G. Hyde (SOS), L. Casey (8), D. Platt (2), K. Atkinson (SOS), J. Fairbank (8), J. Fieldhouse (SOS)	8
Rochdale H.	3	R. Marsden (2), D. Lonergan (2), L. Edwards (8)	6
Runcorn H.	3	P. Beckett (2), P. Southward (8), T. Rose (8)	6
Ryedale-York	7	B. Ake (SOS), S. Bleakley (1, 4), P. Hutchinson (2, 1), I. Paver (2), B. Carlyle (2)	9
St. Helens	6	R. Haggerty (4), S. Evans (4), S. Cooper (NG), L. Quirk (2), P. Groves (3), P. Loughlin (NG)	6
Salford	4	A. Rampling (NG), T. Evans (8), D. Cairns (8), I. Blease (NG)	7
Sheffield E.	3	M. Fleming (6), M. Gamson (NG), M. Aston (8)	8
Swinton	4	M. Sheals (NG), P. Capewell (8, 2), T. Morrison (8)	11
Trafford B.	9	P. Glynn (4), B. Eccles (2, 2), S. Galbraith (2, NG), D. Abrams (2), S. Garner (SOS), M. Hinchcliffe (4), S. Herbert (SOS)	9
Wakefield T.	6	B. Conway (SOS, 3, 2), S. Potts (NG), M. Conway (SOS), C. Perry (2)	7
Warrington	4	T. Burke (2), P. Darbyshire (2), G. Mercer (SOS), P. Cullen (8)	8
Whitehaven	6	F. Johnson (2), M. Fryer (2), N. Lofthouse (4), W. Burns (2), S. Petrie (8), B. Fisher (8)	11
Widnes	6	K. Sorensen (2), P. Moriarty (8), A. Currier (8), J. Grima (8), E. Koloto (NG), P. Hulme (4 to NG)	16
Wigan	8	A. Platt (SOS), K. Iro (NG), S. Edwards (NG), S. Hampson (2, 2, 10), D. Bell (10), I. Lucas (8)	7
Workington T.	8	D. Lowden (3), P. Penrice (2), A. McMullen (4), G. Phillips (NG, 2), K. O'Loughlin (8), M. Mattache (1, 8)	8

In addition, the Disciplinary Committee carried out seven *trials by video*, calling up, after viewing video tapes, players who had not been dismissed by the referee. Gary Charlton of Whitehaven was banned *sine die;* Shane Cooper of St. Helens was given an eight-match ban; Mike O'Neill of Widnes eight matches; Ron Gibbs of Castleford four matches, reduced to two on appeal; Lee Crooks of Leeds two matches; and no action was taken against Mark Conway of Wakefield Trinity.

SPONSORSHIP
This updated sub-section is a record of the sponsorship programme under the control of the Rugby Football League.

1989-90 COMPETITIONS:

Silk Cut Challenge Cup	£275,000
Regal Trophy	£250,000
Stones Bitter Championship and Premiership	£225,000
British Coal Tests	£190,000
CIS Insurance Charity Shield	£ 15,000
Rodstock War of the Roses	£ 5,000

	£960,000
Awards:	£ 30,000
Miscellaneous:	£ 60,000
GRAND TOTAL	£1,050,000

COMPETITION SPONSORSHIP
The following is a review of sponsorship of the game's major competitions.

SILK CUT CHALLENGE CUP

	Prel.	1st	2nd	3rd	S.F.	R.U.	Winners	Development Fund	Total
	£	£	£	£	£	£	£	£	£
1979	—	750	1,160	2,000	3,555	6,555	12,555	4,500	60,000
1980	—	750	1,160	2,000	3,555	6,555	12,555	19,500	75,000
1981	—	750	1,160	2,000	3,555	6,555	12,555	29,500	85,000
1982	1,000	1,000	1,400	2,400	4,325	8,000	14,555	30,000	100,000
1983	1,000	1,000	1,400	2,400	4,325	8,000	14,555	40,000	110,000
1984	1,000	1,000	1,400	2,400	4,325	8,000	14,555	48,000	120,000
1985	1,100	1,100	1,500	2,500	4,500	9,000	16,000	47,600	130,000
1986	1,100	1,100	1,500	2,500	4,500	9,000	16,000	57,600	140,000
1987	1,200	1,200	1,650	2,750	4,500	9,000	16,000	58,200	150,000
1988	1,200	1,200	1,800	3,000	5,000	10,000	18,000	62,000	160,000
1989	1,300	1,300	2,000	3,250	5,500	11,000	20,000	62,600	170,000
1990	2,000	2,000	3,250	5,000	8,500	16,000	30,000	111,000	275,000

● Sponsored by State Express 1979-84

INTERNATIONAL

Great Britain v Australia Tests 1978
Forward Chemicals: £17,500

Great Britain v Australia Tests 1982
Dominion Insurance: £40,000

Great Britain v France Tests 1983 and 1984
Dominion Insurance: £10,000

Great Britain Tour 1984
Modern Maintenance Products: £100,000

Great Britain 1985-89
Whitbread Trophy Bitter: £330,000

Great Britain 1989-93
British Coal: £750,000

REGAL TROPHY

	Prel.	1st	2nd	3rd	S.F.	R.U.	Winners	Development Fund	Total
	£	£	£	£	£	£	£	£	£
1971-72	—	—	—	—	1,000	2,500	5,000	—	9,500
1972-73	—	150	300	450	1,000	2,500	5,000	—	16,100
1973-74	—	150	300	450	1,000	2,500	5,000	—	16,100
1974-75	—	150	300	450	1,000	2,500	5,000	—	16,100
1975-76	—	300	450	600	1,500	3,000	6,000	—	22,800
1976-77	—	400	550	700	1,500	3,000	6,000	—	25,600
1977-78	—	450	600	750	1,750	3,500	8,000	—	30,000
1978-79	—	550	700	900	1,750	3,500	8,000	—	33,000
1979-80	—	600	800	1,000	2,000	4,000	8,500	—	36,500
1980-81	—	600	800	1,000	2,000	4,000	8,500	3,500	40,000
1981-82	700	700	900	1,175	2,500	4,500	9,000	7,000	50,000
1982-83	700	700	900	1,175	2,500	5,000	10,000	10,500	55,000
1983-84	700	700	900	1,175	2,500	5,000	10,000	15,500	60,000
1984-85	750	750	1,000	1,500	2,500	5,000	10,000	20,000	75,000
1985-86	750	750	1,000	1,500	2,750	5,500	11,000	26,000	80,000
1986-87	800	800	1,100	1,700	3,000	6,000	12,000	26,200	85,000
1987-88	1,100	1,100	1,600	2,825	4,750	9,000	16,000	65,000	150,000
1988-89	1,250	1,250	1,850	3,175	5,250	10,000	18,000	74,000	170,000
1989-90	1,740	1,745	2,750	4,800	8,250	15,500	28,000	100,000	250,000

● Under the John Player banner from 1971-1989

STONES BITTER

	Championship winners	R.U.	2nd Division winners	R.U.	Premiership winners	R.U.	2nd Division Premiership winners	R.U.	Development Fund	Total
	£	£	£	£	£	£	£	£	£	£
1980-81	6,000	—	3,000	—	4,000	—	—	—	42,000	55,000
1981-82	10,000	—	6,000	—	6,000	—	—	—	48,000	70,000
1982-83	12,000	—	7,000	—	7,000	—	—	—	54,000	80,000
1983-84	12,000	—	7,000	—	7,000	—	—	—	59,000	85,000
1984-85	13,000	—	9,000	—	8,000	—	—	—	60,000	90,000
1985-86	13,000	—	9,000	—	8,000	—	—	—	65,000	95,000
1986-87	20,000	8,000	10,000	4,000	9,000	3,500	4,000	1,500	60,000	120,000
1987-88	20,000	8,000	10,000	4,000	9,000	3,500	4,000	1,500	70,000	123,000
1988-89	25,000	10,000	12,000	5,000	10,000	4,000	5,000	2,000	77,000	150,000
1989-90	40,000	15,000	18,000	7,500	15,000	6,000	8,000	3,000	112,500	225,000

● Sponsored by Slalom Lager from 1980-86

GRUNHALLE LAGER LANCASHIRE CUP

	Winners £	Total £
1976	1,000	4,000
1977	1,500	5,000
1978	1,800	5,500
1979	1,900	6,000
1980	2,530	10,000
1981	2,700	11,000
1982	3,000	11,500
1983	3,200	12,500
1984	3,400	13,250
1985	3,400	13,250
1986	4,300	17,000
1987	4,600	18,600
1988	5,000	19,000
1989	5,000	21,000

● Sponsored by Burtonwood Brewery 1976-85

YORKSHIRE CUP

	Sponsor	Winners £	Total £
1972	Esso	800	4,000
1973	Esso	1,500	6,000
1974	Esso	1,400	6,000
1975	Esso	1,200	6,000
1976	Esso	1,200	6,000
1977	Esso	1,600	8,000
1978	Esso	2,000	9,000
1979	Esso	2,000	9,500
1980	Websters Brewery	2,750	13,000
1981	Websters Brewery	3,000	14,000
1982	Websters Brewery	2,500	15,000
1983	Philips Video	2,500	15,000
1984	Philips Video	2,500	15,000
1985	John Smiths	2,500	5,000
1986	John Smiths	2,500	12,500
1987	John Smiths	3,000	12,500
1988	John Smiths	3,500	27,500
1989	John Smiths	5,000	35,000

QUEEN'S HONOURS

Eight Rugby League players have been awarded the MBE by Her Majesty the Queen for their services to the game.

Player	Awarded MBE	GB Caps	Career	Clubs
Eric Ashton	June 1966	26	1955-69	Wigan
Geoff Gunney	June 1970	11	1951-73	Hunslet
Clive Sullivan	January 1974	17	1961-85	Hull, Hull K.R., Oldham, Doncaster
Chris Hesketh	January 1976	21 + 2	1963-79	Wigan, Salford
Roger Millward	January 1983	28 + 1	1963-80	Castleford, Hull K.R.
Neil Fox	June 1983	29	1956-79	Wakefield T., Bradford N., Hull K.R., York, Bramley, Huddersfield
David Watkins	January 1986	2 + 4	1967-82	Salford, Swinton, Cardiff C.
Ellery Hanley	January 1990	28 + 1	1978-	Bradford N., Wigan

ATTENDANCES

CLUB ATTENDANCE REVIEW

The following is a review of clubs' home attendances for league matches from 1981-82.

The main figure is the individual club's average gate for league games during that season. The figure in brackets indicates an upward or downward trend compared with the previous season.

Also indicated is the division the club competed in that season, i.e.

1 — First Division, 2 — Second Division.

Club	81-82	82-83	83-84	84-85	85-86	86-87	87-88	88-89	89-90
Barrow	1 4162 (+97)	1 3852 (−310)	2 3218 (−450)	1 2728 (−490)	2 1926 (−802)	1 2664 (+738)	2 1624 (−1040)	2 1594 (−30)	1 1997 (+403)
Batley	2 1052 (−277)	2 916 (−136)	2 864 (−52)	2 1015 (+151)	2 930 (−85)	2 744 (−186)	2 859 (+115)	2 924 (+65)	2 1506 (+582)
Bradford N.	1 5816 (−289)	1 4920 (−896)	1 5316 (+386)	1 4251 (−1065)	1 3975 (−276)	1 4312 (+377)	1 4723 (+411)	1 4969 (+246)	1 5584 (+615)
Bramley	2 928 (−122)	2 809 (−119)	2 759 (−50)	2 858 (+99)	2 831 (−27)	2 737 (−94)	2 858 (+121)	2 1004 (+146)	2 982 (−22)
Bridgend	2 2008 —	2 854 (−1154)	2 581 (−273)	2 510 (−70)	—	—	—	—	—
Carlisle	2 2950 (−1026)	1 1924 (−1172)	2 752 (+244)	2 986 (−368)	2 618 (+171)	2 789 (+171)	2 763 (−26)	2 678 (−85)	2 574 (−104)
Castleford	1 3791 (−821)	1 3548 (−243)	1 4288 (+740)	1 3217 (−1071)	1 3701 (+430)	1 4758 (+1057)	1 4520 (−238)	1 6580 (+2060)	1 6428 (−152)
Chorley	—	—	—	—	—	—	—	—	2 806
Dewsbury	2 1048 (−329)	2 779 (−269)	2 706 (−73)	2 995 (+189)	1 1819 (+824)	2 669 (−1150)	2 658 (−41)	2 772 (+114)	2 1227 (+455)
Doncaster	2 556 (−72)	2 441 (−115)	2 255 (−186)	2 266 (+11)	2 689 (+423)	2 1543 (+854)	2 1450 (−93)	2 1906 (+456)	2 1965 (+59)
Featherstone R.	1 2806 (−201)	1 2647 (−159)	1 3032 (+385)	1 2541 (−491)	1 2320 (−221)	1 2606 (+286)	2 1879 (−727)	1 4379 (+2500)	1 4269 (−110)
Fulham	1 4321 (−1775)	2 2688 (−1633)	1 2238 (−450)	2 949 (−1289)	2 817 (−132)	2 684 (−133)	2 615 (−69)	2 588 (−27)	2 841 (+253)
Halifax	2 2818 (−1272)	1 2270 (−548)	2 1254 (−1016)	1 3497 (+2243)	1 4944 (+1447)	1 4891 (−53)	1 6521 (+1630)	1 8022 (+1501)	2 5921 (−2101)
Huddersfield	2 1185 (−584)	2 776 (−409)	2 699 (−77)	2 905 (+206)	2 678 (−227)	2 524 (−154)	2 601 (+77)	2 1114 (+513)	2 1634 (+520)
Hull	1 13190 (+1479)	1 11525 (−1665)	1 10679 (−846)	1 8525 (−2154)	1 6245 (−1280)	1 5538 (−707)	1 5111 (−427)	1 6804 (+1693)	1 6218 (−586)
Hull K. R.	1 8723 (−181)	1 7379 (−1344)	1 6966 (−413)	1 6715 (−215)	1 4855 (−1860)	1 4651 (−204)	1 4186 (−465)	1 5298 (+1111)	2 4851 (−447)
Hunslet	2 744 (−177)	2 1195 (+451)	2 1338 (+143)	1 2246 (+908)	2 722 (−1524)	1 1050 (+338)	1 2678 (+1050)	2 947 (−1731)	2 1046 (+99)

Club	81-82	82-83	83-84	84-85	85-86	86-87	87-88	88-89	89-90
Keighley	2 1576 (−36)	2 1085 (−491)	2 734 (−351)	2 822 (+88)	2 685 (−137)	2 445 (−240)	2 958 (+503)	2 961 (+3)	2 936 (−25)
Leeds	1 5599 (−335)	1 5893 (+294)	1 6542 (+649)	1 7330 (+788)	1 6928 (−402)	1 6393 (−535)	1 9911 (+3518)	1 12060 (+2149)	1 12251 (+191)
Leigh	1 5939 (+1441)	1 4617 (−1322)	1 4434 (−183)	1 3822 (−612)	2 2710 (−1112)	1 4232 (+1522)	1 4516 (+284)	2 2346 (−2170)	1 4568 (+2222)
Nottingham C.	—	—	—	2 1020 (—)	2 487 (−553)	2 368 (−119)	2 368 (—)	2 560 (+192)	2 577 (+17)
Oldham	1 2395 (−825)	1 3721 (+1326)	1 4138 (+417)	1 4562 (+424)	1 4333 (−229)	1 3915 (−418)	2 3790 (−125)	1 5759 (+1696)	2 4401 (−1358)
Rochdale H.	2 888 (−261)	2 619 (−269)	2 538 (−81)	2 542 (+4)	2 1267 (+725)	2 877 (−390)	2 1106 (+229)	2 1027 (−79)	2 2510 (+1483)
Runcorn H.	2 385 (+115)	2 224 (−161)	2 172 (−52)	2 509 (+337)	2 363 (−146)	2 331 (−35)	2 515 (+184)	2 298 (−217)	2 453 (+155)
Ryedale-York	1 3677 (−150)	2 1685 (−1992)	2 1215 (−470)	2 1528 (+313)	1 2828 (+1300)	2 1520 (−1380)	2 1406 (−114)	2 2021 (+615)	2 2495 (+474)
St. Helens	1 4862 (−72)	1 4543 (−319)	1 4656 (+113)	1 7336 (+2680)	1 6022 (−1314)	1 7341 (+1391)	1 8417 (+1076)	1 9514 (+1097)	1 8555 (−959)
Salford	2 2404 (−1054)	2 1928 (−476)	1 2399 (+471)	2 1795 (−604)	1 2520 (+725)	1 2826 (+306)	1 3747 (+921)	1 5470 (+1723)	1 3720 (−1750)
Sheffield E.	—	—	—	2 885 (—)	2 698 (−187)	2 708 (+10)	2 847 (+139)	2 838 (−9)	1 4038 (+3200)
Southend Invicta	—	—	2 731 (—)	2 216 (−515)	—	—	—	—	—
Swinton	2 1567 (−368)	2 1314 (−253)	2 1077 (−237)	2 1590 (+513)	1 2706 (+1116)	2 1622 (−1084)	1 2987 (+1365)	2 1435 (−1543)	2 1678 (+243)
Trafford B.	2 768 (+84)	2 679 (−89)	2 625 (−54)	2 555 (−70)	2 534 (−21)	2 475 (−59)	2 922 (+447)	2 512 (−410)	2 780 (+294)
Wakefield T.	1 3716 (−1098)	2 2344 (−1372)	1 3483 (+1139)	2 1568 (−1915)	2 1714 (+146)	1 2637 (+923)	2 2416 (−221)	1 5151 (+2735)	1 5428 (+277)
Warrington	1 3838 (−1079)	1 3824 (−14)	1 4059 (+235)	1 3801 (−258)	1 3618 (−183)	1 4172 (+554)	1 4974 (+820)	1 4893 (−81)	1 5412 (+519)
Whitehaven	1 2710 (−23)	2 1742 (−968)	1 1639 (−103)	2 1540 (−99)	2 1878 (+333)	2 1800 (−78)	2 1772 (−28)	2 1310 (−462)	2 961 (−349)
Widnes	1 5485 (+179)	1 4703 (−782)	1 4687 (−16)	1 4266 (−421)	1 4019 (−247)	1 3840 (−179)	1 6262 (+2422)	1 8648 (+2386)	1 7858 (−790)
Wigan	1 5497 (+804)	1 7426 (+1929)	1 7479 (+53)	1 10056 (+2577)	1 12515 (+2459)	1 12732 (+217)	1 13021 (+289)	1 14543 (+1519)	1 13973 (−570)
Workington T.	2 1969 (−219)	1 1470 (−499)	2 934 (−536)	1 920 (−14)	2 702 (−218)	2 653 (−49)	2 737 (+84)	2 774 (+37)	2 691 (−83)

COMPETITION ATTENDANCE REVIEW

		81-82	82-83	83-84	84-85	85-86	86-87	87-88	88-89	89-90
FIRST	Total	1,264,520	1,113,915	1,140,548	1,137,195	1,100,329	1,162,666	1,060,296	1,327,192	1,173,815
DIVISION	Av.	5,268	4,641	4,752	4,738	4,585	4,844	5,826	7,292	6,450
SECOND	Total	403,652	321,226	279,673	266,730	310,311	217,552	381,825	298,776	515,687
DIVISION	Av.	1,484	1,181	914	953	1,014	863	1,364	1,067	1,754
LEAGUE TOTALS (1st & 2nd)	Total	1,668,172	1,435,141	1,420,221	1,403,925	1,410,640	1,380,218	1,442,121	1,625,968	1,689,502
	Av.	3,258	2,803	2,601	2,700	2,584	2,805	3,121	3,519	3,549
R.L. CUP	Av.	11,388	8,355	8,399	8,497	8,280	6,965	8,764	8,666	7,339
REGAL	Av.	5,590	4,219	3,893	4,881	4,232	4,122	3,570	4,987	4,876
PREMIER	Av.	9,454	10,099	8,136	10,115	9,273	15,154	13,462	15,856	16,796
10,000+ (No. of)		36	37	26	27	36	43	46	59	54

20,000-plus crowds . . . . A 10-year review
All matches except the Rugby League Challenge Cup final at Wembley

25,245	Hull v. Hull K.R.	John Player final	Leeds	23 Jan. 1982
21,207	Hull v. Castleford	RL Cup semi-final	Leeds	27 Mar. 1982
41,171	Hull v. Widnes	RL Cup final replay	Elland Rd, Leeds	19 May 1982
26,771	Britain v. Australia	First Test	Hull C. FC	30 Oct. 1982
23,216	Britain v. Australia	Second Test	Wigan	20 Nov. 1982
26,031	Hull v. Castleford	RL Cup semi-final	Elland Rd, Leeds	2 Apr. 1983
20,569	Hull v. Hull K.R.	Division One	Hull	8 Apr. 1983
20,077	St. Helens v. Wigan	RL Cup round 3	St. Helens	11 Mar. 1984
25,237	Hull v. Hull K.R.	Yorks Cup final	Hull C. FC	27 Oct. 1984
26,074	St. Helens v. Wigan	Lancs Cup final	Wigan	28 Oct. 1984
25,326	Hull v. Hull K.R.	John Player final	Hull C. FC	26 Jan. 1985
20,982	Hull v. Castleford	RL Cup semi-final	Leeds	6 Apr. 1985
20,968	Hull v. Castleford	RL Cup semi-final replay	Leeds	10 Apr. 1985
22,209	Britain v. New Zealand	Third Test	Elland Rd, Leeds	9 Nov. 1985
21,813	Wigan v. St. Helens	Division One	Wigan	26 Dec. 1985
23,866	Hull K.R. v. Leeds	RL Cup semi-final	Elland Rd, Leeds	29 Mar. 1986
32,485	Hull K.R. v. Leeds	RL Cup semi-final replay	Elland Rd, Leeds	3 Apr. 1986
28,252	Wigan v. St. Helens	Lancs Cup semi-final	Wigan	1 Oct. 1986
30,622	Wigan v. Australia	Tour	Wigan	12 Oct. 1986
20,180	Oldham v. Wigan	Lancs Cup final	St. Helens	19 Oct. 1986
50,583	Britain v. Australia	First Test	Manchester U. FC	25 Oct. 1986
30,808	Britain v. Australia	Second Test	Elland Rd, Leeds	8 Nov. 1986
20,169	Britain v. Australia	Third Test	Wigan	22 Nov. 1986
21,214	St. Helens v. Wigan	Division One	St. Helens	26 Dec. 1986
21,144	Warrington v. Wigan	John Player final	Bolton W. FC	10 Jan. 1987
20,355	Wigan v. St. Helens	Division One	Wigan	17 Apr. 1987

(continued)

22,457	Wigan v. Halifax	Premiership semi-final	Wigan	10 May 1987
38,756	Warrington v. Wigan	Premiership final	Manchester U. FC	17 May 1987
36,895	Wigan v. Manly	World Club Challenge	Wigan	7 Oct. 1987
20,234	Wigan v. Warrington	Lancs Cup final	St. Helens	11 Oct. 1987
23,809	Wigan v. St. Helens	Division One	Wigan	27 Dec. 1987
25,110	Wigan v. Leeds	RL Cup round 2	Wigan	14 Feb. 1988
20,783	Salford v. Wigan	RL Cup semi-final	Bolton W. FC	12 Mar. 1988
20,534	Halifax v. Hull	RL Cup semi-final	Leeds	26 Mar. 1988
25,117	Hull v. Halifax	RL Cup semi-final replay	Elland Rd, Leeds	30 Mar. 1988
21,812	St. Helens v. Wigan	Division One	St. Helens	1 Apr. 1988
35,252	St. Helens v. Widnes	Premiership final	Manchester U. FC	15 May 1988
22,968	Castleford v. Leeds	Yorks Cup final	Elland Rd, Leeds	16 Oct. 1988
20,709	Widnes v. Wigan	John Player final	Bolton W. FC	7 Jan. 1989
26,080	Leeds v. Widnes	RL Cup round 2	Leeds	26 Feb. 1989
26,529	Warrington v. Wigan	RL Cup semi-final	Manchester C. FC	25 Mar. 1989
21,076	Wigan v. St. Helens	Division One	Wigan	12 Apr. 1989
40,194	Hull v. Widnes	Premiership final	Manchester U. FC	14 May 1989
30,786	Widnes v. Canberra	World Club Challenge	Manchester U. FC	4 Oct. 1989
20,346	Britain v. New Zealand	Third Test	Wigan	11 Nov. 1989
27,075	Wigan v. St. Helens	Division One	Wigan	26 Dec 1989
23,570	Leeds v. Wigan	Division One	Leeds	4 Mar 1990
26,489	St. Helens v. Wigan	R.L. Cup semi-final	Manchester U. FC	10 Mar 1990
24,462	Wigan v. Leeds	Division One	Wigan	10 Apr. 1990
40,796	Bradford N. v. Widnes	Premiership final	Manchester U. FC	13 May 1990

1989-90 ATTENDANCE ANALYSIS

FIRST DIVISION

Total............................ 1,173,815
Average 6,450

Wigan topped the gates chart for the sixth successive season with an average home attendance of 13,973, Leeds again commanding second spot with an average of 12,251. Half of the 14 clubs recorded an increase in gates, headed by newly-promoted Sheffield Eagles who nearly trebled their turnout. Gates fell by 11 per cent compared with the 1988-89 figures of 1,327,192 and 7,292.

SECOND DIVISION

Total.......................... 515,687
Average.......................... 1,754

Halifax, despite missing promotion, were the best supported Second Division club, ahead of promoted trio Hull K.R., Oldham and Rochdale Hornets. Rejuvenated Hornets celebrated a move to neighbouring soccer ground Spotland by recording a 144 per cent rise in attendances. Eleven of the 21 clubs attracted gate increases, particularly the Kirklees trio of Batley, Dewsbury and Huddersfield. Attendances went up by 64 per cent compared with the 1988-89 average of 1,067.

LEAGUE CHAMPIONSHIP

> Aggregate..................... 1,689,502
> Average 3,549

The average attendance for the 35 clubs in both divisions, staging a total of 476 matches, was up 0.85 per cent compared with the previous figure of 3,519.

SILK CUT CHALLENGE CUP

The 1990 Challenge Cup trail attracted a total of 286,230 to the 39 ties, including two replays, providing the season's top gate of 77,726 for the Wembley final. The average of 7,339 was a 15 per cent decrease on the 1989 figure of 8,666.

REGAL TROPHY

Previously titled the John Player Special Trophy, the tournament attracted a total of 190,172 fans to 39 games, including two replays. The average gate of 4,876 was two per cent down on the previous figure of 4,987.

STONES BITTER PREMIERSHIP

The end of season top-eight competition was attended by a total of 117,578 spectators, the average gate for the seven ties being 16,796. This was a six per cent increase on the 1989 figures of 110,992 and 15,856. The 1990 tournamant featured a new record attendance for the Premiership final of 40,796 at Manchester United's Old Trafford ground.

SECOND DIVISION PREMIERSHIP

There was a massive 93 per cent increase in the six ties, including a replay, leading up to the Old Trafford doubleheader final. The total turnout of 23,632 provided an average gate of 3,938, compared with the 1989 figure of 2,039.

GRUNHALLE LAGER LANCASHIRE CUP

Gates for the 16-tie competition went down by 21 per cent, the 1989-90 total being 79,237 for an average gate of 4,952, compared with the previous returns of 94,107 and 6,274.

JOHN SMITHS YORKSHIRE CUP

The White Rose county competition featured 19 matches, including two replays. There was a total turnout of 190,172, an average gate of 5,633, which was eight per cent down on the previous average of 6,145.

FIVE-FIGURE CROWDS

There were a total of 54 five-figure gates, the second best since the reintroduction of two divisions in 1973. Once again the top gate was at Wembley for the Silk Cut Challenge Cup final, while the Stones Bitter Premiership doubleheader at Manchester United's Old Trafford created a new record gate for the second successive year. The reintroduction of the Foster's World Club Challenge, staged for the first time at Old Trafford, pulled the third best attendance of the season, 30,786. Five-figure crowds were attracted for all three British Coal Tests between Great Britain and New Zealand, the decider at Wigan breaking the 20,000-mark. The 10,000-plus gates were divided into the following categories:

> League 28
> Challenge Cup............................ 6
> Premiership Trophy 5
> Regal Trophy............................ 4
> New Zealand Tour..................... 4
> Yorkshire Cup 3
> Lancashire Cup 1
> Charity Shield........................... 1
> World Club Challenge 1
> War of the Roses...................... 1

STONES BITTER CHAMPIONSHIP

	1989-90 Average	Annual Difference
Wigan	13973	(−570)
Leeds	12251	(+191)
St. Helens	8555	(−959)
Widnes	7858	(−790)
Castleford	6428	(−152)
Hull	6218	(−586)
Bradford Northern	5584	(+615)
Wakefield Trinity	5428	(+277)
Warrington	5412	(+519)
*Leigh	4568	(+2222)
Featherstone Rovers	4269	(−110)
*Sheffield Eagles	4038	(+3200)
Salford	3720	(−1750)
*Barrow	1997	(+403)

Promoted 1988-89

SECOND DIVISION

	1989-90 Average	Annual Difference
*Halifax	5921	(−2101)
*Hull Kingston Rovers	4851	(−447)
*Oldham	4401	(−1358)
Rochdale Hornets	2510	(+1483)
Ryedale-York	2495	(+474)
Doncaster	1965	(+59)
Swinton	1678	(+243)
Huddersfield	1634	(+520)
Batley	1506	(+582)
Dewsbury	1227	(+455)
Hunslet	1046	(+99)
Bramley	982	(−22)
Whitehaven	961	(−349)
Keighley	936	(−25)
Fulham	841	(+253)
Chorley	806	(−)
Trafford Borough	780	(+268)
Workington Town	691	(−83)
Nottingham City	577	(+17)
Carlisle	574	(−104)
Runcorn Highfield	453	(+155)

Relegated 1988-89

FIXTURES

PRINCIPAL DATES 1990-91

1990

19 August	CIS Insurance Charity Shield (Vetch Field, Swansea)
26 August	County Cup Competitions (1)
2 September	County Cup Competitions (2)
12 September	County Cup Competitions (SF)
23 September	John Smiths Yorkshire Cup (F)
29/30 September	Greenalls Lancashire Cup (F)
27 October	British Coal Test: Great Britain v. Australia (1) (Wembley)
10 November	British Coal Test: Great Britain v. Australia (2) (Old Trafford, Manchester)
24 November	British Coal Test: Great Britain v. Australia (3) (Elland Road, Leeds)
1 December	Regal Trophy (1)
8 December	Regal Trophy (2)
15 December	Regal Trophy (3)
22 December	Regal Trophy (SF1)
29 December	Regal Trophy (SF2)

1991

12 January	Regal Trophy (F)
26 January	France v. Great Britain Under-21s (Limoux)
27 January	British Coal Test: France v. Great Britain (Perpignan)
9 February	Silk Cut Challenge Cup (1)
15 February	Great Britain v. France Under-21s
16 February	British Coal Test: Great Britain v. France
23 February	Silk Cut Challenge Cup (2)
9 March	Silk Cut Challenge Cup (3)
23 March	Silk Cut Challenge Cup (SF1)
30 March	Silk Cut Challenge Cup (SF2)
21 April	Stones Bitter Premiership (1)
27 April	Silk Cut Challenge Cup (F) (Wembley)
5 May	Stones Bitter Premiership (SF)
12 May	Stones Bitter Premiership (F)

BRITISH COAL TOUR BY AUSTRALIA 1990

Sunday	7 October	St. Helens
Wednesday	10 October	Wakefield Trinity
Sunday	14 October	Wigan
Wednesday	17 October	Cumbria
Sunday	21 October	Leeds
Saturday	27 October	FIRST BRITISH COAL TEST (Wembley)
Wednesday	31 October	Warrington
Sunday	4 November	Castleford
Tuesday	6 November	Halifax
Saturday	10 November	SECOND BRITISH COAL TEST (Old Trafford, Manchester)
Wednesday	14 November	Hull
Sunday	18 November	Widnes
Saturday	24 November	THIRD BRITISH COAL TEST (Elland Road, Leeds)

STONES BITTER CHAMPIONSHIP 1990-91

SUNDAY, 26th AUGUST, 1990
COUNTY CUPS — ROUND 1

SUNDAY, 2nd SEPTEMBER, 1990
COUNTY CUPS — ROUND 2

SUNDAY, 9th SEPTEMBER, 1990

Bradford N.	v.	Widnes
Featherstone R.	v.	Hull K. R.
Hull	v.	St. Helens
Oldham	v.	Leeds
Wakefield T.	v.	Rochdale H.
Warrington	v.	Castleford
Wigan	v.	Sheffield E.

SUNDAY, 16th SEPTEMBER, 1990

Castleford	v.	Wigan
Hull K. R.	v.	Warrington
Leeds	v.	Hull
Rochdale H.	v.	Sheffield E.
St. Helens	v.	Bradford N.
Wakefield T.	v.	Oldham
Widnes	v.	Featherstone R.

SUNDAY, 23rd SEPTEMBER, 1990

Featherstone R.	v.	Bradford N.
Hull	v.	Widnes
Oldham	v.	Castleford
St. Helens	v.	Hull K. R.
Sheffield E.	v.	Wakefield T.
Warrington	v.	Leeds
Wigan	v.	Rochdale H.

SUNDAY, 30th SEPTEMBER, 1990

Bradford N.	v.	Wigan
Castleford	v.	Featherstone R.
Hull K. R.	v.	Wakefield T.
Leeds	v.	St. Helens
Rochdale H.	v.	Hull
Sheffield E.	v.	Warrington
Widnes	v.	Oldham

SUNDAY 7th OCTOBER, 1990

Bradford N.	v.	Leeds
Featherstone R.	v.	Sheffield E.
Hull	v.	Wigan
Oldham	v.	Hull K. R.
Warrington	v.	Rochdale H.
Widnes	v.	Castleford
St. Helens	v.	AUSTRALIA

WEDNESDAY, 10th OCTOBER, 1990

Wakefield T.	v.	AUSTRALIA

SUNDAY, 14th OCTOBER, 1990

Castleford	v.	Wakefield T.
Hull K. R.	v.	Widnes
Leeds	v.	Featherstone R.
Rochdale H.	v.	Bradford N.
Sheffield E.	v.	Oldham
Warrington	v.	Hull
Wigan	v.	AUSTRALIA

WEDNESDAY, 17th OCTOBER, 1990

Cumbria	v.	AUSTRALIA

SUNDAY, 21st OCTOBER, 1990

Bradford N.	v.	Hull K. R.
Featherstone R.	v.	Rochdale H.
Hull	v.	Sheffield E.
Oldham	v.	Warrington
St. Helens	v.	Castleford
Wakefield T.	v.	Widnes
Leeds	v.	AUSTRALIA

SATURDAY, 27th OCTOBER, 1990
FIRST BRITISH COAL TEST
(at Wembley)
GREAT BRITAIN v. AUSTRALIA
No League programme over this weekend

TUESDAY, 30th OCTOBER, 1990

Sheffield E.	v.	Bradford N.

WEDNESDAY, 31st OCTOBER, 1990

Warrington	v.	AUSTRALIA

SUNDAY, 4th NOVEMBER, 1990

Bradford N.	v.	Warrington
Hull K. R.	v.	Featherstone R.
Rochdale H.	v.	St. Helens
Wakefield T.	v.	Hull
Widnes	v.	Leeds
Wigan	v.	Oldham
Castleford	v.	AUSTRALIA

TUESDAY, 6th NOVEMBER, 1990

Halifax	v.	AUSTRALIA

SUNDAY, 11th NOVEMBER, 1990

Featherstone R.	v.	Castleford
Hull K. R.	v.	Wigan
Leeds	v.	Rochdale H.
Oldham	v.	Bradford N.
St. Helens	v.	Sheffield E.
Warrington	v.	Wakefield T.

WEDNESDAY, 14th NOVEMBER, 1990

Hull	v.	AUSTRALIA

SUNDAY, 18th NOVEMBER, 1990

Bradford N.	v.	St. Helens
Castleford	v.	Oldham
Hull	v.	Warrington
Rochdale H.	v.	Hull K. R.
Sheffield E.	v.	Leeds
Wigan	v.	Featherstone R.
Widnes	v.	AUSTRALIA

SUNDAY, 25th NOVEMBER, 1990

Featherstone R.	v.	Hull
Hull K. R.	v.	Bradford N.
Leeds	v.	Castleford
Oldham	v.	Widnes
St. Helens	v.	Rochdale H.
Wakefield T.	v.	Wigan
Warrington	v.	Sheffield E.

SUNDAY, 2nd DECEMBER, 1990
REGAL TROPHY FIRST ROUND

SUNDAY, 9th DECEMBER, 1990
REGAL TROPHY SECOND ROUND

412

SUNDAY, 16th DECEMBER, 1990

Bradford N.	v.	Wakefield T.
Castleford	v.	Warrington
Hull	v.	Oldham
Rochdale H.	v.	Featherstone R.
Sheffield E.	v.	St. Helens
Widnes	v.	Hull K. R.
Wigan	v.	Leeds

WEDNESDAY, 26th DECEMBER, 1990

Featherstone R.	v.	Wakefield T.
Hull	v.	Castleford
Hull K. R.	v.	Sheffield E.
Leeds	v.	Bradford N.
Oldham	v.	Rochdale H.
St. Helens	v.	Wigan
Warrington	v.	Widnes

1991

TUESDAY, 1st JANUARY, 1991

Castleford	v.	Bradford N.
Hull K. R.	v.	Hull
Leeds	v.	Oldham
Wakefield T.	v.	Featherstone R.
Widnes	v.	St. Helens
Wigan	v.	Warrington

SUNDAY, 6th JANUARY, 1991

Bradford N.	v.	Rochdale H.
Castleford	v.	Widnes
Hull	v.	Leeds
Oldham	v.	Featherstone R.
St. Helens	v.	Wakefield T.
Sheffield E.	v.	Wigan
Warrington	v.	Hull K. R.

SUNDAY, 13th JANUARY, 1991

Featherstone R.	v.	St. Helens
Hull K. R.	v.	Oldham
Leeds	v.	Sheffield E.
Rochdale H.	v.	Castleford
Wakefield T.	v.	Warrington
Widnes	v.	Hull
Wigan	v.	Bradford N.

SUNDAY, 20th JANUARY, 1991

Castleford	v.	Hull K. R.
Hull	v.	Bradford N.
Oldham	v.	Wakefield T.
St. Helens	v.	Leeds
Sheffield E.	v.	Rochdale H.
Warrington	v.	Featherstone R.
Widnes	v.	Wigan

SUNDAY, 27th JANUARY, 1991

Bradford N.	v.	Sheffield E.
Featherstone R.	v.	Oldham
Hull K. R.	v.	St. Helens
Leeds	v.	Warrington
Rochdale H.	v.	Widnes
Wakefield T.	v.	Castleford
Wigan	v.	Hull

SUNDAY, 3rd FEBRUARY, 1991

Castleford	v.	Leeds
Hull	v.	Rochdale H.
Oldham	v.	St. Helens
Sheffield E.	v.	Featherstone R.
Warrington	v.	Bradford N.
Widnes	v.	Wakefield T.
Wigan	v.	Hull K. R.

SUNDAY, 10th FEBRUARY, 1991
SILK CUT CHALLENGE CUP FIRST ROUND

SUNDAY, 17th FEBRUARY, 1991

Bradford N.	v.	Oldham
Featherstone R.	v.	Wigan
Hull K. R.	v.	Castleford
Leeds	v.	Widnes
Rochdale H.	v.	Warrington
St. Helens	v.	Hull
Wakefield T.	v.	Sheffield E.

SUNDAY, 24th FEBRUARY, 1991
SILK CUT CHALLENGE CUP SECOND ROUND

SUNDAY, 3rd MARCH, 1991

Castleford	v.	Rochdale H.
Hull	v.	Featherstone R.
Leeds	v.	Hull K. R.
Warrington	v.	St. Helens
Widnes	v.	Sheffield E.
Wigan	v.	Wakefield T.

SUNDAY, 10th MARCH, 1991

Bradford N.	v.	Hull
Featherstone R.	v.	Warrington
Rochdale H.	v.	Leeds
St. Helens	v.	Oldham
Sheffield E.	v.	Castleford
Wakefield T.	v.	Hull K. R.
Wigan	v.	Widnes

SUNDAY, 17th MARCH, 1991

Hull	v.	Wakefield T.
Hull K. R.	v.	Leeds
Oldham	v.	Sheffield E.
Rochdale H.	v.	Wigan
St. Helens	v.	Featherstone R.
Widnes	v.	Bradford N.

SUNDAY, 24th MARCH, 1991

Castleford	v.	St. Helens
Featherstone R.	v.	Widnes
Hull K. R.	v.	Rochdale H.
Sheffield E.	v.	Hull
Wakefield T.	v.	Bradford N.
Warrington	v.	Wigan

FRIDAY, 29th MARCH, 1991

Bradford N.	v.	Castleford
Hull	v.	Hull K. R.
Leeds	v.	Wakefield T.
Rochdale H.	v.	Oldham
Widnes	v.	Warrington
Wigan	v.	St. Helens

SUNDAY, 31st MARCH, 1991

Sheffield E.	v.	Hull K. R.

MONDAY, 1st APRIL 1991

Castleford	v.	Hull
Oldham	v.	Wigan
St. Helens	v.	Widnes
Wakefield T.	v.	Leeds

SUNDAY, 7th APRIL, 1991

Featherstone R.	v.	Leeds
Sheffield E.	v.	Widnes
Wakefield T.	v.	St. Helens
Warrington	v.	Oldham
Wigan	v.	Castleford

WEDNESDAY, 10th APRIL, 1991
Rochdale H.   v.   Wakefield T.

SUNDAY, 14th APRIL, 1991
Bradford N.   v.   Featherstone R.

Castleford   v.   Sheffield E.
Leeds   v.   Wigan
Oldham   v.   Hull
St. Helens   v.   Warrington
Widnes   v.   Rochdale H.

SECOND DIVISION FIXTURES
Preliminary draft subject to Club amendments

SUNDAY, 9th SEPTEMBER, 1990
Barrow   v.   Salford
Batley   v.   Leigh
Carlisle   v.   Chorley
Doncaster   v.   Hunslet
Halifax   v.   Dewsbury
Huddersfield   v.   Keighley
Ryedale-York   v.   Nottingham C.
Swinton   v.   Whitehaven
Trafford B.   v.   Runcorn H.
Workington T.   v.   Fulham

WEDNESDAY, 12th SEPTEMBER, 1990
Barrow   v.   Ryedale-York
Huddersfield   v.   Doncaster
Hunslet   v.   Leigh
Nottingham C.   v.   Bramley
* Trafford B.   v.   Salford
Whitehaven   v.   Halifax
* Changeable with fixture on 10 April

SUNDAY, 16th SEPTEMBER, 1990
Bramley   v.   Swinton
Chorley   v.   Hunslet
Dewsbury   v.   Carlisle
Fulham   v.   Barrow
Keighley   v.   Batley
Leigh   v.   Halifax
Nottingham C.   v.   Trafford B.
Runcorn H.   v.   Ryedale-York
Salford   v.   Workington T.
Whitehaven   v.   Huddersfield

SUNDAY, 23rd SEPTEMBER, 1990
Barrow   v.   Leigh
Batley   v.   Salford
Carlisle   v.   Runcorn H.
Doncaster   v.   Nottingham C.
Doncaster   v.   Nottingham C.
Fulham   v.   Whitehaven
Hunslet   v.   Trafford B.
Ryedale-York   v.   Chorley
Swinton   v.   Keighley
Workington T.   v.   Dewsbury

SUNDAY, 30th SEPTEMBER, 1990
Bramley   v.   Carlisle
Dewsbury   v.   Fulham
Halifax   v.   Ryedale-York
Keighley   v.   Hunslet
Leigh   v.   Chorley
Nottingham C.   v.   Swinton
Runcorn H.   v.   Huddersfield
Salford   v.   Doncaster
Trafford B.   v.   Workington T.
Whitehaven   v.   Barrow

SUNDAY, 7th OCTOBER, 1990
Barrow   v.   Dewsbury
Batley   v.   Nottingham C.
Chorley   v.   Whitehaven

Doncaster   v.   Keighley
Fulham   v.   Bramley
Huddersfield   v.   Trafford B.
Hunslet   v.   Runcorn H.
Ryedale-York   v.   Salford
Swinton   v.   Halifax
Workington T.   v.   Carlisle

SUNDAY, 14th OCTOBER, 1990
Bramley   v.   Chorley
Carlisle   v.   Ryedale-York
Dewsbury   v.   Swinton
Halifax   v.   Runcorn H.
Keighley   v.   Fulham
Huddersfield   v.   Leigh
Nottingham C.   v.   Workington T.
Salford   v.   Barrow
Trafford B.   v.   Hunslet
Whitehaven   v.   Doncaster

SUNDAY, 21st OCTOBER, 1990
Barrow   v.   Bramley
Batley   v.   Trafford B.
Chorley   v.   Salford
Doncaster   v.   Huddersfield
Hunslet   v.   Dewsbury
Leigh   v.   Nottingham C.
Runcorn H.   v.   Fulham
Ryedale-York   v.   Halifax
Swinton   v.   Carlisle
Workington T.   v.   Keighley

SATURDAY, 27th OCTOBER, 1990
FIRST BRITISH COAL TEST (at WEMBLEY)
GREAT BRITAIN v. AUSTRALIA

SUNDAY, 28th OCTOBER, 1990
Fulham   v.   Batley

SUNDAY, 4th NOVEMBER, 1990
Carlisle   v.   Barrow
Dewsbury   v.   Doncaster
Halifax   v.   Batley
Huddersfield   v.   Workington T.
Keighley   v.   Chorley
Nottingham C.   v.   Ryedale-York
Runcorn H.   v.   Hunslet
Salford   v.   Bramley
Trafford B.   v.   Fulham
Whitehaven   v.   Swinton

TUESDAY, 6th NOVEMBER, 1990
Halifax   v.   Australia

SUNDAY, 11th NOVEMBER, 1990
Barrow   v.   Huddersfield
Batley   v.   Whitehaven
Bramley   v.   Runcorn H.
Chorley   v.   Nottingham C.
Doncaster   v.   Trafford B.
Fulham   v.   Ryedale-York

414

Hunslet	v.	Keighley
Leigh	v.	Carlisle
Swinton	v.	Dewsbury
Workington T.	v.	Halifax

SUNDAY, 18th NOVEMBER, 1990

Carlisle	v.	Batley
Dewsbury	v.	Huddersfield
* Halifax	v.	Bramley
Keighley	v.	Doncaster
Nottingham C.	v.	Leigh
Runcorn H.	v.	Salford
Ryedale-York	v.	Workington T.
Swinton	v.	Fulham
Trafford B.	v.	Barrow
Whitehaven	v.	Hunslet

* Changeable to 23rd September

SUNDAY, 25th NOVEMBER, 1990

Barrow	v.	Halifax
Batley	v.	Ryedale-York
Bramley	v.	Nottingham C.
Chorley	v.	Carlisle
Fulham	v.	Dewsbury
Huddersfield	v.	Runcorn H.
Hunslet	v.	Doncaster
Leigh	v.	Swinton
Salford	v.	Whitehaven
Workington T.	v.	Trafford B.

SUNDAY, 2nd DECEMBER, 1990
REGAL TROPHY FIRST ROUND

SUNDAY, 9th DECEMBER, 1990
REGAL TROPHY SECOND ROUND

SUNDAY, 16th DECEMBER, 1990

Carlisle	v.	Leigh
Dewsbury	v.	Workington T.
Doncaster	v.	Fulham
Halifax	v.	Chorley
Keighley	v.	Nottingham C.
Runcorn H.	v.	Bramley
Ryedale-York	v.	Huddersfield
Swinton	v.	Hunslet
Trafford B.	v.	Batley
Whitehaven	v.	Salford

SUNDAY, 23rd DECEMBER, 1990

Batley	v.	Carlisle
Bramley	v.	Doncaster
Chorley	v.	Keighley
Huddersfield	v.	Whitehaven
Leigh	v.	Barrow
Nottingham C.	v.	Dewsbury
Ryedale-York	v.	Runcorn H.
Workington T.	v.	Hunslet

WEDNESDAY, 26th DECEMBER, 1990

Barrow	v.	Carlisle
* Chorley	v.	Huddersfield
Dewsbury	v.	Batley
Doncaster	v.	Ryedale-York
Hunslet	v.	Bramley
Keighley	v.	Halifax
Leigh	v.	Salford
Swinton	v.	Trafford B.
Whitehaven	v.	Workington T.

* Changeable with fixture on 6th January

1991

TUESDAY, 1st JANUARY, 1991

Batley	v.	Dewsbury
Bramley	v.	Hunslet
Carlisle	v.	Whitehaven
Halifax	v.	Doncaster
Keighley	v.	Huddersfield
Runcorn H.	v.	Leigh
Ryedale-York	v.	Barrow
Salford	v.	Swinton
Trafford B.	v.	Chorley

SUNDAY, 6th JANUARY, 1991

Barrow	v.	Keighley
Dewsbury	v.	Salford
Doncaster	v.	Bramley
Fulham	v.	Trafford B.
Huddersfield	v.	Chorley
Hunslet	v.	Whitehaven
Nottingham C.	v.	Batley
Runcorn H.	v.	Halifax
Swinton	v.	Ryedale-York
Workington T.	v.	Leigh

SUNDAY, 13th JANUARY, 1991

Bramley	v.	Batley
Carlisle	v.	Doncaster
Chorley	v.	Fulham
Halifax	v.	Barrow
Keighley	v.	Workington T.
* Leigh	v.	Hunslet
Ryedale-York	v.	Swinton
Salford	v.	Runcorn H.
Trafford B.	v.	Huddersfield
Whitehaven	v.	Nottingham C.

* Changeable with fixture on 12th September

SUNDAY, 20th JANUARY, 1991

Batley	v.	Halifax
Doncaster	v.	Dewsbury
Fulham	v.	Leigh
Huddersfield	v.	Swinton
Hunslet	v.	Chorley
Keighley	v.	Carlisle
Nottingham C.	v.	Whitehaven
Runcorn H.	v.	Trafford B.
Salford	v.	Ryedale-York
Workington T.	v.	Bramley

SUNDAY, 27th JANUARY, 1991

Bramley	v.	Barrow
Carlisle	v.	Trafford B.
Dewsbury	v.	Chorley
Doncaster	v.	Salford
Halifax	v.	Keighley
Hunslet	v.	Batley
* Leigh	v.	Workington T.
Ryedale-York	v.	Fulham
Swinton	v.	Nottingham C.
Whitehaven	v.	Runcorn H.

* Changeable with fixture on 6th January

SUNDAY, 3rd FEBRUARY, 1991

Barrow	v.	Hunslet
Batley	v.	Bramley
Chorley	v.	Leigh
Fulham	v.	Swinton
Halifax	v.	Whitehaven
Nottingham C.	v.	Keighley

Runcorn H. v. Carlisle
Salford v. Dewsbury
Trafford B. v. Doncaster
Workington T. v. Huddersfield

SUNDAY, 10th FEBRUARY, 1991
SILK CUT CHALLENGE CUP FIRST ROUND

FRIDAY, 15th FEBRUARY, 1991
Salford v. Chorley

SUNDAY, 17th FEBRUARY, 1991
Bramley v. Workington T.
Carlisle v. Swinton
Dewsbury v. Nottingham C.
Doncaster v. Halifax
Huddersfield v. Ryedale-York
Hunslet v. Barrow
Keighley v. Runcorn H.
Leigh v. Fulham
Whitehaven v. Batley

SUNDAY, 24th FEBRUARY, 1991
SILK CUT CHALLENGE CUP SECOND ROUND

SUNDAY, 3rd MARCH, 1991
Batley v. Fulham
Chorley v. Bramley
Doncaster v. Whitehaven
Huddersfield v. Barrow
Keighley v. Salford
Runcorn H. v. Dewsbury
Ryedale-York v. Carlisle
Swinton v. Leigh
Trafford B. v. Halifax
Workington T. v. Nottingham C.

SUNDAY, 10th MARCH, 1991
Barrow v. Trafford B.
Bramley v. Huddersfield
Carlisle v. Keighley
Dewsbury v. Hunslet
Fulham v. Workington T.
Halifax v. Swinton
Leigh v. Doncaster
Nottingham C. v. Runcorn H.
Salford v. Batley
Whitehaven v. Chorley

SUNDAY, 17th MARCH, 1991
Barrow v. Fulham
Batley v. Keighley
Chorley v. Halifax
Doncaster v. Carlisle
Huddersfield v. Dewsbury
Runcorn H. v. Whitehaven
Ryedale-York v. Hunslet
Swinton v. Bramley
Trafford B. v. Nottingham C.
Workington T. v. Salford

SUNDAY, 24th MARCH, 1991
Bramley v. Salford
Chorley v. Ryedale-York
Dewsbury v. Runcorn H.
Halifax v. Workington T.
Hunslet v. Swinton
Keighley v. Barrow
Leigh v. Batley
Nottingham C. v. Doncaster
Trafford B. v. Carlisle
Whitehaven v. Fulham

GOOD FRIDAY, 29th MARCH, 1991
Barrow v. Nottingham C.
Fulham v. Chorley
Huddersfield v. Batley
Runcorn H. v. Keighley
Ryedale-York v. Doncaster
Salford v. Leigh
Trafford B. v. Swinton
Workington T. v. Whitehaven

EASTER MONDAY, 1st APRIL, 1991
Batley v. Huddersfield
Bramley v. Fulham
Carlisle v. Workington T.
Chorley v. Trafford B.
Dewsbury v. Halifax
Hunslet v. Ryedale-York
Leigh v. Runcorn H.
Nottingham C. v. Barrow
Swinton v. Salford

SUNDAY, 7th APRIL, 1991
Barrow v. Whitehaven
Batley v. Hunslet
Carlisle v. Bramley
Chorley v. Dewsbury
Fulham v. Doncaster
Halifax v. Trafford B.
Leigh v. Huddersfield
Keighley v. Swinton
Runcorn H. v. Nottingham C.
Workington T. v. Ryedale-York

WEDNESDAY, 10th APRIL, 1991
Carlisle v. Dewsbury
Fulham v. Keighley
Halifax v. Leigh
Huddersfield v. Bramley
Salford v. Trafford B.

SUNDAY, 14th APRIL, 1991
Bramley v. Halifax
Dewsbury v. Barrow
Doncaster v. Leigh
Fulham v. Runcorn H.
Hunslet v. Workington T.
Nottingham C. v. Chorley
Ryedale-York v. Batley
Salford v. Keighley
Swinton v. Huddersfield
Whitehaven v. Carlisle